The Skills of Helping Individuals and Groups

SECOND EDITION

The
Skills Of
Helping

Individuals and Groups
SECOND EDITION

Lawrence Shulman

Boston University
School of Social Work

F.E. PEACOCK PUBLISHERS, INC.
ITASCA, ILLINOIS 60143

To My Wife Sheila

Contents

ACKNOWLEDGMENTS ix
FOREWORD xi
INTRODUCTION xiii
I. A MODEL OF THE HELPING PROCESS: 1
    WORK WITH INDIVIDUALS AND FAMILIES
    1. AN INTERACTIONAL APPROACH TO HELPING ... 3
        The Client-System Interaction 4
        The Symbiotic Assumption 6
        The Assumption of Strength for Change 8
        Blocks in the Individual-Social Engagement 9
        The Function of the Helping Person 11
        The Integration of Personal and Professional Selves 13

    2. THE PRELIMINARY PHASE OF WORK 17
        Preparatory Empathy 17
        Indirect Communications 20
        Tuning In 22
        Responding Directly to Indirect Cues 25
        Agency Records and Referral Reports 28

    3. BEGINNINGS AND THE CONTRACTING SKILLS .. 33
        The Dynamics of New Relationships 33
        Contracting in First Sessions 37
        Contracting Over Time 41
        Contracting with Resistant Clients 43

    4. SKILLS IN THE WORK PHASE 51
        A Model of the Work Phase Interview 51
        Sessional Tuning in Skills 53
        Sessional Contracting Skills 57
        Elaborating Skills 59
        Empathic Skills 65
        Sharing-Worker's Feelings Skills 71
        Demand-for-Work Skills 77
        Pointing-out Obstacles Skills 85
        Sharing-Data Skills 91
        Sessional-Ending Skills 97

5. ENDINGS AND TRANSITIONS 105
   The Dynamics and Skills of Endings 106
   The Skills of Transitions 115

6. WORKING WITH FAMILIES 125
   Introduction 125
   Family Therapy Theory 127
   Selected Elements of Family Theory 128
   The Two-Clients Concept and the Worker's Role 131
   First Family Session with an Angry Father:
      Child Welfare Setting 134
   Discussion of the First Family Session 136
   Family Support Work Over Time: Bringing
      the Stepfather into the Picture 137
   The Single-Parent Family: Community
      Care Team Setting 143
   Parent Teen Conflict: A Psychiatric Setting 148
   The Impact of Culture and Community: Probation and
      a Native Indian Family 153
   Hiding the Family's Secrets: Dealing
      with Taboo Areas 158
   Summary 159

II. GROUP WORK SKILL 161
   7. THE GROUP AS A MUTUAL AID SYSTEM 163
      The Dynamics of Mutual Aid 164
      Obstacles to Mutual Aid 170
      The Function of the Group Leader 172
      The Fear of Groups Syndrome 173

   8. GROUP FORMATION 177
      Work with the Staff System 177
      Group Composition, Timing, and Structure 185
      Work with Prospective Members 190

   9. THE BEGINNING PHASE WITH GROUPS 195
      The Dynamics of First Group Sessions 195
      The Couples' Group 197

  10. FIRST GROUP SESSIONS: SOME VARIATIONS 215
      First Sessions with Adolescents and Children 215
      The Impact of Authority on the First Session 221
      Client Problem Impact 227
      Impact of the Setting of Service 230

11. THE WORK PHASE IN THE GROUP 239
Sessional Contracting in the Group 240
The Work Phase in a Group Session 252
Sessional Endings and Transitions 262

12. WORKING WITH THE INDIVIDUAL IN THE GROUP 265
The Concept of Role in a Dynamic System 265
The Scapegoat in the Group 267
The Deviant Member 274
The Internal Leader 280
The Gatekeeper 283
The Defensive Member 285
The Quiet Member 286

13. WORKING WITH THE GROUP AS CLIENT 293
The Group as an Organism 293
Developmental Tasks 294
Developing a Group Structure over Time 318
Helping Group Members Negotiate the Environment ... 322

14. SOME VARIANT ELEMENTS IN GROUP PRACTICE 327
The Open-Ended Group 327
The Single-Session Group 329
Activity in Groups 331
Co-Workers 337

15. ENDINGS AND TRANSITIONS WITH GROUPS ... 341
Ending and Transition Summary 341
Ending and Transitions: Group Illustrations 342
A Termination Session: Detailed Analysis 350

III. WORK WITH THE SYSTEM 355
16. HELPING CLIENTS TO NEGOTIATE THE SYSTEM . 357
The Individual-System Interaction 358
Mediating the Individual-System Interaction 359
Confrontation, Social Pressure, and Advocacy 377

17. PROFESSIONAL IMPACT ON THE SYSTEM 391
From Individual Problems to Social Action 393
Professional Impact and Interstaff Relationships 400

EPILOGUE 412
APPENDIX: NOTES ON RESEARCH METHODOLOGY 414
BIBLIOGRAPHY 419
INDEX 425

Acknowledgments

I would like to acknowledge the contribution of the Welfare Grants Directorate of Health and Welfare, Canada, both for their support of two of the research projects cited in this book and for their publication grant which allowed me to complete this manuscript. From this department, I am particularly indebted to J. Evariste Thériault who provided advice and encouragement throught the five years of the social work practice study and the supervision project which followed. I am also indebted to the P. A. Woodward's Foundation and the Ministry of Health of the province of British Columbia for their support of my study of medical practitioners. However, the views expressed in the research report and in this book are solely my responsibility.

I owe a great debt to William Schwartz, whose support as a friend and a colleague has contributed greatly to my work. His theoretical model gave direction to my early curiosity about method, and his published and unpublished works have helped to develop the arguments set forth in this text. Bill's death in 1982 was a great personal loss as well as a loss to the profession. Although we will miss his ongoing contributions, his work will live on as many of his seminal ideas receive wider professional acceptance.

Once again, the content of the book must be my responsibility only. Other colleagues have also helped in the development of this book and my research work. Kloh-Ann Amacher and Hal Goodwin read portions of the manuscript and made many helpful suggestions. Ted Shiner, Henry Maas, and John Crane provided informal advice on methodological questions connected with the social work study.

I was fortunate to have an excellent staff group working on the research project: Manon Nguyen, Mona Propst, Sheila Baslow, Frema Engel, Nilda Hillgartner, Bill Hunt, Robert Lightman, Elsie Shriar, Jeff Jones, Brenda Yarcag, Mary Ann Carbone, Reisa Schneider. Bill Hargartner provided consultation on video and computer programming problems. The project was dependent on the cooperation of the staff, clients, and foster parents of the Children's Aid Society of Ottawa and the Children's Service Centre of Montreal.

I would also like to thank the many workers and students whose recordings of practice have been included in this manuscript. Their material helps to give life to the theory as well as providing abundant evidence of the capacity of dedicated professionals to care for the people they work with. Special thanks to the members of my married couples' group who gave permission for me to use extensive transcript excerpts from the videotapes of our sessions together. Preliminary editing assistance from Chris Burridge was invaluable. Sheila Shulman also helped at key moments when time was short. The manuscript was skillfully typed by April Hamilton and Mrs. M. Visentin. Finally, I would like to thank the staff at Peacock Publishers—Ted Peacock, Joyce Usher, and Marjorie E. Witte for their assistance.

Lawrence Shulman

Foreword

In a paper called "On Psychotherapy," written in 1904, Freud noted that "not one of all those who show an interest in my therapy and pass definite judgments upon it has ever asked me how I actually go about it. There can be but one reason for this, namely, that they think there is nothing to enquire about, that the thing is perfectly obvious."

Freud's complaint has echoed down the years. In 1940, Fenichel recorded his amazement at how little of the psychoanalytic literature was devoted to theories of technique. A generation later, Strupp remarked that considering the importance of the therapist variable, it was astonishing how little research had been conducted on it. Martin Mayer, reporting on schools in America, was surprised to find that even "progressivism," the supposed stronghold of the concern with method, "was always more interested in creating proper attitudes than in developing effective techniques." From an opposite point of vantage, the behaviorist B. F. Skinner also deplored the "extraordinary neglect of method" in American education. In clinical psychology, Blanton commented that "the relationship between knowing and doing has as many puzzles for us today as it had for Socrates." And from the field of social work came Mary Richmond's early avowal that "the investigation is stronger than the treatment." In fact, she said, "after the investigation has been made and recorded, the treatment seems to drop to a lower level almost as suddenly as though it went over the edge of a cliff." Many years later, in the modern era, Helen Harris Perlman reviewed developments in social work method over a ten-year period and concluded that "the what and the how of carrying knowledge and belief into action—these are yet to be formulated." In *The Quest for Certainty,* John Dewey accused the philosophers and intellectuals of depreciating action, assigning menial status to the tasks of "doing and making," and trying to escape from their feelings of uncertainty by "changing the self in emotion and idea," rather than "changing the world through action."

All human relations practitioners know that goals, concepts, attitudes, commitments, and intentions are important to their work; these "emotions and ideas" provide the impetus and energy for their engagement with people in need. But they also know from their experience that knowing and believing and intending do not translate automatically into effective action. Knowledge in itself is not power; fine attitudes do not convert themselves easily into skillful doing; and objectives, no matter how worthy, do not carry within themselves the means of achievement. Given all the knowledge there is, the noblest intentions, and the best-laid plans, it is still true that if one is to know what to do, he must learn what to do.

The neglect of means has produced a professional literature that is extremely thin in its descriptions of practice. It is largely concerned with diagnosis, conceptual analysis, philosophy, and abstract discussion. If records of process are still being written, the journals show few signs of them; since supervision has come to be regarded as fostering dependency, the records are gone and the supervisory literature has shrunk to almost nothing; practice research, despite the proliferation of new theoretical systems, is as rare as ever. It becomes increasingly difficult to find out what it is that social workers *do* to help people in need, how they implement and deepen the services of a social agency, and what makes their skills so unique as to require a long period of training.

In view of all this, Dr. Shulman's book is a happy event in the profession; with it, social work takes a long and energetic step in the right direction. It is one of the very few systematic attempts to show how theory, research, scholarship, and the experience of practice can be put together to define and describe the social work method in action. It is rich in practice examples—many of them taken from his own work with clients—and leaves the reader in no doubt as to what he means when he illustrates a theoretical point with an example from practice. One is, of course, free to agree or disagree with a particular technique or way of helping; but it is precisely his achievement that he shifts the terms of debate and discussion from the realms of philosophy and objectives to those of action and professional skill. I am gratified that he has, in the process, put some of my own ideas to the test, and that he has found them useful in working out his presentation of social work function and method.

This is a book that tries to help practitioners fashion knowledge, belief, and compassion into a system of action designed to help complicated people make their way in a complicated world. More of such work is needed in the times to come.

Fordham University
December 1978   William Schwartz

Introduction

This book is about skill. The focus is on method—what professionals do as their part of the helping process. The author believes that the dynamics of giving and taking help are not mysterious processes which defy efforts at explanation. Helping skills can be defined, illustrated, and taught. The process is a complex one, and to present it clearly, it must be broken down into manageable segments. Simple models of the process need to be developed to provide tools for understanding. This is the goal of this book.

A second assumption is that there is an underlying process which can be identified in all helping relationships. This process and its associated set of core skills can be observed whenever one person attempts to help another. Elements of the process may vary according to the particular function of the helping person (e.g., social worker, nurse, child care worker) or the setting for the engagement (e.g., school, hospital, welfare agency).

The client receiving help will also introduce variant elements. However, when the interaction is examined closely, the similarities are what emerge. This book addresses a range of helping situations in the belief that each professional can incorporate the models into his or her own context of work. Although many of the illustrations will be drawn from social work, a liberal use of examples from other settings will help to demonstrate the common elements. In addition, findings drawn from this author's studies of supervision and medical practice, which were conducted after the publication of the first edition of this book, will provide additional research support for the importance of these core skills.[1]

An additional assumption is the existence of common elements in our work with individuals, families, and groups. The skill model developed in this book is illustrated by a range of encounters. The reader will find the core processes and skills which are identified in the chapters on work with individuals reappearing as the discussion shifts to questions involved in group and family work. For example, the contracting skills discussed in the beginning phase of work with individuals are also applied in first group sessions. These skills are common elements. In addition, the unique dynamics of first sessions with groups are presented to illustrate the variant elements.

In a like manner, the common elements of beginning work with different types of groups (e.g., children, unwed mothers, psychiatric patients, ward groups, residential living groups, citizen community action groups) are presented. Unique aspects introduced by the setting and the purpose of the work are also considered.

This book is an effort to conceptualize the elusive generic practice model which has been much sought in recent years. The focus is not on what is common about what we know, value, and aspire to, nor on our common structures for describing clients (as in systems theory), but rather on the common elements and skill of the helping person in action.

Theories and constructs about human behavior, some supported by research and others drawn from experience in practice, will be shared when relevant to specific practice issues. In this way, what we know about the dynamics of helping, group process, family interaction, and so on is directly related to the worker's interactions with the client and relevant systems. Further reading is suggested for those who may wish to explore the areas in more detail.

What the helping person values and seeks to achieve and the guiding ethics of conduct are also shared in the context of practice illustrations which make these important ideas more concrete. In order to simplify this complex task of describing method, historical analysis, surveys of helping frameworks, and descriptions of the settings of practice have been omitted. These have all been discussed elsewhere. A single frame of reference is presented, leaving the reader to make comparisons with other frameworks.

What is left is an attempt to describe a framework of the helping process, a number of models (middle-range descriptions) which provide the important connections between the framework and practice, and the identification of skills needed to put the framework into action. The approach used to guide my understanding of this process was developed by William Schwartz. This colleague's seminal thinking helped to focus my early curiosity about method. Published and unpublished works, conversations about practice, and other collaborative efforts have all contributed to Schwartz's influence on the contents of this book. The author alone, however, must take responsibility for the final shape of the following chapters. While a single framework provides the unifying structure for the book, many of the skills and models can fit comfortably into other frameworks.

The organization of the book begins with work with individuals, and families, examining this process against the backdrop of the phases of work: preliminary, beginning, work, and ending phases. As the helping model is developed, illustrations from a range of settings help to point out the common as well as variant elements of the work. The second part of the book moves into the more complex issues of working with more than one client at a time, focusing especially on groups. The common elements of the model established in Part One of the book are reintroduced in the group context. The special dynamics of working with more than one client are introduced. Part Three of the book explores the skills involved in working with people in the systems important to the client. Conversations with teachers, doctors and politicians help to illustrate effective impact. Although a generic practice approach is presented, the format of presentation (work with individuals, then families, then groups, then systems) was adapted for ease of exposition.

The book is intended to address the needs of the beginning and the experienced practitioner. Because of its structure, the reader with substantial experience in work with individuals but none with groups will discover that the foundation of skill developed in the individual context can be used in group engagements. The novice practitioner will find that explanations proceed logically with each idea building on previous ones. While the entire book will be comprehensible to the beginner, ability to put skills into action will be limited by lack of experience. The book will provide a starting point and an agenda for future work. For the experienced practitioner, the book will provide models which help explain and articulate concepts already developed through experience in practice. Using these models, the practitioner can be more systematic. A clearly developed framework will increase consistency and help to explain more quickly why some sessions go well whereas others do not.

RESEARCH FINDINGS

A four-year study into the helping process, directed by the author, has also contributed to the insights shared in this book. Starting with Schwartz's framework, instruments were developed to measure social work practice skill and relate skill use to effective helping. The findings were then used to analyze the practice approach critically. The findings, which should be viewed as tentative because of the limitations of the study, are shared throughout this book. Findings from the author's more recent studies of supervision and medical practice, as well as those from the social work and related helping professions, are also discussed.

The design of the social work study has been described in detail elsewhere.[2] A brief summary of the design and its limitations is provided here so that the reader may put the findings discussed in the text in proper perspective. A more detailed description of the methodology is provided in the Appendix. The central line of inquiry of the study was to examine social work practice skill and the relationship between what workers did in their interviews and the development of a positive working relationship with clients as well as the worker's helpfulness. One of the instruments developed in the study was the Social Worker Behavior Questionnaire. This consisted of twenty-seven items each describing a particular skill. The questionnaire was designed to be completed by clients who would be reporting on their worker's frequency of use of these behaviors. A second instrument, the Service Satisfaction Questionnaire, obtained clients' perceptions on the content of the work as well as their perceptions of their relationship with the worker ("How satisfied are you with the way you and your worker get along?") and the worker's helpfulness ("In general, how helpful has your worker been?") These two key items were used as dependent variables. The instrument-development stage included testing both questionnaires for reliability and validity. While the results of these tests are summarized in the Appendix, I would caution the reader to consider these instruments as in an embryonic stage requiring further testing and refining.

The total staffs of the two Canadian child welfare agencies participating in the study were included in the sample. The entire case load (active at the time of the study) for each of the 118 workers was identified, and all clients over fourteen years old were sent either a Social Worker Behavior Questionnaire *or* the Service Satisfaction Questionnaire. Random assignment was used to determine which of the two questionnaires a client received, so that each client had an equal chance to report on either their worker's behavior *or* their satisfaction with the relationship and the worker's helpfulness. This procedure was followed so that filling out one questionnaire would not influence the results on the other. Questionnaires were mailed to potential respondents. The return rate was 53 percent with a respondent sample of 1,784. Full details on the worker and client samples are reported in the research reports as well as results of the analyses of the impact of worker and client variables on the outcomes, and the results of a telephone survey which contacted over 50 percent of the nonrespondents.

Average scores were computed from the returns for each worker on each questionnaire. These scores were then assigned as the worker's score. Correlations were computed to determine the association between specific behaviors and the outcome measures of relationship and helpfulness. In addition, a partial correlation procedure allowed for interesting inferences about which skills contributed to relationship building, which ones to helpfulness, and which ones to both. Findings were then used to make inferences about the original practice framework. These findings are reported throughout the text.

In addition, mention is made in this text of the findings of a subdesign of the larger study in which videotapes of the practice of eleven workers in one of the agencies were analyzed by trained raters. The raters used an observation system developed during the study which allowed them to make systematic observations of the interactions between workers and clients, recording their observations every three seconds. From four to six individual sessions of each of the eleven workers were videotaped and analyzed in this manner. The resultant data rated 120 hours of practice and provided over 99,000 discrete entries for computer analysis. The Appendix and the research reports provide further details.

The findings of this study must be considered in light of the limitations of the study design. The study focused on practice in two child welfare agencies and the impact of the setting on the results can be serious. In addition, the study was essentially of client perceptions. Although testing tended to support reliability and validity of client perceptions, further work is needed to increase our confidence. The study was also limited in that it concentrated only on the interactional skills of the worker. Other skills, such as assessment, and other factors such as client strength and motivation, case load, social policy which affects clients (e.g., income support) all play some part in outcome. These limitations and others are reason to consider the findings of this study tentative although useful for developing theoretical constructs for further testing.

NOTES

1. See Lawrence Shulman, *The Skills of Supervision and Staff Management* (Itasca, Ill.: F. E. Peacock Publishers, Inc., 1982); Lawrence Shulman and William Buchan, *The Impact of the Family Physician's Communication, Relationship and Technical Skills on Patient Compliance, Satisfaction, Reassurance, Comprehension and Improvement* (Vancouver: School of Social Work, University of British Columbia, 1982).

2. See Lawrence Shulman, "A Study of Practice Skills," *Social Work* 23 (July 1978): 274-81; for a full report of the study, see Lawrence Shulman, *A Study of the Helping Process* (Vancouver: Social Work Department, University of British Columbia, 1977). For a condensed report of the study, see Lawrence Shulman, *Identifying, Measuring and Teaching the Helping Skills* (New York: Council on Social Work Education, 1981).

I. A Model of the Helping Process:
Work with Individuals and Families

CHAPTER 1

An Interactional Approach to Helping

This chapter sets out some of the central ideas of the practice theory contained in this book. Before beginning, I want to comment on the diversity of practice theories guiding the helping professions. The professions are in what Kühn would describe as a "prescientific stage" in that we have only just begun to use theories to guide empirical research into practice.[1] In a scientific stage, on the other hand, the results of research are used to modify theories, which are then used to guide new research. Since we are just beginning this important process, there is room in the professions for a wide range of views, and this is a healthy state. All practitioners eventually develop their own practice frameworks, some more and some less explicit, and judge them by how well they work in explaining their practice.

The approach described in this book has been most helpful to me in my practice-model building and research. It is neither a religion nor a dogma and will continue to be used as a framework as long as it appears to do the job. Readers should test its ideas against their own sense of reality and use those portions which seem helpful. As stated earlier, many of the skills and intermediate models are not bound by one approach and can easily fit into other structures.

Since I refer to practice theory, models and skills throughout the text, a brief explanation of how I use these terms would be helpful. In developing his framework, Schwartz defined a practice theory as

. . . a system of concepts integrating three conceptual subsystems: one which organizes the appropriate aspects of social reality, as drawn from the findings of science; one which defines and conceptualizes specific values and goals, which we might call the problems of policy; and one which deals with the formulation of interrelated principles of action.[2]

A practice theory, then, should first describe what we know about human behavior and social organization. Based upon these underlying assumptions, a set of specific goals or outcomes desired by the worker should be set out. Finally, a description of the worker's actions to achieve these specific goals completes the practice theory. This approach to theorizing about practice is used throughout the text. For example, when the beginning phase of work is examined, assumptions about how people behave in new situations is related to outcomes the worker wishes to achieve in first sessions. This, in turn, is linked to specific activities of the worker described as contracting.

The term *model* is used to describe a representation of reality. One would construct a model to help simplify the explanation or description of a complex process or object. In this text models are used to describe helping processes (e.g., the dynamics and skills required in a beginning, middle or ending phase session) as well as the entities we work with (e.g., the model of an organism is employed to describe a group or organization).

The term *skill* is used to describe behaviors on the part of the worker which are used in pursuit of the helping purpose. Many of the skills described in this text are core relationship skills, useful in the performance of professional as well as personal tasks. For example, the empathic skills are important for parents, spouses, and friends. My focus will be on their use in relation to professional helping functions.

Finally, although I have begun empirical testing of the hypotheses contained in the practice theory, this work is still at an early stage.[3] Some of the most interesting findings have been those which did not support my initial hypotheses. These were then used to help expand the theoretical constructs. It is in this spirit of tentativeness and evolution that the ideas in this book are shared.

THE CLIENT-SYSTEM INTERACTION

A critical factor in the helping process is the way one views the client.[4] In early attempts to conceptualize the helping process, the helping professions borrowed the medical model developed by physicians. Since the term *medical model*

has also been used in recent years to characterize a view of the client which focuses on illness and pathology, I wish to make clear that I am using it in another sense. The medical model that I refer to is the three-step process of thinking about practice commonly described as study, diagnosis, and treatment. In this framework, the knowing professional studied the client, attempted to make an accurate diagnosis, and then developed a treatment plan. Thus, it is entirely possible that practitioners who are preoccupied with illness or pathology *and* those who use other models of viewing clients (e.g., systems or ecological approaches) may still be employing a medical model in the way they conceptualize their practice. Even practitioners who reject what they term *clinical practice* as "Band-Aid" help, and advocate social action and advocacy, often employ the medical model in their thinking. The only difference, in their case, is that it is the "system" which needs to be studied, diagnosed, and treated.

One of several problems with this model was that it tended to make us think of clients in static terms. The emphasis was on pathology and on attributing descriptive characteristics to the client (e.g., weak, neurotic, resistant). In recent years, the impact of dynamic systems theory on the way helping professions viewed the clients has been profound.[5] One central idea has been the emphasis on viewing a client in interaction with others. Instead of a client being the object of analysis, concentration was on the way in which the client and the client's important systems were interacting. In fact, according to this viewpoint, it is impossible to understand the movements of the client except as they were affected by the movements of others.[6]

An example of this shift in thinking can be illustrated using a middle-aged woman admitted to a psychiatric ward of a hospital suffering from severe depression. One could choose to focus on her depression and other symptoms. An alternative framework would seek to identify those important systems in her life with which she is having to deal. For example, her husband, her children, her job, her peer group, her parents or siblings, and so on. In addition, one could include the hospital, her doctor, ward staff, and fellow patients. A diagrammatic way of viewing this would be (*see* diagram, below):

This important change in perspective leads to a change in the kind of questions the worker mentally asks. Instead of speculating on the state of the patient's mental health, the degree of the depression, and its possible cause (e.g., a depressed mother or early childhood trauma), the worker is more curious about the state of the interactions between the patient and each of the relevant systems. What is the nature of the relationship between the woman and her husband? Can they talk to and listen to each other? How well is the patient integrating into the ward? Is she reaching out to other patients, creating an informal support group, or is she cut off and isolated?

PATIENT◄---------------------►SYSTEMS

                                    Family
                                    Friends
                                    Job
                                    Parents & Siblings
                                    Hospital
                                    Professional Staff
                                    Other Patients

These are not questions the worker will be asking the patient in the early interviews—the structure of first sessions will be discussed later. Rather, they are examples of the potential areas of work upon which the helping process may focus. Furthermore, the worker will not only focus on the patient's part in the interaction. As stated earlier, the patient's movements can only be understood in relation to the movements of those around her. How well do the family, friends, and the other patients reach out to her? Part of the outcome of these interactions will be determined by the patient's input, but other parts will be a result of the system's responses. In fact, the relationship will be cyclical with the movements of each constantly affecting the movements of the others.

In addition, we need to understand the interaction in the context within which it takes place. We are just beginning to understand how our society's stereotypes of women and men affect relationships.[7] In many examples, when one looks beneath the depression of a middle-aged woman one finds an understandable anger, even rage, related to sex role stereotyping and oppression by a largely male-dominated society.

Men are also severely affected in their

relationships with women by societal pressures which define what makes a "real man." Conflict is often experienced between what a man feels and what he thinks he is supposed to feel. Other ecological factors, such as the impact of a depressed economy on employment and job security, may profoundly affect both partners in a relationship. Thus, it is impossible to think of a client's "problem" without understanding the context within which it is expressed.

As the patient-system interactions are identified, the depression takes on new meaning. The sadness and passivity are not the problems; rather they are the symptoms of the breakdown in these important interactions. The depression is not the illness to be cured, but rather a signal that the important areas of interaction in the life of this woman have broken down. The worker's efforts will not be directed to "curing" the patient, but rather to having some impact on the way the patient and these important systems interact. The cure for the "problem" will emerge not from the professional's treatment plan, but rather from the patient's own efforts to find new ways to reach out to these systems that matter to her, or to cut herself off from them and find new sources of support. Similarly, the systems may have to find new ways to reach out to this patient in order to reengage her. Both the patient and the systems may find implementation of this process difficult. Here, the job of the helping person comes in.

At this point, many questions and possibly some objections may have occurred to the reader. What if the client is too weak to deal with the system, doesn't want help, and refuses to work on the interaction? Perhaps the problem is with the system. These and other objections are pursued in some detail in the following

sections. For the moment, just set them aside. At this point, the critical factor is that the person to be helped is viewed as an interactive entity, acting and reacting to the various demands of the systems she must negotiate. The systems will be viewed in this way as well.

Each client is a special case within this general model. The unwed pregnant woman in a child welfare agency might be dealing with the systems of the agency, the child's father, family, friends, societal attitudes, and prejudices towards women and sexuality, and so on. Of equal concern to her may be issues of income (welfare or work), housing, and the medical system. If she lives in a group care home, the houseparents and other residents become part of the active systems in her life. Her feelings about herself as a woman, her reactions to society's norms, and her own, often harsh, judgments of herself may all be part of her agenda—but always in relation to the way in which she deals with those systems which matter to her. Whatever the category of client discussed in this book, whether the child in the residential center, the husband in marital counseling, the schoolchild who is failing, the patient with a terminal illness, or the member of a citizen's community action group—all will be viewed in the context of the interaction with their social surroundings.

THE SYMBIOTIC ASSUMPTION

Now that we have placed clients in interaction with the various systems which impinge upon them, some attention must be given to the nature of this relationship. If we return to the example in the previous section, our view of how we help this woman will depend upon our assumptions about the individual-social engagement. If we examine her interaction with her environment, we can perceive a certain amount of ambivalence. Some part of her will seem to be reaching out, however faintly, towards life and the people around her. On the other hand, her withdrawal, depression, and general communications appear to signal a retreat from life. She may have experienced life as too difficult, her feelings too painful to face, the demands seemingly impossible to meet. A part of her seems to be giving up and saying that the very struggle seems useless. She can be observed placing barriers between herself and these systems, including that part of the system (the worker) which is reaching out to help her. She is simultaneously reaching out for life, growth, and the important systems around her while also moving away from each.

The assumption that a part of us is always striving towards health is at the core of the practice theory formulated by Schwartz.[8] Borrowing a "symbiotic" model of human relationships, he views the individual-social interaction as

... a relationship between the individual and his nurturing group which we would describe as "symbiotic"—each needing the other for its own life and growth, and each reaching out to the other with all the strength it can command at a given moment.[9]

The term *symbiotic* is used to describe the mutual need of individuals and the systems that matter to them. This woman's needs can best be met in interaction with the world around her, not through complete withdrawal from it. In a like manner, society has a stake in maintaining this patient as an active, involved, unique, integrated individual.

Unfortunately, the term *symbiotic* has taken on a professional connotation of unhealthy mutual overdependency, as for example, between a mother and child. Schwartz uses the term to underline our mutual, essential interest in each other. It is a statement of the interdependence which is fundamental to our belief in a social responsibility for the welfare of each individual. It also recognizes that each individual finds life's needs best satisfied in positive relationships with others.

You may be wondering at this point how this assumption of a "symbiotic" model relates to experiences where individual-social interaction appears to be far from symbiotic. Schwartz points out that "in a complex and often distorted society, the individual-social symbosis grows diffuse and obscure in varying degrees, ranging from the normal developmental problems of children growing into their culture to the severe pathology involved in situations where the symbiotic attachment appears to be all but severed."[10]

The very fact that the mutual self-interest of people and their surrounding systems is often obscured creates the working ground for the helping professional. That people and their systems often appear to be acting against each other's self-interest is not an argument against the symbiotic model; rather it is an argument for some helping person to help both regain their sense of mutuality.

The practical implications of this philosophical assumption are important. For example, in the case of our patient, the worker's belief in the importance of helping her to find her connections to people around her and the belief in this woman's partial striving for this connection will cause her to search for faint clues that the woman is still emotionally alive and trying. The worker will not be fooled by the defenses thrown up by the patient and will concentrate instead on the spark of life which still exists, buried under the depression and apathy. The work of the helping person will not be to find ways to remotivate the patient, but rather to find and develop the motivation which is already there.

In a like manner, the worker will search for the part of the family, friends, peer group, and hospital system which is reaching out towards the patient. For instance if, during the family session, the husband appears to turn away from his wife, closing off his feelings, then the worker might reach for the underlying sense of loss and hurt which he attempts to hide even from himself. When the hospital rules, procedures, and services seem to work against the best interest of this patient, the helping person will attempt to influence that part of the system which cares about the people it serves, employing a number of strategies including mediation, brokering, or advocacy.

This powerful idea the reader will find recurring continually throughout this book. In example after example you will observe that the helping person's movements with the client, the moment-by-moment interventions, will be affected by the worker's view of the individual-social relationship. At critical moments in the interactions, connections will be discovered between husbands and wives, parents and children, students and teachers, community groups and politicians, individual group members and the group, and so forth because the helping person was searching for them.

The belief in this "symbiotic" model does not ignore the existence of important tensions and real differences in interest between the individual and the systems. Interactions in life involve conflict and confrontation as well as common elements. All interests are not mutual. The effective helping person will bring out into the open these underlying differences so that the engagement will be

a real human process invested with a range of feelings. This process will be illustrated with examples by which the skilled helper challenges the illusion of agreement between the parties in conflict by reaching for and demanding real work. What the model does is to provide the worker with a sense of the potential common ground upon which both the client and the important life systems can build.

THE ASSUMPTION OF STRENGTH FOR CHANGE

Belief in the existence of symbiotic striving is closely linked to another assumption about the individual-social engagement: that both the individual and the system contain within them the potential strength to implement this mutuality. This assumption depends upon a view of people (and complex systems) as being able to act in their own interest without being bound by their past experiences. An alternative approach considers that people fundamentally act according to the sum of the strengths and skills accummulated by past experiences. Casual links may be even drawn between a person's present immobility and earlier traumatic events.

While it seems logical that learning from past experiences will affect the way in which an individual attempts to negotiate new surroundings, the danger exists, with this view, of prejudging and underestimating a client's strength. Within the framework presented here, the individual is best described by actions and is as strong or as weak as he or she acts in the present moment. The practice implication of this attitude is that the worker must believe that the individual or the system has the capacity to move in its own self-interest, even if only by small steps, and that this movement will lead to increased strength and more change. Therefore, the helping person always places a demand for work before the client. This demand should be reasonable in nature and associated with support.

A familiar expression in this connection is "reach for the client's strength," suggesting that the very act of reaching for strength, that is believing in the potential of the work and refusing to accept even the client's own self-description of weakness, is a central part of what helps a client to act. Possibly the client has reached the present impasse precisely because all the signals received from important "others" have reinforced belief in the client's own impotence. The helping person will be different in this way.

These two assumptions will interact in important ways in the models and examples shared in this book. Workers will always search for subtle connections and will always make a demand that clients and systems people act on their potential for change. This view of practice is built upon a deep investment in the concept of interdependence, a belief in strength, and a preoccupation with health rather than sickness.

This stance does not negate the fact that some clients and some systems, because of a number of complex reasons, will not be able to use the worker's help at a given moment. The helping process is interactional, with workers carrying out their parts as best they can. Clients also have a part to play, and their strength will help to determine the outcome. Social factors may also have a profound impact. For example, income, housing, the economy, may all influence the results. This is all the more reason why helping professionals must be concerned simultaneously with social policies which affect the human situation. Recognizing that a particular client may be unable to

use help at that time, aware of and active on the social policies, the worker will nevertheless always attempt to reach for the client's strength because this is the way in which help is given.

BLOCKS IN THE INDIVIDUAL-SOCIAL ENGAGEMENT

Thus far I have described the client interacting with important environmental systems. Both the individual and the systems are vitally linked through mutual need or symbiosis. Each is seen as reaching out to the other with all the strength available at the moment and with the capacity to reach out more effectively. The next logical question must be: "What goes wrong?"

The mutual dependence can be blocked or obscured by any number of obstacles. One is the problem of a general increase in the complexity of systems. Let us take the family as an illustration of an important system. The relationships between parents and children and husbands and wives has become increasingly difficult. Fundamental changes in the family with the change from extended to nuclear family units have cut people off from important sources of support. Rapid changes in many of society's norms and values force parents to try to reconcile their own beliefs with those of their children. Husbands need to deal with new attitudes towards the role of women, new ideas about what it takes to be a "real man," and confused notions about how fathers should act. The world of work places increasing stress on family stability, making demands on time and energy. Is it any wonder that members of the family may find dealing with each other very complicated?

Recently, we have experienced severe problems in the economy which have had a serious impact on work stability. A seeming acceptance by government of high levels of unemployment have condemned many former wage earners to unemployment and welfare. In this author's current research project in the child welfare area, workers have reported significant increases in the number and severity of child abuse cases which appear to be linked to the stress of the economy—either loss of a job or fear of such a loss. Normal family tensions, such as parent-teen conflicts, become exacerbated when parents are under economic stress as well.

More generally, as the poor collected in cities, as the institutions (welfare, medical, education, etc.) designed to serve then became more complex, the basic relationship between people and these important systems was bound to become blocked. One has to only think of one's reactions to the first day at a new school or to entering a busy hospital in order to remember how strange, overwhelming, and impersonal the system can seem. The obstacles related to complexity are inherent, and emerge less from design than from the realities of the system.

A second set of obstacles is associated with the divergent interest of people and the systems that matter to them. Life does not consist only of mutual interest and interdependence. There are times when self-interest directly conflicts with the interest of others. In fact, each individual, as part of the growth process, must learn to set aside his or her own, immediate sense of need in order to integrate into the social order. For example, in marriage, a husband has some stake in maintaining traditional roles. The rules of behavior, norms, and the traditional structures in a marriage provide some payoffs for the male partner. He will have to pay a price if he wishes to develop a new,

more satisfying relationship with an equal partner. A confident wife who is able to develop a sense of herself differentiated from her husband and her family can be a more interesting wife. She may also be a more frightening one for a husband who is struggling to develop his own sense of self. Obstacles to the symbiotic relationship can be generated by the ambivalence towards change felt by family members. Rapid changes are anxiety producing for all in our society, so we often attempt to maintain the status quo and preserve continuity.

Complex systems are also ambivalent towards the people they serve. Politicians often view community action pressure groups as thorns in their side. As these groups expose important unmet needs, they also reveal problems which are difficult to handle. Government bodies face demands from many sources for a share of the economic pie, and to have this pressure heightened by citizen groups creates new difficulties.

In a general sense, society has a stake in maintaining the poor and in fostering a stereotype which places the blame for their problems on them. It is easy to see how the need for strong, active, community pressure groups as sources of feedback for our society can be obscured by the immediate need for peace and quiet. In a like manner, large institutions such as schools and hospitals find it easier to deal with students and patients who conform, don't make trouble, and go along with the present order. They often fail to realize the price they pay in terms of effective teaching and healing.

A third major set of obstacles relates to the problems of communication. Sharing and understanding painful or taboo thoughts and feelings is hard. People find it difficult to speak of feelings about sex, authority, intimacy, dependency, and so on. The powerful norms of our society are brought to bear in each interpersonal relationship, often making achievement of mutual understanding difficult. Most important conversations between people take place through the use of indirect communications which are extremely hard to decipher. For example, the husband who feels hurt and rejected by his wife's apparent lack of interest in sexual relations may express this through hostile or sarcastic comments in a totally unrelated area. The wife, in turn, may be expressing her own reactions to the husband's continual criticism through refusal to have sexual contact. Each may be feeling a powerful and important need for the other which is obscured by the fund of resentment developed by their immature means of communication.

School children who feel the teacher is always on their backs and does not like them respond with failure, lack of preparation, and cutting classes. The teacher, out of frustration at not being able to reach the children, responds with increased exhortation or punishment. To the children the message is that the teacher does not care. To the teacher, the message is that the children do not care. They are both wrong. Moreover, the children's stake in the successful completion of their education and the teacher's stake in helping students through a difficult learning process may be lost and overwhelmed by their mutual misconceptions. Instead of strengthening the relationship, the children and the teacher appear to turn away from each other, hiding their real feelings.

The parent and child, the hospital ward and patient, the individual and the group members—in each special case of the individual-social engagement—the essential mutual need is fragile and easily obscured by the complexity of the situation,

by divergent needs, or by the difficulty involved in communication. Because of this ever-present possibility of "symbiotic diffusion" Schwartz suggests the need for the helping professional. Our tasks relate directly to the fact that obstacles can easily obscure the mutual dependence between the individual and important systems. When both sides have lost sight of this important connection, a third force is needed to help them regain this understanding. It is this idea of the third force which leads to the general function of mediation described in the next section.

THE FUNCTION OF THE HELPING PERSON

Schwartz discussed the function of the helping person in the context of social work practice. He felt the history of the profession pointed in a unique way toward a special responsibility for acting as a third force between people and their systems. I will be borrowing the core idea of this theory and applying it to a wide range of helping professionals. Recognizing that professionals have different functions in society and that their history may have led to differing focuses for their work, I nonetheless feel that the concept of mediation can provide a starting point for thinking about all underlying helping process.

The child care worker, the nurse, the school counselor, the corrections officer, the doctor, and the teacher all have different jobs to perform with a diverse assortment of people in a range of settings. For each, however, the notion of a client and a system interacting, with a professional as some form of third force attempting to have impact on that interaction, can be helpful. As stated earlier, it is quite possible to use ideas, skills, and submodels contained in this work without adopting whole the theoretical structure.

Schwartz's functional definition for the social work profession is "to mediate the process through which the individual and his society reach out for each other through a mutual need for self-fulfillment."[11] To the earlier diagram of a hypothetical client attempting to deal with a number of important systems, a third force is introduced.[12]

With addition of the worker, the basic triangular model is complete. On the left is the client reaching out with all available strength, attempting to negotiate important systems while often simultaneously throwing up defenses which cut one off from the very systems one needs. On the right are the systems (family, school, hospital staff, etc.) reaching out to incorporate the client but often reaching ambivalently. In the center is the worker, whose sense of function and skills are mobilized in an effort to help client and system overcome the obstacles which block their engagement.

One could argue that this functional statement is too limited. I have already indicated that the term *mediation* is used in a broad sense and can include other activities such as advocacy. There are times when the crucial work in the area between the helping person and the system requires conflict and social pressure. However, even with a broad interpretation of mediation, one might still argue that this functional statement is too limited. The argument in response is that if the helping person is clear about the helping function and that function is specifically defined, then there is a better chance of consistently performing it. Jessie Taft, one of the early leaders of the "functional school" of practice, stressed this view.[13] In addition, the client who understands what the helping person does, the way in which help is given, will be better able to use the worker's services.

Work with couples in marital counseling provides a good illustration. The division between the couple has caused most people they know (family, friends, etc.) to take sides with one or the other. An early, often unstated question on the minds of both husband and wife as they

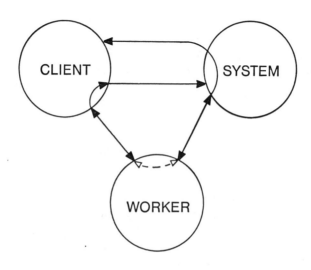

enter the counseling process is, "Whose side will the counselor be on?" Only through explanation and demonstration will the skillful worker help the couple understand that the ability to help them depends upon how well the worker can be on both sides at the same time. Practice experience has taught most workers that the moment they identify with one side versus the other, they have lost their usefulness to the client who feels cut off.

While this example supports the idea of mediation outlined earlier, you may be wondering how generally applicable this assignment can be. The rest of the book explores the answer, drawing illustrations from a range of settings with varying types of individuals, families, and groups. In each example, place yourself in the shoes of the worker. The argument is that the worker's sense of the next step at specific moments of interaction will be vitally affected by an internalized sense of function. These introductory comments alert you to the general model I will be applying in each step of analysis throughout the book. A further elaboration of this function and worker tasks will be shared in the context of practice illustrations.

The Radical Social Work Challenge

This view of practice is often challenged by the segment of our field which calls for a radical social work approach. For some members of this group, direct practice with clients, by definition, is ineffective. All problems are defined in terms of economic, political, or social contexts. These theoreticians point to the very real problems in past approaches to practice which seemed to ignore social realities. The reason they have as powerful an impact on faculty, students, and workers, is that they focus on aspects of our practice in which we are already feeling defensive.

However, practitioners know that it is easy to theorize abstractly, but much more difficult when real clients are involved. Thus, while we need a conception of practice which requires us to act on injustices in our society (and agencies), we simultaneously must provide services to the victims of these injustices. The real task is technical in nature. How can we integrate radical views of society and interpersonal relationships into our ongoing practice and how can we develop the skills to have impact on systems as well as clients. An oversimplified answer which simply rejects practice is of no assistance to people who work in the real world.

Thus, the framework described in this book will attempt to view relationships between clients and their important systems in an ecological context. Real conflicts between clients and systems will be identified, however, an emphasis will be placed upon attempting to identify areas of common ground. Practitioners will be described trying to deal directly with clients, as well as trying to influence families, agencies, political systems, and so on. These practitioners will at times function in different roles—mediating where appropriate, confronting and advocating when necessary. In whichever role they play, however, they will never lose sight of the essential common ground between the individual and society. This is the basis upon which change can be brought about. This is the real challenge for developing a radical social work practice.

THE INTEGRATION OF PERSONAL AND PROFESSIONAL SELVES

Another carry-over from the medical

model borrowed from the doctors, was the importance of one's professional self. Most helping professions stressed the professional role and the need to suppress personal feelings and reactions. For example, in order to work with stressful patients, one might have to keep one's real reactions in check so as to avoid appearing judgmental. A professional worker was described as one who maintained control of emotions and would not become angry or too emotionally involved, would not cry in the presence of a client, and so forth.

This image of professionalism was widely held with many of my social work students starting their careers wondering if they would have problems becoming a social worker because they "felt too much."

The practice model presented in this text will suggest that we have been faced with a false dichotomy when we appeared to have to choose between our personal self and our professional self. In fact, I will argue that we are at our best in our work when we are able to synthesize the two—that is, integrate our personal self into our professional role.

This conflict in view of professional self was brought home dramatically in a workshop I led on direct practice. One hospital social worker described an incident in which a mother appeared at her door after being referred by the attending physician. The mother had just been told that her seven-year-old daughter had a terminal illness. After explaining this to the social worker, the mother broke down and cried.

When I asked the worker what she did, she described how overwhelmed she felt by the mother's grief. All that the worker could do was sit and hold the mother's hand, crying with her. I maintain that while there would be much work to be done in this case (e.g., helping the mother to deal with the dying daughter and her family over the next few months), at this point what the mother needed most was not advice but someone to be with her. In fact, as the worker partially experienced the mother's pain, and shared it with her through her own tears, she was giving that client an important gift of her own feelings. The worker was being professional in the best sense of that word. Other workers, who might not cry as easily with a client, might make the same gift in other ways—facial expressions, a respectful silence, a hand on the shoulder, each worker responding in a way consistent with his or her own personality. The crucial factor would be the worker's willingness to be honest and to share his or her own feelings.

In the case described above, the worker continued her story by telling us that her supervisor passed the open door, called her out, and berated her for unprofessional behavior. The supervisor said: "How could you let yourself break down that way? You can't help your clients if you become overwhelmed yourself." When I asked the worker what she took from the experience, she replied: "I learned to keep my door closed."

While many who hear that story are upset with the supervisor, I am not. I realize that she may have been trained, as I was, in a time when personal expressions of emotion were considered taboo. I encouraged the social worker to talk to her supervisor since I felt it was crucial for her to obtain support from her supervisor and colleagues if she was to continue to provide this kind of help to clients.

I can understand the concern many professionals feel about workers who use the argument of spontaneity to justify acting out with clients. For example, getting inappropriately angry or judgmental, or sharing personal problems ("If you think you have troubles with your wife let me tell you about my marriage"). These examples illustrate a lack of integration of personal and professional selves.

The argument advanced throughout the text will be that each of us brings our own personal style, artistry, background, feelings, values, beliefs, and so on, to our professional practice. Rather than denying or suppressing these, we need to learn more about ourselves in the context of our practice, and learn to use ourself in pursuit of our professional functions. We will make many mistakes along the way, saying things we will later regret, having to apologize to clients, learning from these mistakes, correcting them, and then making more sophisticated mistakes. In other

words, we will be real people carrying out difficult jobs as best we can, rather than paragons of virtue who present an image of perfection.

As we demonstrate to our clients our humanness, vulnerability, willingness to risk, spontaneity, honesty, and our lack of defensiveness (or defensiveness for which we later apologize), we will be modeling the very behaviors we hope to see in our clients. Thus, when workers or students ask me: "Should I be professional or should I be myself?", I reply that the dualism implied in the question does not exist. They must be themselves if they are going to be professional. Fortunately, we have the whole of our professional lives to learn how to effect the synthesis.

NOTES

1. Thomas H. Kühn, *The Structure of Scientific Revolution* (Chicago: University of Chicago Press, 1962).

2. William Schwartz, "Toward a Strategy of Group Work Practice," *Social Service Review* 36 (September 1962), p. 270.

3. See Lawrence Shulman, "A Study of Practice Skills," *Social Work* 23 (July 1978):274-81; for a full report of the study, see Lawrence Shulman, *A Study of the Helping Process* (Vancouver: Social Work Department, University of British Columbia, 1977).

4. For ease of presentation, the term *client* will be used to describe the person receiving help and *worker* to describe the helper.

5. For a discussion of systems theory and its impact on practice thinking, see Gordon Hearn, *Theory Building in Social Work* (Toronto: University of Toronto Press, 1958); Gordon Hearn (ed.), *The General Systems Approach: Contributions toward an Holistic Conception of Social Work* (New York: Council on Social Work Education, 1969); Carel Germain, "Teaching an Ecological Approach to Social Work Practice," in *Teaching for Competence in the Delivery of Direct Services* (New York: Council on Social Work Education,

1977), pp. 31-39; Carel B. Germain and Alex Gitterman, *The Life Model of Social Work Practice* (New York: Columbia University Press, 1980).

6. This view is rooted in a school of thought developed by a number of philosophers and social scientists including John Dewey, *Democracy and Education; An Introduction to the Philosophy of Education* (New York: Free Press, 1916); George Herbert Mead, *Mind, Self and Society* (Chicago: University of Chicago Press, 1934).

7. For a recent publication discussing women's issues, see: Elaine Norman and Arlene Mancuso, *Women's Issues and Social Work Practice* (Itasca, Ill.: F.E. Peacock Publishers, Inc., 1980).

8. William Schwartz, "The Social Worker in the Group," in *New Perspectives on Services to Groups: Theory, Organization, Practice* (New York: National Association of Social Workers, 1961), pp. 7-34. See also *The Social Welfare Forum, 1961* (New York: Columbia University Press, 1961), pp. 146-77.

9. Ibid., p. 15. Schwartz draws his rationale for the symbiotic model from such authors as Peter Kropotkin, *Mutual Aid, A Factor of Ev-*

olution (New York: Alfred A. Knopf, 1925); Muzafer Sherif, *The Psychology of Social Norms* (New York: Harper & Bros., 1936); Gardner Murphy, *Human Potentials* (New York: Basic Books, 1958); James Mark Baldwin, *The Individual and Society: Or, Psychology and Sociology* (Boston: Richard G. Badger, Gorham Press, 1911).

10. Schwartz, "The Social Worker in the Group," p. 15.

11. Ibid.

12. For a more recent description of this function, see William Schwartz, "Social Group Work: The Interactionist Approach," in *En-cyclopedia of Social Work, Vol. 11,* ed. John B. Turner (New York: National Association of Social Workers, 1977), p. 1334. See also: William Schwartz, "Between Client and System: The Mediating Function," in *Theories of Social Work with Groups,* eds Robert W. Roberts and Helen Northen (New York: Columbia University Press, 1976), pp. 171-97.

13. Jessie Taft, "The Relation of Function to Process in Social Casework," in *Training for Skill in Social Casework,* ed. Virginia P. Robinson (Philadelphia: University of Pennsylvania Press, 1942), pp. 1-12.

CHAPTER 2

The Preliminary Phase
of Work

Since the helping process is complex, it helps to analyze it against the backdrop of the phases of work. Each phase of work—preliminary, beginning, work, and ending—has unique dynamics and requires specific skills. Jessie Taft was one of the first to draw attention to the effect of time on practice.[1] Schwartz incorporated this dimension into his work.[2] I will use the phases of work to organize the presentation of this model, starting with the preliminary phase.

PREPARATORY EMPATHY

A major skill in the preliminary phase of work is development of the worker's preparatory empathy. This technique can be employed before contact with the client has begun. Schwartz termed this process "tuning in."[3] It involves the worker's effort to get in touch with potential feelings and concerns which the client may bring to the helping encounter. The purpose of the exercise is to help the worker become a more sensitive receiver of the client's indirect communications in the first sessions. For a number of reasons which are discussed later in this section, some of the most important client

communications are not spoken directly. By tuning in, the worker may be able to hear the client's indirect cues and then respond directly.

An example from practice illustrates the general issues involved before the communication concepts are elaborated. This particular experience has been shared by workers in consultation sessions so often with only slight variations that it probably represents an archetype. The worker was a social worker in a child welfare agency. She was twenty-two, unmarried, and new to the job. Her first interview was with a thirty-eight-year-old mother of seven children who came to the agency's attention because of a neighbor's complaint about her care of the children. Another worker had been meeting with her for four months but was leaving the agency. Our new worker was the replacement, making her first visit. After introductions, they sat in the living room chatting for a few minutes when the client suddenly turned to the worker and said, "By the way, do you have any children?" There was a brief silence after this embarrassing question. Recovering quickly, and hiding her feelings, the worker said to the client: "No, I don't have any children. However, I have taken a number of courses in child psychology." Discussing this incident in a consultation session, the worker reported her internal feelings and her thoughts: "I panicked! I thought, 'Oh my God, she knows I don't have any children—how am I supposed to help her?'"

The conversation in the interview shifted back to the worker's agenda of agency business and didn't return to this area. An important issue had been raised, indirectly, and an unprepared worker had responded defensively. If we analyze the more subtle, indirect communications involved in this incident, we could interpret the client's question in the following manner.

CLIENT: By the way, do you have any children? (unstated—I wonder if this one will be like the other worker. They have all kinds of ideas about how I should raise children and have never changed a dirty diaper themselves. How can they understand what it's like for me?)

There are other interpretations possible; however, I believe that this question is central for all clients in first sessions. The crucial part of the message left unsaid was the client's concern that she would not be understood. The worker's response, a product of her own concern about her capacity to help, only confirmed the client's apprehension. It is quite normal for clients to wonder if a new worker will be like other helping professionals that they might have met—a stereotypical cold, unfeeling "expert" who thinks she has all the answers. This thought was too dangerous to express openly, so it was only hinted at. The worker's reaction was also quite normal, especially for a new worker who had not been prepared for the session.

If the worker had been tuned in to the client's potential concern, not intellectually but by actually trying to get in touch with the way clients in general, and this one in particular, might feel, she might have been able to read the real question behind the question. If she had had some help with her own feelings, from a supervisor or colleagues, she might have been able to consider in advance how *to respond directly to an indirect cue* in this important area. Each worker develops his or her own, unique responses, but one way to deal with that situation might be: "No, I don't have any children. Why do you ask? Are you wondering if I'm going to be able to understand what it's like for you having to raise so many?"

Such a response might have opened up a discussion of the woman's past experiences with workers, when they had helped her and when they had not. The worker might also share her own feelings (without overdoing them) of concern. For example, "I was worried that it might be hard for me really to understand what the difficulties must feel like for you. Perhaps if you tell me about them, it will help." As the client begins the worker's education, the work begins. Instead of the working relationship being closed, the potential exists for this one to begin to grow. If nothing else, the client might end the interview thinking, "This worker is different. Perhaps I can train her."

Although the empathic skills will be discussed in more detail in Chapter 4, it's important to comment here on the issue of genuineness. One of the key reasons for tuning in is to combat the ease with which helping professionals can learn to say the words related to affect without really experiencing the feelings. For example, a popular technique advocated in some texts on practice involves the use of "reflection." That is, the worker reflects back to the client the affective words. If a client said: "I'm really angry at my kids," the worker might repeat: "You're really angry at your kids." If I were the client in that situation, I probably would feel like saying: "Dummy, I just told you I was angry at my kids."

The problem with that response is that it is mechanical and artificial. The worker is not really *feeling* the anger. When I press practitioners on this question, they usually admit that they reflected because they didn't know what else to say. Unfortunately, the client perceives the response as uncaring. The workers would have been better off being honest and saying that they did not know what to say.

An even better response might be to remain silent for a few moments and to try to feel how angry parents can get with their children, and then to respond with reactions which might deepen the conversation. For example, instead of being slightly behind the client, as illustrated in the reflective response, one approach might be to try to be one half step ahead of the client by putting the client's unstated feelings into words: "That's the thing, isn't it; how can you be so angry at the kids and at the same time, love them so much?"

The exact words are not crucial since each of us develops our own personal style and way of expressing our feelings and those of our clients. What is crucial is that the worker really should be feeling something. My students have pointed out that this is easy for me to say, and hard for them to do. The fact is, we have not learned how to deal well with our feelings, and those of others, in most areas of our lives. As one mature student put it: "I have trouble dealing with my kids' feelings, how am I going to help this client deal with hers?"

Fortunately, helping professionals have their whole practice lives to develop their ability to be genuinely empathic. As they listen to clients, trying to tune in, they will discover feelings within themselves that may have been earlier ignored. In the beginning, they will borrow the words of others. It is not uncommon for one of my students to bring the audiotape of an interview into an early class, with the student using my words in his or her efforts to empathize. With some, you can even pick up strains of *my* New York City accent. When this was pointed out by a fellow student, in one case, the mimicking student replied, with some feeling: "I know, and I don't want to be a little Shulman." I try to reassure my students and suggest that they can borrow whatever words they need in the beginning. With continued work at developing their skills, they soon become more comfortable and are able to find and use their own words. This point is elaborated in Chapter 4.

In describing the situation with the young mother and the new worker, I mentioned the term *working relationship*. The concept of a working relationship is central to the model, so a brief explanation is required. A generally accepted model contained in most practice theories suggests that the activities of the helping person can develop a positive relationship with the client; this is a precondition for helping. Something about the way the worker and client talk to and listen to each other, the flow of both positive and negative feelings between them, affects the outcome. I believe that the development of a working relationship is a precondition for helping.

In a later chapter I will include a more specific definition of a working relationship, describe the skills which develop it, and discuss the way it can create conditions for change. I have introduced the concept at this point because the ability of the worker to be tuned in to the unspoken feelings and concerns of the client in the preliminary phase of work contributes to the establishment of a positive working relationship. This underlines the importance of preparatory empathy and the worker's ability to respond directly to indirect cues.

The interview described in the preceding example raised the following three areas for further discussion: the nature of indirect communications; the tuning in skill; and the skill of responding directly to indirect cues. Each of these is explored now in more detail.

INDIRECT COMMUNICATIONS

Human communications can be complex under any circumstances.[4] Let us examine the nature of a single communication. We start with a sender, an individual who has an idea to transmit. This idea must first be "encoded" and then transmitted to the intended receiver through spoken or written words, touch, or body movement. The message must now be received. This involves hearing, reading, seeing, or feeling by the recipient. Next, it must be decoded; that is, translated from symbols to the ideas which they represent. The recipient must then acknowledge the message through some form of feedback to the sender, thus completing the cyclical process.[5]

When one considers how complicated even the most simple communications are, the number of points in the process where meanings can be distorted, it is a wonder that any communication is ever completed. In the helping relationship, additional factors can complicate the process. These obstacles to open communication often result in a client employing indirect methods to express thoughts and feelings.

One obstacle may be the feeling of ambivalence associated with taking help. Our society has a negative response to almost all forms of dependency, stressing instead the norm of independence. A value has been placed on being able to handle things on one's own. Society's pressure is counterbalanced for the client by the urgency of the task at hand. The resulting vector from these conflicting forces is often an ambiguous call for help. Particularly in early sessions, before a working relationship has been established, the client may present concerns in an indirect manner. A worker who is "tuned in" may be able to establish a new norm, more conducive to the helping relationship.

A second area of potential blockage to direct communications is societal taboos, reflecting a general consensus to block or prohibit discussion in areas of sensitivity and deep concern. The client enters the helping relationship with a conscious or unconscious internalizing of these taboos, hindering free speaking. Major taboos in our society discourage "real" talk about sex, dependency, authority, and money. The discomfort clients experience talking about issues and feelings in certain areas may cause them to use indirect methods of communications.

A third obstacle is associated with the feelings that accompany concerns. Feelings may be painful and frightening to the client. The raising of a concern may be blocked by conscious or unconscious defenses which the client uses to block moving into areas with feelings of real or imagined potency. This can lead to clients sharing the facts of an issue, while ignoring their own feelings. Since all issues of concern are invested with both facts and feelings, this represents only a partial communication.

Finally, the context of the contract with the helping person may contribute factors which block real talk. For example, in the case of the new worker and the parent, child welfare workers carry dual functions and in some cases may have to act for the state in apprehending the child. Parents are very aware of the worker's authority and power and thus will be wary of sharing information or feelings which can be used against them. A parole officer who can revoke a parole, a nurse who can make a hospital stay unpleasant, a psychiatrist who can decide when a patient can go home, an adoption worker who can decide if a person gets a child—all these helping people have power over the lives of their clients, and this power may become the most important obstacle to real talk.

The feelings and concerns are present, however, and in spite of the obstacles, which block their open expression, clients will use indirect means to present them as for example, in the classic case of the client who "has a friend with a problem." Hinting is an important indirect cue; the client makes a comment or asks a question which contains a portion of the message. The mother in the earlier example who asks the worker if she has children may be using a question to begin to raise, very tentatively, a more complex and threatening issue. Clients often raise their concerns through their behavior. For example, a child in a residential setting who has not been asked to go home for a family visit over Christmas may let his child care worker know how upset he is by a sudden increase in "acting out" behavior. Adults in counseling sessions who "come on" negatively may be doing the same thing.

Another illustration can be drawn from the child welfare setting. A social worker was visiting a young, single-parent mom, with three children all under the age of four. There had been an abuse com-plaint, and the worker was investigating. As the worker spoke to the harried mother, the youngest child pulled at the mother's leg until the mom said: "Leave me alone, I'm talking now." The child continued to try to engage the mother and she finally grabbed the little girl by the shoulders and shouted: "Leave me alone!"

The worker was stunned and immediately, responding to that part of her function which called for the protection of children, began to counsel the mom: "Mrs. Jones, don't you think there might be other ways in which you can tell your child you wish to be alone?" The mother understood the implied criticism and immediately began to feel tenser and more defensive with this worker.

If the worker could have been tuned in to her own feelings, and those of the mom, and if it was clear to the worker that mom was a client in her own right and not just an instrument for providing service to the child, then she might have recognized the indirect cues of the negative behavior and responded as follows: "Is this what it's like for you all the time—no chance to be alone, to talk to other people without the kids after you?" If said with genuine understanding of the plight of a single mom, who is young, trying to raise kids on her own, probably struggling with an inadequate income, and so on, then there is a good chance that the working relationship might be strengthened by this direct response to the indirect cues. The worker might also acknowledge how hard it must be on the mom to have a social worker come and talk to her about these things.

The crucial point in this discussion is that it is often hard to understand what clients are trying to say because of the indirect nature of their communications. In particular, negative behavior is difficult to understand, particularly for new workers, because it makes them feel on the spot. Developing the capacity to reach behind negative behavior for the real meaning of the client comes with the growth of the worker's sense of professional competency.

Metaphor and allegory can be used by clients as means of indirect communication. As in literature, the intent is to send a message without necessarily expressing its content directly. An example from an interview with a depressed adolescent foster child who has recently lost his parents illustrates this. The youngster is getting ready to leave the care of the agency because he is eighteen and is worried about where he will live. He has had eight changes of residence during the past year. Note both the indirect communications and the means by which the worker uses her preparatory empathy to reach for the underlying message.

Frank asked me if I ever thought of the fact that space never ended. I said I hadn't really. I wondered if he had, and if it worried him somehow. He said it did, because sometimes he felt like a little ball, floating in space, all alone. A little bit higher and more to the right, and bye, bye world—just like a wee birdie. I said he really has been floating in space, moving from place to place, and that he must be feeling all alone. Frank's eyes filled with tears and he said, emphatically, "I am all alone!"

Nonverbal forms of communications can also be used to send important indirect messages. The client who always arrives late or early or who misses sessions after promising to attend may be commenting on his reactions to the process of helping. The children in the family session who arrive looking tense and angry and refuse to take off their coats may be saying something about their feelings about being there. The client who sits back looking angry, with arms firmly folded across his chest, may be saying, "Go ahead, try and change me." These are all important messages; however, the common element is that the clients are not using words.

With communications so complex, how is the worker ever able to hear? This is where the "tuning in" skill can be helpful. It can substantially increase the odds in favor of understanding, particularly in the beginning stage of work when the conversation is usually more indirect. In the next section we examine the skill more closely.

TUNING IN

The tuning in skill is an exercise in which the worker, either alone or with supervisor or colleagues, attempts to develop preparatory empathy with the client. It is a way of putting oneself in the client's shoes and trying to view the world through the client's eyes. There are four important factors to consider when tuning in. First, tuning in must be an affective rather than an intellectual process. Second, the worker's feelings must also be explored. Third, tuning in should be done at a number of levels. Finally, the conclusions of the tuning in process must be tentative. Each of these aspects is explored in the rest of this section.

Affective versus Intellectual Tuning In

To tune in effectively, one must try actually to experience the client's feelings. One way to do this is to recall experiences which have been similar to the client's. The client, for example, is having a first contact with a person in authority. This would be true even if the client is there voluntarily and the helping person has no specific control functions (e.g., protection of children, maintenance of parole). The first encounter is also a new situation, filled with unknown elements. What new experiences or first encounters with people in authority has the worker had? Can the worker remember how it felt, what the concerns were? A new school, a new teacher, the first experience of hospitalization—any of these might serve to remind one and put one in touch with feelings related to those of the client. The important point is that *the worker needs actually to experience these feelings.*

A preparatory supervision session with a nurse, new to a terminal cancer ward and about to meet with family members of the patient, illustrates the difference between intellectual and affective tuning in.

SUPERVISOR: What do you think the family may be feeling towards the medical staff?

NURSE: I think they probably feel a bit angry that we haven't been able to help more—to find a cure.

SUPERVISOR: Try that again, but this time, say I. Put yourself in the role.

NURSE: OK. I'm feeling angry at all of you nurses and doctors—what good are you?

SUPERVISOR: That's closer, but you know, you didn't sound angry. Were you really feeling it?

NURSE: Not really. But that's hard to do—you mean really feel mad?

SUPERVISOR: You know, if you're intellectual about this, not really feeling it, it will come across as artificial and mechanical.

NURSE: God damn it! Why couldn't you doctors and nurses do something about this—and why have you all been lying to me about John?

SUPERVISOR: Any hunches about why you're so angry?

NURSE: Because it hurts so much, it's so hard to accept, I have to let it out somehow. Maybe I'm also feeling a little helpless and impotent myself.

Tuning in to Your Own Feelings

Workers must also get in touch with their own feelings. How we feel can have a great deal to do with how we act. The young worker in the first example could not respond to the client's concerns because of her preoccupation with her own feeling of inadequacy. The nurse in the example above, as she explores her own reactions to working with the terminally ill, may discover many of the same feelings of helplessness and impotency that the family feels. Health professionals often feel quite deeply their inability to save a dying patient. Precisely because the helping person's feelings are similar to the client's, it may be difficult to listen and to respond.

By tuning in to one's own feelings and experiencing them before the engagement, their power to block the worker can be lessened. In many ways, the helping process is one in which workers learn a great deal about their own feelings as they relate to their professional function. One's capacity to understand others and oneself can grow while engaging in this continual process.

This stress on the importance of the worker's own feelings runs counter to many conceptions of professionalism. As pointed out earlier, a central construct of the medical model stresses the hiding of real feelings which are seen as interfering with professional role. In a study I did of the effects on a number of outcomes measures of family physicians' communications and relationship skills, it was interesting to note that the strongest predictor of outcomes, such as patient satisfaction and comprehension, was whether or not the doctor liked the patient.[6] Also, patients were very good perceivers of their doctors' attitudes towards them. The crucial point is that we need to learn to understand and deal with our feelings, instead of pretending to deny their existence.

Levels of Tuning In

Tuning in can be done at a number of different levels. To illustrate, let us take a child care worker at a residential center for delinquent adolescent boys. A first level of tuning in would be to the general category of adolescents. The literature on stages of development and the worker's own experiences can help in this process. The adolescent is going through a time of normative crisis in which he must begin to define himself in a new role. A number of central questions are dominant. He is trying to sort out conflicting messages in our society about the qualities which make a real man. The title of an article by Setleis, "How should we act? How should we be?" poses these questions nicely, and the article itself provides a good illustration of professional literature which can help us to tune in to potential themes of concern to a specific category of clients.[7]

Sensitivity to underlying currents of feelings, to the way in which clients struggle to deal with the normal crisis of life can also be enriched through fictional literature. The adolescent's efforts to develop his sense of differentiation from his family, to further his independence while at the same time trying to maintain some sort of relationship has been explored with great perceptiveness by a number of authors.

Workers must tap their own adolescent experiences in an effort to remember feeling what it was like. Here are some examples from a child care worker's training session as workers attempted to express some of the problems of adolescence.

There are so many things I need to know about sex and how to get along with girls. When I talk to adults about these things, they often make me feel dirty. It's terribly important to me that I get accepted by the guys—be one of the gang. It feels great when we hang out together, kid around, talk about girls, gripe about parents and other adults. I'd be willing to do almost anything, even things I don't feel comfortable about, to be in and not left out.

The second level of tuning in is the specific client, in this case, youngsters who are in trouble with the law. Information on the background of the boys, the nature of the delinquent acts, their relationship with their families, and so forth can all prove useful in attempting to orient oneself to the thoughts and feelings of a specific group of adolescents.

They probably feel that society is starting to define them as outcasts who can't fit in. Their feelings must be mixed.

The hell with them; who wants to be part of all of that crap anyway! Parents, teachers, social workers—they are always pushing you around, telling you what to do. I don't give a damn. . . . What the hell is happening to me? I'm getting deeper and deeper into trouble, people are taking control over my life. Maybe I am a loser—how in the hell am I going to end up?

The third level of tuning in relates to the specific phase of work. For instance, an adolescent has been judged delinquent and is about to enter a new residential setting. What are the feelings, questions, and concerns on his mind about this new experience, and what are some of the indirect ways they may be communicated?

If I were in his shoes, I would be scared stiff but determined not to show it. I would wonder about the workers, what kind of people would they be? "How do they treat kids like me? The other kids, what will they be like? Is it going to be hard to break in?"

Many of the general fears people bring to new situations will be present. For example, the fear of the new demands on him and concerns as to whether he will be up to them or not. At the same time, his feelings may include a sense of hope. "Maybe this place will be OK. Maybe these workers and the kids will accept me, make me feel at home. Maybe I can get some help here." The key element in all tuning in is the recognition of ambivalence. A part of the client is moving towards the service, hopeful but guarded. Another part is using past experiences or hearsay about the service, workers, and so on and defensively holding back.

In the tuning in exercise of workers preparing to meet new clients, I have usually observed that the first efforts at tuning in always pick up the resistance, the defensive side of the ambivalence. This often reflects the worker's frustrating past experiences. It is a statement of the worker's concerns that the client will not want help. This can be a self-fulfilling prophecy unless the worker has a sense of the client's potential for change and a belief in that part of the client reaching out to the worker. Otherwise, the worker's pessimistic stereotype of the client will meet head on with the client's pessimistic stereotype of the worker. The tuning in process is a first step in trying to break this self-defeating cycle.

An important objection often raised to the tuning in skill is that the worker may develop a view of the client which is far removed from what the client actually feels and thinks. The worker may then proceed to make sure the client fits the preconceived picture. This is a very real danger if the tuning in is not tentative. In a sense, the key to the successful use of the tuning in skill rests in the worker putting all hunches aside when beginning the engagement. What the worker responds to in the first contacts are the actual "productions" of the client. By this I mean the direct and indirect cues which emerge in conversation with the client.

For example, if the worker in the residential setting has tuned in to the front a tough kid might put up on the first day and some of the concerns which may underline this front, the worker will have to see evidence of this behavior before acting. The worker reaches only tentatively for indirect messages, prepared to have the client share totally different and unexpected responses. Each client is different, and tuning in is an exercise designed to sensitize the worker to potential concerns and feelings. It does not dictate what they must be. The assumption is that having tuned in both to the client's feelings and your own, there is a better chance that your spontaneous reactions to the client's productions will be more helpful. If it simply produces a new stereotype of the client, it will be self-defeating.

RESPONDING DIRECTLY TO INDIRECT CUES

The importance of tuning in during the preliminary phase lies in preparing the worker to hear indirect cues in the first contacts and to respond to these cues with directness. In the first example given in this chapter, the new worker would have demonstrated this skill if she had said in response to the client's question, "Do you have any children?" something like, "No. Why do you ask? Are you wondering if I'm going to be able to understand what it is like to raise kids?"

The advantage of a direct response in that example is that it opens up an area of important conversation which can then deepen the working relationship. A common criticism is that the worker may "lead" the client by putting words into his or her mouth that are not really there. In addition, the argument goes, even if the worker guesses correctly, the client may not be ready to deal with that particular feeling or concern and may react defensively, be overwhelmed, and not come back. Because of this fear, the worker may be cautioned to withhold hunches and to let it come when the client is ready.

I argue in favor of risking more direct responses early in the first contacts. As the working relationship develops, the client is watching the worker, trying to sense what kind of a helping person this is. Indirect communications are employed because the client is not sure of being able to risk communicating directly some of the more difficult and more taboo feelings. Let us consider what happens when the worker responds directly to the indirect cues, for example, by using a skill called *putting the client's feelings into words.* If the worker's guess is "offbase," the client will usually let it be known. Even if the client goes along reluctantly, hesitation in the voice and lack of affective response will tip the worker off to the artificial agreement. The worker can then respond directly to that cue.

One very common example of the way in which clients communicate indirectly is one in which the client, early in the interview with a new worker, says: "I'm glad to see you. My last worker was really terrible!" There is very little else a client can say which strikes more fear into the heart of a new worker. The usual response is to immediately change the subject. Workers claim to be uncomfortable discussing another professional. In my experience, they are particularly quick to change the subject if they secretly agree that the other worker *is* terrible.

The mistake they make is to think the client is really talking about the previous worker. When in early contacts clients refer to other people, such as social workers and doctors who have not helped, it is usually the new worker they are really talking about, only indirectly. A direct response to this indirect cue might sound as follows: "It sounds like you had a hard time with John. Can you tell me what went wrong so that I can understand what you are expecting from me? I'd like to try to make our relationship a positive one." The discussion of the past relationship is cast in the context of the beginning of this new relationship.

The alternative client statement, even harder for the new worker to hear, often sounds like this: "My last worker, he was really terrific!" Once again, if the new worker can handle his or her own feelings, then a direct response to the indirect cue might be the following: "It sounds like you really got close to John. You must really miss him. Can you tell me why you felt he was terrific? I may not be able to be just like him, because I'm a different person, but it would help to know what you are looking for in a worker." Once again, the ensuing discussion moves the worker and the client quickly into the authority theme—the relationship between the giver and taker of help.

Students and workers have said to me: "That sounds great, but how do you say that when you are scared spitless?" I point out that you usually don't say it, the first time, but if you are good, you catch yourself before the end of the interview, or on the next contact. For example, it might sound as follows: "I was thinking about our last conversation, and I wondered if when you were talking about your problems with John, if you were also thinking about what kind of a worker I'm going to be?"

A second objection raised by workers, particularly those with some elements of mandated authority (e.g., financial aid workers, probation officers), is that they fear the client may say something like: "Well, John, he didn't hassle me. When I needed something extra, he came up with the money." Or they might say: "John wasn't all uptight about every beer I had." If the comment about the last worker is an indirect communication related to how the worker is going to enforce his or her authority, then a direct response opens up the discussion for the worker to be clear about how they will operate—what the client can expect from them, and what they will expect from the client. This is an important part of the contracting process, and getting it on the table early can speed up the work.

One parole officer reported a first session with a recently released con in which they got into a battle of wills over whether or not the con's last worker was too tough. The new parole officer tuned in, between sessions, and inquired during the next session: "Were you really asking what kind of a parole officer I'm going to be?" After a long pause, the ex-con said: "The word back at the pen is that you're a real dink." The parole officer asked what that meant, and the ex-con revealed that he had left the penitentiary with a dossier on the parole officer at least as long as the one the worker had on him. The parolee was beginning with a stereotype of the worker which needed to be dealt with early in the work. Even if the parolee did not have information on this particular parole officer, there would have been a stereotype of parole officers to contend with. In reverse, the worker has to be careful of not being so worried about being "conned" that he or she relates to the client as a stereotype as well.

If the client is not ready to pick up on the worker's statement, because of either lack of trust or lack of readiness to share the concern or feelings, then there is still the option of not responding. The worker must allow that room. The important result of the worker's direct responses is not that they deal with the concern *but that the client knows that the worker understands*. The client hears the worker even though the choice is not to respond. The message received is that the worker is prepared to discuss even tough issues (e.g., authority) or painful themes of concern. In effect, these interventions give the client permission to deal with these issues when ready, while simultaneously showing the worker as a feeling, caring, direct person who can see the world through the client's eyes and does not judge harshly.

The research study I conducted into the helping process supports this view.[8] Although findings in the study are still tentative, they shed some interesting light on this question. I was able to infer whether a specific skill, of the twenty-seven studied, contributed to strengthening the worker-client relationship or to effective help or to both. The result of testing the skill of putting the client's feelings into words was that its essential contribution lay in building the working relationship.[9]

Since this process is begun in the early stages of work, I inferred that workers could use the skill to build a relationship. Instead of holding back on affective hunches and direct responses, I believe the worker should err on the side of being slightly too far ahead of the client rather than being too far behind.

Some additional examples of how this looks in action might help at this point. The following comes from a school counselor's first contact with a sixth-grade child, whom she had observed in the class at the request of the teacher. The child is the class clown and does not do his work, and the teacher does not know how to reach him. Using her hunches, the worker began her conversation with the child as follows:

Class was into their art work. I walked over to Steven and asked if he would come and talk with me. He came along easily. He seemed apprehensive and nervous (the indirect cues). I tried to deal with this by saying *I was not a teacher, and I had not come to check up on him.* I explained that his teacher was concerned because he didn't seem to be enjoying class and has asked me to talk to him. My job was to try to help kids who weren't having fun in school or getting much out of their work. After some further conversation about my role, I said that he seemed quite bright and was able to do the work on math with the class. He agreed. I said I also noticed that when he began to fall behind or things got a bit difficult, he seemed to be really frustrated and just gave up. Steven nodded, smiling, and said that I was right, that's how it happened.

The worker had tuned into his original anxiety and so tried in her opening statement to offer some reassurance. She began to demonstrate her understanding by showing Steven that she could sense his underlying frustration which led to his giving up.

Another example of direct reaching comes from a recording of an interview with an unwed mother who had just returned home to her mother with her baby.

I phoned Linda at her work on the day of the appointment to confirm the time. She said she had "forgotten" but would like to come anyway because she had a few things she wanted to talk to me about. I asked if her concerns involved her parents and the situation at home. She said they did.

[Later] As the interview started, Linda sat stirring her coffee, silent, looking down at the cup. I said, "Linda, you sounded rather upset on the phone. Do you want to talk about the things that are really happening at home?" Linda started to cry and said, with a lot of emotion, "I'm breaking up my parents' marriage. They are fighting all the time. My father is screaming and swearing at both me and the baby and then at my mother."

The worker had tuned into the difficult time the family and Linda were having during her first days at home. She "reached" for this on the phone and then did so again in response to the client's nonverbal clue at the start of the interview.

The worker's signal to Linda allowed the client to move directly into a painful area of discussion. I believe the client is often ready early in the contacts to discuss tough issues, explore taboo subjects, and even deal with the worker-client relationship if only the worker will give the invitation. Workers have said in consultation sessions that they often hesitate because they are not sure *if they* are ready. It is the worker's own ambivalence about exploring an area of work which can produce the block. In the guise of protecting the client, workers are really protecting themselves. As one worker put it, "I don't reach directly for those cues early in the work, because I'm afraid the client may take up my invitation. What will I do with all that feeling if I get it?" This excellent question is explored in more detail in later chapters.

AGENCY RECORDS AND REFERRAL REPORTS

Many helping contacts involve clients who have had prior contact with the particular setting or with other professionals. The agency file system may contain detailed recording on past experiences or a report from an intake worker. Referrals from other professionals often include descriptions of the client, family, problems, and past history. Depending upon how it is used, this prior information can be helpful or can itself become a block to the work.

On the positive side, information about the client may help the worker to develop the preliminary empathy needed to prepare for the first session. A review of past experiences with workers or a report of the intake conversation may reveal potential themes of concern to which the worker can be alert. Understanding the recent strains which have brought the client to the attention of the worker may help in developing a feel for the emotional state to be expected in early sessions. A summary of past experiences may yield insight into the client's attitude towards helping professionals. If the records reveal that the going has been rough, the worker may want to plan how to change the client's stereotype of workers.

On the other hand, if the prior information is used by the worker to develop a stereotype of the client, then the preparatory work can block the development of a working relationship. If the worker begins a contact with, for example, a natural parent in a child welfare setting believing that the client is defensive, resistant, hostile, and not open to help, then this "mind set" may be the start of a self-fulfilling prophecy. One stereotype (the worker's) tries to deal with another stereotype (the client's), and no real communication takes place.

At times, a whole office develops a stereotype of particular, long-term clients, which is quickly passed along informally. For example, the new worker discovers that he or she was given the toughest case in the office, with the following comment from colleagues: "You have the Robinson family? Good luck!"

This can be the start of a self-fulfilling prophecy, or the beginning of the new worker's tuning in to the state of the relationship between the family and this office.

It is helpful to remember that a client described in a report is constantly acting and reacting to systems, including the worker who wrote the report. It is simply not possible to know clients without understanding them in terms of this process. Their actions need to be viewed in relation to the actions of others. I have found it interesting to sit in on case conferences where a client is being discussed. The helping professional will report on a home visit or a contact, describe the client in some detail, review that past history, and then offer a diagnosis of the problem, a prognosis, and a proposal for treatment. If the worker reports that the client was defensive or hostile, this is discussed.

The change in the conversation is quite striking if I suggest we shift from talking about the client as an entity, to the details of the interview between the worker and the client. I ask the worker to describe how the interview began, what was said to the client, and how the client responded. As the detailed description continues, the staff members begin to get a feeling of the client's interaction with this worker. The worker's and client's feelings are explored in the process, and the not-too-surprising fact is that the actions of the client are often quite explainable in relation to the worker's efforts. For example, the worker sensed the underlying resistance but did not respond by directly exploring it. Perhaps the worker read a previous report on the client and began the interview expecting trouble—thereby bringing it about. The worker's own feelings may have made empathy with the client's struggle difficult, thus closing off openings for work.

The end result of such discussion, even when the worker had been skillful in the first interview, is the emergence of a client who is more multidimensional than at first seemed. One sees ambivalence rather than just defensiveness. In addition to the anger, one can sense the underlying hurt, distrust, and bitterness that may have resulted from poor past experiences with professionals. The important point is that what might have seemed like a *hopeless* case changes under our hands to a *hard* case with some important openings for work.

If the worker using prior record material or referral material can keep in mind not only the tentativeness of the information but also the need to see the client in interaction rather than as a static entity, then this material can be helpful in the preparation process. As will be seen in the next chapter on beginnings, the important point is that as the first interview begins, the worker needs to clear all of these facts, opinions, and even the worker's own tentative tuning in guesses from the mind. The preparatory work has helped to get ready; now skill will be demonstrated in responding not to what was expected but to the actual productions of the client.

NOTES

1. Jessie Taft, "Time as the Medium of the Helping Process," *Jewish Social Service Quarterly* 26 (December 1949):230-43.

2. William Schwartz, "On the Use of Groups in Social Work Practice," in *The Practice of Group Work,* ed. William Schwartz and Serapio Zalba (New York: Columbia University Press, 1971), pp. 3-24.

3. The skills of tuning in and responding directly to indirect cues have been described by Schwartz in some detail. For example, see William Schwartz, "Between Client and System: The Mediating Function," in *Theories of Social Work with Groups,* eds. Robert R. Roberts and Helen Northen (New York: Columbia University Press, 1976), pp. 186-88.

4. For previous publications by this author on this subject, see Lawrence Shulman, *A Casebook of Social Work with Groups: The Mediating Model* (New York: Council on Social Work Education, 1968); Lawrence Shulman, "Social Work Still: The Anatomy of a Helping Act," in *Social Work Practice, 1969* (New York: Columbia University Press, 1969), pp. 29-48.

5. For an elaboration of the idea of communication as a "transmission," see Jurgen Reusch, *Disturbed Communications* (New York: W.W. Norton and Co., 1957).

6. Lawrence Shulman and William Buchan, *The Impact of the Family Physician's Communication, Relationship and Technical Skills on Patient Compliance, Satisfaction, Reassurance, Comprehension and Improvement* (Vancouver: School of Social Work, University of British Columbia, 1982).

7. Lloyd Setleis, "How Should We Act? How Should We Be?" *Journal of Social Work Process* 35 (1967):139-58.

8. Throughout the course of the text I have integrated findings from this study. The reader should note that these findings are tentative, and an early review of the summary of the research design contained in the Appendix is recommended. As described in the Introduction, the study was of the associations between the use of twenty-seven skills and the development of effective working relationships as well as the helpfulness of workers. Client perception measures were used to obtain data on these variables. Reliability and validity testing was undertaken on these instruments (see Appendix); however, they are still viewed as being in an embryonic stage. The study was undertaken in two child welfare agencies with 118 workers and 1,784 clients participating. Findings should be

considered in light of the limitations outlined in the summary of the research methodology.

9. Lawrence Shulman, "A Study of Practice Skills," *Social Work* 23 (July 1978):278.

CHAPTER 3

Beginnings and the Contracting Skills

During a first interview, a twenty-five-year-old client put his social worker through an indirect test to see if she would be honest with him. The worker, responding directly to the indirect cues, asked, "Did I pass?" After acknowledging that she had passed, the client said, "I had to see where we stand. The first meeting is really important, you know."

First meetings in all helping relationships are important. If handled well, they can lay a foundation for productive work and begin the process of strengthening the working relationship between client and worker. If handled badly, they can turn the client away from the service offered. This chapter explores the special dynamics associated with new relationships. A set of skills needed to begin the contracting process is described and illustrated. Examples included illustrations of contracting with children and with clients who have been judged resistant or difficult to work with. In addition, the contracting skills of defining mutual expectations are discussed. Finally, skills in the beginning phase, which help to strengthen the early working relationship, are identified.

THE DYNAMICS OF NEW RELATIONSHIPS

All new relationships, particularly those with people in authority, begin somewhat tentatively. Clients perceive workers as "authority people" with power to influence them and often bring with them a fund of past experiences or stereotypes of helping professionals passed on by friends or family. So the first sessions are partly an effort to explore the realities of the situation. Encounters with people in authority usually involve risks, and clients will be careful to test the new situation before they expose themselves.

Ambivalent feelings will be present in any new situation. The client's doubts about adequacy and competency are heightened as are fear of the worker's expectations. The other side of the ambivalence is hope of receiving help. Depending upon the individual and the helping context, one side of the ambivalence may be stronger than the other.

The two major questions on the client's mind are: "What is this going to be all about?" and "What kind of worker is this?" The urgency of these questions stems from the client's fear of the demands to be made. People in authority often have hidden agendas, and the client may fear the worker may try to change him or her. The client's actions will be affected by this suspicion until the two questions are answered. Fear of feelings of dependency will be present until the client can see the helping person, not in the imagined role as the all-powerful authority, but as someone with skills to help the client work on the client's own concerns.

In the illustrative interview which follows, some of the concerns of the beginning phase are evident in the client's indirect communication. The worker heightens the feelings of concern by not addressing the questions of the purpose of the session and the role of the worker. The setting is a hospital, and the patient a forty-three-year-old woman with three young children. Although laboratory tests have been negative, persistence of symptoms necessitated exploratory surgery and a possible diagnosis of cervical disc disease. Referral to the social worker was made because a long convalescence would be required and house duties and child care would be impossible. In his written introduction to the recording of the interview, the worker described his purpose as exploring after-care possibilities and determining if homemaker or alternative services might be necessary.

WORKER: Good day, Mrs. Tunney. I'm Mr. Franks from the social service department. Your doctor asked me to visit you and to see in what way we could be of help.

PATIENT: Is this a habit? Do you visit all the patients or only me? (She was smiling, but seemed anxious.)

WORKER: We interview patients whenever it seems to be indicated, when there is such a medical request.

The patient was asking: What's this all about? and expressing a natural anxiety.

She might be wondering but not saying, "Oh my God! It must be more serious than they told me." The worker's response does not answer this question and does little to address the concern. Instead of clarifying the reasons for the referral, such as concern over the possible need for homemaking services, the patient is left in the dark. She responds with an unusually direct demand.

PATIENT: All right, in what way do you think you can help me? I am in the hospital for the second day. My children are being looked after by their father. Most probably I will be operated on in the near future. You know this started because I felt I had arthritis. I had difficulty in moving my hands and fingers, so I decided to come here and see what I really have. (Occasionally she works on her crocheting while she speaks.)

WORKER: I would like to ask a few questions, Mrs. Tunney. But first, tell me, do you feel more comfortable talking while you are working?

PATIENT: Perhaps, I always do something.... I have to....

Once again the worker has not responded to a direct question. The worker is proceeding according to his agenda, conducting a fact-gathering interview. The client is left out of the process. As long as the patient is unclear why this worker is talking to her and what his purpose and role as a social worker are, she will be unable to use him effectively. The client will experience the interview as being "acted on" by the worker. Her sense of dependency will be heightened, and her fears of intrusion into her personal life increased. She will be uncertain of what to say because she has no framework for weighing her responses. The interview continued:

WORKER: You said, Mrs. Tunney, that your husband is taking care of the children. If I am correct, you have three. Is that right?

PATIENT: Yes, but the eight-year-old is a very hard one. He cannot be left alone. Fortunately, my husband's superiors are understanding people, and he can take off time whenever he needs to ... and now he needs it. Usually, he is away on trips, and sometimes he is gone for weeks.

WORKER: I understand your husband is in the army. In what capacity?

It is my guess that the client might be thinking at this point, "Why do you want to know?" The worker's questions are designed to elicit family information for the worker's study. However, the client must wonder how this information is meant to help her. Clients do not usually ask why the worker wants to know. That is not polite in our society. However, as long as the doubt persists, the suspicion and tension will remain.

The interview continued with the worker asking questions about how the pain began, how the husband helped out at home, where the patient was born, and if she had family in this country. The patient's responses became shorter and consisted of direct answers to the worker's questions. When the worker suggested meeting with the husband and the children "to get a clearer picture of how we could be helpful," the client agreed and said, "Jeez! Do you do this for all of the patients?"

The worker's summary of the first interview reported, "Inappropriate, almost childish, smiling and expressions of distress. Distress is covered by rigid attitudes and a compulsive personality. There are 'rules' and consequently a role distribution which for some reason she would not 'negotiate.' "

Another interpretation of the "childish smiling and expressions of distress" would be as signals of her feelings about the interview. These feelings can be expressed in many indirect forms. The new boy at the residential institution who acts out his anxiety by immediately breaking rules and picking fights is one example. The adolescent whose total vocabulary during a first interview consists of the words "yes" and "no" and the natural parent who responds with open hostility are others. When the worker interprets the behaviors as reflecting the client as a fixed entity rather than in dynamic interaction with the worker, the initial behavior often becomes part of a stereotyped view of the client initiating an endless cycle.

There are a number of factors which lead workers into first contacts such as this one. First, the medical paradigm itself, borrowed from the physicians, suggests a four-stage approach to conceptualizing practice. In this model, one studies the client, develops a diagnosis, plans treatment, and then evaluates the results. While this systematic approach has made important contributions to advancing our practice, the emphasis on a first stage of study encourages some workers to see initial interviews as fact-gathering exercises in which the client's function is to provide information. This can lead to an interview somewhat like the extreme example described earlier.

This discussion of the medical paradigm and the three-step process of study, diagnosis, and treatment, always provokes some anxiety on the part of students who may be placed in fieldwork agencies in which this format for a first interview is required. In some situations, workers must complete a detailed intake form which requires them to obtain a "psychosocial history" and then prompts them to provide an initial diagnosis. In some settings, a checklist is provided to guide the worker's responses. These students often ask: "How can I conduct a first interview in the way you described if I'm expected to complete this form?"

Examination of these forms and detailed analyses of such first sessions often reveals the following. First, while protesting the rigidity of the structure, the worker often feels much more comfortable having the form to guide the first interview. The use of the form maintains control in the hands of the worker, allows for predictability in the first session, and allows the worker time to become comfortable. Of course, the opposite is often true for the client.

A second observation, is that with very little effort on the part of the worker, it is possible to design the first interview to both contract with the client, try to help the client feel more at ease, *and* obtain the required information. For example, a worker could say: "There are a number of questions I need to ask you to obtain information for our files, but before I do so, I thought I would explain how I might help, and find out what's on your mind." In example after example, students discovered that this preliminary discussion often yielded much of the information they needed to obtain, only it was provided in an order which fit the client's sense of urgency, instead of the worker's. Time could be left in the second half of the interview for covering missing information by going through the form. The client was often ready to provide the data at that point, especially if the worker explained why it was required (e.g., medical insurance, obtaining a more complete understanding of the families' health experiences).

While students could see how they can change the structure of the interview and still work within the framework provided by their setting, they still had to face

the problem of the diagnosis. Even this could be overcome if one thought of diagnosis as a description of the state of the relationship between the client and the various systems to be negotiated, as well as an assessment of the client's sense of strength and readiness to cope with the problem. Diagnosis could be seen dynamically as something which changed and shifted, often moment to moment, as opposed to a fixed description of a client's "problems." Thus, except in exceptionally rigid settings, students and new workers could adapt more flexible structures for first interviews and diagnosis while still working within the framework of the setting.

A second factor which can contribute to the worker's reluctance to be direct about purpose is the notion that one must "build a relationship" before the work begins. In the model described thus far, the term *working relationship* has been used. The hypothesis advanced now is that the working relationship will develop only after the purpose of the encounter has been clarified and the worker's role explicitly described. A finding of my research project on helping skills was that the skill of clarifying role contributed to developing a positive relationship between worker and client.[1]

A third factor is the worker's tendency to be embarrassed about either the client's problem or the worker's intentions. Having a problem in our society has become identified with weakness and dependency. Workers sometimes feel uncomfortable about mentioning this. Some of the client's difficulties such as a physical or mental handicap are considered so difficult to discuss directly that workers have invented euphemisms to describe them. One group for teenage unwed mothers met for four sessions during which no mention was made of their pregnancy, while their midsections grew with each passing week. Children having great difficulty in school have been brought together by school counselors in "activity groups" for after-school fun activities with no mention of why they were selected. They are not usually fooled, since they all know they are considered to be "the dummies." The worker is embarrassed about mentioning the problem, and so the client gets a message which reinforces reluctance to discuss painful areas.

When workers begin their sessions with hidden agendas, they are equally ill at ease about making a direct statement of purpose. If a worker believes the client's problem is all figured out and the task is now to proceed to change the client's behavior, then reluctance to be direct is understandable.

A final factor leading to difficulty in being direct is our use of professional jargon. When I graduated with a professional degree in social work, my mother asked me at a dinner in my honor, "Now that you're a social worker, tell me, what do you do?" I replied, "I work with people to enhance their social functioning, to facilitate their growth, and to strengthen their egos." She smiled at me and said, "But what do you *do?*"

In fact, I was unclear about how to articulate my professional function. What made it worse was that my fellow graduates appeared to be clear about theirs. I thought, desperately, that perhaps I had missed a key lecture or had not completed a key reading. In reality, all the helping professions have had trouble with direct, functional statements and have obscured this confusion with jargon. If, in training sessions with professionals, I restrict their use of jargon and insist that they describe what they have to offer me as a client in simple, clear sentences, they usually find it difficult to do so. The more

ingenious try to avoid the difficulty by asking me, the client, "What is it that you want?"

In the section which follows, a model is presented which attempts to describe a way in which a first session can be used to clarify purpose and professional role directly and simply, without jargon or embarrassment.

CONTRACTING IN FIRST SESSIONS

The first sessions described in this book take place in the context of an agency or institution. Although many of these concepts of helping are equally relevant to private practice situations, my assumption is that the work takes place in an agency setting. The effect of the context of practice is particularly important in the contracting phase and so needs to be explored.

Social workers, nurses, child care workers, counselors, parole officers, and the like usually work for an agency or institution. The setting is more than a convenient place for help to take place. It has a task in society which means it has a stake in the proceedings. In the societal distribution of tasks, each setting deals with some area of particular concern. The hospital is concerned with the health of patients, the school with the education of students, the family agency with family functioning, the parole agency with assisting released prisoners to function in the outside world, and so on. These tasks are important and affect the helping person's actions.

In the chapter on underlying assumptions, I identified the pressing life tasks that face clients. These included dealing with school, family, work, the welfare or medical systems, and so on. The client sees successfully dealing with these tasks as the immediate necessity. In each case, we were able to describe some life tasks which might be important to the client.

It is these two sets of tasks, that of the agency and of the client, that Schwartz considers in developing the contracting concept.

> The convergence of these two sets of tasks— those of the clients and those of the agency— creates the terms of the *contract* that is made between the client group and the agency. This contract, openly reflecting both stakes, provides the frame of reference for the work that follows, and for understanding when the work is in process, when it is being evaded, and when it is finished.[2]

In the beginning phase of work, the worker's function is one of mediation in searching for the connection between these two sets of tasks. Although there may be many obstacles blocking the mutual interests of the setting and the client (e.g., the authority aspect of the function of the parole board), the worker's search is for the elusive "common ground."

Three critical skills in this phase of work described by Schwartz, are those of *clarifying purpose, clarifying role, and reaching for client feedback* (the client's perception of his or her stake in the process).[3] Although these skills are central to all beginning engagements, there are many variations in their implementation. For example, variant elements are introduced by the setting. The issue of authority, whether the client is voluntary or the worker makes the first contact, can also introduce variations. These skills are described in detail in this section and illustrated in different contexts, and the results of my research on their effect reported.

Given the dynamics of new relationships described earlier in this chapter, the worker must attempt to clarify the purpose of the meeting by a simple, nonjargonized, and direct statement. This statement should openly reflect both the stake of the setting and the possible stake of the client. For example, in the hospital interview described earlier, one way (and there can be many variations) the worker might have begun is, "My name is Mr. Franks and I am a social worker from the social services department. Your doctor asked me to see you to determine if there was any way I could help with some of the difficulties you might be facing in taking care of your children or your home while you're recovering from the operation. I know that can be a difficult time, and I would like to help, if you wish. I would like to discuss this with you to see if you want some help for these problems or any other worries you might have about the operation or your hospital stay."

Such a simple statement of purpose sets the stage for the discussion which follows. The client does not have to test to find out why the worker is there. The purpose of the visit is to discuss the service and to see how that fits with what the client feels she needs. With this simple framework in place, the client's energies can be involved in examining areas of possible work. With a clear boundary in place, the client does not have to worry about what the worker is there for. Conversation and the questions of the worker which follow should be related to this task, a mutual exploration of areas of potential service.

The worker also needs to be prepared for the client's inevitable question about how the worker can help. In this example, clarifying the worker's role might consist of spelling out a number of possible forms of assistance. For example: "I can help you examine what you may be facing when you return home, and if you think you need some help, I can connect you to some homemaking resources in the community." Another form could be in relation to the family: "If you're worried about your husband's ability to help at this time, I can meet with the two of you and try to sort this out," or, in relation to the hospital and the illness, "when you're in a big, busy hospital like this, you sometimes have questions and concerns about your illness, medication, and the operation which are not always answered; if you do, you can share these with me and I can see if I can get the staff's attention so that they can help out, or, perhaps I can do so myself."

Each of these simple statements defines a potential service the client may wish to use immediately or at some future date. They may seem overly simple, but for a troubled patient on the ward, these simple statements provide orientation to services of which she may simply not be aware.

Contracting is a negotiating period in which both the client and the worker are involved. The skill of reaching for client feedback is essential. In the last example, this skill might sound like this: "Are any of these of concern to you, and would you like to discuss how I might help?" It is quite possible that in the feedback stage the client may raise issues which were not part of the worker's tuning in process. The agenda for work can expand. The only limitation is that the area of service offered is bounded by the tasks of the setting. The worker cannot offer services which are not relevant to those tasks. For example, this social worker would not get involved in long-term marital counseling with this woman and her husband, even if early contacts indicated that this was needed. Instead, he might make a referral to an appropriate family counseling agency.

The boundaries to the work created by the agency service and the need of the client help the worker to focus and also relieve the client's anxiety that possibly private areas may be intruded on. Contracts are negotiated continuously and can be openly changed as the work proceeds. Often a client, not fully trusting the worker, will only risk "near problems" in the early interviews. When the working relationship strengthens, areas of concern which were not part of the initial agreement may enter the working contract.

The procedure is not mechanistic; variations in the first sessions are often required. The helping person who is contacted by a client for help may begin the first interview by indicating a wish to understand what brought the client to the agency, to know what is on the client's mind. As the client shares concerns, the worker tries to connect these to potential service areas and to explain available help. The important point is not the order of skill use, but the fact that the contracting is started, that it be an open process, and that both parties are involved. Some illustrations of statements of purpose and role from a range of settings might help at this point.

Marriage Counselor

"Living together over a long period of time can be tough—with many ups and downs. You have been describing a crisis in your marriage, which I am sure is a frightening time. It's also an opportunity for change, perhaps to make a new marriage out of the one you already have. One of the ways I may be able to help is by assisting both of you to talk and listen to each other about the problems you are having. I can help you tell each other how you are feeling, try to help you figure out how you get into trouble, and do some thinking about what each of you can do to strengthen the relationship. I'll throw in some of my own ideas about living together as we work, and some of these may be helpful."

School Counselor

"Your teacher told me you were having trouble in her class and that she thought school was not much fun for you. My job at the school is to meet with kids like you to see if we can figure out, together, what's going wrong for you at school and to see if there are things we can do to make it better. How about it, how is school for you right now?" After some discussion of the problems, the worker tried to define her role. "If you really feel Mrs. T. [the teacher] is down on you, maybe I could talk to her a bit about how you feel and help her understand that it makes it harder for you to work. With so many kids, she may just not understand that you feel that way."

Child Care Worker

(First contact with new resident) "I thought I should tell you what I do around here so if there is any way I can help, you can let me know. Part of my job is seeing that things run smoothly at the house, clean up after meals, etc., but I'm also interested in how you guys are making out. For example, right now, you're new to the house and that can be a scary time; if there is some way I can help you get connected with the other staff, the kids, or to answer any of your questions about the place, I'd be happy to." In the course of the conversation, other functions can be clarified. "Sometimes you may have troubles on your mind and you need someone to talk to about them. For example, if it's not going well at school, or you're having problems with the guys in

the house or your family when you visit, or you're mad at the staff or the rules— I'll be around to listen to your troubles, if you want me to, and to try to help you figure out how you might handle them."

Nurse

(To a new patient on the ward) "Coming into a hospital with an illness can be a very stressful time. There are so many people to deal with, questions you may have about the ward routine or your illness, and problems getting settled in. If I can help in any way, I would like to. For example, if you're feeling down about what's going on and you need someone to talk to about it, you can call on me. If you're not sure what's going on with your doctor or the tests or the medicine, I might be able to give you some answers or find someone who can. In addition, if your family is concerned about what's happening, I could talk to them about it."

Child Welfare Worker

(With a young unmarried mother who is rejected by her family) "I know it's tough when you're young, pregnant, and feeling very alone. We could meet each week and talk about some of the things on your mind right now. Perhaps I can help you think them through and figure out some answers to some of your concerns. Such as, if you're having trouble with your parents or your boyfriend, or if you're trying hard to decide whether you can make it if you keep the baby or if you need to give the baby up. How about it, are some of these things on your mind right now?"

These illustrations show how contracting can be fashioned to reflect the particular service of the setting and possible needs of the specific clients. This is where the tuning in process can be helpful. In my research project on the helping process, the skill of clarifying role was significantly related to developing a positive working relationship with the client. This finding supported the idea that early clarification of role can free the client's energy for work. Similar findings on the importance of clarifying mutual role expectations were reported by Charles Garvin in his study of social work groups.[4]

In my study, the skill of reaching for feedback about purpose had a significant relationship to the worker's ability to be helpful.[5] This supports the concept that the areas of work in which the worker can be most effective are those in which the client can perceive some stake.

CONTRACTING OVER TIME

The discussion thus far is focused on the initial contact with the client and the beginning of the contracting process. In reality, the contracting process takes place over time with both the worker and client deepening their understanding of the content to be covered and of the expectations each can have of the other. For example, clients often share "near problems" in the early sessions as a way of testing a worker. If the worker deals with these in a way which helps the client to lower defenses, then more serious (and often frightening) themes may emerge. For the worker's part, even a clearly stated description of purpose and role may not be heard nor remembered by a client overwhelmed with anxiety on a first session. Thus, contracting should be understood as a process which, in some ways, may continue throughout the life of the relationship.

The worker can also feel overwhelmed in a first session, and as a result, miss or skip over clues to crucial issues related to contracting. In the following example, a client uses the device described earlier of referring to a former helping professional who was not helpful as an indirect cue to her concerns about this new worker. The strength of her feelings frightens the worker, a student with some counseling experience, who ducks the issue. The client also raises her past suicide attempts, further upsetting the student. The student starts to catch her mistakes at the end of the first session and then continues to clarify the contracting at the start of her second meeting.

Right at the beginning of our first session, Mary indicated that she had been to see a psychiatrist over a year ago, shortly after her husband had left her. When I asked if that experience had been helpful she described at length how terrible it had been. She stated laughingly that if she was violent she would like to go and punch him out right now. I failed to respond to this message by relating it to me, and instead, asked her to elaborate.

MARY: He told me more or less that I was just feeling sorry for myself and that the relationship had ended, and that I had to accept it and get on with my life. I knew I was feeling sorry for myself, but I couldn't help it. I didn't need him to tell me what I already knew. I just wanted an assist—not for him to solve my problems. He wanted to give me pills but I wouldn't take them. I was afraid enough of myself that I would do something stupid—like I have . . .

WORKER: Like you have?

MARY: Ya, I'ver tried to commit suicide a few times—a number of times—lots of times (pause—a strange laugh)—and one of these days I'm going to succeed.

WORKER: Have you been thinking of suicide lately?

MARY: (silence) Ya, that's a good question. I think I hit the age of twelve and I really felt like I was 195 in my mind.

The client continued to talk indirectly about suicide, describing how she wasn't afraid to die, how nobody would miss her, and so on. The worker changed the subject by picking up on the problems the client faced. The worker described her feelings as follows:

I felt that Mary was trying to manipulate me into feeling sorry for her and I was angry at her for doing this. I also felt a little bit nervous at what I'd gotten myself into—this was my first client at field placement number three (my first two did not work out). All I needed was someone to commit suicide on me. I wasn't able to empathize with Mary since I was caught up with my own feelings.

I had heard her message loud and clear that she was desperate for help, however, I didn't let her know that I'd heard or that I was prepared to help. I didn't realize at the time this was her way of saying: "Hey, are you sure you can handle me?" Although I didn't reassure her at the beginning that I was prepared to take her on, because I was feeling ambivalent myself, I had my opportunity at the end of the interview.

As we were leaving at the end of the session, Mary suddenly stated: "You know I once called a crisis centre and told the person I felt like killing myself. They told me I might as well go ahead and do it."

WORKER: I'm wondering if you are worried that I might tell you something like that. I guess you're worried about if I'm going to be able to help you. You know, I can't decide for you if you want to live or die—that's something only you can decide. But if you want to live, I can help you to begin sorting through some of your problems, one step at a time. I don't have any magic cures to help you feel better—I wish I did because I know you're feeling pretty low right now. It'll take lots of hard work for both of us. I'll try my hardest if you want to continue. (long silence).

MARY: Ya, I guess that's fair. At least I can talk to you.

I had some anxieties about whether or not Mary would show up the following week. She was ten minutes late and I was on pins and needles thinking the worst had happened. I couldn't believe how relieved I felt when she finally arrived. I tried to own up to my mistake, declare myself as human, and return to some of Mary's concerns I had missed last week.

WORKER: Mary, you know I was going over the tape of last week's session and I think a lot of what you were trying to tell me went right over my head. It seems like you were quite worried that you wouldn't be able to get the kind of help you needed. Who wouldn't be after the experience you had with the psychiatrist? I guess I first want to let you know that I am going to make mistakes too and I'm probably going to say things that you don't agree with, so you're going to have to let me know if you feel I've screwed up. It'll be hard, but please don't keep it in.

MARY: Well, at least you seem real and I'm glad you're not a guy. I didn't trust him. It was all a big game of verbal semantics with him trying to guess what I was thinking and feeling and me going along with him, because I wanted to give the right answers, I wanted him to like me. I didn't realize it at the time.

WORKER: Do you find it hard to say things sometimes, because you're afraid the person won't like you?

MARY: Ya, I think I do that, especially with men.

When I asked her to elaborate she described her relationship with men, her fear of making demands, how she gets angry and "starts acting like a bitch." When I asked if that was what was happening with her current boyfriend right now, she elaborated in some detail, and we spent the remainder of the session on this theme.

The contracting process is not completed in this example. Both worker and client will have to come back to discussions of both their way of working, as well as expansions of the content (themes of concern) of their work. The worker has laid the groundwork for the discussion of their process by letting the client know she will make mistakes and that it is the client's responsibility to help keep her honest. The worker's job will be to try to create the conditions which will help the client to do just that.

The discussion thus far has described contracting work with clients who appear open to help or who have sought it out. What about work with clients who are resistant? How can you find common ground when the client appears defensive and not open to your intervention? How can you contract with a client when you carry a function which includes authority over the client's life (e.g., parole, protection in child welfare)? The next section explores this variation on the contract theme. The analysis of first sessions expands to include discussion of the skills required to begin to strengthen the working relationship.

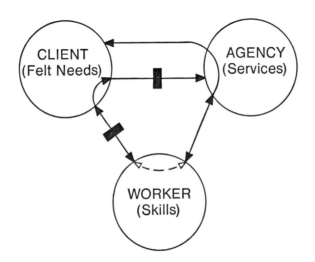

CONTRACTING WITH RESISTANT CLIENTS

All clients bring some ambivalence towards taking help into the first interview. Resistance to the worker may be very strong for some clients, because of either their past experiences with professionals or their particular concerns or the problems created by the authority of the helping person. It may be expressed passively, as for example by an apathetic response during the interview, or by open hostility. Whatever the specific reasons or the form of expression, an obstacle sits squarely on the line between worker and client (see diagram). Therefore, the worker's efforts to turn the client towards the service must be integrated with efforts to deal with this obstacle.

The first step in this process begins with the worker honestly facing his or her own feelings about the engagement. Workers are human, and the thought of meeting a new client who does not appear to want help or who has a reputation for being hostile (or one whom the worker anticipates may be hostile) can cause the worker to hold back on efforts to reach for the client. Workers experience difficulty in offering help in the face of possible rejection. In this situation the worker's offer of service contains the same elements of ambivalence as the client's attitude towards taking help. This can easily lead to a self-fulfilling prophecy where the first engagement breaks down.

The skills of beginning discussion with a resistant client are the same as those described earlier: clarifying purpose, clarifying role, and reaching for feedback. A negotiating process is taking place, but this time the potential obstacles to a working relationship must be part of discussion. In effect, the worker is asking the client if they can work together in spite of the barriers that may block their efforts. Often, when an obstacle has been identified and explored, the client and the worker are free to move past it into a deepening relationship.

To illustrate how this might work, let us take an example of a first session in a child welfare agency. The client, Mr. Gregory, is twenty-five-years-old. He has recently separated from his wife. She has applied to place their three children in temporary care of the agency. Mr. Gregory has a long record with the agency in which different workers have consistently characterized him as hostile and defensive. This worker described the purpose of her first interview as informing him of his legal rights, describing the meaning of the agency's intervention, having him sign consent forms, and seeing if some help could be offered to him for his own concerns. The interview began with the worker's efforts to clarify purpose.

WORKER: You know that your wife has signed forms to place your children under the care of this agency. I wanted to meet with you to have you sign agreements, but before that, to discuss what this means for you and your children. I know it can be an upsetting time,

and I thought you might also have things on your mind you want to discuss.

MR. GREGORY: For how long are my kids going to be in care?

The worker's opening statement clarified the purpose of the interview, placing a strong emphasis on the offer of service to the client—not just as someone called in to sign forms, but as someone with feelings and concerns in his own right. In a sense, her direct reaching for him as a client represents a form of skill called *making a demand for work*. This is discussed in some detail in the next chapter, but in the present context it means the worker is gently attempting to involve the client actively in the engagement. The demand is synthesized with the worker's ability to express some genuine *empathy* with the client's situation. This is demonstrated in the sentence, "I know it can be an upsetting time. . . ." (The use of empathic skills is also discussed in detail in the next chapter.) In the client's response we see a shift back to the children—a polite way for him to refuse her offer. The interview continued with the worker responding to the direct question but also refusing to be put off by the client's first refusal.

WORKER: Your wife has signed forms for six months. That means that we are responsible to look after your children for that time, but with twenty-four-hours notice you or your wife can have your children home at any time. If you wish, after six months, the time can be extended.

MR. GREGORY: It's a long time for the kids.

WORKER: Yes, it is *and for you also.*

MR. GREGORY: Yah, I haven't seen them yet, but I hear they're doing fine.

WORKER: Would you like to see them?

MR. GREGORY: I thought I wasn't allowed to.

WORKER: Sure you are. You have the right to see your children whenever you wish.

MR. GREGORY: I was told that it would upset the kids, especially Alan, to see me, so it would be better not to.

WORKER: Sure it will upset him. It will upset you, too. It's hard to see someone you love and can't be with.

The worker's continued "empathic demand" is contained in the phrase "and for you also." In response, the client began to explore the visiting issue. The worker continued her emphasis on his feelings with the comment, "It will upset you, too. It's hard to see someone you love and can't be with." This persistence resulted in his beginning to explore the difficult feelings surrounding visiting. In the next segment, the worker opened up this area by using the skill of *putting the client's feelings into words.* She used her "tuning in" preparation to articulate the underlying difficulty clients face in visiting children who have been placed in care.

MR. GREGORY: Yah, Alan has been in care before, and he's confused and sad.

WORKER: *Yes, that must make it hard on you to see him.*

MR. GREGORY: Yah. Like what do I say to him?

WORKER: Like when he asks "when do I come home?"

MR. GREGORY: Well, yah.

WORKER: What do you say?

MR. GREGORY: Oh, I change the subject and cheer him up.

WORKER: Does it work?

MR. GREGORY: Not really.

WORKER: What do you want to say?

MR. GREGORY: Well, I don't know when he's coming home.

WORKER: I guess that hurts you.

MR. GREGORY: Well, kids don't understand.

WORKER: Have you tried telling him?

MR. GREGORY: No, not really.

WORKER: I think it's hard to tell your child you don't know when he's coming home, but clearing that up might make it easier for you both once it's discussed.

MR. GREGORY: Yah, I won't feel like I'm holding out. But I won't be seeing him until he comes to my wife on the weekend. Can I do that?

The worker's persistent and genuine concern with *his feelings* caused the client to begin to open up and deal with a real concern. When she responded to his comment, "Like what do I say to him?" by saying "Like when he asks, 'When do I come home?' " she effectively opened the door for him to explore one of the roughest issues facing parents who place children in care, the guilt they feel which often results in difficulty in visiting. Even in these first few minutes the relationship has opened up, disturbing the client. Before he can allow himself to go further, he had to clarify how things stand between them. The next excerpt demonstrates how this discussion emerged.

WORKER: Whatever visiting arrangements you want to make will be done. I have to know in advance to help plan and to know where he is, since he's our responsibility. Seeing him at your wife's place is fine if your wife wants that.

MR. GREGORY: I want to know something. Are you going to be my social worker? I know you see my wife and you help her. So how does it work? Are you are her side or mine or do I get another social worker?

The directness of the client, which workers in the past may have confused with aggressiveness, is apparent. It is interesting to consider the effect of this question on the worker. This interview was analyzed in a videotaped discussion between William Schwartz and a group of social work students and professional workers.[6] When asked about her reactions to the client's question, the worker admitted to being taken aback and feeling put on the spot by his assertiveness. Clients often ask questions or make statements that throw a worker off balance. This worker responded to her own feelings of defensiveness by delivering a substantial lecture which contrasts with her earlier terse reactions.

> **WORKER:** I'm on no one's side. I try to help your wife with what's on her mind. I'm here to help you with whatever you want. I do this so you can both come to the point of finally making a decision about your children — do you want them home? If yes, when and how many of them? Whatever we discuss is confidential, and the same goes for your wife and me. When the two of you will make decisions that will affect each other, we'll do it together. Then I won't take sides but try to help the two of you talk to each other and work together on arriving at a decision. (Quiet)

The silence which followed this speech was important, since it contained a message for the worker. The client was probably confused by the words and felt that he really was not getting an answer to his question. In the next segment the worker is seen demonstrating an important skill called *reaching inside of silences*. This is the worker's effort to explore the meaning of the silence to understand better what the client is thinking or feeling.

In my research project, over 120 hours of videotaped social work practice was viewed and rated according to an observation system we developed. Silences seemed to occur most often just after the worker appeared to misunderstand the client's concern.[7] They were often, but not always, a message that the client felt cut off. In this study, workers responded to silences most often by changing the topic of discussion. Workers often experience silences as uncomfortable because they sense negative feedback. Silences can, of course, mean other things as well. For example, the client may be reflecting on the worker's comments or he may be experiencing strong emotions. These will be discussed in the next chapter.

As illustrated in the next segment, by reaching inside the silence, this worker demonstrated skill in catching her mistake exactly as she was making it. Workers often have the mistaken notion that in good practice one never makes mistakes. In reality, good practice involves spontaneity on the worker's part, and so mistakes will be a natural part of the work. If workers always wait for the exactly right thing to say, they will always be thinking and analyzing while the client is working well ahead of them. This was a key moment in the interview, and this skilled and experienced worker proved up to it.

> (Silence)
> **WORKER:** Why did you ask? It sounds like you may have had trouble with social workers before?
> **MR. GREGORY:** I did. All the other social workers seemed to be with my wife and against me. I was always the bad one.
> **WORKER:** And you're worried that I might do the same thing?
> **MR. GREGORY:** Well, yah, you might.
> **WORKER:** I try to help the two of you decide to do what's best for you and the children. If you feel I'm siding or if you don't like how things are going with me, I want you to tell me because I want to help you both.
> **MR. GREGORY:** Don't worry, you'll know. Are you new at this job?

As a result of her "tuning in," the worker correctly guessed the meaning of his earlier question. "Are you on her side or mine?..." She knew that his past experiences might well have led to the development of a stereotype about social workers and that at some point she would have to deal with this. By reaching directly for this in her comment, "It sounds like you may have had trouble with social workers before," she gave him permission to talk directly about what some clients would consider a taboo subject.

Workers sometimes express concern about exploring such a question. They feel it would be unprofessional to discuss other workers or other professionals. They say that they might be perceived as "not identifying with the agency" or as simply "trying to get on the client's side." If one views most discussion of other helping professionals as the client's way of indirectly exploring the *present working relationship,* then the dilemma is nonexistent. This worker picked up the indirect cue and reached for his present concerns with her comment, "And you're worried I might do the same thing?"

This client responded directly and acknowledged that this was what he meant. Many clients who lack this strength and ability to be direct might have held back at this point. Since the obstacles are powerful ones, they needed to be explored openly in first sessions. The worker needs to push, gently, a bit harder for these concerns. For example, in response to a client who says, "Oh no, I wasn't worried about you," the worker might continue, "It would be easy to understand how you might be concerned about me. After all, I'm a social worker, too, and you have had some tough experiences. How about it, perhaps you are just slightly concerned?" The client will often sense, in this second invitation, that the worker really means that it is all right to talk about their relationship. If not, the worker can let things be and try to return to this topic at another time when the client's trust has developed a bit more strongly. Meanwhile, the client has the message

that this issue can be discussed when he or she feels ready. In a first group session described in Part II of this book, the process of accepting a second invitation is clearly illustrated.

Returning to the interview, we have the interesting question by the client, "Are you new at this job?" When students discussed the possible meaning of the client's question, a number of alternatives were considered: "Maybe he was trying to figure out what kind of worker you are, because you don't talk like a social worker." "Maybe he was thinking after you have been around for a while, you'll change." This time, in contrast to her reactions to the earlier direct question, the worker tried to explore its meaning. This involved the *skill of elaboration,* inviting the client to expand on the meaning of his comment or question.

WORKER: No, I've been here for a while. Why do you ask?

MR. GREGORY: Well, the last worker I had was really green. She knew nothing. She took me to court—didn't get anywhere, but what a mess.

WORKER: Are you wondering if I'll take you to court?

MR. GREGORY: Oh, no. And if you did, I'd go and fight.

Once again, the worker reached for the implications for the here and now of their relationship from his description of past experiences. In the next excerpt, she tries to clarify some of the terms of their working relationship in the context of the agency and her dual responsibility of trying to offer him a service while still carrying statutory responsibility for the protection of his children. This is part of the contracting process. The terms of the relationship must be defined openly. The client may be able to overcome the obstacle posed by the worker's dual function if there is an honest discussion of it and a clear definition of the worker's responsibilities. This is just as true with the child care worker who must define responsibility for supervising the home, the parole officer who must spell out legal responsibilities, and the adoption social worker who must make a report on the suitability of the prospective parents. When these realities are openly discussed in the first sessions, when the responsibilities and mutual expectations are clearly defined for both the client and the worker, the client is often able to overcome the obstacles they pose. The worker in this illustration attempted to define this part of the contract.

WORKER: I think it's important for me to let you know under what conditions I'd go to court. Children can be in care of the agency either by court custody or voluntary agreement. In your case, it's voluntary, so there is no court involvement. But if I see the kids harmed when they're with your wife or you while visiting—by harmed I mean beaten, black and blue, bones broken, or not fed or supervised for the whole weekend home, then I go to court. But only under those circumstances, beaten or neglected.

MR. GREGORY: What if I want to take my kids home? Can you stop me, go to court and stop me?

WORKER: No. You can take your children whenever you want.

MR. GREGORY: That can't be. What if I'm not working, can't care for them, you won't let them come home.

WORKER: I can't stop them. If, however, once they're home and they don't get fed, clothed, taken care of, then I can go to court and bring them back.

MR. GREGORY: [*Smiling*] I really knew the answers to this, but I was misinformed by other people in the past. I used to sort of test my last worker to see if she would tell the truth.

WORKER: *Did I pass?*

MR. GREGORY: Not you, her. [*Quiet*] Yah, you passed [*he smiled*]. I had to do it to see where we stand. *The first meeting is really important, you know.*

WORKER: Yes, it is. And it is also scary, since you don't know what to expect.

MR. GREGORY: Yah, but it looks okay.

They talked some more about procedures, rules, regulations, arranged a next meeting, and then summed up.

When we have reviewed this interview, a number of students and workers have commented on the client's directness. They have even asked, with a touch of hopefulness in their voices, whether clients like this come into agencies often. The key point is that he seems like such a good client *only* because the worker was able to respond to him with skill. Another worker, and even this worker in her training days, would have been put off by an assertive client such as this. The interview might have had a much different ring to it if the worker had not "tuned in" and prepared herself to reach for the part of this client which, in spite of his ambivalence, was still reaching out to the agency, the worker, and his children. The directness and anger were actually a sign of his caring.

A similar analysis could be presented of a nurse dealing with a new, constantly complaining patient on the ward or a child care worker reaching past the bravado which is part of the front put up by the tough teenager, or an alcohol addiction counselor who faces a client whose arms are tightly folded across his chest, thus expressing visually his feelings about being referred to the program by his boss.

In each case, the worker must "tune in" to prepare for indirect cues and to get in touch with his or her own feelings about the engagement. A clear statement of purpose and role, one that incorporates the client's potential sense of urgency, is needed. An opportunity for client feedback about purpose must be given in addition to the exploration of the potential obstacles to developing a working relationship.

As with any client, the worker begins in the first session to use skills to start development of a positive working relationship while the contracting process is taking place. These skills include elaboration, reaching inside of silence, empathizing with expressed feelings, and articulating unexpressed feelings slightly ahead of the client.

The worker attempts to carry out the helper part as well as abilities permit, making mistakes along the way but correcting them as soon as possible. The client also has a part in the proceedings: the decision to use this worker, to trust, to take some responsibility for part of the problems. If worker and client are both up to their interdependent tasks, then a foundation may be laid in the first sessions for movement into the work phase. This phase is examined in the next chapter, with a more complete discussion of many of the skills mentioned in this one.[8]

NOTES

1. Lawrence Shulman, "A Study of Practice Skills," *Social Work* 23 (July 1978): 279.

2. William Schwartz, "On the Use of Groups in Social Work Practice," in *The Practice of Group Work,* ed. William Schwartz and Serapio Zalba (New York: Columbia University Press, 1971), p. 8.

3. William Schwartz, "Between Client and System: The Mediating Function," in *Theories of Social Work with Groups,* eds. Robert R. Roberts and Helen Northen (New York: Columbia University Press, 1976), pp. 188-90.

4. Charles Garvin, "Complementarity of Role Expectations in Groups: The Member-Worker Contract," in *Social Work Practice, 1969* (New York: Columbia University Press, 1969), pp. 127-45.

5. Shulman, "A Study of Practice Skills," p. 278.

6. This videotape program was one of six produced to describe the practice model and the research project. Lawrence Shulman (Producer), "Social Work Theory and Practice—Program One, Part Two," in *The Helping Process in Social Work: Theory, Practice and Research* (Montreal: Instructional Communi-

cations Centre, McGill University, 1976). In the United States, information on the tapes can be obtained from: Film Rental Center, Syracuse University, 1455 East Colvin St., Syracuse, NY 13210.

7. Lawrence Shulman, *A Study of the Helping Process* (Vancouver: Social Work Dept., University of British Columbia, 1977), p. 356; see also Lawrence Shulman, *Identifying, Measuring and Teaching the Helping Skills* (New York: Council on Social Work Education, 1981.)

8. For readings which deal with the beginning phase of work, see Norman Polansky and Jacob Kounin, "Clients' Reactions to Initial Interviews," *Human Relations* 9 (1956):237-64; Virginia Satir, *Conjoint Family Therapy* (Palo Alto, Calif.: Science and Behavior Books, Inc., 1967), pp. 91-160; Frances Stark, "Barriers to Client-Worker Communications at Intake," *Social Casework* 40 (April 1959):177-83; Allen Pincus and Anne Minahan, *Social Work Practice: Model and Method* (Itasca, Ill.: F.E. Peacock, Publishers, Inc., 1973), pp. 141-61; Max Siporin, *Introduction to Social Work Practice* (New York: Macmillan, 1975), pp. 192-218.

CHAPTER 4

Skills in the Work Phase

In the course of a training workshop, a psychiatric nurse expressed her feelings about the work phase in a manner which summed up the feeling of many helping professionals: "I'm good at beginnings and I can even deal with the problems involved in endings, but I'm at a loss when it comes to what happens in the middle." After a session of discussion with child care workers about the problems of contracting clearly with children in a group home, one of the participants echoed the nurse's sentiments: "I'm afraid that if I make a direct and clear offer to help the kids with their problems, they might take me up on it. What in the hell would I do then?"

This chapter explores the answer to the question, "What do I do then?" It picks up after beginning, tentative clarity about contract and worker role has been achieved, as discussed in the previous chapter on the beginning phase. To simplify the presentation, the processes of the middle phase are also examined against the phases of work: tuning in, beginning, work, ending, and transitions. This time these phases are applied to each session.

A simplified, general model of a work-phase interview is presented first to give the reader a grasp of the whole of the

chapter. This is followed by a detailed analysis of each segment of the work-phase interview. Specific skills are identified and illustrated by examples from a variety of practice situations. Findings from my research project and those of others are discussed where relevant.

A MODEL OF THE WORK PHASE INTERVIEW

Schwartz addressed the problem of defining the workers' professional skills required in the work phase. In a monograph on group work in public welfare settings, he described the specific skills required after adolescent group members accepted their workers' invitations to discuss "bad" feelings and anxieties. These skills were:

... to break down large problems into smaller, more manageable pieces of work; to reach for the details of a problem and help others in the group add to the inventory from their own experiences; to ask for *more* of the feeling, both negative and positive, and help the members support each other in its expression; to help them try out new ideas in public and rehearse new ways of handling old problems; to help them generalize from their experiences and others; to ask them to define their realities, without underplaying or overplaying the difficulties; to hold them to their work; to help them talk to and listen to each other; to invest their own (workers') compassion and spontaneity without losing their special helping role; and other moves designed to help the youngsters examine their world in detail and teach each other some new ways of handling it.[1]

In this chapter, the skills of the work phase have been grouped into general categories called *skill factors* in order to simplify their description. A skill factor consists of a set of closely related behaviors. The common element of the behaviors is the general intent of the worker using the skill. For example, in this model all behaviors associated with the efforts of the worker to deal with client affect are grouped together under the rubric "empathic skills."

Table 4.1 lists the skill factors included in this work phase model.

TABLE 4.1

1. Sessional Tuning in Skills
2. Sessional Contracting Skills
3. Elaborating Skills
4. Empathic Skills
5. Sharing-Worker-Feelings Skills
6. Demand-for-Work Skills
7. Pointing-out-Obstacle Skills
8. Sharing-Data Skills
9. Sessional-Ending Skills

In the preliminary phase prior to each session, the worker attempts to sensitize himself or herself to potential themes which *may* emerge during the work. A review of the previous session, information passed on by the client or others, the identification of subtle patterns emerging in the work may all serve to alert the worker to the client's potential current concerns.

In the beginning phase of each session, the central task of the worker is to find out what the client is concerned about at the moment. Sessional contracting skills are used to clarify the immediate work at hand. In some cases, the worker may bring issues which need to be addressed, and these will then be included in the contracting discussion. Since clients often use indirect communications to indicate their concerns, care has to be taken to determine the client's agenda before moving quickly into the work. Elaborating skills are important in this phase to help the client tell the story.

When the sessional contract has been tentatively identified, the process shifts into the work phase of the session. A priority in this phase is the worker's use of empathic skills to help the client share the affective part of the message. The worker must also be ready to share his or her own feelings as spontaneously as possible.

As the work progresses, it is not unusual to encounter some resistance from the client who is often of two minds about proceeding. A part of the person is always reaching out for growth and change, but another part is pulling back and holding on to what is comfortable and known. This ambivalence often emerges just as the work in the session starts to go well. It can be seen in evasive reactions (e.g., jumping from one concern to another) or defensiveness or expressions of hopelessness or in other forms. A premium is placed on the ability of the worker to "read" this resistance and to make a demand for work which can help the client mobilize to take the important next steps. The important point is that resistance is normal and to be expected. It is a sign that the work is going well.

As the work phase proceeds, obstacles may emerge which will frustrate the client's efforts on his or her own behalf. For example, the flow of feeling between the client and the worker may itself become an obstacle. As the worker makes demands for work, the client may react to the worker, and this reaction in turn will have an effect on the working relationship. Attention has to be paid to this obstacle as well as others which may emerge to block the client's work. Since the worker-client relationship is similar to others the client must deal with, discussion of these feelings can contribute to the client's understanding.

The client must also be allowed to have access to the worker's own relevant data. Sharing data such as facts, opinions, and value judgments is an important part of the helping process. The worker must take care to do so openly and to leave the client free to accept or reject the worker's views.

Endings of sessions have important dynamics and require the worker's attention. In addition, issues which have been raised indirectly throughout the session may emerge with some force when the client is about to leave (the classic "doorknob therapy" phenomenon). Finally, transitions need to be made to next sessions and future actions.

In an effort to describe this complex process in simple terms, I have had to oversimplify the central ideas. The work session does not proceed as neatly as outlined. The skill categories are not mutually exclusive. For example, as the sessional contracting proceeds, the worker will use elaborating, emphathic, and demand-for-work skills. The advantage of describing this complex process in an oversimplified form is that you can now use this model to orient yourself as you explore each phase and each skill factor in further detail.

SESSIONAL TUNING IN SKILLS

All the principles of tuning in described in the chapter on the preliminary phase of work are equally applicable to each encounter with the client. This process involves an effort by the worker of self-sensitization to potential concerns and feelings which may emerge during the session. The worker must also tune in to his or her own feelings about the encounter. This is also a time when one can draw upon one's fund of experience, the literature on human behavior, or colleagues and supervisors to deepen understanding of the client's struggle and, especially, of the symbiotic connection between the client and the people and systems that matter. Each of these types of preparatory work is now explored.

Tuning in to the Client's Sense of Urgency

Because the client's communications are often indirect, the worker significantly increases the chances of catching the crucial issue early in the work by being prepared to "hear" it. The worker is often made aware of events which take place between sessions which may affect the client's sense of urgency. For example, a child care worker who starts an evening shift might be informed by daytime staff of an incident in the house which had been difficult for a resident or some traumatic news received during the day.

In one illustration, a child care worker was told that a teenager had just heard about the death of his father, necessitating leaving the residence the next day to return home for the funeral. The youngster had appeared to take the news badly but handled it by withdrawing. The child care worker tuned in to the effect this had on the resident. He did this by getting in touch with his own feelings about the death of a close relative. He thought of the mixed feelings that must exist: on the one hand, wanting to be alone and not to talk about the hurt, and on the other, desperately wanting to share the feelings with another person. He thought about the boy's need to cry, in relation to the societal injunction that crying is not manly. He worked hard to be in touch with his own sense of sadness so that he would be sure not to run from the sadness of this youngster.

He guessed that the cues would be indirect. In this case the youngster was hanging around in the lounge, looking sad but not saying anything. In other cases, the cues might emerge in provocative behavior as the resident tried to hide the hurt and deal with it by acting out the anger. So he prepared to reach for the feelings and make an offer to talk while still respecting the youngster's right to be left alone. Even if the youngster did not take him up immediately, or at all, at least he would know the worker cared.

At an appropriate time, he made his offer. "I heard about your father's death, and I wanted you to know how sorry I am. I think I can understand how much it must hurt. If you want to talk with me about it, or just spend some time together this evening, I'd be glad to. If you just feel like being alone for a while, I'd understand that as well." In this case, the youngster had said he wanted to be left alone. He had heard the message, however, and at bedtime when the worker stopped by to say goodnight, he began to cry. The worker sat for a while, at first crying with him, sharing some of the hurt and then listening as the youngster spoke of his father.

When the incident is traumatic, the worker can strategize to reach for it directly in the sessional contracting stage. If a number of less urgent themes are possible, the worker can be alert to their potential emergence. When the session starts, the worker will clear them from the mind and listen to and watch the client. In another example, the nurse on the ward may be more sensitive to patient concerns by tuning in to the variety of feelings patients will experience upon hearing they will be discharged. The patient who has experienced a serious illness or a long period of hospitalization may be worried about the lack of medical support on returning home or how the family will react to this new condition. These concerns may well be expressed indirectly, sometimes in the form of testiness and short temper.

Tuning in to the Worker's Own Feelings

The worker's feelings can be used to facilitate the work or can block a concern from emerging. For example, after thinking about an interview the reaction may be that the worker has "blown" it by not listening to the client, attempting to impose an agenda, and turning the client off by attempting to preach. The worker can easily tune in to the client's feelings of frustration and anger at finding another professional who thinks he or she has all the answers. The worker may plan to begin again by apologizing, pointing out how the worker had "missed" the client, and inviting the client to discuss reactions.

It would be important in this case for the worker to tune in to his or her own feelings about receiving this negative feedback. For inexperienced workers, reaching for negative feedback is one of the hardest skills. How will it feel for the client to accept the invitation and provide negative feedback? But if the worker can get in touch with his or her own feelings of doubt, insecurity about the work, and possible panic if the client were actually to get angry, that worker will have a better chance of avoiding defensiveness. This can then be the start of the development of a new idea about what makes a professional. Instead of believing that a professional is always right and never makes mistakes, the worker can begin to be more comfortable with the notion of a professional as someone who can own up to mistakes.

Another illustration might be an interview where the helping person anticipates having to set limits or carry out the part of the helping function which involves control over the client. For example, the probation officer who finds out the client has lied and is breaking an agreed rule. If it is a client with whom the officer has developed a good relationship, it would not be surprising if the probation officer feels hurt and disappointed by the client's actions. The worker wonders if the client has "conned" him or her all along, and this possibility can increase the anger.

Helping professionals are just as vulnerable as clients and will often refuse to take risks because of their fear of being emotionally taken for a ride. If the probation officer can get in touch with his or her own feelings, then there is a better chance of using this incident as a critical turning point in the relationship rather than feeling that it signals an end to the work. Breaking rules can be an indirect signal to the helping person of another problem or of some difficulty in the helping relationship or a way of testing limits. With the officer's own feelings clear, a plan might be worked out to deal with the issue of limit setting while simultaneously reaching for possible work. Demands might be made on the client without losing the capacity for empathy. The feelings of disappointment might also be used to deepen the working relationship.

The line of argument I am pursuing is

that the worker is a human being, like the client, with a special function and skills to put that function into action. The worker's feelings can have as profound an impact on actions as the client's do. For example, it is not unusual for a child welfare worker who has developed a beginning relationship with a mother to dread the interview following a neighbor's report of neglect of her child. As one worker put it, "I feel like a rat. I have encouraged this woman to open up to me, to share her feelings, now I may have to take her kid away." This feeling can lead the worker to harden him or herself, to put up a front, and at the time in the work when the most help is needed, cut him or herself off from the very feelings needed in being helpful.

Tuning in to the Meaning of the Client's Struggle

As patterns emerge in work with a client, the worker must often step back and attempt to understand the client's struggles in a new way. For example, consider the worker meeting with a father who is attempting to deal with his seventeen-year-old son's efforts to break away. The battle is a classic one, but the worker must consider what the special meaning of the struggle might be for this father. Understanding the stage of life development which the father may be going through can be helpful in getting at the unique qualities of this particular father-son engagement. The literature on midlife crisis tells us something of men's struggle in their late thirties to work on their own sense of differentiation as individuals in their marriage.[2] The father may be seeing the signs of rebellion in his son which mirror some of his own feelings that he is still trying to deal with.

The worker who sensitizes himself or

herself to the father's potential conflict will be better able to "hear" this theme if it emerges in discussion. Helping the father face his own crisis may often be the best way to help him understand and deal with his son's experience. The worker's understanding can be gained through life experience, work experience, professional literature, and fiction.[3] In many ways, the work experience is an education about life, and the worker is an eager learner. Each client will teach the worker something new. If the worker is listening and feeling, then every encounter with a client will involve some change.

One particularly important aspect of the tuning in process in the mediating practice approach is the worker's ability to find the threads of the common ground when the parties are frustrated by obstacles. In developing his practice approach, Schwartz described method as the means by which the worker implements the helping function. He identified five general tasks of the worker which constitute method. The first of these is:

1. The task of searching out the common ground between the client's perception of his own need and the aspect of social demand with which he is faced.[4]

There are a number of ways in which the worker carries out this task, but in the immediate context of this discussion, the connection between the father and the son would need to be explored. I have already pointed out one possible connection—the son's struggle may not be so different from that of the father. Let us explore others. For example, as a young man pursues independence, some part of him will also want to hold on to the security of home, parents, and people who still care about him. The connection between the son's need for security as he

moves into adulthood and the father's concern about his son's budding independence may be only partial, hard for the father or the son to perceive, but there nevertheless.

On the other side of the coin is the father's hopes and aspirations for his son's growth into manhood. What connections exist between these aspirations and the son's effort to find some form of independence? It must be obvious that these connections are subtle and can easily be lost by both parties as they become overwhelmed by the obstacles related to their ambivalent feelings. This is why the worker must tune in to the common ground to be sensitive to it when it emerges. Under the anger and recriminations of both is a fund of feelings for each other which needs to be identified and nurtured. It will not make the son's struggle for independence or the father's struggle to let go an easy one, for both are always difficult. It may, however, allow the parties to hang on to what is important between them in the process.

Tuning in and Time

Workers often say to me, "It sounds great, but who can take the time?" Having time to prepare for a session is often prevented by the size of the caseload or the speed with which things happen. It is not possible to prepare for each encounter if caseloads are too heavy. When the action occurs in a group home, the child care worker needs to respond on the spur of the moment and may not have time to tune in.

For workers with the heavy caseload, the answer is to tune in whenever possible and to recognize the limits to their ability to provide service for all their clients.[5] Workers will often admit they have time to connect with some of their clients while they drive home or as they review the work of the week. The real barrier, they say, is unwillingness to expend that much emotional energy. It means feeling for their clients in some difficult situations. Child care workers will readily admit there is often time after an incident to use this skill to prepare to pick up the work again or to be ready for the next opportunity.

Self-Awareness

In my view, a worker's capacity for empathy expands with use. This is the exciting part of the worker's growth which comes from the engagement. Within limits, the worker can feel more often, more accurately, and more deeply what the clients are experiencing. Life and work experience contributes to understanding. This understanding can be drawn upon when needed. Workers discover their own feelings about many of the issues their clients deal with, many of which may touch on unresolved concerns in their own lives. Young workers still close to the battle for independence often discover how their own feelings lead to identifying with the child in the struggle with the parent. Older workers, moving through personal crises of their own, may learn a great deal about their own lives as they struggle to help the parent.

This is one sense in which the work is interactive, with the feelings of the client affecting the feelings of the worker. This idea is easier to understand when one views the professional worker not as someone who has worked out all of the answers to life's problems—and is now prepared to share them with the client—but rather as a fellow learner with a special functional role and a number of skills for implementing that function.

SESSIONAL CONTRACTING SKILLS

One portion of my research project examining social work practice skill involved videotaping over 120 hours of individual and group practice.[6] With the client's permission, interviews were recorded by a videotape camera. Although the clients knew that these tapes would be analyzed at the university by some unknown researchers, the client and the worker were alone in the room with the camera.

One videotape illustrated dramatically the issues related to sessional contracting. As the session began, the client touched upon a concern she was feeling about her child in a slightly indirect manner—hinting at it instead of raising it directly. The worker listened to the concern, but it soon became obvious that she had her own agenda for the session as her questions attempted to lead the client to other issues. After a few minutes the client hinted again, making a second offering of her concern, this time a little more strongly and clearly. The worker still did not "hear," since she was preoccupied with her own agenda. The client made a third attempt a few minutes later which the worker once again missed. At this point, with a look of complete frustration, the client turned to the video camera and said, "Do you understand?"

This interview illustrates the problems that occur when the client and the worker are operating on two different agendas. It also raises the larger issue of control over the interview. This, in turn, is directly related to the paradigm or model which guides the helping professional in thinking about the worker's work. The sessional contracting skill provides a good opportunity to elaborate the general issue.

In an interactional approach, clients are

seen as attempting to work on those is-sues of importance to them as best they can. Clients will find that their sense of urgency about problems shifts from week to week depending upon the realities of their lives. A major assumption of Schwartz's practice theory is that clients will only invest in those areas of concern that they feel are important. The worker's task is not to decide what the client *should be* working on. Instead, using sessional contracting skills, the worker attempts to discover what the client *is* working on.

I have already discussed some of the difficulties clients experience in commun-icating their thoughts and feelings direct-ly, especially at the beginning of each session. Clients often raise their concerns ambivalently and express this ambiva-lence in indirect forms of communica-tion. For example, a client may begin a session describing how great things have been that week while really facing a terrific problem. An example from a couples' group illustrates this situation.

WORKER: Does anyone have anything they would like raised?
FRAN: We've had no problems this week; it has been really great. We have been com-municating with each other better than ever before. (Silence). We had a problem last week which I used to get really angry about, but I think I was more helpful to Ted this time (looking over to her husband).
WORKER: Can you tell us a bit about it?
FRAN: It was a problem that had to do with our sexual relations (looking nervously over at Ted now), but I'm not sure Ted wants to discuss it.

Further discussion revealed the con-cern was over Ted's premature ejacula-tions, a major concern for this couple now being raised for the first time. This client offered her concern for the first time by emphasizing the opposite to the true state of affairs.

In another example, an eighteen-year-old young man, a foster child about to leave the care of the child welfare agency, introduces a discussion of his feelings of rootlessness and terrible loneliness by using a metaphor.

CLIENT: Have you ever thought about space, about space never ending?
WORKER: Yes, I have. Have you thought about it, and does it bother you?
CLIENT: Sometimes I imagine that I'm a little bird and that I'm a little bird and that I'm floating up into never-ending space. A little bit higher and a little bit to the right, and it's "bye, bye world."
WORKER: You have been floating in space this year, with all of the changes you've made.

The client responded by detailing with great feeling all of the places he has stayed during the year (eight), the deaths of his mother and an uncle, and his feelings of being alone in the world. The discussion continued with a poignant description of what it was like to spend important fami-ly holidays, such as Christmas, alone in a movie theater.

Examples of the indirect first offerings of concerns could be endless. A parent who is dreadfully worried about how her child is making out and feeling guilty about her own parenting may raise the concern by attacking the worker's com-petency to help her child. A child in the residential treatment center, who the week before Christmas holidays finds out his parents are not taking him home for a visit, may act out his feelings by getting into fights with other residents and staff.

In each case, the clients are working on important issues. Sometimes they are aware of the concern but have difficulty saying it. Other times the feelings are there, just below the surface, but the clients themselves are unaware of the central theme. Whatever the case, the clients' offerings are present, but they are hard to understand in their early forms. Because of the complexity of communication, a worker often feels that the client is not working and so decides to take over the task of determining the client's agenda. As in the example which opened this chapter, there is little possibility of the worker understanding the client's agenda without actively attempting to determine what it is.

One of the findings of a subdesign of the research project concerned the question of sessional contracting. It was based upon the practice of eleven workers, out of the 118 in the major study, who agreed to have their practice videotaped and analyzed. It would be a mistake to generalize the findings beyond this sample. However, in my experience as a consultant in a number of settings, I have found this pattern persisting.

Each videotape was analyzed by a trained rater who scored a number representing a category of behavior (e.g., clarifying purpose, encouraging elaboration, dealing with feelings) every three seconds. A numerical record of the session was available for computer analysis. Over 120 hours of individual, family, and group practice were analyzed in this manner.

It was also possible to judge whether workers were relating to the client's concerns, as judged by the raters, or working on their own agendas. According to this analysis, workers related to the client's concerns only 60 percent of the time.[7]

We further analyzed separately each third of every session. This roughly approximated the beginning, middle, and end phases of work. Workers began by relating to client concerns 65 percent of the time but dropped to 58 percent in the middle and ending phases.[8] This finding

was interpreted as suggesting a high incidence of unsuccessful sessional contracting in the beginning phase.

Earlier, I suggested the question of sessional contracting was related to the larger questions of control of the interview and the paradigm of the helping process guiding the worker. I believe that some of these workers operated from a paradigm of helping which placed the central responsibility for determining the agenda on the worker. A good worker was one who controlled the interview so as to reach selected goals for the clients. Workers operating from this model would find it impossible to hear the clients' indirect efforts to communicate their own sense of urgency.

It becomes clear that even as we discuss specific skills, such as sessional contracting, the worker's sense of function needs to be considered. If one believes that the worker's tasks include selecting the agenda for the work, then sessional contracting is impossible. On the contrary, if one believes that this is the task of the client, and one has faith in the client's ability to do this, with help from the worker, then all beginnings are tentative. The worker begins each session by listening for the client's concern, and the question of control of the interview is settled. The interview belongs to the person receiving help, not the one who is giving it.

ELABORATING SKILLS

When a client begins to share a particular concern, the first presentations of the problem are usually fragmentary. These initial offerings provide a handle which the worker can use to deepen the work. The elaborating skills are important in this stage, since they help clients tell their own story. The focus of the worker's questions and comments is on helping the client to elaborate and clarify specific concerns. Some examples of elaborating skills explored in this section include moving from the general to the specific; containment; focused listening; questioning; and reaching inside of silences.

Moving from the General to the Specific

Clients often raise a general concern which is related to a specific event. The general statement can be seen as a first offering. It may be presented in universal terms because the client experiences it that way at the moment. The general nature of its expression may also represent the ambivalence the client may feel about dealing with it in depth.

One example of this process is the mother at the beginning of an interview who states, "It's impossible to raise teenagers these days." The worker who responds to the general theme may soon be engaging in a discussion of changing mores, peer group pressure, and so on. An example of moving from the general to the specific would be, "Did you have a tough time with Sue this week?" The client's response in this case was to describe a fight she had with her fifteen-year-old daughter who had returned home after 2 A.M. and refused to say where she had been. This second offering of the concern is a somewhat more specific and a manageable piece of work. By this I mean that the general problem of raising teenagers is pressing in our society, but this client and this worker will not be able to do much about it. However, this mother's relationship with her daughter is open to change.

Behind most early general statements is a specific hurt. If the worker does not encourage elaboration, the concern might emerge at the end of the session as a "doorknob" comment (as the client is leaving the office). The teenager in the living room of the group home who casually comments during a general discussion that "parents just don't understand" may be reacting to a letter or phone call received that morning. The patient on the ward who mentions to the nurse that "doctors must work hard because they always seem so busy" may still be reacting to terse comments overheard during rounds which the patient was too frightened or overwhelmed to inquire about. In each case, the skill would involve reaching for a possible specific incident.

Helping professionals have suggested to me two major reasons why they might refrain from reaching for the specifics behind the general comments. First, they have not been clear about how specific work must be. By that I mean that help can be given on the *details* of the problem. One cannot help a parent with the problems of dealing with teenagers through general discussion alone. The learning will take place through the discussion of the specific interactions between parent and child. The worker can help the parent develop general principles about her relationship to her daughter which emerge from the discussions of the specific events. Without the specific discussion, the worker's attempts to generalize may be perceived by the mother as theoretical advice.

For example, the parent in the earlier encounter might describe a conversation with her daughter in which she did not level about her distress and hurt but instead gave way to the surface feelings of anger. After a while, the worker may be able to help the client see how, in incident after incident, she finds it hard to be open with her daughter about certain feelings. The client may be able to understand this point because of the discussion of specific incidents. The discussion should develop an experiential base upon which the client can build the new understanding. It is the lack of understanding of the power of specific discussion which may lead the worker to omit using this elaboration skill.

The second reason why workers do not reach for the specifics, even when they sense the concrete problem conected to the client's general offering, is that they are not sure they want to deal with it. Child care workers may wonder, "Is that my job?" Nurses suggest they do not reach for the patients' comments about busy doctors because they are not sure what they can do about it. As one put it, "I find the doctors too busy to answer my questions, so how can I help the patient?" The source of the worker's ambivalence may vary, but the presence of the ambivalence is common. My belief is that when workers feel more confident about offering help, they find themselves reaching more easily for the specifics. Discussion in later sections of this chapter and later chapters will deal in more detail with the child care workers' and nurses' questions raised above.

Containment

As clients begin to tell their story, it is not at all uncommon for workers to begin to "help" before the whole story is told. This problem is especially true for people who are new to helping. The desire to be of help is so strong that they will often rush in with suggestions which are not helpful, since they are not directed at the client's actual concerns. The elaborating skill of containment is an interesting one, since it suggests that *not acting*, that is, a worker containing himself or herself, is an active skill.

In the following example, we see a new worker in a public welfare setting failing to contain herself in response to a mother whose children have grown up and who is interested in pursuing a career.

CLIENT: I've been thinking that now that the kids are older, perhaps I can find a job. But you know, finding jobs is difficult these days.

WORKER: I think that's a great idea. You know we have a job-finding service, and I bet if you speak to one of the workers, he could come up with something for you.

CLIENT: (hesitantly) That sounds like a good idea.

WORKER: Let's set up an appointment. How about next Wednesday at three?

The client agreed to the appointment and then did not show up. At the next interview, the disappointed worker asked the client why she missed the appointment. The client said that she forgot, and this time the worker contained herself and did not make a new appointment. Instead, she attempted to explore further the client's perception of what was involved in taking a job.

WORKER: I was thinking about this business of taking a job, and it struck me that it might not be so easy for you after so many years at home.

CLIENT: That's what I'm worried about; I'm not sure I can handle work again—you know, I've been away so long. I'm even nervous about what to say at a job interview.

Feelings of fear and ambivalence are usually associated with most concerns. Workers who attempt to find simple solutions often discover that if the solutions were indeed that simple, then the client could have found them alone without the help of the worker.

Focused Listening

Listening is something we do all the time; however, focused listening involves an attempt to concentrate on a specific part of the client's message. I discussed earlier how complex even the most simple interchange of communication can be. In complex communications at the beginning of sessions, it is essential that the worker focus the listening on whatever the client is working on at that particular moment. By listening to the early communications with this purpose in mind, the worker has a better chance of hearing the message.

A simple analogy is the difficulty of hearing two simultaneous conversations at a crowded social occasion. One can listen in a general way and all one hears is a loud buzz. If one then attempts to focus on one particular conversation, it begins to stand out clearly, the buzzing noise in the background. In the same way, the "noise" of the client's early communications may make it difficult to understand the single strand representing the basic concern. Focused listening, directed to determine the concern, often makes the theme stand out in bold relief.

Questioning

Questioning in the elaboration process involves requests for more information as to the nature of the problem. For example, in the earlier illustration of working with the mother and daughter, we left the process at the point where the client responded to the worker's effort to move from the general to the specific by describing a fight with her daughter. Picking up the process at that point, we can see that the worker's questions are designed to elicit more details of the encounter.

CLIENT: We had some row last night when Sue came home at 2 A.M.

WORKER: What happened?

CLIENT: She had told me she was going to a movie with a friend, but when she didn't get home by 11, I was really worried.

WORKER: You were afraid something might have happened to her?

CLIENT: Well, you know we have had some problems in the neighborhood with men.

WORKER: What did you say to Sue when she came home?

CLIENT: I let her have it good. I told her she was irresponsible and that I was going to keep her home for two weeks.

WORKER: What did she say back to you?

As the conversation proceeded, the worker helped the client to elaborate on the details of the interaction. In other situations the questioning may be directed at getting a fuller picture of the client's concern. To return to the example of the woman considering going back to work, the worker could simply inquire about her concerns in returning to the work force.

Reaching Inside of Silences

A silence during a helping interview may be an important form of communication. The difficulty with silences is that it is often difficult to understand exactly what the client is "saying." In one situation the client may be thinking and reflecting on the implications of the conversation. In another, a discussion may have released powerful emotions in the client which are struggling to surface. The client may be at the critical point of experiencing suppressed and painful feelings. Silence can indicate a moment of ambivalence as the client pauses, and tries to decide if he should plunge headlong into a difficult area of work. This is not uncommon when the conversation deals with an area generally experienced as taboo in our society. Silence may also be a signal that the worker's preceding response was "off base" in relation to the client's expressed concern. The worker has "missed" the client, and the silence is the client's polite way of saying so. The client may be angry at the worker. Frequent silence in an interview may reflect a systematic attempt to express this anger passively.

Since silences have a variety of different meanings, the worker's response must vary accordingly. An important aid is the worker's own feelings during the silence. For example, if the silence does represent the emergence of difficult feelings, the worker may have anticipated this reaction from the content of the conversation or from the nonverbal communications sent by the client. Posture, facial expression, body tension—all speak loudly to the observing worker and can trigger empathic responses. The worker may experience the same emergence of feeling as the client. At moments like this, the worker can respond to silence with silence or with nonverbal expressions of support and in some cases, through physical contact such as an arm around a shoulder. All these responses offer some support to the client while still giving time to experience the feelings.

If the worker senses that the client is thinking about an important point of the discussion or considering a related problem, then to respond with silence allows the client room to think. Silence demonstrates respect for the client's work. However, a problem can be created if the worker extends the silence over a period of time. Silence can be particularly troublesome if the worker does not understand it or if it is used to communicate either a negative reaction or passive resistance. In such cases, the client may

experience the silence as a battle. What started as one form of communication may quickly change to a situation where the client is saying, "I won't speak unless you speak first." In this battle both worker and client are always losers. During these kinds of silences the skill described by Schwartz as reaching inside the silence is most important.

This skill involves attempts to explore the meaning of the silence. For example, the worker who responds to a silence by saying, "You've grown quiet in the last few moments. What are you thinking about?" is encouraging the client to share the thoughts. In another case, the worker could try to articulate what the silence may be saying. For example, the client who hesitates as he describes a particularly different experience might be offered this response: "I can see this is hard for you to talk about." Once again, it is the worker's own feelings which guide attempts to explore or acknowledge the silence. The worker must be open to the fact that the guess may be wrong and must encourage the client to feel free to say so.

It is not unusual for workers to find silences in interviews to be difficult moments. They have been affected by societal norms which create the feeling that a silence in a conversation is embarrassing and may feel that the most helpful thing to do is fill the gap. When one works with clients in different cultures one is struck by the differences in these social norms. For example, native Indian clients describe how hard it is to talk to non-Indian workers because they never keep quiet. As one native worker said to me, "The problem with white workers is that they never stop 'nattering.'" She went on to point out that Indian culture respected silence as a time to reflect but non-Indian workers would continue to talk ("natter") because of their own anxiety without giving the Indian a chance to think. In some cases, the native Indian might simply be trying to translate the non-Indian worker's English into the Indian language and then trying to translate back to English.

In the research project on practice, the skill of reaching inside silences was one of the five skills used least often of the twenty-seven studied.[9] But another analysis showed it to be the one of the most significant. The fifteen workers with the most positive overall skill scores were compared to those workers with the most negative overall skill scores. The group with the positive skill scores were found to have more positive working relationships and were more helpful than those with the negative scores.[10] The practice skill profiles of these two groups of workers was compared according to their scores on the twenty-seven specific skills. The skill of reaching inside silences was one of the three most important in which the positive skill group of workers differed from the negative skill group.[11] These findings tentatively support the notion that there are important communications within silences which can lead to more effective work connected to silences.

Another finding from a separate design of the study yielded additional evidence that this important skill may often be lacking. In this part of the study, the practice interviews of eleven volunteer workers were videotaped and then analyzed by trained raters using a system developed by research project staff. It was possible to analyze which behaviors of the workers most often followed silences of three seconds or more. In an analysis of thirty-two interviews, raters scored the worker's or the client's behavior by entering a number describing the interaction at least every three seconds. A total of 40,248 individual observations were scored and then analyzed by computer.

The findings were striking. Of all of the entries scored, only 1,742 (4 percent) indicated that a silence of three seconds or more had taken place.[12] Raters found that silences were followed by client comments only 38 percent of the time. A three-second silence was followed by another three-second silence 26 percent of the time. Workers' active comments in response to silences were noted 36 percent of the time. When these were examined more closely, they revealed the following results. When workers actively intervened after a silence, they attempted to encourage elaboration 31 percent of the time. Their efforts to deal with the client's feelings or share their own feelings were noted in only 4 percent of their responses. The most common active action in response to silence *was to direct the client away from the client's presented theme of concern.* This occurred 49 percent of the time.

Review the Appendix again for a fuller discussion of the research project. In particular, the limitations of the project should be kept in mind when assessing this data. For example, this finding is based on one small subdesign of the project which analyzed the practice of only eleven workers in one child welfare agency with a variety of training and experience, each of whom was under the unusual pressure of being videotaped as part of a research project. My attempt to generalize from these findings to other settings or workers is tentative, supported, however, by my observations as a training consultant.

The findings are shared because they reflect statistically my own observations that workers often seen reluctant to explore silences. In addition to the reasons already advanced, workers have suggested when discussing these findings how they often perceive silences as representing a problem in the interview. If there is silence, then the worker must have done something wrong. The worker often sees silence as negative feedback, even in those cases when it may stand for other things. A worker's willingness to reach inside the silence when there is a possible negative response is directly related to feelings of comfort in the work and willingness to deal with negative feedback. This aspect of the process will be discussed more fully under the skill factor called "pointing out obstacles." Understandably a worker may be unsure about what to do with the feelings and concerns which may live within the silence and may choose to change the subject rather than reach inside the silence. At this point, after the worker has successfully helped the client elaborate concerns, the discussion needs to move to the question of feelings and how to deal with them.

EMPATHIC SKILLS

As clients tell their stories, workers use a number of skills designed to keep the discussion meaningful by having clients invest it with feelings. Clients often share difficult experiences while seeming to deny the affect associated with them. For some, the experience may be so painful that they have suppressed the emotion so that their own feelings are not clear to themselves. For others, the emotions may seem strange or unacceptable, and they are fearful of admitting their existence to the worker.

Whatever the reason, the affect is there, and it will exert a powerful force on the client until it can be acknowledged and dealt with. The client's sharing of feelings with the worker can release an important source of energy. The client can also learn how emotions directly affect actions, can develop skills in understanding the sen-

sations, accepting them without harsh self-judgment, and disclosing them to those who matter. Taft was one of the early social work theorists to acknowledge the power of feelings:

There is no factor of personality which is so expressive of individuality as emotion. . . . The personality is impoverished as feeling is denied, and the penalty for sitting on the lid of angry feelings or feelings of fear is the inevitable blunting of capacity to feel love and desire. For to feel is to live, but to reject feeling through fear is to reject the life process itself.[13]

Rogers stressed the importance of the helping person listening for the affective component of the communication.

Real communication occurs when the evaluative tendency is avoided, when we listen with understanding. . . . It means to see the expressed idea and attitude from the other person's point of view, to sense how it feels to him, to achieve his frame of reference in regard to the thing he is talking about.[14]

As the worker allows himself or herself to get closer to the client, to experience the client realistically and not necessarily as the client has presented himself or herself, the worker also gives the client permission to be natural. The acceptance and understanding of emotions and the worker's willingness to share them by experiencing them frees a client to drop some defenses and to allow the worker and the client more access to the real person. The worker also serves as a model of an adult with empathic ability. The client can learn to develop powers of empathy to be used in turn with those who need support.

There are a number of reasons why it can be difficult for a worker to express empathy with the client. The capacity to be in touch with the client's feelings is related to the worker's ability to acknowledge his or her own. Before a worker can understand the power of emotion in the life of the client, it is necessary to discover its importance in the worker's own experience. Workers will often have difficulty in expressing empathy with the feelings of the client in specific areas which touch upon their own lives. Workers are human, facing all of the stresses and difficulties associated with daily living including periods of life crisis. When a worker hears his or her own difficult feelings being expressed by a client in an interview, the capacity for empathy can be blunted. Another major block to empathy can be the worker's authority over the client. For example, a worker who has apprehended a child in an abuse situation may find empathic responses to the client blocked at the time when they may be most needed.

The following example effectively illustrates this difficulty and shows how it can lead to a relationship devoid of feeling, cold and apparently uncaring. The excerpt is from a recorded interview with a mother who has undergone psychiatric treatment for a time and is separated from her husband. Her nine-year-old adopted and only daughter came into care of the agency one year before this interview because the mother had found her unmanageable. A short time into the interview there was a pause followed by this comment:

CLIENT: You know, I'm afraid of you.
WORKER: Why?
CLIENT: Because you are sitting in judgment of me. You're only human—you might make a mistake.
WORKER: I'm only judging how we can help you—help you to improve ...
CLIENT: No, you are judging whether or not I can be a mother to Fran—whether I can have my child back.

(Silence)
I feel at the moment I am not capable of caring for Fran on a full-time basis—I know that. ... (tape garbled) Don't you understand— I'm grieving—I'm grieving for Fran. Wouldn't you be upset and worried and confused?
WORKER: I'm worried about other things as well.

The worker was not in tune with the client's feelings. She regarded the child as her client and did not respond to the mother as a client in her own right. After some further discussion in which the worker indicated that the client was not working hard enough in her contacts with her psychiatrist, the worker asked how long she had been seeing the doctor.

CLIENT: I'm not sure—I don't remember— (with tremendous feeling)—It's absolutely terrible not to be able to remember. It makes me feel incompetent, incapable—(silence)— There are some things in my head I know can't be real—(silence)—but I feel I can be competent and capable of looking after Fran— or I wouldn't want to—because I know she is a problem to look after. But I love her even with her faults.
WORKER: When you think of Fran, what do you think of most—her faults?
CLIENT: No! Fran wants to laugh—enjoy people—not to analyze them. She's a baby bird, full of life, receptive, loving people. I may seem aloof, but I'm really just shy.
WORKER: You say Fran is sociable, but before, you told me she had no friends.

The worker ignored the client's productions, her self-depreciation and her expression of feelings of loss and guilt. Her capacity to help this mother was minimal, since she saw her intellectually, not affectively. Smalley has described this process:

The self of another cannot be known through intellectual assessment alone. Within a human, compassionate, and caring relationship, selves "open up," dare to become what they may be, so that the self which is known by a worker, a worker at once human, caring, and skillful, is a different self from that diagnosed by one who removes himself in feeling from the relationship in an attempt to be a dispassionate observer and problem solver. As an adolescent girl once said to her new social worker, in referring to a former worker, "She knew all about me, but she didn't know me."[15]

Because of the difficulty involved in the area of this skill, workers must develop over time their ability to empathize. The capacity for empathy appears to grow with experience. The worker who is open to this learning can learn more about life from each client dealt with. This will aid in better understanding the next client. One also learns more about one's own feelings, and true reactions to the plight of others. Awareness of the sensitive areas in one's own emotional armor will help to avoid denying or intellectualizing difficult emotions when they are presented. The worker will more readily allow a client to share more difficult emotions as the worker becomes comfortable with their effect, particularly with negative affect, both worker's and client's, which is a natural part of any helping relationship.

The three empathic skills described in this section are: reaching for feelings, displaying understanding of client's feelings, and putting the client's feelings into words. They will be illustrated by excerpts from practice with a mother whose child is about to be apprehended because of parental abuse. This example provides a contrast to the earlier one and demonstrates how the functions of protection and caring can be integrated.

Reaching for Feelings

This is the skill of asking the client to share the affective portion of the message. It is important to clarify one point before proceeding. This process can be handled superficially in a ritualistic manner, thus negating its usefulness. The worker who routinely asks a client, "How do you feel?" while not really being open to experiencing the feeling, may be perceived by the client as not really caring. Genuine empathy involves stepping into the client's shoes and summoning an affective response which comes as close as possible to the experience of the other.

With the emergence of technique-centered training programs focusing on developing a patterned response by the worker, the danger of artificial response is increased. One worker described how she had been taught by one program to reflect back the clients' feelings with the phrase, "I hear you saying that . . ." When she used this technique in one interview, her client looked aghast and replied, "You heard *me* saying *that!*" The reaching for feelings must be genuine.

In the illustration which follows, a worker talks with a mother about her reactions to one of her five children being taken into the care of the agency after being admitted to the hospital with bruises. In discussions with the hospital social worker the mother had admitted that the child had been beaten. The child welfare social worker discussed the placement with the mother.

WORKER: We have to be honest with you, Mrs. Green. Did the hospital social worker talk to you about the possibility of your child being placed?
CLIENT: Yes, but not with my mother. Anywhere else but there.
WORKER: I guess your mother has enough kids already.

CLIENT: It's not that; it's that we don't get along.

WORKER: Can you think of anyone else your son can live with?

CLIENT: I have a friend, Sara, who helped me when my husband died and when I had my baby.

WORKER: This must be a hard time. How are you feeling about the possibility of your son being placed?

CLIENT: I can't stand the idea. I don't want the other children with me if John is placed. I have often said this to the kids when I was angry at them—I told them I would place them all, and the kids remember that.

Displaying Understanding of Client's Feelings

The skill of displaying understanding of client's feelings involves indicating through words, gestures, expression, physical posture, or touch the worker's comprehension of the expressed affect. The worker attempts to understand how the client experiences the feelings even while perhaps believing that the reality of the situation does not warrant the reaction. The worker may believe that the client is being too self-punishing or taking too much responsibility for a particular problem. The worker needs to resist the natural urge to rush in with reassurances and attempts to help the client feel better. The worker may feel the client *shouldn't* feel so guilty, but the client *does* feel that way. Efforts at a reassurance are often interpreted by the client as the worker's failure to understand. As one client put it, "If you really understood how badly I felt you wouldn't be trying to cheer me up."

We return to the interview with the mother at the point she has commented that "—I told them [the children] I would place them all, and the kids remember that."

WORKER: We often say things when we are hurt or angry that we regret later.

CLIENT: I told the hospital social worker that if John was placed, all of the kids might have to be placed. I feel very strongly about this. It will hurt me to lose my kids, but I can't bear to think about getting up in the morning and only counting four heads instead of five.

WORKER: You mean that together you are a family and if one is missing, you're not? (She nodded when I said this and began to cry softly).

The worker's gentle restatement of the client's feelings has communicated to the client the worker's understanding and compassion. The emotions are expressed through the tears. This is an important form of communication between worker and client. Part of the healing process includes the client's sharing of feelings with a caring person. Workers often express their fear of strong emotions. They are concerned that a client might become too depressed and that the worker's effort to bring the emotions to the fore could result in more problems. Some workers worry they will be overwhelmed by the client's feelings and feel equally depressed and hopeless, thereby losing their ability to be effective. For many workers the ultimate fear is that they might trigger such deep expression of emotion that the client might be overwhelmed and turn to a drastic act such as suicide.

The assumption here is that it is not the emotions themselves that create the problems, but rather clients' inability to be in touch with their feelings or to share them with someone important. The power which feelings can have over clients may be dissipated when these feelings are expressed and dealt with. The greater danger is not in the facing of feelings but in their denial. The only thing worse than living with strong emotions is the feeling that one is alone and that no one can understand.

As for the worker's fear of being overwhelmed by the emotions, this can be alleviated somewhat if the worker is clear about the function and purpose of the engagement. The worker's sense of function requires making a demand for work on the clients. This important skill is dealt with in some detail in the next section, but it must be noted at this point in the discussion. No matter how strong the client's feelings of hopelessness are, there is always some next step that can be taken. The worker needs at one and the same time to experience the client's feelings of being overwhelmed (the empathy) while still indicating a clear expectation that the client will do something (the demand) about the situation, even in those cases where doing something means coming to grips with the reality (e.g., the death of someone close) and picking up and beginning again (e.g., searching out new significant relationships). The worker can make this demand because of a belief in the client's strength.

With clarity of purpose in mind, the worker can help the client find the connections between the emotions and the purpose of the discussion. This is also explored in the next section under the skill of connecting feelings to purpose. The central point is that significant work with clients in painful areas can only be done after the expression and acknowledgment of feelings. The flow of affect and understanding between worker and client is a necessary precondition for the movement to follow. Workers who attempt to make demands upon clients without first having experienced the affect with them will be perceived as "not understanding," and their demands will be experienced by the client as harsh and uncaring.

Putting the Client's Feelings into Words

Thus far I have described how a worker might reach for feelings and acknowledge those which have already been stated. There are times, however, when a client comes close to expression of an emotion but stops just short. The client might not fully understand the feeling and thus be unable to articulate it. In other cases, the client might not be sure it is all right to have such a feeling or to share it with the worker. The use of this skill involves the worker articulating the client's affect, in the words of Schwartz, "Just one half step ahead of the client." This occurs when the worker's tuning in and intense efforts to empathize during the session result in emotional associations as the client elaborates a concern.

Returning to the previous example to illustrate this point, the worker had said, "You mean that together you are a family and if one is missing, you're not?" and the client had responded by crying softly. The worker gave the client a Kleenex and waited a few minutes. The client was just sitting looking at the floor.

WORKER: You must be feeling like a terrible mother right now. (The client just nodded.) I said it must be really rough with all of the problems with the house, everything breaking down on you, having these hassles every day, and five kids also must make it pretty rough some times.

The client had not said anything about her parenting or about the guilt which must be present under the circumstances, but by articulating this emotion, the worker gives permission to the client to discuss her own feelings about herself. Often, as in the first illustration in this section, the worker is so busy trying to communicate, indirectly, disapproval of the client's actions that she cannot hear the client's own harsh judgment of herself. The assumption here is that how we feel about ourselves has a great deal of influence upon how we act. The way to begin to help this mother is to break a vicious cycle where her own guilt leads to feelings of helplessness and hopelessness which in turn leads to poor parenting, which in turn . . . and so on. The ability to articulate and face her feelings, sharing them with a caring and yet demanding worker, can be a beginning. The worker's acceptance of the client, including her feelings, can be the starting point for the client's acceptance of herself.

Research Findings on Empathy

The empathic skills have consistently been identified as important in helping relationships. Working in the field of psychotherapy, Truax found a relationship between therapist empathy, warmth and genuineness, and personality change.[16] Rogers has pointed to a number of studies in which empathy was found to be central to the worker's effectiveness.[17] In the field of educational research, Flanders found empathy to be an important skill for teachers in improving student performance.[18] There is a growing body of evidence which suggests this is one of the core skills which applies to all helping functions.

The findings of my own research studies supported these earlier findings. The skill of acknowledging the client's feelings appeared to contribute substantially to the development of a good working relationship between worker and client as well as contributing to the worker's ability to be helpful.[19] It was the second most powerful skill, ranking only behind the skill of sharing worker's feelings which is discussed in a later section. This finding was replicated in both my study of supervision skill and the study of family doctors.

The findings on the specific skill of putting client's feelings into words also indicated a strong relationship between it and building a relationship. It was also associated with helpfulness; however, the analysis suggested that its contribution to helpfulness lay in its strengthening of the relationship.[20] As suggested earlier in this book, this skill appears to be of particular importance early in the helping relationship. It is important to underline that the findings from my study refer to client perception of skill, relationship, and helpfulness. A review of the Appendix will indicate the evidence in support of the reliability of client perceptions of these variables.

In examining the skill profile of the average worker, I found that the worker was able to acknowledge client feelings (rated between often and fairly often), but was less able to articulate client feelings before they were expressed (rated fairly often).[21]

Data drawn from the observers' scores after rating the videotaped segments of practice (sixty-two sessions) indicated less concern with affect on the part of workers than the overall study suggested. Workers appeared to share their own feelings or to deal with client feelings in only 2.3 percent of their interventions in the individual sessions and in 5.3 percent of their interventions in the group sessions.[22] When total interactions in the sessions were analyzed, including the times when the client was speaking and the worker listening, the total interventions dealing with the affect in the group sessions dropped to 1.4 percent. This figure is very close to Flander's results when he analyzed teaching behaviors.[23]

The findings on lower frequency of use of these skills in some areas may indicate the difficulty workers face in dealing with client affect. My experience has been that a worker's capacity to respond empathically to client is somewhat related to how well the worker's own affective needs are met. In the supervision and teaching process, for example, the ability of the trainer to deal with the worker's feelings in relation to the work can have an important effect on the worker's growth. I have noted elsewhere that the teacher and supervisor is in many ways a role model of the helping person in action.[24] Colleagues can also provide important support. Whatever the source, support through empathic responses to the worker's feelings can free energies to invest the same empathic responses in work with clients.

This hypotheses of a parallel process between supervisors and workers was advanced in the first edition of this book. The suggestion was that a worker's relationship with clients might parallel the supervisor's relationship with the worker. A first step in examining this process was undertaken in my subsequent study of supervision. We found that the core skills of practice, described in this text, were also the core skills of supervision. In addition, supervisors who were described by their workers as being able to understand their feelings, were also supervisors who described their administrators as providing empathic support to them.

In my major study of child welfare practice currently under way, the complete hypotheses will be tested. That is, the belief that the way in which staff members in a system are treated, at all levels, flows through the system and affects line workers in their work with clients.

Stated simply, administrators need to be supportive of supervisors, if supervisors are to be supportive of workers, who in turn need to be supportive of their clients.

In a training workshop for experienced workers one worker put it succinctly: "If I'm going to be able to give to clients, who is going to give to me?" This is a crucial question which must be considered by teachers, supervisors, administrators, and public officials at all levels.

SHARING-WORKER'S FEELINGS SKILLS

An essential skill is related to the worker's ability to present himself or herself to the client as a real human being. Some theories of the helping process which have borrowed their model from the medical paradigm have presented the worker as an objective, clinical, detached, and knowledgeable professional. Direct expression of the worker's real feelings (e.g., anger, fear, love, and ambivalence) has been described as "unprofessional." This has resulted in a concept of professionalism which asks the worker to choose between the personal and the professional self. One worker, an example described earlier, illustrated the effect of this attempt to dichotomize the personal and the professional during a training workshop. She described her experience as a student working with a woman who had just discovered her child was dying of cancer. As the woman spoke, she was overcome with grief and began to cry. The worker experienced her own feelings of compassion and found herself holding the woman's hand and crying with her. A supervisor, passing by the open door, called the worker out and complained of her "unprofessional" behavior.

My view is that the worker was helping at that moment in one of the most important and meaningful ways we know.

She was sharing the pain with the client and, in expressing her own sorrow was making a gift to the client of her feelings. This worker was responding in a deeply personal way, yet at the same time was carrying out her helping function. Schwartz's practice theory suggests that the helping person is an effective helper only when able to synthesize real feelings with professional function. Without such a synthesis of "personal" and "professional" the result is a loss of spontaneity, with the worker appearing as a guarded professional, unwilling to allow clients across to themselves and their feelings. The irony is apparent, for the professional asks the client to share feelings while in the name of professionalism hides his or her own. The result is often the "mechanical" worker who appears to be always under-self-control, who has everything worked out, and who is never at a loss or flustered, in short, an impossible person to relate to in any real way.

The client does not need a perfect, unruffled worker who has worked out all life's problems but instead a real human being, like the client, who cares deeply about the client's success at work, expresses the client's own sense of urgency, and openly acknowledges feelings. As the client experiences the worker as a real person, the worker and the helping function can be utilized more effectively. If the worker is presented without signs of any humanity, the client will either be constantly testing to find the flaws in the facade or idealizing the worker as the answer to all problems. The client who does not know, at all times, where the worker stands will find trusting that worker hard. If the worker is angry at the client, then it is much better for the client to have the anger out in the open where it can be dealt with honestly. Workers who fear the expression of angry feelings as signs

of their "aggressiveness" often suppress them, only to have them emerge indirectly in ways to which the client finds it harder to respond. Professional expressions of anger, for example, through an unfeeling interpretation of a client's behavior, can be more hurtful than an honest statement of the feeling.

Direct expression of feelings is as important for the worker's sake as it is for the client's. A worker who suppresses feelings must use energy to do so. This energy can be an important source of help to the client if it can be freed for empathic responses. The worker cannot both withhold feelings and experience those of the client at the same time. The worker may also become cut off from important forms of indirect communications in which the client uses the worker's feelings to express his or her own. Consider the following example of this process. A child care worker in a residential center for children was confronted by an angry parent after an incident on an excursion in which the child was left on a bus and lost for a period of time. This child had been apprehended by the agency because of numerous complaints of neglect and abuse. The parent was on a visit to the center and began a loud, angry tirade directed at the worker.

CLIENT: What kind of a place do you run here anyway? He's only been here three weeks, and already he's sick, had a bump on his head, and you jerks lost him on a bus.
WORKER: (Obviously upset but trying to control himself) Look, Mr. Frank, we do the best we can. You know with fifteen kids on the bus, I just lost track.
CLIENT: Lost track! For God's sake (his voice getting louder), you mothers are paid to keep track, not lose track of my kid. Do you realize what could have happened to him on that bus alone? (The client screams the last question out. The worker is feeling embar-

rassed, overwhelmed, backed against the wall, is conscious of the other workers and the kids watching, and angry at the client.)

WORKER: (With great control in his voice.) You know, we simply can't tolerate this behavior in the house. You're upsetting all of the children, and if you don't calm down, I'm going to have to stop your visiting.

The truth of the matter is that the client was upsetting the worker who did not know what to do about it. His anger was expressed in a controlled fashion, turning it into an attempt to exert his authority on the client. He tried to tame the client by using his ability to influence access to the child. The calmer and more controlled the worker seemed, the angrier the client became. With his own feelings racing away in all directions, the worker's efforts to put up a calm front actually cut him off from a professional response. He has no way of understanding, at this point, that parents who have had children apprehended also often feel guilty, embarrassed, overwhelmed, backed against the wall, and very conscious of the reactions of their children. The client was unconsciously using the incident to make the worker feel exactly how he himself has felt for the past three weeks. In this sense, the client's feelings were projected onto the worker and the attack was also a form of indirect communication. Unfortunately, the worker expended his energy on defending himself and suppressing his anger. He was not able to work with this client in a meaningful way as long as he blocked expression of his own feelings. The client needed to keep pushing him until he got some reaction. Returning to the interview, we see that the worker's attempt to "read the riot act" to the client resulted in an escalation on the client's part.

CLIENT: You can't stop me from seeing my kid. I'm going to call my lawyer and bring charges against you and the agency for incompetency.

WORKER: (Finally losing his temper.) Well, God damn it, go ahead. I'm tired of hearing you complaining all the time. Do you think it's easy to deal with your kid? Frankly, I'm sick and tired of your telling me what a lousy worker I am.

CLIENT: (With equal intensity) Well, how the hell do you think I feel?
(Silence)

WORKER: (A deep sigh as the worker seems to be catching his breath.) I guess as frustrated, angry, and guilty as I do. You've been feeling this way ever since they took Jim away from you, haven't you?

CLIENT: (Subdued, but still angry.) It's no picnic having your kid taken out of your house and then being told you're an unfit parent.

WORKER: Look, we can start all over. I felt angry, guilty, and very defensive when you put me on the spot, and that's why I threatened you about the visiting business. I guess I just didn't know how else to handle you. You know, we really need to get along better in spite of your being angry at the agency, for your sake, for mine, and especially for Jimmy's. How about it? (Silence)

CLIENT: I guess I was a little rough on you, but you know, I worry about the kid a lot and when he's not with me, I feel—(struggling for the right word).

WORKER: —powerless to help him, isn't that it?

The worker's expression of his own feeling freed his energy to respond to the client's question, "Well, how the hell do you think I feel?" The results of this important step were threefold. First, the worker began to strengthen the working relationship between himself and the child's parent. This parent cared, and his anger and assertiveness could make him an excellent client to work with. Second, it allowed the worker to begin to respond empathically to the client, a crucial skill in the helping process. Finally, it demonstrated an openness on the part of the worker to admitting feelings and mistakes. The client perceived an adult, a helping professional, who understood the connection between his own feelings and his actions. It is precisely this kind of openness to self-examination that the father will need to develop if the family relationship is to be strengthened.

In the two illustrations thus far, we have seen how the worker's feelings of both caring and anger, when expressed openly, can be helpful to clients. This honest and spontaneous expression of feelings extends to a broad range of worker affective responses. Another example is the feeling of investment a worker can have in a client's progress. For some reason, the idea of "self-determination" has been interpreted to mean that the helping person cannot share a stake in the client's progress and growth. Workers sometimes watch a client struggle towards change and at the points in the process when clients feel most hopeless and ready to quit, workers suppress their own feelings of disappointment. This is a misguided attempt not to influence unduly the client's choices. The following example illustrates the importance of direct expression of a worker's feelings of hope and expectation. The illustration is of a nurse working with a paraplegic young adult in a rehabilitation center. A relationship has developed over months as the nurse has helped the patient deal with his feelings about this sudden change in his life. The exercise program to help the patient develop some limited functioning in his limbs has gone slowly and painfully, and with no signs of a quick recovery. The patient is disappointed by the pace of his progress and becomes depressed and apathetic, refusing to continue. It is at this point the illustration begins.

PATIENT: It's no use continuing, I quit!

NURSE: Look, I know it's been terribly frustrating and damn painful—and that you don't feel you're getting anywhere—but I think you are improving and you have to keep it up.

PATIENT: (With anger) What the hell do you know about it? It's easy for you to say, but I have to do it. I'm not going to get anywhere, so that's that.

NURSE: (With rising emotion) It's not the same for me. I'm not sitting in that wheelchair, but you know, working with you for the past three months has not been a picnic. Half the time you're feeling sorry for yourself and just not willing to work. I've invested a lot of time, energy, and caring in my work with you because I thought you could do it—and I'm not about to see you quit on me. It would hurt me like hell to see you quit because the going gets rough.

The patient did not respond immediately to the "demand for work" expressed in the nurse's affective response. However, the next day, after some time for the feelings to work through, he appeared for physiotherapy without a word about the previous conversation. Once again, we see how a worker's statement of feeling can integrate a highly personal and at the same time, highly professional response. The worker's feelings are the most important tool in the professional tool kit, and any efforts to blunt them results in a working relationship which lacks real substance. Even as I write this statement, I can remember the many objections raised by workers when I have advanced this argument in workshops. Let us take some time to examine these.

Issues in Sharing Worker's Feelings

The first concern relates to the boundaries within which personal feelings can be shared. I believe that if a worker is clear about the purpose of the work with the client (the contract) and the particular professional function, then these will offer important direction and protection. For example, if a client begins an interview by describing a problem with his mother-in-law, the worker would not respond by saying, "You think you have problems with your mother-in-law? Let me tell you about mine!" The client and worker have not come together to discuss the worker's problems, and an attempt by the worker to introduce personal concerns, even those related to the contract area, is an outright subversion of the contract. The client seeks help from the worker, and the worker's feelings about personal relationships can be shared only in ways which relate them directly to the client's immediate concerns. For example, take a situation where a worker feels the client is misinterpreting someone's response because of private feelings. The worker who has experienced that problem might share briefly the experience as a way of providing the client with a new way of understanding a concern.

A second area of major concern for workers is that in sharing their feelings spontaneously, that is without first monitoring all their reactions to see if they are "correct," they risk making inappropriate responses. They are worried that they will make a mistake, act out their own concerns, perhaps hurt a client irretrievably. There is some basis for this fear because we do often respond to clients because of our own needs rather than theirs. A young worker may get angry at an adolescent client's mother because the mother seems as overprotective as the young worker's own. Another worker experiences great frustration with a client who does not respond immediately to an offer of help but moves slowly through the process of change. Although the client makes progress at a reasonable pace, it still makes the worker feel ineffective.

A child care worker misses a number of indirect cues from a resident about a serious problem with his family, whom the child is about to visit over the Christmas vacation. The worker then responds to the child's acting out the feelings by imposing angry punishment instead of hearing the hidden message. Spontaneous expression of feeling will lead to all these mistakes and others. In fact, a helping professional's entire working experience will inevitably consist of making such mistakes, catching them as soon as possible and then rectifying them. A good worker will learn from these experiences something about his or her personal feelings and reactions to people and situations. As this learning deepens, these early "mistakes" will become less frequent. The worker now becomes conscious of new, more sophisticated "mistakes."

Teachers, supervisors, theorists, and colleagues who convey the idea that one tries during interviews to monitor continuously one's feelings, to think clearly before acting, to conduct the perfect interview simply set up blocks to the worker's growth. Only through continuous analysis of some portion of one's work *after* the interview has taken place can workers develop the ability to learn from their mistakes. The more skilled workers, who are truly spontaneous, can catch the mistakes during the interviews—not by withdrawing and thinking, but by using their own feelings and by reaching for the cues in the client's responses. What is often not realized is that clients can forgive a mistake more easily than the image of perfection. They are truly relieved by a worker owning up to having "blown" an interview or not having understood what the client was saying or feeling or overreacting and being angry with a client because of inappropriate responses. An admission of a mistake serves the simultaneous functions of humanizing the worker and indirectly giving the client permission to do the same. Workers who feel clients will lose respect for their "expertise" if they reveal human flaws simply misunderstand the nature of helping. Workers are not "experts" with the "solutions" for clients' problems. The expertise workers bring relates to skills in helping clients work on developing their own solutions to their problems. One of the most important of these skills is the ability to be personally and professionally honest.

Finally, there are some worker feelings which are experienced as potentially too harmful to be expressed. I can understand and agree with this view while feeling that these types of feelings are very few in number. For example, there are many feelings of warmth, caring, and loving which may flow between a worker and a client. These positive feelings are important and constitute a key dynamic which helps to power the helping process. Under certain circumstances, feelings of intimacy may be associated with strong sexual attractions. When the ages and circumstances are right, these mutual attractions are understandable and normal. However, it could be very difficult for a client to handle a worker who honestly shared the sexual attraction. This would be one example of a feeling I would not want to share with a client. While expressing this attraction might be helpful for the worker, I am of the belief that it can be too tough for the client to handle.

Workers sometimes feel in a bind if clients begin to act seductively towards them and even directly request some response from the worker. For example, a young and attractive female worker described her reactions to the "come on" of her paraplegic male client in a rehabilitation setting as "stimulating." She felt somewhat ashamed of her feelings, since she thought they revealed a lack of "professionalism." Most workers in the consultation group where this illustration was presented reported that they, too, had experienced these feelings at times. They had not discussed them with colleagues, supervisors, or teachers because they felt a professional "taboo" against doing so. When the discussion returned to the interaction in the interview with the paraplegic, I asked them to tune in to the meaning of the sexual "come on" in the context of the contract. Speculation began as to the fear of a young client in this situation as to his sexual attractiveness as a "cripple." With a new handle for approaching the issue, it was clear to the worker that the client's feelings and fears about his sexual attractiveness might be a central issue for work which the worker would miss if overwhelmed by her own feelings. A discussion of their mutual sexual attraction might easily avoid a potentially significant area of work. It would be important for workers to feel free to discuss this kind of feeling, as well as others of this type, with their colleagues and supervisors rather than using the helping interviews to work them through.

Research on Sharing Feelings

Research on sharing of feelings has been undertaken in a number of helping professions. The findings have indicated that this skill plays as an important part in the helping process as the empathic skills described earlier.[25] The skill has been described as *self-disclosure, genuineness,* and other labels. The findings on this skill in my own research were among the strongest in the study. The worker's ability to "share personal thoughts and feelings" ranked first as a powerful correlate to developing working relationships and to being helpful.[26] Further analysis of the research data suggested that the use of this skill contributed equally to the work of developing the working relationship and the ability of the worker to be helpful.

It may be that the worker in sharing personal thoughts and feelings breaks down the barriers which clients experience when they are faced with their feelings of dependency implied by taking help. As the worker becomes more "multidimensional," more than just a professional helping person, there is more "person" available for a client to relate to. In addition, thoughts and feelings of a personal nature appear to provide substantive data for the client's tasks and therefore contribute to the helpfulness factor. Perhaps it is the personal nature of the data which makes it appear more relevant to the client, easier to use and to incorporate into a sense of reality. This skill, like many others, may simultaneously serve two functions. A worker shares feelings freely and at the same time effectively strengthens the working relationship (the process) while contributing important ideas for the client's work (the content).

When the profile of the average worker in the study was examined. I found such a worker less able to share thoughts and feelings than to understand and to verbalize client's feelings.[27] These findings were shared with workers in a number of training groups following the completion of the study. They always provoked some of the most important discussions, exploring the reasons why they found it difficult to reveal themselves to clients. The first response was to cite a supervisor, a book, or a former teacher who had made it clear that sharing feelings was unprofessional. After a discussion of these injunctions and their impact on the workers, I would offer to lift them as barriers to the free sharing of feelings. I would say, " Based upon my research, my practice experience, my expertise, I am now telling you that it is no longer 'unprofessional' to be honest with clients and to make your feelings part of your work." I would then inquire how this new freedom would affect their work the next day. After a long silence, a typical response from a worker would be, "You have just made things a lot tougher. Now I'm going to have to face the fact that it's my own feelings which make it hard for me to be honest. I'm not really sure how much of myself I want to share." At this point in the discussions the work usually became real. Developing the ability to be honest in sharing feelings is difficult, but it is possible; we ask clients to do it all the time. Its importance can be underlined by a client's written comment in response to our research questionnaire. She expressed, in her own words, the essence of the statistical finding on sharing feelings: "I like Mrs. Tracy. She's not like a social worker, she's like a real person."

DEMAND-FOR-WORK SKILLS

In constructing this model of the helping process, I have underlined the importance of a clear contract, of identifying the client's agenda, of helping the client to elaborate concerns, of making sure the client invests the work with feeling, and of the worker sharing feelings. At this point in the model-building process, it is important to examine the question of ambivalence and resistance. Clients will be of two minds about proceeding with their work. A part of them, representing their strength, will move towards understanding and growth. The other part of them, representing the resistance, will pull back from what is perceived as a difficult process.

Work often requires discussing painful subjects, experiencing difficult feelings, recognizing one's own contribution to the problem, taking responsibility for one's actions, and lowering long-established defenses. Logical next steps may require a client to tackle a difficult task, to confront someone directly, or to put off immediate satisfactions. Whatever the difficulty involved, a client will show some degree of ambivalence. The amount of movement towards the work (the strength) as compared with the movement away from the work (the resistance) will vary with each individual and the nature of the problem.

Perlman described client ambivalence as follows:

To know one's feelings is to know what they are often many-sided and mixed and that they may pull in two directions at once. Everyone has experienced this duality of wanting something strongly yet drawing back from it, making up one's mind but somehow not carrying out the planned action. This is part of what is meant by ambivalence. A person may be subject to two opposing forces within himself at the same moment—one that says, "Yes, I will," and the other that says, "No, I won't"; one that says, "I want," and the other, "Not really"; one affirming and the other negating.[28]

Relating client ambivalence to the relationship with the worker and the process of taking help, Strean describes resistance as follows:

Recognizing that every client has some resistance to the idea and process of being helped should alert the social-work interviewer to the fact that not every part of every interview can flow smoothly. Most clients at one time or another will find participation difficult or may even refuse to talk at all; others will habitually come late and some may be quite negative toward the agency, the social-work profession, and the social worker.[29]

An example of this ambivalence at work is found in the following videotaped interview with an adolescent foster boy. Early in the interview the eighteen-year-old youngster indirectly hinted at his feelings about leaving a group home and particularly about the warm feelings he had established for the head child care worker. The worker missed the first cues, since she was preoccupied with her written agenda resting on the table between them. Catching her mistake during the session, the worker moved her agenda aside and began to listen systematically to this theme, to encouraging the client to elaborate, and reaching for and articulating his feelings. The following excerpt picks up the interview at the point where the worker responded to the client's second offering of this concern.

WORKER: Is it going to be hard to say good-bye to Tom? (the child care worker)

CLIENT: It's not going to be hard to say good-bye to Tom, but I'll miss the little kittens that sleep with me. Last night one dug his claws into me and I screamed and screamed and yelled to Tom—"Come and get this God damn kitten—do you think I'm going to go around ruptured all my life?" (At this point the client had told the story with such exuberance that the worker was laughing along with him. The client quickly reached over to the table for the worker's written agenda and said, "OK, what's next?")[30]

When the worker was distracted by the agenda, the client continually offered indirect cues related to this important theme. As the worker began to deal seriously with the theme, that part of the client which feared the discussion and the feelings which went along with it found a way to put the worker off using her own agenda.

The important thing to remember is that resistance is quite normal. In fact, a lack of resistance may mean the progress of the work is an illusion with the real issues still unexplored. If this client could have easily dealt with his feelings about terminating his relationship with Tom, he would not have needed the worker's help. Termination feelings are at the core of the work for foster children who must struggle to find ways of investing in new, meaningful relationships in spite of the deep feelings of rejection they feel. When the worker approaches the core area of feeling it would be surprising if resistance didn't appear.

A lack of understanding that *resistance is a part of the work* leads less experienced workers to back off from an important area. Their own confidence in what they are doing is fragile, and so when the client shows signs of defensiveness or unwillingness to deal with a tough problem, they allow themselves to be put off. This is especially true if workers experience ambivalence about dealing with the area themselves. Communication of ambivalence in tough areas can be seen as the client's way of saying, "This is tough for me to talk about." It can also be a question to the worker, "Are you really prepared to talk with me about this?" It is one of those life situations in which the other person says no, hoping you won't really believe him. The surface message seems to say, "Leave me alone in this area," while the real message is, "Don't let me put you off." These are the moments in interviews when the skills of the demand for work are crucial.

The notion of a demand for work is one of Schwartz's most important contributions to our understanding of the helping process. He described it:

The worker also represents what might be called the *demand for work,* in which role he tries to enforce not only the substantive aspects of the contract—what we are here for—but the conditions of work as well. This demand is, in fact, the only one the worker makes—not for certain perceived results, or approved attitudes, or learned behaviors, but for the work itself. That is, he is continually challenging the client to address himself resolutely and with energy to what he came to do.[31]

The construct of demand for work is not limited to a single action or even a single group of skills, but rather it pervades all the work. For example, the process of open and direct contracting in the beginning phase of work represents a form of demand for work. The attempts of the worker to bring the client and feelings into the process is another form of a demand for work. The earlier illustration of the first interview with the angry father in which the worker kept coming back to *his* feelings in the situation is a good example. Similarly, in the interview with the foster child just described, the youngster was discussing, at one point, the feeling that has grown between Tom (the child care worker) and himself, and he said to the worker, "How does it hit people like him?" The worker's response was, "How does it hit you?" This is another illustration of the demand for work. It is important to note that this demand can be gentle and coupled with support. It is not necessarily confrontative in nature.

There are a number of specific skills which lend themselves to being grouped under the category of demand skills. Each is related to specific dynamics in interview situations which could be interpreted as forms of resistance. These are reviewed in the balance of this section. It is important to note that the consistent use of demand skills can only be effective when they are accompanied by the empathic skills described earlier. As the workers express their genuine caring for the client through their ability to empathize, they build up a fund of positive affect which is part of the construct "working relationship." Only when clients perceive that their worker does understand and is not judging them harshly, are they able to respond to the demands.

The argument advanced here is that workers who have the capacity to empathize with clients can develop a positive working relationship but not necessarily be helpful. Workers who only make demands upon their clients, without the empathy and working relationship, will be experienced by clients as harsh, judgmental, and unhelpful. The most effective help will be offered by workers who are able to synthesize, each in their own way, caring and demand. This is not easy to do either in the helping relationship or in life. There is a general tendency to dichotomize these two aspects of relationship—caring about someone, expressing it through empathy, but getting nowhere. This frustration leads to anger and demands with an associated hardening of empathic response. Precisely at this point, when crucial demands are made on the client, the capacity for empathy is most important. With this stipulation clearly in mind, the next section describes four demand-for-work skills.

Partializing Client Concerns

Clients often experience their concerns as overwhelming. A worker may find that a client's response to an offer of help in the contracting phase consists of a flood of problems, each having some impact on the other. The feeling of helplessness experienced by the client is as much related to the apparent difficulty of tackling so many problems as it is to the nature of the problems themselves. The client feels immobilized and does not know how or where to begin. In addition, maintaining problems in this form can represent resistance. If the problems are overwhelming, the client can justify the impossibility of doing anything about them.

Partializing is essentially a problem-solving skill. The only way to tackle complex problems is to break them down into their component parts and to address them one at a time. The way to move past feelings of being immobilized is to begin by taking one small step on one part of the problem. This is the sense in which the worker makes a demand for work. While listening to the concerns of the client, while attempting to understand and acknowledge the client's feelings of being overwhelmed, the worker simultaneously begins the task of helping the client to reduce the problem to smaller, manageable proportions. This skill is illustrated in the following excerpt of an interview with a single parent.

WORKER: You seem really upset by your son's fight yesterday. Can you tell me more about what's upsetting you?

CLIENT: All hell broke loose after that fight. Mrs. Lewis is furious because he gave her son a black eye and is threatening to call the police on me. She complained to the landlord, and he's threatening to throw me out if the kids don't straighten up. I tried to talk to Frankie about it, but I got nowhere. He just screamed at me and ran out of the house. I'm really afraid he has done it this time, and I'm feeling sick about the whole thing. Where will I go if they kick me out—I can't afford another place. And you know the cops gave Frankie a warning last time. I'm scared about what will happen if Mrs. Lewis does complain. I just don't know what to do.

WORKER: It really does sound like quite a mess; no wonder you feel up against the wall. Look, maybe it would help if we looked at one problem at a time. Mrs. Lewis is very angry, and you need to deal with her. Your landlord is important, too, and we should think about what you might be able to say to him to get him to back off while you try to deal with Frankie on this. And I guess that's the big question, what can you say to Frankie since this has made things rougher for the two of you? Mrs. Lewis, the landlord, and Frankie—where should we start?

The demand implied in the worker's statement is gentle and yet firm. The worker can sense the client's feelings of being overwhelmed, but she will not allow the work to stop there. One can see clearly two sets of tasks, those of the worker and those of the client in this illustration. The client raises the concerns, and the worker helps her to partialize her problems. The client must begin to work on them according to her sense of urgency. This is the sense in which work is interactional, with the worker's tasks and those of the client interacting with each other.

The research finding in my study on this skill was most interesting. Partializing was the only one of the four demand-for-work skills in this section which indicated a positive correlation with both relationship building and helpfulness to clients.[32] In a further analysis which allowed me to infer whether the skill of partializing contributed more to building the working relationship or to helpfulness, the surprising finding was that its essential contribution was to relationship building.[33] I would have expected the reverse. A finding such as this one forces the researcher to rethink his hypothesis and to speculate on the meaning of the apparent anomaly. As with all of the findings reported in this study, the nature of the research and its limitations argue for caution in interpretation. This result could be an accident which will not be repeated in future studies.

An alternative explanation may relate to the secondary effect the use of such a skill has on the client. In addition to actually helping in the problem solving, the worker's use of the partializing skill conveys a number of important ideas to the client. First, the worker believes the tasks facing the client are manageable. There has to be some positive affect flowing towards a worker who takes a complex problem and helps to sort it out in this way. Second, the worker conveys the belief that the client can take some next step; that is, that the client has the strength to deal with the problem when properly partialized. The conveying of a secondary message of positive esteem on the worker's part towards the client is then an essential part of a positive working relationship. Finally, another secondary benefit may flow from the worker's focus on the work rather than on the client. A popular public conception of helping is some form of "therapy" in which the problem lies with the client who needs to be "changed." Some support was cited earlier for the positive impact that the clarification of role had on developing the working relationship. Since partializing also serves to focus the work clearly, it may be another form of clarifying role and purpose. The particular finding on the partializing skill suggests that workers might concentrate in the early sessions on helping clients to identify clearly the component parts of the concerns they bring to the worker.

Holding to Focus

As a client begins to deal with a specific concern, associations with other related issues often result in a form of rambling with great difficulty in concentrating on one issue at a time. Once again, the skill of asking the client to stay on one question represents the use of a problem-solving skill incorporating a demand for work. Moving from concern to concern can be an evasion of work—that is, if I don't stay with one issue, then I do not have to deal with the associated feelings. Holding to focus sends the message to the client that the worker means to discuss the tougher feelings and concerns. This skill can be illustrated in the earlier interview with the single parent. After the client decided to deal with Mrs. Lewis first, because of her fear of police involvement, the discussion continued.

CLIENT: When Mrs. Lewis came to the door, all she did was scream at me about how my Frankie was a criminal and that she would not let him beat up her son again.
WORKER: You must have been frightened and upset. What did you say to her?
CLIENT: I just screamed back at her and told her that her son was no bargain and that he probably asked for it. I was really upset because I could see the landlord's door opening, and I know he must be listening. You know he warned me that he wouldn't stand for all of this commotion any more. What can I do if he really kicks me out on the street?
WORKER: Can we stay with Mrs. Lewis for a minute and then get back to the landlord? I can see how angry and frightened you must have felt. Do you have any ideas about how Mrs. Lewis was feeling?

Checking for Underlying Ambivalence

One of the dangers in a helping situation is that a client may choose to go along with the worker, expressing an artificial consensus or agreement, while really feeling very ambivalent about a point of view or a decision to take a next step. A client who feels the worker has an investment in the "solution" may not feel like upsetting the worker by voicing doubts. The client may also be unaware at this moment of the doubts that may

appear later on when implementation of the difficult action is attempted. The client may also withhold concerns as a means of putting off dealing with the core of the issue. In this sense, it is another form of resistance, a very subtle form, since it is expressed passively.

Sometimes workers are aware of the underlying doubts, fears, and concerns but simply pass over them. They believe that raising these issues may cause the client to decide not to take the next step. They believe that positive thinking is required, and they do not wish to heighten the client's ambivalence by discussing it. The reverse is true. When a client has an opportunity to express ambivalence, the worker has access to the client's real feelings and can be of help. The power of the negative feelings can be diminished through the process of discussing them with the worker. Perhaps the client is overestimating the difficulties involved, and the worker can help to clarify the reality of the situation. In other cases, it will indeed be a difficult next step. The worker's help consists of empathic understanding of the difficulty and expression of faith in the client's strength in the face of these feelings. There are any number of reasons for hesitations, but whatever they are, they must be explored, so that they do not work their effect on the client outside of the session.

Workers need to struggle against a sense of elation when they hear clients agreeing to take an important next step. Schwartz described this particular move on the workers' part as "looking for trouble when everything is going your way." The next illustration, drawn from work with a single mother on welfare, helps to illustrate the problem. The mother's younger child was about to finish high school. During an interview with her financial assistance worker, she had raised the possibility of returning to the work force.

WORKER: I think that would be a terrific idea. You could get off welfare, start to earn your own living, and begin to feel a lot better about yourself. You know it's going to be awful lonely after Johnnie leaves home, and having a job can help a lot.
CLIENT: I thought of that, but you know, (hesitantly) jobs are tough to find these days.
WORKER: That's true, but we have an excellent employment counseling program. I'm sure if you met with the employment worker, he could help to match up your interests with available jobs. How about it, will you meet with him?
CLIENT: I guess that would be a first step.
WORKER: Great! I can arrange an appointment for Tuesday afternoon. Would that be all right?
CLIENT: I guess so. I think I'm free that day.

The client did not show up for the agreed appointment. In an analysis of the interview the worker admitted to sensing the client's hesitancy but also to feeling that she could encourage her to take the next steps. In a follow-up interview, the woman apologized profusely for missing the appointment which she said she had simply forgotten. The worker backtracked as follows: "You know I thought about last week, and I think I really rushed you. You have been out of the work force now for twenty years. I guess the idea of going back to work must be a litle scary." The client responded with a flood of feelings about her capacity to work, how employers would view her, whether she could just pick up where she had left off. She continued by saying she was frightened of the idea of going for an interview. This worker was skillful enough to catch her mistake only one week after she had made it. The demand for work in the first interview would have speeded the process up.

When the mother appeared to agree to the interview, she could have simply said that she wondered how the woman would feel about returning to work.

This example provides a good opportunity to elaborate on the earlier comment that resistance is part of the work. It would be a mistake simply to think of client resistance as an obstacle blocking progress. Resistance is not only explored for the purpose of freeing the client to proceed. There are important "handles for work" within the resistance itself. In this example, as the worker explores the client's resistance, a number of important work themes emerge: her capacity for work, how employers would view her, and so on. One colleague of mine described an example in which a young university student, who had been admitted to a psychiatric unit after a suicide attempt, announced early in the first interview that she would not discuss her boyfriend or her family because that would be like blaming them. This is simultaneously resistance and the expression of one of her central concerns related to her guilt over her feelings of anger and resentment. Exploring why she does not want to discuss them could lead directly into a central theme of concern.

Challenging the Illusion of Work

One of the greatest threats to effective helping lies in the ability of the client to create an illusion of work. Much of the helping process I have been describing takes place through an exchange of words (although helping can be achieved through nonverbal means, through touch, and so on). We have all developed the capacity to engage in conversations which are empty and which have no meaning. It is easy to see how this ability to talk a great deal without saying much can be integrated into the helping interaction. This represents a subtle form of resistance because by creating the illusion of work, the client can avoid the pain of struggle and growth while still appearing to work. But for the illusion to take place, it is necessary to have two partners in the ritual. The worker must be willing to *allow* the illusion to be created, thus participating actively in its maintenance. Workers have reported helping relationships with clients that have spanned months, even years, in which the worker always knew, deep down inside, that it was all illusion.

Schwartz described the illusion of work when writing about the practice of group work.

Not only must the worker be able to help people talk but he must help them talk to each other; the talk must be purposeful, related to the contract that holds them together; it must have feeling in it, for without affect there is no investment; and it must be about real things, not a charade, or a false consensus, or a game designed to produce the illusion of work without raising anything in the process.[34]

The skill involves detecting the pattern of illusion, perhaps over a period of time, and confronting the client with the reality. An example from marriage counseling illustrates this process. The couple had requested help for problems in their marriage. As the sessions proceeded, the worker noted that most of the conversation related to problems they were having at work, with their parents, and with their children. Some connection was made to the impact of their marriage; however, they seemed to have created an unspoken alliance not to deal with the details of their relationship. No matter how hard the worker tried to find the connections to how they got along, they always seemed to evade him. Finally, the worker said, "You know when we started out, you both felt you wanted help with the problems in your marriage, how you got along with each other. It seems to me, however, that all we ever talk about is how you get along with other people. You seem to be avoiding the tough stuff. How come? Are you worried it might be too tough to handle?" The worker's challenge to the illusion brought a quick response as the couple explored some of their fears about what would happen if they really began to work. This challenge to the illusion was needed to help the couple begin the difficult process of risking. In addition, their response illustrates how the resistance itself reveals a great deal about the underlying problems.

Research Findings

The findings on the demand-for-work skills were most interesting because of their lack of significance. With the exception of partializing, the specific skills described in this section were not found to be associated with relationship building or helpfulness.[35] Once again, a finding which does not support a researcher's hypothesis can be distressing, but it can also be an opportunity for further thinking about the theoretical assumptions underlying the work. A few possibilities occurred to me. First, the skills were looked at in isolation. It may well be that these skills, holding to focus, checking for underlying ambivalence, and challenging the illusion of work, since they are skills of confrontation, require simultaneous use with the empathic skills. If so, then this finding raises interesting questions about the types of demand for work made by the worker. Since an element of criticism is inherent in these demands, perhaps they have to be made "softly" and made with understanding. The client needs to sense the demand and at the same time not feel that the worker is judging the ambivalence harshly. This question of "soft" versus "hard" demands, the conjoint influence of demand skills and support skills, offers interesting ideas for future research and theorizing. Research findings in psychotherapy have already pointed to a positive association between the use of "facilitative confrontation" skills and effectiveness.[36]

A striking finding in this area, which did support the researcher's hypothesis, was that demand skills such as these were among some of the least used skills by the average worker in the study.[37] The frequency of use was related to the difficulty in making the demand. Workers were able to partialize effectively, but less able to hold to focus. Checking for underlying ambivalence and challenging the illusion of work were the two least used skills. While there is a strong possibility this may have been a result of the wording on the questionnaire, since there was some evidence of lack of reliability on these items, nevertheless, I believe these findings are an accurate reflection of the difficulty workers experience in using these skills. They may sense the potential threats to the relationship involved in making demands and therefore refrain. This is the way in which the worker and the client both contribute to the illusion of work through their mutual refusal to risk their real thoughts and feelings.

POINTING-OUT OBSTACLES SKILLS

When developing his theory of the mediation function for social work, Schwartz broke down the function into five general sets of tasks. One of these was the task of searching out the common ground between the client and the systems to be negotiated. This task is evident when the worker attempts to contract with clients, that is, find the connections between the felt needs of the client and the services of the agency. It is also apparent when the worker attempts to alert himself or herself to the subtle connections between the needs of a teenager for independence and the desire of the parents to see their youngsters grow. These are just a few of the many moments when the common ground between the individual and the system may appear to each to be diffused, unclear, even totally absent.

Because of the complexity of relationships and the potential for the common ground to be obscured Schwartz elaborates his mediation function with a second set of important activites, the task of "detecting and challenging the obstacles to work as these obstacles arise."[38] Like all Schwartz's tasks this one is not a single activity but one which is repeated, moment by moment, in each and every helping encounter. Two of the major obstacles which tend to frustrate people as they work on their own self-interest are the blocking effects of social taboos and the effect of the "authority theme," the relationship between the person who gives help and the one who takes it.

Supporting Clients in Taboo Areas

In moving into a helping relationship the client brings along a sense of the societal culture which includes taboos against open discussion in certain sensitive areas. For example, we are taught from childhood that direct questions and discussions about sex are frowned upon. Other areas in which we are subtly encouraged not to acknowledge our true feelings include dependency, authority, and money. To feel dependent is equated with feeling weak. The image of a "real man" is of one who is independent, able to stand on his own feet, and competent to deal with life's problems by himself. This does not match reality. In the real world life is so complex that we are always dependent and interdependent upon others. The bind we experience is that of feeling one way, consciously or not, but thinking we *should* feel another way. The norms of our culture include a clear taboo which makes real talk in such areas difficult.

Money is considered a taboo subject as well. Many families resent deeply questions related to their financial affairs. Having enough money is equated with competency in our society, and the admisssion of poverty is considered embarrassing. Reluctance to discuss fees with professionals is another example of the effect of the taboo against open discussion about money. Many professionals have developed a system whereby money is discussed by their nurse or assistant. It would be beneath their dignity to discuss it directly with the client. Clients will often accept services without asking about the fee, feeling that it would be embarrassing to inquire.

One of the most powerful taboos relates to feelings towards authority. Parents, teachers, and other authority figures do not generally encourage feedback from children in the nature of the relationship. We learn early on that commenting on this relationship, especially if the reactions are negative, is fraught with danger. People in authority have power to hurt us, and therefore, we will, at best, hint at our feelings and reactions. It is almost as hard to reveal positive feelings to people in authority, since our peer group has taught us that this is considered demeaning. This taboo creates an important problem in the working relationship between the worker and the client as I will demonstrate in the next section.

A worker who is to help a client discuss feelings and concerns in these areas and others experienced as taboo will have to create an unique "culture" in the helping interview. In this culture it will become acceptable to discuss feelings and concerns which the client may experience as taboo elsewhere. The taboo is not going to be removed for all situations. There are some good reasons for us not to talk freely and intimately on all occasions about our feelings in taboo areas. The purpose of the discussion of the taboo in the interview is not to change the client's attitudes forever, only to allow work in the immediate situation. The way the worker does this is to monitor the interaction of the work with the client and to listen for clues which may reveal a block in the process related to a taboo. The worker's past experiences with clients and the tuning in process may heighten sensitivity to a taboo which is just beneath the surface of the interivew. On recognizing the taboo, the worker brings it out in the open and begins the negotiation of a new norm of behavior for the interview situation. The following illustration is from an interview between a nurse and a male, forty-eight-year-old patient. It demonstrates how a helping professional can support a client in discussing a taboo subject.

PATIENT: I've been feeling lousy for a long time. It's been especially bad since my wife and I have been arguing so much.

NURSE: Tell me more about the arguments.

PATIENT: They've been about lots of things—she complains I drink too much, I'm not home often enough, and that I always seem too tired to spend time with her. (At this point, the nurse senses the patient's difficulty in talking. His hesitation and an inability to look directly at her are the cues).

NURSE: Often when there is a lot of

difficulty like this, it spills over into the sexual area.

PATIENT: (After a long pause) There have been some problems around sex as well.

NURSE: You know I realize that it's tough to talk about something as intimate as sex, particularly for a man to discuss it with a woman. It's really not something one can do easily.

PATIENT: It is a bit embarrassing.

NURSE: Perhaps you can speak about it in spite of your embarrassment. You know there is not much I haven't heard already, and I won't mind hearing what you have to say. Anyway, we can't do much about the problems if we can't discuss them.

PATIENT: I've been tired lately with a lot of worries. Sometimes I have too much to drink as well. Anyway, I've been having trouble getting it up for the past few months.

NURSE: Is this the first time this has happened?

PATIENT: The first time, I usually have no trouble at all.

NURSE: It must have come as quite a shock to you. I guess this has hit you and your wife hard.

The discussion continued in more detail about the nature of the problem. Other symptoms were described, and the nurse suggested that a complete physical was in order. She pointed out that it was not at all unusual for these things to happen to men of this age and that often there were physiological reasons. At the end of the interview the nurse reinforced the development of the new norm in her working relationship by commenting, "I know how hard it was for you to speak to me about this. It was important, however, and I hope this discussion will help you to feel free to talk about whatever is on your mind." The patient answered that he felt better now that he had been able to get it off his chest.

It is important to stress that identifying the taboo or any other obstacle which obstructs the process of work with a client is done for the purpose of freeing the client's energy to work on the negotiated contract. Sometimes all that is necessary is for the obstacle to be named to release the client from its power. In other situations, some exploration of the obstacle may be needed before its impact on the work can be reduced. For example, a client might need to talk briefly about the difficulty he felt in discussing issues related to sex. His family norms might have added to the normal pressures against such open discussion. The worker needs to guard against a subtle subversion of the contract which can easily occur if the discussion of the obstacle becomes the focus of the work. The purpose of the helping encounter is not to examine the reasons why the taboo exists nor is it to free the client from its power in all situations. The importance and power of clarity of purpose and function is best demonstrated when they assist the worker in avoiding the trap of becoming so engrossed in the analysis of the process that the original task becomes lost.

Research Findings

The research finding on this skill suggested that it was important in contributing to the development of a working relationship as well as helpfulness.[39] In comparing the correlations between the skills and relationship/helpfulness, we found that this skill was tenth in importance in developing working relationships and third in correlating with helpfulness.[40] While these findings must be viewed with great tentativeness, they did support the notion that workers need to pay special attention to the skills required in helping clients overcome their reluctance to discuss taboo subjects. In the profile of the average worker in the study, one finds that this skill is less used than many of the others.[41] In another analysis in the study, fifteen workers with the best overall average on their skill use scores were compared with fifteen with the lowest overall average.[42] Those workers with the best overall average scores were found to have better working relationships and to be more helpful, as judged by their clients, than the fifteen with the lower behavior scores. When one compares the individual skills of the two groups, one finds that supporting in taboo areas is one of the skills with the largest difference in scores.

Another aspect of the general study provided additional information which relates to the importance of this skill. An effort was made to examine the content of the discussions between workers and clients. Clients were asked to rate how important they felt it was to discuss a number of specific concerns with their workers. They were also asked to indicate how often they actually did discuss these concerns. It was interesting to note that clients indicated their desire to discuss many of the more sensitive areas. In addition, they reported the lack of such discussion in their meetings with workers. These were many of the same subjects which workers had indicated to me they felt clients were reluctant to discuss. When this was explored in consultation workshops, it became clear that workers picked up the ambivalent messages their clients sent about taboo areas. Since workers were just as much conditioned by the societal injunctions as their clients, the worker's own ambivalence often led to a response to the part of the message indicating reluctance to proceed. It became clear that very little help had been given workers in exploring their own feelings about discussing sex, authority, dependency, death, and other difficult subjects.

In the subtle communication which passes between worker and client, clients must have sensed their workers' hesitancy to enter the taboo area, a hesitancy which mirrored their own.

Dealing with the Authority Theme

The authority theme refers to "the familiar struggle to resolve the relationship with a nurturing and demanding figure who is both a personal symbol and a representative of a powerful institution."[43] As the client uses the worker's help to deal with this task, positive and negative affect will be generated. There will be times when the client thinks fondly of this caring and supportive figure. There will be other times when the client feels anger for a worker who makes demands to take responsibility for the client's own part in the events of his life. Workers are not perfect individuals who never make mistakes. Even the most skilled worker will miss a client's communications or lose track of the real function and begin to sermonize or judge the client harshly without compassion for real struggles. Reactions and feelings on the part of the client will result. As one enters a helping relationship, problems with the authority theme should be anticipated as a normal part of the work. In fact, the energy flow between worker and client can provide the driving force which helps to power the work.

Two processes which are central in the authority them are "transference" and "countertransference." Strean describes their effects on the worker-client relationship, drawing upon the psychoanalytic theory of Freud.[44]

This relationship has many facets: subtle and overt, conscious and unconscious, progressive and regressive, positive and negative. Both client and worker experience themselves and each other not only in terms of objective reality, but in terms of how each wishes the other to be and fears he might be. The phenomena of "transference" and "countertransference" exists in every relationship between two or more people, professional or nonprofessional, and must be taken into account in every social-worker-client encounter. By "transference" is meant the feelings, wishes, fears, and defenses of the client deriving from reactions to significant persons in the past (parents, siblings, extended family, teachers), that influence his current perceptions of social worker. "Countertransference" similarly refers to aspects of the social worker's history of feelings, wishes, fears, and so on, all of which influence his perceptions of the client.[45]

Unfortunately, the authority theme is one of the most powerfully taboo areas in our society. Clients have as much difficulty talking about their reactions and feelings towards their workers as they do discussing subjects such as sex. When these feelings and reactions are generated but not brought to the surface, the helping relationship is in trouble. These strong feelings operate just below the surface and emerge in many indirect forms. The client becomes apathetic or is late for appointments or can't seem to follow up on commitments. The worker searches for answers to the questions raised by the client's behavior by attempting to understand it in terms of the client's "personality." The answers to the worker's questions are often much closer to home and more accessible than the intangible notion of "personality." The answers may often be found in the interactional process between the worker and client.

The skill of dealing with the authority theme involves the worker's continual monitoring of the relationship. A worker who senses that the work seems unreal or is blocked can call attention to the existence of the obstacle and try to respond directly if the source of the trouble may be the authority theme. Once again, as with other taboo subjects, the worker is trying to create a "culture" in this situation in which the client perceives a new norm: "It is all right to treat the worker like a real person and to say what you think about how he deals with you." The worker can begin the process in the contracting stages, as pointed out in Chapter 3, in responding directly to the early cues that the client wants some discussion about what kind of worker this will be. The new "culture" will develop slowly as the client tests this strange kind of authority person who seems to invite direct feedback, even the negative kind. As the client perceives the worker will not punish, then the ability to feed responses back to the worker more quickly will grow. As an important side product, the client is exposed to a worker who is nondefensive and is demonstrating the capacity to examine his or her own behavior and to be open to change, exactly what the worker will be asking the client to do.

The following illustration demonstrates the skill in action. It describes a brief interaction between a child care worker and a fourteen-year-old male resident in a group home. The resident had been disciplined by the worker that afternoon for a fight he appeared to have provoked with another resident. The worker's one-sided intervention had shifted the fight to a battle of wills between John and himself which then escalated until he finally imposed strict consequences. John had been quiet and sullen throughout dinner and the early evening. The worker approached him in the lounge.

WORKER: John, you have been looking mad all evening, ever since the fight. Let's talk about it.

CLIENT: F—k off!

WORKER: Look, I know you're mad as hell at me, but it won't help to just sit there and keep it in. It will be miserable for both of us if you do. If you think I wasn't fair to you, I want to hear about it. You know I'm human, and I can make a mistake, too. So how about it, what's bugging you?

CLIENT: You're just like all the rest. The minute I get into trouble, you blame me. It's always my fault, never the other kids'. You took Jerry's side in that fight without ever asking me why I was beating up on him.

WORKER: (Short silence) I guess I did come down hard on you quickly. You know you're probably right about my figuring it was your fault when you get in trouble—probably because you get into trouble so often. I think I was also a little tired this afternoon and maybe not up to handling a fight on my shift. Look, let's start again. OK? I think I can listen now. What happened?

The discussion carried on about the fight and the issues which led up to it. It became clear that there were some ongoing questions between John and Jerry which needed to be argued out. The worker suggested another meeting with Jerry present at which time he would try not to take sides and try to help both John and Jerry work this out. John indicated some willingness to try but with a great deal of skepticism. The interview continued and the worker returned to the authority theme.

WORKER: You know, I really wasn't helpful to you this afternoon, and I'm sorry about that. But you know, I'm only human, and that is going to happen sometimes. What I'd like you to do, if it happens again, is not just sit around upset but to call me on it. If you do, I may catch myself sooner. Do you think you can do that?

CLIENT: Don't worry, I'll let you know if you get out of line.

WORKER: I guess this kind of thing happens a lot to you, I mean with the other staff here and maybe even the teachers at school.

CLIENT: You bet it does! Mr. Fredericks is always on my back, the minute I turn around in my seat.

In this illustration the worker was able to catch his mistake and to have an important discussion about the *way which they worked together.* His willingness to own up to his own mistake and to take negative feedback contributed to a change in the subtle rules which have governed this child's reaction to adults in authority. The worker was very conscious that one of the most important outcomes of the youngster's stay in the group home may be his development of greater skill dealing with authority people who are not always conscious of their effect on him. In many ways, the helping relationship itself is a training ground in which the client develops new skills at dealing with authority people and that in itself is a major achievement. For some clients, particularly children in alternative care facilities, their ability to trust adults and to risk themselves is so limited that a profound change would be embodied in their ability to relate in a new way to the workers. It becomes a first step in developing their skills at dealing with the outside world which may not always be as skillful in dealing with them as this worker had been.

The worker also demonstrated an advanced level of skill by the move at the end of the illustration when he deftly integrated process and task. Part of his work with John involves helping him to deal with the other systems of his life, like the school. By generalizing to another situation, the worker found the work element, related to their contract, which was contained in the process. Dealing with the authority theme is not only a requirement for maintaining a positive working relationship; it may also provide important material for helping clients to work on the substance of the contract. In another example of this idea of the possible synthesis of process and task, a social worker used her discussion with a foster teenager about the termination of service to open up a discussion of the difficulty the youngster had in making new relationships after so many had ended badly. Their own ending provided an important opportunity for substantive work on how he could deal with new relationships now that he was leaving the care of the agency. In a final example, one worker explored the difficulty a married client was having in allowing himself to feel dependent upon the worker and the discomfort he felt at expressing his need for help. The difficulty seemed related to many of his notions of what a "real man" should feel. The work on the authority theme led directly to discussions of how hard it was for him to let his wife know how much he needed her. In each of these examples, dealing with the authority theme served two distant functions. It freed the working relationship from a potential obstacle and led directly to important substantive work on the contract.

Research Findings

The profile of the average worker in the study indicated a general willingness to invite feedback.[46] This was another of the skills on which the group of workers with positive skill scores differed from the group with negative scores.[47] The finding that the average worker in the study did appear open to feedback was somewhat surprising. I had expected, based upon my consulting work with workers, that accepting negative feedback might be one of the more advanced skills which workers developed with experience and a growing confidence in their

ability. A possible alternative interpretation of this finding may relate to the selectivity in the responses to the study. While over 2,000 clients participated, there seemed to be a smaller rate of return from clients who were contesting agency actions and were thus assumed to be angrier and more critical. No evidence was found to indicate that those contesting clients who did respond answered strikingly differently from respondents who were not contesting; however, the possibility exists that this particular finding may have been more open to influence by a mellow sample (one with less angry clients).

In summary, this section has identified two of the major obstacles which may impede the work of the client. I have argued that paying attention to such obstacles, that is the process of work, is crucial to the accomplishments of the tasks. Detecting, challenging, and exploring taboos will free a client to use the worker's help in sensitive areas. Maintaining open communication on the nature of the working relationship, the authority theme, will help to strengthen the relationship.

SHARING-DATA SKILLS

Data is defined as facts, ideas, values, and beliefs which workers have accumulated from their own experiences and which they make available to clients.

Schwartz argues,

The worker's grasp of social reality is one of the important attributes that fit him to his functions. While his life experiences cannot be transferred intact to other human beings, the products of these experiences can be immensely valuable to those who are moving through their own struggles and stages of mastery.[48]

Not only is it important for workers to share data because of the potential usefulness to the client, but the process of sharing the data is also important in building a working relationship. The client looks to the worker as a source of help in difficult areas. If the client senses that the worker is withholding data, for whatever reason, the withholding can be experienced as a form of rejection. As a client might put it, "If you really cared about me, you would share what you know."

I remember an experience during my social work training when a fellow student, majoring in group work, described his work with a group of teenaged boys in a residential institution. They were planning their first party and were obviously without any sense of the quantities of food and drink required. The soda pop they ordered, for example, would not last given the number of people present. When I asked if he had pointed this out to them, he replied that he had not interfered, since they would learn something important about planning. I was shocked and felt that if they ever found out he knew they were underestimating quantities and had not told them, their significant learning would be about him. While the skills of sharing data may sound simple, a number of misconceptions about how people learn and a lack of clarity about the helping function have served to make a simple act complex. The problems can be seen in the actions of workers who have important information for the client but withhold it because the client must "learn it for himself." These problems are also apparent in the actions of workers who claim to be allowing clients to "learn for themselves" while they indirectly "slip in" their ideas. This is most easily recognizable in interviews where the worker leads a client to the answer that the worker already has in mind. The belief is that

learning takes place if the client speaks the words the worker wants to hear. In the balance of this section I will identify some of the skills involved in sharing data and discuss some of the issues which often lead workers to be less than direct.

Providing Relevant Data

The skill is the direct sharing of the worker's facts, ideas, values, and beliefs which are related to the client's immediate task at hand. The two key requirements suggested by Schwartz are that the data be related to the working contract and that it is needed by the client for the immediate work. If the worker is clear about the purpose of the encounter and that purpose has been openly negotiated with the client, then the worker has a guideline as to what data is appropriate to share. A problem is created when the worker wants to "teach" something indirectly to the client and uses the interchange to "slip in" personal ideas. This mistaken sense of function on the worker's part is rooted in a model in which the worker can "change" the client by skillfully presenting "good" ideas. The problem is that the client soon senses that the worker has a "hidden agenda" and instead of using the worker as a resource for the client's own agenda, must begin to weigh the worker's words to see what is "up his or her sleeve." This hidden purpose often creates a dilemma for a worker in sharing data directly. A part of the worker is uncomfortable about efforts to impose an ideology on the client, thus treating the client as an object to be molded. This ambivalence comes out in the indirectness in which the ideas are shared. If data are related to an openly agreed upon purpose, then the worker is free to share them directly.

The second requirement for directly

sharing data is that the data be connected to the client's immediate sense of concern. Clients will not learn something which the worker feels may be of use to them at some future date, even if it is related to the working contract. The attraction people feel towards objects (e.g., ideas, values) is related to their sense of their usefulness at the time. One reason for the importance of sessional contracting is that the worker needs to determine the client's current sense of urgency and must share data which the client perceives as helpful. An example of sharing data which are not immediately relevant is a practice I have observed in work with preadoptive couples in child welfare agencies. Individual or group work is often employed for the dual purposes of evaluating the couples' suitability as adoptive parents and helping them discuss the adoption. It is not unusual for the worker to prepare a well-developed agenda for group meetings touching on all the issues that workers feel the couples will need to face as adoptive parents. Unfortunately, such an agenda may often miss the immediate concerns preadoptive parents have about adoption and about agency procedures for the accepting and rejecting of parents. In the following illustration adoptive couples in a second group session respond to the worker's request: "Should one tell adoptive children they were adopted? If yes, when and how?" The important point to remember is that these couples are still waiting to hear if they are going to get children and are all expecting infants. The issue of whether to tell is one which will not present itself until a few years after the child is adopted.

MR. FRANKS: I think you have to tell the child or you won't be honest.

MR. BECK: But if you tell him, then he probably will always wonder about his real parents and that may make him feel less like you are his parents.

(This comment starts a vigorous discussion between the men about how a child feels towards his adoptive parents. The worker uses this opportunity to contribute her own views indirectly; she already has an "acceptable" answer to her question.)

WORKER: I wonder, Mr. Beck, how you think the child might feel if you didn't tell him and he found out later.

MR. BECK: (Recognizing that he may have given the wrong answer to the worker who will also judge his suitability to be an adoptive parent.) You know, I hadn't really looked at it that way. I guess you're right, it would be easier to tell right away.

When the group had apparently reached the consensus that the worker had intended from the start, she shifted the discussion to the question of when and how to tell. Unfortunately, the urgency of the issue of "telling" was not an immediate one. Preadoptive couples are more concerned with how *they* will feel towards their adoptive child. This is a very sensitive subject, particularly since preadoptive couples are not sure about the agency's criteria for acceptance. They worry that they may be rejected if they don't express the "right" attitudes and feelings. This cuts them off from a supportive experience in which they might discover that most preadoptive parents are "in the same boat," that it is normal for them to have doubts, and that the agency will not hold that against them. In fact, parents who are in touch with their feelings, including such feelings as these, are often the ones who make excellent adoptive parents. Because the worker was so occupied by "teaching" ideas for future use, she missed the most important issue. Compare the earlier example with the following excerpt. In this case, the parents raised the question of "should one tell?" and the worker listened for cues to the present concern.

MR. FRIEDMAN: (Responding to a group member's argument that the kids would not feel they were their real parents.) I can't agree with that. I think the real parent is the one that raises you, and the kids will know that's you even if they are adopted.

WORKER: You have all been working quite hard on this question of how your adopted child will feel towards you, but I wonder if you aren't also concerned about how you will feel towards the child?

(Silence)

MR. FRIEDMAN: I don't understand what you mean.

WORKER: Each of you are getting ready to adopt a child who was born to another set of parents. In my experience it is quite normal and usual for a couple at this stage to wonder sometimes about how they will feel towards the child. "Will I be able to love this child as if it were my own?" is not an uncommon question and a perfectly reasonable one in my view.

MRS. REID: My husband and I have talked about that at home—and we feel we can love our child as if he were our own.

WORKER: You know we would like the group to be a place where you can talk about your real concerns. Frankly, if you're wondering and have doubts and concerns such as this, that doesn't eliminate you from consideration as an adoptive parent. Being able to face your real concerns and feelings is very much in your favor. You folks wouldn't be in this group if we hadn't already felt you would make good adoptive parents. It would be the rare situation in which we would have to reconsider.

The worker shared some important data with these clients that was relevant both to the general contract of the group and to their immediate sense of urgency. They learned that their feelings, doubts, and concerns were not unusual, that the agency did not eliminate prospective adoptive parents for being human and having normal worries, that the group was a place to discuss these feelings, and finally, that their presence in the group indicated that they were all considered good applicants. This comment was followed by a deeper discussion of their feelings toward their prospective child and the adoption. These included their concern over the possibility of getting a child from a "bad seed," their fears as to the reactions of friends and family, and some of their real feelings of anger about the delays and procedures involved in dealing with the agency. The data shared by the worker in these areas was more meaningful to these parents than information about future problems. Agencies often offer follow-up groups for adoptive parents at key moments along the child's developmental path which can focus more clearly on issues that are only theoretical in the preadoptive stage.

Providing Data in a Way That Is Open to Examination

Workers are sometimes fearful of sharing their own fears, values, and so forth because of a genuine concern over influencing clients who need to make a difficult decision. The unwed mother, for example, trying to decide whether to abort her child, to have it and keep it, or to have it and give it up for adoption faces some agonizing decisions, none of which will be easy. In each case there will be important implications for her life which she will have to live with. The skillful worker will help such a client explore these implications and the underlying feelings of ambivalence which may be associated with them in detail. During this work the client may turn to the worker at some point and say, "If you were me, what would you do?" Workers often have opinions about questions such as these but hold them back, usually responding to the question with a question of their own. I believe it is better for workers to share their feelings about revealing their opinions and then to allow the client access to their views representing one source of reality. For example:

When you ask me that question, you really put me on the spot. I'm not you, and no matter how hard I try, I can't be you, since I won't have to live with the consequences. For what it's worth, I think the way you have spelled it out, it's going to be an awfully tough go for you if you keep the baby. I probably would place the child for adoption. Now, having said that, you know it's still possible that you can pull it off, and only you know what you're ready for right now. So I guess my answer doesn't solve a thing for you, does it?

Workers who withhold their opinion are concerned that the client will adopt it as the only source of reality. Rather than holding back I believe that a worker should simultaneously allow the client access to his or her opinions while guarding against the client's tendency to use them to avoid difficult work. Schwartz describes this consideration which guides the worker's movements as follows:

The first [consideration] is his awareness that his offering represents only a fragment of available social experience. If he comes to be regarded as the fountainhead of social reality, he will then have fallen into the error of presenting himself as the object of learning rather than as an accessory to it. Thus, there is an important distinction to be made between lending his knowledge to those who can use it in the performance of their own tasks and projecting himself as a text to be learned.[49]

Thus far I have described how a worker can provide data to clients in a way which is open to examination by making sure that the client uses this data as just one source of reality. An additional consideration is to make sure that what is shared is seen as the worker's own opinion, belief, values, or whatever rather than as fact. This is one of the most difficult ideas for many workers to comprehend, since it contradicts the normal pattern in society for exchanging ideas. Workers have an investment in their own views and will often attempt to convince the client of their validity. We are used to arguing our viewpoint by using every means possible to substantiate it as fact. New workers in particular feel it is essential to present their credentials to clients in order to convince them that they know what they are talking about. In actual fact, our ideas about life, our values, and even our "facts" are constantly changing and evolving. A cursory reading of child-rearing manuals would convince anyone that the hard and fast rules of yesterday are often reversed by the theories of today. I have found that workers are often most dogmatic in relation to areas where they feel most uncertain.

The skill of sharing data in a way that is open for examination means that the worker must qualify statements in order to help the client sort out the difference between reality and the worker's sense of reality. Rather than being a salesperson for an idea, the worker should present it with all of its limitations. A consistent and honest use of such expressions as "this is the way I see it" or "this is what I believe, which doesn't mean it's true" or "many people believe" will begin to convey to the client that tentativeness of the worker's beliefs. The worker must encourage the client to challenge these ideas when they do not ring true to the client. Any nonverbal signals of disagreement mean that the worker needs to reach for the underlying questions. For example, "You don't look like you agree with what I just said. How do you see it?" The client's different opinions need to be respected and valued. Even if all the experts support the idea, fact, or value at issue, it will only have meaning for the client if and when the client finds it useful. In many ways the worker is a model of someone who is still involved in a search for reality. Every idea, no matter how strongly held, needs to be open to challenge by the evidence of the senses. The worker is asking the client to do the same in relation to life, and the client should not expect any less of the worker. Schwartz sums this up:

As he [the worker] helps them to evaluate the evidence they derive from other sources—their own experiences, the experiences of others, and their collaboration in ideas—so must he submit his own evidence to the process of critical examination. When the worker understands that he is but a single element in the totality of the [group] member's experience, and when he is able to use this truth rather than attempt to conquer it, he has taken the first step toward helping the member to free himself from authority without rejecting it.[50]

Research Finding

The research finding on the skill of providing data indicated it contributed to both relationship building and helpfulness, apparently more significantly to the former.[51] While this finding was not a strong one, it offered some support for the notion that the most important aspect of sharing data is the access the client gains to the worker.

Viewing Systems People in New Ways

A specific form of data was viewed as important enough to be included as a separate skill. This is the skill in which the worker offers a perception of the important person or system in the client's life (e.g., husband, parent, the school) different from the one held by the client. Clients have developed their view of life subjectively. Given the difficulties involved in communications, they quite possibly distort other people's actions. By posing an alternative view, the worker attempts to identify the part of the system or the important person that may still be reaching out to the client. In a way, the worker plays the role of the missing person in the interview articulating what might be the thoughts and feelings beneath the surface. For example, here is an excerpt from an interview between a school counselor and an adolescent who is having trouble in a class.

CLIENT: Mr. Brown is always after me, always putting me down when I'm late with my work. I think he hates me.
COUNSELOR: You know, it could be that Mr. Brown knows that you're having trouble keeping up and is really worried about your failing. He may be keeping after you to try to get you going again.
CLIENT: Well, it doesn't help. All it makes me do is want to miss his class.
COUNSELOR: He might not realize that what he says makes you feel so badly. Maybe it would help if I could let him know that you feel he is really mad at you.

The work continued with a discussion of the student's fears of what might happen if the counselor talked to the teacher and the counselor's reassurance about how he would handle it. Mr. Brown was surprised at the student's feelings. He had been frustrated because he felt the student didn't care about school. A joint meeting was held to begin to discuss what each really felt in relation to the child's schoolwork. This started to open doors for collaboration.

After a period of bad experiences the blocks in the reality of the relationship become the client's (and sometimes the system's) only view of reality itself. At these moments a worker offers the possibility of hope and some next step by being able to share a view of the system's person which allows the client to glimpse some possibility of mutual attraction. This is only possible when workers themselves see these possibilities which have been described earlier as the areas of common ground. The worker who can help the teenager see that his parents' setting of curfew limits may be a reflection of caring for him as well as a recognition that he is growing up has not solved the problem. However, at least he has put a new light on the interaction. The child care worker who helps a resident see that a parent who misses visits may not be saying that he doesn't care for the child but rather that he really cares too much also holds out the possibility of reconciliation.

The finding of my research on this particular skill was not strong; however, it correlated with helping to develop a working relationship,[52] perhaps indicating that the importance of sharing new ways to see a systems person is not in its content but rather in its impact on the relationship with the worker. The client will have to revise some thinking about people and systems which are important in his or her own time and based upon personal experiences. It takes many years to build up stereotypes of parents, systems, and people in authority, and it will take more than the worker's words to change them. In expressing these alternative views which help the client see strengths and mutual attraction, the worker is making an important statement about views of life. The willingness to see the positive side in people's behavior and not to be a harsh judge of people's weaknesses may say a great deal to clients about how the worker might view them. This could contribute to strengthening the working relationship.

SESSIONAL-ENDING SKILLS

As with beginnings and middles, endings contain their own unique dynamics and special requirements for worker skills. I have described this phase elsewhere as the "resolution stage."[53] It is not unusual to find workers carrying out their sessional contracting, demonstrating sensitive work with clients on their concerns, and then ending a session without a resolution of the work. By resolution of the work I am not suggesting that each session end neatly, all issues fully discussed, ambivalences gone, and next steps carefully planned. A sign of advanced skill is a worker's tolerance for ambiguity and uncertainness which may accompany the end of a session dealing with difficult work. If uncertainty is present for a client at the end of a session, then the resolution stage might consist of identifying the status of the discussion. The five skills discussed in the balance of this section include summarizing, generalizing, identifying next steps, rehearsal, and identifying "doorknob" communications.

Before describing these skills, it is important to comment on the question of client activity between sessions. Workers sometimes believe that clients have no life between sessions. They review an individual counseling session or a group meeting and then prepare to pick up the next session "where we left off." Schwartz comments on the continuity of client experience in the group context:

...the meeting does not end when it is over, but moves, via the informal system, into an interim phase of communication in which the difference is that the worker is not present. This is another way of saying that the life of a group does not proceed in quantum jumps, but in a continuous and unbroken process, with the meetings constituting a special—but not isolated—event in that process. Thus, in a group that meets weekly for ten weeks, there is considerable difference in whether the life of the group is regarded as ten meetings or ten weeks.[54]

The individual client, as well, also has life experiences, contacts with other helping systems (e.g., family, friends), new problems which may emerge during the week, and has had some time to think about problems discussed. It would be a mistake not to recognize and legitimate these between session activities. That is one of the reasons for the importance of the sessional contracting skill described at the beginning of this chapter.

The Skill of Summarizing

In many ways, the client is learning about life and trying to develop new skills for managing it in more satisfying ways. It can be important to use the last moments of a session to help the client identify the learnings. How does the client add up the experiences? What are the new insights the client has in understanding relationships to others? What has the client identified as the next, most urgent set of tasks? What are the areas the client feels hopeless about, at a loss about what to do, and needing to continue to discuss? I believe the process of summarizing can help a client secure the grasp of learning. Sometimes the client may summarize the work; other times the worker may try, and sometimes they can do it together. It is important to note that summarizing is not required in all sessions. This is not an automatic ritual, but rather, a skill to be employed at key moments.

The skill is illustrated in the following excerpt from an interview with a mildly retarded, sixteen-year-old boy who is discussing a relationship with his mother who he feels is overprotective. After a painful session in which the worker has asked the youngster to examine his own part in maintaining the problem, the resolution stage begins.

WORKER: (John paused and seemed thoughtful.) This hasn't been easy, John; it's never easy to take a look at your own actions this way. Tell me, what do you think about this now?
(Silence)
JOHN: I guess you're right. As long as I act like a baby, my mother is going to treat me like a baby. I know I shouldn't feel like such a dummy, that I can do some things real well—but you know that's hard to do.
WORKER: What makes it hard, John?
JOHN: I have felt like a dummy for so long, it's hard to change now. I think what was important to me was when you said I have to take responsibility for myself now. I think that's right.
WORKER: If you did, John, then maybe your mother might see how much you have grown up.

The Skill of Generalizing

In an earlier discussion, I underlined the importance of moving from the general to the specific as a way of facilitating the immediate work of the client. As clients deal with life, problem by problem, system by system, it is often possible to generalize the learning from one experience to a whole category of experiences. This is a key skill of living, since it equips the client to continue without the worker and to use the newfound skills to deal with novel and unexpected experiences. This skill is demonstrated in the continuation of the interview with the mildly retarded adolescent. The discussion has moved to the importance of talking more honestly with his mother about his feelings. He balks and expresses doubts about being able to do this.

JOHN: I could never tell her how I felt, I just couldn't.
WORKER: Why not? What would make it hard?
JOHN: I don't know why, I just couldn't.
WORKER: Is it anything like what you felt when we discussed talking to your teacher, Mr. Tracy, about how dumb he sometimes makes you feel in class?
JOHN: I guess so, I guess I'm afraid of what she would say.
WORKER: You were afraid then that he would get angry at you or laugh at you, do you remember?
JOHN: Yah, I remember. He didn't get mad. He told me he hadn't realized I felt that way. He has been nicer to me since then.
WORKER: Maybe it's also like that with other people, even your mother. If you could find a way to tell her how you felt, she could understand better. Do you remember how proud you were of yourself after you did it, even though you were scared?

The Skill of Identifying Next Steps

We have all experienced at one time or another the frustration of participating in some form of work which goes for naught because of lack of follow-up. A good example is a committee meeting in which decisions are made, but the division of labor for implementing the decisions is overlooked and no action follows. Conscious effort must be made by the worker to help the client identify the next steps involved in the work. No matter what the situation, no matter how impossible it may seem, there is some next step possible, and the worker will ask the client to discuss it. Next steps must be specific; that is, the general goal the client wishes to achieve must be broken down into

manageable parts. In the example used in this section thus far, next steps included helping the youngster to plan to spend some time thinking of some of the things he could do differently to help his mother see another side of him, identifying what he felt about the relationship, and deciding to confront his mother with his true feelings.

The next step for an unemployed mother on welfare who wishes to find a job might include exploring day care centers for her child and meeting with an employment counselor. The next step for a couple in marital counseling, who feel their relationship is worsening and they don't seem to be getting anywhere, might be to identify specific areas that are most difficult for discussion the following week. In essence, the identification of next steps represents another demand for work on the client. Lack of planning by the client does not always represent poor life management skill. It may also be another form of resistance. It may have been difficult to talk about a tough subject, but it can be even more difficult to do something about it. By demanding attention to future, specific actions, the worker may surface another level of fear, ambivalence, and resistance which needs to be dealt with. Sometimes the expression of understanding, support, and expectation by the worker is all the client needs to mobilize resources. There may be no easy way for the client to undertake the task, no simple solution, no easy resolution when two genuinely conflicting needs are evident. For the client, verbalizing the dilemma to an understanding and yet demanding worker may be the key to movement. At other times, the specifics of how to carry out the act may require help. For example, the client may need some information about community resources. In the example of our mildly retarded adolescent, where the next step involved implementing some difficult interpersonal strategy, the next skill was crucial.

The Skill of Rehearsal

Talking about confronting another person around difficult, interpersonal material is one thing, but actually doing it is quite another. A client who protests, "I don't know what to say" may be putting a finger on an important source of blockage. A worker can help by offering the safe confines of the interview situation for the client to rehearse; that is, practice exactly what to say. The worker takes the role of the other person (boss, teacher, husband, mother, doctor, etc.) and feeds back to the client the reactions to the client's efforts. All too often the worker skips this simple and yet powerful device for aiding a client by saying, "When the time comes, you will know what to say." Words do not come easily for us, especially in relation to our most difficult feelings. With the help of a worker, a client may be able to find a way of saying what must be said and with some successful rehearsal under the belt, may feel a bit more confident about doing it. We return to the illustration at the point the teenager says that he does not know what to say.

WORKER: Look, John, perhaps it would be easier for you if you practiced what you would say to your mother. I'll be your mother, and you say it to me. I can tell you how it sounds.

JOHN: You will be my mother? That's crazy! (laughing)

WORKER: It's not so crazy. I'll pretend I'm your mother. Come on, give it a try.

JOHN: (With a lot of anger) You have to stop treating me like a baby! Is that what you mean, is that what I should say?

WORKER: Yes, that's what I mean. Now if I was your mother I could tell you were really angry at me, but I'm not sure I understand why. I might think to myself, "That's just like John, he always runs around hollering like that." Maybe you could begin a bit calmer and tell me what you want to talk about.

JOHN: I don't understand.

WORKER: Let me try. I'll be you for a minute. "Mom, there is something I want to talk to you about—about the way we get along. It's something that really bothers me, makes me sad and sometimes angry." Now I don't know, perhaps that's not so good either. What do you think?

JOHN: I see what you mean. Tell her I want to talk to her about how we get along. That's good, but I don't like the part about being sad.

WORKER: Why not? It's true, isn't it?

JOHN: I don't like to admit that to her.

WORKER: You mean you don't want to let her know how much it hurts you? (John nods) How will she ever understand if you don't tell her? Maybe there are things she would like to tell you, but she feels the same way.

As the conversation continued, the worker and John explored the difficult problem of real communications between a teenager and his mother, with this case a special variation on the theme because of the mild retardation. John tried to formulate what he would say, using some of the worker's ideas and incorporating some of his own. The worker offered to speak to John's mother or to be there during the discussion if John wished. The illustration underlines the preparation value of rehearsal but in addition to the way in which an instant role play can reveal additional blocks to the client's ability to deal with important people in his life. A worker who thinks a marvelous job has been done in helping a client achieve a new level of understanding and readiness to deal effectively with an important person may find additional work to be done when the client formulates the words to be used.

The Skill of Identifying "Doorknob" Communications

A "doorknob" communication is shared as the client leaves the office with his or her hand on the doorknob. This commonly observed phenomenon, described in the literature of psychotherapy, actually refers to any comments of significance raised by the client towards the end of a session when there is too little time to deal with them. We have all experienced a session with a client, or a conversation with a friend, when after a relatively innocuous discussion they say, "There is just one thing that happened this week." Then we hear that he lost his job or found out that his girlfriend was pregnant or received an eviction notice or has noticed a strange lump in his groin. When reflecting on the session, the worker may see where the first clues to the concern were presented indirectly in the beginning phase. It is also possible that there were no clues at all.

A "doorknob" comment is a signal to the worker of the client's ambivalence about discussing an area of work. The concern is raised at the time when it surely cannot be fully discussed. It may be a taboo area or one experienced as too painful to talk about. Whatever the reason, the desire to deal with the concern finally overwhelms the forces of resistance. Time has its impact on the interview and the urgency of the concern, coupled with the pressures created by the lack of time, finally results in the expression of the issue. This kind of comment is actually a special case of the general problem of obstacles blocking the client's ability to work. As with all forms of resistance, it is a

natural part of the process and provides the worker with an opportunity to educate the client about the client's way of working.

The skill would involve the worker identifying the process for the client. For example, in a session with a young woman concerned about her marriage, at the end of the second session she directly revealed a difficult sexual problem between herself and her husband. The worker responded directly:

WORKER: You know you have just raised a really important issue which we will not have time to talk about. You raised it at the end of a session. Were you feeling it was too tough to talk about, too uncomfortable?

CLIENT: (Brief silence) It is embarrassing to talk like this to a stranger.

WORKER: I can understand how it would be hard to discuss sex, I mean really talk about it, with anyone. You know, it's quite common for people to be reluctant to discuss this subject directly, and they often raise these kinds of difficult areas right at the end of the session, just like you did. (The client smiles at this.) Would it help if we started next session talking a bit about what makes it so hard for you to talk about sex? That might make it easier for us to discuss this important area. What do you think?

CLIENT: That sounds OK to me. This is a hard one for me, and I would like to discuss it.

WORKER: I think you are making a good start even raising it at the end.

The worker did not "blame" the client for her difficulty and, instead, offered support for the strength she had shown in raising the issue. By identifying the "doorknob" nature of the comment, she is starting to build into the interview comments on the way in which the two of them work. The client's sophistication about how she works will increase, and after a number of such incidents, she can begin to understand and control how she introduces material into the interviews. In addition, the discussion of the source of the embarrassment in the interview will open up related feelings about the difficulty of discussing sex in our society and the problems in open communication in this area for the couple. The discussion of the process in the interview will lead directly into work on the content.

This discussion of the sessional-ending skills brings to a close the analysis of the work phase. The purpose has been to identify some of the key dynamics in giving and taking help which follow the negotiation of a joint working contract. The discussion of "doorknob" comments is an appropriate one to serve as a transition to the next chapter on the skills of the ending and transition phase. In many ways the last portion of the work with a client may have a "doorknob" quality in that some of the most important and hard-to-discuss issues may make their appearance at this time. This phase of work provides an opportunity for the most powerful learning of the entire encounter. It does not always happen that way, however, and in the next chapter I will discuss why the ending phase can create problems if not handled well or solve others if the worker is skillful.

NOTES

1. William Schwartz, "Group Work in Public Welfare," *Public Welfare* 26 (October 1968), p. 334.

2. For examples of efforts to understand normative life crises, see Jack Block and Norman Haan, *Lives through Time* (Berkeley, Calif.: Bancroft Books, 1971); Erik H. Erikson, *Childhood and Society* (New York: W.W. Norton, 1950); Barbara Fried, *The Middle-Age Crisis* (New York: Harper & Row, 1967); and Joan Huber (ed.), *Changing Women in a Changing Society* (Chicago: University of Chicago Press, 1973).

3. One example of an author who has explored this universal struggle between a father and a son is Chaim Potok. See *My Name Is Asher Lev* (New York: Alfred A. Knopf, Inc. 1976); *The Chosen* (New York: Alfred A. Knopf, Inc. 1976).

4. William Schwartz, "The Social Worker in the Group" in *New Perspectives on Services to Groups* (New York: National Association of Social Workers, 1961), p. 17.

5. It is important to acknowledge the need for workers, administrators, researchers, and clients to work to change the conditions of work which often leave large populations of clients without adequate levels of service.

6. A discussion of the observation system and the findings from its implementation in the larger study can be found in Lawrence Shulman, *Identifying, Measuring and Teaching the Helping Skills* (New York: Council on Social Work Education and the Canadian Association of Schools of Social Work, 1979), Chapter Three; Lawrence Shulman, *A Study of the Helping Process* (Vancouver: School of Social Work, University of British Columbia, 1977), Chapter Eight.

7. Shulman, *A Study of the Helping Process,* p. 337. (Note: citations for findings in the text may be made to one of two publications. When findings have been discussed in the more widely available journal article, "A Study of Practice Skills," *Social Work* 23 (July 1978):274-81, this citation is used. For other findings, the reader is referred to the major report, *The Study of the Helping Process.* The purpose of this note is to caution the reader that titles and page numbers of the two separate publications are similar.)

8. Ibid., p. 347.

9. Shulman, *A Study of the Helping Process,* p. 273.

10. Ibid., p. 293.

11. Ibid., p. 294.

12. Ibid., p. 354.

13. Jessie Taft, "Living and Feeling," *Child Study* 10 (1933):105.

14. Carl R. Rogers, *On Becoming a Person* (Boston: Houghton-Mifflin and Co., 1961), pp. 331-32.

15. Ruth E. Smalley, *Theory for Social Work Practice* (New York: Columbia University Press, 1967), p. 86.

16. S. B. Truax, "Therapist Empathy, Warmth, and Genuineness, and Patient Personality Change in Group Psychotherapy: A Comparison Between Interaction Unit Measures, Time Sample Measures, and Patient Perception Measures," *Journal of Clinical Psychology* 71 (1966):1-9.

17. Carl R. Rogers, *Freedom to Learn* (Columbus: Charles E. Merrill, 1969).

18. Ned A. Flanders, *Analyzing Teaching Behaviors* (Reading, Mass.: Addison-Wesley Publishing Co., 1970).

19. Shulman, "A Study of Practice Skills," p. 278. See also: Shulman, Robinson and Luckyj, *A Study of the Content, Context and Skills of Supervision;* and, Shulman and Buchan, *The Impact of the Family Physician's Communication, Relationship and Technical Skills on Patient Compliance, Satisfaction, Reassurance, Comprehension and Improvement.*

20. Ibid.

21. Shulman, *A Study of the Helping Process,* p. 273.

22. Ibid., p. 342.

23. Flanders, *Analyzing Teaching Behaviors.*

24. See Shulman, *Identifying, Measuring and Teaching the Helping Skills,* Chapter Four.

25. See Robert R. Carkhuff, *Helping and Human Relations: A Primer for Lay and Professional Helpers,* Vol. 1, *Selection and Training* (New York: Holt, Rinehart and Winston, 1969), p. 38. For an excellent view of research of practice skills, including the core relationship skills, see Ray Thomlison, "Outcome Effectiveness, Research and Its Implications for Social Work Educations," *Canadian Journal of Social Work Education* 7 (1981):55–92.

26. Shulman, "A Study of Practice Skills," p. 278.

27. Shulman, *A Study of the Helping Process,* p. 273.

28. Helen Harris Perlman, *Social Casework, A Problem-solving Process* (Chicago: The University of Chicago Press, 1957), p. 121.

29. Herbert S. Strean, *Clinical Social Work Theory and Practice* (New York: The Free Press, 1978), p. 62.

30. Videotaped excerpts from this interview, which illustrates the ambivalence, are found in Program Five, Part One, of the video series, Lawrence Shulman, *The Helping Process in Social Work: Theory, Practice and Research* (Montreal: Instructional Communications Centre, McGill University, 1976).

31. Schwartz, "On the Use of Groups in Social Work Practice," in *The Practice of Group Work,* ed. William Schwartz and Serapio Zalba (New York: Columbia Univ. Press, 1971), p.11.

32. Shulman, *A Study of the Helping Process,* p. 201.

33. Ibid., p. 218.

34. Schwartz, "On the Use of Groups," p. 12.

35. Shulman, *A Study of the Helping Process,* p. 212.

36. See Robert R. Carkhuff, *Helping and Human Relations: A Primer For Lay and Professional Helpers, Vol. 1* (New York: Holt, Rinehart, and Winston, 1969), p. 38.

37. Op. cit. Shulman, *A Study of Practice Skills,* p. 273.

38. Schwartz, "On the Use of Groups," p. 16.

39. Shulman, "A Study of Practice Skills," p. 279.

40. Pearson Product Moment r (relationship, r=.24; helpfulness, r=.33).

41. Shulman, *A Study of the Helping Process,* p. 273.

42. Ibid., p. 294.

43. Schwartz, "On the Use of Groups," p. 11.

44. Sigmund Freud, "Freud's Psychoanalytic Method," in Standard Edition, Vol. 7 (London: Hogarth Press, 1953).

45. Herbert S. Strean, *Clinical Social Work Theory and Practice,* p. 193. See also Florence Hollis, *Casework: A Psychosocial Therapy* (New York: Random House, 1964), pp. 154-55.

46. Shulman, *A Study of the Helping Process,* p. 273.

47. Ibid., p. 294.

48. Schwartz, "The Social Worker in the Group," p. 23.
49. Ibid., p. 24.
50. Ibid., p. 25.
51. Shulman, *A Study of the Helping Process,* pp. 201, 212.
52. Ibid., p. 201.
53. Shulman, "Social Work Skill: The Anat-omy of a Helping Act," *Social Work Practice, 1969* (New York: Columbia University Press, 1969), pp. 44, 45.
54. William Schwartz, "Between Client and System: The Mediating Function," in *Theories of Social Work with Groups,* eds. Robert W. Roberts and Helen Northen (New York: Columbia University Press, 1976), p. 192.

CHAPTER 5

Endings and Transitions

The ending phase offers the greatest potential for powerful and important work. Clients feel a sense of urgency as they realize there is little time left, and this can lead to the introduction of some of the more difficult and important themes of concern. The dynamics between worker and client are also heightened in this phase as each prepares to move away from the other. Termination of the relationship can evoke powerful feelings in both client and worker, and discussion of these can often be connected by the worker to the client's general concerns and tasks. While the ending phase has this tremendous potential for work, the irony is that this phase is often the least effective. Missed appointments, lateness, apathy, acting out, and regressions to earlier, less mature patterns of behavior are often characteristic. Moreover, these behaviors can be observed in the actions of the worker as well as the client.

In many ways the ending sessions are the most difficult ones for both worker and client. The source of the strain stems from our general problem of dealing with the ending of important relationships. The worker-client association is a specific example of this larger problem. It can be painful to terminate a close relationship; when you have invested yourself meaningfully in a relationship, have shared some of your most important feelings, and have given and taken help from another human being, the bond that develops is strong. This is true with friends, family, working colleagues—in fact with all relationships. Our society has done little to train us how to handle a separation; in fact, the general norm is to deny feelings associated with it. For example, when a valued colleague leaves an agency, the farewell party is often an attempt, usually unsuccessful, to cover the sadness with fun. The laughter at such parties is usually a bit flat. Similarly, children and counselors who have developed an intimate, living relationship in summer camps usually end by resolving to meet again at a winter reunion—a reunion that often does not take place.

Strean has described the difficulties involved in terminating a close working relationship:

Whether a social worker-client relationship consists of five interviews or a hundred, if the worker has truly related to the client's expectations, perceptions of himself, and transactions with his social orbit, the client will experience the encounter as meaningful and the worker as someone significant; therefore, separation from this "significant other" will inevitably arouse complex and ambivalent feelings. Still, a long-term relationship with a social worker will probably include more intense emotions at termination than a short-term one. A prolonged relationship has usually stimulated dependency needs and wishes, transference reactions, revelation of secrets, embarrassing moments, exhilaration, sadness, and gladness. The encounter has become part of the client's weekly life, so that ending it can seem like saying goodbye to a valued family member or friend.[1]

The extreme illustration of this general difficulty in dealing with endings is in death and dying, and the process of grief. Kübler-Ross has written with great sensitivity about the phases of dying and how people react to the most permanent separation.[2] The ending of any intimate relationship may resemble, in a less powerful way, the ending process described in her book. Her phases of dying can usefully be adapted to all separations. The ending process in a helping relationship can trigger feelings of the deepest kind in both worker and client. This is the reason why there is potential for powerful work during this phase as well as ineffective work if the feelings are not dealt with. This chapter will explore the dynamics of this ending process, identify some of the central skills required to make effective endings, and discuss how workers can help clients make transitions to new experiences.

THE DYNAMICS AND SKILLS OF ENDINGS

Schwartz described this phase in the group context:

In the final phase of work—that which I have called "transitions and endings"—the worker's skills are needed to help the members use him and each other to deal with the problem of moving from one experience to another. For the worker it means moving *off* the track of the members' experience and life process, as he has, in the beginning, moved *onto* it. . . . The point is that beginnings and endings are hard for people to manage; they often call out deep feeling in both worker and members; and much skill is needed to help people to help each other through these times.[3]

One of the dynamics which makes endings hard has already been mentioned. This is the pain associated with bringing to an end a relationship into which one has invested a great deal.

In addition to the pain there is a form of guilt where the clients may feel that if they had worked harder in the relationship, played their parts more effectively, and risked more, then perhaps they could have done a better job. This guilt sometimes emerges indirectly with their saying, "Can't I have more time?" As with many of the feelings in the ending phase, this sense of guilt is often shared by the worker who may feel that he or she should have been more helpful to the client. Perhaps if the worker had been more experienced, more capable, he or she could have been more helpful about some of the unresolved issues. Rather than recognizing the fact of being just a part of the client's life, the worker tends at this time to feel responsible for the client. Instead of understanding that the client will need to work continually on life's problems, the worker feels guilty at not having "solved" them all.

One worker presenting an example of his work introduced the difficulty that he had had in ending a relationship with a client in a hospital outpatient setting. When I asked how long he had been seeing him, he replied seven years. Further discussion revealed that the worker was still upset over an ending with another patient a number of years back. The patient had committed suicide shortly afterwards, and the worker held himself responsible, an unrealistic but yet not unusual reaction. The worker feared that if he ended his relationship with his present client before everything was "all worked out," he might have another suicide on his hands.

The flow of affect between worker and client is heightened during the ending phase. Because of the general difficulty in talking about negative and positive feedback, both worker and client may have many unstated feelings which need to be dealt with in the final phase. Things may have been left unsaid because of taboos against honest talk about the role of authority. This theme needs to be discussed before the relationship can properly end. For example, there may be things the worker did and said which made the client angry. The reverse might also be true with the worker somewhat frustrated over the client's inability to progress in certain important areas. Providing this feedback can serve to clear the air. Even if a client and worker have not been able to get along together and both face the impending separation with a sense of relief, the discussion at the end should be real. What was it about the worker that the client could not relate to? In turn, the client should know what made it difficult for the worker. There may have been misconceptions on the part of either or both parties, and discussing these can help to clear them up. This could be very helpful to the client who may choose to enter another helping relationship at another time. The importance of feedback to the worker is also obvious. In addition, if the negative feelings are not dealt with, it is not unusual to find a client transferring them to his next worker in the way that we have seen in some of the examples in Chapter 3 on beginnings.

Even more difficult for worker and client to handle than the negative feelings may be the positive ones. It is not easy for any of us to tell someone close to us, particularly someone in authority, that they have meant a great deal to us. Accepting these feelings gracefully is something many workers find extremely hard. I have repeatedly observed workers responding to a client's genuine expression of thanks for all that he has done with the comment, "It wasn't really me, I didn't do that much, it was really all your work." One student in a social work training program asked during a class if it was all right for her to accept a fruitcake offered to her by an elderly client at the end of their work together. This was not a case in which a client was trying to pay a worker for her services which were normally free. It was simply this old woman's way of saying "thank you" to a worker who cared.

When I press workers as to the cause of their embarrassment when clients express positive feelings, they usually point to the general cultural barriers which make this seem immodest as well as to their belief that they could not have *really* given that much help. The second response reflects an underestimation of the effect of the help given. Clients respond with great feeling to a caring, honest worker. They are not usually as critical about what the worker might have done as the worker is self-critical. The mutual sharing of the positive feelings is important at the end of a relationship, cultural barriers notwithstanding, because this enables both client and worker to value what has taken place between them and to bring it properly to an end. Both client and worker can carry feelings of regret for unspoken words long after they have stopped seeing each other, thus making the actual ending process protracted and more difficult. The problem with long-delayed endings is that both parties need to invest their energy in new relationships.

The timing of this phase is dependent upon the length of the relationship. For example, in weekly counseling over the period of one year, approximately the last eight weeks constitute the ending process. In short-term work, for example six sessions, evidence of feelings about endings may emerge in the fourth or fifth session as the worker receives subtle cues to the client's reactions. While these cues mark the beginning of the ending phase, thoughts about the end are present even in the beginning. It is not unusual for a client to enquire after a session which was helpful, how long the sessions will continue. Time is an important factor, and clients will orient themselves accordingly. A long break in the work phase, whether caused by the worker's illness, a vacation, or perhaps the Christmas season, can provoke ending feelings as the client associates the break in the work with the ending to come. It is not uncommon to observe apathy, withdrawal, and other premature ending symptoms immediately after such a break.

Schwartz has outlined the stages of the ending process as follows: denial, indirect and direct expressions of anger, mourning, trying it on for size," and finally, the "farewell-party syndrome."[4] Each of these is discussed now in more detail, and the required worker skills, as suggested by Schwartz, are identified and illustrated.

The Denial Phase

Because of the general difficulty in facing feelings associated with the ending of important relationships, the first stage is often marked by evidence of denial. The client neither admits to the impending ending or to his feelings about it. This first phase may be characterized by the client's refusal to discuss the ending or by insistence on a nonexistent agreement with the worker to continue the sessions long past the ending date or by forgetting that an ending date has been set or by requesting that sessions be prolonged because the client feels that "unready." Unless the worker raises the ending issue, the client may simply ignore it right up until the last session. Workers also may handle their feelings towards endings through denial and avoidance as, for example, when they leave a job. Many clients have greeted a new worker with stories of how their former workers had simply told them that they were leaving the agency during their last session. These clients are often left with the feeling that their workers did not care about them. In reality, these workers' denials are often rooted in the fact that they cared very much but were not in touch with their own feelings.

It is important that the ending process provide enough time for the worker and client to sort out their feelings and use this phase productively. A sudden ending will be difficult for both worker and client and will cut short necessary work. Since the worker wants the ending to be experienced as a process rather than as a sharp closure, the *skill of pointing out endings* should be employed some time before the relationship is to end. At the appropriate time, given the length of the relationship, the worker will remind the client of the impending ending. An example from a child welfare setting helps to illustrate this skill. The client was a young man who had been a ward of the agency for eight years. The worker had been in contact with him for the past two years. Since the client was approaching his eighteenth birthday in two months, he would be leaving the care of the agency.

The worker set the process in motion by reminding him of the ending date.

WORKER: Before we start to talk about that job interview next week, I wanted to remind you that we only have eight more weeks before you leave the agency. You have been with the "Aid" [the term used by clients to describe the Children's Aid Society] for a long time, and I thought you might want to talk about the change.

CLIENT: Only eight weeks? I hadn't realized it was coming so soon. That's great! After eight years I'm finally on my own; no more checking in, no more "Aid" on my back. You know, I'm going to really need that job now, and I'm worried about the interview.

WORKER: What's worrying you?

By commenting on the limited time the worker set the process in motion. The client's reaction was in part denial of the impact of the ending and in part recognition of its importance. Schwartz has described the "graduation quality" of endings where the client feels excited and ready to test his ability to make it on his own.[5] The quick switch from the ending topic to the job interview represented resistance. The client did not want to talk about it right then. The worker was also reluctant to discuss it and so allowed it to be dropped easily. In addition, he had identified the issue of ending only in terms of the agency, instead of also in relation to themselves. This evasion by the worker is a signal of his own ambivalence. The statement of the impending ending is enough to set the process in motion.

In the example which follows, the worker presses for the ending feelings but the client resists.

JANE: I will be leaving the office at the beginning of May which gives us four more times together. I thought we might want to talk about this.

THELMA: I don't understand, why are you leaving?

JANE: I'm not sure if you remember, Thelma, but I mentioned to you last October that I was a student, which means I will be leaving my placement in early May. (Silence.)

JANE: Thelma, you have turned quiet, what are you thinking about?

THELMA: (after some pause) I don't know what I am going to do now, I don't understand why you have to go.

JANE: Are you worried about what is going to happen with you after I leave? (Silence.)

THELMA: Yes, but you are not leaving for a month, right?

JANE: Yes. I know that we have been seeing each other for many months now, and talking about my leaving is hard, it is hard for me too—but we both need to share our feelings and thoughts about this. (Silence.)

JANE: I know that I am feeling a little sad, we have been through some tough times together.—It's tough letting go.

THELMA: (looking down ... picked up a piece of her child's schoolwork) Hey, did you know that Gladys will be going into grade 2 next year. Ivan and I went up to the parent-teacher meeting last Friday and the teacher told us then. She even showed us some of her schoolwork. She is doing so well.

I tried to have Thelma elaborate on her feelings about the ending of our sessions but she denied and avoided the opportunities, and the remainder of the session covered some superficial topics and how her children were doing.

Indirect and Direct Expressions of Anger

The denial stage in ending is often followed by the indirect or direct expression of anger by the client towards the worker. The circumstances of the endings may vary; for example, the worker may be leaving the agency as opposed to the client ending contact. While these circumstances may affect the intensity of the angry feelings, these are usually present even in those situations where the ending seems perfectly reasonable. The anger may be expressed directly, by the client challenging the worker who has changed jobs, "How could you leave if you really cared for me?" The ending is perceived as a form of rejection, and the worker must be careful to face these feelings directly and not try to avoid them. Alternatively, the cues to the underlying feelings may be communicated indirectly, for example, by lateness or missed sessions. Conversations with clients may take on an element of antagonism, and the worker may sense the hostility. Sarcasm, battles over minor issues, or indications by the client of being glad to see the relationship finally end may also be evidence of this reaction. However, under the angry feelings are often sad feelings. It is therefore important to allow the expression of anger and to acknowledge it even though the worker's instincts make it hard to do so.

The skill involved here, as with all stages of the ending process, calls for the worker *to respond directly to the indirect cues to ending stages.* The worker, perceiving these signals, should point out the dynamics of the stage to the client. In the case of anger, the worker should reach past the indirect cue and encourage the client to express any feelings directly. The worker should also acknowledge the validity of the feelings and not attempt to talk the client into feeling differently. This direct acknowledgment is important even if the client does not take up the worker's invitation to discuss the anger and instead denies its existence. By the worker's pointing out of each stage of the process, the client can increase understanding of the experience. This can then free ener-

gies to participate productively in the ending-phase work. It is important for the worker to be honest in sharing any personal reactions to the client's anger.

The following illustration shows a child care worker who is changing jobs and leaving a residential setting for teenage boys. He had told the boys of his impending departure and had reached unsuccessfully for their reactions. One evening, the worker noticed a current of edginess among the boys in the living room. One youngster, John, to whom he had become very close, seemed to be provoking another youngster into a fight. When this appeared to be close to blows, the worker intervened as he had in the past to help sort out the difficulty.

WORKER: What's going on here, guys? John, you've been edgy all night. How come?

JOHN: (with great anger) Why don't you keep your God damn nose out of this! It's none of your business.

WORKER: What goes on between you guys *is* my business. Wow, John, you're jumping on everyone tonight, even me. What's up?

JOHN: This is between Frank and me, and you have nothing to do with it anymore.

WORKER: (Silence) You mean because I'm leaving. Is that it? Are you angry because I'm going?

JOHN: I'll be glad to see you gone! (John leaves the room.)

John did not pick up on the anger issue. However, he had heard the worker's comment, and it had an impact. He was too angry to acknowledge his feelings, for this would have been an admission to the worker that he was really hurt by his leaving. This came later. By identifying this stage of the process the worker helped the client begin to take control of it.

In the following example, the anger is expressed indirectly towards the agency.

This meeting had involved a single mother, Debbie, her twelve-year-old son, Mike, and a special care worker, Liz, who will be working with Mike in school. I had been involved with Debbie on a regular basis since October and we have four more meetings planned. Both Liz and Mike had left and Debbie and I had been discussing future plans for Mike. I initiated the discussion on ending.

WORKER: I've been thinking that we have just four more meetings together, I'll be finished school—the time seems to be going quickly.

DEBBIE: What do you mean, I didn't know that you were in school. Are you not coming after you're finished school? (Debbie sounded shocked; it surprised me that she actually said that she didn't know I was a student as she'd regularly asked me how school was going.)

WORKER: Seems like I shocked you and you shocked me right back when you said that you didn't know I was in school.

DEBBIE: Yeah, I know you're in school, it's just a surprise that the year has gone so fast.

WORKER: I'm feeling both happy and sad—I'm happy about the way things have worked out and I'm sad that I won't be coming after April.

DEBBIE: (started to speak angrily) Those jerks, you just get someone who you can talk to and then they take them away. Now I have to start all over again with someone else. You know Mike used to say . . . you know . . . when Trudy (previous worker) would be coming over but with you he's always wondering what we're going to do and he likes to see you.

I could feel and accept Debbie's anger at me for leaving and realized how frustrated she'd be starting over again. She'd paid me quite a compliment and I appreciated it.

WORKER: I remember our first meetings, Debbie, when I wasn't sure if we could work together at all. I feel that we've come through a great deal together and it's been rough at times to talk about some of the things we've talked about. Thank you for telling me about Mike—he and you have made me feel welcome in your home. I've gotten to like you both very much and I'm going to miss you.

DEBBIE: Then why are you leaving? (Debbie said this quickly, then added abruptly) I know you have to leave, who will be my new worker?

WORKER: That's something I've been wondering about. You've said that you've had a hard time whenever a new worker is involved. Do you think our experience together has given you any ideas about getting to know and work with a new social worker?

DEBBIE: Yup—if I thing he's a jerk I'm going to tell him right away instead of waiting for three months and burning up inside. I'm not going to fool around like I used to.

WORKER: That's one of the things I really like about working with you, you give it to me straight. I was honoured last week when you told me that you trusted me and saw how hard that was for you—that's when you added "almost."

DEBBIE: Well, I do trust you. (She laughed and added) Almost.

WORKER: What do you want to be able to do with your new worker?

DEBBIE: I guess I'll want someone to talk over what happens with Liz and Mike and also how things are going at home for me with Mike—you know, just as things come up.

I explained how cases got assigned at the office and that Sue most likely would be the new worker. Debbie had spoken with Sue a couple of times on another matter but said she didn't know her all that well.

We talked a bit more about some of the issues we'd tackled, how things had progressed, fallen back and continued on. As I was walking down the front steps, Debbie called out, "At least I'll see you until the end of April" and I felt warm and sad at the same time.

The Mourning Period

Under the feelings of anger expressed by the client are often those of sadness. When these emerge, the client begins the mourning stage of the ending process. During this stage the client experiences fully the feelings he may have been struggling hard to suppress. When this happens, some clients are able to express their feelings directly to the worker. For others the feelings emerge indirectly. A normally active and involved client suddenly seems apathetic and lethargic. Interviews are marked by long periods of silence, slow starts followed by minimal activity, and conversations which seem to trail off rather than end. One worker described arriving at a woman's home to find the blinds drawn in midday and a general, gloomy feeling pervading the usually bright room. In part, the difficulty in working reflects the client's unwillingness to open up new areas just when the work seems about to end. In addition, the work left to the end is often the most difficult for the client, adding to the ambivalence. Essentially, the feeling is one of sadness over the ending of a meaningful relationship. The denial and anger are past, and the ending must now be faced.

Two important skills in this phase involve *acknowledging the client's ending feelings* and *sharing the worker's ending feelings*. The skills of acknowledging and sharing worker feelings have already been identified as crucial to the helping process but also difficult for workers to employ. In the ending phase, the difficulty is compounded by the intensity of feelings and the societal taboos against their direct expression. Workers have suggested that even when they did pick up the cues to the sadness, they did not acknowledge the feelings because they felt somewhat embarrassed. "How can I tell clients I

think they are sad because we won't be seeing each other anymore? It sounds like I'm taking my impact on the client and blowing it out of proportion. And anyway, how will it feel if the client says I'm all wet?" The worker feels vulnerable to the risks of commenting on the importance of the relationship. This also holds the worker back from expressing personal feelings towards the client. As one worker said, "It doesn't sound professional for me to tell a client I will miss him. He will think I'm just putting him on. Won't that be encouraging dependency?"

In most cases the reluctance to share feelings stems from the difficulty workers have in coming to grips with their own sadness when separating from a valued client. The flow of affect between the two has first created and then strengthened a bond which workers value. It is important that this relationship be recognized as it comes to an end. Often workers must risk their own feelings first for the clients to feel free to risk themselves. Both may feel vulnerable, but it is part of the worker's function and a measure of professional skill to be able to take this first, hard step. Let us return now to the earlier illustration of the eighteen-year-old foster child about to leave the care of the agency.

WORKER: You seem quiet and reserved today, don't seem to have much to say.
CLIENT: I guess I'm just tired.
WORKER: And then, again, this is almost our last session together. I've been thinking a lot about that, and I have mixed feelings. I'm glad to see you getting ready to go out on your own, but I'm really going to miss you. We've been through an awful lot together in the past two years. (Silence) How about you? Are you a little down about our ending too?
CLIENT: (Long silence) I guess we have gotten close. You've been my best worker— although sometimes you were a real pain.

WORKER: Why do you feel I was your best worker? It can be important to talk about this.

After the mutual acknowledgment of feelings, the worker takes another step by asking the client to reflect upon the relationship. The client has had many important close relationships and has seen them broken, sometimes experiencing sharp rejections. Understanding this worker-client relationship can be an important aid to the client in his future efforts to make close contacts. This part of the work is discussed further in the "Transitions" section of this chapter. In the following process recording, a worker describes the difficulty in sharing her own feelings.

Beginning termination was a difficult and emotional process for both myself and my client, Debbie. As I attempted to discuss the ending of our relationship, Debbie stated that she wanted her next income assistance cheque mailed to her home address. I asked her why. Debbie replied that by doing so, she would no longer have to go into the office for her cheque.

WORKER: Debbie, I don't really understand that. You've always picked your cheques up. In fact, you preferred it that way, didn't you?

DEBBIE: Well yah, but I'm getting tired of seeing the same people, and I think they're tired of seeing me every month. (Silence. Debbie looking away.)

WORKER: Debbie, is it that you don't want to see me at the end of this month? (Silence) Cheque days have been our "hi/keep in touch days." I feel like you want to avoid seeing me on my last cheque day here.

DEBBIE: Maria, what am I going to do without you?

WORKER: Debbie, do you feel you really need me?

DEBBIE: I need somebody to talk to. Well, sometimes I feel like I don't. Other times I feel like I'm going to fall apart. I don't know what I'm going to do without you.

WORKER: Debbie, I know we've been through a lot and shared a lot together, but to be honest, I feel you're much stronger now than you were in the beginning, and I feel you can make it without me. That's not to say I think things will be easy for you, but I've seen a growth in your own self-confidence. You're beginning to take more risks, make your own decisions.

DEBBIE: Yah, my self-confidence has increased slightly hasn't it?

WORKER: It really has, Debbie. I know it's going to feel weird and empty without me, but you know you've made a lot of new friends in the past few months at the center, at your new place. Sherri has been a real support and a good friend for you, hasn't she?

DEBBIE: Yah she has, she really has. But, it won't be the same. I just know it.

WORKER: It won't be the same for me either, Debbie. You know I've never had an ongoing involvement with any client before. It feels weird to think that I won't be your worker after May. Right now ... I can't describe exactly how I feel, but I know it's going to feel weird without you. I know I'm going to keep thinking about you, about how you're doing. I know I'm going to miss you and Don (her son). (Debbie silent; looking down). I feel you'll make your goal (to be self-dependent, off of income assistance [I.A.]). It'll be slow and you'll have to take a lot of steps, but I really feel you'll do it. I wish I could be there to see that.

I then offered my phone number as a means of keeping in touch.

DEBBIE: Yah, I'm going to make it!

WORKER: You sound determined. That's another change I've noticed.

DEBBIE: Yah, I am more determined. I have to get off I.A. (income assistance) The changes in me have been because of you.

WORKER: Well, I may have helped you, but the changes came from you (Debbie shrugged her shoulders) ... Debbie, what kind of a worker have I been for you?

Debbie stated: (1) that I was the first worker that ever shared personal feelings with her. She felt that this made it easier for her to discuss problems and to relate to me; (2) that I expressed a great deal of concern for her, but at times Debbie felt I was too overly concerned; (3) that in the first term I seemed to think I was always right whereas in the second term I was easier to talk to, more relaxed, more open . . . ; (4) that whenever I was late, Debbie felt I was treating her like "scum," even though I did apologize to her each time. As Debbie began to know me better, she realized that my apologies were genuine, that I really did care for her . . . I also relayed my feelings to her regarding our relationship. For example: (1) I struggled with her resistance associated to the authority theme; (2) that as I noticed more strength and confidence in herself, I felt threatened; I wanted to keep "protecting" her; (3) that I've learned a great deal about single parenthood, the hardships and difficulties associated with sole child rearing, with no outside support. . . . Near the end of the session, we began to discuss Debbie's feelings regarding new beginnings with a new worker in a new office. Debbie stated that prior to myself, she had had two good workers. Both these workers were older and had had children of their own. Debbie hoped that her new worker would also be older; she felt this would facilitate new beginnings. This issue was tabled for our next session. As I was leaving, Debbie stated that she would like my phone number, and she would come to get it from me on cheque issue day.

"Trying It on for Size"

Earlier I referred to the graduation quality of the ending. As the client moves to the final sessions, the worker often senses an effort to test out new skills and ability to do things independently. It is not unusual to have a client come to a session with a report of having tackled a tough problem or dealt with an issue which, prior to this time, would have first been discussed with the worker. The worker senses the client's positive feelings of accomplishment and employs the *skill of*

crediting the client. This consists of a direct acknowledgment of the client's ability to "go it alone." In those situations when the client remains with the service and the worker leaves, discussion of the new worker often begins to dominate the conversation. Who will that be, and what will the person be like? This can also represent a "trying the change on for size" as well as being one form of expression of anger towards the worker. I have experienced this process during my classes when I have worked with students over a long period of time. Our class/group relationship and the students' relationship with me is, in some ways, a model of the process we study, although both the content and my function differ from that found in social work practice. Nevertheless, I can remember times when I found it impossible to get into the class conversation. I would make a comment on the work under discussion, the students would look at me briefly, and then continue to talk *as if I were not there*. After a few such attempts to enter the conversation, I felt as if I were not in the classroom. As I sat back and listened, I could hear the students carrying on important discussion and analysis of practice within the peer group and without my help. This was a part of our ending process.

The "Farewell-Party" Syndrome

Schwartz uses this term to refer to the tendency to "pad" ending discussions by concentrating only on the positive aspects of the relationship. All working relationships have both positive and negative aspects to them. It is important for the worker not to allow the ending discussion to get so caught up in the positive feelings that an honest analysis of the content and process is bypassed. The worker should use the skill of *reaching for negative evaluation* to encourage the client not to hold a "farewell party."

Thus far I have detailed some dynamics and skills involved in the ending process with individuals. Part II of the book will provide further illustrations in the group context as well as address itself to some of the differences in the dynamics. In addition to the *process* of ending, it is important that the worker pay attention to the *substantive content* which can make the ending important for the client's learning. In the next section of this chapter I will review those skills of the ending phase which serve to help the client use the experience with the worker to make an effective transition to the new situations which may be faced alone.

THE SKILLS OF TRANSITIONS

It is important to remember that a new beginning is inherent in the ending of a working relationship. As the young adult, the former foster child, leaves the care of the agency, he begins a phase of his life facing a new set of demands. Some of these are similar to those faced by any young person of the same age, but others are unique to someone who has been the ward of an agency. The ex-con who is completing the term of parole begins to function in society without the supervision and support offered by the parole officer. The patient who is leaving the rehabilitation center must face the experience of negotiating the outside world, perhaps still limited by the effects of the accident or illness. The former narcotics addict who leaves the treatment center must deal with many of the same pressures and demands on the street which helped lead to the addiction. This time, the ex-addict needs to make it without the support of either the worker or the

drugs. The adolescent delinquent leaving the protection of the wilderness camp may be dealing again with a family which has changed little during the time away. For each of these clients, the time of ending is also the time of a powerful beginning.

The worker needs to pay attention to this process of transition during the ending phase by focusing on the substance of the work together as well as on the process of ending. In work that has gone well, clients may have found out new things about themselves, their strengths and weaknesses, their patterns of behavior under pressure, and their abilities to handle problems. They may also have gained new ways to view some of the important people and systems they must deal with. Ending should be a time for adding up what has been learned. Since the work is never finished, clients end with new ideas as an agenda of future issues. This agenda needs to be identified. As with all phases of the relationship, the interaction between workers and clients offers fertile areas of learning related to the contract. Workers can use the dynamics of the ending process to help clients generalize from their learning to new experiences. And, finally, workers can help clients make direct transitions to those new experiences and to other workers and alternative sources of support which may be available for their use. These tasks of the ending phase are examined in this part of this chapter.

Identification of Major Learnings

Endings are a time for systematically adding up the experience by the worker asking the client to reflect on their work together and to identify some of the things that have been learned. One week before the final session the worker could ask the client to prepare to share these important ideas the last week. In the first session, the worker asked the client for feedback on the issue that seemed to be of concern. Now that they are ending, they need to review jointly where things stand on these issues. The worker's demand must be for specifics, since a general summing up is not enough. When the client says that the sessions with the worker were valuable because the client has learned so much about himself or herself, the worker might respond, "Exactly what was it you learned that was important to you?" This process helps the client to consolidate the learning. A second benefit accrues from the client's recognition of new abilities that have been developed. This can strengthen the client in preparing to end. The worker can participate in this process as well, since in any real interactive experience, the worker will learn from the client. What has the worker understood differently about the problems faced by the client, and about his or her personal and professional self? The summing up should include discussion of what both worker and client are taking away with them from the experience. The example which follows illustrates this adding-up process.

Christine came in because she felt so bad that she hit her oldest daughter whenever she became angry. It was established that she wanted techniques of parenting that would prevent her from hitting her child. We openly discussed her lack of bonding with this oldest daughter, and the poor marital situation Christine found herself in. Christine tried but could not get her family to participate. This was to be the second to last session (fourth) with a follow-up in February (two months).

JOHN: Let's review a little where we started and where we are now.
CHRIS: The reason I came was because I had been hitting Raphaelle, much more than I felt good about. But things have been going very well. In the beginning I thought that if I can stop hitting her altogether, I would feel really happy about it. Well, I haven't struck her once, and I don't even feel like it. It is going very well.
JOHN: And it's been about three months.
CHRIS: It almost seems so far away now.
JOHN: You mean from the time we started?
CHRIS: Yes, it seems almost a little unreal, do you know what I mean . . . a little embarrassing.
JOHN: Well, it has been some time since October, but it was all very real then.
CHRIS: No kidding. But it feels good to end, because I don't feel I need it anymore—things are going well. But it does feel good that I can come back in February.
JOHN: Why did you say it is embarrassing?
CHRIS: It was embarrassing to even come in and state that I was hitting my children. I had to talk to my family doctor and explain it all to him. I wish I could have solved it within the family without outside help (condensed).
JOHN: I guess it seems all so easy to solve this hitting now, eh?
CHRIS: Well this is it, but I am glad I came because I might still be hitting Raphaelle. You know just the commitment of getting help was the biggest factor.
JOHN: Asking for help makes you vulnerable but ironically it also makes you stronger.
JOHN: Sure . . . . Is there anything else that's different for you and Raphaelle?
CHRIS: For some reason I look at her a little different. I see her having some problems, but I see her also as older. Remember how you said that she is becoming a teenager and won't take hitting anymore. I also think like she could be gone in five years. Where have all the years gone? (Showing sadness.)
JOHN: What is happening for you right now? (Some discussion followed about Raphaelle.)
CHRIS: . . . No, I don't really think that either, but it was just a little thought of what could happen—I should say what could have happened. I guess I also feel that things aren't

going so well between my husband and I. I suppose that will always be there.

JOHN: Well, you know I always did feel it was a shame that you couldn't get him to participate in these sessions. But maybe that's for another time and under different circumstances. Have things deteriorated between you two? I guess I am asking if you need to spend some time on this issue even though he won't come in?

CHRIS: No, not really. I guess I don't really want to dwell on the negative. I am glad for me and as you said, that's what counts.

JOHN: Sure, but the door is open. I don't know how aware you were but a couple of times I really pushed hard for you to bring your husband into these sessions.

CHRIS: (Laughing) Oh, I felt it! (This was followed with some discussion about this issue.)

JOHN: You seem to have consolidated some strengths and determination. You seem to put your foot down. I guess it will take some adjustment for your relationship (with husband). Somehow you have to find a way to support each other. You do tend, it seems to me, to walk a bit of a tightrope sometimes and as a result, you end up having to give quite a bit, even when you need to be given to.

CHRIS: You know how you said, last time, that I am a giving person. My husband just thinks I am a selfish manipulator. I think he is more right. But it sure is nice to hear.

JOHN: You mean that you are a giving person?

CHRIS: Yes (a little teary). (I followed this with some examples of her giving.)

JOHN: It's hard to hear, isn't it?

CHRIS: It's just not something I heard before. My husband says I do some nice things but doesn't say I am a nice person. I don't think of myself as a nice person.

JOHN: It can be your little secret that you are a nice person.

CHRIS: (Laughing) What do you mean?

JOHN: Well, we'll say goodbye and we'll see each other only one more time in the end of February, but you'll remain a nice person, even though I won't say it anymore.

CHRIS: It's nice of you to say so and it's funny but you have to hear it to believe it, but I have also thought about it as well and that makes a difference. (We reviewed some of the main themes of the sessions and discussed what was helpful and what wasn't. We contracted to see each other at the end of February. We planned to have a short session in February to see if things are still doing okay with her and Raphaelle.)

The end of the last session in February. A short half-hour session in which Christine brought in a little book as a gift.

JOHN: Well, maybe we can just say goodbye?

CHRIS: Goodbye, John, and thank you.

JOHN: You're welcome; goodbye, Christine, good luck to you and your family. It's funny but I feel a little sad about saying goodbye.

CHRIS: I feel a little bit sad as well. Just a little sad but I am also happy that I came and now I don't feel I need to come anymore. I felt good about having this six weeks to see if I could keep it up.

JOHN: In retrospect, that does seem like it was good. Anyway, you have our telephone number and don't hesitate to call even if it is to say hello.

CHRIS: Yes, thanks a lot for that. Bye, John and good luck with your studies. You're not a bad social worker (laughing).

JOHN: Thanks, goodbye, Christine . . . and of course thanks for that beautiful little book.

Identification of Areas for Future Work

It is important to convey to the client that the work will continue after the ending. It is all right to have unanswered questions, to be faced with unsolved problems, and not to have life all figured out. The client began the experience with certain problems or life tasks and has learned how to handle some of these more effectively than at the beginning. The experience ends with other problems or life tasks ahead. The difference now is that the client has learned how to deal better with these concerns. If some of the uncertainties and the ambiguity which are still present are detailed, the worker must resist the temptation to "jump in" and try to "solve" these last-minute concerns. Part of the learning experience involves being able to live with some uncertainties. The worker's task is to help the client to inventory these, to create an agenda for future work, and to use their experience together to determine how the client can continue to work on these concerns. The worker must also resist the temptation to reassure the client who expresses doubts about competency. Acknowledging and understanding these fears of not being able to continue alone is more helpful. It is important for the worker to convey a belief in the client's potential to tackle future tasks without in any way attempting to minimize the feeling that the going may be rough. Let us return to the ending sessions of the eighteen-year-old about to leave the care of the child welfare agency to illustrate this point. The worker had asked the client to identify those things he had learned as well as those areas he still felt he needed to consider. This excerpt from the last session begins as they review what the client has learned.

WORKER: What ideas hit you hard during our discussions together? What will stay with you?

CLIENT: I learned that I have to be more responsible for myself. That was important to me.

WORKER: Exactly what do you mean by that?

CLIENT: Well, I used to walk around wilth a chip on my shoulder. All my problems were someone else's fault. I was angry at my mother for giving up on me; it was always my foster parents who were the cause of my fights; and the "Aid," well, I hated the place.

WORKER: And how do you see it now?

CLIENT: Well, I did have it tough. It wasn't easy moving from home to home, never having the kinds of things normal kids had. But I think I understand better that what happens to me from now on is pretty much up to me. I can't blame everyone else anymore. And the "Aid," well, for all my complaining, with all the changes in foster homes, the "Aid" has been the only place I can call home.

WORKER: I guess you have a lot of mixed feelings about this place, but now that you're leaving, a part of you is going to miss it.

CLIENT: (Silence) With all the complaining and all the crap I had to take, I'm still going to miss it. You know, I'm scared about being on my own.

WORKER: Sure it's scary. What exactly are you afraid of?

CLIENT: I'm going to have to make it on my own now. I'm starting this new job, and I'm worried about how I'm going to do. And what if I don't make any friends in the rooming house? There are other people my age there, but it's hard to get to know them. It's not like a group home where you spend a lot of time together and you always have the houseparents to talk with.

WORKER: So there are the questions of how to make it on the job and how to make some new friends that you need to work on.

The two critical tasks identified in this discussion are major ones for any young adult and quite appropriate to this client's phase of life. As he moves into adulthood, he must tackle issues related to how he will fit into the world of work and he must also begin to shift his relationships from parental figures to his peer group. These tasks are made more difficult for a client who has moved through the child welfare system. His life has been marked by so many broken relationships, so many times that he has invested himself and then been hurt, that a major barrier is his willingness to risk himself again. In the next segment we will follow this illustration to demonstrate how the worker-client ending process can be directly related to the content of the work.

Synthesizing the Ending Process and Content

If we keep in mind that the worker-client relationship is one of many the client deals with in life, and is in fact just a special case among all relationships, then the experience can be used to illustrate important themes. The relationship can be viewed as a training ground for the client. Skills which have been developed in dealing with the worker are transferable to other situations. The astute worker can use "tuning in" to identify connections between the worker's own interaction with the client at the ending. For example, to return to our illustration, this client had had to overcome his guardedness to establish a close relationship with the worker. It was a long time before the client allowed himself to be vulnerable, to risk being hurt. In effect, the client needed to learn what we must all learn: for our life to have meaning, we must risk getting close to people, even though this may mean getting hurt sometimes. If we go through life remembering only the hurt, then we may build a wall between ourselves and people who represent sources of comfort and support. The typical "graduate" of the child welfare system has been hurt so often that new relationships often begin with the expectation that they will not work out. Such children may seek out close ties (e.g., marry early) but will hold back on really investing themselves. This worker recognized that intimacy is a central issue for clients who must now risk themselves with their peers in the rooming house and elsewhere. Eventually they will face the same problem as they consider marriage.

Let us return to the interview as the worker tries to help the client learn from their experience together. This is an example of trying to synthesize process and content.

WORKER: You know, I think what we have gone through together might offer you some ideas about how to handle this friendship question. Do you remember how it was with us when we first met?

CLIENT: Yeah, I thought you would be just another worker. I wondered how long you would stick around.

WORKER: As I remember it, you made it pretty tough on me at the beginning. I had the feeling you wouldn't let me get close to you because you figured it wouldn't last too long anyway.

CLIENT: That's right! I didn't build it too high 'cause I knew it was only temporary.

WORKER: It was frustrating for me at first because I couldn't seem to get anywhere with you. You seemed determined not to let anything get going between us. Somehow, it worked out. Because I feel real close to you, it's going to hurt now not to be seeing you all the time. I knew from the first day that someday we would have to say good-bye and it would be painful. No matter how much it hurts now, I wouldn't want to have missed knowing you this way. It was something special for me, and I will remember you.

CLIENT: (Silence—obviously struggling with emotion.) I'm glad you stuck with me. You're the only worker who really did.

WORKER: What can you take out of our experience that relates to you and the people at the rooming house, or wherever you meet friends—at work, the Y?

CLIENT: You mean the same thing could happen there? If I build the walls too high, they might not get through?

WORKER: You said before that you had discovered how responsible you are for a lot of what happens. I think that's true in this case as well. If you're afraid of risking yourself, of being rejected, of getting close to these people and then losing them, then you will be alone. Maybe the most important thing you have learned is that you can get close if you want to, that it does hurt when you say good-bye, but that's life. You pick yourself up and find new people to get close to again.

CLIENT: You mean like the kids at the rooming house?

WORKER: Right! And on the job, and maybe at the Y, or other places where you can meet people your own age.

CLIENT: So it's up to me.

WORKER: It usually is.

In many ways the worker is sharing his own learning with the client. Every time the worker starts with a new client and finds himself investing feeling, he must do so with the knowledge that it will hurt to say good-bye. This is the gift a worker can give to a client. The best way for workers to handle their own feelings of loss is to share them in the ending and then begin with a new client.

Transitions to New Experiences and Support Systems

As the worker brings the relationship to a close, it helps to identify what it is about their work together that the client valued and to discuss how the client can continue to receive this support. The previous illustration demonstrated a worker helping a client think about how he might shift his need for support to a peer group. This suggestion made sense for his stage of development. In another case, a worker might help the client identify family or friends who could offer help if the client will use them, employing the skills developed while using the worker. In cases where a transfer is made to a new worker, some discussion of the strengths and weaknesses of the present working relationship can aid a client to develop a strategy for using the new worker more effectively. Community resources for social, vocational and counseling needs can also

be identified. The worker can, in addition, convey to the client a sense of having used the worker for important work at a particular time of life and to feel that there might be a desire to use help at other times when the going gets rough. The counseling process is not necessarily a one-time experience which leaves the client capable of facing all of life's crises. It was an aid for a particular period of life and can be one again at some future time. The notion of a client moving in and out of supportive experiences at different points in life is a much more realistic one than one of seeking help once and never needing it again.

Finally, a physical transition can also be made to the new situation. For example, a joint session with the new worker can ease the change. In another example, a child care worker from a residential center might accompany a resident on visits to a new foster home. In many circumstances, concrete steps can be taken in addition to conversation about endings and transitions.

The following record material provides a complete illustration of a session when a worker in a psychiatric residential setting tells a teenage client that she is leaving the agency. Their relationship has been very positive, using dance therapy as a medium for helping the client express her thoughts and feelings. Even as the worker began to deal with her own feelings and those of the client, she incorporated first steps for effecting a transfer of the work to other support staff.

Sandra arrives in a good mood and with a bouncy step and says "I've been looking forward to this"—"I'm glad to get back." She is talkative and indicates she didn't have enough activity or exercise over Christmas, felt sluggish—had difficulty with her feelings. She says Christmas was hard for her, missed me while I was on holidays, and tried not to get into anything too heavy.

As we are talking I began to put on the videotape, and Sandra notices the video equipment. I ask whether she's really energetic, saying, "We've been away for a while. Is it difficult to start again?" Sandra says it is a bit scary—not sure how deep she wants to get in—we were working on some very frightening things—wants to get into it but feels safer if she avoids it, too. I said, "Sounds right on—you've been taking lots of risks with me and our dance work has been getting deeper and deeper." I point out that safety is a must if she is to go on with it, and we must build and establish that important trust. I said, "This is really important, Sandra, and we have to be honest with each other and not take things for granted." I stopped working on the equipment and said, "Before we go on, I've got something to tell you first—we have to talk about it—I'm going to be leaving in two months, on April 2." I choked a little as I said this and revealed feeling in my voice, and a tear ran down my face. I stopped for a moment and Sandra stepped forward to me and put her arms around me in a hug, and I put my arms around her. We held each other for several moments. She stepped back and looked me directly in the eyes and said, "But *why* are you going? *Why?*" I answered, "Sometimes that's a hard question to answer." I said that we'd have six weeks together to complete our work and to say good-bye, but stopped talking when I saw that Sandra's feelings were still back at the sense of loss. She said, "Just like that—you're walking out just like that!" I said, "It's been very hard for me to come and tell you. I knew it would hurt. It just seems when things start going for you, somebody important leaves. I want you to know it's not you, what we've been doing together is very important, and you're doing very well—I know it's a bad time for me to have to go. We're not finished, and we're at a critical point in your treatment. I feel terrible." She, as if in a trance, said, "Then *why* are you going? I don't understand. Are you going to a new job? Did you get fired?" The questions came like a barrage demanding to be answered, insisting on a response as her anger mounted. She became more direct, and her contact and communication became more personal and intimate.

My own feelings were stirred, and I grasped in my mind for an answer that would sound "right." I replied, "I am tired, my job has been demanding, and I feel I need a change. My husband and I will be having his family to visit us this summer, and we're thinking we might want a family of our own. I would like to be at home for a while."

Sandra said brightly, "That's nice that you want your own family—you're the same age as my mother." To which I replied, "But I'll be leaving you and that will be hard—I'll really miss you—we've become very close and you've shared a very private and special part of yourself with me." Sandra visually appeared to sag—at which I took her by the arm and said, "Let's sit down together." She sat down and tears formed in her eyes. I gave her a handkerchief from my purse and she wiped her eyes and began twisting the cloth. I asked, "What are you feeling now—can you get it out?" She replied initially as if not hearing me, "*Why?* How can you do this to me? It's like I'm losing my best friend, or my dog— You're just like my mother and now you're leaving." I said, "Like your real mother or your adoptive mother?" She said, "Like the real mother I never had—you're what I would like my real mother to be like, as I imagine her." I said, "You've been very special to me too, Sandra—I'd be proud to have a daughter like you." She said, "Not one as mixed up as me." I said, "You're putting yourself down again. Didn't you hear what I said? You've given me a lot too—but you are not my daughter, and I am not your mother, and we must not lie about that. We must look each other in the eye and treasure the real things between us." Sandra looked up and said, "I don't know if I can, it's too hard and it hurts too much. You're the person I've really cared about here. I've never told you that. What will happen to me when you go?" I replied, "That's very honest, Sandy—I believe you can make it, but we'll have to work on it. There is lots to do yet. Do you think we can use the next five sessions to do that?" She weakly replied, "Only five left—they're disappearing already. It's all happening too fast." So she added, "We'd better get busy. I want to get as much as I can before you go. I do want to get through my fears." I hugged her and said, "You're a very determined young lady when you make up your mind, aren't you!" She replied, "That's what you've taught me, to say what I want and I'm determined toward that!"

I cautioned her, "But we probably won't finish everything—and in a couple of weeks you may need to close down, you may want to stop, but as long as you can and as long as it is safe to keep going—we'll keep working—but you must keep me informed on how you're doing and how much you can handle—you must take some control of the safety and I'll watch closely—that must be our bargain. I want to leave you with support and with staff who can understand, but we will have to bring our work together to a safe finish."

Sandy agreed, saying, "Let's get started—I don't want to lose a day." I said, "And as if that's not enough, I have one other thing to say. You've asked me to be confidential on some of the really scary things until you felt safer to talk about it. Well, we've got to begin sharing the material with cottage staff." Sandra said, "Not yet, don't ask me this now, this is too much." I replied, "I must. I want to show your videotape to staff from your cottage. We can't keep secrets. They won't understand, and you'll need them. I'd like your permission to show the tape, and I want you to know that this material must be shared." Sandra became quite vulnerable and said, "They'll think it's ugly. I'm scared of what they'll think about me, I'll feel like something inside has been violated!" I paused and said, "I know—I'm asking a lot, maybe too much of you all at once, but I'm asking you to keep

your trust in our work, that I'll treat the material as we have in these sessions with love, with care and with dignity, as something beautiful and a part of your inner world." Sandy shrugged her shoulders and said, "Now *you're* determined, aren't you?" to which I replied, "I am, and this sharing is part of our work. It would be wrong and hurtful to both of us to keep it to ourselves. You know I've talked to your cottage staff about what we're doing, but they have not seen the videotapes." (Long pause) Sandy said, "Oh, go ahead, you'll do it anyway, I don't feel very good about it, but you can show them if you want to." I replied, "If I would do it anyway, I wouldn't be talking to you now—we must be together on these things—that's our bargain—I would like your permission." She said, "I agree, but I don't have to like it." We both looked at each other, and I laughed, saying, "That's a deal, but I promise I'll give you time to get mad at me." Sandy replied, "I won't get mad—I like you," to which I replied, "It [the anger] will come, but we'll work on it when it comes."

As we cleared up at the end of the session, Sandy claimed, "If I'd only known what was waiting for me when I came today!" I said, "It has been a really hard session for me, too. Are you feeling OK to go back to the cottage?" She replied, "I'm feeling OK now, but I feel a bit low." I said, "You've really struggled with hard things today. I don't expect you to be singing, but if you start to feel bad, talk to Fran or Rhonda. They'll be available for you." I walked her back to the cottage arm-in-arm and said good-bye. She replied, "It sounds so final." I said, "It does, but we've got to start—and I'll see you next week."

NOTES

1. Herbert S. Strean, *Clinical Social Work Theory and Practice* (New York: The Free Press, 1978), pp. 227–28; for a seminal article on the use of time in social work practice see: Jessie Taft, "Time as the Medium of Helping Process," *Jewish Social Service Quarterly* 26 (1949); see also Ruth Elizabeth Smalley, *Theory For Social Work Practice* (New York: Columbia University Press, 1967), pp. 147–50.

2. Elizabeth Kübler-Ross, *On Death and Dying* (New York: Macmillan, 1969).

3. William Schwartz, "On the Use of Groups

in Social Work Practice," in *The Practice of Group Work*, ed. William Schwartz and Serapio Zalba (New York: Columbia University Press, 1971), pp. 17–18.

4. William Schwartz, "Between Client and System: The Mediating Function," in *Theo-* *ries of Social Work with Groups*, eds. Robert W. Roberts and Helen Northen (New York: Columbia University Press, 1976), pp. 191–94.

5. Ibid.

CHAPTER 6

Working with Families

INTRODUCTION

In the first five chapters of this book, a model of the core dynamics and skills of the helping process was described and illustrated. Even as these ideas were presented as constant elements of a helping model, variant elements were introduced by the setting of practice as well as the particular client being served. One's work with individuals might look somewhat different in a child welfare agency as compared to a hospital, and additional variations would be introduced if one worked with an adolescent or a senior citizen.

In addition to setting and population factors, modality of practice also introduces significant variant elements to our work. This chapter is designed to build upon the first five chapters by examining the variant elements of the helping model introduced by working with families and family problems. While the core elements of the model are the same, the phases of work concept, the importance of contracting, the skills required to build a positive working relationship, and so on, there are significant differences when one attempts to provide help to families and family members. Some of these differences are addressed in this chapter to assist the reader in making the transi-

tion from work with one to work with more than one in the family context. In Part II of this book, the variant elements in work with groups are examined while Part III focuses on the variant elements in working with the system.

In addition to describing what this chapter is intended to do, it is important to note what it is *not* attempting. It is not meant as an introduction to what is traditionally called *family therapy*. The reader is referred to any one of a number excellent publications devoted to this topic.[1] While the chapter will refer to and draw upon models of family therapy, it will focus on the element of working with families which is more familiar to most helping professionals who do not, strictly speaking, carry out long-term, intensive family therapy. Social workers have a long history of working with families which predates the emergence of family therapy as a practice modality. This type of work with families falls into two general categories. In the first, the practice is often called *family support work* or *family counseling*. This practice is usually short term in nature, and is designed to help families facing normative crises (e.g., the first child reaching the teen years or a crisis provoked by a new baby). The focus of the work is on helping a relatively healthy family get through a difficult time, using the experience to strengthen rather than erode the family system. In those families in which the crisis leads to the revelation of deeper, more long-term problems, it is not unusual for short-term, family support work to involve working to help the family identify the real problems (e.g., abandon the use of a family scapegoat as the identified patient), creating a working relationship so that the family sees helping professionals in a positive way, and then referring the family for more traditional forms of long-term, family therapy. The family support worker, by definition of his or her job, does not undertake the long-term, intensive family therapy task.

The second major set of circumstances in which most workers find themselves working with families, is in the provision of help to families or family members which are directly connected to the specific services of their agency.

For example, in child welfare, a social worker might work with a family, over a period of time, in helping the parents strengthen their child-rearing skills and to cope more effectively with aspects of their life which are making parenting more difficult. Just as the worker would try to make effective referrals to other services for alcohol counseling, job counseling, and so on, he or she would also make such a referral for ongoing marital counseling or intensive family therapy. The focus of the work would be directed by the agency's mandate to work with families with children at risk. In another example, a hospital social worker in a medical setting might work with family members on their adjustment to a patient's illness (e.g., living with cancer, paraplegics and the problems of dependency). In a third example, a school social worker might undertake family work in helping parents and a teen-

ager deal with serious school failure problems. In each of these examples, the child welfare, hospital or school social worker, it is crucial that the focus of work be guided by the specific agency function and not turn, under the hands of the worker, into family therapy. This is often precisely what the clients fear most, and a major cause for defensiveness and resistance in early sessions.

The client's fears are not completely unfounded. Workers who are not clear about the importance of agency function in limiting their practice can and often do use the initial purpose for contact as an entry for family therapy. In one extreme example, a family support worker, working for a child welfare agency, described her work with a couple around their sexual dysfunctioning problems. While originally referred to the family to help with their parenting problems which had led to suspected child abuse, the mandated concern of her agency, the sessions with the couple had revealed sexual problems and the worker had undertaken to provide sexual dysfunctioning counseling.

When I enquired as to the connection between this work and her mandate, she admitted it was not there. She went on to say that she had taken a neat course in counseling people with sexual problems, and this seemed like a good chance to practice. While there were many reasons this worker's subversion of the working contract was inappropriate, not the least was that while she was busy doing sexual counseling, she was ignoring the work that was in her domain. Workers have argued that in rural areas, with few services, they often must be all things to all people. The problem is a real one, and I can appreciate the dilemma. In some cases, workers may have to provide a range of services as the "only game in town." Even in these situations, I believe there is a responsibility for working to close the gap in services through professional impact on the community. This is discussed in more detail, in Part III of this book. The argument here, is that in trying to provide all services, we often end up not providing those which are our responsibility.

This chapter, than, will focus on family work—helping families through normative crises, creating the conditions for effective referrals to long-term, intensive family therapy for more troubled families, working with families and family-related problems in the context of other services (such as child welfare, medical, psychiatric, corrections, and school). It is hoped that this focus will help the reader see how the ideas of the first five chapters can be useful in the family modality, as well as helping workers in many different settings understand how work with families can be an extension of their ongoing tasks as opposed to the introduction of a completely different service. While ideas and techniques found useful in family therapy approaches were borrowed in developing this chapter, no one model of family therapy is adopted whole as the working approach.

FAMILY THERAPY THEORY

There are a number of factors to be taken into account when one works with families. For example, families have a history which goes back a number of generations. The impact of family members beyond the nuclear family, both dead and alive, can often be felt in the present. The impact of the nuclear family's relationship or lack of relationship, to the extended family or the community may play a large part in its functioning. There is a power differential between family members. For example, children (or a spouse)

may face serious threats of retribution when family members return to their ongoing, between-counseling-sessions life. The fact that the stereotypes, roles, communications patterns—the whole family structure—has developed and been reinforced on a daily basis, twenty-four hours a day, over many years, can create strong resistances to the "unfreezing" process needed for change. The family has had years to develop a "facade," which represents its presentation to outsiders, and each family member has also had time to create the external role which they present to the other family members. One of the major advantages of seeing whole families, as opposed to working with one member of a family at a time, is that it is possible to observe many of these factors in the family interaction (e.g., who sits where, who speaks for the family). Family therapy theory can be helpful to us in better understanding family dynamics and how workers can effectively intervene.

An early contributor to family therapy theory, whose work influenced many of the current theorists, was Ackerman.[2] I will draw upon his framework for viewing a family and many of his practice strategies for describing the role of the worker in carrying out family work, while also integrating concepts from other, more recent theorists. There are many widely different views about how families function and what to do when one tries to help. Unfortunately, only a few of the family therapy theorists have integrated a formal research stance into their work, and in some of these cases, the research is limited to special population groups (e.g., work with anorexics).[3] Therefore, the practitioner is often left to evaluate ideas based upon his or her own practice experiences.

In considering constructs which might

be useful, I have selected ideas and strategies which lend themselves to integration into the general model described in this book. In particular, I have excluded a whole range of approaches which argue for "indirect" forms of influence. Of all modalities of practice, the family therapy area seems to be most advanced in developing approaches in which the therapists influence family members without their knowing what is happening to them. Thus, family members may find themselves faced with suggestions from therapists for outrageous actions which they are not really meant to undertake. Or in another example, one member of a co-therapy team may seem to be involved in other activities (e.g., rummaging through a desk) while actually listening intently, throwing in occasional comments designed to undercut defenses. In yet another approach, the family members are put through exercises under the "direction" of the therapists which are designed to produce outcomes which are only known to the therapists.

While many of these interventions are dramatic and artful, and in fact do accomplish their underlying goals (e.g., upsetting defenses to help families reorganize their structures), the price paid may be too high. Central to the model of practice presented in this book is the importance of trust, and the crucial role played by the helping professional's honesty in developing client confidence. The danger in the use of indirect approaches is that clients may invest a great deal of energy in trying to figure out what the therapist is trying to do to them. If anything, I believe the use of these techniques may tend to heighten client defenses. And yet, practice experience seems to indicate that for some families, these techniques prove effective in influencing change. However, concepts selected for inclusion in this book

must pass the test of whether or not the helping professional is acting "with" or acting "on" the client.

SELECTED ELEMENTS OF FAMILY THEORY

Ackerman views family work as a special method of treatment of emotional disorders based upon dynamically oriented interviews with the whole family.[4] The family is seen as a natural living unit including all those persons who share identity with the family and are influenced by it in a circular exchange of emotions. The family has a potential for mutual support which can be blocked because of problems of communication and the anxieties of individual members. This leads to family disorders and the family's inability to carry out its task.

Although Ackerman does not specifically define the function of the helping person as mediation, many of his treatment skills can be explained as implementing this function in action. For example, he recognizes that treatment usually begins at a time of crisis when the emotional equilibrium of the family has been upset. In the beginning stages of work, after contracting to help the family members work together to improve their communications and deal with the family problems troubling them, his worker would employ the skill of observation to identify the idiosyncratic language of the family. Using personal emotions, stirred by the feelings of the family members towards each other and herself or himself, the worker tests hunches about the family and its feelings by sharing them with family members. In this way, the worker helps the family move past the facade presented in the first stage to a more honest disclosure of their interpersonal conflicts. One example of this would be helping the family move beyond viewing the family problem as concerning a single child (the identified patient) who may be serving as a family scapegoat.

The worker would identify these patterns and roles and point them out to the family members. Roles might include scapegoat, victim, persecutor, and so on. Confrontation (similar to the demand for work) is used to break the vicious cycle of blame and punishment that usually characterizes family relationships. The worker challenges the illusion of work using the "here-and-now" of the family session to bring out the central issues. The process of the family session is directly synthesized with the content of the work, since the family acts out its dysfunctional patterns in front of the therapist. The therapist, in Ackerman's model, controls interpersonal danger, selectively supports family members, and finally, attempts at all times to present a model of interpersonal functioning.

Another theorist whose ideas are helpful in understanding and working with families is Bowen.[5] He has stressed the intergenerational aspect of the family as a system. Without needing to adopt the model whole, it is possible to borrow concepts and techniques which can be integrated into effective family work at any level. Freeman's work has been particularly useful in explicating Bowen's theoretical model and describing and illustrating the techniques involved.[6] In particular, his use of time in organizing his discussion of family work (beginning family therapy, the family therapy process: beyond the first interview, and the terminating stage: letting go) makes it easy to fit useful concepts within the model presented in this book.

Freeman points out that the family therapy process begins before the first interview as the helping professional responds to the call to set an appointment. Rather than rigidly requiring all members of the family to attend a first session, he demonstrates how a skillful and sensitive telephone discussion with the caller, usually the person who most often takes responsibility for dealing with the family's problems, can provide important information about who is involved in the problem and clues as to who would be best to attend the first sessions. Rather than challenging the caller's definition of who should attend, the therapist respects the feelings of the caller and would agree, if needed, to seeing the parents alone, at first, to help develop the working relationship which would encourage the parents to allow the therapist entry into the family. He points out how the discussion of who the caller sees as involved can be the beginning of helping the family members to redefine who is involved in the problem and who should attend the sessions.

Freeman describes four phases in the first interview. These include "warming-up," "defining the problem," "reframing the family's thinking about the problem," and obtaining "the commitment to work as a family." The warming-up stage helps to reduce family members' anxiety. The defining the problem phase involves a form of contracting, trying to understand how all family members perceive the problem. The reframing phase involves helping the family to see the problem in new ways (e.g., as a family problem, not just a result of the behaviors of the identified patient). And finally, the commitment work phase which lays the groundwork for the future sessions.

It is in the middle phase of work that Bowen's theory adds its special emphasis on intergenerational work. As individuals take more responsibility for their own actions, and the sessions are marked by less blaming and reactive behavior, the relative calm in the family sessions allows for identification of subsystems "within the intrafamilial and extrafamilial networks to which the family can direct their attention." It is at these points that the multigenerational concepts are used to help families expand their boundaries. An effort is made to help the family members use the extended family as a source of support and understand the impact of the family history. For example, in one of the illustrations which follow, the active involvement of a stepfather in dealing with a teenage stepdaughter in a family session leads to his revealing for the first time his own childhood experiences as a stepchild. The telling of his story has an important impact on the family's ability to find areas of common ground.

Another family therapy theory, termed *the person centered approach,* builds upon the ideas developed from the early work of Rogers.[7] In this approach, the therapist works on establishing a healthy psychological climate "...which the family members can use to establish realness in family relationships, express true feelings, remain separate and yet identify with the family, develop effective two-way communication, start a healthy process for family development and problem-solving, and clarify societal effects on the family as well as clarify conflicts, seek solutions, explore values, make decisions, experiment with new behaviors, and develop a family model/direction unique to its needs and wants."[8]

The followers of this approach focus on the core helping skills which have been demonstrated repeatedly to create facilitative conditions for change. These components of a healthy psychological climate include: the therapist's genuineness (being real as a person); the therapist's caring and prizing of family members (unconditional positive regard for family members); and the therapist's willingness to listen carefully to what family members have to say (hearing and understanding family members' needs, wants, conflicts, fears, joys, loves, goals, values, hates, disappointment, dreams, sorrows, and their worlds or realities). These core conditions will be familiar to the reader from their discussion in Part I of this book.

Many of the core ideas in family therapy cut across theories. For example, multigenerational issues are important in most models, with Satir interested in "family fact chronology," and Keith and Whitaker referring to a "longitudinally integrated, intra-psychic family of three generations."[9] The core issue of integration and differentiation, how to be part of a family and at the same time, a separate individual, appears in most formulations although the terms used may differ (e.g., Keith and Whitaker refer to *unification* and *separation*). All theorists recognize the problem of "triangles," the effort of one party to gain the allegiance of a second party, in the struggle with a third party (e.g., the parents and the therapists versus the child; the mother and an older child versus the father). Where they tend to differ is in their views of how to avoid the trap, change the pattern, or make strategic use of being the third party in the situation. The importance of developing a safe atmosphere is also stressed, although theories differ sharply in their timing and methods of confrontation designed to upset the dysfunctional patterns.

In the sections which follow, a number of constructs borrowed from the family therapy theorists whose work was described in this section will be discussed and illustrated with examples of family work drawn from a variety of settings.

THE TWO-CLIENTS CONCEPT AND THE WORKER'S ROLE

One of the major differences in working with families and couples is that the worker is dealing with more than one person at a time. In most of the examples in Part I of this book, workers had before them a single client. Even though the model called for conceptualizing the client in interaction with important systems, the worker usually had only one person to deal with at a time. As soon as the helping unit expands to more than two (worker and client) it becomes more complex, introducing new problems, new possibilities, and new demands upon the worker's skills. One of the most common problems observed in family work results from worker identification with a subunit of the family system.

Perhaps the best way to describe the problem is to give an example of how it typically emerges in workshops I conduct for helping professionals. The workshop participant in this case was presenting an example of a general problem: "How do you work with a family if the father is umotivated and very defensive?" In response to my request, the worker described the family as containing middle-aged parents, the father an immigrant from Europe, a fifteen-year-old daughter (the identified patient—the I.P.—whom the parents felt was the problem), and an eleven-year-old son who was no problem at all. The parents had called indicating they could not control the daughter and wanted the child welfare agency to "straighten her out or get her out." While the particulars may differ, this type of situation and the conversation which follows is typical of hundreds of workshops.

After the description of the family and the circumstances of the worker's involvement, I asked for the details of the first session (word for word) as best as the worker could recall. He described the interaction with the father angrily taking the lead in confronting the daughter with accusations of misbehavior. These were directed at the worker almost as a prosecuting attorney might speak to a judge. When I enquired what the daughter was doing, the worker said: "She was just sitting there, her head hanging down, very close to tears." When I asked for the worker's feelings at the moment, he replied: "I felt badly for her and could easily understand why she had trouble dealing with that father. He didn't seem to have any sense of how upset she was." I replied: "You must have also felt angry at him for his insensitivity. You were feeling her hurt and pain, and he seemed closed to her." The worker agreed.

At one point the worker described the father berating his daughter for running around with girls who "...came in late, dressed like sluts, smoked dope and didn't listen to their parents." I asked how the worker responded and he said: "I asked Maria [the daughter] if it hurt her to hear her father say those things, and she just nodded. I asked if she could tell her father that, and she just sat there, unable to speak and about to start crying." I said to the worker: "You wanted the father to understand her hurt. Did it seem to get through to him?" The worker replied that the father was so dense, he couldn't hear a thing. He simply escalated the anger, and said: "In Europe children listen to their parents and respect them." I said: "Which made you even angrier. What did you say to him?" The worker replied: "I told him that I thought he had to understand that he was in the United States now, and that teenagers here were quite different in many ways from the old country. I don't think it helped much, because he just sat there and glared at me. How do you get through to a guy like that?"

It is at moments such as these that it is possible to help workers see the problem in a new way. Using the three circles illustrated below, I asked

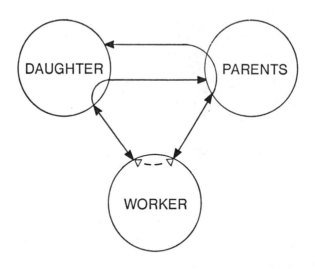

if the worker could put himself back into that moment and tell us where he was in respect to his emotional identification. Pointing to the daughter's circle I said: "It would be quite understandable if you were really with the daughter." The worker replied that I was right. I then ask the workshop group: "Who was with the father?" After a few moments of silence, someone said: "He was all alone."

This is the moment when the "two-client" idea, proposed by Schwartz in the context of group work, becomes helpful in understanding the worker's function in work with families. In order to effectively mediate the individual-social engagement, in the special case of the family, the worker must understand the importance of conceptualizing and identifying with two clients simultaneously. The first client is the individual and the second is the family system. Thus, in the conflict example just described, if the worker was to be helpful at all, he must find a way to emotionally identify (be with) both the daughter and the parents in the family system. By identifying with the daughter, however understandable the reaction may be, the worker cut himself off from the parents, in particular the father, just at the moment he needed him the most. His response to the daughter was helpful in that he recognized her pain and articulated her feelings. If at the very same moment he could have understood the father's feelings, and responded (with genuine empathy) the conversation might have sounded as follows:

FATHER: In Europe children listen to their parents and respect them.

WORKER: So it makes it hard for you to understand what's going on now—why it doesn't seem to work the same way here in the United States.

It's important to underline the genuineness that must be present if the worker uses these words at this moment. The worker *must be feeling* something of the father's struggle to figure out how to be a good parent when the world seems turned upside down from the way in which he was raised. As indicated in the previous section on family therapy theory, the worker will work in this first session to reframe the family's thinking about the problem, trying to help them shift from blaming of the daughter and confrontation, to seeing the problem as one facing the whole family system. However, at this moment, the worker needs to be able to develop his working relationship with the parents, particularly this father. In fact, as will be apparent in the first full example described next, the father's behavior is in part an effort on his part to find out just what kind of worker this is going to be. Since he is already feeling guilty about his parenting, something he may not even admit to himself, he probably began the session assuming that the worker would be on his daughter's side. When the father saw the worker's informal dress and guessed at the worker's age, a part of him said: "He's not much older than she is. How is he going to understand?" When the worker responded with the lecture on American culture, he knew he had been right.

The worker was suffering from an advanced case of "functional diffusion." Fortunately, this is not a terminal illness and can be overcome with a dose of functional clarity. If the worker is there to mediate the individual-social engagement, and the worker can understand his responsibility to the two clients, each individual family member (including the father) and the family-as-whole, then he can be with both clients simultaneously. The importance of this can be seen clearly if one realizes that in the example as presented by the worker, at precisely the moment he was trying to get the father to understand the daughter's feelings, he was demonstrating his complete inability to

feel with the father. Since the worker demonstrates a model of personal functioning, what Schwartz has described as "lending a vision," he said more to that father by his actions than through his words. He wanted the father to understand the daughter's behaviors, even those the father experienced as "deviant," but he was having difficulty in reaching behind the father's deviant behavior to understand the message he was sending.

In reality, even with functional clarity in hand, workers will continuously find themselves overidentifying with one part of the family system and cutting them off from another. The countertransference process, that is, workers relating to clients as substitutes for important people in their own lives, and attributing to clients feelings and reactions from their own experiences, is never stronger than in work with families. Younger workers, some not far removed from situations similar to those experienced by the teenager in the family, must work hard to deal with their own feelings towards authoritative fathers or mothers if they are ever to begin to relate to these parental types as individuals instead of as cardboard caricatures. This is a lifelong task, as described in Chapter 1, with workers using their professional experiences to better understand their own personal lives, and using their personal experiences to better understand their professional practice. In this sense, each family we work with represents an opportunity to learn more about our own families of origin. As our own work in coming to grips with our relationships to our families proceeds, it can have a profound impact on our work with clients.

In the example which follows we see a worker dealing with a family not unlike the one just described—with an angry, volatile father, and a 14-year-old son. It is an illustration of how one can catch a mistake during the session. This worker is in a family support worker role in a large child welfare agency. Because of a complaint of physical abuse of the teenager, the social worker with the protection responsibility had made the first contact. The family support worker was called in to provide family counseling to see if the family could be helped to deal with the problem while keeping the child at home.

FIRST FAMILY SESSION WITH AN ANGRY FATHER (CHILD WELFARE SETTING)

THE "C" FAMILY

FATHER: Greek, a storeowner. Described to me as an angry, volatile, and violent man. Those who had tried to work with him described him as "a write-off," unworkable. He held very definite ideas of family life—including roles, expectations, etc. He came from a family where his father hit him often when disciplining. Obedience was valued.

MOTHER: German, teacher. A quiet, soft-spoken woman from an upper middle-class background.

SON: 14 years old, defiant towards his father. Smoked in front of him in direct contravention to the father's orders. He performed well in school; no apparent peer problems.

Precipitating Incident. Mother sought help after her husband repeatedly hit her son with his fist and once with a board. (Mother was not present during this incident. The story was shared by the son.) Father denies he hit the boy with anything other than an open hand.

History
Professional/Family Friends. During previous contacts with professionals and family friends, they scolded—in one form or another—the father for his behavior and showed sympathy for the boy. The most recent con-

tact with a social worker was similar, with the additional threat to remove the boy from the house (which the mother was planning to do at the time of this meeting, and did do the following day against the father's wishes). He believed the family and its functioning was his responsibility.

Family. Both the husband and wife said that their marriage prior to the birth of their son was fine, though Mrs. C's voice was tentative. Discord arose shortly after the child's birth. From Mr. C's point of view his wife was too soft; from her point of view he was too hard. Throughout the child's life they could not agree on parenting procedures.

Mr. C was the boss in the house. What he said was done. His wife was able to modify these edicts to a moderate degree in regard to herself, but only to a minor degree in regard to her son.

At times of discipline the father took command—often in a physical way. While this was happening, Mrs. C would not become involved unless she felt that her son would be *seriously* hurt. However, after Mr. C finished she would take her son aside (in Mr. C's absence), calm him, cuddle him, and in most instances contradict or modify what Mr. C had said.

These actions on Mrs. C's part were a constant irritant in the couple's relationship. She felt it was necessary to her son's development. He felt it was undermining his authority, and was the reason the boy was acting the way he was.

I gave the above history to indicate how—from the father's point of view and in reality—he had been undermined, excluded and put down, and at the same time how his son was "sided with" (coalition)—against him—by family friends, social workers, his family doctor, and his wife.

The Interview. The family had just been introduced to me by the above-mentioned social worker. The boy walked into the interview room smoking a cigarette.

I introduced myself and began to give a brief introduction of myself and my role in the agency. As I was about two minutes into the introduction the father began admonishing the boy for smoking. The boy said nothing at first. The father kept shouting. His statements became more derogatory and turned into a general attack on the boy's attitude. Mrs. C, under her breath, said her husband's name, thereby asking him to stop.

I asked her if this is how the fights between her husband and her son often began.

Mr. C glared at me, at his wife, and then continued attacking his son (verbally).

Throughout the next ten or fifteen minutes I made numerous attempts at connecting with individual family members by empathizing, understanding, etc. I connected easily with Mrs. C and her son, but was unable to do so with Mr. C. In fact, he was becoming more and more angry each time I spoke, regardless of whom I spoke to. But he was most hostile while I was speaking with the boy. Each time I began speaking to the boy, the father would, in a voice louder than mine, accuse the boy of some transgression. They would then get into a loud argument.

After a while, this pattern changed. Now each time I spoke to the boy, Mr. C would start arguing with the boy, but ended up shouting at me. At first I did not realize this change; I only realized that I was beginning to understand what my colleague had warned me about. I was becoming impatient and angry with this "jerk." Almost mechanically, I said, "You are angry with me?" There was little or no concern in my voice and it must have sounded completely monotone.

The nonverbal cues did not seem to matter. The quality of anger changed. He was now focused on me, but he was not angry with me. For the next fifteen minutes he angrily related the years of no one understanding him, the sincere attempts he had made and was making to help his son grow up properly, the repeated incidents of "people" siding with his son against him after he had disciplined his son and how that had created the present situation, and how his wife and he could not get close because of it.

I said something like: "And that makes it even more difficult, doesn't it?" in a sincere manner.

But he just continued letting it out. There was a pregnant silence—a very pregnant silence.

I began to get uncomfortable and wanted to find something appropriate to say. Something that would summarize what he was trying to say. But I couldn't think of anything.

Then a sentence came to mind: "And you think I'm going to be like all the rest."

"THAT'S RIGHT!" he shouted, almost coming out of his seat. He went on for a few minutes about this concern about when I was talking to his son. I was acting just like the others.

There was a long silence. I was nodding, admitting to both of us that he was right. I apologized, and told him that what I had done was not what I was trying to do. I went on to say that it was my job to be helpful to both of them, and if I wasn't then I wasn't doing my job the way I wanted to.

I asked him to do me a favor. If he noticed me doing that again—to anyone in the family—to please let me know. I would appreciate it.

The remaining ten to fifteen minutes of the meeting were spent, to a large degree, discussing "old" parenting issues (between Mr. and Mrs. C)—nothing significant. What *was* significant was that they were talking on a topic which they had avoided—except in argument—for many years.

I asked them if they wanted another appointment. After a few moments' discussion they decided they did—as a family.

On their way out I said goodbye to the boy. He was a little less "cocky," but not very different.

Mrs. C felt quiet, not quite at ease, but it looked like the universe she had been carrying around on her shoulders was reduced to a solar system.

The biggest change was in Mr. C. He shook my hand with both hands, looked me in the eyes and said, "Thank you .. thank you ... thank you very much." There were tears in his eyes.

I put my other hand on his and said, "You're welcome." Tears welled up in my eyes.

When I walked into the front office after

they left, some of the office staff shook their heads, thereby referring to what I must have gone through and what a "jerk" he was. (It seems that he had been quite gruff to the receptionist on the way in.)

I told them that he was quite a nice guy. Pregnant silence.

DISCUSSION OF THE FIRST FAMILY SESSION

In a first session with a family, as with an individual counseling session, contracting is crucial. The key questions on the minds of all of the family members are: "Who is this worker, what kind of worker will he or she be, and what will happen here?" Because of the prior experiences which the family has had with other helpers, they begin with a stereotype of the worker which must be dealt with head on. Even though the worker has tuned in to the potential feelings and concerns of the family members, and is sensitive to the past experiences as described in the brief history, when the father explodes at the son all of the worker's best plans, opening statements, strategies, etc., go up in smoke. His first reactions are quite normal for a new worker. His skill is revealed in the quickness in which he catches the mistake in the same session and begins to address the real issues raised by the boy, who enters with a cigarette, the mother who displays her passive form of intervention, and the father who says: "If you want to see what it's like around this family, just watch."

The worker has been set up by previous workers (even the office staff) to see the father as the stereotype he presented. The father is ready to see the worker as a stereotype as well. By responding directly to the anger, and the implied question about how he was going to help, the worker broke the pattern. Previous work-

ers had found this father hard to work with because of his anger. As the worker reaches past the cardboard character presented by the father, and responds to the process of the session rather than just the content, he makes a start on developing the working relationship with one of the most important family members, revealing a side to the father that probably has been hidden from previous workers and the family members. In fact, the father's open expression of anger will make him an easier client to work with, in some ways, than if he had hidden his real reactions, participated in an illusion of work, while all the time really feeling: "He's just like all of the rest of those workers; against me, and with the kid."

Because of the urgency of dealing with the father, and the "which side are you on?" issue, other steps were left undone. For example, the worker will need to be clearer about the purpose of these meetings, and the specific role he will play. He starts this process by trying to say he wants to help all of them, and not take sides. At a next session, he might want to say something about helping the family members to talk to each other about how they operate as a family, and helping them to understand how the other family members really feel. In addition, he will need to make sure that in his effort to be with the father, that he not lose sight of the mother and the son. The eleven-year-old child will also need to be brought into the picture.

He will need to help them reframe the problem as well. At this point they are meeting to discuss their "problem" teenager. However, even in the first session the problem with the son quickly leads to the problem between the parents. It is not unusual for a family needing help to use a teenage child as a "ticket of admisson" to the helping agency. The struggle over authority and the role of the father in the family is just as much an issue for the husband and wife—only the wife has found it easier to deal with that struggle through the child. It is important for the worker to stay focused on how the parental struggle relates to their ability to parent effectively, helping them to see the connections to their general relationship, but not embarking on a course of general marital counseling—which would be outside of the agency-family working contract. Reassurance on this point may make it safer for both the husband and the wife to drop the "family facade."

Another issue which was not directly dealt with in this interview was the question of confidentiality. There was a child welfare agency involved, and already a threat to apprehend (take into care) the teenage son had been expressed. The worker will need to deal honestly with this issue, since as a staff member of the agency, the worker carries a responsibility to report to the social worker on the case information related to serious child abuse. This issue was just under the surface of the first interview and must be raised and clarified. Under what conditions might the family support worker have to report child abuse to the social worker in the case? Avoiding such a discussion will not make the authority issue go away, rather, it will invest it with more power to block the work. In summary, the worker has made a start with developing a working relationship with the family, especially its most potentially resistant member. There is much work to be done, and the outcome of the work will depend somewhat on how the worker handles his part, and how ready the family members are to tackle their responsibilities.

FAMILY SUPPORT WORK OVER TIME: BRINGING THE STEP-FATHER INTO THE PICTURE

In the example which follows, a family support worker is brought in by a child welfare agency social worker to help a family in which a twelve-year-old son is having trouble staying in school. The family has a two-and-a-half year history of difficult times with the agency staff and is seen as "hard to work with." As the worker's tuning in comments indicated, he was aware of the past history and of the need to deal with it at the beginning of the relationship. In this case, a fifteen-year-old daughter raised the question for the family. He was also aware of the family's concern over the session turning into marital counseling between the mother and her common-law husband of five years. The work demonstrates how he tried to develop a working contract which respected the family's concerns, and then redefined the contract, as it became clear that the parents wanted help in sorting out how they dealt with the children. A central issue, not uncommon in families with stepparents, is how involved shall the non-biological parent be? Often, the stepparent is wary about "butting in," and the biological parent is concerned about not burdening the other partner. In the early sessions, the mother indirectly chooses to exclude the stepfather. After confidence grows in the new family support worker, mom and dad are more open to including their relationship in the working contract.

RECORD OF SERVICE: FAMILY
Family: Smiths.
Time period: November–April
Agency: Child Welfare
Composition: Natural mother Linda 35, common-law husband of five years Brian 29, Marie 15, Mike 12, and foster child 15.

Problem Area: Linda's relationship with the agency and her need for Brian's help with Mike.

Problem Statement. Linda was in a bind; she had turned to the Agency for assistance but was very hesitant to work with an agency which she felt wasn't responsive to her needs. Both Linda and her previous worker of years had seen each other as adversaries, each trying to do what they thought was best for Mike. My record will follow how I worked to develop a culture in which Linda and the Agency could identify their common ground of getting Mike back into school.

How the Problem Came to My Attention. The Smith family was my first chance to get working with a family and Jane, the previous worker, went over the file with me. It soon became clear that the Agency and Linda went through a definite pattern whenever the social worker found a facility that would consider taking Mike. The worker would find a facility, set up intake interviews, inform Linda, she'd agree to attend the interviews but always ended up by saying it wouldn't work. Mike would initially attend the program but after about a month, he wouldn't show up. In frustration the worker would tell Linda that Mike had been missing and she'd confirm that she knew this. Mike would always stop attending the facility close to the times that there were to be "family sessions" and Linda's perception of these was a time when her relationship with Brian would be examined and they would be blamed for Mike's problems.

People in the Home. Linda, 35, natural mother of Mike and Marie, was from a very unhappy background, having an alcoholic father, being abused by him, and living in fear. School was a bad experience and she prides herself on being very financially successful with only a grade 6 education. She believes that Mike can do just as well if he can learn the basic three R's. Brian, 29, had lived with Linda for the past five years as her common-law husband. He was born and raised in Europe, and immigrated to the United States when he was 15 years old and works successfully with a small business. He only gets involved with the chil-

dren if Linda is desperate. His family which lives in town feels that Linda has led him into a sinful life and he visits them on his own. He cannot accept the fact that Mike has a severe learning disability and feels that he must be made to sit down and learn. Brian had not spoken to the previous worker in 2 1/2 years except to exchange hellos. Marie, 15, was in the process of dropping out of school and trying to get into an accelerated programme in order to get school finished quickly. Sally, 15, joined the household in January, had been Marie's best friend previously and couldn't manage living with her own family. Mike, 12, had been at numerous resources and was expelled from school as he'd threatened several teachers and beaten up different children at the school. The special teacher later supplied had threatened to resign if she was required to tutor Mike. When I contacted the last resource he'd been in, I was informed that the family and Mike were "unworkable." Combined with the information at the office, I was more than a little wary about being involved.

In preparation I did some resource hunting and came up with some possible placements from the description of what Linda wanted from conversations we'd had by telephone.

I Did Some Preliminary Tuning in (or How to Stay Alive Planning)

In considering the work to follow, I came up with several taboo areas:

1. Telling Linda about parenting techniques.
2. Trying to probe Linda and Brian's relationship.
3. Trying to do a sales pitch for a resource.
4. Trying to steer Linda where I thought she should go.

I realized that:

1. Things must be getting desperate for Linda to call for help.
2. Linda had been through the routine many times and knew the ropes much better than I.
3. I had to level about my agenda.
4. I had to do a lot of work on the negatives before we could move.

5. I had to let the family know that there might be nothing available for Mike.

The First Meeting (I Was Nervous) —Clarifying Role

I was let in the door by Linda who seemed tired, looked as if she were in pain, and flustered. They'd just finished supper and another social worker who was seeing Sally had left about 20 minutes previously. Linda offered me a seat in the living room, turned off the TV and called Mike who sat next to me on the couch. To my amazement Mike was a pleasant looking 12-year-old who spoke as I'd expect a fellow his age would. I relaxed a bit figuring he must either have been well-drilled beforehand or a top-blower. Marie sat about six feet away looking at a book but was all ears. Brian sat at the far end of the dining room reading and looked up occasionally. I opened the meeting by establishing role and purpose.

SELF: Linda, you and I have spoken on the telephone and I'm wondering if the others know why I'm here tonight? What have you told them?

LINDA: Well, I told these guys that we're having a new social worker to find a place for Mike to go to school. He's 12 now and needs to get something—anything so that he'll know how to read, do some math and get a job. We need someone to find out where he can go and still be able to stay at home.

Linda continued speaking and Brian had stopped his reading and looked interested so I asked him what he thought about plans for Mike. He agreed that Mike needed to be in school and hoped that I could find a place. Linda jumped in suddenly, "Brian works really hard and I do all the kids' schoolwork planning, you know." It seemed like Linda was trying to shut me off from talking with Brian but I fought the urge to try to override her. Linda said, "Brian, why don't you make us some coffee?" He slowly disappeared into the kitchen and only appeared to deliver coffee, then returned to the kitchen. I wondered why Linda wanted Brian out of the discussion but didn't feel comfortable asking so I turned to Mike and asked him what he'd like.

MIKE: The same things you've been talking about.

SELF: Some regular schoolwork and some things to do with your hands like mechanics and carpentry?

MIKE: Yeah, I'd really like that. I fix my bike all the time and I've made things, you know. Would you like to see something?

LINDA: Show Frank your blue vase.

Mike got a blue ceramic vase from the knick-knack shelf and proudly showed it. It was a good job and I told him that I liked it. Marie was getting fidgety and I thought she wanted to get in so I asked her what she thought about plans for Mike. She spoke angrily.

MARIE: I don't want to talk about that. I want to talk about social workers and how they don't care about people. All they care about is making money and themselves.

She gave a rundown on all the things that had been tried, failed and a list of social workers' faults. I was glad for our classwork on checking out previous experiences and felt Marie's strength in speaking out.

SELF: (Moving from the general to the specific) Boy (I sighed), from what you've said I'm sure you must be wondering if I'll be just like all the rest? I do want to find out exactly what Mike wants as I know that there's no point in trying to force something on Mike that he doesn't want and that everyone doesn't agree to try. I hope that Mike and Linda will tell me like you have when I've missed the point or am not listening.

MARIE: Well, you are different. You're the first person who's asked Mike what he wants and not just come here and told us what to do.

I thanked Marie, felt like she'd done a lot of work for me as everyone agreed to let me know if I was missing their point. I told them that I'd let them know if I thought they were missing my point or assuming without checking. This led into a discussion about years of misunderstandings and the frustrations involved. (Focused listening.)

Progress Was Slow and I Became Intent on Pushing for Feelings

As the weeks passed, no facility was available for Mike. Our first meeting in February started with Mike meeting me at the door; he had two friends with him and was eager to talk and leave. I'd been looking for a tutor for Mika and had been unsuccessful.

MIKE: Have you found a tutor for me yet? It's getting to be a long time you know, everyone says they're going to do something and then nothing ever happens.

SELF: No, I haven't found anyone yet. Right now it looks like it could be several weeks before there'll be someone. Bet you're angry waiting to see who'll come.

MIKE: Yeah, you know the longer things go, the worse they'll get; sometimes I just get mad and say to mom—just tell him to stuff it if he can't get someone to help.

SELF: I get really frustrated too, sometimes it seems like forever before there's a worker available. (Sharing worker's feelings). In the kitchen Linda was tallying her day's receipts so I sat down and helped sort them out.

LINDA: No news it sounds like from your call.

SELF: That's right, you sound like you've been through this before, Linda—fed up with the whole waiting business.

With that we got into a discussion about hassles she'd had with the Agency, the school system, and other agencies. She asked if I'd go with her to find out exactly what had happened when Mike had got suspended and I agreed. Brian, who so often barely said two words, came in and sat opposite me at the table and looked as if he wanted to join the conversation.

I Tried to Include Brian and Needed to Recontract If He Were to Be Included

SELF: Do you know what we've been talking about so far, Brian?

BRIAN: Yes, I could hear from the living room and want you to know that it's no good if you get someone for two hours a day. If Mike can get into doing something he wants, then he'll leave the schoolwork and never learn.

Brian went on to explain how he'd learned English, etc., when he arrived from Europe by studying eight hours a day and began to attack Linda's parenting skills and blame her for Mike's failure. I could see Linda freeze up and referred to our contract.

SELF: Linda, Brian is talking now about your differences and we've agreed that you will decide if I'm to be involved in those discussions. (I could see the smoke inside Linda, didn't want to lose Brian's impetus but wasn't going to break my agreement with Linda.)

LINDA: Brian, you know I don't want to talk about this in front of others, it always leads to trouble.

BRIAN: We've got to talk about it or it'll always be the same, nothing's going to change if we don't try something different.

Brian was visibly shaken; he motioned to his chest indicating that he could hardly breathe and stuttered badly while he told me of an old injury which causes this condition when he's angry. I still wanted Linda to have the say as to my participation.

SELF: I still want you to ask me to wait in the living room, Linda, if you want to talk with Brian privately. I am willing to stay if you want, I might be able to help sort out some of the things both you and Brian are saying. This conversation sounds like it's been talked through a number of times without any solutions, just going around in circles with both of you getting really mad at each other.

LINDA: You can stay.

They talked about the differences in their upbringings and their expectations for their own family. They seemed to exaggerate their differences and I pointed out many similarities such as the belief that you have to be tough to survive and at the same time they both wanted warmth and affection. Brian's gasping for breath made it almost impossible to get his words out. At that point it seemed like they both wanted each other's support so badly but couldn't say it.

SELF: You both sound so frustrated and both really want things to be good here. Linda, you sound like you could use some support from Brian. (I missed vice versa.)

Linda looked startled and said, "Yes, I could." Brian was done in, but heard, and excused himself from the room. Linda talked more about how hard it'd been for her and how she felt the kids were biologically hers so she really does have to take all the responsibility for them. I told her we could talk more about that and thanked Brian on the way out for telling his part.

Because conversations between the husband and wife had broken down and turned to blaming and recriminations, Linda had feared opening up the "taboo" area. And yet, if the family system was going to work effectively, she would need all the help she could get from the whole family to tackle their problems—Brian included. By creating a positive and safe working relationship, and focusing on the part of their relationship dealing with the children, this worker helped set the stage for Linda agreeing to open the door on this important area of work. The exchange of their different cultural backgrounds and family histories can be used to help them understand both their commonalities and differences. It is only a beginning, but a rather important one in reframing the problem.

Another interesting observation is how the worker sat down with Linda and helped her sort her receipts. Workers often complain of the difficulty in getting a family's attention, with so much going on. This worker did not feel the need to ask Linda to stop what she was doing, and instead, sat with her and helped. In another case, he carried out an excellent interview with a single-parent mom while helping her fold laundry. These ongoing family activities are often a signal to the worker of the stress the family feels about the session, and at times, it may be easier to work within the activity, than to try to bring it to a formal stop.

In the excerpt which follows, the worker brings a tutor into the situation and meets with her and Linda and Mike to discuss their working contract. When the tutor mentions the possibility of a family meeting to discuss Mike's school progress, both Mike and his mother go off into "flight," in an effort to escape the uncomfortable subject. The worker responds to the process of the session and calls everyone's attention to what happened. This allows the concerns about "family sessions" to be aired and the contract clarified. In the second excerpt, we see the worker beginning the phase of transitions and endings, getting ready to connect the family members to new sources of help after he leaves.

I Offer the Opportunity for Linda and Mike to Set a Contract

By March, I was able to get a tutor for Mike—Betty who had worked with him two years before and the only worker the Smiths had identified as being helpful in our first meetings. We met together to draw up Betty's contract. Mike was eager to have Betty to work with him.

SELF: Now, what do you two want Betty to work on with her time with Mike?

There was silence, many shrugs, looks at the ceiling and "I don't knows"; then Linda asked me, "What do you think should go down there?" referring to the contract.

BETTY: No, no, no—it's not up to Frank to say what you want, it's up to you and Mike. There's no way I can work with you unless we agree on the contract. We can change as we go along but you have to say what you want.

After more silence, Linda listed what she wanted. Betty added a weekly family meeting to discuss how things were going at school and at home for Mike and Linda. Suddenly Mike started talking about the paint on the ceiling and he and Linda spoke at full speed about the ceiling paint.

SELF: Wait a minute, wait a minute—what's going on here? All of a sudden you two took off and I don't know what's happening. What just happened here? (Responding to indirect cues.)

LINDA: Oh, nothing, I'm sorry.

SELF: Mike, do you know what happened to you, you started looking at the ceiling all of a sudden?

MIKE: It's the family meetings—she doesn't like them, that's what happened before, she didn't want to go to them. (Linda looked shell-shocked.)

SELF: What happened when you didn't have the sessions, Mike?

MIKE: I got kicked out.

SELF: Are you worried that the same thing might happen again? (Supporting Mike in a taboo area.)

Mike went on to say that he wanted to have the school work out for him. Linda explained to him what she'd disliked about previous family meetings. After some clarification of Betty's role and purpose in the meetings, Mike thought it would work and was first to sign the agreement, looking proud of playing his part. Betty and I told them that they'd both taken big steps in leveling with us and each other. (Crediting work done.)

I Wanted to Talk about Endings and Start Transitions

At a regular evening meeting in early April we'd been talking about endings and Linda had been shocked at first that the time was so short and then angry at me for leaving and frustrated about having to start all over again with another worker.

SELF: I remember our first meetings, Linda, I wasn't sure if we'd be able to work together at all. I feel that we've come through a great deal together and it's been pretty shaky at times—you know when the times we've both got pissed off. You've all made me feel welcome in your home, I've come to like you very much and I'm going to miss you.

LINDA: Then why are you leaving? I know, you have to leave. Who will be my new worker?

SELF: That's something I've been checking out. You've said that you've had a hard time whenever a new worker is involved.

Linda agreed and said that she wouldn't fool around and be nice to a new worker she didn't like.

SELF: That's one of the things I really like about working with you, you give it to me straight. I was always confident when I felt like I'd blown it that you'd tell me. That's a feeling I enjoy. Also I was honored last week when you told me that you trusted me—I knew that was hard for you to say—that's when you added "almost."

LINDA: Well, I do trust you. (She laughed and added), "almost."

I explained that I'd talked to my supervisor to find out who'd be getting the Smiths after I left and we talked about getting together in order to clarify what would be happening. The conversation continued around some of the snags we'd hit, how things were resolved and what obstacles might come up. It hadn't occurred to me how much I'd become involved with the family until that evening and the conversation about leaving really hit me.

Where It Stands Now. Linda has begun to see the Agency as an ally and took the opportunity to suggest a joint meeting with Debbie who'll be the new worker in order to establish a working contract. Brian has joined in the last four out of five meetings and has said that he's willing to help with Mike when Linda asks. She's agreed to include Brian in the weekly family sessions.

Specific Next Steps.

1. Betty will continue working with Mike until the end of June and will be available in September for schoolwork and family sessions.

2. Debbie and I will follow up on our meeting to discuss future plans and she'll be available to the Smiths and Betty.

3. Linda, Mike, Betty, and I will visit another possible resource this week and discuss future plans.

THE SINGLE-PARENT FAMILY: COMMUNITY CARE TEAM SETTING

Our view of the average family as a working father, a mother at home, and two to three children is fast becoming more of a myth than reality. The rate of growth of single-parent families is increasing (as is the major change in women's involvement in the work force). At one of my speaking engagements on the subject of working with single parents, I asked the audience, all helping professionals, how many of them were single parents, had been children in homes of single parents, or had close relations who were involved in single parenting. Almost two thirds of the five hundred of the audience raised their hands.

Although there are many similarities between single-parent and two-parent families, there are also some differences which need to be noted by helping professionals. Single parents have to face many of the same normative crises faced by other families (e.g., children becoming teenagers), however, they have to face them alone. Most single parents are women, and a large percentage of these have to either work (often in low-pay, low-status, dead-end jobs) or depend upon welfare. For many, the lack of affordable day-care facilities makes it impossible to work and improve their financial situation. Between low pay and welfare, most single-parent women are trying to live on income levels below the accepted poverty level—a factor which significantly adds to the stress of raising a family alone.

Housing is another major area of distress for single parents. Many housing options are not open to them, and as a result, they need to pay more of their income than the general population. A female single parent quickly discovers that her credit rating left her with her husband, even if she had a positive relationship with her local bank over the years of her marriage. She may suddenly find herself in a "catch 22" situation, needing a positive credit record to get credit, and needing credit to obtain a positive credit record. Thus, if she wished to purchase a home, she may run into discrimination cutting her off from this avenue of improving her housing situation.

The problem of dealing with friends can also be a serious one. Many single parents report changes in attitudes towards them after a split in the marriage with former close friends seeming to take sides. Another common factor is sometimes referred to as the "Noah's Ark syndrome," in which friends seem to be operating under the general belief that people should come "two by two." Old friends seem to slip away and new friends seem to be harder to find. This problem, often compounded by the single parent's depression and lack of effort to create new support groups, leads to further isolation and loneliness. With all of these added pressures, a single parent often finds it hard to have time for her personal needs, trying to balance these with the demands of the children. Dealing with school meetings, dental appointments, homework, etc., is difficult enough for two parents. In addition, dealing with the feelings of one's children when one is so vulnerable can be too hard to do alone. As a result, barriers start to grow in a family and certain areas become "taboo." One crucial one may be the feelings of the children about the absent parent and the rejection they feel. As one woman said in a group I led for single parents, "It's hard for me to help my kids face their rejection because I still haven't been able to face mine." The guilt felt by the remaining single parent often makes it hard to open up honest discussion with the children in the family. If the children show signs of their distress, through behavior cues appropriate to their age (e.g., young children regressing and bedwetting; latency age children cutting themselves off from friends, having school trouble, getting into fights; teenagers getting into trouble with the law), the parent often senses the cause; however, their guilt creates a significant communications blockage.

Ongoing relations with the ex-spouse can also take its toll on the parent and the children. Often, the battles of the marriage or the leftover feelings over the split emerge around custody issues, financial support issues, and struggles over loyalty. Children already hurt by a split between their parents, which they sometimes feel responsible for, are further distressed by feeling they must take sides and cannot be loyal to both parents at the same time.

A number of these problems emerge in the example of practice which follows. In this case, the setting is a community care team, with the single-parent mom, age thirty-two, coming for help in coping with her family of five children, aged two to fourteen. Kurt, the ten-year-old, is the "ticket of admission" for the family.

Name (disguised): Jane (mother)
Time Period: February 26–April 4
Agency: Community Care Team
System: Family *Age:* 32
Family Members: Judy, 14; Robert 13; Kurt, 10—First marriage, divorce. Arn, 5; and Bobby, 2—Second marriage, separated (to Len).

Problem. Jane is a 32-year-old woman, a single parent with five children. She is a very reserved, dignified person who finds it difficult to ask for help, to open herself up, and share her feelings. She came in identifying her problem as depression. She also has difficulty managing her family and communicating well with

them. One child, Kurt, has become the I.P. [identified patient] and has been acting out with attention-seeking behavior by stealing at school, setting fires, and eventually breaking into homes and stealing. Jane needs help in dealing with her own depression and in dealing with her family situation.

How the Problem Came to My Attention. During our first interview, Jane spoke of how difficult it was for her to come to the Team and ask for help. She only came when she was desperate and felt there was no other way she could help herself. Jane had not been able to tell any other person the problems she was having with being depressed and in handling the children. Much of this seems to have to do with Jane being a single parent and having to take care of the children by herself. After a few family sessions, I discovered that the children too were responding in the same way as Jane, keeping their feelings inside except for Kurt who overtly displays his unacceptable behavior. I could see that they both needed to learn how to express their feelings and perhaps could help each other by learning how to do this together. Jane and the children need to learn how to respond directly to each other as a way to help their communication. The problems with Kurt brought the situation out into the open as Jane was not able to handle him or know how to respond to him.

Summary of Work (Note: Entries are not in chronological order.)
March 14

1. I gave Jane a chance to express some of her feelings to me which she finds difficult to admit even to herself. I had a guess that Jane was not only feeling depressed but also angry and was keeping this anger inside. This came out very clearly when Kurt ran away one day when he was in trouble after setting a fire in the school. Jane was very upset and kept saying how depressed she was over what had happened. I reached into what she was saying and said, "I imagine this makes you pretty angry too?" Jane said, "I do all I can and I get no thanks; I know they're only children but they're all I have. (Silence.) They are quite a burden to handle." She cried a little. She began to say how angry she was that Kurt would do this to her. "I have no life of my own; they're all I have." For Jane to be able to express anger in this way was something new for her. After we had talked she was then able to gain some control of herself and begin to organize some search parties to go out and look for Kurt.

Jane also has a lot of angry feelings about being abandoned by her two husbands and also by her parents when she was a child. "I am sick of being walked on by him. When we got married, I went out to work to help put him through school and then he just dumped all of us. He just walked out. And now he makes all these demands (to see the kids). Now we have to jump just cause he says to. And I really resent it. I'm really bitter about it. It's not fair." Jane's first expression of feelings to me were depression over having been abandoned by her husband. She slowly was able to turn this expression of depression into an expression of anger. Getting her to admit these feelings was a beginning step.

2. I began to help Jane try to understand some of the feelings the children were having, especially Kurt. In the first excerpt [above] after Jane had a chance to express some of her anger, I began to try to point out how badly Kurt must have been feeling to run away. She said she knew how desperately he was asking for help. I asked her to go over in detail what had happened in the family the night before or earlier that morning. She told of how she had been awakened early by Kurt and Arn fighting. Later Arn told her Kurt had said, "I'm going to kill myself." I pointed out to Jane how badly Kurt must have been feeling that morning. I asked about school and what was going on there that could be upsetting him. Jane suddenly remembered that today was report card day and that the teacher had told him that if he didn't stop stealing (he had been stealing from the class) that he would get a bad report card. Jane began to tune into some of Kurt's fears of getting a bad report card and how worried he probably was. She also began to tell some of the reasons why Kurt is picked on by the other children and isn't liked. Jane seemed to be more under-

standing of Kurt at that point and could see a little why he was behaving like he did.
March 24

Helping Jane to tune into Kurt's feelings occurred a number of times. In another instance when Kurt stole from the school and was suspended, Jane first began expressing her own feelings of depression about what he had done. I asked her how she thought Kurt was feeling and she said pretty badly. She told me how he had confessed to her what he had done, had started crying, and wanted to strangle himself. Because Jane was able to express this to me, she began to really feel for him and tears rolled down her face. "I feel badly that he feels so bad." We talked of how depressed Kurt is underneath and asking for help in his own way.
April 2

Another example occurred when Jane was telling me about her second marriage to Len and how he wanted a child of his own. I began to question her about how Kurt had felt at that time because he was the baby (5 years old). Jane began to describe how hurt Kurt was over Len's rejection of him when their new baby came. Len had wanted to put all three older children in a foster home to get rid of them. I pointed out to Jane how this still must be an influence on Kurt today and he probably has lots of feelings from what happened then. Through having Jane discuss these three incidents in detail, she was able to understand some of Kurt's feelings and begin to understand what the world is like from his eyes.
March 19

3. Through family sessions, we (the children and family worker who leads the family sessions, John and I) were able to help Jane express some of her thoughts and feelings directly to the children. This began to open up for the family a communication pattern of talking directly to each other. An example of this occurred in our second family session. Jane came in looking obviously upset. John asked her about this and she said, "I'd rather not talk about it; it doesn't concern the kids." John said, "the subject matter doesn't concern them; your upset concerns them." John asked the kids how they feel when their mom gets upset. Kurt said worried. The other kids agreed; they were curious. Jane then said that if it was going to upset them, then she would tell them. It had to do with her second husband calling her that morning. After Jane put that out we were able to deal with two important issues: (1) the kids should know why she's upset so they don't think that they're the cause of her depression, and (2) how the kids should respond to her when she's depressed. Jane had been afraid to share her feelings with the children but found that it helped them not be worried by doing so.

April 4

Another example of this occurred at our family session after Kurt had been breaking into homes and stealing. John said, "Did you [to Jane] and Kurt have a talk last night?" Jane said, "A little. I thought it was better not to say too much. I didn't know what to say to him." John said, "Do you have any idea today what you'd like to say to him?" Jane said, "No, I don't know what to say to him; I'm at a loss." John had to persuade her to try and think of what she should say. Jane finally turned to Kurt directly and said, "I want to know why you did that." The conversation didn't end up so well. Kurt cried and Jane yelled at him unmercifully. A better intervention here would have been to help her understand some of his feelings first and then begin to have them talk directly. Because she came down so hard on Kurt, we were not able to get him then to respond back to her.

4. We are able to point out the difficulties they were having in their communications with each other. During the first family session, Bobby was receiving a great deal of attention by crying, demanding his own way, and generally disrupting the family session. I asked whether this occurs at home. The kids all agreed with me on this. Robert said that Bobby demands a lot of time at home. Judy says he is always getting into something, you have to pick it up, and he's into something else. Kurt says that he keeps on getting up at night and this keeps his mom up so she's tired during the day and doesn't have time for anyone else. Jane agrees with all this. Everyone decided to leave Bobby with a babysitter so that the rest of the family could enjoy the family sessions.

March 27

At a later family session, John was able to point out some communication problems the family seemed to be having. The boys were talking about the neighborhood hockey game that they play. Arn said, "Can we have a hockey game today, mom?" Robert jumped in with "no." Jane said, "You and Kurt have things to do first." John said, "Does that mean that he can do it after?" Mom said yes. John asked Arn if this is what he had understood it to mean, or that he couldn't do it at all. Arn said that he thought he couldn't do it at all. John pointed out that sometimes people mean one thing and other people can take another meaning from it. The family seemed to think this happened quite often with them.

During this same family session John was also able to point out how Jane's anger was an obstacle to communication in the family sessions. John asked the kids how they can get on the good side of their mom. They were answering with some joking about what their mom likes and how they can win her over to their side. Jane's face was very serious and John asked what was happening with her. Jane said, "I'm mad at these two" [to Arn and Kurt]. John said, "What brought that on? Did you just get angry all of a sudden?" Jane said no. She had been angry all day because she can't get the kids to do anything at home. John told her that was a real shame 'cause she had not been enjoying what had been happening with the family. She had been missing out on that opportunity. We then were able to talk about her anger and begin to help her deal with the source of the anger. Often Jane's feelings are an obstacle in ways similar to this when she will not put them out in the open and tries to hide them.

Later on in this session, John had asked the family to give things they liked about the family as a way of ending the session. Kurt said to Jane, "Good job," and patted her hand. Jane was silent. John asked her if she had heard Kurt say that. She said, "I guess I didn't." Kurt said, "Yes, you did." Jane was silent again. John pointed out to her that is the way people often respond when they hear a compliment because they think the person is trying to flatter them. "But that's the way you really see it, isn't it, Kurt?" said John. Kurt agreed. John told Jane that "one way to keep a depression going is to not hear the good things. From Kurt's point of view, you were doing a good job." One of Jane's obstacles to improving communication in the family is her own unwillingness to hear the good about herself. These obstacles to communication encourage denial and repression of feelings instead of the open and honest communication the family needs to function.

February 26

5. I tried to point out to Jane how the kids are concerned about her and that they have a common concern for each other. During the first family session this concern came out in a natural way without my intervention. When we asked the children why they were here, Kurt promptly replied, "Because my mom cares what happens to the family." Later on in that session we were talking about what it's like for the kids not to have a father in the home. Kurt replied that his mom is twice as busy 'cause she has to be both mom and dad. Jane had a startled look come over her face as she realized how deeply Kurt understood her feelings. At the end Jane said that she had appreciated what Kurt had to say as she had never realized this herself. This was a beginning step in drawing Kurt and Jane together as she took his understanding of her as genuine concern.

March 19

In a later family session we had asked the kids to try to think of options of what they could do to help their mom since she is so down. The suggestion was offered that the three oldest go live somewhere else for awhile to give their mom a break. Robert said, "If it will make her feel better, or if she'll recover by the time we come back, then I wouldn't mind." The kids discussed this for awhile. Jane said, "I wouldn't consider that as an option. I think that's all that's keeping me going, to keep the kids together." John said, "I bet the kids were glad to hear that, that they meant

that much to their mom." Jane then said, "Well, maybe they'd rather do that." John asked her what she heard them saying. She said [about Robert] "that he wouldn't mind living somewhere else." John asked her what she thought his preference was. She didn't know so he told her to ask him. Jane said, "Do you want to go live somewhere else?" Robert said, "I wouldn't rather, but if it's better for you, I would." John said that it sounded like he was really considering her first, and would sacrifice for her if necessary. This began to show Jane that the kids do care about her and she about them. The obstacle of her not really listening (or not wanting to listen) is what hurts her communication with the children.

April 4

In a later family session, Kurt had been talking about how bad he felt for not having a father. He had been crying and was expressing his deep hurt over being rejected by his real dad and his stepdad. John said, "It seems like you've been shortchanged in the dad department and not had very good luck. And you, Jane, you've been shortchanged in the husband department." In this way he was trying to draw attention to the common ground between them—they've both been shortchanged and it's rough for them. The need that they have for each other and the help that they can give each other is the message we tried to get through to them.

6. We gave Jane alternatives for dealing with the children when she asked for help in knowing what to do.

February 27

In the first family session the kids described the things they miss about not having a dad. The two older boys said that they missed having a dad to be involved with them in sports. Jane said that she finds it difficult to work with the boys. When I asked her to clarify this she said that she finds it overwhelming, finds herself inadequate for sports, etc. This theme of concern was raised several times so I suggested that she try to find a "big brother" for each of the boys, someone who she knew that would take a special interest in them and give them a little attention. I told her that this was especially important for Kurt whose behavior indicated that he wanted more attention. Jane has never carried through with this suggestion even though I tried to pin her down on it several times. It seems as though this is "my" idea rather than hers.

April 25

7. As a result of pointing out and identifying feelings with Jane (her own and Kurt's), she has been able to speak more directly with her children, especially Kurt. Jane had been telling me how her second husband was trying to get custody of the two youngest children. We had been discussing the legal details and implications of this for about a half hour. I said to Jane, "It must be hard on you having Bobby and Arn look like their dad. It must remind you of him." Jane said, "Yes, I suppose that's why it's so hard to stop caring for someone. Arn and Bobby are more special to me." I said, "Is that because they're Len's kids?" She said she guessed so. I told her that was not an easy thing for her to be saying. I asked her if she thought the other three children could sense how she felt. She said she didn't know. Maybe they could. A week later Jane told me this: "I've asked Kurt what's going on inside of him. . . . I asked him if he thought I didn't love him or if he thought I didn't love him as much as the other kids. And he said yes. I asked him how long he felt like that, to see if it goes back a long ways to when Arn was born and Len rejected him. He said, a couple of months. I tried to explain to him that he has friends that he likes more than others, or that he gets along with better. I said I love you. It's taken me a long time to figure that all out 'cause I do love them all the same but I get along much better with Robert, Arn, and Judy. For Kurt and I, it's a real effort to get along." For Jane to speak this directly and openly with Kurt is something new. It shows her concern, her realization of mistakes in the past, and how she is trying now to share her feelings and thoughts with Kurt.

Where It Stands Now. Jane still appears depressed a good deal of the time and she and the family have only made beginning steps in their relationships together. It seems that Jane is learning that it isn't easy to share her feelings with another person but it can be rewarding. This past week she was able to tell a friend all about the family problems. That person became a real source of help to her. I pointed out that because she had been willing to open up, this person then was able to help her. Jane has also begun to get out of the house two afternoons a week while a homemaker comes there. It seems that as she begins to develop a life outside of her children, that it will help lift some of her depression and give her more quality time when she is home. She and Kurt still have difficulty in getting along with each other but they have made a few positive steps in trying to understand each other.

Specific Next Steps.

1. Explore the common area both mom and children have in not having a husband or father. Probably this is one of the areas that is most difficult for them to express their feelings about.

2. Help the family begin to support each other as they express feelings. Jane especially needs to learn how to listen and support the kids as they open up to her.

3. Support Jane in her efforts to develop her "own life" away from the children. Help Jane to structure her limited free time away from the home so that she is able to accomplish some of her personal goals.

4. Point out to Jane the pattern of response that she has with the children.

5. Deal with ending and who will continue work with Jane.

PARENT-TEEN CONFLICT: A PSYCHIATRIC SETTING

In the following example, a fifteen-year-old native Indian teenager is in conflict with her mother and stepfather. Her family included eight children, and her natural father had been sent to prison two years before. Recently, she had outbursts of uncontrollable aggressive and destructive behavior which had led to her being committed to the psychiatric department of a large urban hospital. The social worker, in this setting, worked with the patient and their families in trying to identify family issues and prepare the family for the patient's return home. In separate interviews, first with the teenager and then her parents, the worker started to develop a working relationship and tuned into the issues for both. In his work with the teenager, it became clear she missed her natural father and consistently made negative comparisons with her new "dad." In the session with the parents, the worker described how the mother, Mrs. Smith, continually interrupted and answered for her husband. An example from the first interview follows:

My first session with Janet's parents contributed even more to my understanding of the problems they faced. My purpose for seeing them was partially upon the doctor's request for a social history but I also wanted to give them a chance to talk about the concerns they had about Janet. During this meeting they shared their fears of not knowing how to handle their daughter without making her angry, the feeling that they were always walking on "eggshells" around her, and that they were losing total control of her. Mrs. Smith was definitely the dominant personality. Mr. Smith on the other hand seemed content with taking more of a backseat role, allowing his wife to speak for them. However, in my zeal to understand their situation (and acquire the necessary information), I neglected the process of the interaction which graphically illustrated several problems: (1) that Mr. Smith found it hard to share his personal feelings about Janet; and (2) Mrs. Smith generally bailed him out by doing the talking for him. The following is a very brief excerpt which illustrates these dynamics. I was focusing on their response to their daughter's anger and had explored in considerable depth the mother's reactions and feelings in those circumstances. The course of the conversation began to drift into an unrelated issue and I made a deliberate attempt to draw it back in order to concentrate on the father's feelings (maintaining focus and reaching for feelings).

WORKER: Before we leave this area of Janet's anger, I wonder, Mr. Smith, whether you can share with us what it is like for you when your daughter gets really angry with you and defies your authority.

MR. S.: (He began very slowly) Well, you know it's really frustrating . . . (his voice trailed off and for a brief moment there was silence as he pondered the question).

MRS. S.: (Almost immediately). It's usually worse when we are trying to get her to do the dishes or some other chore. I notice that this was when Henry finds it most difficult to handle her. He gets angry, yells and then kind of clams up almost like he is giving up. (Looking to her husband) Isn't that right, dear?

MR. SMITH: Simply nodded his head and Mrs. Smith carried on.

It wasn't until after the interview while I was reviewing the audiotape that I noticed how often Mrs. Smith spoke for her husband when I asked him about his feelings and how often I had missed it. In spite of this mistake we clarified some common areas of concern and laid the groundwork for the first family session.

In the following excerpt the worker meets the teenager and her parents together for the first time. He attempts to establish a working contract and to underline the mutual concern for each other that is not apparent to the parties in conflict. In addition, he points out the pattern, observed earlier, of Mrs. Smith answering for her husband. This brings a strong response from the daughter and sets a new set of ground rules for the discussion.

This session took place while Janet was still in the hospital. I greeted each one of them as they walked into the room and during the first few minutes as we were settling into our chairs and informally chatting, I sensed an air of tension which had not been present to the same degree when I met with them separately. Even their laughing lacked spontaneity and seemed to be filled with anxiety (tuning in). I asked them whether they were feeling a little anxious about this session. Mrs. Smith was the first to agree while Janet just smiled trying to avoid eye contact with anyone in the room. Mr. Smith just nodded in agreement with his wife. I asked Janet whether that smile meant that she too was a little nervous. (Reaching for feelings.) She indicated that it did. I shared with them that I was also a little anxious. (Worker sharing feelings.) This brought a smile to each of their faces. I wanted to go further with this, sensing it was part of the beginning work, so I asked them what it was about this session which was making them feel anxious. There was a silence. Mrs. Smith eventually spoke up by suggesting that possibly everyone was unsure about what to say or what might come out of the meeting. *I asked if that's how she was feeling.* She said she was, so I tried to find out what she was afraid might happen. She replied that her fear was that the family would not get back together. Sensing that Mrs. Smith was trying to reach out to her daughter early in the session in her own way I said that it appeared that she cared very deeply for Janet and that to lose her would really hurt. For a moment Janet looked at her mother and then quickly returned her gaze to the floor. There was another silence. I went to Janet and asked her what it was about the meeting that made her nervous. After a brief moment of contemplation she shrugged her shoulders and said I guess the same as mom. *I tried to highlight the common concern* which I saw by saying that being part of the family appeared to mean a great deal to her too. Finally, I went to Mr. Smith but he was unable to articulate what he was nervous about. I shared that it was natural to feel this way when dealing with something as important as this.

In the next few months I tried to clarify for each of them my understanding of why they were there, and what I saw my role as. I said that from previous meetings with them individually they had indicated a need to look at what made it difficult for them to live with each other, talk to each other, and to be understood by each other, and that they wanted to give things another try. I attempted to check this out with them. (Reaching for feedback.)

Mrs. Smith said that they needed a chance to really sit down and work out some of their differences because life had been becoming unbearable prior to Janet coming into the hospital. I agreed saying that it had been hard on all of them, but that in spite of that they continued to care about each other. I indicated that I would try to help them to say the things they wanted to say to each other.

Very early in the interview I noticed the pattern begin to develop once again where Mrs. Smith would speak for her husband, especially in situations where he found it difficult to share his feelings.

We were looking at what it was like for them at home and what kinds of things made it difficult for them to get along with each other. Mrs. Smith had just shared how crowded and inadequate their living conditions were and how much easier it was for them to get on each other's nerves under such circumstances. *I asked if the others could relate to what was being said.* Mr. Smith said that the same thing was true for him and that sometimes after a hard day at work it was impossible to find that much-needed time to himself. But before he could really answer for himself his wife interrupted and without as much as a pause began to talk about how she saw her husband react. The following is a verbatim account of the conversation.

MRS. SMITH: (looking to me) Well, I know it is hard on Henry because he gets very irritable and then yells at the kids and often frightens them. I know he doesn't mean to because he just isn't that kind of person.

WORKER: Mrs. Smith, I have noticed that whenever I ask your husband how he feels about a certain situation that you quite often answer for him. I wonder whether you were aware of that? (There was a brief pause where both parents looked to each other. Mrs. Smith seemed somewhat startled at my comment and then both began to chuckle.) (Highlighting process.)

MRS. SMITH: No, I wasn't aware that I was doing that.

WORKER: Mr. Smith, were you aware that your wife often answers for you?

MR. SMITH: No, I hadn't noticed it either.

(At that point Janet seemed to come to life.)

JANET: Yes, you do, mom. You do speak for dad lots of times. Sometimes you speak for me too.

WORKER: What is that like for you?

JANET: Sometimes it's ok and sometimes it makes me angry.

WORKER: When does it make you angry?

JANET: When I have something important to say.

WORKER: Like to dad?

JANET: Ya maybe, or anyone.

WORKER: Could you tell your mom what it is like for you and how you want her to change that?

JANET: (For a minute she laughed at the awkwardness of having to speak directly to her mother, but then became more serious and demonstrated more strength than I had previously seen) If I have something to say I will say it on my own.

WORKER: Mrs. Smith, what is going on with you as you listen to this?

MRS. SMITH: Well, this is the first time I am hearing this from her, but now that I know I'll try to be more aware of what I do.

WORKER: I know that your intentions are to be as helpful as you can, but I am very interested in what your husband and daughter are feeling in some of these areas and so I would like them to answer for themselves. I don't want you to take that the wrong way because I value what you think about things as well. Can you go along with that?

MRS. SMITH: Yes, of course. I'll try to catch myself from now on.

After this exchange the session began to open up in a greater way and I was able to draw Mr. Smith into the discussions much more readily. Overall, it helped the work to progress much more rapidly.

In retrospect, I could have been more open with Mrs. Smith by expressing my concern that she might feel I was putting her down by implying I didn't care about what she had to say, and that I was afraid of alienating her. Second, it probably could have been useful to explore why she spoke for her husband and daughter, and what it was like for her to see them struggle to share their own feelings.

As the work continued, the worker tried to encourage the stepfather, Mr. Smith, to show more of his feelings about how difficult it was for him to be the father of a family with eight children, none of whom were his own. Because of a number of factors, some related to an unrealistic sense of what a "real man" should be like, others related to cultural factors, it is not easy for fathers to share with their children the side of them which is tender, caring, and vulnerable. As the worker provides the opportunity and the demand for Mr. Smith to increase his participation, the stereotype of the uncaring and cold father starts to break down. As this process proceeds, it leads to Mr. Smith sharing his own experiences with his father which have had a powerful impact in shaping his views and his feelings. Through the medium of discussing his own family history, he is able to communicate a greater sensitivity to the feelings of his teenage stepdaughter. Since the family moved away from the city when the daughter was discharged, the worker also made efforts to encourage a transition to another worker as part of the ending process.

I tried to explore some of Mr. Smith's feelings about how difficult it was for him to be the father of a family with eight children who were not his own.

To see Mr. Smith with his rough, unkempt, unshaven exterior one could be fooled into thinking he was a callous, uncaring man. But behind that was a man who was frightened by his responsibility and struggling to hold on to what little self-worth he had left. He was faced by stresses on every side. Our conversation had shifted to Mr. Smith's role in the family.

MR. S.: Right now I am barely making enough to make ends meet. That really makes it hard to satisfy the needs of the children let alone anything extra on top of that. I don't know if Janet really understands how hard it is for us to give her any spending money. She complains that we are stingy and never give her any money to go to the movies, but she just doesn't understand.

WORKER: Mr. Smith, could you tell Janet what it is like for you when you have to tell her she can't go to the movies and then she calls you stingy or gets angry with you.

MR. S.: Janet, it makes me angry.

WORKER: What else besides angry? (Reaching for underlying feelings.)

MR. S.: (After a long pause, and in a quiet voice) A little hurt too.

WORKER: Like you're not really appreciated?

MR. S.: Ya, I guess.

WORKER: Janet, has your dad ever shared with you how much it hurts him besides the anger you see?

JANET: No, he never tells me that part. He just says no and doesn't give a reason, so of course I get mad and then he gets mad and then it's over.

MRS. S.: We've told you before how hard it is for us, you should know.

JANET: You have maybe once but dad never has.

WORKER: Are you saying you would be more willing to understand if your dad would take more time to explain these things to you?

JANET: (She nodded her head in agreement and said) At least that way I know.

This exchange represented a crucial point in the sessions because Janet was starting to see her stepfather as someone with more than just feelings of anger.

In between sessions, Janet went home on a weekend pass with her family. She had been making considerable progress in the hospital and there were plans of her discharge in the following week. I briefly talked with her about what it had been like at home. She said that things had gone well, everyone had been happy to see her and even her stepfather had been much nicer. She was looking forward to the time when she could finally go home.

Although Janet and her mother were quite close from the beginning I noticed a lessening of the distance between Janet and her stepfather. We began to deal with an issue in the final session which had been briefly touched on in previous sessions.

I raised the issue of Janet's natural father. It was an area that I tried to deal with in previous sessions but up to this point they had not been ready to look at it with the exception of Mrs. Smith. Janet and her mother had been talking about an event in the family's past. Janet made reference to her natural father with a degree of fondness. I said to her that it appeared she had a lot of good memories of him. She said that she did but had not seen him for several years. I asked her what it was like not to have seen him for so long. She paused and then replied she was getting used to it. I commented that it must still hurt anyway. (Putting client's feelings into words.) Mrs. Smith joined the conversation saying that Janet had been closest to him, and for this reason was taking it hardest of all the children. Janet retorted that she wasn't taking it hard. There was silence. Mr. Smith tried in his own way to reach out to Janet by saying that he could understand why she would find it hard to forget her real dad and accept him. I asked him to say a little more about that. Janet sat with her head down and tears in her eyes. Mr. Smith said that the kids probably didn't know it but he too had a stepfather when he was growing up. Sensing this was probably a common experience which could draw them together, *I tried to pursue it further.* In the next few moments he described a very painful part of his own past that in many ways seemed to parallel what Janet was going through at this point. He shared with us how at the age of eight he was taken by his own father to live with his cousins because his father couldn't make ends meet. He was told by his father that he would return to get him as soon as possible. But he never did and hasn't seen him to this day. I tried to find out what it was like for him when he finally realized that his father was not coming back. He just avoided the feelings by saying that he waited and waited but he just didn't come back. I said it must have been a very painful time for him. He didn't acknowledge the pain and I could see it was hard for him to talk about. I asked him what it was like to talk about this part of his life. He just said, "well it's over now." I told him that I thought it took courage to share this with Janet (crediting client) and that he could probably understand quite well what she was going through right now. I asked him where his stepfather came into the picture. He continued to relate his story to us, but carefully avoided the feelings associated with it. Janet was quiet throughout and seemed to be listening intently. He talked about how hard it was for him to get along with his stepfather, and that he was never able to talk much with him. I asked Janet if she could relate to anything that was being said. She nodded her head to say yes but refused to elaborate. We continued with it for a while longer and then I suggested that they could continue to share more about this in the future with each other. We spent the rest of the session talking about their transition to another helping person in the community.

THE IMPACT OF CULTURE AND COMMUNITY: PROBATION AND A NATIVE INDIAN FAMILY

One of the greatest tragedies in North America has been the impact of the white society on its "first peoples," the native Indians. A strong family and community tradition, a whole culture and way of life was systematically stripped from a people in what has been described as a case of cultural genocide. This problem is a special case of the struggle each minority group faces, whether aboriginals or immigrants. Each must find a way of preserving what is of value to their own culture and still come to grips with a surrounding and dominating culture. When the group is of another race, Indian, black, Chicano, etc., the struggle is usually intensified by a persistent racism, sometimes subtle in nature, other times open and direct.

In the native Indian community, from which the family in this example is drawn, years of neglect, discrimination, and exploitation have often led to a breakdown in individual, family, and community functioning. Once proud cultural traditions have been lost for many of the community's members. In particular, teenagers must go through a crucial step in their normative development in which they struggle to understand who they are, and how they shall be. The separation and integration issue is just as important in relation to one's culture and community, as it is in relation to the immediate family. In fact, the two struggles become intertwined in important ways. The ambivalent feelings are pronounced when the subculture, the peer group for a teenager, encourages and supports deviant behavior (the extensive use of alcohol, criminal activity, etc.) and the future appears to be bleak. When a teenager looks around and sees members of the adult community who appear to give up, it is not hard to understand an internal struggle which can lead to complete alienation from the larger society, or in a shockingly large number of cases, teenage suicide. The alternative choice of facing the problems, finding the strength to cope, accepting the role model of many of the adult members of the community who have refused to surrender to years of oppression, is also an option. For the teenagers in this situation to make this transition, they will need all the help they can get from family, community (the local band), and their cultural heritage.

In the example which follows, culture and community are key issues as Jim, a fourteen-year-old native Indian teenager, struggles with this crucial, transitional crisis. Father is forty and stepmother is twenty-nine.

Jim, in the throes of puberty, is searching very hard to establish his identity. Most of all, he wants to feel and be proud of his Native Indian heritage but the conflicting messages he has internalized about "being Indian" do not allow him to do so positively. His anger and confusion manifest themselves by his acting out: he has committed seven B&Es [Breaking and Entering] on the reserve, two of them specifically focusing on the Indian Band office. He has developed an alcohol problem. His acting out has alienated him from the elders of the Band who refuse to be involved in helping him with the court process, as is usually the case for juvenile delinquents of this Band. I perceive his B&Es as cries for help with his home situation.

Jim's parents are disheartened and upset. They feel they have tried their best and have failed. They are considering sending him away to a residential school. Their medium of communication and major stumbling block between Jim and his parents is discussion of native Indian identity: all emotions, conflict, and disagreement are discussed under the heading "Indian." In my efforts to help this family, I must also deal with their feelings about me—a white female probation officer. I realize I will have to become more than just a symbol of white authority.

How the Problem Came to my Attention. My first meeting with Jim and his parents was to discuss the B&E charges in the hope of sparing Jim court appearances. I had great difficulty keeping the session on focus: it was too painful a topic for everyone to discuss directly. Actually, Jim and his parents reenacted their communication pattern in front of me: the war was on. Jim's mother said angrily that these B&Es were "crazy Indian stuff." I tried to reach for the feelings of pain and disappointment behind the anger and said, "Jim's B&Es are hard on the family, right now, they would be for any family, Indian or not." Jim's father said, "I knew nothing about them Indians." Jim didn't give me a chance to say anything and counterattacked by angrily saying that his parents are Honkies in disguise but *he* is an Indian, he is a super dancer and carver and can drink and fight with the bigger guys

on the reserve any day. I said that his parents might be proud about his dancing and carving. Jim's mother said, "Honkies or not Honkies, they know that Jim is a no good Indian." The energy they put out fighting made me believe that there was a lot of concern and care hidden behind the anger. Their faces were painted with pain.

Work

1. I tuned into Jim's feelings and tried to put his feelings into words. Jim had a tough look on his face. He slid himself down into a chair, his knees up close to his chest as if to protect himself. I said, "You look angry as hell today." No response. I waited out his silence. He said with a tone devoid of affect that he had a big fight last night after Indian dancing and that it lasted until 4 in the morning. I asked him if he'd got hurt (*empathizing*). He said no, he never gets hurt. He was drunk anyway. I was lucky he was sober this afternoon. I said, "Alcohol dims the pain. A 14-year-old drunk is a sad story to me." He said he knew. Jim said he had also siphoned gas out of a car last night. I said "It is a lot for one night. Are you trying to tell me how bad you can be?" Jim looked at me intently. I said that behind his tough facade I thought there was a lot of pain. His voice changed. With a defensive tone he said "Pain about what?" I said, "Maybe it was painful to feel you have to act like a hellion to get attention. He giggled and said I wasn't funny. I said, "I agree, it's not funny, it hurts." He cocked his head down. I waited out his silence. He said suddenly, "Nothing ever hurts anymore. Nobody cares about me anymore." I said, "Are you talking about home?" *(recognizing his indirect communication).* He said simply yeah.

2. I recognized his indirect communication and tried to help him go from general to specific concerns. Jim had done a rerun of the above two weeks in a row; that is, enumerating all the "bad" behaviours he had got into. I said it was the third weekend that he had asked me to give him hell. He said that if I didn't nobody would. I asked him if that's what he wanted his parents to do. He said, "No, I want them to understand me." I said that I knew things were rough for everyone at home right now, could he tell me what had taken place at home that hurt. He looked away and said in a low voice, "They called me a rotten Indian." The affect of pain was so strong that he could not elaborate on his feelings or the specific circumstances. I said, "It hurts a lot doesn't it? I wish I could take the pain away from you."

3. *I tried to share my feelings openly.* Jim said that he was sick and tired of being called a dirty Indian at home. The affect was anger. I tried to reach for the specific but got nowhere. He said that all his parents talked about was "Dirty Indians this, silly Indians that. Who do they think they are anyway?" I said that "It may hurt to hear the word Indian coming from your own parents as a curse word." He asked me if I thought he was a dirty Indian. I said no, he was Indian alright, "but the two words together were a terrible combination." He said, "What about a silly Indian?" I reached for his indirect communication and said, "You're checking out if I'm prejudiced aren't you?" He said, "Yup." I said it was for him to judge. He said I would be on probation for awhile. I said I knew. He said in a low voice that he doesn't think I can understand. I said gently "Do you feel you can't win: you can't be right and you can't be Indian." *(Putting the client's feelings into words.)* He said suddenly, "I don't know what 'Indian' means. How am I supposed to grow up okay?" I put my arms around him and said that he was right. I wasn't sure I could understand fully what it means to grow up as an Indian. I said that his hurt was choking me up right now.

4. *I tried to help Jim view his parents in new ways.* Jim said that his parents put him through a grinder whenever he is home. I said that it sounds horrible, what does he mean *(reaching for elaboration).* He said that his parents hassle him about every little detail about what he does at night. I jokingly said, "It's not such a horrible grinder after all!" He laughed. He said that really they don't care about him, they just want him on a leash. I said "And you want to be more independent, don't you?" *(recognizing the metaphor.)* He said, "Yup." I asked him to give me an example of the

grinder. He said that last night he came home at midnight. They just had to know who he was with, where he had been. I said that "sounds to me like they care about you. They worry about you and frankly at midnight I would worry too." Jim pouted. I waited out his silence. He said "I don't think they care. They're just angry." I said that maybe they felt both—fear and anger. Did he think that they had any reason to be angry last night? He said, "Maybe so. Midnight is kind of late." I agreed. I asked him if he knew what his parents felt waiting for him. He said that "they always assumed the worst. That's dumb." I said, "We all do that when we're worried." He said, "I guess I give them reasons to be angry and I don't like it." I said sadly— "and they don't either. I bet they feel just as bad as you do about yesterday."

5. *I supported him in a taboo area and tried to stay close to his feelings of anger and rejection.* Jim said that he was going to kill his mother one of these days. She isn't his real mom anyway. I asked him if he was angry about something she had done or angry because she isn't his real mom. *(Trying to partialize his concern.)* He said both. I asked him what his mom had done for him to be so upset. He said, "She is really *unreal;* she had phoned the school to insist that she be warned if he skipped out. It's none of her business. His dad's, sure, but not hers." I kept the issue on focus and said, "not hers because she is your stepmom?" He said, "Yup, I'm not her son. She's got no right on me." I said sadly, "No right to care? She can't win, can she?" Jim said, "No, she can't win. She's the one who made us move from the reserve." I said I knew about that, that she wanted to make a better home for him and his dad. Jim nervously twisted his hair around his fingers and said that he would rather have his mom around than "her" care. I said that he had expressed real and deep feelings. *(Crediting his work.)* "It's real hard to get over one's Mom's death."

6. *I tried to help Jim identify the affect obstacle and offered to mediate with his parents.* Jim said that he doesn't know how to tell his parents to stop calling him names when he does something wrong. Names like "silly In-

dian." When they do, his blood boils and he goes out and gets drunk. He can't say anything. He just walks out. And he does start acting silly. I asked him to tell me what he would like exactly to tell his parents. He said that he just wants them to stop calling him names. But he can't say it to them. I said, "That's their way of criticizing you, isn't it?" He said, "Yeah. It's bad enough being told off when you do something wrong," but then calling him names like that, it's below the belt. I said, "It's like you're nobody all of a sudden." He said, "Yup." He had tears in his eyes. I said, "Do you want me to help you talk to your parents?" He said, "Yeah." He couldn't do it alone. I said that I'd phone his parents and if they agreed we'd try to talk about the name calling and try to understand what is behind it from their side. Jim said that he didn't want to talk about the things he does wrong. I said that he forgets he does a lot of things real well too. We have to take the bad with the good. He said, "Yeah, but I'm far from perfect." I said that perfection is like a rainbow—nobody can reach it, we can only try. He said his parents didn't know that. I said I was sure they did, they just had high expectations for him. He said he didn't believe in high expectations. I laughed and said, "Baloney— you want to be the best about everything." he said, "How do you know?" I said that I had seen some of his carvings. They're beautiful. It was obvious to me that he was trying to be the best. *(Emphasizing the positive).* Jim had a long drawn out "oh." I brought back the conversation on focus and said, "So if your parents are willing we'll talk about both sides." He said he was willing to try but that I was going to get myself into a lot of trouble with his parents. I said, "Because I'm white?" He said, "Yeah." I said I could only try, that things should go easier if I didn't take sides. *(Emphasizing the contract.)*

7. *I tried to tune in to the feelings of ambivalence of the one (Jim) and the many (the family), tried to include everyone in the commonality of the experience and clarified the contract.* At the first meeting I said that they must feel a bit uncomfortable about having a white probation officer coming into their home.

Mr. Jones smiled and said, "You bet, you're the first one we managed to get in here." Mrs. Jones said, matter of fact, that she didn't mind, today she had to clean her home for the health nurse anyway. I recognized her ambivalence and said that I know how it feels, it's a hassle to clean house because a stranger is coming in. She nodded hesitant. I said I felt a bit like an intruder today *(putting my personal feelings into words)* but that I hoped we would feel more comfortable once we know each other better. Jim's eyes were covered by his cap and his arms crossed at his chest. I asked him what he was angry about. He said, "Nothing, leave me alone." Mrs. Jones firmly said that he couldn't talk to me like that. I said it was okay to be angry. Did they (Jim's parents) know what was making Jim so angry? *(beginning to partialize and trying to help the family members help each other.)* Mr. Jones said that Jim is like that around home, not to worry. I said that maybe Jim is afraid that we might all gang up on him. *(Putting client's feelings into words.)* "It's certainly not my intention." I said that I was here to have them talk about a real painful issue: Jim can't stand being called a dirty Indian and it hurts so much that he can't talk about it usually. I got a nasty look from Mr. Jones. Mrs. Jones said she thought it was simple: I should forbid Jim from doing any of that crazy Indian stuff, then she'd stop calling him a crazy Indian. Mr. Jones agreed with her. I said that I know they often worry about Jim but I can't do that. That's not my role and it wouldn't work anyway. Jim nodded sullenly. I said that I felt uncomfortable about the word crazy Indian stuff *(acknowledging feelings).* I asked Jim if he knows what his parents mean by that? He lifted his cap from his eyes and said that he knew for sure "that all Indians are dirty, crazy, violent, and lazy drunks." Mr. Jones said, "Here he goes again, acting crazy. Everyone knows that Indians aren't violent and drunk." Jim giggled and Mr. Jones cracked his knuckles. I said that perhaps Jim was hitting something very painful. That was the prejudice they had to live with day in and day out. Mr. Jones said I was damn right. Mrs. Jones said that's what she worried about, that Jim would become like the rest of them Indians. I said that "You are Indian and you aren't violent, lazy and crazy. Neither is Jim." *(Gentle demand for work).* Mrs. Jones said no, but that's because they'd moved away from the reserve. I said that maybe it was time to look at the positive things of the present rather than the bad things of the past. *(Emphasizing the positive and the potential to work.)*

8. I tried to reach their feelings in their way, to establish contact and help the family members help each other. Jim said that "You can't help but act on impulse, that's what my B&Es are all about." I said, "You forget to pray to the spirit of the bear, don't you?" Mr. Jones nodded and said I was right. He told us an Indian story about a little boy becoming a man becoming a bear. It was the opposite of Jim's progress at this point, but it emphasized his potential. Jim said that the story was OK, but that the elders had better ones. I said to Jim that maybe the story hit home a bit hard. *(Demand for work.)* I got nowhere.

Jim said that he had been kicked out of English today and that he wasn't much more disruptive than some of the white kids. I said that a little more disruption is all it takes to make a difference. Silence. Mr. Jones said that white teachers are racist. Mr. Jones said that females are more racist than men. He would fight with a white man any day, but you can't fight with a white woman. I acknowledged my feelings and said that I was afraid the arrows might start flying towards me. We all laughed, at the relief of tension. Jim said that the Indians only scalp white people who have no honour. Mr. Jones grinned. I recognize their offering and said that it felt good to hear I have honour. Their feelings for me are important to me because I respect them.

9. I tried to put the client's feelings into words for the benefit of the other family members so that they gain a new understanding of each other. Mrs. Jones asked me what I intended to do about Jim's alcoholism. I said Jim was doing his best to stay away from alcohol and the reserve but sometimes he got so depressed about feeling bad about himself that he couldn't help it. Jim said it was right. He can't control himself when his parents call him a

crazy Indian. Mr. Jones said that he and his wife mean well. They just don't know what else to say. I said, "I know, when you're worried words don't come easily." Jim said gently, "When I'm rotten, why don't you just say I let you down, Dad?" Mr. Jones put his arms around his son.

Mrs. Jones said that Jim was wasting his time carving, you can't make a living out of it. I said that I was really impressed by Jim's carving. They are really beautiful. Mrs. Jones said that Jim spends too much time doing that. I said that it takes a lot of time to create a piece of art. Mr. Jones said he knew, because he tried when he was younger and couldn't do half as well as Jim. Jim was beaming. He asked his dad how good an Indian dancer he was when he was younger.

10. I offered to mediate between a system which makes it harder to communicate between Jim and his parents as a result of his delinquencies. Everyone is silent. Mrs. Jones especially looks grim. I asked if I had offended them in any way. Silence. I said, "Anything I have done or said in relation to Jim?" "No," said Mr. Jones, "I guess we are taking it out on you." Jim says that he knows what it's all about. It's about the Band. I recognized the indirect communication. "You wish you were on good terms with the Band, don't you?" Mrs. Jones said it wasn't possible. There is so much politics going on. Mr. Jones said they're arrogant. Jim continued rocking in his chair and looked hurt. I said, noting his eyes, "You feel guilty about it, you want to cry. Your B&Es stand in the way, don't they?" *(Demand for work.)* He nodded. I said that I would talk to the Band office. Maybe they would accept to supervise Jim's probation once I'm gone. Mr. Jones said that they refused in the past, why would they accept now? I said that they had had time to get over the shock, just as Jim had time to do a lot of growing. Jim nodded. *(Crediting client's work.)*

Where It Stands Now. The problem has shifted in urgency. Jim and his parents are starting to be able to discuss the problem of Indian identity with less anger and pain and are starting to be able to discuss other issues without approaching them from a perspective of ethnic origin. Jim's parents are beginning to be able to give positive strokes to Jim for his "native Indian-oriented" achievements. (e.g., his beautiful carvings and his proficiency in Indian dancing). They are striving to live together under the same roof without feeling that it is a battlefield of "good Indians" versus "bad Indians." Jim's anger has lessened, largely because he has regained the support of the Elders in the Band. He has stayed away from committing further delinquencies.

Specific Next Steps

1. For the next white worker, do not shy away from discussing the racial element of the interaction because it is a central element for Jim and his family and permeates all their lives.
2. Continue family work around communication patterns. There are a lot of feelings of anger and sadness connected to Jim's natural mom's death which interfere between Jim and his stepmom.
3. To continue to emphasize Jim's ability and desire to do well and excel rather than Jim's past record of delinquency; to emphasize his parents' desire to be the best parents.

HIDING THE FAMILY'S SECRETS: DEALING WITH TABOO AREAS

Family members often have a secret which they feel is so terrible, no one is willing to talk about it. At times, an unspoken agreement exists in which all family members agree not to deal directly with a sensitive and taboo concern. Family secrets which are kept out of sight and not discussed can have a powerful impact on the ability of the family to function in a healthy manner. The inability to discuss the subject area, the norm of behavior which has declared such discussion as forbidden, works to block the family's ability to deal with the issue and discover its inherent strengths.

In one situation, a young mother suffered from a degenerative illness which had already caused her to go blind. She experienced strokes and memory losses, and the prognosis was for an early death. The father was no longer in the picture, and the family living in the home consisted of the mother (Ruth), her eight-year-old son (Billy), and the maternal grandmother (Millie). A norm of behavior had evolved in which all of the family members agreed, in a covert manner, not to speak of the illness or its symptoms, and in particular, not to speak of the mother's future. The child was seen as too young, and not able to understand. The grandmother worried that discussing the illness would make the young mother more depressed, and perhaps, even trigger a stroke. The young mother worried about the burden the illness placed upon the grandmother and its impact on her health. Both mother and grandmother were deeply concerned about what would happen to Billy if the other died first.

The tensions and stress in the family were carefully covered up. There was no way for the feelings to remain under the surface so that the child, Billy, signaled the underlying problems. His behavior acted out the anxieties he felt about what was happening to his mother and his family. As his behavior problems worsened, and his mother and grandmother were at a loss as how to handle them, they sought help from a child care resource to arrange a temporary placement. The first response of the agency, and the family worker involved, was to respect the grandmother's injunction against getting into the health issues. She involved the workers in a conspiracy of silence on the core issues. Their first efforts were to help the mother and grandmother try to deal with Billy's behavior, and to help Billy control his activities. Since this missed the meaning of the deviant behavior, and played into the family's use of Billy as the identified patient, there was very little progress observed, with both the mother and grandmother expressing feelings of dissatisfaction with the results. The family worker realized the core issue of the family secret and made a number of efforts to open it up. However, at the first sign of resistance, she backed off. Recognizing she would need to confront the family about their conspiracy to keep the family secret, she took her courage in hand, and challenged the obstacle. She confronted the mother and grandmother and tried to support them in opening up discussion between each of them, and then, between them and Billy. Some steps were made in this direction, and the subject was at least out in the open. However, the grandmother refused to continue and closed off further discussions indicating: "When the time comes, we shall deal with it." The mother responded by dealing more openly with Billy on the issue of her death, which helped the situation, but backed off when it came to discussions with her own mother.

Although the worker was unable to help them face the future at this time, a beginning was made on creating the conditions where the unspeakable could be spoken. The denial on the part of both mother and grandmother was strong, but in these circumstances, very understandable. In the last analysis, it was really up to them to pick the time and place for facing a harsh reality.

SUMMARY

This chapter has examined some of the ways the core skills outlined in Chapters 1 through 5 can be applied in working with families. The focus was on family work, as opposed to family therapy, although many of the concepts and strategies developed in family therapy theory were used to both understand family dynamics and strategize as to how to intervene. Illustrations were provided of workers dealing with an angry parent, developing an ongoing working relationship, bringing a stepfather into active family involvement, helping a single-parent family cope with their unique stresses, mediating parent-teen conflict in a psychiatric setting, assisting a native Indian family in dealing with their culture and their community, and helping a family expose and begin to deal with a "family secret," the impending death of the mother. In Part II of this book, I will examine the dynamics of working with clients in groups. Some of that discussion will be applicable, with some modifications, to working with the primary group, the family.

NOTES

1. For an interesting review of major family therapy models, see Arthur M. Horne and Merle M. Ohlsen (eds.), *Family Counseling and Therapy* (Itasca, Ill.: F. E. Peacock Publishers, Inc., 1982).

For examples of the work of a range of family therapy theorists, see Murray Bowen, "The Family as a Unit of Study and Treatment," *American Journal of Orthopsychiatry* 31 (January 1961): 40-60; Virginia Satir, *Conjoint Family Therapy* (Palo Alto, Calif.: Science and Behavior Books, Inc., 1967); Frances H. Scherz, "Theory and Practice of Family Therapy," in *Theories of Social Casework*, ed. Robert W. Roberts and Robert H. Nee (Chicago: The University of Chicago Press, 1970) pp. 219–64; Nathan Ackerman, *The Psychodynamics of Family Life* (New York: Basic Books, 1958); David S. Freeman, *Techniques of Family Ther-*

apy (New York: Jason Aronson, Inc., 1981); Gregory Bateson, Don Jackson, Jay Haley, and John H. Weakland, "Toward a Theory of Schizophrenia," *Behavioral Science* 1 (1956): 251–64; John H. Weakland, Richard Fisch, Paul Watzlawick, and Arthur M. Bodin, "Brief Therapy: Focussed Problem Resolution," *Family Process* 13 (1974): 141–168; Richard Bandler, John Grindler, and Virginia Satir, *Changing with Families* (Palo Alto, Ca.: Science and Behavior Books, 1976); Salvador Minuchin, *Families and Family Therapy* (Cambridge, Mass.: Harvard University Press, 1974); Salvador Minuchin and Herman C. Fishman, *Family Therapy Techniques* (Cambridge, Mass.: Harvard University Press, 1981).

2. Ackerman, *The Psychodynamics of Family Life.*

3. For example, see Salvador Minuchin, Bernice L. Rosman, and Lester Baker, *Psychosomatic Families: Anorexia Nervosa in Context* (Cambridge, Mass.: Harvard University Press, 1978).

4. Ackerman, *The Psychodynamics of Family Life.*

5. Bowen, "The Family as a Unit of Study and Treatment."

6. Freeman, *Techniques of Family Therapy.*

7. Carl R. Rogers, *On Becoming a Person* (Boston: Houghton Mifflin, 1961). See also Louis Thayer, "A Person-Centered Approach to Family Therapy," in *Family Counseling and Therapy,* ed. Arthur M. Horne and Merle M. Ohlsen (Itasca, Ill.: F. E. Peacock Publishers, Inc., 1982), pp. 175–213.

8. Thayer, "A Person-Centered Approach to Family Therapy," p. 192.

9. Satir, *Conjoint Family Therapy;* David V. Keith and Carl A. Whitaker, "Experiential/Symbolic Family Therapy," in *Family Counseling and Therapy,* ed. Arthur M. Horne and Merle M. Ohlsen (Itasca, Ill.: F. E. Peacock Publishers, Inc., 1982), pp. 43–74.

II. Group Work Skill

CHAPTER 7

The Group as a
Mutual Aid System

The approach presented in this book starts with the assumption that a group has the potential of serving as a mutual aid system for its members.[1] Part I focused on the worker's efforts to assist individual clients to negotiate systems which were important to them. In this second part, I will discuss the dynamics which occur when a group of clients with common concerns is brought together for the purpose of helping each other. The reader will find that many of the processes and skills discussed in Part I are equally applicable when employed in the group context. There are also unique features involved in the use of group method, and these will be described and illustrated. I will also briefly introduce the function of the worker in the group, and discuss the feelings often experienced by workers as they prepare to lead their first group.

In discussing earlier the underlying assumptions of the general helping model, the focus was on the client in interaction with the various surrounding systems: family, agency, school, and so on. It is easier to perceive the similarities between individual and group work when one realizes that the helping group is a special case of the general individu-al-social interaction. In a sense, the group represents a microsociety. The potential for the "symbiotic" relationship described in the first part of this book is also present in each small-group encounter. In a seminal article entitled "The Social Worker in the Group" Schwartz defined the helping group:

The group is an enterprise in mutual aid, an alliance of individuals who need each other, in varying degrees, to work on certain common problems. The important fact is that this is a helping system in which the clients need each other as well as the worker. This need to use each other, to create not one but many helping relationships, is a vital ingredient of the group process and constitutes a common need over and above the specific tasks for which the group was formed.[2]

The idea of the group as a "mutual aid system" in which the worker helps people to help each other is an attractive one. However, it raises many questions and doubts in the minds of workers whose experiences in groups, as members and leaders, have led them to question their potential for mutual aid. Exactly how can a group of people sharing the same set of concerns help each other? Isn't it a bit like the blind leading the blind? How will clients be able to talk about their most intimate concerns before a group of strangers? What about the coercive power of the group? How can individuals stand up against the odds? What is the job of the group leader if the members are going to be helping each other? These questions and others are legitimate. They sometimes reflect the workers' past group experiences which may have been hurtful, nonproductive, boring, and far from being enterprises in mutual aid.

My response is that the *potential* for mutual aid exists in the group; simply bringing people together does not guarantee that it will emerge. There are many obstacles which will block the group members' ability to reach out to each other and to offer help. Many of these are similar to the obstacles described in Part I, but their effect can be magnified in the group context. Because all members will bring to the group their own concepts, based upon past experiences of groups (e.g., school, camp, committees), and because many of these past experiences may have been poor ones, the group worker is needed to help the group members create the conditions in which mutual aid can take place. The tasks of the group worker in attempting to help group members develop the required skills are related to these obstacles. Creating a mutual aid group is a difficult process with members having to overcome many of their stereotypes about people in general, groups, and helping. They will need all the help they can get from the group worker. Since the worker has also been affected by past group experiences, one of the early tasks requires facing one's own feelings and examining stereotypes, so that an honest display to the members of a belief in their potential is possible. Faith in the strength of the group will make an important con-

tribution to the group members' success in their struggle.

The balance of this chapter begins to answer the reservations and questions by listing some of the ways in which group members can help each other; these are the processes of mutual aid. The obstacles which can emerge to block this potential are briefly reviewed. An overview of the function of the group worker is then presented. The other chapters in Part II elaborate the model and illustrate the skills of the group worker in action.

THE DYNAMICS OF MUTUAL AID

The mutual aid process is described in detail and illustrated with examples from a range of groups in the chapters which follow. To aid in conceptualizing mutual aid in a general way, a number of illustrations are described here.

Sharing Data

One of the simplest and yet most important ways in which group members can help each other is through the sharing of relevant data. Members have all had different life experiences through which they have accumulated knowledge, views, values, and so forth which can help others in the group. For example, in a married couples' group described in detail in later chapters, one of the couples is in their late sixties. They have experienced many of the normal life crises as well as those imposed by societal pressures (e.g., the Great Depression of the 1930s). As other group members who are in their fifties, forties, thirties, and twenties describe their experiences and problems, this couple is often able to share an insight which comes from having viewed the crisis from the perspective of time. As the group leader, I often find myself learning from the experiences of this couple. We have created in the group a form of the extended family in which one generation passes on its life experiences to the next. In turn, the older couple is able to use the group not only for their immediate problems but also as a place for reviewing their fifty years together. This may be an important part of their ending work.

In another group, working mothers are able to share ideas which have proven helpful in organizing their daily routines. The names of community services which they have discovered are often traded as each mother taps the experiences and the ingenuity of the others. Whether the data consist of specific tips on concrete questions (jobs, available housing, money management, etc.) or values or ideas about relationships, each member can contribute to the common pool. The worker will also contribute data which when combined with that of the others provide a rich resource for the members.

The Dialectical Process

An important debate of ideas can take place as each member shares views on the question under discussion. Group members can risk their tentative ideas and use the group as a sounding board— a place for their views to be challenged and possibly changed. It is not always easy to challenge ideas in the group, and I will discuss later how such a "culture for work" can be developed. When this kind of group "culture" is present, the argument between two or more members takes on a dialectical nature. Group members can listen as one member presents the "thesis" and the other, the "anithesis." As each member listens, they can use the discussion to develop their own "synthesis."

An illustration of this process in the couples' group occurred when one couple in their fifties discussed a problem they were experiencing with their grown married children. They described their negative perception of the way in which their children were handling their marital difficulty and how this was affecting their marriage. As they spoke, I could see the anger in the eyes of a younger couple in their twenties. They were experiencing difficulty with the wife's parents who they felt "meddled" in their life. When I reached for the verbal expression of the nonverbal cues, the battle was on. The older couple had to defend their perceptions against the arguments of the other couple who could see the problem through the eyes of their children. In return, the younger couple had to understand their strained relationships with the wife's parents through the eyes of the older couple who could understand her parents' perspective. For each couple the debate led to some modification of their views and new insights into how the respective children and parents might be feeling. It was obvious from the discussion that other group members were making associations to their own experiences, using the dialogue taking place before them.

It is important to note that confrontation is a part of mutual aid. Instead of being suppressed, differences must be expressed in an arena where they can be used for learning. I believe that group members often present strongly held views on a subject precisely because they have doubts and desperately need a challenging perspective. The skills involved in helping group members to use these conflicts constructively are explored later. This example also illustrates the fact that the group can be a laboratory for developing, among other skills, that of asserting oneself so that the individual members can become more effective in their external relationships. The conversation between the older and younger couples constituted a rehearsal for the important discussion which needed to take place with their respective children and parents. The group members were able to use the experience for this purpose when the leader pointed this out.

Discussing a Taboo Area

Each group member brings to the group the norms of behavior and the taboos which exist in our larger culture. In the beginning phase of work, the group recreates in this microsociety the "culture" the members experienced outside. Thus, direct talk about such subjects as authority, dependency, and sex is experienced as taboo. One of the tasks of the group leader will be to help the group members develop new norms and feel free to challenge some taboos so that the group can be more effective. Each client will feel the urgency of discussing the subject somewhat differently from the others, and each group member will experience the power of the taboo differently. As the work proceeds and the level of comfort in the group increases (the skills for helping this to happen are discussed in later chapters), one member may take the first risk, directly or indirectly, which leads the group into a difficult area of discussion. By being first, the member allows the more fearful and reluctant members to watch as the taboo is violated. As they experience positive work, they are given permission to enter the formerly taboo area. Thus, all the group members are able to benefit from either the particular sense of urgency or the lower level of anxiety or the greater willingness to risk of the member who leads the way.

The "All-in-the-Same-Boat" Phenomenon

After the group enters a formerly taboo area, the members listen to the feelings of the others and often discover emotions of their own that they were not aware of, feelings which may have been having a powerful effect on their lives. They also discover the reassuring fact that they are not alone in their feelings, that group members are "all in the same boat." Knowing that others share your feelings somehow makes them less frightening and easier to deal with. When as a group member one discovers one is not alone in feeling overwhelmed by a problem, or worried about one's sexual adequacy, or wondering who one is and where one comes from (e.g., a foster teenager), one is often better able to mobilize oneself to deal with the problem productively. Discovering that feelings are shared by other members of the group can often be the beginning of freeing a client from their power. Guilt over "evil" thoughts and feelings can be lessened when one discovers they are normal and felt by others. This can be one of the most powerful forces for change resulting from the mutual aid process. There is not the same impact when a worker in individual work tries to reassure the client that the same feelings are shared by others. Hearing them articulated and experiencing the feelings in the group sessions makes an unique impression.

Mutual Support

When the group "culture" supports the open expression of feelings, the capacity of members to empathize with each other is evident. With the group leader setting the tone through expression of personal feelings and understanding of others, each member is able to observe the powerful effect of empathy. Since group members share some common concerns, they are often able to understand each other's feelings in a deeper way than the worker. This expression of empathy is an important healing agent for both the group member who receives it and the one who offers it. As group members understand the feelings of the others, without judging them harshly, they begin to accept their own feelings in new ways. For a member struggling with a specific concern the acceptance and caring of the group can be a source of support during a difficult time.

I have just used the expression "the acceptance and caring of the group" which introduces a new concept to be explored in detail in later chapters. The important term is *the group*, the entity that is created when people are brought together. This entity, to be called the *group-as-a-whole*, involves more than just the simple sum of the parts (members). For example, support in the mutual aid group often has a quality which is different from support received in interaction with a single empathic person. It is more than just a quantitative difference of more people meaning more empathy. At crucial moments in a group one can sense a general tone or atmosphere, displayed through words, expressions, or physical posture which conveys the caring of the "group" for the individual. This seems to have a special meaning and importance to the individual group member. The properties of the group-as-a-whole are described in detail in Chapter 13.

Mutual Demand

In Part I, I described how the helping relationship consisted of both support and demand, synthesized in unique, personal ways. The same is true in the group con-text. Mutual aid is provided through expectation as well as through caring. One illustration is the way group members confront each other. For example, in the couples' group two male members were able to challenge a third who was maintaining that the source of the problem was his wife, that she was the identified "patient," and he was coming to group to "help her out." Both of the confronting group members had taken the same position at our first session and had slowly modified their view. They had lowered their defenses and accepted that the problem was a couple problem. This demand on the third member had a different quality coming from group members rather than the group leader.

As the group "culture" develops, it can include the mutual expectations that members must risk their real thoughts and ideas, listen to each other, put their own concerns aside at times to help another, and so on. These expectations help to develop a productive "culture for work." Another group expectation can be that the members will work on their concerns. At moments when clients feel overwhelmed and hopeless exactly this expectation may help them take a next step. The group cares enough about them not to let them give up. I have witnessed group members take some difficult action, such as confronting a boss or dealing more effectively with a close relative. When the action was discussed the following week, they indicated that one of the factors which pushed them to make the move and take a risk was the thought of returning to the group and admitting that they hadn't acted. Mutual demand, integrated with mutual support, can be a powerful force for change.

Individual Problem Solving

A mutual aid group can be a place where an individual can bring a problem and ask for assistance. For example, in one group a young mother discussed the strained relationship between herself and her mother. Her mother lived nearby and was constantly calling and asking to come over. The group member had been extremely depressed and was going through periods where she neglected her work at home (dishes piling up in the sink, etc.). Each time the mother came over she felt, because of her mother's actions, that she was being reprimanded for being a poor housekeeper and a poor mother to her young children. The strain was difficult and produced many arguments, including some between the husband and wife. The client felt her mother still treated her like a child even though she was twenty-seven.

As the client presented the issue, at first indirectly and later with much feeling and tears, the group members reached out to offer support and understanding. They were able to use their own experiences to share similar feelings. The older members of the group were able to provide a different perspective on the mother's actions. They could identify with her feelings and pointed out how uncertain she might feel about how to help her daughter. Conversations and incidents described by the client were discussed and new interpretations of the interactions offered. It became clear that the client's perceptions were often distorted by her own feelings of inadequacy and her own harsh judgments of herself. The problem was described by the worker from a new perspective, that of a normative crisis in life as the young couple were seeking new ways to relate to her parents and the parents, in turn, struggling to find ways of being close while still letting go. There were other issues involved as well relating to some of the reasons for the client's depression, for example, her feelings about being trapped at home and trapped as a woman. These emerged in later sessions.

It is important to note that as the group members offered help to the individual with the problem, they were also helping themselves. Each group member could make associations to a similar concern. All of them could see how easily the communications between mother and daughter were going astray. As they tried to help the client clarify her own feelings, understand her mother's reactions in new ways, and see how the mutual stereotypes were interfering in the ability to communicate real feelings, the other group members could relate these ideas to their own close relationships. This is one of the important ways in which giving help in a mutual aid group is a form of self-help. It is always easier to see the problem in someone else's relationships than it is to see them in your own. The general learning of the group members can be enhanced through the specific problem-solving work done with each member. The group leader can help by pointing out the underlying common themes.

Rehearsal

Another way in which a mutual aid group can help is by providing a way to try out new ideas or skills. In a sense, the group becomes a safe place to risk new ways of communicating and to practice what the client feels may be hard to do. To continue with the previous example, as the session neared the end, the group leader pointed out that the client seemed hesitant about taking up the issue with her mother. The excerpt from the process recording excerpt starts with the client's response.

ROSE: I'm not sure I can talk with my mother about this. What would I say?

WORKER: That's a good question. How about trying it out right here? I'll pretend to be your mother calling to ask to see you. You can practice how you would respond, and the group can give some ideas about how it sounds. Does that sound all right?

ROSE: (She has stopped crying now and is sitting straight up in her chair with a slight smile on her face.) OK. You call me and tell me you want to have lunch with me and that I should keep the kids home from school so you can see them.

WORKER: (role playing) Hello, Rose, this is Mom.

ROSE: Hi Mom. How are you and Dad feeling?

WORKER: Not so good. You know, Dad gets upset easily, and he has been feeling lousy. (The client had indicated that her mother often used her father's health to try to make her feel guilty.)

ROSE: That's it! That's what she would say to make me feel guilty. (The group members are laughing at this point.)

The discussion picked up with the group members joining in one how easy it is for others to make us feel guilty. The worker inquired how Rose would feel at that point in the conversation. It became clear that the rest of the discussion would consist of her indirect responses to what she perceives as her mother's "laying on a guilt trip." After some discussion of what the mother might have been really feeling and having trouble in saying (e.g., how much she and her father really care about Rose and how much she needs to see her—an admission she might find hard to make), the group strategized with Rose on how to break the usual cycle of indirect communications. The key moment in the role play came when the mother asked Rose to keep the children home for her lunch visit. Rose had complained that the mother never wanted to see her alone, it was always the children. She was always asking to have them at home when she visited. She thought her mother didn't trust her with the kids and was always checking up on her.

WORKER: (speaking as the mother) I wonder, Rose, if part of the reason I always ask to have the kids there is that I'm uncomfortable when we get together. I'm not sure what I would say to you for a whole two hours. I want the kids around to help fill the conversation.

ROSE: You know, I'm not sure what I would say to my mother either. I really don't know what to talk to her about.

FRAN: (another group member) Can you try to tell your mother that you get upset when she asks to keep the kids home because you want to have some time alone with her? Maybe your mother could understand that. (Silence)

WORKER: Rose, do you really want to spend some time with your mother?

ROSE: I'm not so sure I do.

WORKER: Then that's the first step. When you're sure, I think the words will come more easily. If you tell your mother how you really feel, it could be the start of some honest talk between you. Perhaps she could share some of her real feelings in response, instead of always doing it indirectly and in ways which are open to misinterpretation. Maybe if you could do this, then your mother would see this as a sign of your maturity.

Rose tried to articulate her feelings more clearly but was obviously still having difficulty. She reported back the following week that she had talked with her mother about how it made her feel when the mother tried to do things for her (e.g., wash the dishes when she came over), and the mother had responded by describing how she never really knew what to do when she came over: should she help out or not? Rose felt it cleared the air, even though other issues and feelings were not discussed. The interesting thing about the role-playing device as a form of rehearsal is that it often reveals the underlying ambivalence and resistance which the client feels but has not expressed in the discussion. The rehearsal not only offers the client a chance to practice, it also reveals to the group, the worker, and to the client some of the feelings which need to be dealt with if the client is to succeed in the effort.

The "Strength-in-Numbers" Phenomenon

Sometimes it is easier to do things as a group than it would be as an individual. For example, individual tenants in a housing project might find it difficult to stand up to the housing authority on issues of poor maintenance service. When organized into a tenants' group, the "strength-in-numbers" phenomenon works to decrease the individual risk involved thus encouraging the group members to make demands for their rights. An individual's fears and ambivalence can be overcome by participation in a group effort as one's own courage is strengthened by the courage of others.

Summary

A number of examples have been shared to illustrate how the dynamics of the mutual aid process can work. Sharing data, the dialectical process, discussing taboo areas, the "all-in-the-same-boat" phenomenon, mutual support, mutual demand, individual problem solving, rehearsal, and the "strength-in-numbers phenomenon are some of the processes through which mutual aid is offered and taken. It is important to note that this argument is not one which suggests that working in groups is a preferred method. The choice of individual or group work

is influenced by many factors, particularly the comfort of the clients in dealing with their concerns on a one-to-one basis as opposed to a group setting. As I will explain in detail later, it is often helpful for a client to have both individual *and* group work available so that both experiences can be used productively. Each would have a slightly different focus, and each could be expected to provide important stimulation for the other. For many clients the group can offer (under certain circumstances) unique forms of help in dealing with their life problems. In this first section of this chapter I have attempted to identify some of these mutual aid processes. However, groups will not provide this kind of help just because they have been brought together. In the next section I will review some of the obstacles which can make mutual aid a difficult process indeed. These obstacles, and others, will be explored in detail in later chapters.

OBSTACLES TO MUTUAL AID

In the early phases of a group's development, one potential obstacle to mutual aid is the apparently divergent interest each group member brings to the engagement. Even in a group with a narrow, clearly defined purpose, some group members may perceive their sense of urgency differently from the others. Even though the mutual threads of concern may exist, group members may not identify their common ground. Various group members may feel their concerns and feelings are unique and unrelated to those of other members. The "symbiotic attractions" between members may be partial, subtle, and difficult to perceive. In many ways, the group is a microcosm of the larger society, and this diffusion of interest between "self" and "other" reflects the individual social encounter in society. Thus, as each member becomes oriented to the group engagement, that member will be asking, "How am I the same or different from the other members?" One of the early tasks of the group leader will be to help group members begin to identify their mutuality. As the group develops a mature way of relating, individual members can begin to understand that they can learn and grow by giving help as well as receiving it. As each individual member develops the skills required to offer and take help, these same skills will be found to be related to individual concerns. However, at both the beginning stage and periodically during the life of the group, the inability of members to perceive their connections to the others will present an important obstacle.

A second set of obstacles will emerge from the fact that even a small group can be a complex system which must deal with a number of developmental tasks if it is to work productively. As soon as more than one client is involved, a new organism is created, the group-as-a-whole. This group is more than the simple sum of its parts, that is, the individual members. For example, this new organism will have to develop rules and procedures which will allow it to function effectively. Some will be openly discussed, while others may operate beneath the surface by mutual consent of the members. Roles may be subtly distributed to group members, such as scapegoat, deviant member, internal leader, and so on. Some of these role assignments will represent ways by which the group-as-a-whole may avoid dealing directly with a problem. Many of the unstated rules for relating will be counterproductive to the purpose of the group. These factors, and others to be discussed later, are properties of this complex organism

called the group and must be dealt with by the leader if the group is to function effectively.

A final major area of potential problem for the group is the difficulty involved in open communication. I have already discussed some of the barriers which make it difficult for clients to express their real feelings and concerns. These are related to the culture in our society which has implicitly and explicitly developed a number of norms of behavior and identified taboo areas in which honest communication is hard to achieve. Each group member brings a part of this culture into the group so that the group culture, in early phases of work, resembles the culture of the social surroundings. This often makes it difficult for group members to talk to and listen to each other in areas of central concern. With the group leader's help, group members will need to develop a new culture in which norms are modified and taboos lose their power, so that members are free to use each other.

I have just outlined three major areas of potential obstacles to mutual aid: the difficulty individual members have in identifying their self-interest with that of the other group members, the complex tasks involved in creating a mutual aid system, and the difficulties in communicating honestly. The existence of these potential obstacles helps to define the job of the group leader. These problems are not arguments against the use of groups as mutual aid systems. They represent an agenda for the group worker. If groups were not faced with these problems, if people could easily join together to offer aid and support, then we would not need the group worker. Essentially, what we find in the small group, which is a special case of the larger individual-social engagement described in Chapter 1, is the same potential for diffusion of the "symbiotic" relationship. I will once again use the functional role of mediation as a starting point for describing the tasks of the helping person, this time, however, in the context of group work.

THE FUNCTION OF THE GROUP LEADER

In my earlier discussion of Schwartz's mediation practice theory, the function of the helping person was illustrated by three circles. The client was on the left, the systems to be negotiated on the right, and the worker in the middle. Since the group is a specific case of this larger engagement, the same diagram can be drawn with the individual on the left and the group on the right.

The general function of mediating the individual-social engagement is now translated into mediating the individual-group interaction. This leads Schwartz to argue one of his most central and exciting ideas about group work: that the group worker always has "two clients," the individual and the group. The function of the worker is to mediate the engagement between these two clients. As the group process unfolds, the worker is constantly concerned both with each individual member and with the other client, the group. For example, as an individual member raises a specific concern, the worker will help the member share that concern with the group. The discussion in Chapter 4 on the work phase detailed how difficult it often can be for clients to describe their concerns. All the worker skills described earlier (e.g., reading indirect communications, helping clients move from the general to the specific) will now be employed to help individuals express their concerns to the group. As the leader helps the one (the individual)

talk to the many (the group), the interaction will also be monitored to see if the members appear to be listening and relating to the individual. If they seem to be turned off, the worker will explore their feelings and reactions. Perhaps the individual's problem is painful to the group members, raising related feelings of their own and making it hard for them to listen. Whatever the realities may be, the group worker, with a clear sense of function, will pay attention to both "clients" at exactly the same time.

Attention to the second client, the group, will require that the worker help group members to deal with the obstacles described earlier. For example, if the group culture is making members' discussion of their real feelings about a specific issue difficult, then the worker can call this to the attention of the group members. An effort to bring the obstacle out in the open is a first step in helping the group members become more conscious of their own processes. With the assistance of the group worker, group members can discuss how the blockage of open communication in a sensitive area frustrates their work. With understanding may come growth as the group becomes more sophisticated about its way of working. A new agreement, including new norms that are more productive, can be openly reached. In many ways the group worker serves as a guide for the group members faced with the complex task of developing an effective mutual aid system. The important point is that this is the members' group, the work to strengthen it is theirs, and the group worker is there to help them to do it.

In a general way, these two areas of work characterize the group leader's responsibilities: helping the individual and the group relate effectively to each other and helping the organism called the group

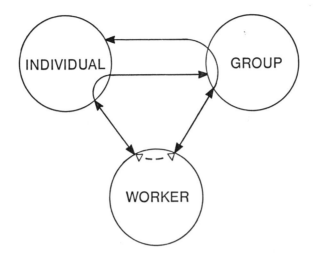

become more sophisticated about its way of working, so that it releases the potential for mutual aid. Of course, this process is more complicated than this simple explanation implies. The balance of Part II of this book will explore the underlying assumptions about how mutual aid groups work and the tasks and skills required of the group worker. Once again, the process will be analyzed step by step. The chapter on the preparatory phase will include a discussion on setting up a group, dealing with questions of group composition, recruitment, and the important work required with fellow staff members to gain their support and avoid possible "sabotage." The dynamics of initial group meetings will be discussed and illustrated by examples from a number of groups. The discussion of the work phase will include a chapter on the individual-group interaction. A second chapter will explore the individual role in the group and a third will examine the tasks of the group-as-a-whole and how the worker assists in its development. A fourth chapter will illustrate variations on the central ideas with groups from a wide range of settings. A

consideration of group endings and transitions will complete Part II.

THE FEAR OF GROUPS SYNDROME

In every group work training workshop I have led, there is a moment, usually early in the first morning, when I can sense a general unease in the group. Sometimes, the first clue of the fear of a groups syndrome emerges in the introductions when participants will indicate they have never led a group in a tone of voice which indicates that if they had it their way, they never would lead one. When I explore these clues, I often hear that the worker was sent by an administrator or supervisor who decided that group work would be a good idea.

Whether the participants are in the workshop voluntarily, or were volunteered, whether they are experienced workers or new workers, the underlying feelings are often the same: they are scared stiff of the idea of being responsible for leading a group. As one experienced social worker said in one of these workshops: "There are so many of them (the clients) and only one of me!"

A common concern is of having to practice with a group of people who are judging your work. Group work practice is seen as more exposed than individual work. If a client does not return after a few interviews, workers can always hide their feelings by chalking it up to "lack of motivation." However, if ten clients don't return to a group session, the worker feels he or she has failed.

Another concern relates to direct negative feedback from clients. Anger from a single client or couple is one thing, but facing an angry group is something else. Of even greater concern is the possibility of a boring group. Workers feel completely responsible for the success of a group and dread the possibility of long silences, rambling conversations, individuals who dominate the discussion, or the sight of ten pairs of eyes glazing over.

Lack of control is often cited as a fear by beginning group workers. One workshop participant put it this way: "When I'm conducting an individual interview I know where it is going and can keep track of what is happening. In a group session, the members seem to take the control of the session away from me. It feels like I am on my motorcycle, pumping the starter to get going, and the group members are already roaring down the road." It takes some experience for a new group worker to realize that it is exactly at moments such as these, when the group members take over the group, that the worker can relax in the knowledge that the group is well on its way to success. One of the benefits of caseworkers doing groups is that they begin to realize they can also let go of the control in their one to one interviews.

The complexity of group work also intimidates workers. Where before they needed to concentrate on the relationship between themselves and the client, they now have to also concentrate on the relationships between group members. As they gain group work experience they become more conscious of the entity called the group-as-a-whole, which I will discuss in detail in a later chapter. In their one-to-one interviews they just had to concentrate on the individual, now they must also pay attention to the group, and somehow develop the ability to observe both the one and the many at the same time.

All of these concerns are understandable. However, with some reflection, experienced practitioners soon realize these concerns are similar to those they experienced when they first began to practice. Skills in work with individuals, which they now take for granted, seemed out of reach in their first interviews. They are continually learning more about the dynamics of the relationships between themselves and clients, as well as the dynamics of family relationships or couples. With some confidence in the skills they have, they are less concerned about those they need to learn and are more able to tolerate areas of ambiguity. The difference with group work is that they are often starting with no confidence at all.

I try to reassure these workers that they already know more about group work than they realize. Much of what they have learned about helping can be applied in the group situation, as will be illustrated in the chapters which follow. The areas of uncertainty represent exciting areas for new learning which they have the rest of their professional lives to explore.

For the new worker or student, I suggest starting with individual work to develop some beginning confidence in basic practice skills and then broadening these in the group context. This does not mean students cannot begin their learning with group work practice. I have seen many students develop quickly working in the group medium. However, for their own comfort in the beginning of their practice, it is often easier to start by talking to one client at a time. If this can be supplemented with an opportunity to work as a co-leader with a more experienced group worker, then the learner has the best of all learning possibilities.

With both the new and the experienced worker I try to point out that the root of their fear is a misconception about their complete responsibility for the group work process. In fact, it is when they realize that they only have responsibility for their part, and in fact, some of the most important helping in the group will be done by group members, that they can put their group work into proper perspective. Certainly they will be more helpful to groups they lead later in their careers, as they develop an increased understanding of group processes, more skill and greater confidence. They can, however, still give a great deal to their first groups as they develop their group work skills.

New group workers tend to underestimate the amount of help they can give to their group members in the same way they did when they began their work in the one-to-one context. Continued group experiences will do a lot to correct this misconception, and the marvelous feeling a worker gets when he or she sees the power of mutual aid that can be released in group work practice helps to make up for the worker's anxiety along the way.

NOTES

1. The mutual aid model of group work practice is used to organize the discussion in this book. Schwartz draws upon the seminal work of Kropotkin in developing the "mutual aid" concept. See: P. Kropotkin, *Mutual Aid, A Factor of Evolution* (New York: Knopf, 1925). For examples of other orientations towards groups, most of which include mutual aid within their models, see Margaret Hartford, *Groups in Social Work* (New York: Columbia University Press, 1972); Baruch Levine, *Fundamentals of Group Treatment* (Chicago: Whitehall Press, 1967); Gesela Konopka, *Social Group Work: A Helping Process* (Englewood Cliffs, N.J.: Prentice-Hall, Inc., 1971); Alan F. Klein, *Effective Group Work* (New York: Association Press, 1972); Helen Northen, *Social Work with Groups* (New York: Columbia University Press, 1969); Helen Phillips, *Essentials of Social Group Work Skill* (New York: Association Press, 1957); Robert D. Vinter (ed.), *Readings in Group Work Practice* (Ann Arbor, Mich.: Campus Publishers, 1967); Saul Bernstein (ed.), *Further Explorations in Group Work* (Boston: Boston University School of Social Work, 1970); Sheldon D. Rose, *Group Therapy: A Behavioral Approach* (Englewood Cliffs, N.J.: Prentice-Hall, Inc., 1977).

2. William Schwartz, "The Social Worker in the Group," in *New Perspectives on Services to Groups* (New York: National Association of Social Workers, 1961), p. 18.

CHAPTER 8

Group Formation

The preparatory phase can be one of the most complex in work with groups. There are a number of crucial issues which must be dealt with before the first meeting takes place. The literature on group work pays surprisingly little attention to the problems of this phase, other than discussion of questions of group structure (e.g., frequency and number of sessions), group composition, and so on. As one example of a problem often ignored, it is not unusual for a worker to decide that a group would be helpful for clients and then to approach colleagues for appropriate referrals. General agreement may be reached at a staff meeting to support the group; however, the worker waits two months and does not get a single referral. In analyzing examples of this kind, I have consistently found that the worker had left out the important step of involving the colleagues in a meaningful way. I could often determine the moment in the staff meeting when the groundwork was laid for the frustration that followed.

In like manner, a worker may launch a group and prepare for a first meeting with ten group members who have given assurance of their attendance. The evening of the meeting arrives, and after waiting thirty-five long and painful minutes for latecomers, the worker must face the reality that only two members have come. Once again, the source of the disappointment can often be traced to steps which were left out in the preparatory work with clients as the worker or other workers began the referral process. In analysis of interviews and telephone conversations it is often possible to identify the moment the worker sensed the ambivalence of the prospective group member but did not reach for it.

The remainder of this chapter will explore in detail the steps required to establish a group and to increase the chances of its success. Work with the staff system is dealt with first, since much that follows depends upon these first efforts. Next, questions related to group formation (timing, composition, etc.) are explored. This is followed by the problems of recruitment. Finally, we return to the tuning in skill, this time adding the additional component of a first session in the group context.

WORK WITH THE STAFF SYSTEM

An important first principle is to recognize that a group in an agency or institution must be related to the service. If a worker attempts to establish a group

177

because of a desire to develop new skills or because of a decision that there is a need for such a group without involving the rest of the staff, the work may be doomed to failure. A common example is the student placed in an agency for practicum experience who takes a course at school in group work practice. A requirement for the class is to have a group, so the student endeavors to set one up in the field. Quite often the group never even has its first meeting because the student's need for it is not a sound reason for developing a group. The idea for a group must begin with the identification of an area of clients' unmet needs, a missing piece in the service which the group method may be able to meet. The group must reflect the consensus of the department or team involved so that it is not seen as being personally "owned" by the group worker.

The difficulty or ease involved in establishing a group may depend upon the group experience of the agency. In those settings where groups are a common form of service and where all staff members take their turn at leadership, many of the problems of formation may be minimized. In other agencies, where groups are unusual as a form of service, these problems may be intensified. For example, a worker who attempts to introduce group work into a setting which has not had groups before must recognize that a threatening situation may be created for other staff. Many workers are frightened by the idea of facing more than one client at a time. If they do not have a fund of good experiences to draw upon or if they unsuccessfully attempted to establish a group when they were students, they may be hesitant about working with groups. The worker attempting to initiate a group service must recognize that, on some level, colleagues may wonder whether, if the

service is successful, they will be asked to carry a group next. This is a fear which is often expressed indirectly (e.g., "Groups would be great in this agency, but do we really have the time?") The development of group service can have an important impact on the staff system, and the worker should make use of the tuning in skill in preparing to negotiate the establishment of the group. In the rest of this section, excerpts from an effort by a hospital social worker to establish a ward group are used to illustrate the dynamics and the skills involved in work with staff.

Achieving Consensus on the Service

There are many ways by which the idea of a group may emerge in an agency: client feedback, a worker discovering a common concern among a number of individual clients, or a staff team discovering an important gap in the service. Wherever the idea of a group is initiated, it is important that all staff involved have the opportunity to comment honestly on the potential service. A common mistake is for a worker to decide on the need for a group and then to set about "selling" colleagues on the idea. Rather than presenting their own views on the need for it and inviting feedback and discussion, workers may set about trying to influence their colleagues, creating the illusion that they are involving others in the process. In the following illustration a young social worker, relatively new to the hospital, approaches a long-time head nurse about the possibility of forming a group on the ward. She had been warned that the nurse has a reputation for being tough and uncooperative on projects such as this and has therefore steeled herself for the task of convincing the nurse of the need for the group. The illustration demonstrates the problems generated when one tries to "sell" an idea.

I said to Miss Ford that I had been doing some thinking which I would like to share with her. I told her that I had been on the ward quite a bit and felt quite at home on it. I said to her that I, as everyone else on the ward, am here to try to service the patients to the best of my ability. I then asked her what she thought of a group having any value on the ward. She said that it has been suggested before, so that it was nothing new. She said that the room full of ladies could do with something of that sort but that that's the only ladies' room there is. I asked if she thought that only ladies could benefit from a group experience and she said "no," but that she was thinking in terms of room number 1403. She asked what the group would be about and for. I said that I'm open to suggestions but that perhaps the basic purpose could be for the patients to discuss their hospitalization, frustrations, etc. It would be open to all patients.

Although the worker said she wanted to explore the nurse's views, she really did not mean it. The nurse quickly sensed her purpose when she did not explore the suggestion that the patients in room 1403 might benefit from a group. The worker was still reacting, on an emotional level, to the nurse's first comment that "it had been suggested before, so that it was nothing new." Had the worker not been so set on convincing the nurse, she could have asked for an elaboration of the comment. What had that effort been like? Had there been any problems? The worker is new on the ward, and the nurse might have shared some of her past experiences which could have provided helpful feedback. However, since the worker began with a stereotype of the nurse as being "resistant," she did not reach past this first comment. The same lack of genuine interest in the nurse's views is demonstrated when the worker challenges her suggestion that the ladies in room 1403 might need the help. As the worker will find out at a later

date, this room contains patients with terminal cancer. It represents a room full of problems for which the nursing staff has genuine concern but few ideas of how to help. It could represent an important area of missing service, but the worker does not know this because she has cut off the nursing supervisor's participation in the process.

After the nurse received the signals confirming the stereotype of workers as outsiders who do not really appreciate the problems of the ward, she responded rather perfunctorily asking questions sharply and crisply about the *worker's group*.

Miss Ford asked how the patients would know or how I would tell them. I told her that in order to make it a voluntary thing, perhaps written invitations to each patient would be a good idea. She asked when and where it would be held. I told her that I hoped she could help make that decision, especially the time, because I realize they are busy. As far as the room goes, perhaps an empty bedroom or the sunroom. She said that by October 16th all rooms should be filled up. I suggested we could decide on that at a later date. I asked if she could, however, talk to the doctors and staff about this, get some ideas, and we could discuss it again next week at rounds. She said that would be fine.

At the end of the worker's process recording she included the following comment:

Miss Ford did not seem too enthusiastic and was quite resistant (mentioning no rooms, how would patients know, etc.). However, I feel she can see some value in a ward group. Next week I plan to give her some examples of why I can see a need for the group.

If the worker had done that, it is likely she would have met the same resistance. If she continued to accept the nurse's superficial agreement, her artificial consensus, she would have proceeded to set up her group and, most likely, been surprised on the day of her first meeting. Either the room would have been unavailable or the worker would have discovered that half the patients she had selected for the group session had been "inadvertently" scheduled for blood tests, x-rays, or other medical procedures which took them off the ward. There would have been profuse apologies by the nursing staff, and the problem would have repeated itself the following week. The worker would eventually give up, adding one more story to the collection of examples of how "resistant" Miss Ford was to any new ideas.

The missing skill in this interview was described in Part I as "looking for trouble when everything seems to be going your way." In this case, the worker sensed the underlying negative reaction in the interview but did not reach for it. For example, she could have said, "Miss Ford, you don't seem too enthusiastic about this group. Why not?" This direct response to the indirect cue would have opened up Miss Ford's real feelings and reactions and might have turned a one-way selling job into an honest exploration of mutual thoughts about a new service. In many ways, the nurse's relative directness about her feelings should have been an aid to the worker. At least her feelings were almost out in the open. In contrast, in many instances, for example a worker describing a group to fellow workers at a team meeting, the worker might find an artificial agreement expressed through apparently unqualified support. Once again, the skilled worker would not leave the session without first reaching for underlying reservations. For example, "You know it's great to see such quick support for my idea, but you know, it's going to cause some problems and

inconveniences for the rest of you. Don't you think we should also talk about these?"

The worker often senses, as did the worker with the head nurse, the underlying resistance but fears to reach for it. The belief is that if one leaves the negatives unexpressed, they will perhaps go away. They never do. These reservations, negative reactions, fears, and the like all come back to haunt the worker in the form of conscious or unconscious sabotage of the worker's plans. If the group is to take place, the worker must insist it be a service of the team, the agency, or whatever, not just the worker's personal group which happens to be taking place in the setting. Without this real support the worker will be alone when problems emerge. I have seen excellent work done with school principals, for example, when after the principal has given perfunctory agreement to allow a group to meet in the school, the worker has asked, "Would you be very upset if we couldn't offer this group to your kids?" After a moment's pause, the principal responded, "The only reason I OK these groups is that the people at the board like to see them in the schools. Actually, staff and I often find they are more trouble than they are worth." Only at this point does the real discussion begin, and the worker can start serious contracting with the agency or setting. If it is skipped over in the worker's eagerness to gain a toehold, then the lack of real investment will hurt when the going gets rough in the group.

Fortunately, as with work with clients, workers usually have the opportunity to go back after making a mistake and to try again. After some consultation and discussion of the first process recording of the interview with the nurse, the worker strategized to return to Miss Ford and instead of trying to convince her, own up to her mistake and try to start all over again. You will notice the change in the nurse's attitude as the discussion becomes real.

I told Miss Ford that I felt I may have been too pushy about the ward group. I said that I had asked for her participation and interest, yet I hadn't given her a chance to express herself, and I wasn't really listening to her. I then apologized and suggested that we might go back to the beginning. I said I was interested in knowing her true feelings regarding the group. She said she thought the group would be very good for most patients, but she was worried about the manpower of nurses. She said it was difficult enough to get all the nurses to attend her ward conference without having them attend a patients' group. I asked if she was thinking in terms of all the nurses going to the group at once. She said she didn't know and wondered what I thought. I said that the decision of nurses was up to her. I suggested that it might be just as effective to have one nurse drop in on the group or have the nurses rotate.

This may have been the issue on the head nurse's mind when she commented on the group having been tried before. It is important that the worker pay attention to the problems created by the group for the ongoing system. The worker has to be able to empathize genuinely with the day-to-day difficulties of other staff members. Often, the recognition of these problems can lead to alternative solutions or to the willingness of the staff to extend themselves. As in all human relationships, it is important that the worker really understand how the other staff member feels. The discussion in the interview turned to the issue of purpose and contract.

I suggested that one important gap existed between patients and doctors or patients and nurses. I explained further that I believed that if a patient could release some of his anxieties or fears about his medical problems or share his hostilities in the group, he might be an easier patient to cope with. Rather than expressing his feelings in an undesirable way, he might be happier on the ward and easier to deal with. Miss Ford agreed with this and then asked about the resident on the ward. How could we keep him involved? We discussed this for a while.

Although the worker's contract statement is still a bit unclear, reflecting her own lack of clarity, the general sense of the group dealing with issues related to hospital and illness and with communication between patient and staff is clearly suggested. This is important, since workers who propose groups in a setting without connecting the purpose of the group to the general service of the agency are often seen as simply requesting space. When administrators and staff members perceive the connection between their service and the purpose of the group, they will be more likely to invest themselves in the group's development. A worker offering to lead a group for children identified by teachers as having trouble at school will be more easily accepted by the staff than one asking to lead groups for general discussion (e.g., "I would like to work with children who need a 'socialization' experience.")

As the discussion with Miss Ford continued, note her more active involvement:

Miss Ford asked how the patients would know about the group, who would go, etc. I suggested that the nurses see all the patients, and they could tell who could benefit from a group experience, who was ready to go. She asked how patients would find out about the group. I suggested we stick notices to their bedside tables. She said it would not be a good idea because the tables must be washed. She suggested we put them in the bathrooms where the beauty salon advertises. I said it was a good idea, and we went to the bathroom to select the best spot. I then brought up the subject of confidentiality.

The worker had used her "tuning in" preparation to anticipate another sensitive area for discussion—the issue of confidentiality. Although the nurse had not raised this issue, it is a good bet that she was wondering what would happen if patients complained about the nursing staff. This issue is often a difficult one for workers. It is often an important underlying negative when a worker proposes a group in a setting (e.g., hospital, school, or residential setting) or when the worker is sharing clients with another worker and the worker will continue to see the client on an individual basis. The group worker often suggests the need to maintain confidentiality to staff, not reporting group discussion, so that the group members will feel free to talk. In my experience, when group members talk negatively about staff, they are often hopeful the worker will help improve a bad situation. It is true that they are concerned about how the information will be used (e.g., the possibility of retribution from the teacher, nurse, etc.) They are not, however, raising the concerns just for the sake of ventilating feelings.

From the point of view of the helping function outlined in this book, the mediating approach, acting as a communication bridge between clients and the agency system, is very much a part of the work. If the worker begins work with staff by stating they will not be included in discussion of group content, their fears and anxieties may lead to direct or indirect efforts at sabotage. In one such case, a worker in a home for unmarried mothers had completely ignored the housemother in negotiating for the group—particularly her fears of complaints—and had indi-

cated that all discussions would be confidential. When the worker arrived, the housemother rang a bell and shouted, to the worker's consternation, "Group therapy time." In other examples, the worker's colleagues have described the group to their individual clients in a way which helped to heighten the clients' fears of involvement. For example, "We are going to offer this group for single mothers, but you don't have to go if you don't want to."

If the worker's sense of function involves a commitment to helping in the process between client and system, including the agency, then this must be part of the contract. Nurses, child care workers, teachers, and other counselors must be viewed as colleagues with each having a part in the operation. Discussions should focus on how both the group worker and the other staff members will handle feedback. The meaning of the feedback and the way in which clients might use either the individual worker or the group worker as a channel must be recognized. The agreement can include ways to achieve the optimum outcome in which each will attempt to asist the clients' efforts to provide direct feedback to the other. I have found that this discussion often takes much of the threat out of the fear of negative feedback and, instead, turns it into an important technical issue for both workers. The details of how the fears of the group members can be handled and how a worker can effectively share feedback with other staff will be dealt with in later chapters.

When I explore why workers are reluctant to follow this course of action, that is, treat other system people as colleagues and work out agreements for mutual sharing of relevant information, they usually express concern about the client's acceptance of such a contract. While there is some basis to this concern, I often find, in addition, their own fears about confronting a colleague with "bad news." How do you tell a fellow staff member, with whom you have coffee each day, that his client doesn't feel he understands him? Confidentiality can then serve as a protection for the group worker. Often workers reveal that they have developed stereotypes of their colleagues and feel that they are "lousy" workers (poor teachers, insensitive doctors, etc.), so what good would sharing be? I can understand their reticence to take on this function. However, if the group worker accepts that the nurse on the ward, the teacher, a fellow social worker, or whomever, is actually closed to change, such acceptance means that an important part of the service to clients will no longer be available. The worker will inevitably be in a serious quandary when the strength-in-numbers phenomenon leads the group members to share their real feelings. The situation will have been set up to make it impossible to do anything about the problem except empathize, ignore the problems, or defend the system. This often leads to apathy and loss of involvement on the part of the group members.

The question of confidentiality has changed during this discussion to a much larger issue: the function of the helping person within his or her own helping system. This will be explored in detail in Part III of this book. For now, I would summarize my view as being that this concern may be a central issue for other staff members when group formation is discussed. I would want it out in the open, and I would want to contract with both staff and group members for freedom of communication of group content in a responsible manner. Returning to the interview, we find that this is precisely what our worker on the hospital ward does.

I then brought up the subject of confidentiality. I asked how Miss Ford felt it should be handled. For example, if one patient or more complained about a certain nurse or herself, would she like to know or not? Rather than directly answering, she told me about a patient on the ward who would complain of different shifts of staff and play one against the other. I asked her if the gist of her story was that it was better to know the complaints so that they can be investigated and dealt with. She said "yes." I told her I felt the same way and that I would like to know when patients made complaints about me.

We then talked about where the group could be held. I again suggested the sunporch. This time, Miss Ford said that it would be all right because patients used it anyway. We then discussed further clearances in the hospital and set up a meeting with the nursing staff to clarify the group purpose and to select members.

Group versus Individual Work with Clients

Another issue which can create problems for the group worker is the compatibility of group and individual work. Some group workers take the position that group members should not be seen individually because that will lessen the intensity of the group experience. Individual counselors as well are often worried that clients will use their group session to discuss central issues. This can lead to a struggle over "who owns the client," a misunderstanding of the interdependence of individual and group work, and an attitude to client participation in decisions about service which I do not accept.

On the first issue, clients may use both individual and/or group help for different issues as they see fit. For example, as the group works on the concern of a particular member, the discussion may raise a similar concern for the client who may want a chance to discuss a special case of the general problem and may not have enough time in the group to do this. Individual sessions can provide this opportunity. Group discussion, rather than robbing the individual work of its vitality, will often enrich the content of the individual counseling sessions. As clients listen to issues, as they understand how others are experiencing problems, they may be put in touch with feelings of their own which were not previously evident. Finding out that others have fears related to taboo areas, for example sex, may greatly speed up clients' willingness to discuss their own concerns in individual work.

In like manner, the work in the individual sessions can strengthen a client to raise a personal concern in the group. For some clients it may be too difficult to start to talk in a group context about some of their most private feelings and concerns. As they find they can share these with an individual counselor and not be harshly judged, then this may strengthen them to share these feelings in the group. Thus, the group and individual work can be parallel and interdependent, with the client free to choose where and when to use these resources for work. The question of client choice raises the second issue. In my view, these choices, at any particular moment, rest with the client. Feeling comfortable about dealing with issues in one context or the other, the client will make these decisions. I may share my opinions, offer support, and even provide concrete help (e.g., role playing in an individual session to show how the client might raise an issue in the group).

With two and possibly more helping people working with the same client, good communications between the helpers become essential. Structures should be established that guarantee regular communication so that each understands how the client is choosing to deal with issue

and so that each can help the other staff member in their related work. For example, in a couples' group that I have led, two co-leaders sat in on each session. They were seeing most of the couples on an individual counseling basis. In the "tuning in" session we held prior to each group meeting, they summarized the specific concerns dealt with in the individual sessions. We used this preparatory work to anticipate potential group issues. I hold to a policy of not directly raising concerns in the group which were discussed in the individual work unless the couples wish them raised. Through the tuning in process, I became more effective at picking up their indirect cues. Since co-leaders sat in on the sessions, they were able to incorporate content from the group experience into the individual work. If they were not able to sit in, I shared copies of my group process and couple summary reports so that they would be aware of the couples' progress. When sessions were videotaped, the tapes were also available for their use. Rather than competing for client ownership, we have two professionals, each providing a service through different modalities. As pointed out in the earlier discussion on confidentiality, without freedom to share information this open communication would not have taken place.

Agency Support for Groups

In addition to support from colleagues, help from the agency administration may also be needed. For example, special expenses may be incurred in carrying out a group program. Mothers' groups held during the daytime may require baby-sitting services. Recruitment publicity, transportation expenses, coffee, and other items may be involved in some group programs. In addition, the worker developing a group may need support in the form of a reduced individual caseload and group work consultation from an outside consultant if one is not available on staff. These issues should be discussed as the group is formed.

In some settings, where groups have not been an integral part of the service, the approach to group work programs may require that the worker take personal responsibility for their implementation. For example, workers are encouraged to develop groups, if they can do so "on their own time." Many workers, eager to see the service begin or to develop new skills in work with clients, accept this responsibility and soon regret it. If a service is part of the agency function, it should not have to be carried as a personal "hobby" by the worker. Groups take time, and if workers do not see that the group is viewed as a part of their responsibilities, the additional demands upon them and their feelings about these will often affect their work with the group.

When agencies do support the development of group services, they sometimes do so for the wrong reasons. Administrators may believe that seeing clients in groups can save time and so encourage a swing to group programs as a way of providing more service to clients with the same staff. There are some situations where seeing clients in groups does save time. For example, orientation meetings for prospective adoptive parents or new foster parents can be an effective way of starting communications with more than one person at a time. However, more often than not the development of group services tends to increase the workload, since new issues and concerns may be discovered that require additional individual work. Groups can be an important service in their own right rather than as a service substitute. A worker in

a group will need time to follow up with individual members, to meet with other staff, to develop a system for recording the group work for agency accountability, and for personal learning.

To start a group service on a sound agency footing is better, even though the process may be slower and frustrating. Time taken by the group worker to interpret the group purpose as well as identify the special needs and potential problems related to instituting new group services will pay off in the long run. In those cases where doubts exist about the benefits of group practice, the worker can propose the group as an agency experimental service to be closely evaluated. Records can be kept on the costs and benefits. The agency staff and administration can use the first groups as a way of developing experience with a new form of service. The important point is that the service be the agency's, not the personal project of a concerned worker. With the latter, it is not unusual to have a good first group only to discover that the service dies when the worker is no longer able or willing to provide it personally.

GROUP COMPOSITION, TIMING, AND STRUCTURE

A conversation I had with a group of students and health professionals helps to illustrate some of the myths and questions involved in planning a group. I led a group for five couples in marital difficulty which was videotaped and simultaneously observed on a monitor in another room. After each session, I met with the observers and my co-leaders to discuss the session. At the end of a first session, which was marked by excellent group member involvement (excerpts from transcripts of this group are shared in later chapters), I was peppered by questions on how the group had been formed. The first request was for my principles of group composition which had led to such a lively, interactive group. One couple was in their twenties, another in their thirties, a third in their forties, a fourth in their fifties, and the oldest couple in their late sixties and early seventies. I explained, much to the disappointment of the group, that these were the only five couples referred for the group.

Another student asked how I had decided on five couples. I pointed out that we were using a studio, and with myself and my co-leaders, there was only room for five couples. Another effort to tease out principles followed as they inquired how we decided on the number of sessions. I pointed out that there were many long-standing issues involved, and a short-term group did not seem to offer enough time. "How did you settle on exactly twenty-three sessions?" was the next question. Once again I disappointed the group by explaining that we decided we couldn't do the advance work needed to start the group before October 15. We simply counted the weeks until the end of the academic year. We then went on to discuss the differences between what I felt to be the myth of scientific group composition versus the reality of how decisions were made. The students wanted prescriptions and rules, and I argued, a bit more strongly than perhaps was needed, that the rules were not really that clear.

The position I took then was that each setting must develop its own rules, based upon its experiences as well as those of others. The literature provides a fund of observations on questions of group composition and structure, but unfortunately it also provides conflicting scientific evidence in support of rules.[1] For example, there are conflicting studies on the optimum size for effective discussion groups

with support for different numbers argued persuasively. Given this reality, a worker must address a number of questions, using the experiences of colleagues and of other settings, to develop some tentative answers. Each group represents an experiment which can contribute to the fund of experience which workers will draw upon in starting new groups. Some of the questions requiring discussion are highlighted in the remainder of this section. What I hope to provide is not the answers to these questions, but rather, a way of finding answers.

Group Member Selection

The crucial factor in selection of members is that there be some common ground between their individual needs and the purpose of the group. Whether this purpose has been defined broadly or narrowly, each member must be able to find some connection between a personal sense of urgency and the work involved. Even if this common ground is not apparent to the prospective member at the start, the worker should have some sense of its existence. In the example of the couples' group, each couple was having severe problems in their marital relationship. Another point in common was that all five couples had some commitment at the start to trying to strengthen their marriages. Couples who had already decided to separate but who needed help in doing so without additionally hurting each other or their families would not have belonged in this group. In organizing a community action group, the fact that members live in the same community, share the same services, and use the same institutions (e.g., schools) can help bind them together and create the mutual need.

As the group leader considers the purpose of the group and considers potential

members, common sense can help to identify potential differences which might create difficulty in reaching group consensus
on the focus of the work. For example,
although twelve-year-old foster adolescents may have their wardship status in
common with seventeen-year-old wards,
their issues and concerns may be quite
different. Combining these two age-
groups in a group to discuss life problems
and issues related to being "foster" could
create unnecessary obstacles. On the other
hand, I have seen groups developed by a
child welfare agency to promote better
communications between teens and staff
and to provide social and recreational activities in which a wide age difference
between teens appeared to have a less
negative impact. The older teens provided leadership for the group and looked
upon themselves as "big brothers" and
"big sisters" to the younger ones.

Group purpose will be important in
thinking about age and group composition. For example, in the couples' group
described earlier, the differences in the
ages of the five couples provided unexpected dividends. Each couple was experiencing the crises associated with their
particular phase of life and phase of their
marriage; however, there were common
themes cutting across all phases. In many
ways, the older couples were able to share
their experiences and perspectives with
the younger ones as the group often took
on the appearance of an extended family.
After one session in which some of the
problems associated with the older couples' life phases were clearly delineated,
the husband in the youngest couple said
good humoredly, "I'm beginning to wonder if this is what I have to look forward
to going through!" The wife of the oldest
couple, who had been married forty-nine
years, responded, "But you will have the
advantage of having had this group to

help as you face these problems." Whether
to include males, females, or both will
similarly have to be determined according to the group purpose. Some of the
other factors often discussed when deciding on group membership, such as judgments about a member's "personality,"
are somewhat questionable to me. For
example, I have seen a group meticulous-
ly assembled with a proper number of
relatively passive schoolchildren balanced by a manageable number of active
ones. The theory was to guarantee interaction with the active members stimulating the passive ones. In addition, some
limit on active members was thought to
help the leader with potential problems
of control. Unfortunately, nobody informed the group members about their
expected roles. The leader was observed
in the first session desperately trying to
deal with the acting out behaviors of the
"passive members" while the "active
members" looked on in shock and amuse-
ment. The fact of the matter is that clients do not act the same in each situation.
A passive client in an individual interview or a classroom may act quite
differently when exposed to a new context. Clients simply will not remain in
the "diagnosed" box long enough to be
clearly identified. Their reactions will be
somewhat dependent upon the actions of
those around them, particularly the group
leader.

Group Timing

There are a number of factors related
to time to consider in setting up a group.
How often will the group meet? How long
will the meetings last? For how long will
the group meet (e.g., six sessions, four
months)? Once again, each of these answers must draw upon common sense,
the experience of the agency, and the lit-

erature, and all must be related to group purpose. In the married couples' group we chose to meet once each week, for two hours each session, for a period of twenty-three weeks. Meetings had to be held in the evening so that working partners could attend. The group was designed to provide long-term support to the couples as they dealt with their marital problems. The alternate option of intensive weekends, for example, was not considered. For such couples in crisis, it seemed that the intensive, short-term experience might open up more problems while leaving the couples unable to deal with them. On the other hand, weekend workshops for marital enrichment groups, in which the relationships are strong to begin with, may be beneficial as education and skill-development experiences.

The decision to meet weekly recognized that longer breaks between meetings might diffuse the intensity of the experience, each session seeming like a new beginning. Two hours seemed to be enough time to allow for the development of central themes and issues in the beginning phase of each meeting, yet leaving enough time to deal effectively with specific individual and group concerns. More than two hours might be wearying for both group members and group workers.

Whatever the decision reached for a particular group, discussing and clarifying it with group members is important. Group members have a sense of the group's time frame and will be affected by the particular phase of a meeting or the phase in the life of the group. As pointed out earlier, the "doorknob" phenomenon can accelerate the presentation of important issues; however, the members need to know when the time to reach for the door is close at hand. It is possible for group members to work more effectively if they have less time to carry out their tasks. Reid and Shyne, for example, have discussed the impact of time on both the worker and the client in their work on short-term treatment.[2] There is a limit, however, to how much can be dealt with, so a judicious balance needs to be developed, allowing enough sessions to deal with the anticipated themes of concern. This limit will come from experience as an agency evaluates each group, using the group members as part of the evaluation process. Group members can be used quite effectively in setting up the initial parameters by exploring their reactions to time proposals before the group is established. Feedback on the day of the week or the specific time for starting may help a group worker to avoid unnecessary conflicts.

Group Structure

There are a number of questions related to group structure in the formation stage. For example, the place for meeting needs consideration. Ease of access by public and private transportation might be a factor. Holding a session on sensitive and potentially embarrassing work (e.g., child abuse) in a public setting where members might fear being identified could be a mistake. The room itself should offer group members face-to-face seating (e.g., in a circle or around a table) and privacy. Comfortable chairs and surroundings often add to the group members' comfort during the first sessions. Work with children, on the other hand, where activity is going to be part of the work, may require facilities which are relatively "activity proof," so that members and the group worker can relax without constant worries about order and decorum.

Structure also raises questions about the type of group. For example, will it be a group of fixed membership meeting over a period of time, or will it be what is called an "open-ended group" where different members arrive and leave each week? There are special problems and dynamics associated with such groups which are discussed in later chapters; however, for some purposes and settings they provide a better alternative than a fixed-membership group. One ward group in a hospital consisted of women who arrived for a two-day preparatory stay, a one-day exploratory operation to determine the possibility of cancer, and a two-day recovery period. Participation of both pre- and postoperation patients lent itself to the mutual aid process as those who had just gone through the experience were helpful to those preparing for it, and those who were new began the process of preparing to leave the hospital by helping those who were leaving.

Groups are sometimes formed from ongoing natural groups such as in a living setting. A residential group home is a good example, since it represents a living group, operating seven days a week, twenty-four hours each day. For two hours twice each week house meetings are held as special times within the ongoing group life to focus on the issues of group living as for example, problems between residents and between residents and staff. These meetings represent structured incidents in the life of the ongoing group designed to improve the ability of all concerned to live and work together.

Another issue related to the content of the group meeting. People can provide mutual aid through means other than just talking. I have written elsewhere on the use of activities in group work practice.[3] For example, senior citizens in a residential center might use activities which they have developed to structure their time, provide enjoyment or education, give them the opportunity to develop new skills, or just to enjoy the company of others. I will discuss the place of program activities in the life of the group and the worker's tasks in a later chapter. In the formation stage it is important to consider whether interaction through activity represents an important part of the purpose of the group and is within the general function of the setting. A ward group in a psychiatric hospital involved in planning recreational activities for patients may be an example where activities relate to both patients' need and the service of the setting. On the other hand community-center-type activities offered during schooltime to a group of children who are not doing well in their classes may be viewed by the school staff as a "reward" for acting badly, even if the worker argues they are indirectly helped. When these activities are used in work with children as a substitute for discussions about class problems or because the worker is concerned that the youngsters would not come to a "talk group," they may frustrate the essential work rather than to assist it. This issue will be discussed in some detail in the section on work with children, but for now the important point is that a decision on group type (talk, activity, both) needs to relate directly to both the service of the agency *and* the needs of the group members.

Finally, the area of group "rules" needs clarification prior to the first group meeting. For example, limits on physical activity may be set with children's groups. Even with some adult groups it may be necessary to clarify the boundary on the use of physical force. Expectations about attendance are important. The expectations the members have of the agency and the group and those the worker has of the members should be discussed. In addition, what can each member expect from the others (e.g., confidentiality of material shared)? In my couples' group, for example, the three rules discussed in the first session are that each member is expected to come each week as long as they are not ill, that a couple wanting to quit the group will come back for one additional week to discuss it, and that confidentiality will be respected by group members. These are many differences of opinions on the question of group rules. For example, some would argue that group members should not have contact with each other outside the meetings. The field of group work is far from the point where we can come to agreement on these questions. My general bias is that group members own their own lives and that my group is simply an incident in their week (although I hope an important incident). I would, therefore, have difficulty insisting on a rule preventing them from having contacts outside the group. In fact, in many groups the bonds of mutual aid which have developed through telephone calls and informal contacts outside the group have been powerful supports for individual members. Workers in some groups, who fear that group members may get involved in "acting out" outside of the group (having sexual contact for example), appear to me to take more responsibility for their lives of the members than they should. In addition, group members should be free to bring their outside interactions into the group if they wish, since they can represent an important entry into the content of the group work. In general, the rules stated in the beginning of the group should be firmly rooted to the reality of the situation rather than the arbitrary authority or personal treatment preferences of the group leader. They should be seen by group members as emerging from the necessities of the work.

Summary

A number of issues related to group composition, timing, and structure has been raised in these sections for the purpose of alerting you to questions requiring consideration prior to the start of the group. My opinions on these questions have been shared not as the truth, but rather as an illustration of how one practitioner develops his own views from his experiences and those of others. As with all the ideas shared in this book, you have to test them against your own sense of reality, your ongoing group experiences, so that for your setting and your particular collection of clients you can write your own book.

WORK WITH PROSPECTIVE MEMBERS

After agency administration and staff support have been mobilized, the potential obstacles to cooperation identified and discussed, and decisions made on the formation questions, then one more step remains—the recruitment of group members. This process can also be complex, since clients feel the general ambivalence about taking help described in Part I as well as unique concerns related to the group context. I should point out that there are workers who deal with groups in settings less focused on personal problems, for example community centers or community organization agencies, which do not have to deal with the same reluctance to join a group activity. However, some degree of ambivalence is usually present in joining any group. I will focus this discussion on examples of mutual aid groups designed to deal with problems of living (e.g., marital difficulties, parenting skill, alcohol or drug addiction, school difficulties) in the belief that some of the principles can be applied to the other groups as well.

Clients may become prospective group members by identifying themselves in response to posters, newspaper stories, letters from the agency, or other means of publicizing the existence of a group service. The steps involved in making potential group members aware of the group can help, if handled well, to turn the potential client towards the service. For example, posters or letters should be worded clearly, without jargon, so that the prospective member has a clear idea of the group purpose. It may be helpful to identify some of the themes of concern which may be related to the client's sense of urgency. If the embarrassment of the workers, discussed in the chapter on contracting with individuals, results in the use of euphemisms, or if the workers have "changing the client up their sleeve" and try to hide this by general and vague offers of service, prospective group members can be turned away. It is helpful to test the letters or posters with colleagues and clients to get their sense of the meaning and suggestions as to how to make the wording direct but still nonthreatening.

Other clients are referred by colleagues or other helping professionals or are selected by workers from their caseloads. Whatever the case may be, even when the client has initiated the contact, the gap between thinking about joining a group and arriving at the first meeting can be a big one. Many of the skills already identified can be helpful in increasing the chances of a successful start. Two areas I will now examine are work with colleagues after they have agreed to recruit group members (a real agreement), and telephone or in-person contacts between the worker and prospective members.

Strategizing for Effective Referrals

A worker may have done an effective job with fellow staff members on the establishment of a group and still be disappointed by a relatively low number of referrals. An important question often overlooked is how the colleague will conduct a referral interview. It is a mistake to assume that even a motivated colleague will be able to make an effective referral without some joint work and strategizing as to how it might be done. For example, the colleague may have a general sense of the group contract but be unable to articulate it clearly. One who has not worked with groups oneself may not be sensitive to some of the underlying feelings and ambivalence which the client may share indirectly, thereby missing a chance to help overcome some of the obstacles blocking access to the group. I have found it helpful to suggest a "tuning in" session, either individually or with a staff group, in which we pool our efforts to sensitize ourselves to the concerns clients may have about joining the group and the indirect ways these may emerge. Staff can then share strategies for reaching for the underlying concerns. In addition, a brief role play of the referral interview may reveal to the group worker that the colleagues are not able to articulate purpose, and work can then be done on this skill. Such a process may also bring to the surface ambivalent feelings on the part of the worker or unanswered questions which need to be dealt with before the actual referral interviews.

An example of this process is a referral workshop which I conducted for social service professionals in connection with the establishment of a new, experimental group service for men who had physically abused their wives or mates. Recognizing the importance of professional referrals to launch the program and knowing that the referral process might be extremely difficult in this situation, we provided an opportunity for "tuning in" and joint strategizing. To keep the discussion focused on skills, I asked for examples of difficult referrals of a similar nature. One worker described from memory a referral he had recently attempted with the common-law husband of a client. The client was a prostitute who had been beaten by the husband who was also her pimp but refused to report the incident or leave him (the existence of many situations such as this had led to the project to establish mutual aid groups for the men involved). As the worker's interaction with the husband was analyzed, it became clear that he had never mentioned the physical abuse, attempting instead to lead the husband indirectly to agree to seek help. When this was mentioned during the analysis of the example, the worker revealed that he feared angering the husband and that the husband might then take the anger out on the wife. An important discussion followed in which other workers spoke of their fears of retribution if they were direct. Their dilemma was discussed and strategies developed for broaching the subject directly but without putting the husband on the defensive. Without this preparatory work, I believe workers would have been blocked, thus indirectly offering this group because of their fears.

Let us consider another example from this group of the problem of stating group purpose. In a role play it became clear that one of the workers was describing the group in a way which would lead the prospective member to believe his worst fears—that it would be a group designed to chastise him for his antisocial behavior and to educate him to appreciate his impact on his woman. When I pointed out that the worker seemed angry at the prospective group member, my comment released a flood of feelings, echoed by many in the room, of anger at the men. Although all had agreed earlier that these groups could not be effective unless the men could see them as *their* groups, helping them to deal with the problems and pressures which led to the use of violence, including discussion of their internalized views on what "manliness" was all about, this intellectual agreement evaporated in the role play. It was replaced with a punitive and thereby ineffective offer of service. The ability for the workers to discuss and be in touch with these natural yet often denied feelings might help ensure a presentation of the group that might turn prospective members towards the service rather than reinforce their resistance. Although this group example may be an extreme one, I believe that in most cases the worker forming a group would be well advised to take some time with colleagues to discuss the technical aspects of making the referral.

Skills of the Initial Interviews

Group workers often have initial contacts with individual members, in person or by phone, to discuss their participation in the group. These interviews can be seen as part of the exploratory process in which the worker describes what the group has to offer and checks with the client to determine what may be needed. The skills described in Part I of clarifying purpose, clarifying role, and reaching for feedback are useful in this interview. Describing the structure of the group (how it will work) as well as timing helps to provide the information needed for the prospective member to make a decision about using the service.

In addition to the normal "tuning in"

to the client's feelings about beginning a new relationship, it is also important to "tune in" to the specific concerns related to beginning in a group. The general population has been exposed to a number of reports on groups ranging from "group psychotherapy" to "encounter." In addition, clients may bring stereotypes of groups based upon their past experiences (e.g., class groups at school, camp experiences) which will have some effect on their feelings about attending. Questions about how people with the same problems can help each other will also be on their minds. Much of this hesitancy and fear may be just beneath the surface. It can be expressed in indirect ways, and the worker must listen for it and reach directly for the indirect cues. In the following example, a worker has been describing a foster parents' group to an agency foster parent and has found the parent apparently receptive. The cues emerge when the worker gets specific about the dates.

WORKER: We are going to have our first meeting in two weeks, on a Wednesday night. Can I expect you there?
FOSTER PARENT: (long pause) Well, it sounds good. I'll try to make it if things aren't too hectic that week at work.

If the worker quits right there and accepts the illusion of acceptance, she may be guaranteeing that the parent will not show up. Even though workers can sense the ambivalence in the client's voice, they often refrain for reaching for the negative attitude. When I have inquired why workers refrain from exploring such cues of uncertainty, they tell me that they are afraid that if they bring the doubts out in the open, they will reinforce them. The belief is that the less said the better. In reality, these doubts and questions are valid, and the worker is missing an opportunity to help the client explore them.

Without this exploration, the client may simply not show up at the first meeting even though promising to attend. When the worker later calls, there is much guilt on the client's part and profuse explanation of his absence (e.g., "I really meant to come, only it got so hectic that day it just slipped my mind.")

Returning to the interview with the foster parent, note the turn in the work when the worker reaches for the cue.

WORKER: You sound a bit hesitant. Are you concerned about attending the group? It wouldn't be unusual; most people have a lot of questions about groups.
FOSTER PARENT: Well, you know I never do too well in groups. I find I have a lot of trouble talking in front of strangers.
WORKER: Are you worried that you would have to speak up and be put on the spot?
FOSTER PARENT: I don't mind talking about fostering; it's just that I get tongue-tied in a group.
WORKER: I can appreciate your concern. A lot of people feel that way. I can tell you right now that except for sharing your name, no one will put you on the spot to speak. Some people always talk a lot at the early meetings while others get a good deal out of listening. You can listen until you feel comfortable about speaking. If you want, I can help you to begin to talk in the group, but only when you're ready. I do this all the time with people who feel this way.
FOSTER PARENT: You mean it's not just me who feels this way?
WORKER: Not at all. It's quite common and natural. By the way, are there any other concerns you might have about the group?
FOSTER PARENT: Not really. That was the biggest one. Actually, it doesn't sound like a bad idea at all.

Once again we see the importance of exploring the indirect cue so that the worker has a clearer idea about the source of the ambivalence. Many workers would hesitate exploring the cue because they would feel it was a sign of polite rejection of the group (and the worker). When asked why they assume this unnecessarily, they often reply that they are unsure themselves about their own competency and the quality of the group. They respond to the client's ambivalence with their own feelings. In the case just cited, the fear of speaking in the group needed to be discussed. Knowing that the worker understands and that it is all right to feel this way can strengthen the client to overcome an obstacle to undertaking group experiences. In other cases, it may be memories of past group experience, or horror stories recounted by friends or relatives about harsh and confronting group

encounters, or embarrassment about sharing personal details with strangers. The workers need to clarify the reality when possible, empathize genuinely with the fears, and still attempt to help the client take the first difficult step. With this kind of help from the worker, many prospective group members will be able to overcome their fears and doubts and give the group a try. A source of great support for the client is knowing that the worker understands the feelings.

Now that the worker has completed the group-formation tasks and the clients are ready to attend, the worker needs to turn attention to beginnings and the dynamics of first sessions. These topics are explored in the next chapter.

NOTES

1. For discussion of group formation issues, see Margaret Hartford, *Groups in Social Work* (New York: Columbia University Press, 1972), Chapters 4, 5, and 6; Gesela Konopka, *Social Group Work: A Helping Process* (Englewood Cliffs, N.J.: Prentice-Hall, Inc. 1971), Chapter 6; Dorothy Stock Whitaker and Morton A. Lieberman, *Psychotherapy through the Group Process* (New York: Atherton Press, 1964), Chapter One.

2. William J. Reid and Ann W. Shyne, *Brief and Extended Casework* (New York: Columbia University Press, 1969).

3. Lawrence Shulman, " 'Program' in Group Work: Another Look," in *The Practice of Group Work,* ed. William Schwartz and Serapio Zalba (New York: Columbia University Press, 1971), pp. 221–40.

CHAPTER 9

The Beginning Phase with Groups

Many of the issues related to beginning described in Chapter 3 are equally applicable to first sessions with groups but with an important difference: the individual client must also deal with a new system—the group. The first two central questions for the client in the individual context were "What are we doing here together?" and "What kind of person will this worker be?" In the group context a third question is added: "What kind of people will these other group members be?" Many of the uncertainties and fears associated with new beginnings will be present in a first group session, but they will be increased by the public nature of the engagement. For example, the client's fear of being manipulated by someone in authority may be heightened by the thought that any potential inadequacy in the situation and the resultant humiliation may be witnessed by peers. For this reason, among others, special attention to first sessions is important, so that a proper stage can be set for the work to follow.

In this chapter I present an overview of the general structure of a first group meeting, reviewing some of the underlying assumptions outlined in Chapter 3 and considering some of the unique dynamics associated with group work. The tasks of both the group members and the group worker are outlined and a number of specific skills identified. With this overview as a backdrop, I then illustrate the process by a detailed analysis of a first session of a married couples' group. Chapter 10 addresses the variant elements introduced into the beginning process by the nature of the setting (e.g., hospital ward, residential group home, community action, agency, educational context), the nature of the particular group members (children, preadoptive parents, husbands who have battered their wives), or the particular structure of the group (e.g., single-session information meeting, open-ended group). You will note that as examples introduce variant elements which affect the group worker's movements, they also underline those core elements of group process and worker skill which are present in all group beginnings.[1]

THE DYNAMICS OF FIRST GROUP SESSIONS

Clients begin first group meetings, as they do all new encounters with people in authority, with a certain tentativeness.

Their normal concerns about adequacy and being up to the demands about to be made upon them can be heightened by the fact that the encounter is taking place in public view. Most clients bring to first meetings an extensive fund of group experience (e.g., classrooms, summer camp), many of which are associated with painful memories. We have all either witnessed or experienced the excruciatingly difficult moments in a classroom when an individual student has been singled out to answer a question, solve a math problem on the board, or give some indication of having completed the assignment. One could feel the embarassment of a classmate when exposed to sarcasm as a punitive weapon in the hands of an insensitive teacher. In fact, whereas new encounters in a one-to-one counseling situation generate fears of the unknown, new group encounters tend to reawaken old fears from early experiences.

The requirement of early clarification of purpose, described in individual work, is also central in the group context. The clients' first question will be, "What are we here for?" Once the boundary of the group experience has been clearly described, it will be easier for members to select appropriate responses. Once the expectations of the group worker and the setting or agency within which the group takes place are clear, then the group members' feelings of safety can increase. If purpose remains ambiguous, then all the fears of inadequacy will be increased. As the group starts, the group members will watch the group worker with keen interest. Having experienced the impact of pqwerful people in authority, they know it is important to "size up" this new authority figure as soon as possible. This leads to the clients' second central question, "What kind of person will the worker be?" Until the group members can understand clearly how this worker operates and the way in which they will be affected, they will need to test the worker directly or indirectly. Defenses will remain in position until members are certain that their individual safety is ensured.

All these dynamics are similar to the ones described in Chapter 3 on the beginning of any new helping relationship. However, the major difference now is the presence of other clients. As the group session proceeds, each group member will also be appraising the others. Questions will be many. Who are these other people? Do they have the same problems as I do? Will I be embarassed by finding myself less competent than they? Do they seem sympathetic and supportive, or are there people in this group who may be attacking and confronting? While the client's primary concern in the first session is the group leader, questions about fellow members follow closely behind. Not only do members wonder what they can get out of the experience to meet their own needs, but they also wonder why it is necessary to get help in a group, "How can other people who supposedly have the same problems as I have help me?"

With some of these issues in mind, the worker should design the structure of first meetings to meet certain specific objectives.

(a) To introduce group members to each other.

(b) To make a brief, simple opening statement which tries to clarify the agency's or institution's stake in providing the group service as well as the potential issues and concerns that group members feel urgently about.

(c) To obtain feedback from the group members on their sense of the fit (the contract) between their ideas of their needs and the agency's view of the service.

(d) To clarify the job of the group worker, the worker's task and method of attempting to help the group members' work.

(e) To deal directly with any specific obstacles which may be involved in this particular group's effort to function effectively. For example, dealing with stereotypes group members may bring of either group work, helping people in authority, or dealing with their feelings of anger if the group is involuntary.

(f) To begin to encourage intermember interaction rather than discussion only between the group leader and the group members.

(g) To begin to develop a supporting culture in the group in which members can feel safe.

(h) To help group members develop a tentative agenda for future work.

(i) To clarify the mutual expectations of the agency and the group members. For example, what can group members expect from the worker? In addition, what expectations for their involvement does the worker have for the members (e.g., regular attendance, meeting starting on time)? Such rules and regulations concerning structure are part of the working contract.

(j) To gain some consensus on the part of group members as to the specific next steps; for example, Are these central themes or issues with which they wish to begin the following week's discussion?

(k) To start to encourage honest feedback and evaluation of the effectiveness of the group.

At first glance this list of objectives for a first meeting must appear overwhelming. Actually, many of them can be dealt with quickly, and most are interdependent in that work on one objective simultaneously affects the others. Obviously,

however, these objectives cannot be achieved in the first session unless a clear structure for work is provided. The approach to creating such a structure, which I will illustrate in detail in the remainder of the chapter, is offered as a general statement recognizing that the order of elements and the emphasis may vary depending on the worker, the group members, and the setting.

In the next section I will illustrate a first meeting using excerpts from a videotape recording of the first session of a married couples' group. The next chapter will examine some of the variations which occur on this basic structural theme.

THE COUPLES' GROUP

The group was conducted under the auspices of a community mental health setting.[2] Five couples were referred from a variety of sources. All had experienced problems in their marital relationships, and in each of the five couples, one partner was identified as the "patient." The youngest couple were John and Louise, in their twenties, with two young children. Rick and Fran were in their thirties and had been married for seven years with no children. Len and Sally were in their late forties, had been married for twenty years, and had children in their late teens and early twenties. Frank and Jane were recently married, both having had prior marriages and divorces. Jane's teenage boys were living with them at this point. Finally, Lou and Rose were in their sixties with a number of married children, who in turn, had children of their own. Louise and Rose had recently been inpatients at a psychiatric hospital. Sally had been seen at the hospital and was considering entering as an inpatient. Frank and Jane and Rick and Fran had been referred to the group for marital counseling. Each of the couples had been interviewed individually by one of my two co-workers in the group; however, they were meeting the senior group worker for the first time that evening. My two co-workers, one male and one female, were also present.

The Initial Stage

The group meeting room was carpeted and had comfortable chairs set in a circle. The session was recorded on video cameras placed in an adjoining studio. Cameras and cameramen were on the other side of one-way glass partitions. The couples had met the co-workers in another part of the clinic and had been escorted to the meeting room so that they all arrived at once. The purpose of the videotaping had been explained to the couples, and they had signed written consents prior to the first session. The group workers had tuned in to the impact of the videotaping and had therefore strategized to reach for their reactions at the beginning of the session. As the couples arrived, I met them at the door, introducing myself to each partner and encouraging them to take a seat. Len, Sally's husband, had to miss the first session, as he was out of town on business. Frank and Jane, who had expressed the most ambivalence and uncertainty about attending the group during the week, were not there at the beginning of the session. After everyone was comfortably settled, I began by suggesting that we go around the room so that the members could share their names, how long they had been married, and whether they had any children. I said this would be a way for us to get to know each other.

LOUISE: I am Louise Lewis. We have been married six years, and we have two children.
WORKER: Go ahead, John (speaking to Louise's husband sitting next to her) please share it with the group members. (Point to the rest of the group.)
JOHN: My name is John. (pause)
WORKER: (Smiling) With the same kids!
JOHN: (Laughing along with the rest of the group) Yes, I hope so.

The group members continued around the circle, giving their names and the data on their families. The advantage of introductions is that they help group members break the ice and begin to speak right from the beginning of the group. In addition, the worker conveys to them the sense that knowing each other will be important. Often during these introductions someone will make a humorous comment followed by nervous laughter; however, even these first contributions can help the members settle down. It is important that the minimum of relevant information be asked for at this point, since discussion of contract has not taken place. Group members will have the opportunity later to share the reasons why they have come. This will come after clarification of group purpose which will provide the necessary structure. An alternative approach would be to make a brief statement of purpose before asking for introductions. This could be particularly important if group members had no idea of the purpose of the group.

Following the introductions, I brought up the videotaping issue.

WORKER: I realize you discussed the taping with my co-workers, but I thought I would like to repeat the reasons for taping these sessions and also to give you another opportunity to share your reactions. As you know, this is a training institution and we are involved in teaching other health professionals a number of skills, including how to work with groups. We find it helpful to use videotapes of groups such as these so that new group leaders can have examples to assist them in their learning. In addition, the co-leaders and myself will use these tapes each week as a way of trying to figure out how to be more effective in helping this group work well.

I went on to explain that if segments of the tape were kept, they would have an opportunity to view them and could decide if they wanted them erased. I asked if there was any response, and after a few moments of silence and some verbal agreement that there was no problem, I proceeded. I believed the tapes were still on their minds and would come up again; however, they were not quite ready at this point to accept my invitation.

With this acknowledgement of the taping issue, I moved to begin the contracting process. The first skills involved were similar to those described in Chapter Three: clarifying purpose, clarifying role, and reaching for client feedback. I had prepared an opening statement in which I had attempted to explain the stake the clinic had in providing the group, to identify their potential interest in the work of the group, and to state our roles as workers. This statement had been reworded a number of times with the assistance of my co-leaders until we felt it was jargon-free, short, and direct.

WORKER: I thought I would begin by explaining how we view the purpose of this group and the role that we would be playing, and to get some feedback from you on what you see the sessions to be all about. All of the couples in the group, and there may be one more here later this evening, are experiencing some difficulties in their marriages. This is a time of crisis and not an easy time. The way we see it, however, is that it is also an opportunity for change, for growth, and a chance to make a new marriage right within the one you pres-

ently have. Now we know that isn't easy; learning to live together can be tough. That is why we have this group organized. Essentially, the way we see it, it will be a chance for you to help each other, a sort of a mutual aid group. As you listen to each other, as you share some of the problems, some of the feelings, and some of the concerns, and as you try to help each other, we think you will learn a great deal which may be helpful in your own marriages. So that's pretty much the purpose of the group. Now, for our role as group leaders, we have a couple of jobs. The first is that we are going to try to help you talk to and listen to each other, since it's not always easy to do that, particularly with people you don't know. Secondly, we will be sharing our own ideas along the way about close relationships, some of which may be helpful to you. Does that make sense? Do any of you have any questions about that? Does that sound like what you thought you were coming to? (Most heads were nodding up and down, there were murmurs of yes, John took it a bit further.)

JOHN: That's pretty well what I thought it was. By the way, are those cameras running now? (There was a laugh at this point on the part of all the group members, including John, as tension seemed to be released.)

WORKER: Yes, they are. There are cameras over there, over there, and over there.

JOHN: You shouldn't have pointed them out to me.

WORKER: You know what I find? At the beginning, everyone is very conscious of the cameras, even myself. But after the group gets going for a while, you tend to forget they're there. How about you, John, are you worried about them right now?

JOHN: No! Well, I have thought about them once in a while.

John's acknowledgment of his nervousness about the cameras seemed to help members of the group relax. Sometimes simply identifying the presence of an obstacle such as this one can be helpful in relieving its pressure. It would be a mistake, however, to discuss it in some depth unless the group members pick up on it themselves. It seemed essential to me that they understood that I knew that it wasn't easy to do this work and that I was conscious of their feelings. After there were no other responses to my questions, I decided to move us into the problem-swapping and feedback stage.

WORKER: I thought to get us started, it would be worthwhile to take some time to do some problem swapping. What I would like you to do is to share with each other, for a little while, some of the problems and difficulties you have found between you as couples. I would like you also to share some of the things you would like to see different. How would you like the relationship to be? We can take some time to find out the kinds of issues that you're concerned about and then move from there. Would someone like to start?

The purpose of the problem swapping is twofold. First, it provides the feedback necessary to begin to develop the client's side of the working contract. These are the issues and concerns which will be the starting point for the work of the group. It is quite possible that in the initial stage, group members will share "near" problems which do not bear directly on some of the more difficult and hard-to-talk-about issues. This is their way of testing, of trying to determine how safe it is to use the group. The group worker has to respect and understand their defenses as an appropriate way to begin a new experience. The second function of the problem-swapping exercise is to encourage intermember interaction. For most of their lives clients have participated in groups where the discussion has essentially been between the group member and the leader, the person in authority. This is a long-standing habit. They will need to learn new ways of relating in a group, and the problem-swapping exercise is a good way to start.

As each individual member shares a problem or a concern, the group worker pays attention to his two clients. The first client is the individual who is speaking at the moment. The second client is the group. Attention is paid to the group by monitoring their reactions from their eyes, their posture, and so on. The mediation function of the group worker can be seen in action during this exercise as he encourages individual members to speak to the group and share the concerns they are bringing to the forefront and at the same time helps group members respond to the individual. As group members hear others describing problems, they become better able to identify those issues for themselves. In addition, when they hear their own concerns echoed by other group members, there is some relief at finding out that they are "all in the same boat." The onus that each member may feel over having somehow failed as a human being and as a partner in a marital relationship can begin to lift as they discover that their feelings and their concerns are shared by others.

Silence is not unusual at this point in the first group session. This silence can represent a number of communications, a different one for each group member. Some may be thinking of what they are willing to share with the group at that time. Others may be shy and afraid to be the first one to speak. Still others are expressing their wariness of being put on the spot if they raise a concern, since they do not know how other group members or the leader will react. These are the moments that inexperienced group leaders dread. The silence, they feel, is the beginning of a recurring nightmare they have had about their first group session. They are worried that after making their opening statement and inviting feedback, nobody will speak. It is not unusual for group leaders to take over the group at this point and to offer subjects for discussion or, in some cases, present prepared films or presentations. This, of course, leads to a self-fulfilling prophecy, where the message conveyed to the members by the worker is that although their participation is being asked for, there is no willingness to wait for it.

In the case of the couples' group, Lou, the member in his sixties, had a strong sense of urgency about beginning to work and was ready to jump right in. He was seated directly to the left of the central group worker. As he spoke, he directed his conversation to the other members. He began by describing the problem as his wife's depression. The effect was flat in his voice, and his wife sat next to him stonefaced, without any change in expression. This is a position she held throughout the session, almost until the end, not saying a word, although she appeared to be hearing everything said by others. As Lou spoke, the rest of the group listened intently, obviously relieved that he had started.

LOU: To begin with, as you heard, we have been married for forty-five years. Our relationship has been on a rocky road due in a great degree to tragedies that have happened to our family. While that was a real contributing factor, social conditions, economic conditions, and family relationships were also contributing factors. I'm making this very brief because most of this will come out later on. I think the outline on this will be enough for us to get our teeth into. As a result of the things I have mentioned, Rose, particularly, went into some real depressions. All the threads of her family seemed to go. As a result, it became difficult for her to operate. The problems were so strong, she decided she had to go to a psychiatrist. She went and I went with her for two and one-half years. The psychiatrist opened up some doors for her but not enough to really make her free to operate. The

unfortunate thing about her depression is that it developed into hostility towards me and the children. Now as soon as the depression lifted, as far as she was concerned, things straightened out. As soon as her depression lifted, we had no problems. (This is said emphatically, facing the group worker.) We had differences of opinion, but we had no problems.

WORKER: It sounds like it has been tough for her and also tough for you.

LOU: Oh yes! The unfortunate thing as far as we were concerned is that we did not have a psychiatrist who understood what the relationship was. He took our problems as a family problem. His suggestion after a while was that if we weren't getting along together, we should separate. I felt I really didn't like that because I knew that wasn't the problem. The problem was getting Rose out of her depression.

Lou had begun presenting the problem the way one partner often does in a couples' group. The problem was essentially the other partner who, in some way, needed to be "fixed up." This is the way one partner often experiences things, and it is important that the group worker attempt to understand and express that understanding of the members' feelings as they are presented. In addition, it was obvious that other group members were listening to what Lou had to say and did not mind his going on at some length. Group members begin first sessions with various patterns of behavior. Those who are used to being quiet and withdrawn in new situations will begin that way. Those who are used to speaking and jumping in quickly, such as Lou, will begin that way. Each member is entitled to his own defenses in the beginning, and it is important that the group leader respect them. When a group member speaks for a period of time, keeping to the subject, usually only the leader feels nervous. The other group members are often relieved that someone else has begun the discussion. In this case, the tuning in work from the individual session had alerted us to Lou's strong feelings towards helping professionals who he felt had not been helpful. I had strategized to reach directly if I felt there were indirect cues relating to us, the group workers. I did so at this point in the following way:

WORKER: Are you worried that I and the other group leaders might take the same position with you and Rose?

LOU: Well, I don't know (voice slightly rising with annoyance). I'm not worried; I'm past that stage (accompanied with a harsh laugh). I'm just relating what happened, because I know where I'm at (said emphatically). To be very frank, my opinion of psychiatrists is very low, and I can cite two hours of experiences of what I have been through, my friends have been through, to show you exactly what I mean. This was a good case in point, his making a suggestion that we should separate because of the problem.

WORKER: After forty-five years I can imagine that must have hit you as a terrible blow.

LOU: Well, sure it did.

WORKER: Lou, do you think we could move around the circle a bit and also hear from the others as to what they see some of the problems to be?

In retrospect, I think Lou responded somewhat angrily partly because of the way I made my statement "Are you worried that I and the other group leaders might take the same position with you and Rose?" I wanted to open up Lou's concerns about what kind of workers we would be, however, my attempt was not direct or clear enough. Instead of asking for further elaboration from Lou, or perhaps, asking if others in the group had similar experiences or reactions, I suggested we allow others to exchange problems by "moving around the circle." It is

important to encourage such an exchange of problems, what Schwartz has called "problem swapping;" however, further exploration of the authority theme was also important. Fortunately I had an opportunity to "catch my mistake" later in the session when I returned to the initial concerns raised by Lou. Lou responded to my suggestion that we "hear from the others" by turning to his wife.

LOU: Sure, you're on. Go ahead, dear. (He turns to his wife.)

ROSE: I think I'll pass right now (said in a slow, even way, with no evidence of affect).

WORKER: That's fine. How about some others? You don't have to go in order, and you know, you can also respond to what Lou just said if you like, as well as adding some of your own issues. We won't solve all of the problems tonight; I hope you realize that. (Some laughter by the group members.) But what we would like to try and do is get a feel for how they seem to you right now. That can help us get a sense of what we need to talk about, and I think Lou has helped us get started. (At this point, John takes off his coat and seems to settle back in his chair.)

LOUISE: (John's wife who is now speaking directly to Lou.) I can understand what Lou means because depression has been our problem as well. I have gotten into such a state of depression that I can't function as a mother or a wife. I feel I have lost my identity. (This is all said with a very flat affect.) And I don't think that separation is the answer either. And I have had some pretty bad psychiatrists as well, so I can really feel for you when you say that, Lou. I can understand that. But the problem is to be able to sort out and find out what feelings I really have and recognize them for what they are and try to get myself out of the hole that I fell into, and that's the tough part.

WORKER: How does it affect your relationship with John?

LOUISE: It's very strenuous. There is a lot of strain and tension when I'm sick and down and I put the responsibility for taking care of the household on John's shoulders. There is a breaking point for him somewhere there; I want to catch it before we get there. (Pause, worker is nodding and other members are listening intently.) That's about it. (Brief silence.)

JOHN: Our biggest problem, or Louise's biggest problem, is due to her migraine headaches. She's had them ever since she was five years old. This is where the whole problem stemmed from, those migraine headaches. And this new depression which she seems to have gotten in the last few months.

WORKER: Anything special happen within the last few months?

JOHN: No, it has been actually a very quiet time this summer.

LOUISE: I think it is things that have been festering for a long time.

WORKER: For example?

LOUISE: I don't know. I can't put my finger on what they are.

WORKER: (Speaking to John) This depression came as a surprise to you, did it?

JOHN: Yes, it did.

WORKER: How do you see the problem, John? What would you like to see different in the relationship?

John goes on to describe how they don't do much together as a couple anymore and that he would like to see Louise get back on her feet so they can have some fun the way they use to. Discussion continued around the circle with Fran and Rick looking at each other as if to ask who would go first. I verbalized this, and Fran begged off, saying that she didn't feel comfortable starting right away and that she would get in a bit later. Her husband, Rick, responded to my question by saying he was wondering why he was there because he knows that he has, or rather, they have, a problem, but what the problem is, is hard to define. Fran coached him at this point by whispering in his ear the word "communication." They seemed to agree that that's the problem, and when I asked for elaboration, Rick said, "That's

not my problem, that's Fran's problem." Rick then took a further step for the group by entering a taboo area.

RICK: I guess if you get right down to basics, it would have to be sexual intimacy. I have been going along for a little over seven years, and now I find that I'm all alone. Fran's gone on a trip, and we're really in the very rocky stages of breaking up. (Some shaky emotion in his voice as he is speaking.) For the last six months, we have sort of been trying to recover, but it's still pretty shaky.

WORKER: It must feel pretty dicey for you right now.

RICK: Right. (With resignation in his voice.)

WORKER: What would you like to be different? What would you like to see changed in your marriage?

RICK: (After a deep sigh to get his breath.) There are times when everything is just fine, it seems to be going along smoothly, but just to say what I would like would be tough to put my finger on.

WORKER: How would you like the relationship to be with Fran?

RICK: I think I would like it to be peaceful at all times. We have been getting into a lot of fights and just recently we have been getting into a lot of physical fights. A peaceful relationship, that's what I would really go for.

WORKER: How about you, Fran, do you have any ideas now?

FRAN: No, can we come back to me?

WORKER: Sure.

The discussion continued with Sally talking about her marriage. This was difficult because her husband, Len, was not present. She described it from her perspective. Her description was filled with interpretations which had obviously been gleaned from years of involvement in various forms of analysis. The group listened intently to her stories. She also responded to Louise's comments about migraine headaches, mentioning that she had had them as well, and then she and Louise exchanged some mutual understanding. After Sally finished her description, there was a long silence as the group seemed unsure about where to go.

WORKER: (Turning to Lou) I didn't mean to stop you before, Lou, if you want to get in again.

LOU: No, that's OK (laughing). I could go on for hours.

WORKER: Oh, they won't mind, you know (pointing to the group), they would be glad. (Most of the group members laugh at this.)

LOU: I want to give others the opportunity to speak because, after all, I have been married over forty-five years, so I have an accumulation of incidents.

At this point, I picked up the theme that had been common to many of the presentations: helping people who have not really helped. I had reached for this theme in terms of myself and the other workers earlier in the session, but Lou had not accepted my invitation. I believe the relationship between the group and the group leader is a central question at the beginning of each new group. Some discussion needs to take place on this issue in order to begin to work on what was called in Part I the "authority theme," the relationship between the person who offers help and the person who takes help. It is a powerful factor in the first group session and for the group to develop properly, the worker must begin to deal with it.

During the problem-swapping exercise, I had attempted to express my empathic responses to the concerns as they were raised, taking care not to express judgments on their feelings and actions. Even this brief period had built up a sufficient fund of positive relationship that I was able to reach for some discussion on this difficult theme. If the group was

to start to develop as a healthy organism, it would need to begin to sort out its relationship to me as the leader and the person in authority. Since this is a taboo subject, it would require considerable effort on my part to make it clear that it was open to discussion. I decided to return to the theme of helping people who had not helped. It is important to note that I returned to this issue directly by pointing out to the group members that I thought such a discussion might be important, so that they could be involved with full knowledge of the process. The group discussion which followed, led by Lou who was an internal leader on this issue, was a critical factor contributing to a striking change in the group atmosphere and to its successful beginning.

WORKER: I have noticed a theme that has cut across a number of your presentations which I think is important for us to talk about. A number of you have commented on helping people who have not been very successful, psychiatrists you have had in the past, doctors, etc. (Group members all nod, saying yes.) Can you stay on that for a minute in terms of the things in your experiences you found difficult? The reason I think it is important is because it would be a way of your letting myself and my co-leaders know what you would not find helpful from us.

This is the second time I reached for some comments about the group members' concern about us. This time, since a relationship was beginning, and since I reached in a way that was less threatening, they were ready to take me up. Lou volunteered to begin the discussion. He took us back to the year 1940 when he had his own business. He described some of the pressures on him concerning economic conditions and a rash he developed on his leg. His doctor referred him to a psychiatrist who was brand new at the hospital. It was his first job. Lou's enthusiasm and feelings while describing this experience captured the attention of the group. They smiled and nodded agreement with his comments as he continued his story. As he was about to describe his encounter, the door to the group room opened and the fifth couple, Frank and Jane, arrived late. It is not unusual for group members to arrive late for a first session. It usually presents a dilemma for the group worker: What do I do? In this case, I had the new couple introduce themselve and the other couples give their names as well. I then briefly summarized the contract, explaining that we had been hearing some problems to help get a feel for the concerns that brought the couples to this session, and pointed out that one theme that kept recurring had to do with helping people who had not been very helpful. I said that we were focusing on this right now and that just before they had entered, we had been with Lou in 1940. With that, I turned back to Lou to continue, and the group picked up where it left off. I think that it is important to recognize the entrance of the new group members and help them connect to the group but, at the same time, I think it would be a mistake to take a great deal of time to start again. As will become clear later in the group session, these group members were late for a reason; their lateness was their way of handling a new and frightening experience.

Lou continued his story of his first encounter with the young psychiatrist, indicating that the psychiatrist had tried to lead him indirectly to recognizing that he had a marital problem. As Lou put it, "I was talking about the economic conditions and the problems of the time, and he kept coming back to the wife and the kids, and the wife and the kids, and the wife and the kids . . . until I said to him, 'Are you trying to tell me my problem is with my wife and my kids?' " Lou went on to say that when the psychiatrist indicated it was, he stood up, called him a charlatan and quickly got out of the office as the enraged psychiatrist came out from behind the desk shaking his fist at him.

LOU: OK. I knew that my wife and my family were part of the problem, but I also know that they were not at the core of the problem. They were a contributing factor because of the social and economic conditions. I went to this guy to get rid of this rash on my leg and not to have him tell me that my wife and my kids were giving me the problem. It took a while for the rash to go away, but eventually it did. That was item number one. I am going to skip a lot of the intervening incidents that had to do with families, and I will go to the one which we just experienced recently. We went to a psychiatrist in the community for two and one-half years (and then with emphasis) *two and one-half years!* I knew I had to go with her to give her some support plus I wanted to find out what made her tick. I couldn't understand her depression. I had been down in the dumps and felt blue, but I had never felt depressed as she seemed to feel. He asked her a lot of questions, asked me a lot of questions, tried to have us do some play acting and had us try and discuss the problems. "You're not communicating" was his term. I didn't know what he was talking about when he said we didn't communicate, so we tried to communicate. But nothing really came of it because we saw we weren't communicating.

As Lou related his experiences, he was describing a number of techniques which appeared to have been used to try to help him and his wife deal with their problems. The central theme appeared to be that of a helping person who had decided what the problem was and was now acting in order to educate them as to its nature.

Lou was resentful of this and resisted

it in most of the sessions. And yet, part of him deep inside knew that there was a problem which he attempted to try to deal with in his own way. He described an incident when he had taken a tape recorder home and recorded a conversation with his wife, listening to it later. His description of the aftermath of this tape recording contained the first overt expression of the sadness and pain the couple had felt but were not ready to share. In this case, I believe it was necessary for Lou to share first the anger and the frustration at the helping people who had not understood him before he was willing to share his hurt and pain.

LOU: We talked for about fifteen minutes, and I realized when we played the tape back, that I was screaming at Rose. Now I never realized that I was screaming at her. But I heard my voice (Lou clears his throat at this point and began to choke up, obviously feeling emotions and trying to fight back his tears.) This is a little rough for me, can I have some water?

WORKER: (Getting a glass of water from the decanter) Sure you can, Lou, take your time.

LOU: It's kind of tough to get over the fact that I was screaming at her. Then I realized that when I was screaming at her, I was treating her like a kid. I took this tape to the psychiatrist, and he couldn't hear the screaming. He got nothing out of it.

WORKER: He didn't seem to understand how it felt to you to hear yourself screaming?

LOU: That's right. He didn't even hear me screaming. The other thing he tried to get us to do which I found really devastating is he tried to get us to reverse roles; she should be me and I should be her. OK, we tried it. But while we were doing it, I was thinking to myself: "Now, if that isn't stupid, I don't know what is." (Turning to me at this point.) But you're a psychiatrist, you know what the score is. How can you reverse roles when I'm not feeling like she's feeling and she doesn't feel like I do? How can I communicate? Well, it

was things like that that had been going on for *two and one-half years*, and when we had finished, I was nowhere nearer being helped to be able to live with Rose than I was when we started. *Now that's two and one-half years!* It isn't that we didn't try; both of us used to discuss this. Rose went back to the doctor, but I said I wouldn't go because I found I was just getting more frustrated.

At this point, there was some discussion on the part of group members about the use of the tape recorder. Rick thought it was a good idea and wondered if Lou had tried it again. Lou said he hadn't. The conversation returned to his feelings of frustration and his sense of not being helped.

LOU: I felt stupid. The psychiatrist kept telling me something, and no matter how hard I tried, I simply couldn't understand.

WORKER: You also seem to be saying, not only couldn't you understand him, but he didn't seem to be understanding you.

LOU: Well, yes. Peculiarly enough, that thought had not occurred to me. I felt, well you are a professional (facing the worker at this point), so what you're doing, you're doing on purpose. You know what you're supposed to be doing. And whether you understand me or not is immaterial. That's not what the game is. It's my responsibility to understand what you, if you are the psychiatrist, are saying. (There was anger in his voice.)

WORKER: If you're asking us (referring to the other co-workers) in this group, that's not the way I see it. I think that if we can be of any help to you or the other group members, the help will be in our listening and in our trying to understand exactly how you see it. The gimmicks and the things that seem to get tried on you is not my idea of how we can help. You'll have to wait to see if I mean that.

LOU: Yah, we'll see.

WORKER: I think you folks have a powerful lot of help to give each other. And essentially, what I will try and do is to help you do that. And I'll share my own ideas along the way. But I have no answers or simple solutions.

LOU: Then, well, OK.

(General silence in the group as the members appear to be taking in the meaning of the words.)

CO-WORKER: I'd like to know, Lou, as we go along, how you see things. So, if you're feeling stupid or whatever, you'll let us know.

WORKER: It might be because we're said something dumb (some subdued laughter in the group).

Although I had described the group as a mutual aid group in the opening statement, it was only at this point that the members really began to have a sense of how the group might work. Also, the clarification of the group worker's role contained in this exchange was actually "heard." Lou, playing the role of an internal group leader, was able to articulate the fears and concerns that group members felt about the potential power invested in the group worker's role. He provided the opportunity for an initial clarification of who we were as group leaders and what it is that we did. Skills of accepting and understanding his feelings and his frustrations, and of helping to connect his past experiences to the present moment were crucial in this session. The feeling in the group was that we had moved past the first step in building our relationship. The authority theme was not finished as a topic of discussion; however, one could sense that an important start had been made. Following this exchange, the group members were able to move into work on their contract with more energy, involvement, and intermember interaction.

The Work Continues

With a two-hour session it was possible to move past problem swapping and clarification of purpose and worker role into beginning efforts to focus on an example of what the work might consist of. Interestingly enough, Frank and Jane, the couple who had arrived late, provided an opportunity to do this. Frank began to share, with some elaborative assistance from the group worker, a problem that they were experiencing in relation to his wife's teenage sons living with them at home. It was an interesting example of a group member raising a problem tentatively, moving quickly back and forth between the implications of the difficulty for the couple and his relationship to the children. He spoke of the sexual difficulty they had, while attributing most of it to a medical problem he was having treated and also to the lack of privacy in their home. The bedroom door was not locked at any time, and the children would wander in without notice. As Frank was sharing this dilemma, he phrased it in terms of his problem with the sons, but one could hear throughout the discussion hints of the implications for his relationship to his wife. Each time the worker would acknowledge, even gently, the implication for the relationship, Frank would back off slightly and both he and Jane would be quick to reassure the group of the positive nature of their communications.

It is not unusual for group members to use the early sessions to raise "near" problems in a way which presents them as issues and at the same time defends them from discussion. This matter was discussed in Part I relating to the ambivalence of the client to deal with real concerns. It is also necessary for the group members to test the reaction of a group worker and the other members. Group members often feel it would be unwise to rush right in until they know how their feelings and thoughts are going to be treated, whether they will be met with support or confrontation, and whether it is OK to share the real feelings and concerns. Not only must the members in this group be worried about the worker and the other members, they must also be concerned about their partners. Each of the couples has developed a "culture" in their marriage which has included certain norms, behaviors, taboo areas, rules for interaction, and so on. The group will in many ways be a place for them to learn how to change that culture or at least those parts of it which are not conducive to strengthening their marriage. However, with so many factors to consider, it is not unusual for group members to come close to a concern while watching to see how the partner, the other group members, and the group workers react. Timing is important in a first session, and it would therefore be a mistake for a group worker to attack defenses at a point when the group member greatly needs them.

As Frank began to describe his efforts to deal with the children about this issue of privacy, the worker suggested that they might use this as an example of one of the ways in which they might help each other (speaking to the group): "Perhaps we can use this as an example of how we can be helpful. Frank can describe the conversation he had with his son, and the rest of the group members might respond by suggesting how they would have reacted if they had been the son. We could do some thinking with Frank about how he might handle this kind of an issue." The group members agreed, and Frank went into some details of a conversation when he sarcastically implied to the son that they needed some privacy. After a number of group members supported his right to privacy, the co-worker pointed out that it would be difficult to take his comments seriously because he always seemed to be joking as he described things

and never seemed as if he could really get angry. This triggered a response on the part of his wife, Jane.

JANE: Aha! That's it exactly. Frank has trouble getting angry. Ever since he has been a kid, he has been afraid to be direct and angry with people. I keep telling him, why don't you let yourself get angry and blow off steam? He says that he feels that it is just not the thing to do. You just don't do it. I do it all the time. I didn't use to, but now I do, and I get angry at least a couple of times a day.

FRANK: You know the kids are scared of you because you get angry so much.

WORKER: (Noticing that Sally appears to want to say something) Go ahead, Sally, get in.

SALLY: (Laughing as she speaks to Frank) You've got to meet my Len! (The whole group, including Frank, erupts in a great roar of laughter.) You sound like two of the same kind, and you're hard to live with.

WORKER: Frank, what made it hard for you to speak seriously to your son right then?

FRANK: I don't know. Well, you know the image of a stepfather like in the fairy-tale book, he is like a monster. I've got a nice thing starting to build with these boys, and I don't want to ruin it.

WORKER: You are afraid they would get angry if you were direct and honest.

JANE: (Laughing, but with a touch of anger) It's all up in your head.

WORKER: You know, Jane, I think Frank really is worried about that.

FRANK: I do worry about that. I really do.

In response to the worker's question, "What are you afraid might happen?" Frank goes on to describe the relationship the children had with Jane's former husband, of some of his fears of being unable to prevent the continuation of the same coldness and the problems that he envisioned in that relationship.

FRANK: It was because I didn't want to hurt that relationship that I more or less . . . symbolized what I really meant.

WORKER: You kind of hinted at what you felt rather than saying it directly.

FRANK: Well, it's like you are in a washroom and you saw a fellow peeing on the floor. You would probably say, "Hey you missed, fella." (Group members roar with laughter at his story.)

Frank went on the describe how he finally had to speak directly with the son. He described, much to his wife's surprise, a very direct conversation in which he explained the problem to the son. Frank's point was that since that time, the son had been much more understanding about not interrupting. At this point in the group session, Lou, who had been listening intently, moved in and took responsibility for the group process. In a striking illustration of internal leadership at an early stage in the group development, Lou moved directly from the general discussion of anger and indirect communication to the implications for each couple. The worker had noticed during the discussion that on a number of occasions Lou had attempted to whisper to his wife, Rose, and to ask her a question but she had refused to respond, and instead had sat impassive and expressionless. Lou now used the group and this theme to deal with his concern, a concern which was common to all members. I believe that he was able to make this direct intervention and assume some leadership responsibility in the group because the way had been cleared through our earlier discussion of the role of the worker. This was an example of Lou taking the worker's invitation for the group members to begin to own their own group.

WORKER: (Noting Lou's indirect communication of his desire to get into the discussion) Were you going to say something, Lou?

LOU: Something has come up here which I would like each couple in turn to answer if

they can. (Turning to John, he asks his name which John gives him.) I would like each couple to add to this in turn if they can. John, do you get really mad at Louise? I mean really mad, peed off? Do you yell at her, do you tell her off?

JOHN: Not really.

LOU: Why not?

JOHN: That's my style, that's the way I have been all my life.

LOU: Louise, how about you?

LOUISE: I'll probably hold back until as long as possible and then usually end up to where I'm in tears, or slam cupboards or dishes, or give John a cold shoulder rather than coming right out and saying that I'm angry. (As Louise is speaking, Lou is nodding and saying yes.)

LOU: Why? By the way, I am referring to Rose and myself right now when I'm asking this question and I . . . want to . . . hear from everyone.

JOHN: It happens sometimes, but it is really rare that we actually yell at each other. (Louise shaking her head and agreeing.)

LOU: Are you *afraid* to get angry, either one of you?

JOHN: I don't think I'm afraid. I don't have a problem yelling at other people. It's kinda strange. I don't know why.

LOU: How about you, Frank and Jane?

Jane and Frank both discussed her getting angry regularly, blowing her top all the time. She indicated that it worried her. Frank said he had trouble getting angry directly at Jane and gave an example of her not sharing her load of chores (they are both working) and that he had been getting angry at that because it was setting a bad example for the kids, but that he had not told her. He paused when he said that, and then said, "I guess I hadn't said that to you until tonight." As the conversation went on, the group worker was monitoring the members, making sure they were involved and paying attention. Occasionally he would comment on some of the feelings which were associated with the comments.

LOU: (Directly to Jane) You have no aversions about getting mad, I mean spontaneously mad?

JANE: What other way is there to get mad?

LOU: You don't build anything up and then have it boil over?

JANE: Not any more, not now.

After a pause, the worker turned to Lou and said, "Stay with it." Lou responded, "Fine, because something is happening here that happens to us (pointing to his silent wife, Rose) and I would like to hear from everyone in the group on this." At that point he asked Fran, who had declined to speak thus far, if she got mad.

FRAN: I hold it for a little while, and then I start and I pick, and I can't stop at the issue. Often I can't even determine what the issue is at the time. Since I can't figure out what it is, I go through the whole gamut to make sure I get to the right one. And—maybe I should let Rick speak for himself—my opinion is that he's quiet. He listens to all of this without a comment back. That really drives me out of my mind. I can't stand the silence. If only he would yell! Even if I'm wrong, then I know I'm wrong. But like I said, I go over the whole ball park because I know I may hit the right one, since the right one is in there somewhere. There's not much of a reaction, because Rick is the quiet type. He doesn't like to argue or fight. And the quieter he seems to get, the angrier I get. I have to push even harder. It's just recently, the last couple of months, that we've started to fight physically. We've been married for seven years, and this is just coming out now. Well, I didn't think that Rick had a breaking point and that he could get that mad. And I wasn't even aware that I could get that mad, but I can. I'm the pusher, I'm the one—the things that I could say could definitely curl your hair.

RICK: She basically said it all for me.

FRAN: And that's usual, too.

LOU: (Smiling in a supportive way) Your hair looks pretty straight to me, Rick.

RICK: (Sighing) It's been a long day. Yes, I am the quiet type, and I have a very long fuse, but once it gets to the end, look out. I've done some stupid things in my time, and they usually end up costing me. I guess I just reach my breaking point and take the frustration out somewhere. If it happens that Fran is taking hers out on me, I try and cool it as long as I can, but then I can only take so much of that, and we end up going at each other. That's about it.

LOU: Let me ask you a question, Rick. When Fran is at you like she does, is it that you don't want to or are you afraid of hurting her feelings so that she'll come back at you again and this thing will snowball, or is it that you have a reluctance and you feel you'll let her get it off her chest and then things will calm down again? Which of these is it?

RICK: I guess I'm just hoping that she'll get it off her chest and things will calm down again. But it doesn't work that way.

WORKER: (Turning to Lou) If I can just ask Rick this before you go on, Lou—what's going on inside of your guts when Fran is pushing that way? What do you feel?

RICK: (Takes a big sigh before he speaks) Well, I guess I'm trying to just block everything out of my mind. That's the reason I become quiet, even go to the point of reading the newspaper and just completely try to wipe it out.

WORKER: Because it hurts?

RICK: Right.

Lou continued, turning to Sally, who also described how she saw herself in Fran since her husband, Len, is like Rick, the quiet type. She described a number of similar examples, finally ending by saying, "I don't think I have ever found his boiling point. Heaven help me if I ever do."

WORKER: That must be as hard as having found it.

SALLY: Yes, I guess it is. The problem is

that you hoard the hurts and when you get a chance, zap, you give them right back. The sad part is that I really don't think Len has a mean bone in his body.

There is a long silence after this as the group waits in anticipation. The next speaker should be Rose, Lou's wife, who has not said a word nor changed her expression during the entire session. She has been watching and listening intently. Because of her silence, her comments at this point have a stunning impact on the group members as well as the group worker.

ROSE: Well, I think there is a common thread running through with everyone and part of it is anger, and there may be some recriminations amongst the couples here. Some people have learned to live with it, but obviously, those of us here have not. And no matter how long you're married, it's still something you don't know how to handle. I found that I got very angry here and . . .

WORKER: You mean here tonight?

ROSE: Yes, but I wasn't going to interrupt my husband to tell him that I didn't want him to say that or I didn't like what he was saying. So, I'm back to zero not just one. I can pack my bags and go back to the hospital. (At this comment, her husband, Lou, flinches almost if in pain and looked towards the worker.) And I don't feel comfortable talking about it.

WORKER: It's hard even now, isn't it?

ROSE: Yes, but I made up my mind I was at the point where I would pack my bags or talk.

WORKER: I'm glad you talked.

LOU: (His face brightening) Well, I have been thinking that that was about the only way I could get Rose to talk and to burst open.

ROSE: Sure, well, I knew that's what was going on.

LOU: She wasn't going to say anything to me. I asked her during the group if she was mad, and she said she was. I asked if she would say something, and she said no.

ROSE: Right, I said no.

LOU: Plus the fact that what goes on is that all our lives both of us have always been afraid of hurting each other.

ROSE: So, we kept quiet. Or else one spoke and said too much, I always felt that Lou had spoken lots more than I did. Now I had an opportunity to do a lot of speaking at the hospital for five weeks, and certainly I found it helped me quite a bit. I told myself and the people there that I was going to try and remember to use everything they taught me. And there's really no way. Because different things come up and, say they're not in the book that I went by.

WORKER: I guess you have to write your own book then.

ROSE: That's right. I'm not very quick on my feet, and I don't think my mind operates very quickly either. But how to deal with anger seems to be everyone's particular problem. (A pause in the group as Rose's words sink in.)

WORKER: It's close to the end of our session, and I wonder if what we haven't done is identify a common theme and issue that we might want to look at in more depth next week. Perhaps you could be prepared to share some of the incidents and difficulties, because I think if you can bring some of those arguments from the outside into here, where it is a little safer, and where there are people around to help, maybe it's possible to learn to do what Rose did just now without hurting. Perhaps it is possible to say what you are really thinking and what you're feeling without having to store up the hurts. My own feeling is that any real, intimate relationship has to have both some loving and some fighting. That comes with the territory. But it's a hard thing to do. We simply haven't learned how to do it. So maybe this could be a safe area to test it out. Does that make any sense to the rest of you? (Group members nodding.) Maybe we could pick up on this next week as something that we're interested in. How do you find a way of saying what you're really thinking and feeling towards each other without wiping each other out?

JANE: Is there a way to do that?

WORKER: I think so, but why don't we test that out here in the group? If there isn't, though, then I think we're in trouble, because I don't think you could really care for each other if you can't also get angry at each other. Does that make some sense to the whole group? (Once again, there is some nodding in agreement.) What we could do is different couples could bring some examples. Maybe you'll have a hard time during the week that's tough to handle. Well, we could go over that with you here in the group and see if we can find a way of helping you identify what you were really feeling and also be able to say it directly and clearly in a way that keeps communication open. I think this is the way it would work. Even if one couple raises a specific example, the rest of us could learn in helping them with that example. So, you would get something out of each week's session even if you weren't talking about your own marriages.

With a clear contract and some work in the beginning of the session which helped create the safe conditions within the group, group members felt free to begin to risk themselves. The group has moved directly to one of the core issues in marital relationships. What is striking is the way the group members themselves directed the emergence of this theme. Each group is different, since it reflects the strengths and experiences as well as the weaknesses of its members. Lou brought a sense of urgency and a willingness to risk himself to the group that helped it not only tackle the issue of authority directly and constructively but also helped it to move past its early defenses into the common concerns they had about their relationships with each other. Although this particular way in which this group worked during its first session is unique, I do not believe the level of its work or the speed with which it began is at all unusual. I believe it reflected the urgency of the group members, the clarity of group purpose and worker role. The member's willingness to attack the issue of authori-

ty directly, and the worker's consistent efforts to articulate the feelings expressed by the group members, even being slightly ahead of them. Given these core conditions, the impetus of the group members carried them towards productive work.

The Ending and Transition Stage

Now that the session was nearly over and a consensus had been reached on a theme for additional work, the ending and transition phase of this session continued with an opportunity for evaluative comments. The worker wished in the first session to encourage members to talk about the way the group was working.

WORKER: We have five minutes left. This was our first session. I would like you to take a few minutes to share with each other and with us what your reactions are. What are your feelings and your thoughts? How has this session hit you? What will you be saying to each other on your way home in the car about this evening's session? It's important that you say it now.

ROSE: Well, I have the feeling that the first thing out the door, Lou is going to ask me what it is he said that made me angry. I can't define it right now. I'd have to pull it out of my head.

LOUISE: That's tough. That's really tough trying to figure out what it is that makes you angry. I feel that way, too. When I was an inpatient and someone showed me that I was angry at a resident and why I was angry, well that was fine; I was able to do a little bit of yelling and get it off my chest. But it's not always easy to put my finger on what it is I'm feeling.

WORKER: Maybe that's what we can do here—help you figure out what those feelings are. (Turning to Lou) What's your reaction? I'm really interested in your reaction because I have a feeling that you came in here thinking about all of the people in the past who haven't been helpful. Where do we stand so far?

LOU: So far I feel that we're beginning to break a little new ground. Actually, the most important thing that happened to me tonight was Rose getting mad.

WORKER: Is it easier to handle it when you know where she stands?

LOU: No, not really, I don't know where she stands. I knew she was mad; I asked her to tell me what she's mad about, but she said no. The reason I am feeling good about this is that she has just gone through five weeks as an inpatient, and I can assure you (voice cracking) I've just gone through the same five weeks.

WORKER: I think these things change step by small step and perhaps tonight made a beginning. Perhaps if you aren't too harsh with yourself and demand too much, you have a chance of doing it. I am glad it hit you that way. How about the others, what will your reactions be tonight?

FRANK: Whew!

JANE: (Laughing) I think we were so apprehensive about what would happen here tonight it wasn't funny.

WORKER: What were you afraid of?

JANE: Well, I guess it was the fear of the unknown, and yet when we got here, we immediately started to sense that here are people who are concerned, who care, and this came right to the fore.

LOU: Larry, I'd like to make a comment here. Our youngest son is thirty-six, and one of the things he complained about to us was that "You never taught me how to argue with my wife." I wondered where in the world did he get the idea that it was necessary to argue with each other. As time went on, I realized that we used to argue and keep things on the inside. My son today is having problems, and he even called me last night on the very same subject. The important thing he said was, "You haven't taught us how to argue," oh, yes . . . not only that but "you haven't taught us how to argue and to win the argument." (The group roared with laughter.)

Other members of the group were given a chance to comment. Frank pointed out that he and Jane were late partly because they were ambivalent about coming. He had been telling the co-worker all week that he wasn't sure whether he really belonged here. As he described his conversations, he laughed along with the other members of the group. They all acknowledged that coming to the first session was frightening. Frank went on to say that what impressed him was the people in the group; they all seemed to be a really "super bunch," and that helped a lot. Louise commented that it was reassuring to find out that she wasn't alone and that others had the same feelings.

After some additional positive comments, I pointed out that it would also be important to share their negative reactions or questions; these were tough to share but were also important. Sally indicated her concern about whether or not the group would really help, if anything would really change. She was also worried about her husband Len having missed the first meeting. We talked about this, and I asked the group to strategize how we might bring Len into the second meeting quickly, since he would be feeling a bit like an outsider, having missed this first session. I then told Sally that there were no promises, no sure answers or easy solutions. Marriage is hard work, as she knew, but perhaps through the group we might be able to offer some support and help with their difficult tasks. She nodded in agreement. Fran and Rick responded that they had felt a bit shy and found it difficult to talk in the group. John and Louise jumped in and reassured them, saying that they thought they had participated quite a bit. I pointed out that they had risked some very difficult and hard-to-talk-about subjects in the discussion with the group and gave them credit for that. Rick said that after a week or two he would probably find it easier getting in; I told him to take his time, that he would get in as he felt comfortable.

As the evaluation seemed to be coming to an end, I pointed out that there were three rules we would follow in the group. I explained that members were expected to come each week and that it was OK to come even if your partner could not make it because of illness or some other reason. I said that material they shared with each other should be treated as confidential so that they could all feel that the other couples in the group would not be talking about them to outsiders. I also asked that if they wanted to drop out of the group at any time before the twenty-three sessions we had planned were over, they would agree to come back and discuss it with the group before quitting. All agreed that these seemed to be reasonable rules. I then complimented them on what I thought was an excellent start. I told them I could understand how nervous they must have felt at the beginning, since I felt a little of that nervousness, too, but that I thought they were off on some important work, and that boded well for our future. The session ended at this point but people did not leave immediately; instead they milled around talking to other members and the workers. Then, slowly, the group members left the room.

This has been a detailed description of the first session of one kind of group. Many of you will be immediately thinking about some of the differences in the groups you lead. For example, these were generally articulate group members. They had volunteered to come to the group session and were not there under duress. The group leaders carried no additional functional responsibilities in relation to them, (e.g., a child welfare protective function). Of course, there are differences between groups depending upon the setting, the members, the purpose, and so forth. Some of these are illustrated in the next chapter with brief excerpts from first sessions of groups from different contexts. Nonetheless, I believe the basic dynamics and skills involved in effective beginnings with groups cut across these differences. You will find in the illustrations which follow that when the principles I have outlined are respected, they more often than not lead to an effective start. When these principles are ignored, they haunt both the group leader and the group members. First sessions are important because they lay a foundation, a groundwork for difficult tasks to follow. If handled well, they can provide a fund of positive feeling as well as a clear framework, both of which will have important influence on the remaining sessions.

NOTES

1. For discussion of contracting in groups, see Alex Gitterman, "Group Work in the Public Schools," in *The Practice of Group Work,* ed. William Schwartz and Serapio Zalba (New York: Columbia University Press, 1971), pp. 45–72; Charles Garvin, "Complementarity of Role Expectations in Groups: The Member-Worker Contract," *Social Work Practice, 1969* (New York: Columbia University Press, 1969); Louise P. Shoemaker, "The Use of Group Work Skill with Short Term Groups," *Social Work with Groups* (New York: National Association of Social Workers, 1960), pp. 37–51.

2. The setting, names of the members, and some of the details of the discussion have been changed to protect the confidentiality of group members. The process is described as it was recorded on a videotape record of the group maintained for teaching purposes with the permission of the members.

CHAPTER 10

First Group Sessions:
Some Variations

The previous chapter identified a number of common dynamics and skills related to first group meetings. However, not all groups are composed of articulate adults attending voluntarily. I will now consider the most important variant elements which may affect the workers' strategy. Basically, these can be broken down into the following five categories: the age and relative articulateness of the members, the authority of the worker, the specific concerns of the clients, the setting of the encounter, and the impact of time. Each of these variations is illustrated with extracts from first sessions of appropriate groups. Thus, I have used work with adolescents and grade-school children to illustrate the first category; work with women on welfare and prospective adoptive parents to illustrate the impact of authority; groups of parents of children with cerebral palsy, foster parents, depressed psychiatric outpatients, and widows in a community center program for the effect of specific purpose; a residential lounge committee, a ward group in a general hospital, and a newly formed tenants' group for the importance of setting; and finally, the first session of a short-term group with single

parents. Throughout these very different examples a common theme runs through them all: the need for the worker to contract clearly with the group, even with a group such as the last, which has its own, elected internal leader, a chairperson.

The examples also serve to show some of the events which can occur for which the worker is not always prepared (e.g., when only one client arrives on time and the others show up at twenty-minute intervals). The first sessions included demonstrate a range of worker skill levels to provide contrast, to illustrate how one can catch mistakes, and to reassure readers who are new to group work and who might be intimidated by first sessions that seem to go too easily.

FIRST SESSIONS WITH
ADOLESCENTS AND CHILDREN

The problem of lack of clarity of purpose or embarrassment about making a direct statement of purpose, discussed in Part I, is even more common in the group context. The presence of more than one client may increase the reluctance of the worker to be direct. In this extract, note the worker's reliance on safe and generalized topics in her opening statement to a group of foster adolescents in a child welfare agency:

I opened the discussion by telling all the members that what was said in these groups would remain confidential. Neither workers nor foster parents would ever know what was being discussed. In addition, I pointed out that the same sort of commitment would be required on their part. I then mentioned the kinds of things we could discuss; for example, such as the trouble they have making their allowances stretch and whether or not the clothing allowance was sufficient. There followed a great period of silence, at which point I suggested that if they could think of nothing else, perhaps they would like to talk about the lack of conversation (which seemed to be a little too far advanced for the group to handle).

Nothing in the worker's statement recognized that they were all foster children. The examples she used could have been drawn from any discussion group for teenagers, and yet they all knew that they were foster and that this group was sponsored by a child welfare agency. The worker omitted any comment about her role in the proceedings. The silence probably reflected their confusion about the group purpose and their reluctance to begin. The worker's comment about the silence could reflect her own anxiety about their lack of immediate enthusiasm. In the rest of this session the discussion was marked by the wide shifts in subject matter with youngsters talking both about related topics (e.g., trouble with foster parents) and totally unrelated ones (e.g., TV shows). In an illustration from another group, we see how the lack of clear contracting in the opening of a session came back to haunt the group leader. In this case the group consisted of older teens who had recently left the care of foster parents or group homes and were starting

to live on their own (although still legally wards of the agency) or who were about to do so. The age and relaxed attitude of the members encouraged spontaneous conversation that lulled the worker into skipping the contracting work:

There was no official opening as the group began prior to the arrival of the last member. They discussed common issues such as Grade 13, schools, and then talking somewhat about their present life styles—living in a foster home or living on their own. When Frank entered late, he picked up on the flow of the conversation. Because of the easy flow, I did not intervene with an official contract, preferring to encourage them to interact with one another.

CONNIE: How long have you been in care?
DIANE: Since I was three.
CONNIE: That is a long time.
CAROL: Since I was fifteen. I just made it, because I was almost sixteen years old. (A short silence followed.)
WORKER: And you, Connie?
CONNIE: I'm not sure. I came and then went again. About six years old, I guess. (Discussion followed about where they lived and how they felt about their foster parents.)
CONNIE: Did you notice those ads on TV asking for foster homes?
WORKER: How did they strike you?
CONNIE: What do you mean?
WORKER: Well, you are a foster child. I was wondering if they affected you?
CONNIE: I think it's a good idea. If you need a foster home, that's a good way to get one.

The discussion continued, covering many issues without staying on any one for very long. The worker's request that Connie elaborate on the effect of the TV ads was politely declined because she had no way of knowing why he was asking. The issue of contract became explicit at the "doorknob" as the worker attempted to end the meeting.

WORKER: What about next week?.

DIANE: I want to come back. I have a lot to learn about loans and money and how to manage. We could meet until we are tired of meetings or don't have anything else to say, but I don't want it to be like last year in a group where we really didn't talk about anything. It got boring.

JOHN: Well, I don't know. I like to hear from the other kids, but I don't have any real problems since I was discharged.

DIANE: Well, what is the purpose of this group? Why are we coming?

WORKER: We thought you might be having some problems because of your discharges, and we wanted to give you a chance to help each other. We were concerned with how you are coping with this problem.

CAROL: At first I thought maybe you were checking up on us to find out how we were doing.

WORKER: Sounds like you were rather suspicious.

CAROL: Yes. (Laughter followed.)

WORKER: No, we really do care. We just want to help you in any way we can.

CAROL: Yes, I can see that now.

The worker could have eased their concern about the purpose early in the session by interrupting their conversation with these brief words about purpose. Only at the end of the session did members have a clear framework for selecting their responses and understanding why the worker asked certain questions. This worker caught her mistake in the same session. Sometimes, however, it is necessary to come back at a later session and initiate the contracting discussion. In the following illustration a worker recontracted during the second session of a discussion group for adolescents attending a training workshop which dealt with work-related problems. The first meeting had been difficult, marked by acting out behavior from the members with the worker finding herself playing a police role. The

acting out behavior, in fact, reflected their lack of understanding about the purpose of this mandatory group and their resultant anxiety.

WORKER: OK. Let's get started. I overheard Roy sigh as he sat down and said, "Boy, is this boring." (Roy grinned and looked surprised.)

WORKER: I don't think he is the only one who feels this way. Last week, after our meeting, Jimmy expressed doubts about whether this could be a good group. (Silence)

JIMMY: I just meant that Lou could make us shut up and stop fooling around if he were here.

WORKER: Is that what you want me to do?

JIMMY: Well, yah. (Others agreed with him.)

WORKER: I don't think it's the leader's job to force everyone to listen and get involved. I'll help but not take that on entirely as my own job.

JAMES: You know what we need in the workshop—filing cabinets to store the cards in. (Everyone agreed and they all started talking at once.)

WORKER: Things are getting out of hand again. (Silence)

ROY: Say something, will you!

WORKER: What do you want me to say?

ROY: Anything!

WORKER: I guess it's hard for us to get down to what we are really here to do.

ROY: Well, what are we here to do? I didn't even know about this until last week when Dennis told me it was time to go to the group about the workshop.

JAMES: I know why we are having the meetings. To get the filing cabinets and stuff like that.

WORKER: I think that's part of it, James. But there is another part to these meetings. It's a place where we can talk about what is going on in the workshop, what some of the problems might be for you down there, and also make connections from the workshop experience to the world of work outside. That is where you are all going eventually. You can relate past experiences you have had out there to what is going on here.

(They all agreed this would be a good idea.)

JAMES: I'm here 'cause I got fired for always coming in late.

And so the work began as soon as the members had some clarity about the purpose and an idea of what the worker was *not* going to do (i.e., serve as a police officer). In the next example the contrast is sharp. The worker began with a clear statement about group purpose and her role. The group members, adolescent unmarried mothers residing in a shelter awaiting the birth of their babies, took up her offer immediately.

I started off the group session by welcoming everybody. I also asked their permission to use the tape recorder for my own learning (they agreed). I said that they were probably wondering what the group was all about. We had found that upon entering the home, many girls became more aware of the difficulties of their pregnancy and the decisions they had to make. We believed that by talking about common problems together, they could help each other. I said that I was there to help them get started and to clarify agency policy. This was their group—I wondered where they wanted to start.

Carol (she had been told she had to attend the group) immediately jumped in. She wanted to know if it was true that there were financial resources available to help you keep your child. I said that the city welfare and mothers' allowance were available. Leslie said that she had looked into this and she proceeded to explain how this operated. I asked Carol if she was thinking of keeping her baby. She said she wanted to, but she also wanted to attend school. I wondered who would care for her child while she attended school. Carol said probably a day care center. An animated discussion began about day care. Andrea said she was giving up her child because she did not feel that you should keep your child if you were not home to care for it. Kate said she

was planning to give up her child because she was not ready to stay home with it. I wondered if Carol was saying that this was a very difficult decision and that she felt like keeping and relinquishing her child at the same time. Carol said that she was not responsible enough to care for a child and that a child limited your life. Andrea felt that you might grow to resent the child which would be unfair. She did not feel ready to be a parent. Carol said that she could be quite rational about the baby, but she was afraid of the emotional appeal of the baby. I wondered if others in the group felt the same way. There was some nodding of heads, and Andrea and Kate said out loud that this scared them. I said that I could understand this feeling. Carol said she should have gone on the Pill. She proceeded to explain that the youth of today are sexually active. She said she kept putting it off (taking the Pill). Several of the girls said together, "It couldn't happen to me." Everyone laughed or smiled. (Marie, Lisa, and Connie had not said anything, but they appeared interested and laughed with the rest of the girls.) Kate said that she had broached her mother about taking the Pill but had received a cold, negative response. Andrea said she does not know how she could have been so naive and think it would not happen to her. She said that the hard thing now was that her parents were blaming themselves for her pregnancy. She said that she had tried to tell them that she was responsible for her own actions, but she did not think she was successful. She feels to blame now that all of the other kids' freedom in the family would be curtailed because of her. Carol said that her father has not spoken to her since learning of the pregnancy, but her mother has been telling Carol's thirteen-year-old sister not to follow in her sister's footsteps. A discussion followed about why each of the girls came to the home.

As the group members sensed their ability to use this group to deal with their concerns, they quickly accepted the worker's invitation to make it "their group." The worker concentrated on helping them to elaborate their thoughts ("I asked Carol if she was thinking of keeping her baby"), gently confronting them ("I wondered who would care for her child while she attended school"), articulating their feelings, particularly the ambivalence ("I wondered if Carol was saying that this was a very difficult decision and that she felt like keeping and relinquishing her child at the same time"), generalizing to the group ("I wondered if others in the group felt the same way"), and acknowledging their feelings ("I said I could understand this feeling"). As the session drew to an end, the worker identified the themes of concern raised by the members, attempted to develop a consensus on where to start the next session, complimented them for their work, and reached for their evaluation.

I said that we had covered many topics, day care, the Pill, family, abortion, welfare, etc. I said they had worked well. Kate said, "Is it over? It went so fast!" I said that I was pleased that Kate seemed to be saying that she got something out of the group. How did the rest feel?

Carol said it helped her to know that others felt as she did about abortion. She was not the only crazy one. Kate said that it helped to talk. Then, she turned to Linda and said, "How come you didn't say anything?" Andrea said, "That's because you talked too much." I said some people found it easier to talk in a group than others. I wondered where they wanted to start next week. Kate made several halting attempts until she was finally able to say that she was interested in how others would see her after this was all over, particularly men. The agreement to tackle this subject seemed unanimous.

Ambiguity in contracting is common in work with children's groups. A good example is the "activity group" in a school setting for children who are having difficulty with schoolwork or peers. A common problem with such groups results from having borrowed a traditional view of group work from the original group settings which were leisure time agencies, settlement houses, community centers, and the like. In this view, while members attended programs for what seemed like recreational purposes, the group leader actually had a "hidden agenda" related to agency purposes. In the school setting, the group worker might contract with the school administration to lead "clubs" which are to be used as a vehicle for "teaching the youngsters how to get along better with each other and how to manage their own activities." A worker would argue that this would help the children get along better in school. The group would be viewed by the worker as a medium to "change the group members' patterns of behavior." The assumption is that a transfer of training will occur, and the learning from the group experience will make the child a better student. A further assumption is that the worker can influence the group members indirectly using the group activity as a medium for the "real purpose." Both assumptions are questionable.

I have written elsewhere about the ways in which group members can use activities (singing, games, crafts, etc.) as important tools in their work.[1] There are many routes whereby group members can provide mutual aid for each other; certainly, it would be a mistake to view words as the only significant medium of exchange between people. My argument here challenges the view that program activity is the worker's tool for "changing" group members. For instance, workers may withhold the real purpose of the group, leaving the members unclear as to the reason for the activity. However, when the youngsters look around during the first session, they *know* who the other children are and that they are the "losers," the "bad kids," or the "dummies" in the school. Because the contracting is not straightforward and honest, they become more anxious, often acting out their anxiety in disruptive behavior. The worker may assume that this behavior is intended to "test" authority or see it as an example of why the members have been referred in the first place. Early sessions may involve a great deal of limit setting by the worker, resulting in a battle of wills between the leader and the group. An alternative pattern is that the youngsters may involve themselves quickly in the group activities which they say are "a lot more fun than school." The worker then finds it harder to deal with school problems directly. Since the worker's promise to the teachers and the principal was that the group would "change" the child's school behavior, the worker may be in trouble with the school staff when this does not happen and may then have to defend the rationale for the group against attacks by staff who view the group activities as "rewards for the kids for bad behavior."

By honestly contracting with the school and the children from the beginning, much of this difficulty can be avoided. Group work is not magic. The youngsters cannot be "cured." The group worker can help children who are having difficulty making it in the school by providing them with an opportunity to talk about whatever goes on in school that makes it hard for them. For example, students often feel their teacher is "down" on them or does not like them. Efforts by the teacher to encourage better levels of work may be experienced by the students as "being picked on." The group might provide a means for helping the members to see the teacher's actions in new ways and a place where they can figure out how to talk to

the teacher more directly about their feelings. In turn, the group worker can meet with the teachers to help them understand the students' perspective. This might help the teachers reach out in a different way to these particular children. The group worker has a part in these proceedings, the teachers have a role to play, and most important, the children will also have to work on improving their situation at school. Other issues may include peer relationships (e.g., fights or feelings of rejection which interfere with school activity) or the impact of the family (e.g., how hard it is to concentrate in the mornings when you have just had an argument with your mother and the teacher does not understand how upset you are).

The important point is that both the school staff and the group members understand that the group is formed to help them use school more effectively and to make learning more fun. When teachers see that this focus is central to the work, they are more willing to accept that change may come slowly. They can see the group as essentially related to their educational purposes and therefore worth an investment of time and effort. When group members are clear about the real purpose of the group, they are better able to use both it and the worker to deal directly with their school concerns. In some cases, group activities may be part of the way the group operates, and the leader can contract to help the members see how their attitude to issues in the group (e.g., cooperation on projects) often reflects the patterns they have developed in the classroom and which get them into trouble. In the following example, a new group worker started to clarify purpose directly with a group of twelve-year-old grade-school boys who are in trouble in their school.

WORKER: I'm Frank, a social worker with the Riverview Youth Services. We try to help kids who are having troubles with their school and their families. The reason I'm meeting with you guys is that your teachers feel you're not having as much fun out of school as you can. I thought we might be able to help by talking about some of the problems and seeing if we could figure out a way of making school more fun. What do you think?

KEVIN: Yeah, I know what you mean.

WORKER: This is going to be your group. You guys will make the decision about what we talk about and what we do, and you will have to come up with the answers to your problems yourself. I make suggestions and I'll make sure we don't go flying all over the place so that nobody gets hurt.

GEORGE: (Smiling) Like if we get into a rumble?

WORKER: Yeah, I'll make sure no one gets thrown through the window (the members laugh). What we will talk about is how to make school more fun.

KEVIN: I was in a group last year. A few of us used to go to a classroom, and Mr. K. used to help us with our math.

WORKER: This group won't be like that. I'm not a teacher, so I won't be teaching you math or spelling or anything like that. But what we can do is talk about problems you might be having with teachers or with other kids that are making it hard for you to learn.

DAVE: I was having problems in my class. I had the same teacher as my older sister and she used to always get A's.

WORKER: And you don't.

DAVE: Yeah!

WORKER: It must be hard having the same teacher when she expects you to do the same as your sister.

DAVE: Yeah, 'cause I'm different.

The group members were trying to sort out what type of group this would be and what kind of authority person this leader would be. They attempted to match this experience with others in their lives. The worker used this to help describe what

they would do. Further clarification might consist of examples of how the help could work in the group. For instance, the worker can prepare a sample problem, a hypothetical situation for them to discuss (e.g., suppose you had a fight with a kid during recess because he was bugging you in class, only the teacher didn't see that part, she only saw you hit him back). The examples help the youngsters get a sense of the type of problems they might bring to the group and how other group members and the worker can help them "think it through and come up with some ideas about what to do." In the group just described, the discussion moved to the issue of confidentiality as the worker discussed the importance of his being able to share information with teachers and the principal. Group members expressed fears which he explored, working out an agreement as to how he would communicate and how they could be involved in deciding on what teachers and their principal needed to hear. They agreed that it would not do much good if their complaints were not heard, and the worker assured them that he would try to do it in a way that did not get them into more trouble. Part III of this book discusses systems work and some of the dynamics involved in providing feedback to teachers, doctors, and other system representatives.

THE IMPACT OF AUTHORITY ON THE FIRST SESSION

The authority of the worker is always an issue in the first session. In some settings it can take on increased importance when the agency, and therefore the worker, carries functional responsibilities that may have a profound impact on the client. Examples of workers with these additional functions include parole officers, child welfare workers in abuse situations, welfare workers dealing with income assistance, and adoptive workers who make judgments about who can and who cannot receive a child. Normal concerns about the authority of the worker are heightened by fears of sanctions, and these fears can create a powerful obstacle which may block effective work. As with other obstacles, if the worker can reveal their existence and explore them with the group members, then the power of the obstacle can often be diminished. In the following example, a public welfare worker leads a group for welfare mothers for the purpose of providing mutual aid on the problems of living on welfare. After some angry discussion about husbands who leave them all the bills and courts that garnish their wages if they work, they finally get to the authority issue. Once again, the relationship to the group worker is raised indirectly by referring to another social worker.

MRS. S.: I didn't know about legal aid until I got involved in the welfare rights group.

MRS. M.: Your caseworker doesn't tell you anything. They always say they don't know. Well, what do they know? They're supposed to be trained and have an education.

MRS. S.: They (caseworkers) are too young; they're not mature, and they are not exposed to life. What do they know about life and especially our problems?

MRS. B.: How can I tell that child (the caseworker) my real problems if I don't think she cares?

MRS. S.: (to the worker) Can't you get some older people to work instead of those young children?

WORKER: Are you saying that because your caseworker is young, she is not capable of being a good caseworker? (Silence)

WORKER: Sometimes, you know, it's harder to teach an older dog new tricks. We find that young people are not as set in their ways. Of course there are exceptions to this rule.

(Silence—a long one)

WORKER: Are you trying to say something to me that you really have not stated?

MRS. M.: She (the caseworker) is prejudiced. She doesn't like Blacks.

The worker caught her own initial defensiveness towards the anger directed at the other worker and reached inside the silence for the unstated communication. Other group members countered Mrs. M.'s opinion of this worker, offering examples of where she had been helpful. Most of these were younger women. The group members had risked a powerful issue in sharing her feelings about the worker's prejudice. The group worker was also black, and this may have been the reason for the honesty. The group worker remained defensive, however, and began to challenge Mrs. M., thus cutting off an important area for discussion.

WORKER: Have you ever discussed this with your caseworker?

MRS. M.: I sure did. I told her off good.

WORKER: In the same manner in which you're speaking now?

MRS. M.: I sure didn't bite my tongue.

WORKER: Then you were rude to her, yes? (Silence)

WORKER: How would you feel if you were the caseworker and she spoke to you in that manner? (Silence) Respect has nothing to do with age or color; it's a two-way street. (Silence).

One of the members commented to Mrs. M. that she thought she was wrong about the worker and this statement was followed by a quick change in the discussion. The group worker had not allowed this difficult area to be opened up and had not demonstrated an understanding of the client's perception. She felt required to identify with the other worker, and perhaps even more so because she was black and the other worker was white. In addition, she did not reach for the implied question about her role and her authority. The discussion continued with complaints about the amount of money available, the difficulty of making ends meet, and so on. As each theme emerged, the worker responded with a lecture or some advice which was followed by silence. Each silence contained the message: You really don't understand. However, the group members sensed the worker's honesty and directness, and they began to take her on. For example, when they complained about making ends meet, the worker asked them if they made out a list of what they needed at the end of the month before they went shopping. The response was, "I need everything by the end of the month; the cupboard is bare. I don't need a list!" This was said with good nature, and the group members laughed in agreement. Their energy level was high, and as the worker accepted their comments about her suggestions, laughing with them rather than getting angry, they warmed to her and took her on with even more gusto. Finally, after one piece of advice near the end of the meeting there was a silence and the following exchange:

MRS. S.: You see, Mrs. P., you just don't understand.
WORKER: I was wondering when someone was going to say that. (The group members all broke up in laughter.)

Even though the worker responded defensively at times, and missed the indirect cues about her authority, the group members seemed to sense her honesty and her genuine concern for them. Her willingness to enter exchanges with them to give and to take in the discussions, and to maintain her humor helped to over-

come her early efforts at preaching and sermonizing. The group continued to meet, and as the worker became clearer about her function and demonstrated her capacity for empathy, the work improved. The important point is that group members can forgive a worker's mistakes if they sense a genuine concern and honesty.

However, it is not always necessary to discuss the worker's authority in the first session. For instance, in the example which follows, the worker's direct offer to use the group as a means of improving communication between welfare clients and the agency was accepted quickly without a discussion of her authority. The members moved quickly past the problems of policy to other issues they shared in common. The problem swapping revealed a range of more personal concerns, setting a broader agenda for future discussions. The worker with this group was white and the group members were black; however, the session demonstrated that each group is unique, and anticipated problems may not always arise in a first session.

Our first meeting was held at the local welfare director's office. I began the meeting by stating that everyone was familiar with who I was, and then I asked each person to give her name and tell us how many children she had. Each member of the group was aware of what the group was all about, because I had previously discussed it with them. After the introductions I said, "I'm concerned because I don't think there is any communication between the welfare board and the people. I'm hoping that our getting together will help us to overcome this. Before we go any further, I want to say that it's important to keep to ourselves what is said here. This goes for me as well as you. I've noticed that many of my clients are concerned with budgeting, the new revisions which went into effect in March, and the food stamp program." Before I could go any further, Mrs. D. jumped in with, "I think the food stamps stink. You can't buy toilet paper or napkins or tissues." Mrs. M. stated that she thought they helped her. Mrs. S. said she didn't use them because she could get her friends to take her to wholesale houses where she could get her meats and canned goods so much cheaper. Besides, she didn't like to shop in the neighborhood supermarkets because around the first of the month, the prices went up. The other two women agreed with this. Then Mrs. M. brought up the fact that in predominantly black neighborhoods, foods that are usually eaten by blacks are much higher priced. I had a puzzled look on my face, and Mrs. M. told me that it is a known fact that blacks like okra and black-eyed peas. Mrs. S. said she noticed the higher prices, too. The group then began talking about how much it costs to feed growing boys and girls. Then Mrs. D. said, "Something else that's been bugging me lately is the drug business with the kids. I'm so afraid that my children are going to try it someday." Everyone then launched into a discussion of raising children. All three felt that if you give a child love and respect, they'll turn out OK. Mrs. M. stated that she wished she could find a man to marry so her sons could have a father. Mrs. S. said she had been single for so long that she didn't want a man around. Mrs. D. stated that she would like to marry someone again, but she was afraid.

At this point, the meeting had gone for over an hour, so I stopped the discussion and said that I thought we'd better close the meeting. I asked them how they felt about continuing this. Mrs. M. stated she would like to because she wants to participate in things like this and see how other people manage their problems. Mrs. D. said it felt good to blow off steam. Mrs. S. sat there and smiled. We all decided we would like to make our group a little larger, and I said I would try to find more people who were interested. We decided to meet again in two weeks. Mrs. S. asked if I could explain at the next meeting what would happen to her monthly check if she started working. The other two said they would be interested in that also. I agreed and the meeting was adjourned.

One of the areas in which the impact of authority is evident is in work with prospective adoptive parents. When requests outnumber the available children, particularly if couples want "a little white girl with blue eyes and intelligent parents," preadoption groups are often experienced as one of the hurdles to be overcome. Rather than viewing it as a potential source of mutual aid, couples approach the group with trepidation and fear. Spouses will caution each other on the way to the first meeting "not to say anything dumb" which would disqualify them as applicants. Competition can often be sensed as couples silently eye each other, measuring their own chances in comparison. The difficulty can also exist for the group leader who has the dual function of leading a mutual aid group and assessing the prospective parents. Workers feel deeply their responsibility towards the child, and the thought of making mistakes which could lead to an adoption breakdown at a future date is often a fear. Unless the issue of "being judged" is dealt with at the start of the first session, the discussion in the groups may become an illusion of work in which the members vie to say what they perceive the worker wants to hear. In the following excerpt the worker contracts but does not reach directly for the unstated concern.

WORKER: We at the agency felt this might be a hard time for you and that you might have a number of concerns and questions about adoption. The group would be an opportunity for you to discuss these concerns with other people who are in the same situation. I realize this is not always easy to do, and I would be here to help you.

Because the question of the worker's authority was not raised, the group began a generalized discussion of how to tell the child about being adopted, whether the child's biological parents or the environment they create would affect the child more, how husbands would help their wives (they were adopting infants), and concerns about "how the agency matches the children to the parents." Each of these issues, as will be discussed later, is related to a real concern these couples have about the adoption procedure and their future child. However, they are not sure whether they can raise their real feelings because they do not know by what criteria they will be judged. Discussion remains on the intellectual level of "biology" versus "environment" because that is safer, at this point, than discussing their fears about the possibility of receiving a child from a "bad seed." As the session ends, their discussion about matching finally leads to the central issue of the authority theme in the following way:

Mrs. Epstein said that by watching the parents in the group, we really couldn't determine what kind of parents we will make. I agreed that was not my role. Mr. W. said that people might decide they do not want to adopt, but how does the agency reject people? I said, "I guess you may be wondering if you're accepted yet?"

The worker discussed their status and reassured them that they wouldn't have gotten this far if the agency did not feel they were good prospective adoptive parents. The discussion was dropped, however, and the conversation continued in a superficial manner. As an alternative response the worker could have opened up the whole question of criteria used for making such decisions. For example, it would be a great relief if the couples knew that having doubts, questions, and fears (e.g., the bad seed) was not unusual and certainly did not disqualify them. In fact, the worker might underline the value of

prospective parents who were "in touch" with how they felt. Workers often duck this discussion because they are also unclear about criteria. In addition, the worker could clarify under what circumstances she might have to raise questions about their suitability. Note the difference in the opening comments in another preadoption group:

Mrs. O'H. spilt her coffee and went into the other office for paper towels. Within a minute Mr. O'H. followed her. I recognized that he was uncomfortable in the group and talked with him while his wife was cleaning up. I went with them to rejoin the group. I also recognized that Mr. and Mrs. T., who were one of the last couples to arrive, seemed tense and flustered. Mrs. T. said her husband hadn't come home for supper and had met her at the door. I commented about whether he might be working late as we were entering—Mr. T. looked a little sheepish. Mr. A. arrived and apologized to the group. I opened by welcoming everyone and requesting that we all introduce ourselves and give the following information: whether you have children, if adopted or natural, age and sex; child desired—age, sex, anything else specific. Everyone responded quite comfortably to this, with the men speaking for both (as is usually the case).

I explained the purpose of the meeting as being an opportunity for them to share thoughts and feelings about adoption. Discussion in a group might be helpful to them in sorting out what their attitudes are, what they're comfortable with, and whether adoption is for them. I wondered if they might be feeling uneasy about sharing their concerns with us. We recognize their feelings about this and it being part of our getting to know them. We're not looking for perfect people, but we want to get to know them and what they are suited for. They might find it helpful to discuss questions with others who may be having the same concerns.

The information from previous visits with them is confidential, and what they share of what they've told us is up to them. It's their group. Our role as co-leaders is to see that we stay on topics related to adoption and to clarify policy matters, but we hope that they'll be free in talking about what's on their mind. I asked the group's permission to take notes of tonight's meeting. The purpose of this recording was to use it in a group learning session on how to work with groups. Confidentiality of the group members was noted—they would be identified by initials. Staff members from other departments—unmarried parents, workers, etc., are also present. Through this learning session we hoped to improve in how we work with groups.

Mr. A. wondered if what they said was confidential or part of the assessment of them. I replied that the groups are part of the total study and process of getting to know them, but the recording as we would use it would not identify anyone. It will be about how we work in a group and not thoughts and feelings they were expressing. The group laughed. I asked if they felt free to move ahead. They nodded heads and said yes.

Mr. T. began by asking how long it takes to get a child and what the ratio of applicants to children is. Mrs. T. followed his question by asking when they would know if they were approved. I explained that we try to let people know what we are thinking all along. Adoption brings happiness to many, but it's not right for everyone. There was also an explanation of our contacts with our client and what happens following the group sessions.

The group members' response to this opening was to move immediately into questions of criteria and procedures involved in adopting. After some discussion, the focus shifted once again to a more general discussion rather than the specific concerns of the couples. In addition to dealing with the authority theme, the worker must stress that the purpose of the group is to deal with the concerns and feelings of the preadoptive parents. Sometimes, group leaders have a different purpose and view the group as a medium for "educating" the parents. They then develop set agendas for a preadoptive parent "curriculum." For example, such a worker might begin by discussing "how to tell your child he is adopted" even though all the couples are awaiting infants who will not need to be told for a number of years. As one listens to such discussions with an ear for the themes important to these couples in their immediate situation, one can often hear subtle undercurrents. For example, when they discuss whether the child will love them as parents once the child knows about being adopted, they are often expressing their own concerns about how *they* will feel towards an adopted child. Even though the worker has been honest about the judging function, the group will still need help to enter taboo areas. They will need support to open up potentially difficult and dangerous subjects, and yet these are precisely the concerns they need to share to discover that they are "all in the same boat." Once the worker is clear that the group is offered to the couples as *clients in their own right,* then concentration can turn to their concerns. In the next example, the worker's empathic responses open up an important discussion about how friends and relatives respond to the adoption. The supportive atmosphere set by the worker has encouraged members to share problems rather than to attempt to convince the worker that everything is going well.

MRS. T.: We have a problem with a grandmother who is against the idea of adoption, but we feel that once a child is placed with us, she'll love the child the same as she does the others.

MRS. C.: People can change their opinions also. When my husband's grandmother first heard of me being adopted, she regarded it very hush-hush. Now that she knows that we are adopting a child, she things it's great—she's going to be a great-grandmother, and she is very thrilled about that.

MR. C.: At work, many people are asking me how the adoption is proceeding.

WORKER: What do you say?

MR. C.: I say that we're going to more meetings. (Laughter)

MRS. K.: It's a necessary thing in getting ready for adoptive parenthood.

WORKER: Are many of you feeling that this is a hard way to get a baby?

MR. K.: It's more difficult; it's easier to have your own.

MRS. K.: For you men, maybe. (Laughter)

MRS. C.: What I find so difficult is not knowing how long we'll have to wait. When a woman is pregnant, she knows it's nine months, but this way, it's unknown just how long it will be.

MRS. G.: I was taking a friend's baby for a walk, and someone said to me, "Don't you wish it was yours?"

WORKER: How do you feel when people say things like that?

MRS. G.: It bugs me.

MRS. T.: They're giving you a dig, don't you think? People ask at work, When are you having a family? and Are you pregnant? It bothers and hurts me, too, but they don't seem to realize it.

MR. G.: Even my brothers-in-law, who are really good fellows, they tease me about why we aren't having any children. I know that they're kidding, but on a down day, it can hurt.

MRS. T.: Have you told anyone it hurts? I told a friend that it hurt me when he kept asking about us having children. He is a reference for us, and now he is the most interested and considerate person to talk to about our adoption. He's always asking me how things are going with the adoption, and he seems to really care.

MRS. K.: I like the way you said that.

WORKER: I think it's good that you were able to say that it does hurt.

MRS. T.: It's a door closed if a couple are not able to have children born to them. You feel so alone and that you're the only person that this has ever happened to. My husband and I both love children so much and we've always wanted to have children, and when we think of a life ahead of us with just the two of us, it seems so shallow. We have to adopt, and that's why we are nervous. We were nervous when Mrs. G. came to our home because we want to be accepted—this is our only way.

CLIENT PROBLEM IMPACT

The specific concern facing the group members needs to be stated clearly and without embarrassment in the opening statement of the group worker. It is helpful to provide examples which serve as "handles" for the group members. In the next example, a worker begins a group for parents of children with cerebral palsy.

Everybody had already introduced themselves, so I began by saying I wanted to give them an idea of what the group was about and then find out what they thought. I said that bringing up a teenager can be difficult, but when the teenager has cerebral palsy, a whole new set of difficulties and problems arises. In this group we are bringing parents together who are in a similar situation to discuss these problems. Hopefully, this will enable you to go back to your children with some new ideas of ways of coping with them. I also said that when I was talking to parents on the phone, they had mentioned several areas which were important to them right now. For example, what about starting high school? At this point Mrs. B. jumped in and said, "You know, that's exactly what I've been thinking about." She went on to describe her ambivalence about whether or not to send Stevie to a regular high school (he's twelve). She talked about her desire for him to be with normal children, but she didn't really know if he'd be able to do it—it was a hard decision. She talked about this for quite a while. Finally, I said that the whole idea of the future for her son seemed to be an important thing to her now. She said, yes, it just began to be important in the last six months or so when she realized that he was getting older.

In the following excerpts the worker contracts with a foster parent group under difficult circumstances. Only one couple was present at the starting time although six were expected. The worker must have experienced a terrible, sinking feeling as she waited for additional members.

I welcomed them and after chatting for a few minutes, I said that we were obviously going to be late in starting the meeting, as no one else had arrived. Name tags for six couples were on a small table. Mr. L. examined the names carefully and read them aloud to his wife. They recognized one couple's name, who had also taken part in the May orientation meeting. I said the name tags were for the six couples who had said pretty definitely that they would attend. Mrs. L. said she wondered where they all were. I said it would be disappointing if there were not enough people present to go ahead with the meeting as planned. Mrs. C. arrived, breathless and apologizing for being late. I welcomed her and said we could begin by reviewing the purpose of the meeting. I said it was hoped the meetings would provide an opportunity for new foster parents to meet each other, to identify and share their common concerns, to plan with them an agenda for the subsequent three meetings; that we had resource people in the agency who were willing to meet with the group; that we might also consider using audiovisual resources like films or tapes. Mrs. C. said she enjoyed the meetings and that it was a shame the others had not come. Mrs. L. said it was too bad, that a foster parent group needed more than three people. Mr. L. got up and took another look at the name tags and began intoning their names again. Mrs. P. arrived, flustered and breathless. She said her husband had been driving around for half an hour trying to park. Finally, he dropped her off and was still trying to find a parking place. I welcomed her and introduced the others.

Mrs. P. said she had gotten the impression there would be more people. I said I had, too, and there was some laughter. I began to feel more relaxed. There was a general interchange at this point about each other's families, their own children and foster children.

The worker's good-natured response to the member's question about the low attendance helped everyone to relax. It is important to acknowledge feelings of disappointment to help members discuss their reactions when attendance is low, whether at a first meeting or any other meeting. At the same time, it is also important to convey a sense of willingness to go on with the work in spite of the low attendance. The people who have arrived have come because of their need for the group. It would be a mistake to spend the entire evening discussing why other members have not shown up.

In the next extract a worker contracts with a group of patients from an outpatient clinic of a psychiatric department in a general hospital. All of the group members have suffered severe depression and are isolated in the community. The worker is thrown off balance a little when, in response to her opening statement, a group member expressed reservations about the group.

The members came in and sat down. They were early. They looked anxious and did not speak to each other. I brought some coffee in, and Mr. C. immediately got up and served everybody. After people were settled, Miss N. said, "After this comes the chicken." I said, "I see you're expecting a party." She replied, "Isn't it a party?" I began the meeting by introducing myself and suggesting the others say who they were. I then stated the contract: "We are here for two reasons. First, to discuss the problems which result from your loneliness and depression in order to gain some understanding of these problems. Second, we are going to try to find solutions to these problems." Mr. C. began to talk about what he thought having a good time was. That consisted of being together with people and not getting too personal. Then he talked about how much he enjoyed playing cards. Miss N. talked about how much she enjoyed cards, too, and they had quite a discussion about this. I asked the group for their reactions. Mr. Mc. said he hadn't come here to play cards or to talk about cards. He had come to gain some understanding of his problems and for the group members to be honest with each other. Mrs. W. backed this up and said there were plenty of other groups they could join to play cards, and Miss N. and Mr. C. could join them if they wanted. Miss N. seemed taken aback by this.

The worker had made a direct offer, and Mr. C. and Miss N. have expressed reservations. Other members of the group used the worker's invitation to attack directly the position of the first two members. The worker used her tuning in to the anxiety felt by all group members at a first meeting to search out immediately the connection between these two subgroups. She did this by recognizing that Mr. C. and Miss N. were simply expressing the concerns they are feeling about the starting in a group.

I said I feel both sides are right. On the one hand Mr. Mc. and Mrs. W. were saying they are here to talk about problems, and Miss N. and Mr. C. are basically saying how hard it is to do this. I then made a few comments about how anxious people must feel coming to a first meeting like this. Mr. C. said, "You're right, it is hard. It's like walking down the street and telling the first guy you meet all your problems." I said, "It takes time to get to know one another." Mr. Mc. said, "Let me make a suggestion. Maybe everyone could tell a little bit about himself, and then we would be one step further." The group agreed and began talking about their problems of loneliness and sadness. I was somewhat taken aback at how fast things were proceeding but figured they wouldn't share anything they didn't want the group to hear.

The worker's directness in her opening and the skill she demonstrated in understanding the meaning of the early resistance to discussion helped free the group members to begin. Her feeling of being taken aback is related to the process by which the group members were taking over the group and quickly making it their own. Workers often feel lost when this happens, out of control, and unsure of themselves. One worker described the feeling as follows: "I feel I'm on my motorcycle, hitting the starter bar with my foot and unable to start the engine, while all my group members have started theirs and they're off down the road zooming away." It is exactly at this moment, when the worker feels the group has taken over, that he or she can feel a good start has been made. Group members are often able to move quickly into expressions of deep emotion while the worker is more concerned than the members about the speed of the evolution of group feeling. In the first session of the following community center group for widows, the opening statement brought one member to tears as she reexperienced the pain associated with the loss of her husband.

I explained with detail how the idea of such a program had developed here at the YWCA, the different phases of the program stressing the fact that what was most important in this program was the participation they were to give. The YWCA designed this program to meet their needs. I said that widows are inclined to be self-absorbed, and in order to restore their balance, a group in which they can socialize helps them a great deal. I said that it enables them to express pain and dissatisfaction and to receive acceptance.

I mentioned that every person here was at a different stage of widowhood and that the very recent widows could be helped by the experience of others. I said that the age group was varied but that the widows under thirty-five could contribute their youth to the group and share the experiences of the elders. Mrs. P., a six-year widow who had mentioned over the phone that she had accepted her condition and had no problems but would join only to be with a friend already registered, broke down in tears saying, "Where were you when I lost my husband six years ago?" "You would have liked to talk with someone then?" I asked. "Oh yes, yes," she added.

Immediately I had the feeling that a current of sympathy spread among the entire group and half-crying they began to ask questions. Mrs. A. asked Mrs. P. if after six years she felt things were easier, to which she agreed saying she had become very aggressive though, to protect herself from the ones who seemed to take advantage of her being alone. I asked if others felt this way; several shared this opinion but others mentioned that everybody was nice. "The ones who had this attitude," replied Mrs. S., "must have very good characters." "You don't think you have good character?" I asked. She explained that her family thinks she is made of iron. "My brother disagrees with me all the time," she continued. "He would never go out with my eight-year-old son, he cannot understand he should be a father to him," and she expressed anger and disappointment towards her relatives. Mrs. T. said she understood her as she herself was very unhappy because her own sister-in-law, when she baby-sits for her, takes away the affection her children have for her. "They don't understand," explained Mrs. C., a sixty-year-old widow. "When I lost my first husband many years ago, I had the same problems." A discussion followed on the relatives' attitudes towards widows and the difficulty for widows to express their feelings in front of them. They agreed that being able to express something here in a group helped. The difficulty of going out alone, the discomfort in being with groups of relatives who give them "pity and overprotection," their own inexperience, their isolation, etc., came out gradually and brought them closer to one another.

A member crying in a group may be experienced by the others as an uncomfortable and embarrassing situation. In this group, where mourning was central to their work, the crying did not seem strange. In other groups, particularly in a first session, it would be important for the worker to reassure the member and the group that the expression of strong feelings was natural and appropriate. In understanding and accepting these feelings, the worker demonstrates a way of working that will help the group members create a new "culture" in which all the emotions of sadness, anger, joy, and so forth can be freely expressed. When a group has begun with a particularly strong first session, in terms of emotion and quickly getting to core issues, it is important for the worker to use some time at the end of the session to discuss the members' reactions. At times, members will feel embarrassed *after* a session at having expressed strong feelings or ideas which they may feel are only theirs. Some attention to this issue often results in other group members reassuring the exposed members that they are not alone.

IMPACT OF THE SETTING OF SERVICE

The setting of service will have some impact on the nature of the group contract. In this first illustration, a social worker in a hospital contracts with a patient ward group to discuss their illness and hospitalization. He views the hospital as a complex system which patients must negotiate and the group as a vehicle for helping them do that.

I introduced myself to patients and asked them to go around and introduce themselves, which they did. I asked whether they have been told anything about this group. They hadn't. I told them we get together to discuss what it means to be a patient in the hospital, how it feels being in a strange place away from family and friends. I said that often patients found it difficult getting used to a hospital experience, and sometimes it helped to talk with other patients. Often they have the same feelings of anxiety, fear, and uncertainty; we get together as a group so that we can freely talk about hospital experiences and feelings around being a patient. I mentioned that they will probably notice that I take notes from time to time, the reason being so that I can look back on the session to see where I could have been more helpful to them. Mrs. J. began talking about the doctors and how they change, just after you get used to one doctor. I said that it must be a frustrating and anxious time when the doctors change. She agreed. Mrs. B. said that this is her first hospital experience and it was upsetting. Mrs. C. said that she's used to hospitals and she felt she adapted well. Mrs. V. said that the system didn't bother her. I asked Mrs. B. why she felt so upset about the hospital. She said it was strange and she felt all alone. If it hadn't been for Mrs. C. "adopting" her, she would never have stayed after the first hour. I remarked that it must have been terribly frightening, this being her first time here and her not knowing the ropes. She agreed.

Mrs. C. said that the hospital system didn't bother her, but she's scared they won't find out what's wrong with her. She was very sick at home, and she's hoped they'll be able to do something. I said that it's a natural feeling to worry about one's illness, particularly when the diagnosis is not known. At this point an orderly came to take Mrs. J. to X-ray.

Mrs. C. said that when you're not told what's happening, you feel bad. I asked in what way she felt bad. She answered that all of a sudden you're told to go through a difficult test or examination, about which you know nothing and you feel horrible. I remarked that you need time to adjust to the idea of a test and prepare yourself for it. She agreed. I asked whether the others had similar experiences. Mrs. B. said one day a doctor came in for a heart examination. She was very upset because nobody told her anything about it and she was thinking she had a heart condition; otherwise why would she have to have this

examination? The nurse explained that this is just routine and that every patient who is on the ward gets cardiac and respiration examinations while they're here, and it certainly does not mean that there is anything wrong with her. I asked Mrs. B. how she felt now, knowing that it's a routine examination—she said much easier; she would have felt less upset had she known this before.

In addition to helping the patients adjust to the difficult situation and clarify their concerns, the worker can use this group as a vehicle for change within the hospital. Involving staff can help to bridge the gap between the providers and consumers of service. In Part III of this book I will explore ways in which a worker can use patient feedback to affect the way in which the system relates to the client.

In the next example, a worker meets with a somewhat reluctant group of boys who are living in a residential institution. They have been elected by a resident executive committee to serve as a lounge committee, whose purpose is to provide feedback to the administration on ways in which the new lounge could be run more effectively. They were apathetic because they felt powerless to affect the institution.

I began this meeting by explaining why I felt an active lounge committee was needed. I said that the guys probably had a lot of beefs regarding the lounge and that this was an opportunity to do something about it. Billy agreed that there were a lot of beefs but felt little could be done about them. I asked why he felt this way. The boys shared their feeling that the administration was really inflexible and uninterested in their views. Their past experiences had confirmed this. I said I could appreciate why they felt a bit hopeless; however, this lounge committee was a new attempt which the administration was supporting. It might still be impossible; on the other hand, if they acted together as a group, I thought they could accomplish something. If no ideas and suggestions were forthcoming, how could the administration act on them?

I encouraged them to try it out, and if they found it was hopeless, we could simply quit. At this point their beefs about the lounge emerged.

In the last example the focus of the work shifted from individual personal needs and concerns to tasks related to the benefit of the group. This is also true in work with community action or tenants' groups where the focus is not on mutual aid for meeting individual needs, but rather mutual aid for impact on systems related to group needs. For example, in a group for immigrant parents designed to assist them in dealing with the school system, it would be inappropriate for members to discuss their marital problems or other areas of concern that might be personally important but are unrelated to the contract. If the group contracts to band together to improve communications with the school staff, then this boundary serves to guard their contract. The worker can offer to refer members to other services for help in other areas. Nonetheless, as they work on their social action tasks, all of the principles of group dynamics, process, and the requirements for worker skill are just as relevant in these groups as for those designed to deal with personal problems.

I believe that the central function of the group worker is the same, whether a leader of a hospital ward group or an organizer of a public housing tenants' group. The method used to pursue that function and the interactional skills required are also equivalent. Of course, working in a community setting, the worker will also need other areas of knowledge (e.g., how political power systems operate) and specific skills (e.g., procedures for dealing with the press). Each setting requires certain specific knowledge and specific skills. However, the core ideas of function and the interactional skills are the same. In the following example, a social worker contracts at a first meeting of public housing tenants he is attempting to organize. He has done his preliminary phase work through door-to-door contacts and interviews, thereby gaining a sense of the issues of concern to the tenants. A meeting has been publicized by circulars and posters. Natural leaders in the housing complex have been identified through the interviews, and the worker has requested their help in getting a turnout for this first session. Since the first session began without a structure in place, the worker made the opening statement—to a room full of forty-five tenants.

After introducing myself, I explained that I was a community worker employed by the local neighborhood house and that my job was to work with citizens' groups to help them organize themselves to improve their community—that included their housing, schools, recreational services for kids, etc. After spending some time in this housing project, it became clear to me that the tenants had a number of gripes which they felt the management was not doing anything about. The purpose of tonight's meeting was to discuss these gripes and to see if they felt it would help to organize a tenants' group to deal with the management more effectively. I would try to help them get started, and would stick with the group to try to help it operate effectively. However, it would have to be their group, since I couldn't do anything for them by myself. I asked what they thought about that.

The discussion began with group members starting to identify complaints about maintenance, the general haughty attitude of the administrator, ignoring simple requests, and so on. There was a great deal of anger in the room which the worker acknowledged while he kept track of the issues raised. He did little to intervene other than to assist the group members to speak in some order, and, at times, to encourage members to respond to each other when it seemed appropriate. After a while, the members were speaking more to each other than to the chair. The discussion also moved into complaints tenants had about each other (e.g., noise at night, loud radios, littering) and about gaps in services for kids (e.g., a safe place to play). The discussion was animated. When the list seemed complete, the worker returned to the question of his role.

You have a number of issues here which I think can be dealt with if you organize yourselves as a group. There are issues with management, issues between each other, and new services you feel are needed. Now I told you at the beginning that I was getting you started but that you would have to form your own group to deal with these concerns. I would like to recommend that you select a steering committee tonight that could meet to discuss next steps. For example, they could discuss whether you need an association, if yes, what kind should you have, etc. What about it? There were murmurs of agreement. I then asked for volunteers and was greeted by silence.

As another demonstration of the importance of process in dealing with groups and the importance of using the skills described thus far, the remainder of the excerpt illustrates how the worker reached into this silence for the underlying concern to which he had tuned in prior to the meeting. If it were easy to get together as a group to take on these problems, why hadn't the tenants done so on their own? The worker had tuned in to the possible fear of reprisals if they became identified as "trouble makers" in the housing project and decided to reach for it at this point.

As the silence continued, I asked why they seemed hesitant to volunteer. With no response, I risked my hunch and said, "You know, I was thinking about this before the meeting, and I wondered if you might be concerned about reprisals if you get organized. You know you are dependent on this place for housing, and if you were afraid that management might be upset, I could understand that." Mrs. C., who has been identified as one of the community leaders, spoke up at this point, "You know Mr. B. used to raise a ruckus and complain all the time. He got drunk a while back and they used that to get him." I asked if they were afraid that this might happen to them. Discussion began to explore what might happen, their mutual fears, etc. Mrs. C. finally said, "I guess we do take a chance, but if I knew you other folks would stand behind me and not run for cover if it got hot around here, I would think about doing it." At this point, others indicated they would help out on the committee. I said, "It seems like some of your neighbors are willing to take some responsibility for leading this off and getting the group organized, but they want to know that you will back them up." Another member, a tall, older man with grey hair who hadn't spoken all evening said, "It's about damn time we stood up to the bastards!" Laughter broke the tension of the moment, and one could sense an agreement had been reached. I wanted to complete my contracting on my role before I finished the evening. "I want to be clear that I will help you folks get yourselves organized and help you work together, but it will have to be your group. You will need your own chairperson, you will have to make your own decisions." Group members murmured agreement to this. "We can discuss this later, but perhaps I might be able to speak to management at a later point and help them see how the group could be in their interest as well." The meeting ended as I complimented them for making a great start and set a brief meeting with the steering committee to get ourselves organized.

The principles of contracting, clarifying purpose, clarifying role, and reaching for feedback were central to the effective start of this group. In a later chapter, I will discuss the ongoing work of the group worker with such a group when there is a clearly elected chairperson and other leaders as well. In addition to the contracting skills, the worker's tuning in and effective elaborating and empathy skills helped the group members to examine and overcome a major obstacle to their formation. I would argue that if the worker had ignored their fears, tried to overcome them with a lecture on "strength in numbers," or simply jumped in and agreed to take the responsibility for the next steps *for them* instead of *with them,* then the group development which is central to the worker's purpose would have been seriously delayed. Instead, his empathy and demand for work helped them to find their own strength.

The Impact of Time

Time can have an important impact on the worker's activities in the first session. For example, some groups meet for a single session and must incorporate the beginning, work and ending/transition phases in that time frame. This type of group is discussed in Chapter 14. In this section, I discuss the variations in a first session of a short-term group—one designed to meet for only a few sessions.

In the first session of the married couples' group described in the previous chapter, I could use the entire session for contracting and setting the stage for work in the knowledge that we had many sessions to follow. My work was affected by this knowledge, as was the work of the group members. For example, I did not feel the need to confront defenses and instead, could concentrate on providing a clear framework and as much support as possible. The group members could take their time, as well, starting with "near problems," designed to test the waters until they felt safe.

This contrasts with another group I led, for single parents, in which the entire group experience needed to be contained in three, three-hour sessions, consisting of one evening and a full day. I will use this group to illustrate the differences in a first session when time is limited.

The group was set up by community professionals in a small rural town. They felt the need for a mutual aid group for single parents and I was invited to fly into the town to spend one evening and one day. A number of the professionals also attended the group with two purposes in mind. First, they could provide ongoing services to the group members after the sessions were over. I felt it was important that resources be readily available to pick up with clients on issues which might be raised through the group meetings. Their second purpose was to observe my group leadership so that they might be better equipped to start mutual aid groups of their own. The group was advertised as open to the public and a number of community professionals suggested it to their clients. I met the fifteen group members who attended for the first time on the night of the first session. In this section I will focus on the implications for the first session only.

I had tuned in to the possible themes of concern prior to the group meeting and had prepared an opening statement which I had hoped would focus us quickly on their most central concerns. I also tuned into the difficulty involved in getting started in such a new group, in a small town where people tended to know about each other, with an "expert" from out of town (who would not be around long), and the difficulty in opening up issues in a short-term context. I decided

I needed to move quickly from the problem-swapping stage into work on a specific issues since we did not have the luxury of a long contracting phase. In addition, I felt we needed to demonstrate how helpful the group could be, quickly, if I expected members to risk. Finally, I prepared by tuning in to my own hesitations about risking in a first session and prepared to raise the issue directly with the group when and if I sensed defensiveness and/or the illusion of work. The following is from my recording of the session dictated immediately following the meeting.

I explained the purpose of the group as an opportunity for single parents to discuss with each other some of the special problems they faced because they were alone. I explained that my role was not as an expert with answers for them, but rather, I would try to help them to talk and to listen to each other, and to provide help to each other from their own experiences. In addition, I would throw in any ideas I had which might be helpful. I then offered a few examples of possible concerns around dealing with friends and relatives after the split in the relationship, problems in relating to the ex-spouse, the financial strains, and problems which often accompanied being a single parent and the difficulties presented by the children. There was much head nodding as I spoke. I finished by describing briefly the phases which both parents and children commonly go through after a separation (denial, anger, mourning, and finally, coming to terms with it). I then invited the participants to share their own experiences and suggested that these could form an agenda for our work that evening and the next day.

There was a brief silence and then Rene asked how long it took to go through the phases. I asked her why she was asking and she said it was three years since her separation and she doesn't think she has passed through all of them yet. The group members laughed in acknowledgment of the meaning of the comment. I said I thought there must

have been a great deal of pain and sadness, at the time of the split and since then, for it to still hurt after three years. I asked Rene if she could speak some more about this and she continued, in a more serious tone, by describing her ongoing depression. She described days in which she feels she is finally getting over things and picking herself up, followed by days she feels right back to square one. Others in the group agreed and shared their own experiences as I encouraged them to respond to Rene's comments. I told them it might help just to know that they were "in the same boat" with their feelings.

I then asked if the group members could be more specific about what made it difficult. This resulted in a number of areas raised by members which I kept track of in my written notes. They included most of the problems I had raised in my opening statement. There was much emotionally laden discussion of the first area, problems with friends and family, with a great deal of anger expressed towards others who "didn't understand" and related to them in ways which hurt.

Dick, a young man in his mid-twenties, spoke with great agitation about his wife who had left him with their six-month-old baby only six weeks before. The group seemed to focus on Dick who expressed a very strong sense of urgency and was clearly still in a state of shock and crisis. I had earlier noted that Dick was the first to arrive that evening and during the premeeting chatter, he had told the person next to him all of the crises he had gone through just to get there that night. I pointed out to the group that it seemed that Dick was feeling this concern about friends and relatives rather strongly, and in fact he had had a great deal of difficulty even getting here tonight. I asked if they would like to focus on problems with friends and relatives first, using Dick's example to get us started. They all agreed it would be helpful, including Dick.

My effort to move us more quickly into the work began with my contracting statement and continued when I responded to Irene's joking comment about "not getting through the phases yet" by reaching for the underlying hurt and bitterness. If we were to move quickly in the group, I felt I had to send an early message that I was ready to deal with the difficult feelings as soon as they were. The group responded by immediately moving into the painful feelings as well as the anger. Feeling the need to get into substantive work early in this first session, I moved to obtain group consensus on an initial theme of concern and to bring Dick's urgency to the group members' attention. Thus, we were moving into the work phase in less than an hour after my opening statement. In the continuation of the first session description which follows, Dick's resistance to taking personal responsibility for his problems emerges. I responded with a demand for work, pointing out that we had very little time in which to work.

After Dick described the details of his separation and his current living situation with the six-month-old child, he went on to describe the problems. He emphasized the difficulty of living in a small town, and in his particular case, being in a personal service occupation which put him in daily contact with many town residents. He said: "Sure I feel lousy, depressed, and alone. But some days, I feel I'm getting over things a bit, feeling a little bit up, and everywhere I go people constantly stop me to tell me how terrible things are. If I didn't feel lousy before I went out, I sure do by the time I get home."

Dick added a further complication, in that the baby had a serious case of colic and was crying all the time. He told the group that everyone was always criticizing how he handled the baby and even his mother was telling him he wasn't competent and should move back home with her. He continued by saying he was so depressed by this that he had taken to not talking to anyone anymore, avoiding his friends, staying home alone at night, and going out of his mind. Others in the group

shared similar versions of this experience. I said to Dick: "And that's the dilemma, isn't it? Just at the time you really need help the most, you feel you have to cut yourself off from it to maintain your sense of personal integrity and sanity. You would like some help, because the going is rough, but you're not sure you want to have to depend on all of these people, and you're not sure you like the costs involved." Dick nodded, and the other group members agreed.

After providing recognition and support for these feelings, I tried to move the group members into examining what they could do about them in terms of how they handled their conversations with friends and relatives. I encountered a good deal of resistance to this idea, with Dick balking each time I tried to get him to look at how he might have handled a conversation differently. He evaded this by jumping quickly to other comments or examples, or by expressions which seem to say: "If you only knew my Mother/friends you would realize it is hopeless." When Rose, a member of the group in her early fifties, confronted him from the perspective of his mother—she had children close in age to him—he rejected her comments.

I pointed out what was happening. I said: "It seems to me that when I or a group member suggest that you (Dick) look at your part in the proceedings, you won't take in what we are saying." I said I only had a day and a half with the group, so I really couldn't pussy foot around with them. I wondered if it was tough for Dick, and all of them, to take responsibility for their part in their problems. Dick smiled, and admitted that it was hard. He already felt lousy enough. Others joined in on how easy it was to blame everyone else and how hard it was to accept any blame themselves. I agreed that it was tough, but I didn't think I would be of any help to them if I just sat here for a day and a half agreeing about how tough things were for them. The group members laughed and a number said they didn't want that.

At this point, Dorris, one of the three workers participating in the group, surprised us all by saying that she had intended to listen and not talk during the session, but that listening to Dick's problem made her want to share hers. She said she had come to the group as an observer, however, she was pregnant, and unmarried, and therefore, was about to become a single parent. She thought she was having the same problem in communicating with her mother as Dick was having with his. It was a classic example of a conflict between a mother who is hurt and embarrassed, and a daughter who feels rejected at a critical moment in her life. At my suggestion, Rose offered to role play the mother as Dorris tried to find a new way to talk to her mother. The group was supportive, but at the same time, following my example, they also became quite confrontative with each other, in a healthy way.

Dick listened and participated in the work on Dorris's problem, and as is often the case, was able to learn something about his own situation as he watched someone else struggling with the same concerns. When I asked him later if he had taken something from it, he said it had helped him a lot to see how he was holding back his real feelings from friends and his own mother. I pointed out to all of the group members what a shock their situation was to their friends and close relatives, and how, at first contact, they could not respond in a way which met their needs. I said: "This does not mean they don't love you. It just means that they have feelings and aren't always able to express them. Your mixed messages also make it difficult."

Cerrise, another worker/observer in the group, joined the discussion at this point and described how she had felt when close friends had split up their marriage. She realized now that it had taken her a couple of months to get over being so angry at them for ending their marriage, because she loved them both. She hadn't been able to reach out to them to support them, but she was lucky, because they had not given up on her and she had been able to work it out. Dick said that hearing that helped a lot. That was what was probably going on with some of his friends.

Carrie, who was both an unmarried parent and a worker in the community, described her own experiences with her mother when she split up. She shared how she had involved

her mother in the process, had let her know her feelings, and that she wanted her mother's love and support, but felt she had to handle the problems herself. Dick listened closely and said that this was probably what he had not been able to do. We did some role play on how Dick could handle the conversation with his mother—how he could articulate his real feelings. The group was supportive and helpful.

When I asked the group how they felt about this discussion, thus far, Dorris said it was helpful because I kept stressing the positive aspect, the reaching out and caring between people. Most of them were so upset, they could only see the negatives. The discussion turned to how much they needed others to talk to about what they were going through. As the session neared the end, in typical "door knob" fashion, Dick revealed that a close male friend of his, in a similar situation with a young child, had told him he was considering committing suicide. He went on to tell us, with tears in his eyes, that the friend had just killed himself. I said: "It must have hit you very hard, when that happened, and you must have wondered if you could have done something more to help." Dick agreed that was so, and the group members offered him support. After some time, I asked Dick if he was worried about his own situation, since he had many of the same feelings as his friend. He said he was worried, but that he thought he would be strong enough to keep going, to have a goal in life, to make it for his child. I told him he had shown a lot of strength just coming to the group and working so hard on his problem. Carrie said that he was not alone, and that he could call her if he needed someone to talk to—as a friend, or as a worker. Rose pointed out that there was a single-parent social group at the church, and Dick said he had not realized that. Others in the group also offered support. I asked Dick how he felt now, and he said: "I feel a lot better. I realize, now, that I'm not so alone." Irene, who had opened the discussion by saying she had not yet gone through all of the phases, summarized the evening's work when she said: "I guess we are all struggling to find ways of saying to friends and close relatives, 'Please love me now, I need you.'" The discussion ended and we agreed to pick up again in the morning.

Summary

In this chapter we have seen a number of examples of contracting in first sessions. The age and relative articulateness of the members, the authority of the worker, the specific concerns of the clients, and the impact of the setting and time have added their own variation to the central theme. In addition, each worker brought a unique personal style to the beginning. The common elements, however, should also be clear at this point. These common elements represent the science of our work. In the chapters to follow the core dynamics of groups at work will be examined and illustrated as will be the specific function and skills of the group worker. The next chapters attempt to answer the queston of what to do after the first session.

NOTES

1. Lawrence Shulman, " 'Program' in Group Work: A Second Look," in *The Practice of Group Work,* eds. William Schwartz and Serapio Zalba (New York: Columbia University Press, 1971).

CHAPTER 11

The Work Phase in the Group

A common problem raised by beginning group workers, particularly those with experience in working with individuals, is that in an attempt to deal with an individual's concern, they find themselves doing "casework in the group." Suppose, for example, a member raises an issue at the start of a session and the worker responds with appropriate elaborative and empathic skills. The group member expands the concern, and the worker tries to help deal with the problem—while the other group members listen. When this problem seems to be finished, the worker then begins with another client as the others patiently wait their turn. After the meeting, the worker worries about having done casework in front of an audience. In reaction to this feeling of uneasiness, the worker strategizes not to be trapped this way during the next session, thereby making a different kind of mistake. Vowing to pay attention to the "group" aspect of group work, the worker attempts to do so by refusing to respond with elaborating skills when an individual opens the session with a direct or indirect offering of a concern. For example, one member of a parent group says, "It's really hard to raise teenagers these days, what with all the changing values." The worker quickly responds

by inquiring if other members of the group find this to be true. One by one they comment on the general difficulty of raising teenagers. The discussion soon becomes overly general and superficial, and meanwhile the first group member is anxiously waiting with a specific concern about a fight with her daughter the evening before.

In an attempt to deal with individual concerns workers sometimes find themselves doing "casework in the group." When trying to pay attention to the group, workers find themselves leading an over-generalized discussion. Both maladaptive patterns reflect the worker's difficulty in both conceptualizing the group as a system for mutual aid and understanding the often subtle connections between individual concerns and the general work of the group. Schwartz's notion of the "two clients," discussed earlier, can help to resolve the apparent dilemma. He suggests that the worker must pay simultaneous attention to two clients, the individual and the group, and the field of action is concerned with interaction between the two. Thus, instead of choosing between the "one" or the "many," the worker's function is focused on mediating the engagement between these two clients. This is a special case of the general helping function defined in Part I and illustrated below.

This chapter focuses upon the interaction between the individual and the group and the way in which the group worker mediates the engagement. Using time as an organizing principle, the beginning phase of group sessions is examined emphasizing the way in which the worker helps individuals present their concerns to the group and simultaneously assists the group members to respond. The section of this chapter on the work phase illustrates the dynamics of mutual aid and the way in which group members can help individuals and themselves at the same time. The discussion of the ending phase stresses the importance of resolution and transition to next steps or next meetings. Each of these phases and the skills required are illustrated with record material from a range of settings. While the focus of this chapter is on the individual-group interaction, it is important to recognize that both the entities involved, the individual and the group, require further examination. The next chapter analyzes the individual's role in the group, while the succeeding chapter concentrates on the group-as-a-whole.

SESSIONAL CONTRACTING IN THE GROUP

In Chapter 1, I described some of the barriers which make open communication difficult in the helping situation. These included ambivalence towards taking help because of the resultant feelings of dependency, societal taboos against discussion of certain topics (e.g., sex), the client's painful feelings associated with particular issues, and the context of the helping setting (e.g., the impact of the helping person's authority). These blocks often result in a client's using an indirect form of communication when sharing a problem or concern. For example, clients might hint at a concern (stating a specific problem in a very general way), or act it out (begin a session by being angry at the worker or other group members, using the anger to cover up the pain), use metaphor or allegory as a means of presenting an issue (e.g., telling a seemingly unrelat-

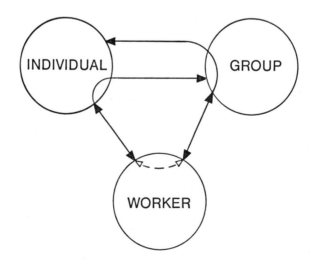

ed story), or send the message nonverbally (e.g., sitting quietly with a pained expression or sitting apart from the group). The indirectness of these communications may cause the group members and the worker to miss important cues in the early part of the session. Alternatively, a member might raise a concern but do it in such a way as to hide the depth of feeling associated with it thereby turning off the other group members. The worker's function is to provide assistance in this process.

Reaching For Individual Communication in the Group

Because of the problems involved in individual-group communication, the worker should concentrate efforts in the early stages of each meeting on helping individual members present their concerns to the group. The beginning of each group session should be seen as a tentative, slow form of feeling out the group, endeavoring to determine which member or members are attempting to capture the group's attention for their own issues, and how these issues may represent a theme of concern for the group. In a like manner, the group itself may be approaching a major theme of concern for that week, and the individual offerings may thus present specific examples of the concern of the group. Whether the concern originates with the one or is an expression of the feelings of the many, the worker's tasks in the early stages should be focused on answering the question, "What are we working on this session?" It would be a mistake for workers to rush in with their own agenda simply because the first productions of the group members are unclear. Likewise, it would be an error for the worker to believe that simply because the group had agreed to

deal with a specific issue or an individual's concern at the end of the previous meeting, that this will be the issue for the current session. Even if the discussion picks up exactly where the members agreed it would, the worker should monitor the conversation in the early part of the session with an ear either for confirmation of the theme or hints that members are going through the motions.

The important point is that the worker believe that even though the conversation may not *seem* directed towards the group's purpose, it is always purposeful. For clarity of exposition, I will focus here on examples where the early discussion is directed towards presenting a specific theme of concern. In Chapter 13, however, I will explore examples where the purpose of the early conversation is to raise an issue concerning the working of the group or the leader. In both cases the worker should be asking himself during the early discussion, "How does this conversation connect to our work?" or "What is troubling this particular member?" By doing so, there is a better chance of helping the individual relate a concern to the group.

An illustration from the couples' group described in Chapter 9 can demonstrate this process as well as the importance of sessional tuning in. The session was the eighteenth. At the previous one, Louise, who was present without her husband John, had revealed that he had a drinking problem. There was general agreement to pursue this concern with John present the next week. In my tuning in session with co-leaders prior to the start of the session, I had learned that Fran and Rick had had a particularly difficult week and had threatened separation during their individual counseling session. Rick had questioned returning to the group. The couple previously had made substantial progress in the group and in a related sexual therapy group program but had hit a critical point and were regressing. Over the course of the sessions I had observed that this couple had a characteristic pattern of presenting their concerns in the group: Fran would express her own concerns and fears indirectly as she responded to other couples in the group, and Rick would physically retreat. Having accomplished the preparatory work, we strategized to reach for Fran's indirect cues if they were evident and were prepared to help the group discuss priorities for this session. The session began with some hints from the group about the ending process, a topic that I had planned to respond to directly. After I acknowledged the group's sadness and my own about ending and the members briefly discussed their feelings, there was a silence which was broken by John:

JOHN: I know about your discussion about my drinking last week, since I met with Larry [the worker] and he filled me in. If you have any questions, let me have them.

At this point there was some relaxation of tension, and group members offered supportive comments for John for his having raised this difficult concern. I noticed that Fran and Rick had turned their chairs so that they faced apart from each other. Rick was staring into space with a blank expression. Fran turned to face John:

FRAN: I want you to know, John, that I think it's great that you have come here prepared to talk about this problem. It takes a lot of courage on your part. It would have been a lot easier if you simply stayed away or refused to discuss it. That would have been the coward's way out.
WORKER: Fran, I wonder if that's what you think Rick is doing right now, in relation

to you? His chair is turned away from you and you seem to be upset with each other.
FRAN: (after a period of silence) I don't understand how you do this, how you read my mind this way. It must be a form of magic. (Pause) But you're right, we had a really bad fight this week, and we're not over it. Rick didn't want to come this week, and he won't talk to me about it (Fran shows signs of becoming upset emotionally).
WORKER: How do you see it, Rick?

After Rick's confirmation of the seriousness of the situation, both he and Fran state they are concerned because this was supposed to be the week for John and Louise. I raised the issue with the whole group and they decided to stay with Rick and Fran because of the degree of urgency in their situation. John and Louise felt they could wait another week. The session turned out to be an important turning point for the couple (Rick and Fran), as well as one which yielded important insights for the other couples into their own relationships.

There was no magic in picking up Fran's cues; tuning in and the identifying of a pattern over time had helped. Also important was the recognition that often early comments from members are indirect efforts to raise themes of concern. Another example from the same group was the issue raised by Lou, the member of the group in his sixties. In this illustration, the problem of identifying the issue was compounded, since the nature of the concern was not clear to the member and was presented indirectly as part of an angry attack upon the group leaders. In the previous session, a videotaped segment of a meeting when one of the couples had blown up at each other had been viewed by the group with the couple's consent. Lou was upset that this painful exchange had been replayed in the group. He began with an angry attack on helping professionals concentrating on "the way they played games with people's lives." He was extremely upset at the way workers encouraged the expression of bitter feelings between couples, feeling that this tore them apart emotionally. He argued that this was not necessary. I reached for the specific meaning of his opening comments.

WORKER: Lou, I think you're talking about us and last week's session—when we watched the tape. (I had missed this session due to an accident but had reviewed the videotape. The session had been led by my co-leaders.)

LOU: Of course I am! I've never been more upset. It tore my guts watching what you people put them through.

Lou went on to attack the helping professions in general as well as us in particular. The workers responded by attempting to explain what they had done. We were generally made to feel defensive and incompetent. Group members will often make the workers feel exactly the way they feel themselves. When they are unaware of or unable to express their own pain and the hurt under their anger, one way to deal with it is to project it upon the leaders or other members. Bion described this process as "projective identification," in which the client communicates his feelings by stimulating the same feelings in the worker.[1] The difficulty for the worker is that there always is some element of truth in the attack which is usually aimed at an area where the worker feels less confident. In this situation we stayed with the issue raised by Lou:

WORKER: Lou, you're angry with us and also feeling that we really hurt Len and Sally last week. Obviously we missed how hard it hit you to see their pain. Why don't you ask them how they felt?

LOU: Well, am I right? Wasn't that terrible for you to go through?

LEN: It wasn't easy, and it hurt, but I think it helped to get it out in the open. It also helped to have all of you care about us and feel the pain with us.

LOU: But there must be some way to do this without having to tear your guts out. (Lou seemed a bit taken aback by Len's comments which were echoed by his wife.)

WORKER: When you attacked us, Lou, I have to admit it hit me hard. A part of me doesn't want to get at the anger and pain that you all feel, and yet another part of me feels it's the way back to a stronger relationship. I have to admit you shook me.

ROSE: (Lou's wife) I think you have to understand this has been a hard week for us.

WORKER: How come?

ROSE: We just got word that Lesley, our granddaughter who lives in London, is splitting up with her husband.

Lou and Rose have spoken before in the group about their children and the pain it has caused them to see each of them experience difficulties in their marriages. Lou has been particularly angry with helping professionals who have helped neither him nor his family members. This was the first grandchild to experience marital problems and signified to Lou and Rose the continuation of the family instability into another generation. Under much of the anger is their pain as well as their feelings of defensiveness and doubt to which Rose responded by clarifying Lou's signal.

WORKER: It must have hit you very hard, Lou, having the first grandchild experience marital problems.

LOU: (Seeming deflated, the anger gone, slumped in his chair, speaking with a tone of resignation and bitterness) After forty-five years you learn you have to live with these things. It's just another notch that you have to add to all of the other hurts.

The discussion continued with Lou and Rose explaining their feelings of helplessness as they watched their family disintegrating and their desire to show the children that it doesn't have to be that way. The group members commiserated as they described impotence they felt to affect the lives of their children and their grandchildren.

In the first illustration with Fran and in the second with Lou, the individual was reaching out to the group indirectly through the opening comments. With Fran the concern was presented in the guise of a response to a group member, while with Lou it appeared as an attack upon the leaders. In both cases the communication had two meanings. The first was the actual statement of fact while the second was a disguised call for help. Unless workers are tuned in, listen hard for potential offerings from group members, and are clear about their own function in the group, it is easy to miss the early indirect productions of group members. Of course, the member will often present a concern more directly, thus making it easier for the group to hear. And sometimes an issue may emerge at a later point in the meeting. In the following excerpt, a member moves from the general group discussion to a specific concern. The conversation in the group and the feelings expressed generated a spontaneous response from a group member which, with the worker's help, evolved into a specific issue. The group was a support group for men who batter their wives or the women they live with. This mutual aid group was set up in recognition of the fact that the men involved in family violence need some form of help in breaking the cycle of destructive relationships with their wives and women in general. The group was formed to help them discuss their common concerns, concentrating on their relationship with women. In this illustration, the general topic of relationship to children triggered Frank's specific concern which the worker helped him elaborate.

Frank said he was having a hard time finding things to do on his own. He had gone, alone, to see the movie *Short Eyes* the other night. He had left half or three-quarters of an hour into the movie. He said it was about prisons, and it had really made him uncomfortable. The movie had made him feel "boxed." Sid then said, "I feel confined in other ways." Frank said that he got the feeling that his wife had felt confined as well. Sid nodded and said that might often be true in relationships. He, Sid, had felt there were certain ways he had to be when he was in a relationship. I asked him what he meant. Sid said he felt that he "had to hold out in expressing certain feelings." He meant, he explained, that there were certain feelings he couldn't express. Frank said that he had felt the same way. But now, his marriage was over, and he was finding it a lot harder than he thought it would be to get over it. He said he knew it was finished but that didn't make it easier to accept. I said to Frank that it had taken me longer than it had my wife to get over the marriage ending.

Rod said to Frank, "It'll pass." I said to him, "What do you mean?" Rod said, "You only remember the good times." I started to ask him about that, but Sid interjected, telling Rod that he felt Rod made large "encompassing statements." Rod gave a small shrug and said, "I left that 3,000 miles away."

Rod went on to discuss how he took the few dollars he had and his three children and packed up and crossed the country to begin again. They celebrated Christmas decorating a tree with tin cans and by exchanging food wrapped as presents. However, the family had good memories of these hard times and talked about the fun involved. The other members were fascinated with the story. It was at this point that Frank moved to his specific concern about his family.

Frank used this as a means of bringing up something which had been worrying him over the last week. It seems his wife had taken in two young men (about seventeen) who were friends of his daughters (aged thirteen and fourteen). Rod didn't feel this was a good situation and wanted to know what Frank could do about it. He looked particularly at me and asked if I knew what he could do. I said I would have to know what was going on in more detail. Rod was very interested in this situation, taking the stance that children were all-important to him and that he "would do anything, anything, to keep mine." He said that he had even spent a night in jail, charged with five counts of kidnapping. Gerry had appeared upset while Frank and Rod were speaking; he had been told that he could be charged with kidnapping if he attempted to remove his son from his wife's custody. Rod's response was that all Gerry had to do was cross the provincial border and he would be OK.

I explained that generally the parent who had the most involvement with the child or children was the one who received custody. Unless there was evidence of unfitness, this generally meant the mother. Rod was nodding away at Frank who said several times to him, "You don't know how bound I am," referring to the legal restraints applied to him by family court. I went on to say that the legal system was now changing somewhat and that either parent was denied access only on rare occasions, that even if one parent had custody, the other wasn't totally without rights.

I told Frank that if he were really concerned about the situation, I would be willing to help him talk to his court worker about it. He felt reassured about this and said that maybe he would try some things on his own. He went on to say that until he had become involved in this group, he would have responded differently to the situation. I asked him how he would have handled it before. He said that he would have just charged right into a confrontation with his wife and probably achieved nothing except to raise bad feelings.

Gerry appeared to be calmer by now. I asked him if he were still upset. He said that when he and his wife separated, he was really concerned about what would happen to his son. He was afraid that if his wife took up with another guy, his son would somehow be damaged. Frank and Ron both were nodding at Gerry. I asked Gerry if he were still afraid of this. He said no, that he and his wife were still working on things but they were getting along OK.

As one individual begins to explore a concern, associated feelings and issues will often be triggered for other members. It is important for the worker to recognize these issues and feelings as they emerge but, at the same time, to keep the group focused on the original concern raised by the first member. In this case, it is important to come back as the worker did to Frank for further elaboration.

Frank looked at Sid and Gerry and said that he wanted to know if they felt that being brought up in families where separations had occurred had affected them. He wanted to know what it had been like for them. I asked him if he were concerned about his children and he said yes.

Sid and Gerry talked about their perceptions of growing up in separated families. Both indicated that it hadn't been any real big deal. Gerry said his mother tended to "bad mouth" his father but not vice versa. Frank seemed a bit upset at that, saying that was probably to be expected. Sid indicated that he had had contact with his biological father only twice, once when he was in his teens and then when he sought him out several years ago. He said he was the only one of the children to have contact with their biological father. Frank was thoughtful after hearing this. I asked him what was going on. He said that he was concerned about his future relationship with his son and daughters.

The process had been a slow one, but with some help. Frank was able to begin to talk about an area of concern that struck at the heart of his feelings of guilt at having "abandoned" his children. As will be illustrated in a later chapter when further illustrations are drawn from this group, a central theme throughout the work was the difficulty these men had in dealing with their feelings of tenderness and the associated feelings of dependency. The worker who led this group, a new experience for him, learned a great deal about the underlying feelings of men who use violence, aiding his ability to "hear" more clearly the indirect offerings of members in the next group he led. In this sense, each group is an educational experience for the worker, and the ability to understand the themes expressed will increase with experience.

The emphasis in this first section has been on helping the individual reach out to the group. In many cases, particularly when the feelings expressed reflect those held by the group members, the worker's second client, the group, paradoxically appears to turn away from the individual. The next section discusses the meaning of this dynamic.

Reaching for the Group Response to the Individual

It is easy to see how a worker can become identified with a particular client's feelings as a theme of concern is raised. If strong emotions are expressed, the worker may feel supportive and protective. Not surprisingly, if the other group members do not appear to respond to the individual, a common reaction from workers is to feel upset and angry. The worker is shocked and surprised to see group members apparently not listening, to see their eyes glazing over as they appear to be lost in their own thoughts, or to witness a sudden change in subject or

a direct rebuff to the client who has bared some innermost feelings. At moments such as these the worker's clarity of function and the notion of "two clients" can be most critical. Instead of getting angry, the worker should view the group members' responses as a signal—not that they are uninterested in what is being said—but that the theme may be having a powerful impact on them. The tasks of the mediation function, as outlined by Schwartz, call for the worker to search out the common ground between the individual and the group at the point where they seem most cut off from each other. This clear sense of function directs the worker to empathize with the group members' feelings underlying their apparent resistance at precisely the same time as expressing empathy with the individual client. The group leader must be with both clients at the same time. The following illustration of this process is drawn from group work with fourteen- and fifteen-year-old boys in a residential treatment center. One of the members, Jay, tries to use the group for some help in discussing his feelings about his parents. In this first excerpt, he is shocked when his brother (a member) tells him that he has just heard from a relative a family rumor that their father may not be in fact Jay's biological father. As Jay attempts to come to terms with his reactions, the worker has to pay close attention to the part of the group which has difficulty in dealing with this issue. The group discussion has been general thus far, dealing with questions about prostitutes.

J.: Right. Take my mother for instance. We—we know that she's ... she's married and going out with some guy. ... My old man knows it. She left him once you see ... and now she's back again.

F.: (J's brother) J, you want to know something? (hesistant) I don't want to bother you but—I heard—from someone—I don't want to say who—

J.: (impatient) Ahh, come on.

F.: That you—

J.: (interested, wants to hear) Yeah.

F.: Aren't—er—that it was Mom and some other man. . . . I'm not saying it's true or anything—

J.: You don't think . . .

F.: Oh, I'm not believing it—

J.: (jumps in) Oh, I wouldn't doubt it—my mother knew Bill (her boyfriend) before my old man and her were married. Bill had already given it to her before.

M.: Maybe your old man doesn't know.

J.: For all my old man knows she could have said he was drunk one night . . . and what could he say?

M.: (who had started to get restless) Let's do something else, let's listen to some music for a while now.

WORKER: Why do you want to do that?

J.: Why? Why? Why does M. want to stop? (The others mumble something, a few yeahs.)

M.: We'll talk about it afterwards.

J.: (angry) Why? You only get in here once a week. God, I'm not going to quit. You can quit if you want.

M.: Not quit!

J.: If I found out that my old man . . . that Bill (his mother's boyfriend) was my real father . . .

F.: (interrupts, soft voice) How would you feel?

J.: (Pause) I'd go see him. I'd go see him—and talk it over with him—and find out what happened. I'd really want to know—I mean, that's—that's a really good thought. I never thought of that.

M.: Who told you? (to F.)

J.: Yeah, who told you (to F.). I mean, I might as well know, I know most of it all now. (Cross talk for a couple of seconds. Meanwhile, M. had not been paying any attention.)

WORKER: M., you don't seem to want to talk about any of this.

M.: Well, it's none of my business.

While Jay was speaking the worker was watching the group members, particularly their facial reactions. This is the skill of "monitoring the group." When she spotted the signal of M. turning away, she reached for it directly. In some ways, M. was expressing the discomfort felt by all the boys as they explored a sensitive and personal area which hit home to them as well. The worker acknowledged this as a potential obstacle thereby freeing the process.

WORKER: I think it's hard to listen to such a personal problem. What makes it even tougher is that all of you have a lot of mixed feelings about your folks. But you know, this is what the group is all about, and I think Jay really needs some help on this one.

J.: But I want you to listen. (said very emphatically) At least—at least—

D.: (interrupts) You can get some ideas.

J.: I can get some ideas—what I should do. What would you do if you found out your old man wasn't really your old man?

M.: Like you were—sort of like a bastard?

J.: No . . . Well, let's say—that your mother had got it from another man. He wasn't your real father. What would you do?

M.: You, you were an illegitimate child (half statement, half question).

F.: Yeah.

J.: What would you do? (Pause)

WORKER: How would you feel?

D.: (emphatically) I'd feel rotten.

M.: I, I, I, I'd feel—I'd feel dirty.

F.: I'd feel so— (Pause)

WORKER: How would you feel, J.?

J.: I don't know what I'd feel really. I think I'd really feel—I mean, really feel . . .

M.: (interrupts) J.?

J.: . . . Bad. I—you know, um, I'm um, I don't know what I'd really do if I ever found out that this wasn't really my father.

M.: What do you feel like right now?

F.: (interrupts) But J., just think back, in a way . . . it could be true.

J.: The way I think it is, it could be true,—the time I was born was when my parents really started to break up—that they really started to have fights and all that stuff. And—and after I had a heart attack as a baby—then—

M.: (interrupts) You did? (Group talks about J.'s heart attack and illnesses for a few minutes.)

J.: But he's the worst off guy of all of us, this guy right here. (points to D., whose parents are both dead.)

The subject is changed and the meeting ends shortly thereafter.

The worker was unable to help at this point beyond assisting Jay to share his concerns with the group members and to help the group members stay with him. She tried to help Jay explore his feelings, and the boys in the group commiserated with him. This, in itself, was helpful; however, neither the worker nor the group members knew where to go at this point. The subject was dropped and did not pick up again for three sessions. At the start of the next session, the worker noticed that Jay was unusually quiet and commented on it. Jay was reluctant to take up the worker's offer, and the group members seemed ready to drop the issue. However, the worker persisted, reminding the group of how they had helped Jay the last time. Jay finally revealed that his mother was leaving home.

J.: (Points at F.) You know what it's all about. (Pause. D. and F. say they think they know.)

J.: Ma's leaving home again. It's the second time. She's leaving home again. She told—I heard—a while ago I—I heard her talking about it. (Pause)

F.: Your father's house is up for sale. (Pause) That would give her a chance to leave anyway. (Pause)

F.: She's leaving now—she said in two weeks. (The boys talk for a few minutes about the woman she is going to stay with. J. looks at the books, lies down on the floor.)

WORKER: (to the group) You're not helping J.

F.: (quickly) Oh, I'm thinking about it.

M.: Get it off your chest, J.

D.: That's how you go crazy, if you don't.

M.: It's just going to build up and you'll explode and become a paranoid, or schizophrenic—right, Joanne (the worker)? Do you know what a paranoid or schizophrenic is? (Worker answers, "Yes").

F.: (to J.) You didn't feel that bad about it last time.

J.: (Talks very low, can hardly be heard.) Then I wasn't old enough to really understand—but this time for some reason—(F. talks about what it was like when his father walked out. M., too.)

M.: J., I've just found an article you should read. It's called "How to deal with your tensions." (Laughs. Everyone ignores this)

WORKER: M., I think it's hard for you to stay with J.'s feelings because they hit you hard as well.

F.: When you get older, you realize more—you think and put the pieces together.

J.: When you're older, you think about the future, not the past.

F.: Sometimes it haunts you—the future. You're scared. (Pause. J. quiet.)

WORKER: You told J. to get it all off his chest. It looks like it's very much still there.

C.: I think you should find out the truth . . . and ask.

J.: I don't want to do that. I'm afraid to find out what happened—that my father might not be—my real father. I don't know what I would do. I've never lost my temper—but there's always a first time.

WORKER: You're afraid of what you'd feel. (half question, half statement)

J.: If this guy was my father . . . he's rotten . . . he broke up my family. (Silence) Maybe the others aren't interested. I don't want to bore them. (Worker asked what the others said to that. They denied it.)

J.: They can say that but they may not feel that inside—they got their own problems.

C.: I don't find it boring. I'm just trying to think of a solution.

D.: It's my problem, too.

C.: Same here. I—you don't know what's going to happen if you ask something.

D.: I think it's better to find out the truth, because sooner or later it's going to hit you. The more you wait the harder it's going to hit.

C.: I think so, too. Just then the bell rang, indicating the end of the meeting. Before everyone left the worker asked them if they wanted to continue talking on this the next time, and they said yes.)

As I have described the sessional contracting phase of a group meeting, many of the dynamics and skills discussed in the first part of this book have reappeared. The worker's sessional tuning in, sessional contracting, elaborating, empathy, and demand-for-work skills are as important in helping the individual present concerns in the group session as they were in individual work. This is the common core of practice skill, the generic element. The worker's function is also the same, since the work is focused on helping the client negotiate important systems in life. The variant elements of the work derive from the presence of one of these important systems—the group—and the need for the worker to pay attention to its responses. The core skills are important in implementing this aspect of the functional role as well.

Reaching for the Work when Obstacles Threaten

In the analysis of work with individuals, the connections between the way of working (process) and the content were explored. For example, the flow of affect between the worker and the client, the authority theme, was identified as a potential obstacle to work. Attention needed to be paid to these feelings; they had to be acknowledged if the work were to proceed. This same issue was highlighted in the analysis of first group sessions when

the importance of discussing the worker-group relationship was underlined. In the group context one also has to deal with the interchange which takes place between the members, what Schwartz refers to as the "intimacy" theme. While both of these issues, authority and intimacy, are discussed more fully in the next two chapters, they need to be mentioned now in the context of sessional contracting. For example, it may be important to discuss the process between members as a way of freeing individuals to trust the group enough to offer concerns in painful and sensitive areas. In the example which follows, a youngster in a group for boys at a residential center wants to discuss a difficult issue but is hesitant about revealing himself to the group. By pausing and encouraging the group to discuss briefly the intimacy theme, the worker frees the member to continue.

I began the meeting by asking if there was anything that anybody wanted to ask or say before we got started. Mike said, "Well, I have some things, but I am not sure that I want to talk about all of it." I said that Mike wanted to get at what was bothering him but he wasn't going to be able to do it right away. Perhaps he needed to test the group a bit to see if he could trust them? He said, "I don't know if I can always trust people." Terry came in here and said that, "This is our group here, and we can say what we want to. What goes on in here does not go outside to others, isn't that right? If we have something that we want to talk about, something really personal, we won't let it out of our own group, right?" Terry got verbal approval from all of the boys in the group. I also felt that Terry was demonstrating the basis of our contract. I said that I agreed with what Terry had said. To clarify the point further, I said that I saw our purpose as being able to talk about some of the feelings that we have around being here in the Boys' Centre and that out of this might come family problems, work problems, and the problems of what is going to become of me, for example, am I really worth anything? Steve elaborated this aspect by referring to his willingness to share his feelings with the group.

The next move by the worker was important. After acknowledging the problem and restating the contract, the worker re turned to Mike and his specific issue. This demonstrates the importance of not getting lost in a discussion of process. There are times when it is necessary to discuss obstacles and to explore them in depth, as will be illustrated later; however, in most cases the recognition of the obstacle is all that is needed. Workers can be "seduced" into expanding the discussion of the obstacle unnecessarily, thus subverting the contract of the group and substituting a focus of group members attempting to understand how they work as a group rather than discussing their concerns. This worker properly returned to the member, Mike.

After this brief return to the contracting, I asked Mike if he thought he might feel like sharing some of the things he had said at the start of the meeting that were bothering him. He said that he thought that he could talk about part of it. John M. said that he thought that he knew what it was that was bothering him. I let this hang. I wanted to see if Mike would respond to John or if the others would respond to either John or Mike to help us work on what Mike had come up with. Terry reiterated what he had said earlier, "What is said in the group is for the group." John said, "I think that it is about your family, isn't it, Mike?" Mike: "Yes, that's part of it." I asked John what he meant by Mike's family. John: "Well, Mike doesn't have any parents, and we are all the time talking about troubles with our family, or we always have some place to go if we make a weekend [receive permission to take a weekend away]." Mike: "Yah, that's part of it. Like I make a weekend and I stay here."

Another way in which process and content are synthesized was described earlier in the discussion of the meaning of resistance. For example, the client may appear to hold back from entering a difficult area of work, and the worker senses the reluctance to proceed. Such resistance was viewed as central to the work and a possible sign that the client was verging on an important area. The need to explore the resistance was suggested. A group may also resist by launching a tacit conspiracy to avoid painful areas. This is often the reason a group or individuals hold back in the early stages of a group meeting. Once again, the worker's task involves bringing the obstacle out in the open in order to free the group members from its power. In the following example of work with mothers of children who have been diagnosed as hyperactive, the early themes had centered on the parents' anger toward school officials, teachers, neighbors, and other children, all of whom did not understand. They also acknowledged their own anger at their children. The worker empathized by saying, "It is terribly frustrating for you. You want to be able to let your anger out, but you feel that if you do so, it will make things worse." After a few comments, the conversation (as the worker pointed out) became general again:

I told the group members that they seemed to be talking in generalities again. Martha said it seemed they didn't want to talk about painful things. I agreed that this appeared to be hard. Every time they got on a painful subject they took off onto something safer. I wondered if the last session had been very painful for them. Martha said that it was a hard session, they had come very close, and she had a lot to think about over the weekend. Lilly said that she felt very wound up over the last session, so much so that she had had trouble sleeping at night. I asked her to tell us what made it so upsetting for her. She said that she had felt so helpless when they had been talking about the school boards and the lack of help for children like her own. Doreen said it really wasn't so helpless. She had talked to a principal and had found out some new information.

It is interesting to note that when the worker asked, "What made it so upsetting?" the answer to the question designed to explore the resistance brought the group back to its work. Later in the same session, the worker picked up on the acknowledgment of their own anger towards the child and the difficulty in talking about that with similar results. It is easier for workers to explore resistance if they do not view it as a commentary on their lack of skill.

One final connection between process and task has to do with the power of specific examples in the work of the group. We saw earlier how the skill of elaboration, called "moving from the general to the specific," could also have a powerful impact on deepening work with individuals. It is an even more essential skill in work with groups. Because of its numbers, a group can sustain a general discussion about problems to an extraordinary length. The group work problem identified at the beginning of this chapter, that of responding to a member's general comment by asking all the other group members if they too feel that way, is one of the most common problems in the sessional contracting phase of group work. In the following example the group is for mothers of sixth-grade boys who were underachieving. The purpose was to discuss how they could more effectively help the youngsters with their schoolwork. After general discussion of their feelings when faced with their children's resistance to homework, their own memories

of failure at school, their identification with their children's feelings, and their recognition that they sometimes push their children because of their own need for success, the worker realized the importance of more specificity in the work. She began by focusing the members on the need to deal with specific methods.

I said that I thought it would be useful if they described what actually happens at home concerning the issue of homework—how they handle getting the kids started on and completing assignments, and then discuss the pros and cons of the various ways of handling this. . . .

I told them that they had come up with some good ideas during the past meetings and that if they could apply these with their own children, they might begin to resolve some of the difficulties they had been describing. I said that it seems to me that they already have found some alternate ways of dealing with their children related to schoolwork and homework, and it is just a matter of seeing where they can be applied in their own particular situations.

And then, she made a direct demand for work.

I asked that each describe as fully as possible what goes on in each of their homes concerning getting the children to get started on the homework and also to describe the means they may use to get them to complete it.

The members needed this help at this point to get into the details of their experiences, and it is only in analysis of the specific details that the worker and the group can provide the required help.

In summary, I have described how individuals reach out, often indirectly, to raise their concerns with the group. I have also illustrated the group's ambivalent responses. The worker's function in mediating this engagement and the importance of paying attention to the process in the group have been analyzed, concentrating on such problem areas as the feelings of members about the trust they have in the group, or the resistance which sets in when the work gets difficult, or the difficulties involved in helping in general terms, rather than specifically. In the next section of this chapter I will focus on the mutual aid process in the middle stages of sessions and examine how individuals and the group are helped and what the tasks of the worker are in this process.

THE WORK PHASE IN A GROUP SESSION

A number of mutual aid processes were described in Chapter 7, including sharing data, the dialectical process, exploring taboo areas, the "all-in-the-same-boat" phenomenon, mutual support, mutual demand, individual problem solving, rehearsal, and the strength-in-numbers dynamic. The following section illustrates some of these processes using recordings from work-phase sessions of groups. In the first set of excerpts the way general themes of concern are presented and discussed over a period of time is illustrated, emphasizing how individuals use the general discussion for help with their specific concerns. In the second set of illustrations, we will see how individual problem solving can influence the general concerns held by group members.

It is important to note that work in a group is not neat and orderly, with general themes or specific problems presented at the start of the meeting, worked on in the middle segment, and then neatly resolved towards the end. In reality, themes and problems may emerge only partially in early sessions and then reemerge later in new forms as group members become more comfortable with each other and the worker. For example, in the early ses-

sions of an unmarried mothers' group, most of the conversation involved sharing the hurt and bitterness the young women felt over the reactions of the child's father, their own parents, friends, and others. It was only as trust developed in the group and these feelings were accepted and understood that the members began to face their own feelings and considered doing something about their relationships with significant others.

The process of change is a slow one, and group members need to explore their thoughts and feelings at a pace appropriate for them. Difficult issues may take weeks or months of "working through" before the group member is ready to face a problem in a new way. The worker needs to be supportive during this process, but at the same time, a half step ahead of the client, thus presenting a consistent yet gentle demand for work. To provide a sense of time and process, the excerpts in the following section are drawn from an unmarried mothers' group meeting over a period of eight weeks.

Helping the Group Work over Time

Groups for unwed mothers provide a good example of how mutual aid can heal over time. In the following example, the young women are all in their teens and have chosen to stay at a home for unwed mothers during their last stages of pregnancy. Most began at the home feeling uniquely alone, rejected, and depressed. The group meetings were led by workers from a local child welfare agency. The sessions presented an opportunity for the members to talk about their hopes and fears and to discover that they were not alone. The support and caring in the group made the problem easier for them to bear and provided important help as they clarified their thinking about central issues in their lives. After working with many groups of this type, the workers have identified themes of concern which are common to most young women going through this experience. Although the order in which these are raised and the particular variations of the content may change, the themes are basically the same: family relationships, relationship with the father of the child (and other men), relationship to the peer group, the pregnancy and the birth of the baby, legal rights and obligations, the decision to keep or relinquish the child, feelings of loss if they relinquish the child, problems of maintenance if they decide to keep the baby, anticipated relationship problems when they return to the community (e.g., how they will relate to friends), pregnancy-prevention measures, their feelings about sex, and throughout all the discussion their own feelings about themselves.

This group was held in a maternity home sponsored by a religious social service order. It had eleven members and was open ended—that is, new members joined when they entered the home, and others left after they gave birth. These events were incorporated into the work of the group. The young women ranged in age from fourteen to eighteen and were usually of three types: those who are living with their families and enter the home after discussion with parents, those who are living in training schools or are wards of the state, and a smaller number of older young women who feel guilty about their pregnancies and have come to the home to hide. This group was held in the early 1970s, and the excerpts should be viewed in the context of the attitudes, values and mores (e.g., attitudes towards premarital sex, woman's rights, abortion) of the time.

This same group, if held today, would need to deal with women's issues which are closely related to the problems faced by these clients. The worker would need to help the clients see how many of their concerns are really a product of the social context. In the early sessions a common theme was their anger towards the putative father of the child.

Sally had trouble putting her feelings into words, but she wondered how you could get the baby's father "to feel as you do about the baby?" She said her boyfriend was sympathetic and visited her often, but she felt he did things "from his head, not from his heart." I asked the girls if they could help. Sherry said she felt the same about her boyfriend. He even denied that she was pregnant when his mother asked him. The other girls generally felt it was unfair that the boy could act as if nothing had happened. The boys didn't have to come to a home or get fat bellies or feel embarrassed to walk down the street. They agreed, after a question from me, that this made them really angry. I asked Sally if she really understood how her sister felt when she was pregnant (Sally had talked about this in the first session). She agreed that she didn't really know. Maybe her boyfriend would feel differently once the baby was born. No one seemed ready to talk more in response to Sally's question. Lisa thought the boys should take some responsibility. Fay and Bernice thought they'd like to have their boyfriends talk to the social worker. Maybe they'd find it easier to talk to someone else. Fay thought her boyfriend had been very patient with her. She was always in a bad mood when she saw him and was ready to snap his head off. The girls expressed their resentment and anger towards the fathers again but seemed unable or unready to pursue the subject.

The members' anger and resentment towards the fathers is mixed with the hope that their attitudes might change. Perhaps after the birth or a conversation with the worker they might be able to return to the relationship which existed before the pregnancy. The worker's effort to help them understand their boyfriends' difficulty in "understanding" is not picked up because the group members feel too hurt and misunderstood to be able to put themselves in anyone else's shoes. The same hurt and anger was expressed in early discussions about their own parents. The worker attempted to reach for the guilt that she felt underlay their hurt and anger, but the members refused to acknowledge it at this point.

Jane said she'd like to ask a question. Did any of the girls feel closer to their parents since their pregnancy? She said her parents' letters made her cry—they were so beautiful. Bernice and Lisa agreed. Sally, Sherry, and Florence felt closer to their mothers—not their fathers. Nan could talk to her mother, used to talk to father (parents just divorced). Carla said her father told her she had disgraced the family—told her mother she'd have to go away. She thought her mother felt differently but now says her mother is "just acting a part." She told her mother how hurt she was by her father's rejection, and her father tried to be kind when she was at home at Thanksgiving, but he just ignored her pregnancy—acted as if nothing were different. She had always been her father's favorite until now. Jane and Sherry said their fathers were the same—ignored their pregnancy as if it could go away. Jane said her father said they would now be grandparents and he could have been so proud, but he couldn't be now. Sally wished she could tell her step-father and that he should help her and understand, but she was afraid that he might not be kind. I asked if the girls felt guilty about their pregnancy. They denied this. Carla said her father had walked past the maternity home in his noon hour, hoping to see her—her mother told her. Carla wished he had phoned and told her and then she would have gone to meet him. Dolores spoke of her father's reaction, saying "Now you know what I was talking about." This hurt and angered her. Fay spoke at length of her father's stupidity. She and Carla both thought their parents were from the Middle Ages—had no idea of what their lives were like. I asked if they couldn't share with their fathers how they felt.

Carla and Fay thought it would be impossible for them. Lisa thought she would have to make the opening gesture. The girls generally felt they just couldn't talk to their parents.

A central theme for all the group members was the unborn baby. The decision whether to keep or not is always a difficult one. The members feel trapped in that no matter what they decide, they will feel guilty. They want to do what is best for the child and at the same time they recognize their own needs. It is important that they have a chance to explore this decision in depth, to get in touch with their real feelings during the process, to test out their ideas against reality, and to come to an answer for themselves which they can live with. At first, the discussion in this area was superficial as the members attempted to convince themselves that they were clear about what they would do and that the issue was resolved. Nonetheless, they often hinted at their real feelings during conversatons about related subjects, such as the discussion of the adoption process. In the next excerpt group members questioned one member who stated she would like to "forget all about her pregnancy and the baby and start a new life."

Dana said she always thought she was adopted because her own mother didn't love her. The girls wanted to know what adopting parents knew about them apart from height, color of hair and eyes, etc. They wanted us to be sure we'd tell them they loved their babies. Rita wasn't entirely convinced but agreed she wouldn't want to have her child learn about adoption accidentally. Rita said she guessed she just wanted to forget all about her pregnancy and her baby and start a new life afterwards. Once again the girls said she wouldn't be able to forget—explained why they felt this way. They, too, wanted a "new life," but couldn't forget their baby.

In the following excerpt the dilemma of whether to keep or relinquish the baby is challenged by one member who attacks the adoption "dream"—the belief that everything will work out. The worker reaches directly for this underlying feeling.

I asked Sherry to tell the girls about her concerns about adoption. She said she wondered how adoption workers could be sure the adopting parents would carry out the girls' wishes as to their preferences in adoption homes. Several of the girls responded to this. They felt the adopting parents would do what was best for the baby in view of their love for the baby. This didn't satisfy Sherry. She wondered how we would know what was happening when the baby was five or six or so. I asked if Sherry couldn't trust the agency to choose good parents. She said she trusted the agency but maybe not the adopting parents. I wondered if she were really saying she wanted to be the baby's parent. Sherry agreed.

It was important here for the worker to be clear about her helping function because, in so many cases, the worker may feel the client should not keep the child, and if she acts on this feeling, she may cut off the client's ability to explore her true reactions. In those cases where the worker clearly cannot let the client keep the child (such as when the situation raises questions about protection of the infant), she must level with the client about her dual roles. In situations where protection is not an issue, the worker needs to help the clients explore this ambivalent set of feelings, so that the final decision can be made in full recognition of the mixed feelings rather than after denying one part of the client's emotions. Sherry elaborated her concern, and the worker identified the dilemma for all.

She wanted the baby so much but didn't think it was fair to the baby to keep it. She asked if her worker could go ahead with a ten-day hospital placement even if she changed her mind in hospital. She knew she wanted a ten-day placement but feared her emotions would take over and she wouldn't be able to carry through with her plan. I suggested she might need more time than ten days, that babies were adopted up to the three-month period and later. She couldn't accept this. She knew a ten-day placement was best for her baby, but she was frightened for herself. Fay said she'd tell her (Sally) what she really wanted to do if she wavered. (Fay and Sally are expecting on the same date.) Jane (adopted herself) said she was really sold on adoption—knew how carefully applicants were screened. She agreed it would be hard. I said that the decision was a very difficult one because of the girls' mixed feelings, wanting to keep, but feeling adoption in their circumstances best for the baby.

At a later session, the worker attempted to acknowledge the many hurt and angry feelings the group members had expressed about their reactions of others in their lives. The worker also knew, however, that under the anxiety about the harsh judgments by others was the group members' own harsh judgment of themselves. If they were to deal with their boyfriends, their parents, and the decision to keep or relinquish the child, they first needed to face their real feelings. The worker hoped that through the process of mutual aid, they would begin to modify their attitude to themselves. At this point, the worker, using the fund of positive feeling built up in the group during the first weeks and the effective relationship developed through her sympathetic attitude, makes a demand for work:

I reviewed last week's discussion—felt the girls had expressed a lot of anger versus boyfriends, about families, even about adopting parents who would be caring for their babies—felt their anger was justified—it wasn't fair that they received all blame, had the pain of birth while their boyfriends continued normal activity and parents condemned them. I commented that there was a lot of hurt mixed with their anger. The girls agreed, either nodding or commenting. I asked what the girls themselves felt about their pregnancy. This they themselves saw had been missing in last week's discussion, what *they* felt re: pregnancy, baby, and themselves. Carla said she hated her pregnancy—felt she was missing out—not working. Her brother was being married and she was to have been a bridesmaid. How would her parents explain her absence? (Carla close to tears.) Fay said she knew how she felt, because the same thing would have happened to her, but her sister had postponed her wedding. She wondered if Carla were finding it extra hard because her boyfriend was in the hospital and she couldn't visit him. Jane suggested it was harder for the girls who lived in the area because they were afraid someone might see them. Carla said her family was "very well known in the area." Fay said she was ashamed of her pregnancy, but not ashamed of their babies—it wasn't their babies' fault. Jane said she "wasn't going to play house again." Carla said she hated her baby, but then she didn't really mean that. She was close to tears here. Lisa suggested Carla could tell her mother how she felt, and her mother could tell her father so he would understand how she was feeling. Carla felt she was missing her best year—was getting behind in work. Fay said the trouble with Carla was that she "hated" herself, so that anything anyone said to her made her think they were hating her. Carla said she was pleased with the girls' support, she knew who her real friends were, but feared going back in the community afterwards. What would people say? Co-leader suggested people weren't as curious as Carla feared. Fay disagreed. I suggested that they were maturing, had indeed helped each other, noticeably in today's session. I summarized the work, as we were nearing the end.

As trust in the group developed, the conversation became more real and the group members shared feelings, some of which they had not been sure they could safely discuss. How could someone simultaneously love and hate this unborn child? As the group members and the leader accepted these feelings and did not judge the member harshly for them, similar feelings in all the young women were expressed. The worker suggested the use of a film at the next meeting, describing some actual case histories of clients facing a similar decision. The impact of the film was powerful as the group members identified with the unmarried mothers on the screen. The discussion moved to a new level of feeling as the ideas they had discussed, sometimes intellectually, became very real for each of them.

The film was shown in a darkened room, and as the film developed the girls were in tears, and they sat in the darkened room for several minutes afterwards without speaking or moving.

We finally moved to our group session room, and some of the girls started talking while coffee was being served. Lisa said it was hard to believe that her baby was "real." She commented on the film baby's fat legs and pigeon toes. Dina said suddenly her pregnancy was real—she was aware of what she had to face. Carla said she was "mixed up"—Jane, Pam, Rita looked closed in on themselves.

I asked the girls how they were feeling. They answered, "scared, depressed." Jane answered "aware." Fay said she was surer than ever now that it was right to give up her baby "right away." She thought the girl in the film must have been hurt when she gave up right away, and another asked how she could possible bear to do that. Lisa said she thought he girl in the film had been wrong to keep the baby for two years—asked if we'd noticed the baby's bewildered face when he moved toward adopting parents.

After a short silence, the worker acknowledged the pain experienced by the group members as they discussed the film:

I suggested that the film had been painful for them. Sherry said the film made her feel better about adopting parents. Carla said she was different from other girls about her baby—couldn't feel the baby was real. Sally said she felt good about both her pregnancy and her baby. She would likely have to give up her baby, but she always thought pregnant women were beautiful, and she was happy. Sherry said the film made her think about other things she didn't want to think about. I suggested that this was "hurting." Tears came to Sherry's eyes and she ran from the room. We could hear her sobs, and Sally left to be with her. I said it was sad that Sherry couldn't stay with us. There was nothing the matter with tears expressing their feeling. Carla said they tried not to cry in front of each other or everyone would be crying. She said that Dina, her roommate, heard her sniffling sometimes at night.

The worker moved at this point to help the group members explore using each other for mutual support. They have felt alone in their feelings and have not been able to share them with friends, parents, or even the other group members. Attuned to the powerful healing process of mutual aid, the worker encouraged them to use each other in the group, a microcosm of the outside world they would need to draw support from in the future, no matter what their decision finally was:

I wondered if it didn't help to know the other girls were feeling the same way. Carla said it did help to know this, but they were all in the same boat and they kept up for each other. I asked if they felt better after their tears. Carla said she did. I asked how they "hid" their tears. Carla said she got "snappy." Fay made jokes and got "mad," too. I wondered if it might be better to let others know how they really were feeling. Jane and Fay said it didn't

make them feel better to cry. They liked to be alone when they were depressed. Jane said she'd had a bad three days this week, but Dina dragged her out to decorate for Halloween, and she went and was "feeling better." She could understand how hard it was for Jane when she still had two months to go. She'd thought the time would never pass, but now she had only two weeks.

I suggested that this had been a rough session, a painful session. They were becoming more "aware" of the decision they were facing. I asked that someone tell Sherry and Sally that we were sorry—suggested that we break a few minutes early. Carla wasn't ready to stop. She said that she was all mixed up—felt in a daze—didn't know what to do about her baby. Her parents said not to keep, but her girlfriend said she'd help her. She, herself, didn't feel she was ready to take her baby—she wanted to work and have a life of her own. I said she sounded as if she had mixed feelings—suggested we start with this next week. Two or three girls said they wished it were "all over." They wanted to get it over with. I said that it was very hard, but again suggested we wait until next week.

Sally and Sherry came afterwards to say they were sorry to have missed the group. Sherry said she was depressed before the film. She was upset when she thought of her baby. She tried not to feel about it because she knew it was better to give it up.

The worker arrived at the next session to find three of the group members in the hospital, one having given birth, another in labor, and a third with an infection. The early discussion in the group centered on the excitement and the anxiety all of the group members felt at the moment. The home and the group had become like a family, and they all felt an investment in each other. After this early discussion, the worker inquired as to the impact of the film. She felt moved by the reactions of the members, concerned by the depth of feeling evoked, and was uncertain and worried at the power of the feelings and their effect on the members. The group members reassured her and Carla particularly indicated that the week had been spent in important thinking and some resolution.

The girls all spoke in favor of the film. They agreed they were deeply involved with the unmarried mother in the film, related to her feeling of loneliness and loss when she walked along the street at the end of the film. But they all felt that they had become aware of their baby as a real person for the first time. Carla and Dina said they had thought a lot about their decision in the past week. I suggested they were taking responsibility for making the best decision for their baby and also for themselves. For example, Carla had suggested this last week when she said she wanted to do what was best for her baby but also wanted a life of her own, to work, to date, to be a normal teenager. Carla agreed with my comment. She said she thought adoption was the best for her baby, and she planned to return to her home and to her job.

Sherry told the group that she and her boyfriend have decided to get married and keep the baby. The worker acknowledged her excitement and told her that she was happy for her. Other group members indicated that the last session had helped them in making their decision.

Jane, Connie, Carla, Dina, and Rita plan to give up their babies. Each of the girls spoke of their own plans for themselves. Jane goes back to university, Dina, Connie, and Rita back to school, and Carla back to work. I suggested that after a painful session last week, they seemed to have really worked out their decisions.

Sherry explained why she had been upset the week before, and the worker asked the group members to explore the question of the appropriateness of sharing their feelings in the group as well as the issue of being able to use what they have learned outside.

I hoped that the girls felt it was all right to express their feelings of anger and sorrow here. They seemed to feel they could trust the group with their feelings. Carla said this was very true. She felt very close to the girls in the home—felt they accepted her no matter what. I asked if the girls felt they could carry this over to relationships with people outside the maternity home—their parents, their boyfriends. Carla felt it was "safer" in the home, because everyone was in the same boat. Jane said you tried in the "outside world," but people laughed at you or "put you down," and you started to build a wall around yourself, so you wouldn't have to be hurt. Sherry said the reason she could marry her boyfriend was that she could tell him how she felt. She could cry or laugh or dress in old clothes, and he still loved her. They could tell each other how they were really feeling. She thought Sally's problem was that she couldn't be herself with her boyfriend. He was shy and quiet and wanted Sally to be like that. She said Sally kept saying her boyfriend wouldn't recognize her the way she acted in the home. Jane wished there weren't a wall between her and her parents. She wondered how she'd tell them her baby had been born. Would she say, "Look, you're grandparents"? She laughed but was close to tears. I suggested that the girls might help her. Carla thought she might say, "It's all over." Dina wondered if Jane could tell her parents she'd like them to visit her in hospital. Dina said her mother didn't care what happened to her—Carla asked if I would speak to her mother—find out how she was feeling. I asked if it would help if I were to be the middle man. Carla said if I could find out how her mother felt, she would be able to talk to her. Dina, Pam, and Debby would like me to talk to their mothers. I said there was a possibility of a group for parents of girls at the maternity home. All thought this would be a great idea. Connie said her sisters told her their mother said not to mention her pregnancy unless she did. She thought the girls had to make the first move.

The group members have moved from their early feeling that it was hopeless to talk to parents to plan how they might do it or enlisting the aid of the worker. Other sessions included further work on their relationship with their families, discussions of how to handle boys, particularly sexual demands, clarifying their legal rights and learning about adoption procedures (this included a visit to the group by an adoption worker). In one session, three of the members who had given birth returned to discuss the experience with the group members. In the final group session, the members began with a party and a gift for the worker inscribed "Happiness Is Togetherness." The discussion then moved to their thoughts about what would happen after the group.

Dina repeated her concern about her behavior afterwards. She wanted to be herself, but she also wanted to be different. I asked what she meant by "different." She said she wanted to make friends with kids her own age, not older boys. She wanted to be part of a different kind of group. She wanted to act less on impulse but wondered if she could do all this and still be herself. Jane said last week she had suggested that she planned to be "more reserved." That wasn't exactly the right word nor what she meant. She planned to think things through more carefully, make her own decisions rather than just going along with the crowd without thinking where they were leading. Dina was still concerned that she would have to be "different." I asked if anyone else could help Dina.

Pam thought they should be ready to "walk down the street with their heads held high." I wondered if she may be saying they should be feeling good about themselves. Pam agreed and thought then you would be able to be yourself, and your "real friends" would accept you as you were. Pam said she could count on the fingers on one hand the number of "real friends" she had. She said she had lots of acquaintances. I asked what qualities she found in her "real friends." Pam said they were the people with whom you could be yourself, who could accept you, even knowing your faults. She thought a good friend should be honest, that from them you could expect to be told faults and then be able to act on the advice. She gave several examples. Jane, Carla, Helen, and Dina all felt their pregnancies had shown the who their "real friends" were.

Further discussion included practicing specific strategies for handling questions at school and from the family. As the session neared the end, the worker attempted to summarize the process of change over time.

I suggested that they were all expressing mixed feelings—planning to return to their homes and communities, but not yet parted from their group at the maternity home. I attempted to summarize the sessions—the beginning ones when they had raised all the subjects we had been talking about since—the anger expressed against parents and putative fathers in the second session, then their acceptance of the pregnancy, their feeling of responsibility in making the best decision for themselves and their child, the growth I thought was evident in the girls, the better feeling about themselves, so they were getting ready to return to their homes and families, boyfriends, and work or school better able to face new experiences, new problems.

I said they had been a great group and wished them "good luck." I thought they were a "great bunch of kids." Dina said, "At least the leader thinks we're all right." The girls were all very kind in their reaction to the group sessions, thought nothing should be changed in the next group, wondered why we had to stop now. I said it was hard, but with Christmas coming and their Christmas concert, the co-leader and I would be seeing them then, and in interviews. Pam still had questions, was concerned that she had no area worker. I answered briefly, suggested we could go on with these questions in the next group which began in January. Jane, Dina, and Lisa asked to see me afterwards, and the group session ended. Jane was all excited. She had finally had the courage to agree to see the baby's father. She was both excited and scared, but thought it better than facing him first on her return to university.

Dina had been planning to leave the maternity home. She had decided to stay. She was "tired of running away" from her problems. Lisa is to go home for Christmas. Her mother and she are "closer" than ever before.

Focusing the Group on Problem Solving Mutual Aid

The excerpts from the unmarried mothers' group illustrated how group members deal with general themes of concern, the discussion of the general themes having had an impact on their specific concerns. Mutual aid is also offered in relation to specific concerns raised by individual members. As group members help an individual look closely at a particular problem and find a new way of dealing with it, they are helping themselves to deal with similar issues in their own lives. Thus, mutual aid can also start with a specific issue and move to a general concern. This process is now illustrated by excerpts from a group offered in a family agency. The five women and two men in the group were separated, divorced, or widowed. All of them had experienced heavy depression and difficulties in their interpersonal relationships. The group contract was to discuss these concerns and to find some solutions. The session illustrated began with a young woman, S., asking for help. The first response from group members was to offer consolation. The worker asked for elaboration while offering empathic support.

S. suddenly broke in and in a choked voice said, "I am feeling so down tonight." B. quickly responded, "You too?" S. continued that she

had called Don in Toronto; he had been busy and had not wanted to talk to her. I said, "You sound very hurt." Tears filled her eyes, and S. said, "Yes, I am. I blew up and acted like a baby and now I have to apologize when he comes down on Saturday." R. and B. rushed in to support S. saying they would be hurt, too, if they called someone and he was too busy to listen. L. nodded but said nothing. I asked S. why she had called and why she blew up. She softly and sadly replied that she had called Don, as she was lonely. E. questioned if she had told Don this. S. hadn't. B. asked why. S. smiled and said, "That wasn't the only reason I telephoned. I sometimes call to check up and see if he is really working." R. said, "You can't dwell on the fact that he had an affair, and J. is going to have his baby."

S. began to talk about Don and J. and the baby. I suggested, after listening a few minutes, that it seemed to me that S.'s relationship with Don right now was important, rather than again talking about what had happened in the past. I asked the others in the group, "What do you think?"

The worker refused to allow S. to discuss ground already covered in the group. Instead she made a demand for work by focusing S. on the here-and-now details of her discussion with Don. A major step in such work involves asking each group member to take some responsibility for their part in their problems. Our defenses often cause us to explain our problems by projecting the blame onto others in our lives or justifying the present difficulty be describing past reasons. In this case, the worker focused the client and the group on the immediate situation in the belief that this was the only way to help. The client responses elaborated on the specifics of the concern:

S. did not wait for a response and replied directly to me, "I feel so tense. I don't know what to talk to Don about. I don't want it to be like it was before we separated." I said,

"You sound scared to death." S. became very sad and nodded. E. added, "I have felt the same way with Jacques. I was his shadow. When he left and moved in with a girlfriend, I thought I could not exist on my own. I have learned to do so. S., you talk as if you had no life of your own." L. continued, "Do you always do what Don wants?"

S. then revealed the reason she was angry on the telephone with Don. She had earlier thought of going on a trip to England on her own and had wanted Don to say no. He had not, and when financially she had been unable to make the trip, she had called Don expecting him to be very happy that she was staying. He was busy and had not said much. S. then accused him of not caring and had hung up crying.

As the details emerged, so did a fuller picture of the problem. The worker recognized a common problem in intimate relationships—that is, one partner feels that the other should "divine" what she is feeling and wants to hear and then is hurt when it is not forthcoming. This is a specific example of the general problem of the difficulty of risking oneself by sharing real thoughts, feelings, and needs directly with those who are important to us. As a group member began to provide feedback to S. on her part of the proceedings, she cut him off, and the worker moved quickly to point this out.

B. started to say that S. had put Don on the spot, when S. interrupted and continued talking. I stopped her and said to the group, "Did you notice what just happened?" Everyone except S. and B. smiled but said nothing. I said to S., "Bob was trying to say something to you when you cut him off." She cut in to say anxiously, "Did I? I'm sorry, B." B. quietly said, "My God, I didn't even notice. It has happened to me so often, I guess I just expected to be cut off." She picked this up and said Don and B. were alike and that Don let her get away with talking too much and cutting him off. R. commented, "Don seems hard

to get close to," and there followed a few more comments on how Don seemed unapproachable.

The worker then challenged S.'s view of the event and asked her to take responsibility for creating part of the problem. Since the worker had already built a positive working relationship with the group members, S. was able to accept the confrontation and to examine her own actions. As the group members worked on the details of this specific example, it is easy to see how they were also working on their own variations on the theme.

I then went back to S.'s telephone call and asked S. why she had called Don at work when he was likely to be busy, rather than calling him at home. She stumbled around and didn't answer the question. I kept pressing her with the same question and then asked the group if they had any ideas on this. B. said, "I don't know what you are getting at." I said, "Let me check this out with all of you. My feeling is that S. called Don when she knew he would be likely to be busy and set it up so that he would probably be annoyed with her. Once again, she gets very hurt." E. added, "You did that with Don around the trip. Had he told you not to go to England, you would have been angry. If he told you to go, you would have said he did not care. I did the same thing with Jacques, and I never knew what I wanted. I was the little girl who asked father's permission for everything."

S. said, "I guess I set things up so that I am the sad little girl and everyone feels sorry for me, just like I am trying to do tonight. How do I stop?" Bob said, "How do we stop hating ourselves—that is what it comes down to." S. continued thoughtfully, "You know I took the job at the airline so that Don and I could travel, and he really doesn't like traveling. I also bought him a bicycle to go cycling, but then found out he hates it." I said, "It sounds like you assume things about Don but somehow never check them out with him. How come?" There was a short silence, and I continued, "Is it because when, as B. said, we hate ourselves, we are too scared to say what we feel, or want?"

S. talked about how horrible and stupid she feels she is, and the group members gave her much support. They also reminded her of he one area where she feels she has accomplished something—teaching piano. She brightened and talked of her love of music and how she enjoyed teaching.

R. then remarked on how much everyone needs to be told they do some things well. She recounted an incident at work where she had been praised and how pleased she was. The others in the group, except L., agreed. He said it depended on whether or not you believed it. S. agreed and stated it was hard for her to accept praise. E. went back to S.'s relationship with Don, saying S. had given indications that she knew the marriage was breaking up, although she had said Don's decision to separate was a complete surprise. S. said she partly knew, but did not want to admit it to herself. She had been withholding sexually, although they had had good sexual relations prior to marriage. I asked if she often gets angry at Don, and S. replied angrily, "I get furious at him, but I end up being bitchy which I don't like. I am also scared he will leave." As the end of the group session was approaching, the members began making some suggestions around dealing with Don on the weekend. She should be a little more independent, say what she is feeling and not always what she thinks she should say.

As the group members work on a specific problem, workers should share their own thoughts and ideas which may help to place the problem in a new perspective. To do this, they must draw upon their own life experience, the information they have gathered by working with people, individually or in groups, who have had similar concerns, and the professional literature. For example, in this brief excerpt group members were learning something about taking responsibility for one's own actions, the difficulties

involved in interpersonal communications, and specific interactional skills which might be helpful and lead to more effective interpersonal relationships. These agenda items were set in the context of their own experiences as they explored their often mixed feelings about themselves and others. Workers frequently carry out the function of providing data which is unavailable to the client and which may provide help with the problem or issue of the moment. In working with a couples' group, for example, the leader could draw upon communications theory, fair fighting in marriage ideas, developmental life theory, game model theory, gestalt, and other orientations. As workers deepen their own life experience, as they use group experiences to learn more about the complexities of life, and as they use the literature, they can enrich their contributions to the group members' struggle.

SESSIONAL ENDINGS AND TRANSITIONS

Chapter 5 discussed sessional endings and transitions, pointing out that each session required a resolution. A number of skills were identified as helpful in this stage including summarizing, generalizing, identifying next steps, rehearsal, and exploring "doorknob" comments. Each of these skills is just as applicable in the group session as the worker helps members resolve their efforts. Even if the work is not finished this fact should be pointed out. In the illustration which follows, a worker with a group of mothers with children diagnosed as hyperactive helped the members move towards more realistic next steps in their work as a mutual aid group. In making this demand for work, the worker represented an important view of life, suggesting that no matter how hopeless the situation may seem, the group members could begin by taking a step in their own behalf:

There was a lot of exchanging of problem situations with everyone coming out with her problems for the week. There seemed to be some urgency to share their problems, to get some understanding and moral support from the other members. Through their stories themes emerged: an inconsistency in handling their children's behavior (lack of working together with husband); the tendency to be overprotective; and their hesitancy at trusting their children. The issue of "nobody understanding" was again brought up, and I recognized their need to have someone understand just what it was that they were going through. Betty said that her son was never invited to play at the neighbors' houses, because he was a known disturber. Others had the same experiences with neighbors who didn't want their hyperactive son and daughter around. I expressed the hurt they were feeling over this, to which they agreed.

After further discussion about the impact of their children on others (teachers, neighbors, other children) they moved to the impact upon themselves:

There was a discussion of how their children's behavior affected them. Rose said that she ends up constantly nagging; she hates herself for it, but she can't stop. Her son infuriates her so much. Others agreed that they were the biggest naggers in the world. I asked what brought the nagging on. The consensus was that the kids kept at them until they were constantly worn down and they gave in to them. Also if they wanted the children to do something, they had to nag, because the children wouldn't listen. I said that the children really knew them, how they reacted, and also exactly what to do in order to get their own way. They agreed, but said that they couldn't change, they couldn't keep up with the badgering that these children could give out.

The group members have expressed two divergent ideas: on the one hand, they "couldn't change," and on the other they could not "keep up with the badgering." They quickly moved to a discussion of medications as a source of hope for change. The worker pointed out that their hope in this solution was mixed with their recognition that the drugs were addictive and that they could not provide an answer in the long run. This is an example of a process in groups which Bion calls "pairing" when the discussion of the group members appears to raise the hope of some event or person in the future which will solve the problem.[2]

For these group members, drugs provided this hope but also led to the group members avoiding a discussion of what they could do to deal with the problem. In a way, it represented a "primitive" group response attempting to deal with the pain of a problem by not facing it. As the session moved to a close the worker sensed the heaviness and depression of the group members caused by their feelings of hopelessness. She had empathized with these feelings but now needed to make a demand for work on the members, asking them to explore what they could do about the problem. When the members raised another hope for a solution in the form of an outside expert who would help, the worker pointed out their real feelings that no "outsider" could help and that they needed to find the help within themselves. In this way, the worker helped them resolve a difficult and painful discussion by conveying her belief in their strength and her sense of the concrete next steps open to them.

There was further discussion around the children's poor social behavior and the mothers' own worry about how these children will make out as adults. What will become of them? Will they fit in and find a place for themselves in society? I was feeling the heaviness of the group and pointed out what a tremendous burden it was for them. Our time was up, and I made an attempt to end the meeting, but they continued the discussion. I recognized their urgency to solve the problem and the need to talk with each other and get support from each other. Marilyn said that it was good, she came away feeling so much more relieved at being able to talk about how she felt, and she certainly was gaining some new insight into herself. Discussion diverted to the problem with the children and how they were to deal with it. I asked what they wanted to do. Edna suggested they ask a behavior modification therapist to help them work out solutions. Others thought it was a good idea. I said that that was a possibility, but I wondered if in wanting to get an "expert" in they were searching for someone to solve their problems for them. They agreed. I asked if they thought all these experts could do this. They said that it hadn't happened yet. I wondered if we could use the group for the purpose it was set up, to help each other problem solve. I suggested that next week we concentrate on particular problems and work together to see what solutions we could come up with. They seemed delighted with this and decided that they should write down a problem that happened during the week and bring it in. Then we could look at a number of such problems. Consensus was reached as to our next week's agenda, and meeting ended.

With this illustration of one form of sessional ending and transition work, I bring to a close the description of the work phase meeting in a mutual aid group. The purpose of the discussion was to illustrate a number of points: First, how the group worker needs to work with the individual and the group as they reach out to each other in the beginning stages of a session. Second, that mutual aid deals with general themes of concern as well as specific problems of individuals. The examples illustrated how groups can move from the general to the specific and from the specific to the general. The last excerpt illustrated the importance of resolution as meetings draw to an end. Having presented the general model of the individual-group interaction, it is now possible to examine the elements in depth and to explore some variations on the theme. In the next chapter, I examine the individual's role in the group, concentrating on how members are informally assigned to play functional roles such as scapegoat, deviant, and internal leader. Chapter 13 examines the needs of the group as a whole and the way in which the group leader can help the group work on its central tasks. In Chapter 14, a number of variations on the mutual aid theme are illustrated with work from a range of groups.

NOTES

1. William R. Bion, *Experiences in Groups,* (New York: Basic Books, 1961).

2. Ibid.

CHAPTER 12

Working with the Individual in the Group

A central idea in this model has been Schwartz's notion of the "two clients," the individual and the group. In Chapter 11, the interdependence of these two entities was illustrated. In this chapter and the next, an artificial separation of these two clients is employed to deepen our understanding of each in interaction with the other. In this chapter I focus on the individual within the group in order to further the discussion of the way clients bring their personalities to bear in their group interactions. The concept of role is used to help describe how individual personality is translated into group interaction. A number of common patterns of individual-group relationships are described and illustrated (e.g., scapegoats, deviant members, defensive members, quiet members). However, as these individuals are isolated for closer analysis, it will become clear that it is often impossible to understand individual clients without considering them in the context of group interaction.

THE CONCEPT OF ROLE IN A DYNAMIC SYSTEM

Two ideas central to the discussion in this chapter are "role" and "dynamic system." Ackerman described the ways in which the term *role* has been used and proposed his own definition:

Sociology, social psychology, and anthropology approach the problems of role through the use of special concepts and techniques. They apply the term in two distinct ways, meaning either the "role" of the person in a specific, transient, social position or the characteristic "role" of the individual in society as determined by his social class status. Working in the psychodynamic frame of reference, I shall use the term to represent an adaptational unit of personality in action. "Social role" is here conceived as synonymous with the operations of the "social self" or social identity of the person in the context of a defined life situation.[1]

Ackerman suggests that the individual has a private "inner self" and a social "outer self" emphasizing the aspects of his personality which are externally oriented. I shall use this idea of social role in the following way. When clients begin a group, they present their "outer self" as their way of adapting to the pressures and demands of the group context. Their pattern of action represents their "social role."

Ackerman argues that incongruity between the reality of the "inner self" and the "outer self" which is presented can be a source of tension. In many ways, the task of the group worker involves helping individuals find the freedom to express their "inner selves" in the group. For the purpose of this chapter, the central idea is that each individual member brings to the group an established pattern of translating a unique personality into social action.

The second major idea requires that the group be viewed as a "dynamic system" in which the movements of each part (member) are partially affected by the movements of the other parts (other members). This view is rooted in the work of Kurt Lewin, often considered the father of group dynamics.[2] Thus, members bring their "outer self," as described by Ackerman, into this "dynamic system," and the individual's "social role" is his unique manner of adapting to the perceived demands of the group. This process of adaptation is necessary for all group members and the model thus far provides a general description of the individual-social interaction in group. For our purposes, however, I will concentrate on those patterns of interaction which are identified as specific social roles emerging overtime and requiring special attention by the group worker.

Patterned social roles are most easily described by an illustration from a formal, organized group, such as a tenants' association. In order to function effectively, the association usually identifies specific tasks which must be assumed by group members and then assigns these jobs by some form of division of labor. For example, the association may need a chairperson, a secretary, a treasurer, and a program coordinator. The essential idea is that group roles are functionally neces-

sary and are required for productive work. In taking on any of these roles, specific members will bring their own sense of social role to bear. For example, the role of chairperson could be implemented differently by various members, depending upon their experience, their background, their skills, and their sense of social role. Since the group is a dynamic system, the chairperson's implementation of this role will also be somewhat affected by the group and its individual members. The actions of the chairperson can be best described as the product of the interaction between the individual's sense of social role, the role of chairperson as defined by the group, and the particular dynamics of the group and its members.

The roles just described are of a formal nature; in addition, every group creates roles to help in its work even though these may never be openly acknowledged. For example, in a group led by a worker who chairs the discussion as an "external" leader, one or more "internal" leaders may emerge as if they had been formally elected. The individuals who assume internal leadership in a group often bring a concept of social role which includes this function. Group members, by their positive responses to internal leaders, will encourage their assumption of this important role. Other functional roles can emerge in a group that are less constructive and reflect maladaption on the part of the group rather than healthy development. One such role, that of the scapegoat, is discussed in detail in the next section of this chapter. For now, it is enough simply to point out that scapegoats are often selected by the group because they have the personal characteristics which members most dislike or fear in themselves. Thus, a group of young teenage boys who are worried about sexual identity may select the youngster who seems least "manly" or least sure of himself as the group scapegoat. The group members, of course, do not have a formal election for such role. There is no meeting at which volunteers are requested for scapegoats, internal leaders, deviant members, and so on. However, if the group has a need for these roles, they will select members to fill them through a subtle, informal process. The dysfunctional aspect of employing a scapegoat is that it often leads the group members to avoid facing their own concerns and feelings by projecting them upon the scapegoat. The scapegoat, in turn, usually subtly volunteers for this role, since it is consistent with that individual's concept of his or her "social role." Adapting to groups by playing this social role is as dysfunctional for the individual scapegoat as it is for the group as a whole. Once again, the idea of the group as a dynamic system helps us to understand the process of scapegoating in a dynamic way.

In the sections which follow I discuss informal roles developed in groups such as scapegoats, deviant members, internal leaders, and gatekeepers. In addition, I will examine the patterns of social role demonstrated by individuals who are defensive, quiet, or overly verbal. In each case, the focus is on analyzing the dynamics as a reflection of the individual's social role within a group which is a dynamic system. In addition, the skills of the group worker as he or she implements the individualizing part of his work will be discussed and illustrated.

THE SCAPEGOAT IN THE GROUP

The discussion of individual roles in the group begins with the scapegoat because it is both one of the most common and one of the most distressing problems

in work with groups. Whether it is overt scapegoating in children's and teenage groups or the more subtle type experienced in adult groups, the impact on the group members and the worker can be profound. I will deal with this role in some detail as a means of introducing a number of key concepts in conceptualizing social role in the group and the function of the group worker. These central ideas will reemerge as I examine other roles. The discussion can then serve as a general model for analyzing individual role in the group.

This dynamic is discussed by Garland and Kolodny who provide an interesting analysis of the forms of scapegoating prevalent in practice.

No single phenomenon occasions more distress to the outside observer than the act of scapegoating. Frequently violent in its undertones, if not in actual form, it violates every ethical tenet to which our society officially subscribes. As part of that society, the group worker confronted with scapegoating in the midst of interaction often finds himself caught up in a welter of primitive feelings, punitive and pitying, and assailed by morbid reflections on the unfairness of fate which leaves one weak and others strong.[3]

In an early article addressing the scapegoating phenomenon I discussed the common mistake in practice, when faced with these feelings, of moving into the interaction between the scapegoat and group in a way which "preempts" the opportunity for either to deal with the problem.[4] Most often, the worker protects the scapegoat from the force of the group members' attack thus causing the hostility to take more covert forms. Appeals to fairness or requests to give the member a chance do not seem to help, and the worker is usually left feeling frustrated, the scapegoat hurt, and the group members guilty.

The following example from a boys' residential center for teenagers illustrates the dilemma. John was scapegoated by the group members because of his small size, his social discomfort and lack of skills, and his general self-effacing demeanor. The pattern became apparent soon after John arrived; he did little to stop it and sometimes seemed to provoke it. His response was usually to cry and run away. This incident took place in the lounge as John was hanging around trying to get into the general banter of conversation.

LOU: Why the hell don't you buzz off and stop bothering us?

FRANK: Yeah, John, you're such a putz I don't want you hanging around me. I can't stand to see your face. (John doesn't leave, just hangs his head and looks sad.)

WORKER: Come on you guys, stop picking on John. He isn't bothering you. Why do you always jump on him?

LOU: (defensively) He's a creep. You don't understand what he's like. He's a creep in school also, and all the kids hate him.

WORKER: Maybe that's what goes on at school, but it's not going to happen here. (The boys mutter angrily under their breath about "getting him later" and leave the room.)

This is not an untypical exchange. It is seen all the time in classrooms, residences, children's groups, and in more subtle forms in adult groups. When I asked the worker about his feelings during the exchange, he said, "I was mad at the guys for being so hard on John. I felt furious and frustrated because I knew they would just get him later, and I couldn't seem to do anything about it." A diagrammatic way of describing this incident would be:

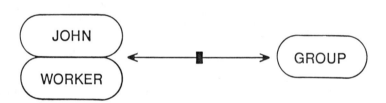

It was the worker and John versus the group. What began as a problem between the group and John had changed to a problem between the group and the worker. When I inquired as to where the worker was, emotionally, he described himself as "with John." My next question greatly affected the worker. "Who was with the group?" Analysis of examples such as this demonstrates that the answer is "no one." In a variation on this theme, if the scapegoat is overtly obnoxious to staff as well as group members and the worker finds himself clearly identifying with the group and its anger towards the scapegoat, then the worker often remains passive or offers subtle support to the group in its attack on the individual. Once again, when I inquire who is with the scapegoat in these situations, the answer is again "no one." It is at moments such as these that a new insight into the scapegoating dynamic and a sense of clarity of function can help the group worker to be "with both clients" at precisely the same time.

First, one must consider the history of scapegoating. The scapegoating idea goes back to an ancient Hebrew ritual when each year, on the Day of Atonement, the chief priest would symbolically lay the sins of the people on the back of a goat and then drive the goat into the wilderness. The death of the goat led to the ritual cleansing of the sins of the people. In a like manner, when group members scapegoat another member, they usually attack the aspect of the other which they most dislike in themselves. One should think of this as a form of communication to the worker of the group members' feelings towards themselves. The boys who are angry at John for his general social ineptness are very much involved in attempting to develop their own sense of social competency. Attacks on a youngster for his behavior often represent a call for help by young men who are struggling to develop their own sense of sexual identity in a society where most adults seem to be too uncomfortable to talk to them about such issues. The anger directed towards the scapegoat is often a signal of the hurt and confusion felt by the group members. In another example, Gitterman describes in detail the work of a group of youngsters, all of whom are having trouble at school, as they pounce upon every defect they can find in one of the group members who is just experiencing a more severe version of their own problems.[5]

Vogel and Bell have described the dynamics of this phenomenon in the family group, emphasizing the functional role played by the scapegoat in maintaining equilibrium in the family by drawing all of the problems into himself.[6] Many scapegoats in groups have been socialized into this social role by their family experiences and are ready to volunteer to play it in each new group they enter. Thus, as we think about scapegoating in the group, the concepts of social role and the group as a dynamic system provides us with clues to the meaning of this interaction. It is impossible to understand the behavior of the scapegoat simply as a manifestation of the person's "personality." Rather it is a result of the interaction between the scapegoat's sense of social role and the group's functional needs. The relationship between the individual role and the group need is clearly evident if he group loses its scapegoat, if, for example, the member leaves the residence or drops out of the group. As though operating on an unconscious command, the group immediately searches for a new candidate to take the scapegoat's place. One member is usually waiting to do so.

Understanding the dynamics, the worker can more easily avoid the trap of siding with either the individual or the group. This natural response misses the essential message: that the group and the scapegoat are using the process as a means of raising a theme of concern. The process can be best understood as an attempt, albeit maladapted, to offer a theme of concern. The worker cannot get too upset with either, since scapegoating may be the only way they know to deal with the feelings. The worker's task involves helping the group and the scapegoat to recognize their patterns and assisting them in finding a new way of dealing with concerns which are common to both. In doing so, the worker can view both the individual and the group as clients in need by better understanding and empathizing with the feelings common to both. Schwartz's mediation idea is helpful here, since it directs the worker to identify and point out areas of common ground between the individual and the group at precisely the moment when, because of the obstacles, they have lost sight of the common ground. As the worker implements this function, the skills described thus far in this book—sessional contracting, elaborating, empathy, sharing feelings, making a demand for work, and so on—should be used in pursuit of this task.

In the following illustration of this process a group worker in a home for unwed mothers deals with the group's attack on a fellow member. In the previous chapter, we saw an example of the same worker in the same house working with members who had the strength to deal directly with their own feelings about giving up their unborn child. With the worker's help, they were able to move past their early, glib acceptance of the need to relinquish the child and face their real feelings of guilt, depression, and loss. In the following illustration, the members were more immature and needy and were less able to face their feelings. The group was not as sophisticated in its ability to offer mutual aid, and the sessions and the living situation were marked by incidents of anger and attack. Individual members expressed their own feelings of hurt by directing anger at each other. The pain of the expected loss was the same; only the means of communicating it was different.

In this group, Susan was one of the youngest (fourteen years old) and least prepared members in terms of her readiness to keep her baby. She was dealing with more extreme versions of the problems facing all of the group members. However, she insisted she would keep the baby. The group members began a concerted campaign, attacking her ability to keep the child and expressing a great deal of anger at her position. When discussing this recording with the worker, I asked how she had felt during the first part of the discussion. She admitted to feeling overwhelmed by Susan's wanting to keep the child, and yet she felt for Susan as she was being put on the spot. She remained passive in the beginning, essentially, because she agreed with the position of the group members and hoped they would convince Susan. She had explained to the group her responsibility to evaluate Susan's plan and that the agency could decide it was not appropriate. The style of the recording reflects the fact that it was written by an observer.

SUSAN: Stated that she intended to finish school and would keep her baby.
JANICE: Stated that such an idea was not feasible.
JUNE: Gave examples of some friends who kept baby and it didn't work out. There was some suspicion of child beating. The husband beat wife and child.
SHAWN: Asked how Susan could possibly study when she had a baby to care for.
SUSAN: Replied that the child would be in a foster home until she completed Grade 10.
DEBBIE: Felt this would not be fair to the child.
SHAWN: Visited her mother weekly as a youngster but never got close to her mother.
JANICE: Expressed her feelings about the importance of a child's first year of development which Susan would miss if the child were placed in a foster home.
SUSAN: Thinking that perhaps she should drop out and get a job.
JANICE: Felt that Grade 10 was not much and wondered what type of work she could do. Said she is giving up her baby and returning to college to complete her education.
SUSAN: Plans to marry boyfriend when she is sixteen (she is fourteen now).
DEBBIE: Felt that Susan would really be shortchanging herself by keeping the baby and not getting more education.
JANICE: Stressed how much they all cared for her and that's why they were trying to make her look at things more reasonably.
SHANNON: Suggested that if Susan wanted to get married at sixteen, that would be fine; in the meantime the child should not suffer but be given a chance at a good life.
SUSAN: Insisted that they weren't going to change her mind. She had thought things through and wants the baby and will do all she can to have a good relationship with the child, something she herself never had because her own mother was in and out of hos-

pital due to nervous breakdowns. She doesn't think that having a child in a foster home for its first year would be harmful.

The more Susan defended her position, the harder the group members pushed her. Susan dug in and refused to listen to their arguments. This often happens when a client is feeling insecure about a position. The more unsure Susan felt, the more difficult it was for her to accept the challenges. The worker sense Susan's discomfort and reached for her feelings in the interaction.

WORKER: Asked Susan how she herself felt about the girls' pouncing on her like this.

SUSAN: Said she is used to it, as they are always trying to get her to change her mind. She is stubborn about wanting the baby and intends to give it a good home. She had a very bad upbringing, and her mother used to get violent with her.

DEBBIE: Expressed the feeling that it was risky with the added responsibility of an infant at such an early age. Her brother was having problems in his marriage.

SHANNON: Pointed out that perhaps staying at home with the baby will make a wife dull, as interests are limited when a wife is preoccupied with child rearing.

SUSAN: Stated she had a good relationship with boyfriend.

JANICE: Made the suggestion that boy-girl relationship can be very different when it becomes husband-wife relationship.

DEBBIE: Said that since Susan's boyfriend was in the army, he would be away a lot and the whole responsibility would be hers.

JANICE: Stressed that keeping baby would be a very limiting thing for Susan; she may not be able to get the beautician course she wants. There are so many opportunities opened to young people, it would really be too bad to limit oneself. It's selfish to want to keep a baby, as she would not be able to offer the child very much while adopting parents had so very much to offer.

SUSAN: Became angry and insisted she could keep her baby.

WORKER: Interpreted the other girls' pouncing on Susan as being an indication of how much they care and are concerned what will happen to Susan and the baby.

The worker tried to protect Susan from the anger of the group while at the same time, she supported the group's position. This is an example of "being with" the feelings of the scapegoat but not those of the group. The group pressure continued.

JANICE: Felt very strongly that it was crazy to consider keeping a baby at fourteen.

SHANNON: Said that Susan's decision was an indication of her immaturity.

SUSAN: Defended herself by saying she was not immature but stubborn.

In the next excerpt the worker regained her sense of function and began to help Susan deal with the group. She tried to assist her in communicating her feelings to the group members. She then pointed out the connection between Susan's feelings and those of the others. The worker did not blame the group members for their angry reactions, but instead expressed her understanding of how hard it would be to hear one's own feelings expressed by someone else. This is an example of being with both clients, Susan and the group, at the same time.

WORKER: Expressed concern that Susan may be feeling that girls were attacking her decision. Perhaps Susan could share feelings as to why she wants to keep the baby.

SUSAN: Feels that she would feel very badly giving baby up, she would always think of it, and feel guilty. She feels so strongly because she has to fight for two, as her boyfriend isn't here to express his feelings.

WORKER: Stressed that the feeling Susan has is one that is common to all the girls. She said that they all initially wanted to keep their child and wondered if it was hard to hear Susan express those same feelings.

DEBBIE: Said she still wants to keep baby but feels adoptive parents can give it more.

SHANNON: Feels that the best thing for her child is to be placed in an adoption home, but she still can't bring herself to signing he papers and won't until after the birth.

The worker's comment allowed the members to begin to express their own deep feelings of hurt which persisted in spite of their expressions of certainty about the decision. In addition, the worker had the task of asking Susan to consider why she was having such a hard time listening to the group members. This is a demand for work on the scapegoat which may be more effective *after* other group members have acknowledged similar feelings. Susan was unable to share her own doubts at this point, but I believe she heard the worker.

SUSAN: Never thought of giving the child up and is upset that girls (Pam and Terry) tried to give her all the negatives.

WORKER: Asked why Susan didn't consider the possibility of some of those problems happening to her. She can appreciate Susan's feeling for her boyfriend. Her life was without much love, so her boyfriend's offer to love her is naturally important. She asked if Susan wanted this so badly it made it hard to face the problems.

JANICE: Stated that she was telling her how she felt because she thinks of Susan as a kid sister, and she sure would be upset if the kid sister made a decision to keep. There was some talk about the fears and anxieties of pregnancy, labor, delivery, the pain involved, fear of needles, etc.

JANICE: Said that she had planned to keep her baby but her family (particularly a sister who is a social worker) made her realize how selfish that would be.

The worker had observed the scapegoating pattern and strategized to pick it up at the next meeting by asking the group members to explore their reactions to the previous session. She planned to ask the group members why they were "so angry" and forced them to examine their own feelings. The worker asked how the group felt about the session last week. She said that they discussed some pretty heavy stuff and she wondered how they were feeling about it. The girls didn't really pick up on the feeling level.

JANICE: Said that there was a good article in *Redbook* on the importance of the child's first three years of life, and she passed it on to Susan to read. She wondered if Susan had bothered to read it.

WORKER: Glanced at article and asked Janice to summarize it for the others.

JANICE: Felt it was too long and had too much in it but stated that it was important for a child to identify with parents at an early age, and moves should be eliminated, as it confuses a child.

WORKER: Again wondered why the girls were so angry last week, explained that their voices were really angry and they sounded a lot like "parents" might.

DEBBIE: Stated that she has a brother that age and feels that she would be very upset and angry if he were in the same situation. She thus identifies Susan with her own brother.

JANICE: Has a sister that age. Knows she would have similar feelings and feel the anger.

DEBBIE: Feels that the girls should ease off and lessen the pressure on Susan to change her mind about keeping the baby.

The members responded by talking about their siblings which still evaded the question of their own feelings. They were, however, beginning to see how counterproductive it was to pressure Susan. The worker then made a demand for work as she once again reached for their feelings.

(Continued references still seemed to be directed at Susan and her unrealistic plan to place the baby in a foster home for one year.)

WORKER: Interjected that perhaps there were other ways to approach the subject with Susan. She asked the girls to put themselves in her place and realize that Susan was being very emotional about keeping her baby and the guilt she would feel at giving it up.

JANICE: Said that they all felt that way.

WORKER: Picked up on this, saying that perhaps it was because they all shared Susan's feeling that they were so angry. They would all like to plan to keep their babies. In addition, Susan wasn't really listening to or answering the girls.

JANICE: Wondered how boyfriend will feel at being trapped so young.

WORKER: Suggested that the girls try to recall how they felt when they first learned of pregnancy besides the feeling of panic.

DEBBIE: Said she felt like Susan, determined to keep her baby.

JANICE: Feeling scared at first.

CAROL: Considered keeping but knew she couldn't.

WORKER: Stated that they all had that feeling in common. They all initially wanted to keep the baby but realized it wasn't feasible. She continued that all the arguments girls were proposing were valid, but they all come on so strong that perhaps a person would hold to an idea just to prove her point, and in Susan's case, an easing off may be more beneficial, as the ultimate decision will have to be made by Susan.

With the pressure off Susan, the members explored their own feelings. Susan was able to listen and for the first time began to share the doubts she felt.

PAM: Feels pregnancy has made her feel old because others in the family have children at a much later age. She feels that panic is the first reaction, followed by grief at the fact that you are stuck and don't know what to do, how to get out of predicament. The feeling of wanting the child is normal. She considered very closely whether she wanted her child to have a father, as he offered to live with her. However, in view of his drinking and running around she doesn't want him back.

WORKER: Stressed that it was an indication that they were moving from the feeling of wanting to keep the baby to considering what was best plan for the baby.

SUSAN: Agreed that they all shared similar emotional and physical stages. She admitted that her boyfriend was away a lot and he himself brought up the idea that perhaps he can give up the army and go into the police corps. He still has four years to go in the army.

WORKER: Suggested that as Susan was raised in an army family, she could share the feelings of what it was like.

SUSAN: Said that it didn't bother her until two years ago when her mother had a nervous breakdown.

WORKER: Asked Susan to consider the stresses she will have in looking after the child. She emphasized that the girls were all working out their own ideas and were interested in helping Susan sort out her feelings even as this was helping them in their decision.

When the common feelings were pointed out between Susan and the other girls, the scapegoating diminished considerably. The challenge to Susan's plan continued off and on, but without the earlier anger. At the end of the sixth session, Susan announced that she had decided to give up her baby. She said the group had "helped" her reach the decision, but she shared with them the feeling that it would not be easy.

Work with the scapegoating pattern includes a number of steps. First, the worker observes the pattern over time. Second, the worker must understand his or her own feelings in the situation to avoid siding with or against the scapegoat. By using the tuning in skill, the worker can attempt to search out the potential connections between the scapegoat and the group. If the worker is not clear about these, the group can be asked to reflect upon the question. The next step involves pointing out the pattern to the group and the scapegoat. Thus, the worker asks the group to look at its *way of working* and to begin the struggle to find a more positive adaptive process. As the worker challenges this obstacle, it is important not to be critical of either the group or the scapegoat for having developed this way of dealing with the underlying feelings. In fact, it is the worker's capacity for empathy and understanding of how hard it is to face these feelings that allows making this demand for work. The two thrusts of the worker's efforts involve asking the group to consider why they scapegoat and also asking the scapegoat to reflect on reasons for volunteering for the role. Discussion of this process is designed to free the members to explore further the underlying feelings. It would be a mistake to turn the sessions into ongoing discussions of the individual's life pattern of being a scapegoat or the group's analysis of its process. When the discussion is honest, invested with feeling, and touching all the members, then the group will no longer need a scapegoat. The discussion may help them to moderate their harsh judgments of themselves which lead to the need for a scapegoat. In turn, the scapegoat may discover these feelings are not unique.

THE DEVIANT MEMBER

One of the most difficult clients for workers to deal with is the deviant member.[7] In this discussion, the term is used broadly to describe a member whose behavior deviates from the general norm of the group. This deviation can range from extremely inappropriate and disconnected behavior (e.g., a participant who attends the first meeting and evinces strikingly bizarre behavior) to one whose actions deviate only mildly or sporadically (e.g., a member who stares out the window while the rest of the group is deeply involved in a discussion). My major assumption is that deviant behavior is *always* a form of communication.

The problem for the worker is that it is often difficult to figure out what the member is saying. This difficulty is compounded by the fact that the deviance is often experienced as directed towards the worker (e.g., acting out behavior in a children's group may be seen as "testing my authority") and thus activates powerful emotions in the worker. A second major assumption, related to the earlier view of the group as a dynamic system, is that deviant behavior in a group *may* be expressing a communication which has meaning for the group as a whole. That is, just as the group may use a scapegoat as a means of dealing with difficult feelings, a deviant member may be serving an important social role for other group members. This section explores these two assumptions.

Deviant Behavior as Communications

I earlier suggested that deviant behavior could be considered on a continuum ranging from extreme to slight deviations from the norm. On the extreme end would be a client or group member who envinces bizarre behavior which is totally inappropriate for the group. This can happen on occasions when meetings are open to the community or screening of prospective members has not taken place. When this happens in a first session the impact on the worker and the group is profound. As the member speaks, one can sense the group shrinking in embarrassment and at times in fear. It is important for the leader to take responsibility for gently, but firmly, asking the member to withhold comment, or in extreme cases, to leave the session. Group members are not prepared, in an early session, to deal with extreme deviance and are dependent upon the group worker to clarify the boundaries and to enforce the limits if needed. In one such example, a woman attending a foster parent recruitment session responded to the worker's opening contract statement and requests for group feedback by beginning a long, and essentially unrelated, tale of personal tragedy. When the worker tried a number of times to clarify the contract or to clarify how the woman's concerns might relate to the discussion, she met with no success. The woman refused to allow others to speak and went on in detail about her personal problems and her fears that people were after her—even that the room was bugged. The discomfort in the eyes of the group members was clear. The worker, herself uncomfortable, finally moved to control the situation.

WORKER: Mrs. P., it is obvious that you're having a tough time right now, but I simply can't let you continue to use this group meeting to discuss it. I'll have to ask you to leave, but I would be glad to talk with you further about your concerns at another time.

MRS. P.: You f——ing workers are all alike. You don't give a s—t about us, you're no different from the rest. You took my kids away, and I want them back.

WORKER: I'm sorry, Mrs. P., I can't talk with you now about that. You will have to leave and I can discuss this with you tomorrow.

Mrs. P. finally left, and the worker turned to the group to acknowledge how upset she was feeling about what had just happened. The group members expressed their own feelings. After emotions had settled, the worker picked up on the group members' reactions to Mrs. P. as a parent of children in the care of the agency. This led to a discussion of parents, their feelings about placements, and contacts between natural parents and foster parents. The worker followed up the next day with Mrs. P. and did get to

see her. There was a long, sometimes rambling and disjointed conversation during which the worker consistently tried to reach Mrs. P. and acknowledge her feelings. Mrs. P. turned to the worker as she left and said; "I'm sorry for what I said last night. You know it's just that I'm so angry—I miss my kids so much." Mrs. P.'s behavior at the meeting was an extreme example of the use of deviant behavior to express deeply held feelings. The worker could not allow the session to be captured by Mrs. P. and, using all of her courage, she acted to protect the group's contract.

Most workers will not experience such extremes of deviant behavior. I have included this example, since workers often fear that such an experience will happen to them and because it demonstrates how even bizarre behavior contains a message for the worker. On the other end of the continuum is an example drawn from another group for foster parents who already had children in their homes. The worker was well into the presentation of introductory material on the agency and fostering policies when a late member arrived. She was dressed elaborately, wore a big hat, and sauntered up to the front of the room. All eyes in the group followed her as she made a grand entrance. The worker was shaken by her entry, but continued to speak. As the woman sat there, the worker noticed what appeared to be a scowl on her face and occasional grimaces in response to the worker's comments. The worker later described how she tended to "speak to this member" as the evening drew on. After the session, unable to contain herself because of the implied negative behavior, the worker inquired why the member seemed so antagonistic. The member, who had not said a word during the evening, was surprised by the worker's question. She explained that she was not angry at all, and that in fact, she was having a really hard time with her new foster child, since it was her first time fostering, and she was looking forward to these sessions for help.

I have been struck by how often group leaders are surprised to find similar reactions and feelings underlying initial deviant behavior which they have felt to be attacks upon them. All that is needed, at times, is to confront the group member directly and to inquire as to the meaning of the behavior. The skills are two-fold in nature. First, is the ability *to tolerate deviant behavior,* and the second is the ability *to reach for the underlying message.* Consider the following example from a group for children who are having trouble in school. The meetings are held at the school in the afternoon, and John starts acting up as he enters the meeting room. He picks a fight with Jim, knocks over the desk, and appears ready to tackle the group worker next.

WORKER: John, what the hell is up? You have been roaring mad since you walked in here.
(John remains silent, glaring, with his fists clenched.) Did you just come from a fight with someone? Or was it Mr. Smith [the teacher]? Did you have an argument with him?
JOHN: (Still angry, but slightly more relaxed) He's always picking on me, the bastard.
WORKER: OK, now slow down and tell me what happened. Maybe we can help you on this one. That's what the group is all about.

The worker was able to reach for the meaning behind this behavior and not get caught up in a "battle of wills" with John because he understood his function, was clear about the purpose of the group, and understood that children often raise their problems indirectly through acting out behavior. The group member does not always immediately respond to the worker's efforts to reach past the behavior; however, I think they understand the worker's meaning and will sometimes pick up the invitation later. Clarity of function is important at times such as this because if the worker is concentrating solely on his limit-setting function (e.g., stopping the fight), he may miss the other part of the work. The skill often involves setting the limit and reaching for the meaning of the behavior at exactly the same time.

The following illustration comes from a living group in a residential center. Frank is a sixteen-year-old resident who has been away from home for a year and is preparing to visit his family over the two-week Christmas break. He had been given a number of hours of community work to do as a result of a conviction on a break-in charge. However, he was slow in fulfilling the requirements of the session, and the worker found himself having to threaten to cancel the visit home. Frank continued to be slow in completing the work as the days progressed, the worker felt backed into a corner and deliberately provoked by Frank. After using a training workshop to tune into the feelings Frank might have about the visit, the worker hunched that he might be using the situation to avoid a difficult encounter. In essence, Frank's behavior signaled a problem. The worker confronted Frank:

I spoke to Frank in the kitchen about how I felt he was using this community service as a cover-up for more important feelings about going home for Christmas. I went on to say that I wasn't going to enforce this consequence and would rather like to help Frank with his hopes and fears about going home, especially since it was a Christmas visit. Frank dropped his peanut butter sandwich and ran out of the kitchen shouting "No way!"

The worker was not deterred by Frank's first response, and in fact, had prepared himself for the possibility of resistance. He approached the youngster later in the evening, in his bedroom, just before lights out. This is often a time when children in a residential center are ready to talk, as the night shift can attest.

I made another invitation to Frank to share his feelings, explaining that I understood it was not an easy area to talk about. He began by showing me the gifts he had bought his dad and his brothers. He asked me if I thought they were appropriate. He then went on to say he was uptight about whether he could act in a consistently mature fashion while at home. Acting his age was always his problem, and although he thought he had grown a lot in the past year, would his dad recognize this? We talked about this for a while and over the next few days; other staff spoke extensively about Christmas and his family with Frank. At one point Frank came to me to ask how I was going to spend Christmas this year, which was a most unusual conversation for him to initiate.

Key moments in time will often bring out specific deviant behavior which the worker can learn to anticipate. In residential centers, holidays are difficult both for youngsters who are visiting their families and those who are not. There is always an increase in acting out behavior at these times. Close examination of the impact of external circumstances often reveals the reason for the deviant behavior. While the thrust of my argument concerns the importance of understanding deviant behavior as a communication, I want to underline that in those circumstances where setting limits is part of the worker's function (e.g., child care work) the worker still needs to set them and implement appropriate consequences. While Frank was allowed to go home for his visit, he still had to meet his responsibility for the hours of community service.

The Deviant as a Functional Role

My second major assumption about deviant behavior was that it may be saying something related to the feelings of the group as a whole. This notion is rooted in the idea of the group as a dynamic system, in which the movement of one member is somewhat affected by the movements of the others. The deviant member can be viewed as simply a member who, for a number of reasons, feels a particular concern or emotion more strongly than the others in the group. This greater sense of urgency causes the deviant member to express the more widely held feeling, often in an indirect manner.

An example which may strike home to the reader and therefore help to illustrate this relates to staff meetings in agencies. When communications between staff and administration are poor, it is often considered taboo to raise certain issues or challenge directly the authority of the staff leader. Under such circumstances, the lack of open communications is dysfunctional for the organization, since serious problems may be ignored or ineffective policies set. It is not unusual for a staff system informally to develop a "deviant" member who directly or indirectly challenges the authority of the leadership. The administrator experiences this staff member as a "problem" and often attributes the attacks to the staff member's "problems with authority." What does not come out is that after the meetings, other staff members have approached the deviant member and passed on words of encouragement. For example, "I'm glad you said that. He really needed to hear it from someone." They may directly or indirectly conspire to encourage a staff member to "speak out" before a group meeting. What the group leader/administrator is missing is that the deviant member actually speaks for many on the staff. This staff member seems like the "enemy" when actually, since open communication is essential to administrative success (even though the administrator may not see this), this staff member is an "ally." If changes do not take place and the deviant member eventually leaves the agency or is fired, the role is filled in a very short time by another member of staff.

Schwartz refers to the function of the deviant member in the client group as follows:

...such clients often play an important role in the group—expressing ideas that others may feel but be afraid to express, catalyzing issues more quickly, bringing out the negatives that need to be examined, etc. This helped us to see that such members should not immediately be thought of as "enemies" of the group, diverting it from its purposes, but as clients with needs of their own, and that these needs are often dramatic and exaggerated versions of those of the other group members.[8]

It is critical, therefore, that the group leader not dismiss a deviant group member too quickly as simply acting out a personal problem. This would constitute the mistake of attempting to understand the movements of a member of a dynamic system (the group) apart from the movements of other members of the system. While it may be true that this member brings this particular social role to bear in all groups, the person cannot be understood simply as a separate entity. The first hypothesis should always be that the member may be speaking for the group as a whole. In the first session of the couples' group, described in detail earlier,

the member who attacked "professionals" was carrying out the important task of dealing with the authority theme, an issue for the whole group. In the following excerpt, a member attacks the purpose of the group in a counseling session at a psychiatric hospital:

MR. W.: (Who had been quiet for most of the first two sessions, although he seemed to have a critical look on his face) You know, I think this is really all a bunch of crap! What the hell is it going to do us any good sitting around and talking like this?

MRS. S.: Well, you know, you really haven't had much to say. Maybe if you spoke up, it would be more worthwhile.

For most inexperienced workers, the force of the attack would be taken personally because the worker feels fully responsible for the success of the group. It would not be unusual for the worker to view Mr. W. as negative, hostile, and resistant, and to set out to challenge him, or encourage the group members to "take him on." For example, "Mr. W. doesn't seem to think the group is too helpful. Do the others feel that way, or do they feel the way Mrs. S. does?" If Mr. W. is viewed in the context of the dynamic interaction, and if the worker sees him as a potential ally, he might instead help him to elaborate.

WORKER: I think it's important that we hear Mr. W. out on this. If there are problems with the group, maybe we can work them out if we can talk about them. What's bothering you about the group?

MR. W.: Well, for one thing, I don't think we are leveling with each other. We're not really saying what's on our mind. Everybody is too busy trying to impress each other to be honest.

WORKER: You know, that often happens in the first few sessions of a new group. People are unsure of what to expect. How about it, have any of the others of you felt that way?

MR. P.: I didn't last week, but this week I thought the discussion was a bit superficial.

By treating the deviant as an ally rather than as an enemy, the worker gave permission for the group to begin a frank discussion of how they were working. Others in the group felt the freedom to express their dissatisfaction, and as a result, the group members began to take responsibility for making their group more effective. This kind of discussion is essential for all groups, but it is often considered impolite to be direct in such areas. Members feel they do not want to "hurt the worker's feelings." As the group proceeded, the worker found that Mr. W., rather than not wanting to work, had a number of pressing issues he wished to deal with. This was the sense of urgency which forced him to speak out. Often in a group, the member who seems most negative and angry is the one who wants to work the hardest. It is easy to understand, however, how the worker's feelings make it hard to see Mr. W. in a more positive way.

Expressions of deviant positions in a group are often a lever for the group leader to deepen a discussion. For example, in one group on parenting skills, a major argument occurred when Mr. T. expressed the view that "all of this talk about worrying about the kids' feelings was nice for social workers but didn't make sense for parents. Sometimes, the back of the hand was what they needed." The other group members literally pounced on Mr. T. and a verbal battle royal ensued. Once again, for new workers who are not clear about their function, the expression by Mr. T. of an idea that ran counter to the worker's view of "good parenting" would arouse a strong reaction. The worker would be particularly angered by the jibe about "social workers" and might set

about to "educate" Mr. T. Instead, this worker saw Mr. T. as expressing a feeling, which in part was true for all the parents but which was not considered "proper" in this group to feel. The worker reached to support Mr. T.

WORKER: You are all attacking Mr. T.'s position quite strongly; however, I have a hunch there must be many times when all of you feel the same way, Am I right? (Silence)
MR. F.: There are times when the only feelings I'm interested in are the ones he has on his behind when I let him have one.

Mr. T., with the worker's help, gave permission for the parents to begin to discuss the reality of parenting which includes the anger, the loss of temper, and the frustrations that are normal for all parents. She continued by asking Mr. T. why he felt he had to express this position so strongly.

WORKER: You know, Mr. T., you come on so strong with this position, and yet you don't strike me as someone who doesn't care about how his kids feel. How come?
MR. T.: (Quietly, looking down as he spoke.) Feelings can hurt too much.
WORKER: What do you mean?
MR. T.: It wasn't easy to talk with my kids when their mother died.
WORKER: (After a silence) You really know what that is like, don't you? (Mr. T. just nodded)
MRS. S.: I've never had to handle something that tough, but I know what you mean about it being hard to listen when your kids are pouring out the hurt.

One final example can be drawn from a community-based citizens' group charged with the responsibility of distributing a portion of community social welfare funds. Mr. F. has developed a reputation in the group for being outspoken, angry, and intimidating, and usually taking a minority conservative point of view on an essential liberal board. The purpose of the board was to represent community opinion in the distribution of funds. On the agenda the evening of the meeting was the funding of a local women's center which is both politically active and providing community social service. As the group worker expected, Mr. F. began by attacking the funding on the grounds that the group was essentially political. The worker, feeling a strong attachment to the work of the women's center, attacked his position by offering additional information in favor of the center. The debate between group members and Mr. F. continued, with his finally losing his vote.

In a retrospective analysis of the process, the worker granted that when Mr. F. spoke, some members were silently nodding in agreement. Other members were obviously disagreeing. It was also clear that the group was uncomfortable about taking Mr. F. on because of the way he argued his point of view. As can easily happen, the worker was so intent on her agenda of getting the center funded that she ignored the communication problem in the group and jumped in to take sides. An alternative line of work would have involved helping other members in the group express the feelings and thoughts behind the nonverbal signals, including those members who agreed with Mr. F. The worker could bring out in the open the difficulty in discussion caused by Mr. F.'s strong presentation but would do so in order to help the group members *and* Mr. F. in their communications. With hindsight, it is easy to see that Mr. F. represented a larger body of opinion in the community, and if the board was to do its job effectively, then decisions had to be made which took into account a broad range of opinions. There was a good chance that some of the most ardent supporters of the women's center had some mixed feelings about funding the political action component, which was clearly outside of their mandate. In turn, Mr. F. and his supporters probably had a sense of the importance of the social service aspect of the center's work. If not, then the discussion would be enriched by a full debate on these ideas in which the worker helped the members from both sides say what they felt, as well as listen to those who disagreed with them. The worker would be free to add her own views on the matter, but she should not abandon the crucial function of group worker. Often, in an attempt to withhold personal views so as "not to influence the group," the worker ends up indirectly attempting to manipulate opinion to the desired outcome. The irony of this is that the same worker may feel and express a deep conviction in the "community decision-making process." Once again, the deviant member, Mr. F., could have been helpful in strengthening the debate on a contentious issue.

In summary, the deviant member who challenges the authority of the leader or who provides negative feedback on the work of the group or who raises a point of view contrary to the group's norm or who fights strongly and with emotion for a position may be playing an important functional role in the dynamic system of the group. The deviant can be an ally for the worker if the worker can deal with personal feelings and then listen to the deviant member as a messenger from the group.

THE INTERNAL LEADER

The internal leader role is played either by a single member or different members at different times.[9] The worker in the group can be considered the external leader: a part of the group but at the same time deriving authority from an external source (the sponsoring agency). The internal leader(s) derive authority from the group members. It is easier to understand this distinction if we consider organized groups in the community (e.g., social action) or recreational groups (e.g., senior citizen clubs). These usually have a formal set of officers who are elected by group members to carry out the internal leadership role. As will be illustrated in a later chapter, the tasks of these leaders are often similar to those of the workers. All groups develop their own internal leaders, even in those situations where there are no elections and the discussions are largely directed by the worker. These leaders help to give voice to the different aspects of the groups' feelings and assist in helping the group resolve its struggles towards growth. They are usually individuals in the group who develop a higher status in the eyes of the members because of their abilities and skills in areas valued by group members. When such leaders take risks, for example move into new areas of emotional expression, other members of the group will often follow their lead.

Group workers who are unsure of their function often experience internal leaders as a threat to their own authority, even viewing them as "deviant members." Actually, if the mutual aid process is central to the work, when workers observe the emergence of an internal leader, then they know the work is going well. This mistake of viewing the internal leader as a deviant is most evident in work with teenagers and children, when the internal leader challenges the authority of the worker. The following excerpt is from a first meeting of a group I led during my first year of professional training. The group consists of acting out adolescents (thirteen and fourteen years old) who were members of a community center club. I had been warned that they were a difficult group and that they had given other workers a tough time in the past. Although the group was set up so that the club members planned their own activities, the agency had structured the first night by planning a mass sports program in the gym. The first issue on the group members' mind was, "What sort of worker will this be?" but my preparation had mistakenly led me to think that I must "demonstrate my authority in the first session and assert myself as leader," which in effect, began the battle of wills.

Only five boys had shown up by 7:45, so we spent the first ten minutes talking about the club last year. At this point, Al showed up and completely changed the tone of our meeting. It seemed as if the first five boys had been waiting for the catalyst that had finally arrived. Al was bubbling over about the school football game he had played in that afternoon. It was their first win in three years. When I asked how it had gone, he described it abruptly. He then wanted to know what we were doing that night. When I explained the preplanned evening program he became very negative about it. "Rope jumping [one of the competitive events] is for girls," he replied. I told him boxers use rope jumping for training, and he replied, "I'm not a boxer, and I'm not a girl." Although the other boys had not been overly enthusiastic about the evening program when I had described it earlier, their tone changed sharply as they agreed with Al.

Lack of clarity of function and initial nervousness led me to defend the program and to see Al as competition. Contracting was unclear, and an important discussion about the role of the worker in relation to the group members was missed because of my own fears and misconceptions. As the meeting proceeded, I got myself deeper into trouble:

I tried to discuss at least next week's program with the guys. Girls from another club started pressing their faces against the window of the door, and before I could stop him, Al was racing to the attack. The contagion was immediate, and what had been a quiet group of boys was now following their leader. I jumped up and asked them to ignore the girls. Instead, they chose to ignore me. I went over to the door, closed it, and politely guided them back to the desk. This time, when they sat down, Al's feet were on the table (one of the wooden finish types). Five more pairs immediately joined Al's (the testing was in full swing). I asked them to remove their feet, since they could damage the table. Joe and Ken responded, but the others didn't. I tried to maintain a light and firm stand. They slowly responded stating that last year's leader let them keep their feet up that way. Another said there were a lot of things their leader let them do last year that I probably would not. I said that I would only allow them to do those things which were acceptable to the agency. One of the boys asked me what an agency was. I explained I meant the center (first week of field work and already I'm overprofessional). It was time to hit the gym for the games (much to my relief).

It is clear that my sense of function, that of "taming the group," led me to miss important issues. The discussion of the last leader's role would have been a helpful one. In addition, for this age group, relationship with girls was an emerging and uncomfortable theme. Al was the only club member to dance with girls later in the evening during the social dance part of the program. He asked about having a party with a girls' group which I put off by saying, "We would need to plan this ahead of time." Al provided leadership in a number of areas, expressing the feelings and concerns of the group, but because I missed the importance of his role, the result was a battle over "who owned the group." Because I missed the signals,

the indirect testing continued. Al led the members in throwing paper around the club room and leaning out of the windows, spitting on other center members as they left. I kept trying to set limits while not allowing myself to get angry (not thought to be professional). Finally, my natural instincts got the better of me.

I said I would like to say a few words before we finished. I was attempting to reestablish the limits I had set earlier, but my own feelings got the best of me. I explained that this evening was really difficult for me and that probably it was so for them too. I said that if we couldn't relax enough to discuss further programs, there probably wouldn't be any. At this point, I said something that surprised me as I said it. I said their behavior better improve, or they could find themselves a new leader. They replied by saying that compared to the group members who hadn't shown up this evening, they were well behaved. My reaction to this group was mild panic.

It is easy to understand my panic in this situation. My idea of being professional was to be able to "handle" the group without losing my temper. Actually, in these moments at the end of the meeting when I revealed my real feelings, I was making a start at developing a working relationship with the group members. After a few more sessions of off-and-on-again testing, I moved to discuss the issue of the authority theme and to help the group members develop their own internal leadership and structure.

I told the boys that since I had been with them for five weeks, they might be interested in hearing what I thought about the group. They perked up at this. Bert said; "You love us," and everyone laughed. I said that during this time I had been able to talk to each one of them individually and seemed to get along well. However, when we got together as a group, we couldn't seem to talk at all, right from the beginning. In spite of what they said, I thought that each one of them was concerned about stealing, acting wise all the time, and being disrespectful. Al said (very seriously this time) that it was different when they were in the group. I asked why that was so. Bert asked all the guys if they had stolen anything, and they all agreed that they had. After some discussion I told them I thought they were really afraid to say what they thought in the group. Bert said he wasn't afraid. I asked about the others. Al mockingly put up his fists and said, "I'm not afraid of anyone in the group." I laughed with the rest and said I thought it was easy to be brave with your fists but that it took a lot more courage to say something you thought the other guys would not like. I said it was their club, and although it was important to me, it was really more important to them. Joel made a wise crack, but he was silenced by Ken who said, "That's just the kind of thing he [the worker] was talking about."

As the discussion continued, the boys explained that they often didn't like my suggestions for activities, and I encouraged them to say so in the future, since it was their club. A surprising amount of feeling emerged about the kidding around in the group, much of it directed at one boy who acted out a great deal but was not present that night. They talked about how they could plan their own programs. The group members suggested that I could bring in ideas from other clubs and that they would then decide what they wanted. At this point, Al suggested they have a president. After some discussion about the respective positions, a president (Al), vice-president (Bert), and treasurer (Ken) were elected. A social committee was also formed to speak with the girls' club to discuss a party.

At this point in the meeting I realized we were actively talking about something with no kidding around and no testing of me. I felt at ease

for the first time. I commented to them about this. Al said; "We won't be able to do this all the time." I said I realized this and that there still would be a lot of kidding around. It would be OK as long as they could pull themselves together at times to get their work done. Al said that would be his job, and that I could help by telling them when they got out of hand. I agreed.

At the end of the process recording I commented that as I left the building, "All of the boys gave me a warm goodbye." From this point on, much of the focus of the work shifted to helping the group members develop their own structure. For example, there were meetings with Al before sessions, at his request, to help him plan the agenda and to discuss his problems in chairing the sessions. For myself, these sessions were a painful initial lesson on the need to clarify my function and the recognition of the group's internal leadership.

THE GATEKEEPER

In the section on the deviant member I pointed out how this client is often the one who feels a sense of urgency more strongly than the other members about a particular issue. In a sense, the deviant behavior is an effort to move the group towards real work. The internal leader often serves this function in a healthier, more direct way. A group can be ambivalent about work in the same way an individual may be, and members can take on the function of expressing that ambivalence for the group. This is sometimes seen in the form of a "gatekeeper" role, in which a member guards the gates through which the group must pass for the work to deepen. It appears as a pattern when as the group gets close to a difficult subject, the gatekeeper continues to divert the discussion. In one group, for example, every time the discussion appeared to approach the issue of the authority of the worker, one female member would light up a foul-smelling cigar or in some other way attract the group's attention (and ire) in her direction. The group would rise to the bait, and the more difficult authority theme would be dropped. The worker pointed out the pattern, describing what he saw: "You know, it seems to me that everytime you folks get close to taking me on, Pat lights up a cigar or says something that gets you onto her back. Am I right about this?" The group rejected the interpretation and turned on the leader with anger, thus beginning to deal with the authority theme. Later in the session, Pat commented that the worker's observation might be accurate, since she had always been fearful of seeing her parents fight and probably did the same thing then. It was not appropriate in this group to discuss the reason for the pattern, either Pat's or the group's, nor was it necessary to have the group members agree with the observation. The mere statement of the pattern offered the group an opportunity to face the worker directly, and Pat no longer needed to carry out this role.

Humor is often used to protect the gates in difficult areas. In the following example, a child care worker picks up directly on the sexual innuendo involved in an apparently casual conversation in the lounge. The boys are young teens.

FRANK: (Watching a television show) Wow! Look at the build on that broad. Boy, I wish I could meet her after the show.

LOU: You wouldn't know what to do with her if you had her, you big jerk. Besides, your pecker isn't big enough.

(At this comment there is general kidding around and teasing of a sexual nature.)

WORKER: You know, you guys kid around a lot about this sex business, but I bet you have a lot of questions on your mind about it—a lot of serious questions.

FRANK: What kind of questions?

WORKER: Well, I'm not sure about your questions, but I bet you are interested in what would make you attractive to women, sexually, and how you actually handle sexual relations as well as other relations with women. It's probably a tough area to talk about seriously.

LOU: My old man never talked to me about sex.

TERRY: (Who has a pattern of clowning in the group) Did you hear the story about the kid who asked his father where he came from? The father gave him a fifteen-minute sex talk, and then the kid said, "That's funny, Jimmy comes from Chicago." (Some of the boys laughed and others groaned) I got another good one. . . .

WORKER: Hold it, Terry! There you go again. Every time we get to some serious discussions in tough areas, you start with the jokes. And the rest of you guys go right along with it. What's wrong? Is it tough to talk about sex without kidding around?

The boys returned to the conversation with a number of serious questions specifically related to sex and others related to the whole question of intimacy with women. Terry sat quietly during the discussion and did not participate. The worker picked up with Terry alone later about his discomfort in such discussions. The worker asked if it was related to some of his difficult sexual experiences. Terry's mother had been a prostitute, and he had been a male prostitute for a time when he was twelve. He could not talk about this in front of the other boys, and the worker had respected this. In most cases the gatekeeper carries out this functional role because he feels the resistance aspect of the group's ambivalence a bit more strongly than the rest of the members. In a sense he is the spokesman for this, in the same way the internal leader or the deviant may speak for the opposite pole.

THE DEFENSIVE MEMBER

Although defensiveness on the part of a group member has already been discussed in connection with other roles, it deserves some special attention. One often notices a group member who seems to be particularly defensive about admitting the existence of problems or accepting responsibility for his own part in the problem or in taking any suggestions or help from the group members after a problem has been raised. The defensiveness often results in the group members increasing their efforts to attack the defense, directly or indirectly, or eventually giving up and ignoring the member. One classic pattern is for a group member to listen to others describe serious difficulties and then have the member exclaim, "I'm not sure what the difficulty is that everyone is having. We don't have that kind of trouble." The reaction of the other group members to such a comment is usually clearly seen in their eyes.

Lewin described a model for change which can be applied on a number of levels (e.g., the individual, the group, the family, the organization).[10] Stated simply, the individual personality in relation to its environment has developed a "quasi-stationary social equilibrium" in which some form of balance has been worked out. For the defensive member, denial has worked as a way of dealing with painful problems. The three steps for change involve "unfreezing" this equilibrium, moving into a phase of disequilibrium, followed by a freezing at a new quasi-stationary equilibrium. The important point is that defenses have value to the individual, and to expect the unfreezing process to be an easy one misses the essence of the dynamics. The more serious the issue, the more deeply the individual feels a challenge to the sense of the core self, the more rigid will be the defenses. Defensiveness on the part of a group member, like resistance, discussed in Part I of this book, is a signal that the work is real. The challenge of the group member or the leader to the individual's position is needed to begin the unfreezing process. However, the individual will need all the support, understanding, and help possible to translate unfreezing into movement into a new level of quasi-equilibrium. Workers often underestimate the difficulty of what they and group members are asking people to do in the way of making substantial changes. The difficulty of this process needs to be respected. It requires a delicate integration of support and demand to create the conditions in which the group members may feel free enough to let down the barriers.

In the example which follows, a father has described a conflict with his eighteen-year-old son which is resulting in the son leaving home with the family in turmoil. As the situation is played out in some detail, a number of other parents point out how the father has been stubborn and failed to listen to what his son is saying. They try to pin him down to alternative ways of relating, but to each, he responds in a typical "yes, but ..." pattern, not able to take in what they were saying. Finally, after a few minutes of this, the group grows silent. The worker intervenes by pointing out the obstacle.

WORKER: It seems to me that what has been going on here is that Ted has raised a problem, you have all been trying to offer some answers, but Ted has been saying, "Yes, but ..." to each of your suggestions. You look like you are about to give up on him. Are you?

ALICE: We don't seem to be getting anywhere. No matter what anyone says, he has an answer.

WORKER: Ted, I think you must feel a bit backed into a corner by the group. You do seem to have a hard time taking in their ideas. How come?

TED: I don't think they can appreciate my problem. It's not the same as theirs. They all seem to be blaming me for the fight, and that's because they don't understand what it really is like.

WORKER: Maybe it would help if you could tell them how this struggle with your son makes you feel.

TED: I gave this kid so much, raised him since he was a baby, and now he treats his mother and me like we don't matter at all. I did the best I could—doesn't he understand that?

WORKER: I think it's tough when you feel you love your child the way you do and you still see him as your kid, but he seems to want to pull away. You still feel responsible for him but you also feel a bit impotent, can't seem to control him anymore. Can any of you appreciate what Ted is feeling right now?

The group members moved to support Ted in his feelings with others recounting similar experiences and feelings. The focus had shifted for a moment to the common feelings between group members rather than the obstacle which seemed to frustrate them. The worker sensed that Ted needed to feel understood and not judged harshly by the other parents, precisely because he tended to judge himself more harshly than any of them. Having established this support, the worker reached for the feelings underlying the resistance.

WORKER: Ted, if I were you, I think I would spend a lot of time wondering what went wrong in the relationship. I would be wondering how this could have happened when I had tried so hard—and if I could have done things differently. Is that true for you?

FRAN: (Ted's wife) He stays up nights these days, can't get to sleep because he is so upset.

TED: Sure it's tough. You try your best, but you always wonder if you should have been around more, worked a little less, had some more time . . . you know?

WORKER: I guess that's what makes it hard for you to believe that anyone else can understand, and you feel so lousy about it yourself. Can the rest of you appreciate that it would be tough to listen if you were in Ted's shoes?

RAY: I think we are in Ted's shoes. When I see him getting stubborn in this group, I see myself and my own defensiveness.

The group discussion focused on how hard it was to take advice in the group, especially when you felt most uncertain yourself. As the conversation shifted, one could sense Ted physically relaxing and listening. After a while, he brought it back to his problem and asked the group to take another crack at it. He said, "This is really tough, but I don't want to lose the kid completely." In some cases defensive members need more time to back off and feel safe enough to "move." Workers will often find that the member has thought deeply about the way he reacted *after* the meeting, and the unfreezing and readiness to change are apparent in a later session. This is the client's part in the procedure, and once again, the worker can only take responsibility for establishing the best possible conditions for change—the rest is up to the client and depends upon many factors. For some clients, the issue may be so loaded, with so much at stake, that they are unable to use the worker or the group's help at that point in their life. While frustrating and often sad, this is a reality.

THE QUIET MEMBER

The quiet member is one who remains noticeably silent over a period of time. In small groups, it takes only a few sessions for the worker and the other group members to notice that someone has said very little or nothing at all. For the group members, a quiet member can create problems, since they do not know what thinking and feeling goes on behind the facade. There is a tendency to believe that the quiet member may be sitting in judgment of them, does not share their problems, or feels that others in the group talk too much. Workers, too, are often uncomfortable in feeling that a member who is not speaking may not be involved. The silence of a member in a group is similar to the silence in an interview. It is a form of communication but, once again, it is hard to know exactly what the message is. For some group members, it may simply mean they are uncomfortable in speaking in the group. This is one of the most common reactions. Others may feel left out or uninvolved in the group because they feel their problems are different. Some may be sitting in judgment of the group's activity (as was the case in one of the deviant member illustrations). However, in my experience, that is the least often stated reason for silence but interestingly is the interpretation most often put on silence by the active group members and the worker and probably reflects their own feelings. Let us examine the quiet member who is afraid to speak, then the quiet member who is left out, and finally, the way in which the worker can help the group when they react to a quiet member.

My first assumption is that it is a mistake to believe that all members need to speak equally. The reality is that social roles developed by individuals include patterns that involve active participation through speech as well as active participation through listening. A member may be getting a great deal out of a discussion without directly participating. The worker who counts interventions and only feels that the group is successful if all members speak equally is, in my view, mistaken. On the other hand, there is a sense of mutual obligation in a small group in which members who risk themselves feel that others should do the same. In fact, the silent member often feels uncomfortable about "taking" and not "giving." In addition, many silent members have been so used to being quiet in groups for so long that they have not developed skills required for intervention. Others will tell you that they are always too slow with their thoughts. The group moves too fast for them, and by the time they can get in, the idea has been stated and the group has moved on. Others say that after they have been quiet in a group for a number of sessions, they are afraid the group members will "fall out of their chairs if I open my mouth." So although all members should be able to move into a group at their own pace and although equal participation is not a goal, the quiet member often needs some assistance in participating in the group.

Workers sometimes try to deal with this problem by direct confrontation or indirect means. Both methods I believe may be a mistake. For example, if a member has been quiet because of discomfort in speaking, a worker who suddenly turns and says, "I notice you haven't spoken yet in the group and wondered what was on your mind?" may find the member even further immobilized. The embarrassment is often great at a moment such as this and simply adds to the original level of discomfort. This direct confrontation is exactly what quiet members may have feared would happen.

The indirect means can be just as devastating. The worker has noticed a member not verbally participating in a discussion and turns and says, "What are your ideas about this question, Fran?" A member who is afraid of speaking anyway often finds that any ideas she did have completely disappear in this moment of panic.

The other indirect technique, of going around the room to get all opinions when it really is only the quiet person's opinion the worker seeks, may be experienced as manipulative and artificial by members.

The task then is to be direct and at the same time non-threatening. My own strategy is based upon the belief that people have a right to their defenses and their characteristic patterns of social interaction. As the worker, my job is to mediate the engagement between each member and the group, so that I would feel a responsibility to check with a quiet member and see how that engagement was going. If there was an obstacle between the member and the group, I could offer to help. The following conversation took place *after* the second meeting of a group. Richard had been particularly silent in both meetings, although his eyes seemed to indicate he was involved.

WORKER: Do you have a second to chat before you go?

RICHARD: Sure, what's up?

WORKER: I noticed you haven't spoken in the group these two sessions, and I thought I would check to see how it was going with you. I know some people take longer than others to get involved, and that's OK. I just wanted to be sure there were no problems.

RICHARD: Well, you caught me.

WORKER: What do you mean?

RICHARD: I managed to get through all of my years in school without ever saying anything in class, and now it looks as if I've been caught.

WORKER: Is it hard for you to speak in a group?

RICHARD: I always feel unsure of what I'm going to say, and by the time I've figured it out, the group has gone past me. Sometimes, it's just hard to get in with everyone speaking at once.

WORKER: Look, I can tell from your eyes that you are actively involved in the discussion. However, after a while, you will probably feel uncomfortable not speaking, and then it will get harder and harder to talk.

RICHARD: That's the way it usually is for me.

WORKER: Not just you, you know. Lots of people feel that way. If you would like, I can help by watching for you and if I sense you want to get into the conversation by the look on your face, or your body, or if you give me the signal, I can reach for you and help you in. Would you like me to do that?

RICHARD: That sounds OK. If I give you a signal, you'll call on me?

WORKER: Exactly! I find that has helped people in the past.

At the next session, Richard avoided the worker's eyes for the first fifteen minutes, probably afraid of giving a false signal. The discussion was heated, and the worker kept watching for Richard. After a while, the worker noticed Richard leaning forward a bit, with his eyebrows arched, looking at the worker. The worker simply said, "Come on in, Richard." The group paused, and Richard began to speak.

Another type of quiet member is one who feels that his particular concerns and issues may not be of interest to the group or that his problems are different from those of the others. Such members do not share problems with the group members and after a while, they feel left out and the group wonders what is happening. In the following example, a woman who has shared some difficult experiences with the group states that she felt let down when the group did not respond to her feelings. Mrs. D., who had been silent in the group, responded to the first mother's comments. The worker reached directly to inquire if Mrs. D. had also felt "let down."

The worker cut in, "Maybe we could hear how Mrs. T. felt let down by the group?" Mrs. T. continued, "I felt that I was not part of the group, that I was not going to get anything out of it." Mrs. D. cut in, "Yeah! We didn't want to listen to other people's troubles because we had enough of our own!" The worker turned to Mrs. D. and said, "Have you felt let down and left out of the group?" "No," said Mrs. D., "I don't feel I have the same situation—they have husbands." (Mrs. B. reached out and touched Mrs. D. on the arm.) The worker asked Mrs. D. how she felt about not having a man. Mrs. D. replied, "Sad, depressed—I wonder if he could be proud of the kids as I am?" She went on to say that maybe things would be different if her husband were alive—maybe they could have made a go of it. The worker said he felt that "Mrs. D. had been cut out of the group for some weeks." Mrs. D. agreed. Mrs. B. said that was probably due to the fact that she had not been able to share with the group and the concerns she had. All agreed. The worker cut in after a silence and said, "I felt the group would like to know what it is like, what it feels like to be alone—what do you need help with?" Mrs. B. cut in, "There you go on that feeling theory again." The worker asked if it worried Mrs. B. when we talked about feelings? "No," she said, "but is it important?" The worker said that it seemed important because everyone in this group was having trouble talking about and sharing feelings while at the same time they were interested in what others were feeling. "Do you see what we have done here? When we began to find out about Mrs. D.'s feelings, someone suggested and we all agreed to avoid it. Let's go back to Mrs. D.'s feelings!" Mrs. D. said, "I feel like a s-h-i-t (spelled out) at home with the kids." The worker cut in and said it was OK with him if she said shit—but why did she feel that way? "It rips me right across here (indicating mid-section) when they are fighting—I've had nothing but fighting all my life—first in my own home—then with my husband—now with my kids." "How do you see the fighting—what does it mean to you?" asked the worker. "I feel on my own, all alone." Mrs. T. cut in, "I know that feeling—I had it with my husband—we used to argue etc., etc.... What can I do? Why is it always me?" The worker asked if Mrs. D. could share a specific problem with the group, and she did. It involved setting limits, then

wavering on them and letting the kids have their own way.

As is often the case, simply acknowledging the lack of involvement by the member is enough to encourage the sharing of her concerns. Sometimes the initiative for reaching out to a quiet member starts with the group. It is not unusual, after a period of time, to have a group member turn to one who has been silent and ask, "What have you been thinking?" Once again, the worker's concern for the two clients and clarity of function can help assist the group and the member in an important discussion.

RAY: I have been thinking about you, Fred. You have not said anything in the group so far. How come? (All eyes turned to Fred.)

FRED: (Looking very uncomfortable) Oh, I've been listening.

WORKER: (Addressing Ray) Does it concern you when Fred doesn't speak?

RAY: Yeah, I begin to wonder if I'm talking too much or he thinks I'm making a real ass out of myself.

WORKER: Have others in the group wondered about that as well? (Nodding of heads.) I think it makes other people uncomfortable when you don't speak much, Fred, because they can't figure out what you're thinking. Could you react to that?

FRED: Actually, I've been sitting here thinking how much all of your problems are just like mine. I've wanted to share some, but I don't feel comfortable talking in a group.

WORKER: This wasn't easy for you right now, was it?

FRED: No, it wasn't easy at all, but I'm glad it came out.

RAY: Maybe if I shut up a bit, you would have more of a chance to talk.

WORKER: I don't think so, Ray. Some people speak more in a group and others do a lot of work by listening. You also seem concerned about what others have to say, so I hope you wouldn't feel you needed to hold back. How about the rest of the group?

LOU: You raise interesting points, Ray, and it helps the group keep going. I would miss you if you just clammed up. (Ray smiles at this.)

WORKER: I can watch the talk in the group, and if I see someone trying to get in, I'll help make room for him. Is that all right? (Members of the group nodded in agreement.)

FRED: I'll get into the conversation. I just need some more time.

RAY: That's OK. Don't feel pressed. You can get in when you feel comfortable.

Once the communications had been clarified, the problem of the silent member receded. Fred did get into the discussion the following week, raising a concern to the group and meeting with a positive response.

This example also brings up the opposite side of the issue: people who talk a great deal. My view is that people who talk a great deal are often more of a problem for the worker than quiet members. In first sessions, in particular, group members are pleased to see someone pick up the discussion. It can become a problem when the person talking does not also listen to others, cuts them off, and creates a negative reaction in the group. The group worker who sees this happening can raise the issue directly. Usually the discussion

between the members and the group helps to ease the problem. If the group worker inquires why the member acts this way in the group, the individual will often reveal that talking is a way of covering up feelings, avoiding a problem, or expressing concern about actions in the group. It often turns out that the overly verbal member's words are a way of handling the same feelings expressed in a quite different manner by the member who is quiet.

Summary

I have used this chapter to examine a number of common examples of individual roles in the group, and the worker's helping role in relation to them. The concept of social role has helped to explain patterned reactions by scapegoats, deviants, internal leaders, gatekeepers, defensive, quiet, and overly verbal members. In each case, as we examined the individual, we found that the view of the group as a dynamic system forced us to attempt to understand the individual member in terms of the dynamics of the group. In the next chapter I will explore in more detail the dynamics of working with this second client, the organism called the group-as-a-whole.

NOTES

1. Nathan Ackerman, *Psychodynamics of Family Life* (New York: Basic Books, 1958), p. 53. For other examples of role in the group, see Lawrence Shulman, "A Game-Model Theory of Inter-Personal Relations," *Social Work* 13 (1968):37–43; Ralph Linton, *The Study of Man* (New York: Appleton-Century-Crofts, 1936), pp. 113–19; Kenneth D. Benne and Paul Sheats, "Functional Roles of Group

Members," *Journal of Social Issues* 4(1948):41–9.

2. Kurt Lewin, *A Dynamic Theory of Personality: Selected Papers of Kurt Lewin* (New York: McGraw-Hill Book Co., Inc., 1935); Kurt Lewin, *Field Theory in Social Science: Selected Theoretical Papers* (New York: Harper & Row, 1961).

3. James A. Garland and Ralph L. Kolodny,

"Characteristics and Resolution of Scapegoating," *Social Work Practice, 1967* (New York: Columbia University Press, 1967) p. 124–36. For discussions of the scapegoat role, see Lawrence Shulman, "Scapegoats, Group Workers, and the Pre-Emptive Intervention," *Social Work* 12 (April 1967):37–43; F. Kräupl Taylor and J. H. Rey, "The Scapegoat Motif in Society and its Manifestations in a Therapeutic Group," *International Journal of Psychoanalysis* 34 (1953):253–64.

4. Shulman, "Scapegoats, Group Workers, and Pre-Emptive Intervention."

5. Alex Gitterman, "Group Work in the Public Schools," in *The Practice of Group Work,* ed. William Schwartz and Serapio Zalba (New York: Columbia University Press, 1971).

6. Norman W. Bell and Ezra F. Vogel, "The Emotionally Disturbed Child as the Family Scapegoat," in *A Modern Introduction to the Family,* ed. Norman W. Bell and Ezra F. Vogel (New York: Free Press of Glencoe, 1960), pp. 382–97.

7. See Earl Rubington and M. S. Weinberg, *Deviance: The Interactionist Perspective* (Toronto: Collier-Macmillan, 1968).

8. William Schwartz, "Group Work in Public Welfare," *Public Welfare* 26 (October 1968), p. 335.

9. See Luigi Petrullo and Bernard M. Bass, *Leadership and Interpersonal Behavior* (New York: Holt, Rinehart and Winston, Inc., 1961).

10. Kurt Lewin, "Field Theory in Social Science," in *Frontiers in Group Dynamics,* ed. Dorwin Cartwright (New York: Harper & Row, 1951), p. 224.

CHAPTER 13

Working with the Group as Client

Throughout this book I have been referring to the worker's second client as the group. This chapter takes a more detailed look at this entity in order to understand its properties and dynamics and to develop a strategy for the intervention of the worker. First, I use the model of an "organism" to describe the group as something more than the sum of its parts. Then, I use a developmental model to describe the tasks of the group as it attempts to deal with the relationships of members to the worker (the authority theme), relationships between members (the intimacy theme), and its internal structure (e.g., culture, communication patterns, roles). Finally, a discussion of the task of the group as it relates to its environment completes the chapter. The role of the worker in assisting this second client, the group, is described and illustrated by examples from practice.

There is a large body of group theory and research available to the practitioner endeavoring to understand a group better. For example, a recent contribution to the literature by Hartford has organized social science theory and research in a way which makes it very accessible to the practitioner.[1] The focus in this chapter is not on describing this body of literature, but rather on the practitioner's use of the-

oretical models and research results to develop his or her own integrated model of group practice. To illustrate this process, I have selected three theoretical models for discussion in relation to the group tasks: developmental (Bennis and Shepard, and Bion) and environmental (Homans).[2] As will be seen in the discussion, each of these theories has ideas relevant to the other group tasks. However, this organization lends itself to ease of exposition. Reference notes provide the reader with a guide for pursuing further the theorists' ideas, for exploring other theoretical models, and reviewing relevant research.

THE GROUP AS AN ORGANISM

When attempting to describe something as complex as a group, it is helpful to use a model. A model is a symbolic representation of a phenomenon which can be perceived. To determine a model for describing a group, an appropriate metaphor must be selected. Two metaphors in common use are the machine and the organism. Many theorists interested in human social systems have adopted the organismic model as the most appropriate.[3] The choice of an organism rather than a machine as a model is influenced by the capacity for growth and emergent behavior. These terms, *growth* and *emergent behavior,* describe a process in which a system transcends itself and creates something new which is more than just the simple sum of its parts.

To apply this idea to the group, we need to identify what is created when a number of people and a worker are brought together that is more than just the sum of each member's contribution. What properties exist which are unique descriptions of the group, rather than describers of the individual members? An example of such a property is the creation of a sense of common interest shared by all the members in the purpose of the group. This common interest is a catalyst for the development of a tie that binds the group members together. A group culture is a second example. As the group process begins, activities in the group are governed by a group culture made up of a number of factors including accepted norms of behavior. In a first session, the culture generally reflects the culture of the larger society from which the members have been drawn. As sessions continue, and with the intervention of the worker, this culture can change, and new norms will emerge to govern the activities of the members. Thus, common interests and group norms of behavior are two examples of properties of the group which transcend the simple sum of its parts, the individual members. A third example is the group's relationship with its environment. As the group is influenced by its environment, for example the agency or the worker as a representative of the agency, it must develop adaptive behaviors in order to maintain itself. This pattern of adaptive behavior is yet another example of a property of the group. Now, of course one cannot actually *see* a group as an entity. That is

why a model, such as the organism, is helpful. What one can see, however, are the activities of a group of people who appear to be influenced by this entity called the group. For example, when group purpose is clear, one can explain the actions of the group members as contributions in pursuit of that purpose. Again, the behaviors of the members are affected by group pressures, expectations, and the members' sense of belonging. The fact that a member's behavior is different as a result of believing in the existence of the group makes the group real. In the balance of the chapter, I refer to the group as an entity, employing the organism as a metaphor, and will focus on *its* developmental and environmental tasks.

DEVELOPMENTAL TASKS

I have already discussed two major group tasks but without having specifically described them as such. It might be helpful at this point to review these as illustrations of how a group can have tasks which are different from the specific tasks of each member. In the chapter on beginnings I addressed what could be called the group's *formation* tasks. The group needed to develop a working contract which reflected the individual members' needs as well as the service stake of the sponsoring agency. In addition, a group consensus needed to be developed. This consensus reflected the common concerns shared by members as well as some agreement as to where the work might start. Reaching consensus on the work is a task unique to work with multiple clients (group, family, couples, etc.), since individual clients simply begin where they wish. Initial clarification of mutual obligations and expectations was also a part of the group's formation task. You can see how the effectiveness of the group is dependent upon how well these formation tasks are dealt with. The skills of the worker in helping the group to work on these formation tasks were described under the rubric of contracting skill.

A second critical group task involves *meeting individual member needs.* For the group to survive it must have individual members. Members feel a part of the group and develop a stake in the work of the group when they can perceive that their own, related needs are being met. If this ceases to be, then members will simply drop out of the group, either by not attending or by not participating. In the chapter on the work phase of the group I pointed out how easy it is for the group to miss the offered concerns of a member or to turn away from these concerns when they hit the group members too hard. In still other examples, individual members did not immediately see the relation between the work of the group and their own sense of urgency. In other examples, in the chapter on the individual and the group, members were seen playing functional roles in the group, some of which cut them off from being able to use the group to meet their own needs. In each of these cases, workers were shown attempting to help the members use the group more effectively or helping the group reach out and offer mutual aid more effectively and usually doing both simultaneously. All these efforts were directed toward helping the group with its task of meeting individual members' needs. Thus, the formation tasks and meeting individual members' needs tasks must be considered if the group is to grow and survive. Other sets of tasks linked to the developmental work of the group are those in which the group works on its *relationship to the worker* (the authority theme) and *relationships between members* (the intimacy theme). Schwartz describes these two critical tasks as follows:

In the culture of the group two main themes come to characterize the member's ways of working together: one, quite familiar to the caseworker, is the theme of *authority* in which the members are occupied with their relationship to the helping person and the ways in which this relationship is instrumental to their purpose; the other, more strange and threatening to the caseworker, is the theme of *intimacy,* in which the members are concerned with their internal relationships and the problems of mutual aid. It is the interplay of these factors—external authority and mutual interdependence—that provides much of the driving force of the group experience.[4]

The group's ability to deal with concerns related to authority and intimacy is closely connected to the development of a *working culture.* Finally, the group needs to develop a *structure for work* which will enable it to carry out its tasks effectively. For example, responsibilities may have to be shared through a division of labor, and roles may need to be formally or informally assigned. Four major task areas— the relationship to the worker, the relationship between members, the development of a working culture, and the development of a structure for work— are now addressed. Obviously, there is a great deal of overlapping of these tasks in that work on one area often includes work on the others. The division is somewhat artificial; nonetheless, it is helpful in the exposition of the argument. As I discuss these tasks, I will draw upon elements of group theory from three major models, focusing on those constructs which seem helpful to my own sense of reality. For example, Bennis and Shepard have addressed the themes of intimacy and authority in their model of group development and a number of their key concepts are useful in explaining group process.[5] Their observations, however, are based upon their work with laboratory training groups (T-groups) in which graduate students studied group dynamics using their own experiences as a group.⁶ As a result, a number of ideas in their theory may be group specific and cannot be generalized to groups of the type discussed in this book. As such, my analysis will illustrate how a practitioner can use what he or she likes from a good theory without adopting it whole.

Dealing with the Relationship to the Worker

In the early phase of the group's development it needs to sort out its relationship to the worker. Much of the beginning energy will be devoted to this theme. An early question has to do with issues of control. The dynamics of "transference" and "countertransference" described in Chapter 4, are also present in the group context. Members will bring their stereotypes or fantasies about group leaders to the first meeting, and these will generate a fear of a powerful authority person "doing something" to them. Thus, in my description of the first session of the couples' group in Chapter 9, Lou raised the issue by sharing his negative experiences with helping people. Open discussion of the implications of this issue for the present workers helped the group members to relax and become more actively involved in the session. But such an open discussion does not "resolve" the question. In fact, the issue of the relationship to the worker is never resolved, in the sense that all the feelings are worked out and all the questions answered. What one does achieve is the ability of the group and the worker to address this issue openly as it emerges. The comfort of the group may increase, but the theme remains. In the second session of the couples' group the members were watching to see if I would carry out the role I had described in the first session. Once again, Lou signaled the members' concern about this issue.

One couple was presenting a problem that they were having which related to the husband's grown children from another marriage. I noticed each spouse was telling the group things about the other, rather than speaking directly to each other. I interrupted Frank and suggested he speak directly to his wife. After a noticeable hesitation, he began to speak to her, but soon returned to speaking to me. I interrupted him again. Once again, he seemed slightly thrown by my action. As this was going on, I noticed that Lou was looking distressed, staring at the floor, and covering his mouth with his hand. After watching this for a time, I reached for the message. "Lou, you look like you have something to say." He responded, "No, that's all right. I can wait till later." I said, "I have the feeling it's important, and I think it has something to do with me." I had been feeling uncomfortable but unaware why. Lou said. "Well, if you want to hear it now, OK. Everytime you interrupt Frank that way, I think he loses his train of thought. And this business of telling him to speak to Jane is just like the stuff I described last week." I was surprised by what he said and remained quiet while I took it in. Frank said, "You know, he's right. You do throw my line of thought every time you interrupt that way." I said, "I guess I ended up doing exactly the kind of thing I said last week I would try not to do. I have not explained to you, Frank, why I think it might help to talk directly with your wife rather than to me. I guess you must feel my comments, since you don't really understand why I'm suggesting this, as sort of pushing you around." Frank said, "Well, a bit." Lou said, "That's exactly what I mean." I responded, "I won't be perfect, Lou. I will also make mistakes. That's why it's so important that you call me on it, the way you just did. Only why wait until I ask?" Lou said, "It's not easy to call you; you're the leader." I said, "I think I can appreciate that, only you can see how it would speed things up if you did."

This second week's discussion was even more important than the first because the members had a chance to see me confronted with a mistake and not only acknowledging it but encouraging Lou to be even more direct. The point made was that they did have rights and that they should not let my authority get in the way. There were many other times when similar discussions arose, for example, about the agenda for our work. When I appeared to return to an area of work without checking on the group's interest, members would participate in an obvious illusion of work. When I challenged the illusion, we were able to discuss why it was harder for them simply to let me know when they thought I was leading them away from their concerns. Issues of control also emerged in connection with responsibility for the effectiveness of the work. The authority theme is one which the worker must also raise with the group members. In this example, there had been an unusually long period when one couple was endlessly discussing an issue without getting to the point. I could see the reactions in the group and inquired as to what was going on.

Fran responded by saying it was getting boring and she was waiting for me to do something. Since this was a middle-phase session, I found myself angry that everyone was waiting for me. I said, "How come you are waiting for me to do something? This is your group, you know, and I think you could take this responsibility, too."

The resulting discussion indicated members felt it was risky to take each other on, and so they left it to me. We were able to sort out, for a time, that members, too, needed to take responsibility for the group's effectiveness. These excerpts help to illustrate the two sides to the members' feelings: on the one hand,

afraid of the worker and the worker's authority and on the other, wanting the worker to take responsibility for the group. These two sets of feelings are attributed by Bennis and Shepard on two types of personalities in the group: the "dependent" member and the "counterdependent" member.[7] They believe that the question of dependency is a major area of uncertainty for members and that the first major phase of group development involves work on this question. They describe three subphases within this first phase. In the first subphase, "dependence-flight," the group is led by the "dependent" leaders who seek to involve the worker more actively in control of the group. In the second subphase, "counterdependence-flight," the "counterdependent" leaders move in to attempt to take over the group. They describe much anger towards the trainer in this phase (in my view a result of overpassivity). Two subgroups develop, one arguing for structure and the other not wanting any. The third subphase is called "resolution-catharsis," in which group leadership is assumed by members who are "unconflicted" or "independent." According to them, this "overthrow" of the trainer leads to each member taking responsibility for the group: the trainer is no longer seen as "magical," and power struggles are replaced by work on shared goals. While many of the specifics of the model are only related to the particular groups observed, the general outline of this struggle over dependency rings true to my experience.

Issues of control are just one aspect of the general theme of relationship with the worker. A second area concerns the worker's place as an outsider to the group. This is practically noticeable in those groups where the worker has not had the life experience central to the group members' themes of concern. For instance, in a group for parents of children who have been diagnosed as hyperactive, the question of whether the worker who has no children can understand them and their problems is a variation on the similar question raised in the discussion of the beginning phase in work with individuals. The following excerpt illustrates this aspect of the authority theme struggle in the group context:

Discussion got back again to causes of hyperactivity. Ann, who had thought it was hereditary, explained that her husband thought that he had been hyperactive as a child, except that nobody gave him the title. Marilyn said that her husband had also said that he had been like her son and had felt that her son would grow out of it. The group picked up on this idea and seemed to like the possibility. I was asked by Betty what I thought. I said I didn't know, that from what I knew, not enough research had been done to really know. The group began throwing questions at me, related to general conditions, medications, and I couldn't answer them. I admitted that I knew very little about hyperactivity. I was certainly nowhere near being the expert that they were. Someone asked if I had children. I said that I didn't. Beatrice wondered what work I had done with hyperactive children and extended this to children with other problems. I answered as honestly as I could. She wondered whether I was overwhelmed by their feelings. I replied that she and others present were really concerned about how I felt towards them, and whether I really understood what it felt like to be the mother of a hyperactive child. She agreed. I added that last week when I had said I was overwhelmed, I was really getting into what it felt like to have such a child. It was pointed out to me that I was the only one in the group who didn't have a hyperactive child, that I was really the outsider. Beatrice offered to lend me her son for a weekend, so that I could really see what it was like. Everyone laughed. (I think they were delighted at this.) I said that they were telling me that it

was important that I understand what it's like, and I wondered whether I was coming across as not understanding. They didn't think so. I said that the more they talked, the better the feeling I got about what they were going through. Towards the end of this there was a lot of subgrouping talking going on, and I waited (thankful for the break).

A third area of the authority theme has to do with the group's reaction to the worker as a person who makes demands. For the group to be effective, the worker must do more than contract clearly and be empathic. The group will often come up against obstacles, many of which are related to the group members' ambivalence about discussion of painful areas. As the worker makes demands, negative feelings will inevitably be generated on the part of the group members. If the worker is good at what he or she does, there should be times when the group members are angry for the worker's refusal to let them off the hook. This is one side of the clients' feelings towards someone in authority who makes demands upon them. The other side, of course, is the positive feelings associated with the worker's empathic nature and the fact that the worker cares enough about the group to make these demands. The angry feelings also need to be expressed; otherwise they can go under the surface and emerge in unconscious expressions such as general apathy. Of course, the worker has to feel comfortable in the role to be willing to deal with this negative feedback. In the same group of parents of hyperactive children the worker picked up the signals of this reaction and reached directly for the negative feedback.

Millie began talking about her son's learning disability. After a little while I cut in and asked the group what was happening here, to the conversation and to the members. (My feeling was that they were way off the track again.) Marilyn said that they had gotten off the subject again, they were supposed to be discussing how they felt, and their attitudes. I added that indeed this was what was happening; it seemed that they were unable to keep on talking about themselves. Millie and Marilyn thought that it was probably because it was hard to accept the fact that they get angry. I started to say something in response to this, and I noticed that Claudette kind of sighed and made a face. I pointed this out to her, and suggested that perhaps she didn't want to discuss some of the things I thought they should. She nodded. I told the group that perhaps this was a good time to talk about how they felt about my forcing them to look at themselves, to keep on the subject, and to talk about what they didn't want to talk about. I said that they must have some feelings about me; perhaps every time I open up my mouth and point this out to them and try to refocus them, they say to themselves, "Why the hell doesn't she get off our backs and let us talk about something easy?" Beatrice said that she had the feeling that was true, every time I brought them back to talking about how they felt, she could feel people moving back in their chairs, as if they were looking for a place to hide, and then they hide by talking about school, teachers, etc. She said that her own behavior has changed considerably with these sessions, and although it has been hard, she's been able to see herself a little more clearly. But not everyone in the group has moved at the same pace; some people are really changing their attitudes because they are willing to risk and look at themselves, and others still hide behind the facade. I said that I agreed. Often I felt how terribly hard it was for them to face things, and I kept pushing them at it. Sometimes I pushed them hard like two sessions ago. And then other times I feel it is too hard, and like last week, I hardly said anything and really let them talk about anything and everything. I don't think that is being helpful to them if I let them do that, even though I can feel their hurt so much, and my own gut reaction is that I should let you alone; it hurts too much to look at yourselves. People nodded agreement.

A fourth issue here is the need for the group to come to grips with the reality of the worker's limitations. Members hope that the worker, or some other expert, will be able to provide the solution. This is, in part, a result of the dependency of the group emerging. When the group members realize the worker has no "solutions," then their own work really begins. However, this realization is painful for the members and often for the workers as well. At the end of one particularly painful and depressing discussion in the same parents' group when the members recognized that the drugs and the professionals were not going to "make the problem go away," a member appealed to the worker to cheer them up.

We were way over our time, and I started to sum up some of the feelings that came out today. I said that they had really been saying all along how helpless they felt that they couldn't do anything to help the children, and how hopeless they were feeling, that there wasn't a solution for them. Marilyn said to me that that's how they felt, depressed and helpless. She said that I always came up with something at the end to make them feel better. I had better come up with something really good today, because they needed it. I said that I was feeling the same way, thinking to myself, "What can I say that's going to take the depression and hurt away?" I told her that I didn't have a magic formula, that I wished that I could suggest something. I knew how much she and all of them wished that I could help them with a solution. Rose said that they were feeling depressed, but they shouldn't blame themselves. I said that perhaps part of the depression was related to the fact that they themselves hadn't been able to help their children more, and they felt terrible about it. She seemed to be so terribly depressed, more than ever before. I know because that's exactly how I felt.

There was not too much discussion on the way out, as I was at a loss to know what to say to them (usually we joke around a bit). Marilyn said to me I let her down, I didn't come up with my little blurb to pep them up. I said that she was feeling very depressed and she looked to me to say something to make things easier. I said that she wanted a solution, and I didn't have one. She said to me that perhaps I had, and I was holding back. I said to her that she was very disappointed in me that I hadn't been able to make things easier. I wished that I did have the magic solution that they all wanted so desperately, but I didn't have one. After this, the members left.

A final aspect of the authority theme requires the group to deal with their reactions to the worker as a caring and giving person. The group members watch as the worker relates to them and to the others in the group. They can see the pain in the worker's face if he or she feels the hurt deeply and, after a while, they can sense the genuineness of the empathy. This is a side of the worker which provokes powerful responses in the group, and a mutual flow of positive affect is the result. An interesting discussion in my couples' group illustrates the awareness of group members of this issue and the importance of this aspect of the authority theme. It was the session before the Christmas break (the eighth), and one member arrived late and distraught. She sat down in the empty chair to the right of me, and for the first time in the group, she shared a frightening problem she was facing. Until then, the member had appeared to be "without problems," since her husband was the identified patient. I comforted her during the telling of her story and tried to help her verbally, nonverbally, and through touch, communicating my empathic responses to her feelings. The group also reached out with support. In the second part of the session, after the immediate issue had been somewhat resolved and the member was in better

shape, we carried out a midpoint evaluation of the group. In discussing the way in which we worked as a group, one of the members raised the authority theme.

Fran said, "I knew that this was Jane's night to get help the minute she walked in the door" (Jane was the member who had been crying). When I inquired how she knew, she said, "Because she sat in the crying chair." She went on to point out that all of the people who had cried in sessions, four of the ten group members, had all sat down in that chair at the beginning of the session. In fact, some had sat apart from their spouses for the first time in the group. Other members nodded in recognition of the accuracy of Fran's observation. I inquired if they had any thoughts about why that was so. Rose said, "Because that's the chair next to you, and we sit there to get some support when the going gets rough." I responded, "Could you talk a bit about what it is about me that causes you to sit there or feel I can support you? This is important as part of our evaluation, but also, it can tell us something about what it is you might want from each other."

The request for specifics was designed to encourage discussion of the members' feelings about the worker reaching out to them with caring. In addition, as is often the case, the process in the group can serve to assist group members in understanding their own relationships more clearly. The record continues:

Louise said, "It's because we can feel free to say anything to you, and you won't judge us. We can tell you our feelings." Rose continued, "And we know you really feel our hurt, it's not phoney—you really care." Lou said, "It's safe next to you. We can share our innermost feelings and know that you won't let us get hurt." As I listened to the members, I felt myself deeply moved by the affect in their voices, and I shared that with them: "You know, it means a great deal to me to have you feel that way—that you can sense my feelings for you. I have grown to care about you quite a bit. It's surprising to me, sometimes, just how hard things in this group hit me—just how important you really have become."

The authority theme is a two-way street, and the worker will have as much feeling towards the members as they have towards the worker. The "counter transference" dynamics described in Chapter 4 are also present in the group. These feelings need to be made a part of the discussion. The honest feelings of the worker, freely expressed, are often the key to aiding the group as it comes to grips with its relationship to the worker. In summary, some aspects of the authority theme to be dealt with during the life of the group include: the worker's control and responsibility and status as an outsider and the group's reactions to the worker's demands, limitations, and caring. Although the phases in which a group deals with issues are never neat and orderly, one can detect a pattern in which as the issues of authority are dealt with, the group becomes more ready to turn to its second major developmental task, the question of the relationships between members (the intimacy theme).

Dealing with the Relationships between Members

Once again, Bennis and Shepard's theory can provide some helpful insights. In addition to concerns about dependency, a second major area of internal uncertainty for group members relates to "interdependence."[8] This has to do with questions of intimacy and the group members' concerns about how close they wish to get to each other. In Bennis and Shepard's model, the group moves from the first phase, concerned with dependence and marked by a preoccupation

with authority relations, to a second phase concerned with "interdependence" and characterized by issues of peer-group relations. The two sets of member personalities which emerge in relation to this issue are the "overpersonal" and "counterpersonal" group members. These parallel the "dependent" and the "counterdependent" personalities of the first phase. Once again, three subphases are identified: the "enchantment-flight" subphase in which good feelings abound and efforts are directed towards healing wounds; the "disenchantment-flight" subphase, in which the "counterpersonals" take over from the "overpersonals" in reaction to the growing intimacy; and finally, the "consensual validation" subphase, in which the "unconflicted" members once again provide the leadership needed for the group to move to a new level of work characterized by honest communication between members.

While the specifics of the model relate most directly to the dynamics of T-groups, ambivalence towards honest communications between members can be observed in most groups. After dealing with the authority themes, it is not unusual to find the group moving through a phase marked by positive feelings between members, not at all unlike the "enchantment-flight" subphase. As the work deepens and members move past simply supporting each other, and they begin to confront each other, more negative feelings and reactions are engendered. As members begin to rub up against each other in their work, these feelings are quite natural and should be an expected part of the process. However, group members have learned from their experiences in other situations (family, groups, classes, etc.) that it is not polite to talk directly about negative reactions to the behavior of others. This conditioning is part of the worker's experience as well, and it is not unusual for the worker and the group to get angry at members but, nonetheless, withhold their reactions. Without direct feedback from the group members, it is difficult for individuals to understand their impact upon the group, to learn from that understanding, and to develop new ways of coping. It is the worker's task to draw these interpersonal obstacles openly to members' attention and to help the group develop the ability to discuss them. Workers often fear "opening up" discussion of the angry feelings they sense in the group because they are concerned that things will "get out of hand," they will be overwhelmed, individuals will be hurt, and the life of the group will be threatened. Actually, the greatest threat to the life of the group is from overpoliteness and the resulting illusion of work. The expression of angry feelings can free the caring and positive feelings that are also part of the intimacy of the group. Of course, the worker needs to take care that the contract of the group does not get subverted so that the discussion becomes centered on intermember relationships, thereby losing sight of the original reason the group was formed. A second possibility that the worker has to be alert to is that the member involved may attempt to use the group to deal with a personal pattern of behaving in groups, another attempt at subversion of group purpose. In the following illustration from a counseling group for college students experiencing difficulty in adjusting to their first year on campus, one member developed a pattern of relating in which she consistently cut off other members, did not really listen to them, and attempted to raise her own questions and concerns directly with the worker. The worker sensed she was relating only to him. The other group members showed increasing nonverbal signals of anger at

her behavior which she did not see. The record starts after a particularly striking example of this behavior:

I noticed all of the group members had physically turned away as Louise was talking. Their faces spoke loudly of their negative reaction. I decided to raise the issue: "There is something happening right now, which seems to happen a lot in this group. Louise is asking a lot of questions, cutting some people off as she does, and I sense that the rest of you aren't too happy about that. Am I right?" There was silence for a moment, and Louise, for the first time, was looking directly at the other group members. I said: "I know this isn't easy to talk about, but I feel if you can't be honest with each other about how we are working together, we don't stand a chance of being an effective group. And I think Louise would want to know if this was true. Am I right about that, Louise?" She answered, "I didn't realize I was doing this. Is it true?" Francine responded, "Frankly Louise, I have been sitting here getting angrier and angrier at you by the minute. You really don't seem to listen to anyone else in the group."

The worker opened the door by pointing out the pattern in the group and breaking the taboo against direct acknowledgment of an interpersonal problem. This freed the members to explore this sensitive area.

After Francine's words there was a moment of silence, and then Louise began to cry and said, "You know, I seem to be doing this in all areas of my life. All of my friends are angry at me, my boyfriend won't speak to me and now, I've done it again. What's wrong with me?" The group seemed stunned by her expression of feeling.

Since this was the first real discussion of an interpersonal issue in the group, it was important that the worker clarify the boundary of the discussion, using the contract as his guide. The group felt guilty and Louise felt a bit overwhelmed. The worker acknowledged both these feelings:

"I guess you all must feel quite concerned over how strongly this is hitting Louise?" Members nodded their heads but no one spoke. I continued, "Louise, I'm afraid this has hit you really hard. I should make it clear that we won't be able to talk about the other areas in your life which you are finding tough right now—that wouldn't be appropriate in this group. I'd be glad to talk to you after the group, however, and maybe, if you want, we could explore other avenues of help. For right now, could you stick to what is happening in this group? How come you seem to be so eager to ask all the questions and why do you seem so cut off from the group?" Louise was thoughtful for a moment and then said to the group, "I guess it's just that I'm feeling really concerned about what's going on here at school and I'm trying to get some help as quickly as possible. I want to make sure I get as much from Sid [the worker] as I can." I paused and looked to the group. Francine responded, "You know that's probably why I got so mad at you, because I'm the same way, and I'm sitting here feeling the same feelings—I want as much as I can get as well." Louise: "Well, at least you were straight with me and I appreciate that. It's much worse when you can sense something is wrong but people won't level with you."

After the exchange between Louise and Francine the group seemed to relax. Louise's readiness to accept this feedback without defensiveness had an impact on the group. In other circumstances, members may feel more vulnerable and would need all the help the worker could give in terms of support. When Louise was able to express the underlying feelings she experienced, other group members were able to identify with her and this freed their affect and concern. Louise could sense

this concern for her, making it easier for her to feel more a part of the group rather than relating only to the worker. The worker proceeded to underline the importance of honest communication between members and then guarded against preoccupation with process by reaching for the implicit work hinted at in the exchange:

"I think it was really tough just now, for Louise and the rest of you. However, if the group is going to be helpful, I think we are going to have to learn how to be honest with each other. As Louise pointed out, it can be tougher not to hear sometimes. I think it is also important that we not lose the threads of our work as we go along. I noticed that both Louise and Francine mentioned their urgency about getting help with their problems right now. Could we pick up by being a bit more specific about what those problems are?"

Francine accepted the invitation by expressing a concern she was having about a specific course. From this point on, Louise was more attentive to the group and appeared a good deal more relaxed. The few times she interrupted, she good-naturedly caught herself and apologized. The worker spoke to her after the session and arranged an appointment for personal counseling. A change in the group was also evident as members appeared more involved and energetic in the discussion.

It is important for a group to develop a climate of trust which will allow members to lower their defenses. A powerful barrier to trust can be raised and maintained by *what is not said* by members. Group members can sense both positive and negative reactions by other members. The effect of these reactions is increased when they remain beneath the surface. On the other hand, open expression of these feelings can free members who will be more confident that they will know where they stand with the group. In the following example, a group for fathers whose children are attending a special clinic for children with behavior problems, the worker had noted a pattern of withdrawal by group members. He had observed indirect cues (such as facial expressions) of feelings towards Mr. A., who had not shared his problems as the others had done. In addition, Mr. W., who had spoken often, had hinted that he feared he might have been speaking too much. At the start of this session there were a number of indirect cues leading the worker to believe members were questioning the way the group operated. After a dispirited opening marked by a rambling discussion, the worker asked the group members to reflect on the way they worked as a group, explaining that he felt the discussion tended to be "impersonal" at times and that he thought they had reactions to each other's way of participating. Mr. W. quickly challenged the view that the group should be personal.

When I asked him to say a little bit more about this, he explained that his feeling was one that he could come here and talk about these things very objectively, but then he was pretty sure that he would never see these men during the week. He was supported very strongly in his feelings about the "impersonal" nature of the group by Mr. L., Mr. A., and Mr. R., with Mr. M. playing a quiet listening role. Mr. M. still seemed to be a little bit confused about where this discussion would lead but said that he would prefer to sort of listen until he got the "hang of things." I encouraged each of the three men, in addition to Mr. W., to talk about how they saw this. All said that there was not much investment of feeling in the group, although each of them said that they certainly liked everyone who came and really looked forward to the sessions. At this point I wondered whether in addition to the feelings of liking and friendship, there might also be some feelings of dis-

like or perhaps some people whom they liked more than others. Mr. R. was the first to comment on this, bringing out a great deal of his feeling while looking at Mr. A. about people who just rambled on about subjects and on the other hand persons who could really talk about themselves but also give a lot of opportunity for other people to identify with them. He said that his preference was for the latter person in the group and then he could recognize that there were times when he wished the former would keep quiet.

Mr. W. responded to this by saying that certainly there were differences in how much one participated or one thought of somebody's participation but that he didn't see this as really being based on competition of any sort. He pointed out that for him there were various ways of participating, that it wasn't always a matter of talking or talking about one's own problem but that one could sit back and listen and get perspective from the way in which other people spoke about their problems. He said that at the beginning, particularly, this allowed him to get help without exposing problem areas that he felt he could not share with the group. Gradually he said as he felt more at ease in the group and really could see where it was helpful to him, he began to share in some of these problems as well. He pointed out that of course his feeling of liking was for a person who could help by talking or commenting on problems which he brought up and that he felt this was rather selfish of him but that after all this was why he was coming to the clinic.

After Mr. W. had spoken, the worker asked if what he had said was true for the others as well—"They weren't always motivated to talk about their own problems, and there were times when they could gain by listening to others." All the members agreed verbally. Mr. W. continued on the question of the impersonality of the group, using as an example that he was not missed when he did not attend a session. He also raised his concern about "talking too much" and was surprised when one member contradicted him. It is as important that group members give each other positive feedback and express their feelings of affection for each other as that they express negative feelings.

Mr. W. said that he was fairly confident that he wasn't really missed and that the group proceeded anyhow, even though when he was there he did a great deal of talking and that perhaps it was even better when he stayed away. To this, Mr. R., with a great deal of feeling, looked right at Mr. W. and said in a fairly strong and loud voice, "I miss you when you're not here, and I can tell when you're not here. It makes for a difference in what we talk about. It's not that I don't get anything when you're not here, because I do, but we talk about different things sometimes when you're not here." I pointed out that, as we talked, they were able to recognize that it was with a great deal of feeling that they came to the group and that these feelings were not related specifically to the content and that they had really an investment in each other as well as in the clinic.

Mr. W. again started off and reacted in a very surprised way to Mr. R.'s statement that he really had missed him and could see in looking back over his own participation in the group that he had similar feelings about people being present or not being present. Mr. A., too, felt that there were differences in how he felt about other men in the group and that while he didn't want to talk specifically about which ones they were, he knew that this was so. He went on to say that, however, in spite of the differences most of his feeling was in a positive direction and he did like most or all of the men in the group. Mr. M. entered the discussion at this time trying hard to make a point. When I recognized him, he said that he could now get an idea of what I had been driving at when I focused the discussion as I did on how people felt about each other in the group.

Mr. M. continued by discussing his role in the group. He explained that he was quiet in the beginning because he "had wanted to make sure that they might have some of the same feelings before he ventured his own opinion." He explained that, at this point, he felt they were enough like him that he was willing to jump in more quickly and risk his ideas. There was further discussion, at the worker's request, of competition in the group which had been mentioned by Mr. M. Mr. W. once again raised his concerns about "talking too much" and the members reassured him that they were interested in what he had to say. As the members of this group began to express some of the feelings they had towards their own participation and the participation of others, their honesty helped Mr. A., a defensive member, to bring his problems to their attention for the first time.

Mr. A. said that now that we had discussed what had happened in the group, he had something else he wanted to bring up. In a very sharp contrast, he said that as long as we were talking about feelings, he wanted the group's opinion about something that he was struggling with. He said that in his contacts with the clinic, he had been "accused" of withholding a great deal of his feeling, particularly in regard to his children. He wasn't quite sure about this and what effect it had on the children, but that he was just wondering if any of the others had ever felt the same way. When I asked what it was tonight that enabled him to ask the group this, Mr. A. replied that he sort of felt that all of the men would really understand and would be able to help him to look at this. Mr. R., Mr. L., and Mr. W. all reacted visibly to this, each looking up, Mr. R. smiling, Mr. L. nodding his head and Mr. W. leaning back in his chair and looking directly at Mr. A. Mr. R. responded first, with a broad grin and in a very pleased and warm tone, welcomed Mr. A. to the group. When Mr. A. wondered what he meant by this, Mr. R. went on to explain that it seems that Mr. A. no longer had to hide the fact that he really has some problems of his own. Mr. R. said that it seemed to him that any time Mr. A. had talked before this, he talked in a very general way and that it was really hard for him to feel that he had any real problems and that now it seemed that he was bringing them out into the open more. Mr. L. confirmed this, saying that if nothing else tonight, he could really tell that Mr. A. was concerned about his feelings with his children as well as "what the book says one should do."

Although previously unspoken, the group's feeling that Mr. A. was remaining outside their work was evident in their reactions to his comments. His lack of emotional and personal involvement had been an obstacle to the group's movement. By pointing out the need to discuss the way the members worked with each other and by holding the group to this discussion, the worker played a key role in helping the members to talk about their relationships. This freed Mr. A. and the other group members to risk ideas in more intimate ways. As the next excerpt reveals, the connections between Mr. A.'s feelings and those of the group became evident.

Mr. W. looked up, paused, and then asked Mr. A. if he could say more about what he meant, to which Mr. A. replied that what he thought he was asking about had to do with the difficulty or the ease with which one really showed how he felt. He said that tonight the group seemed able to do it, and this is what encouraged him to bring his concern and the question that had come from the caseworker and that at this point he wanted really to understand how this might influence his son and his daughter as well and his own participation in his family life. With this, Mr. W. nodded and said this is really what he thought Mr. A. was driving at and that he had a notion that this was something that was not only Mr. A.'s problem, but that as far as he was concerned, this seemed to be the way that most men in the group felt and he asked whether this was not so. He said that for him, this had been and still continues to be somewhat of a concern and that he could feel what Mr. A. was driving at. As Mr. W. stopped talking, he looked up and all of the others in the group very thoughtfully looked at him, looked at each

other, at me, finally at Mr. L. I remarked that if this was so, it gave us something else which could be of some help because as we had discussed that evening, the group was one place where they could really show how they felt and to look at some of these feelings in order to understand better what motivated them. Mr. M. summarized this by saying that he thought that if the group could continue with this topic of discussion, he would have a much better understanding of what role feelings played in the behavior of his children, how these were influenced, what they represented to him and consequently, would give him a much better understanding of how he behaves, as well as what makes his child tick.

The session ended soon after this conversation; the worker acknowledged that the group had worked hard and set an agenda to continue with Mr. A.'s concern. This excerpt demonstrated the need to deal with the intimacy theme as well as the connection between the process of the group and the content of the work, a connection that Mr. M. pointed out in his last comments. I have found that workers experience intermember issues as particularly difficult. Although as they develop group experience, they become proficient at reaching for issues related to the authority theme, it takes longer before they will risk dealing with questions of the intimacy theme. So powerful are the taboos and so strong is their fear of hurting that they will try many indirect routes before finally risking honesty. The reluctance may be partly rooted in the worker's feelings that it is their responsibility to "handle" anything that comes from their reaching for intermember negatives. As has been illustrated in this excerpt, there is strength in a group which has developed even a small fund of positive relationship for handling its own problems. What is needed is the catalyst of the worker's intervention to give them permission and to support them as they enter the formerly taboo area. As I have described the difficulties group members face in dealing with two major developmental tasks, the relationship with the worker and the relationship between members, I have had to refer to a yet more general task, *the development of a culture for work.* The following section explores the question of group culture in more detail.

Developing a Culture for Work

I have been using the term *culture* in its anthropological/sociological sense with a particular emphasis on group norms, taboos, and roles. I have already discussed roles in some detail in Chapter 12 so the focus here will be on norms and taboos. Hare has defined group norms as

rules of behavior, proper ways of acting, which have been accepted as legitimate by members of a group. Norms specify the kinds of behavior that are expected of group members. These rules or standards of behavior to which members are expected to conform are for the most part derived from the goals which a group has set for itself. Given a set of goals, norms define the kind of behavior which is necessary for or consistent with the realization of those goals.[9]

Taboos are commonly associated with primitive tribes which developed sacred prohibitions making certain people or acts untouchable or unmentionable. The term *taboo* in modern cultures refers to social prohibitions which result from conventions or traditions. Norms and taboos are closely related, since a group norm may be one which upholds the tradition of making certain subjects taboo. As groups are formed, each member brings to the micro-society of the group a strongly developed set of norms of behavior and a shared identification of taboo areas. The

early culture of the group is constructed as a reflection of the members' outside culture. As Hare points out, the norms of a group should be consistent with those necessary for realization of its goals. The problem, however, is that the norms of our society and the taboos commonly observed often create obstacles to productive work in the group. A major group task then involves developing a new set of norms and freeing group members to deal with formerly taboo subjects.

I have already been dealing with the problem of helping group members develop their culture for work. For example, the subjects of authority and dependency are generally taboo areas in our culture. One does not talk freely about feelings on these subjects. As one example, group experiences in classrooms over many years have taught us not to challenge authority as well as the dangers involved if one admits feelings of dependency upon a person in authority in front of a peer group. The discussion of the authority theme in the first part of this chapter described the worker's efforts to help the group discuss these taboo areas and to develop a new set of more productive norms; the same was true in the discussion of the intimacy theme. It is important to note that the effort is not directed at changing societal norms or exorcising group members from the power of taboos for all times. There are sound reasons for norms of behavior and many taboos have appropriate places in our lives. The focus of the work is on building a new culture *within the group,* a necessity for effective group functioning. Transfers of this experience outside of the group may or may not be relevant. For example, members in a couples' group have to deal with the taboos against open discussion of sex, an area critical to the work of the group. The frankness of the group discussion freed the members to develop more open communications with each other outside the sessions. This change in the culture of their marriages was important for them to develop and was therefore an appropriate transfer of learning. On the other hand, if the couples used their new-found freedom to discuss problems in sexual functioning at neighborhood cocktail parties, they would quickly discover the power of peer-group pressure. To illustrate the worker's function of helping the group work on these important tasks, I will examine the efforts of a worker to develop a culture for work which encourages the expression of painful feelings. A second example illustrates a group change of culture in relation to expressing feelings of anger. This is followed by an example of discussion of the taboo against open expression of sexual issues. The group theory outlined by Bion is used in this section to illustrate again the way in which practitioners can draw upon the literature to build their own models of group functioning.[10]

For the first illustration I have chosen a worker's report of her efforts to help a group of mothers of hyperactive children share their painful and angry feelings about their children's problems. This group was cited earlier in this chapter in connection with the illustration of the necessity for group members to deal with their feelings towards the worker which resulted from her demands for work. The report is organized through the use of a learning device called "a record of service."[11] In the first entries, the worker describes the problem and how it came to her attention:

The Problem. Members found it very difficult to talk about their own feelings about their hyperactive children. Instead they continually focused on what other people felt about the children such as teachers, neighbors, husbands, relatives. Despite their reluctance to focus on their feelings, they occasionally gave me clues that this was their underlying concern, and as this was also part of the contract, I felt we had to explore their feelings and work on them.

How the Problem Came to My Attention. During the first few meetings, the members continued to talk about how important this group was for them, as it gave them the chance to get together to discuss their problems related to their hyperactive children and get support from each other. The feeling was that no one, not even their husbands, understood what they were going through and how they felt. Anytime they would begin talking about their own feelings, they resorted back to discussing medications, school, etc., in other words, a safe topic. Yet the need to talk about how they felt was always raised by members in different ways. This pattern began in session two when one member raised the question of hyperactivity due to emotional deprivation at an early age—the group superficially touched upon it and dropped the subject, resorting back to something safe. As their pattern of flight became more obvious to me, I was able to help them understand what they were doing, and thus help them deal with their feelings.

Bion is helpful in explaining such difficulties with emotions, a characteristic common to groups.[12] His work was based upon observations of psychotherapy groups, led by himself, in which he played a relatively passive role, concentrating on making interpretations of the members' behaviors. Once again, as with the earlier theory, elements of his model are group specific while other aspects lend themselves nicely to generalizing. A central idea in Bion's work is the existence of the "work group." This consists of the mental activity related to a group's task. When the work group is operating, one can see group members translating their thoughts and feelings into actions which are adaptive to reality. As Bion describes it, the work group represents a "sophisticated" level of group operation. Most groups begin with a more "primitive" culture in which they will resist dealing with painful emotions. Group development is therefore the struggle between the group's primitive instincts to avoid the pain of growth and its need to become more sophisticated and deal with feelings. The primitive culture of the early stages in the group is a mirror of the primitive culture in our larger society where the direct and open expression of feelings is avoided.

In the example of the mothers' group, the worker described how the problem came to her attention, pointing out how the more painful subjects were dropped as the group took "flight" into a discussion of more superficial issues. This conforms to one of Bion's key ideas—the existence of "basic assumption groups." He believes that the work group can be obstructed, diverted, and sometimes assisted by group members experiencing powerful emotional drives. His term *basic assumption group* refers to the idea that group members appear to be acting as if their behavior were motivated by a shared basic assumption about the purpose of the group—an assumption other than the expressed group goal. One of the three basic assumption groups he identifies is the "flight-fight" group. In a primitive group, when the work group gets close to painful feelings, the members will unite in an instantaneous, unconscious process to form the "flight-fight" group, acting from the basic assumption that the group goal is to avoid the pain associated with the work group processes through flight (i.e., an immediate change of subject away from the painful area) or fight (i.e., an argument developing in the group which moves from the emotional level to an

intellectual one). This process in the group context parallels the ambivalence noted in work with individuals when resistance was expressed through an abrupt change of subjects. Bion's strategy for dealing with this problem is to call the group's attention to the behavior in an effort to educate the group so that it can function on a more sophisticated level. As we return to the worker's record of service on this problem, we see that her early efforts were directed at systematically encouraging the expression of feelings and acknowledging these with her own feelings in an effort to build a working relationship. As the pattern developed, the worker drew upon this working relationship to point out the pattern of avoidance and to make a demand for work to the group. The worker has identified her movements (italics) as part of the record-of-service assignment.

Session Three. *I listen to what the members are saying, and I encourage them to talk about their feelings toward their hyperactive children,* e.g., "Marilyn then told us that since she had begun coming to the sessions, she noticed that she had changed her attitude in relation to her hyperactive son, and now he was responding more positively towards her. She had always thought of him in terms of being a normal child, and his not being able to react as normal children do frustrated her. In fact she had set up expectations for him which he couldn't meet. *I encouraged her to continue talking about her feelings toward him.* She said that she supposed she really couldn't accept the fact that he was hyperactive, and then after coming to the meeting she began to accept this. *I asked how she felt now.* (reaching for feelings) She felt better, but the hurt is there.

By the fifth session the group had come close to discussing some of the more difficult underlying feelings but each time had used the flight mechanism to avoid the pain. Some of the feelings experienced by these mothers ran so counter to what they believed they were *expected* to feel that they had great difficulty in admitting the reality to others and at times even to themselves. The worker had developed a fund of relationship during the first sessions through her efforts to understand the meaning of the experience for the members. In the following excerpt, she draws upon that fund and makes a demand for work on the members by pointing out their pattern of flight. Even as she does this, she tries to express her empathy with the difficulty the group experiences in meeting this demand.

Session Five. *The group sometimes picks up on their feelings, and I try to put a demand for work on them; that is, to stick with the subject and to really talk about their feelings. I point out their underlying anger and don't allow them to take flight.* Betty started talking about George and the school again, and the others became very supportive, offering concrete help. She expressed anger at the school but also talked about George and how he didn't fit in—he couldn't read and cope with the courses, and he didn't care. *I detected that some of the anger was directed towards him, and I asked how she felt towards him at this point.* She said that she pitied him. I wondered if she wasn't also feeling somewhat angry at him for causing her so many problems. She denied this. *I continued trying to point out her anger as she talked, and tried to show her that she was really coming across as if she was angry at her son.* The others began talking about their children and the problems they caused. I said that I had felt the undercurrent of anger, and I asked what it was like to have a child such as this. *(Demand for work)* Betty said that it made her mad—she felt like killing him. Marilyn said that he provoked her and she really reacted. I said that it's not easy to talk about how these children make you feel—it's certainly terribly hard to admit that sometimes they provoke you so much that, as Betty said, you want to kill them. *(Acknowledge how hard it is to talk about their feelings, and credit a member for*

revealing how she felt.) I wondered if others felt as she did? *(Finding commonality of feeling)* There was little response, but Denise started talking about the school, and conversation became very lively. I said that I had noticed that whenever they had to talk about how they felt, it was hard, and they always go back to a safe point of how others feel towards their children. *(Point out group's behavior pattern)* Marilyn said that it was true, they always did it, and she supposed it was really hard to talk about how they felt about their children. I agreed that of course it was hard, these are the kinds of things that you don't want to talk about. But they had said that these kids are impossible at times, they're so difficult to handle that it would seem natural to have negative feelings towards them. *(Recognizing the magnitude of the task, and support negative feelings)* I pressed them to tell me what it was like and how these children made them feel. *(Demand for work)* Marilyn said that Jonathan frustrated her so much, and against her better judgment, she reacted like she did this morning—really out of control. Beatrice said that Colin was so difficult, there were times when she was so tired of it—like his room being constantly in a mess—it irritated her so much. I said that there were times when Colin made her very angry. *(Reflect feelings)* Mildred agreed that she reacts negatively, too. . . .

The worker's synthesis of empathy and demand helped the group to modify its culture and to create a new norm in which they would not be judged harshly for their feelings, even those they felt were unreasonable. As the feelings of anger towards the child were expressed, the group moved to a new level of trust and openness. With the help of the worker, they shared the moments they felt like "killing" their child and, under her gentle prodding, they explored how having an "imperfect child" is experienced as a reflection on themselves as bad parents. There is an important connection between their harsh judgments of themselves for having such children and their attitude towards their children. Their attitude, in turn, affects the child's sense of acceptance by his or her parents which can lead to further acting out behavior. Understanding and accepting these feelings is a first step towards breaking this vicious cycle. The worker's comments at the end of the session are designed to acknowledge the important change in the discussion.

I recognize how hard it is to talk about their feelings, and how much pain they feel. I credit them for their work, and try to create a feeling amongst them that I understand. "Denise had been talking about her own feelings about her son, and seemingly had her feelings well under control. She had said that she was very sensitive and had trouble talking about it. I said that perhaps she was saying that she, too, had feelings that the others had mentioned, but she found it very hard to discuss. *(Recognize individual members' feelings, and find commonality to the group)* The others said that it was hard to talk about it, to admit that these children weren't the same as the others, that you wanted to be proud of them but couldn't. I agreed that it was hard—they were living the situation twenty-four hours a day and they had feelings about these children. *(empathy)*

. . .

The members discussed how much they were criticized by their relatives and were very upset. I said that people just did not know what it was like to be a mother of a child like this, and also they did not feel the pain and frustration that they felt. I waited and there was silence. I noticed that our time was long ago up and said that they had done some very hard work. It was not easy to talk as they had today, to share the feelings of depression and hostility towards their children and to admit that they had wanted to kill them at times. I wondered how they felt now. Marilyn said that she couldn't understand everything I tried to get them to do, but I made her think and try new things, and also I made her look at things differently. I said that it wasn't easy for them to do this, I knew that, and I often felt their pain."

We have already seen in an earlier excerpt from this group how the worker needed to help the group articulate its angry feelings in response to her demands for work. Bion might describe those exchanges as examples of the "fight" pattern of reaction in the "fight-flight" group.[13] Another basic assumption group, as described by Bion, is the "dependent group" in which the group appears to be meeting in order to be sustained by the leader. This is another form of avoidance of the "work group" and was illustrated in the earlier excerpt by the group wanting the leader to "cheer them up." The third and final assumption group in Bion's theory is called the "pairing group" in which the group, often through a conversation between two members, avoids the pain of the work by discussing some future great event. The discussion in this group of "new drugs" or "outside experts" who would provide a solution to their problems is an example of the pairing group in action. At the end of the record of service, the worker identifies where she thinks the group stands now in its task of developing a culture for work and strategizes on her specific next steps.

Where It Stands Now. The group is beginning to work on their feelings, although not everyone is as willing to take a good look at themselves. They are starting to share with each other the pain, guilt, and anger they have towards their hyperactive children. Also they're sharing feelings of helplessness, wanting to be the perfect mothers, knowing that they're not, and wanting to find ways to deal with their children better.

Specific Next Steps.
A. Keep the focus, and continue making the demand for work. Continue making this a work group and not a fight group.
B. I feel the deviant member, Denise, in expressing her own resistance to looking at her

feelings, is really expressing what they all feel. Use the deviant member's behavior to point out their own underlying feelings.
C. Continue to recognize their feelings and credit them for their work. In crediting make them aware of their progress, as a means of encouragement.
D. Credit the internal leaders for taking over leadership and focusing the group on the work.
E. Help the group work on solutions to their feelings and problems. The group needs this if they are to lose their feelings of helplessness—they want to learn how they can function better as mothers and help their hyperactive children.
F. Help the group move into the ending and transition stage.

In a second example of a worker helping a group change its norms in order to develop a culture more conducive to work, a worker in a married couples' group (not the one described earlier) notices the group members' reluctance to get involved when couples share very personal and angry feelings. She brings this to their attention:

By the sixth session (following Xmas vacation, during which the group had adjourned for two weeks) most of the group's work seemed to involve each couple presenting problems which had been decided upon by both partners and within limits felt by both to be fairly comfortable. If there was intra-couple disagreement and challenge—even that seemed to be safe—i.e., related to problems of the others in the group or, if pertaining to their own marriage, then almost always at the level of the more reluctant spouse, Don, at the fifth session, challenged Liz directly. Liz responded to his charge that she was "always covering up the truth" by a return challenge—asking him why he had married her—daring him to share with the group the real reason—her pregnancy. When he tried to evade her by deliberately misinterpreting her question, she stuck with it and she said she had always suspected that he had felt an obligation to marry

and had never really loved her. The group seemed reluctant at first to step into this interchange—they seemed to be giving the couple a chance to "unsay" what had been said. I pointed out the difference between their reaction to this problem and others they had picked up on unhesitatingly, and asked if they agreed that there was a difference. A few members did, and I asked why they thought they hadn't wanted to get involved. Most felt it was "extremely intimate," and that made the difference. I agreed that it was and that I felt it really took guts to bring up something intimate. I said that often problems were not brought up because they were so very personal and that we were so used to keeping anything personal as private as possible. The group talked about family and friends and "how far" one could go in these relationships and how this group was different from "out there." Something clicked for Reisa because without even checking it out with Jack, she told the group that she and Jack had been forced to marry because she had been pregnant, too. They talked about her family's reaction and how this affected their marriage and their feelings about their first child.

It is critical that workers pay attention to the group norms and systematically assist the group to examine them and decide which lend themselves to effective work. Research in group dynamics has shown that group norms can have a powerful effect upon group members even in more impersonal laboratory groups established for the experiment. For example, in a study by Sherif and Sherif, subjects were shown a stationary point of light in a darkened room.[14] Because of what is known as the "autokinetic effect," subjects imagine some motion in the light. Each subject estimated the movement and gradually developed a range of estimates. Subjects then had the opportunity to make the estimates in groups of two or three, and then return to the individual estimates. A norm of the range of movements were developed in the small groups which then continued to influence the individual's judgments in individual sessions. In addition, if the first judgments were made in a group, individual judgments converged more rapidly. Another experiment, by Asch, showed the power of group influence on individual judgments.[15] A naive subject was included in a group of seven to nine members made up of "coached" subjects. All were asked to match lines from a card to a standard. The coached subjects gave accurate responses on six of the tries but made unanimous incorrect responses on twelve of the attempts to match the lines. A control group of all naive subjects also made these ratings, but their judgments were written and not shared with each other. Subjects in the experimental group made errors on their matching 37 percent of the times while control group subjects made almost none. In follow-up interviews, subjects described as "yielding" indicated they knew they were wrong in their estimates but did not want to deviate from the group. If laboratory group norms can affect individual participation, then the impact of groups such as the ones described in this book must be powerful.

To complete this discussion of group culture, the problem of taboos must be addressed. I described earlier how the skill of helping individual clients to discuss subjects in taboo areas was important to the work. Because of the social nature of taboos, their impact in the group is magnified. Many of the taboos have their early roots in the first primary groups, such as the family, and can therefore represent a powerful obstacle to group work. Sometimes it is enough for the worker simply to call the group's attention to the existence of the obstacle. However, in the case of some of the stronger taboos, such

as sex, more help may be needed. In the couples' group described in Chapter 9, sexual concerns between members were hinted at in an early session. The hints were at the end of the meeting. I pointed this out to the group members and suggested that we pick up on this at our next session. The group agreed enthusiastically. I did not expect it to be that easy, since the strength of the taboo in this area would still be operating and simply calling the group's attention to the subject probably would be insufficient. At the start of the next session, the members immediately began to discuss an unrelated area. I called their attention to the existence of the taboo:

"At the end of last week we agreed to get into the whole sexual area, and yet we seem to be avoiding it this week. I have a hunch that this is a hard area to discuss in the group. Am I right?" There was a look of relief on their faces and Lou responded, "Yes, I noticed that as well. You know, this is not easy to talk about in public. We're not used to it." I wanted the group to explore what it was about this area that made it hard. "Maybe it would help if we spent some time on what it is about this area, in particular, which makes it tough to discuss. That might make everyone feel a bit more comfortable." Fran responded, "When I was a kid, I got a clear message that this wasn't to be spoken about with my parents. The only thing said to me was that I should watch out because boys had only one thing on their mind—the problem was, I wasn't sure what that thing was." Group members were nodding and smiling at this. Lou: "How many of you had your parents talk to you about sex?" The group members exchanged stories of how sex was first raised with them. In all cases it had been done indirectly, if at all, and with some embarrassment. Those with older children described their own determination to do things differently, but somehow, their actual efforts to talk to their children were still marked by discomfort. At one point, Frank described his concerns as a teenager: "You know from the talk I heard from the other guys, I thought everyone in the neighborhood was getting sex except me. It made me feel something was really wrong with me—and I made sure not to let on that I was really concerned about this." The conversation continued with the group members noting that they had been raised in different generations, and that while some things were different in terms of attitudes towards sex, other things, particularly the taboos, were the same. I could sense a general relaxing as the discussion proceeded, and members discovered that there were many similarities in their experiences. I said, "It's easy to see how these experiences would make it difficult for you to talk freely in this group; however, if we can't get at this critical area, we will be blocked in our work."

By encouraging discussion of the taboo and the reasons for its power, I was helping the members to enter this area. It was important that I did not blame or criticize them for the difficulty in getting started, but at the same time I needed to make a demand to move past the taboo:

"I can imagine that this difficulty in talking about sex must carry over in your marriages as well. I believe that if you can discuss some of the problems you are having here in the group, we might be able to help you talk more freely to each other—and that might be the beginning of a change." Rick responded, "We can never talk to each other about this without ending up in a fight." I asked Rick if he could expand on this. "We have this problem of me wanting more sex than Fran—sometimes we can go for months without sex, and I'm not sure I can take this anymore." Fran responded, "A relationship is more than just sex, you know, and I just can't turn it on or off because you happen to feel like having sex."

The rest of the evening was spent on Fran and Rick's relationship. The group was supportive to both as the couples'

early conversation centered on who was to blame: Fran for her "frigidity" or Rick for his "premature ejaculation." During the next few sessions, the group kept discussing the sexual area as members explored the intricate patterns of action and reaction they had developed which led them to blame each other rather than take responsibility for their own feelings about sex. Once the taboo was breached, and group members found that they were not punished, it lost some of its power and the discussion became more personal. It is again interesting to note that the process and the task are intermixed. As the group members discuss their difficulty in speaking about sex (the process), they are actually beginning to work on their concerns about sex (the task).

Helping Group Members Develop a Structure for Work

As a group develops, it needs to work on the task of building a structure for work. I am using the term *structure* to describe the way the members of the group relate to each other. This is probably easier to conceptualize in a formal group where structure is essential to the operation of the group, for instance, a citizens' antipoverty action group. The group was formed to encourage poor people to use strength in numbers to try to change some of the local welfare and school policies which affected their lives. There were over fifty members who signed up at an initial organizational meeting. The need for structure was evident, since fifty people cannot operate in a cooperative manner without some form of organization. One early task was to identify roles required for effective operation. I am now using roles more narrowly, relying on Hare's definition: "The expectations shared by group members about the behavior associated with some position in a group, no matter what individual fills the position, are called *role*."[16] A small steering committee met to draft an outline of the group's structure and identified functional tasks which needed to be carried by group members: leadership (a chairperson), responsibility for relations with other community groups (a co-chairperson), responsibility for the group's funds (treasurer), and responsibility for maintaining the group's records and correspondence (secretary). As the group developed, other roles became necessary and were created (e.g., committee chairpersons for special projects). By creating these roles, the group was *dividing the labor* among group members, so that each member carries some part of the burden. When division of labor and responsibility are not handled well, as for example, when a chairperson attempts to do all of the work, the overworked member can become overwhelmed while the group members feel angry, left out, and apathetic. The greater the apathy, the more the chairperson feels the need to "take responsibility." In these circumstances the worker's function is crucial. In addition to helping the members develop a structure for effective operations, the worker must monitor how well the structure is working and draw any problems to the attention of the members. In the example of the chairperson who does not share responsibility, the worker's function would be to mediate the engagement between the chairperson and the group. The following example illustrates this work in a steering committee session of an antipoverty action group:

I had gotten signals from a number of members that they were upset with the way things were going and especially with Sid's leadership. He had taken responsibility for a num-

ber of follow-up items and had not handled them well. As a result, the group faced some serious problems on a planned sit-in action that weekend. The meeting began as usual, with Sid reading the agenda and asking for any additions. There were none. Discussion began on a number of minor items. It finally reached the question of the plans for the action, and I could feel the tension growing. Sara began, "Is it true, Sid, that we may not have the buses for Saturday?" Sid replied abruptly, "I'm working on that so don't worry." There was silence. I said, "I think there is something going on here. What's up?" Sara continued, "Look, Sid, I don't want you to take this personally, but there are a number of things screwed up about this Saturday and I'm really worried." Sid responded defensively, "Well, what do you expect? You know I have a lot of responsibility to carry with not very much help." Terry broke in, "Every time we try to give you some help, you turn us down." Sid looked hurt. I intervened, "I think there has been a problem going on for some time, and you folks have not been able to level with each other about it. Sid, you feel you have to carry a lot of the burden around here and the group members don't really appreciate how hard it is for you. Am I right?" Sid nodded in agreement. I turned to the others. "I think the rest of you feel that you would like to pick up a piece, but you sense Sid seems to hang on—so you don't offer. Then you feel angry later when things don't work out." They nodded as well. I said, "Look, I know it's hard, but if we have this out, maybe we can work out a way of sharing the responsibilities that would be more helpful for the group."

The worker needs to be clear that his or her function involves helping group members work on *their* tasks. It is not unusual for workers with such groups to be just as uncomfortable about confrontation as the members. As a result, they may try to use indirect influence, or to take over some of the chairperson's functions, or even try to get the group to replace the chairperson. This reflects a lack of understanding about group developmental tasks. It is not at all unusual for groups to run into such problems in maintaining their structures for work. Indeed, if the group could work easily without such obstacles, it would not need a worker. The real problem for a group such as this one arises when the members cannot openly discuss these difficulties as they emerge. This is the work of the helping professional—not the details of the structure itself, but the way in which group members develop and maintain their structure. In helping the group to explore this area, the worker is conscious that feelings have a great deal to do with most communications problems and that skills in this area can prove helpful.

Although they were uncomfortable, they agreed to take some time to discuss the problem. I asked the group members why they had not leveled with Sid before. Rudy said, "Sid, we all like you a lot. That's why we asked you to be chairman. I didn't want to hurt your feelings. Since you became chairman, you seemed to forget the rest of us—and frankly, I started to get pissed off." I said, "Did you get the feeling, Rudy, that you weren't needed?" Rudy: "That's it! All of a sudden, Sid was going to do the whole ball game himself." I asked Sid how come he felt he had to take all the responsibility. He said: "Look, this is my first time chairing anything. None of us has much experience at this stuff—I'm worried that we will fall on our faces. I've asked some people to do things, and they have screwed up, so I don't ask anymore, I just do it." I said, "Are you worried, Sid, that you're going to fall on your face?" He was silent and then said, "You bet." I waited. Rita said, "I'm probably one of the people you feel let you down, aren't I?" Sid nodded. She continued, "Well, I meant to follow up and hold that subcommittee meeting. I just kept putting it off." I asked, "Have you ever chaired a meeting before?" Rita said "No." I continued, "I guess you were proba-

bly nervous about it." She agreed that she had been nervous. Rudy said to Sid, "Look, Sid, I can understand your feeling worried about the group. We all feel the same way. But you really don't have to carry it all on your back. That's not what we expect of you. We can help out, and if we flop, we all flop." Sid relaxed a bit and said, "It would make it easier if I didn't have to feel completely responsible." I pointed out that the whole group was probably feeling shaky about their jobs and how well they could do them—just like Sid and Rita pointed out. "I don't think that's so unusual—in fact, I think that the fact that you are talking about this is a great sign. At least you can do something about the problem and not let it tear your group apart." They agreed that it was a start and spent the next twenty minutes analyzing the jobs to be done and redistributing the responsibilities.

In addition to division-of-labor problems, groups must develop formal and informal communication patterns. In the example of the community group, decisions had to be made about who reported to whom, how often various subgroups would meet, who would get copies of the minutes, and how communications at meetings would be governed. Another task required the development of a decision-making process which would be efficient and at the same time make sure that individual members felt involved. In addition to the work described on the formal structure, the worker could observe the informal system at work. For example, shortcuts in communications were found which often facilitated the coordination of subgroups within the structure. This had to be monitored because the informal communication system can also serve to subvert the formal system, thus becoming an obstacle in itself. The worker could also observe the informal assignment of status to various members of the group. Members who performed their functions well and demonstrated the most admired skills in the group would be assigned higher status and their contributions to discussion would often carry more weight because of this fact. Differential status can also be a source of friction in the group, and the members' reactions to this also need to be monitored by the worker. In a sense, I have assigned to the worker the special responsibility of paying attention to the way in which the group works on these important structural tasks, monitoring the process to pick up cues signaling the difficulties as they emerge and helping the group members pay attention to these problems. It has been my observation in a number of community groups that workers sometimes ignore these critical group tasks and instead concentrate on a strategy of action in relation to the outside systems (e.g., the welfare department, the school board, government officials). These workers may find that after a period of time, the internal struggles of the group have been so devastating that the strength of the group has declined. This results in a loss of *group cohesion,* the property of the group which describes the mutual attraction members feel for each other. Attempts to develop greater cohesion through social activities (e.g., group parties) or as is even more common by attacking another system and trying to unite members against a common enemy, are only useful in the short run. I believe there are striking similarities between work with community groups and the work carried out with so-called clinical or therapeutic groups. The developmental group tasks are similar, and the skills required by the worker to assist this second client, the group, are similar as well.

Group variables such as role, status, communications patterns, and decision-making processes have received a great deal of study by small-group researchers.

In one of the best known of these, Whyte spent one year as a participant observer with a group of young men (ages early twenties and thirties) he called the "street-corner boys."[17] His findings on group structure indicated that position (rank or status) of the members was related to the degree of origination of group action they contributed. Once a group hierarchy was established, a great deal of energy was invested in maintaining it. In addition, if one could influence the top two or three high status members, one could influence the entire group. Members of this group developed a subtle and complex system of mutual obligations and reciprocities, and position in the group also depended upon how well one discharged these obligations. A member's position in the group was directly related to his resourcefulness, fair-mindedness, and his skills in things valued by the group (e.g., sports).

In a second example, Bavelas worked out an innovative research design in which five-person groups were established to work on a set task. The communication patterns of each group were rigidly controlled by the experimenter.[18] The patterns tested included a circle, a line, a star and a Y pattern. For example, in the Y pattern, communications were organized so that three of the members of the group had to communicate with each other *only* through the fourth member who was located at the branching point of the Y. Groups were tested on their speed at solving the problem, the number of errors they made, the satisfaction of the participants, and their recognition of leadership in their groups. Findings indicated the following: The Y pattern was fastest with the central person identified as the leader. The circle pattern was least productive with no leader. On the other hand, the circle pattern had the highest morale, and the Y pattern had the lowest. In addition, as might be expected, the central people in the patterns had the highest morale and the end people the lowest. One additional finding was that after many trials leadership emerged in the circle groups, and their time on the trials improved.

In a third study by Deutsch, ten groups of five college students each met once per week for five weeks to discuss human-relations problems.[19] After the first week, pairs of students were randomly assigned to groups which were influenced by the experimenter into either cooperative or competitive patterns. His findings indicated that the cooperative groups had stronger individual motivation to complete tasks, a stronger feeling of obligation, greater division of labor, more effective intermember communications, more friendliness, and more group productivity.

Finally, Bales developed a system for observing and analyzing problem-solving behavior in groups called Interaction Process Analysis (I.P.A.) in which observers could record one of twelve categories of interaction taking place in a group.[20] Ad hoc groups of college students were brought together to solve a series of human-relations or construction problems without a formal leader. One of the central findings was that the groups appeared to develop two types of internal leaders—one a "task specialist" and the other a "social-emotional" specialist. The task specialist intervened to help the group complete the test activity while the social-emotional specialist paid attention to problems of group maintenance. The worker function that I have described requires that he integrate these two activities.

Summary

The worker's second client, the organism called the group, must go through a developmental process just as any other growing entity. Early tasks include problems of formation and the satisfaction of individual members' needs. Problems of dealing with the worker as a symbol of authority (authority theme) must be faced, as well as the difficulties involved in peer-group relationships (the intimacy theme). Attention needs to be paid to the culture of the group so that norms which are consistent with the achievement of the group's goals are developed. Taboos which block the group must be challenged and mastered if the discussion is to be meaningful. Finally, a formal or informal structure must be developed. This structure will include assigned roles, assigned status, communication patterns, and a decision-making process. Effective work in the group will develop a sense of cohesion which in turn will strengthen future work.

DEVELOPING A GROUP STRUCTURE OVER TIME

While I have used two chapters to describe working with the two clients, the individual and the group, in reality, it is not possible to deal with them as separate entities. The example which follows is a report of group worker's efforts, over time, to help a group develop a "culture for work." She does this by paying consistent attention to the individual-group connection. The setting is an outpatient clinic at a general hospital and the clients are teenagers referred by their psychiatrists. The time period covered is six weeks.

The Problem. The group members' struggle to share real feelings with each other is an ongoing process. Dave, the deviant group member, expresses the widely held feelings of the group, communicating indirectly by being loud and over-active, and so hiding the deep feelings behind his actions. On occasion he alienates group members. His anxiety and concerns are similar to what each member is feeling, so I had hope I could reach beyond his behaviour to help Dave communicate and relate effectively to the group, and also help the group see past Dave's behaviour to the commonality of their feelings.

1. How the Problem Came to My Attention. At our first session, all the group members were uptight. Dave's uncooperative behaviour was the manifestation of all the members' anxiety. Both verbally and non-verbally, he brought up many of the concerns of the group.

For instance, the day the group started, all members were sitting on cushions on the floor. However, Dave perched on a table and refused to sit on the floor. "I'm here just to listen—I won't be doing any talking. My psychiatrist made me come to this group." Thus Dave started to articulate concerns felt by all members:

The concern of being involved with a psychiatrist—am I nuts?
Is this a group for crazies?
I'm not going to share my feelings with anyone here, it's too risky.
Am I going to be accepted by other group members?
I am here involuntarily.
The authority theme.

I felt that if I could reach beyond the deviant behaviour to bring out the common feelings of all the group members, that Dave could become an important ally to me in the group.

2. Summary of Work

I Tune in to the Group's Feelings and Unasked Questions. The first week of the group, when Dave made his comment, "I'm just here to listen—I won't be doing any talking. My psychiatrist made me come to the group," I was in a dilemma as to which lead to take, he

had given me so many. I turned to him, saying, "Yeah, it's tough, isn't it, when you come into a group like this and you don't know anyone." There was a slight pause, then Dave said yeah. I tried again and said, "I guess all of you were wondering and maybe feeling anxious about what the kids were going to be like in the group." (Expressing commonality of feelings.) Connie jumped in and said, "You know I figured you had to be whacko to be in this group." Wanda agreed, "I really thought this was a group for crazy kids, you know, but when I walked in—you all looked—well, normal." I said that it's hard to come to any group, but especially at a psychiatry clinic, and I could understand them being concerned. Several other members agreed, and Brian said it was easier now that he had met the others.

I Help the Group Deal with the Authority Theme. The concern with the authority theme was especially apparent in our first few weeks. Dave, as usual, had a greater sense of urgency and neatly brought it to the fore. He marched into the group session the second week and said, "Anyone mind if I lead the group today?" No objections. "Good, we won't allow any psychiatrists in." I asked Dave what he meant. "My psychiatrist is about to drive me crazy, I just saw her for an hour." I asked what it was about his psychiatrist that made him feel that way. "Well, she lays trips on me." I asked if other people felt the same way. They all nodded. "I can't talk to my social worker," said Connie. "I can't talk to people who haven't done drugs or gotten drunk," said Gayle. They don't treat us like we know what we're doing," said Chris. I said, "Are you afraid Tom (co-therapist) and I won't treat you as if you know what you're doing?" Silence. I added that it was important that they all understood that this was their group, and we were here to help them talk to each other, and listen, and maybe give suggestions, but not to dump on them. (*Reinforcing contracting.*) The group did not take me up right away on this.

A few weeks later, Tom and I raised the idea of having a parent's night (a Clinic policy), where the parents came and participated in the group. The group was immediately against this, and led by Dave, had a unanimous vote against our suggestion. "This is our group," Dave said, "if we don't want to have a parent's night, we won't have it." I said I'd clear it with the head of the Clinic that we would not plan a parent's night, as the group didn't feel they wanted it. I did so over the next week.

Later, I explored what it was about having parents come that the group didn't like. "I won't say a word," said Gayle, "I can't talk to my parents." Chris said, "I always fight with my parents, and we'll get into a big battle." "My parents won't come," said Tracy. "Sounds like most of you have real difficulties talking to your parents," I said. *(Commonality of experience.)* No kidding, was the generally fervent reply. I asked Gayle to tell us a bit of what goes on at home for her. *(Bringing the problem from the general to the specific.)* Gayle started talking, and led us into an excellent discussion of problems with parents. Several of the members made suggestions to Gayle about how she could do things differently.

I Reach Beyond Dave's Behavior to the Feelings. Dave was attention seeking, singing nursery rhymes into the microphone and being flippant. The group members were trying to ignore him. I confronted him on his behavior. "Dave, it seems you act out just to bug the group, but I'm sure something's going on." *(Pointing out there's something more than behavior.)* Gayle said, "Dave talks too much. He always seems to be doing something. I bet he's not showing his real self." Chris suggested, "Maybe he's insecure." I said, "Dave, I'm sure it bothers you that people are getting angry with you, is it something to do with being accepted in here? Seems you set yourself up to get put down." No reply. Gayle said, "You want us to know you and like you, you won't admit it but it's true." Gayle had hit it beautifully, whereas I had missed the right words. Dave looked at her, then quietly said, "I guess you're right. I guess I feel uptight when I come in here." I then added I was sure each person was feeling what Dave was feeling, he just showed it differently. Gayle said, "Sure, I wonder what you guys think when I talk." I said that perhaps the group could help

each other in that regard. *(Getting the group to make demands on each other.)* I said I thought it was important for them to recognize each one was wondering about each other, and that they were all tense, and each of them understood how hard it was to really express how they were feeling.

Dave was flippant and inappropriate more than usual. He obviously had something on his mind. I confronted Dave, "You're really high today, Dave, bouncing all over the room. What's going on?" The group picked up my use of the word "high" and a discussion ensued on whether Dave was stoned or not. I asked the group to get back to the question. *(Pointing out flight behavior.)* I said maybe it would help for all of us to talk about what was going on for Dave, even if it was hard. The group settled down and waited. I said we knew by now that when Dave had something on his mind he got really hyped and so communicated his uptightness by being noisy, and that we hoped he could feel he could talk to us. *(Demand, support, deviant behaviour explained.)* Chris picked that up and encouraged Dave to talk, "Is something going on, Dave?" Connie said, "What's going on?" *(Pause.)* Dave looked down. Then he said, "I moved yesterday." I encouraged him to continue. "I moved from Franklin House into a foster home." I commented that that was a big move. "Well," Dave said, "I was in Franklin House for eight months. I really liked it there." I tuned into his feelings of loss, "It hurts, doesn't it, when you have to leave someplace familiar. You've had a lot of moves." Chris asked what it was like to move into a foster home. The group began to reach out supportively to Dave ...

I Explore the Obstacles to Working. Ingrid, sitting quietly in the corner, was confronted by Chris about never speaking in the group. Ingrid felt put on the spot, and was able to say so. I asked her what made it hard for her to talk in the group. She said there were too many people around. I guessed she wasn't used to talking in a group, probably not even in school. She said right. Tracy agreed, and said it was easier for her to talk to friends at school who she saw every day. Chris said sometimes she felt her problems weren't very important and not worth talking about. There was a thoughtful silence. Then, Carol, who has a speech difficulty that makes her almost incomprehensible, started talking. It was the first time she had spoken in the group. She said she felt uncomfortable talking in the group because she was afraid she'd get laughed at. There was a long silence. I said, "I guess Carol's really hit the nail on the head for all of us, eh." *(Commonality)* There were nods. Chris said, "No one will laugh, we're here to help each other. I said, "The concerns you have, Carol, are the same as the feelings Ingrid has, but she expresses them by being quiet. Dave on the other hand is loud. You are all wondering how each will react." Gayle asked, "What can we do to make it easier?" Carol said she felt worse because she felt the group couldn't understand her speech. Tom said that if she spoke really slowly that we could all pitch in and help. The group started shouting encouragement to each other. I said I guess they were all feeling the same inside, even if it showed in different ways, and if they knew that, maybe it would be easier to talk, to take the risk. They all laughed and agreed.

I Point Out to the Group That When It's Hard to Talk or Accept What's Being Said, That "Flight Behavior" Can Result, Breaking the Opportunity to Work. Carol, painfully, was talking. She was difficult to understand. Dave decided he wanted to talk about points of interest, rather than difficulties. The group started talking about their various weekends. I said to the group, "How come you changed so quickly from listening to Carol?" There was an uncomfortable silence. I said I had noticed that they became restless when Carol spoke, and it seemed as if they felt uncomfortable listening to her. Carol started crying and said it was the same as at school, no one understood her. Chris asked Carol how long she had had her speech difficulty. Carol said since birth. The group started to reach out for her. Dave said he had a hard time understanding her, and the group agreed. Brian said let's make sure that Carol has the opportunity to speak. Gayle said, "I guess it's hard to talk about difficult things for all of us, but with Carol, it's doubly difficult to talk about difficult

things." I agreed, but said I thought they were doing a great job at this point. *(Crediting the work.)*

I Offer the Opportunity to Work. Connie was having extreme difficulties with her parents, so much so that her social worker was looking for a foster home for her. She was, however, unable to express the deep feelings of pain. As she described her difficulties, I noticed Dave was remarkably quiet. I reached for Dave, "You're in a foster home, maybe you can tell Connie and the group about it." Dave explained the technicalities. I reached for the feelings, "What's it like, Dave, to live in a foster home?" Silence. Dave said, "It's okay." I asked him what that meant. *(Partializing, demand.)* Dave started talking about being kicked out of home and having to go into the foster home. "It's the shits, Connie. I got kicked out, but it sounds like you could still work it out. It's really hard." I said, "And it hurts like hell to have your parents to the point where they're willing to let you go." Connie started to cry. "I'm so scared, I don't know what to do." Chris said she had learned to talk things out at home, and maybe the group could help. Tracy said she was learning to work out problems with her parents. Dave said now he was settling in with his foster parents and things were better for him and he hoped Connie could work it out without having to leave home. I encouraged the discussion of *specific* issues for Connie at home. Honest and deep feelings were shared by all the group.

I Share My Feelings with the Group. Through the weeks, I had been encouraging the group to give feedback to Tom and I. At the fifth session, I said, "Okay, we're half way through our sessions now, and we'd really like some feedback on the group, what we've done, where we're going." *(Alerting group to endings, demanding feedback.)* I said sometimes I felt frustrated at the flight behavior, and sometimes their rambunctious moods. The group started to talk about the help they gave each other and how they felt. A constructive mutual exchange occurred. I said I thought they should know that after the group ended, Tom and I would no longer be at the Clinic. They asked what would be happening. We explained. I said it would be hard for us to leave, and hard for the group to end because I felt really good about the work we had all done together. There was a silence. Then the group began to deal carefully with the ending.

3. *Where It Stands Now.* The group is becoming more at ease sharing real feelings with each other. They are more comfortable in taking each other on. Dave still acts out periodically, but he is doing it less frequently: the group call him on his behaviour and demand to know what's going on. "Hey Dave, what's really going on today?" The more reserved members of the group are becoming more verbal, as each member learns to look beyond behavior to common feelings of anxiety, fear and anger, and to accept and respect different personalities. The group is mutually supportive, and especially protective of Carol, who is encouraged to talk by all members. There are still times when work is avoided and members are not willing to risk. But a culture for work is developing and a common feeling expressed that the group members own the group, are learning to relate effectively with each other and can share common feelings and experiences.

4. Specific Next Steps

1. To continue to point out when hard to talk about issues are raised, fight and flight behavior can result.

2. To continue to reach beyond any deviant behavior for the common feelings.

3. To continue reinforcing Dave for the valuable work he has done: his particular sense of urgency has helped him raise many relevant issues. He is indeed an ally!

4. To continue to demand for work and to keep the work around beyond honest and congruent in feelings.

5. To continue to deal with endings in the group.

HELPING GROUP MEMBERS NEGOTIATE THE ENVIRONMENT

The discussion thus far has focused on the internal task of the group. However, the group does not exist in a vacuum, but is located in an institution or agency or in a community. In the description of the group as an "open social system," presented at the beginning of this chapter, the term *open* was used to imply that the boundary between the group and its environment was not closed. In fact, the activities of the group will have some effect on the relationship between the group and the environment. In turn, the interaction with the environment will have an impact on the internal operations of the group. This section explores this additional group task, that of negotiating the environment.

With the exception of the chapter on contracting, I have been discussing the group almost as if it exists cut off from the external world. In the contracting chapter I focused on finding the common ground between the service of the agency and the needs of the group members. Contact between the group and its external systems continues after the beginning phase and is one of the ongoing realities to which the group must pay some attention. Two aspects of this group-environment interaction are considered in this section. In the first, the group-environment relationship in terms of mutual obligations and expectations is discussed. The example is from a community center setting in which an acting out group of young teens finds itself in trouble with the agency because of its aggressive behavior. The second example concerns a group of sixth graders in an elementary school. Their relationship to the school they are leaving and their fears about beginning a new school illustrate that negotiating the system can be a central theme of work for the group. There are, of course, other examples of group-system relationships, and some of these are discussed in Chapter 16 where I focus on the work carried out with the system and its representatives. For now, these two examples are used to illustrate the interdependence of the group and its environment and the role of the worker in mediating the engagement.

The first example involves the young teenage club described earlier in my discussion of internal leadership in the group. The setting was a middle-class community Y, and the group had a long history of acting out behavior at the center. This group was one of my first as a social work student. I was in the building working on recording one evening when I was told by a staff supervisor to "get the kids in my group in line, since they were acting out in the game room." He was obviously angry at them. My first reaction was panic; I had been working hard to overcome our rocky start together, trying to undo my early mistakes of attempting to impose limits and establish my authority. I had just been getting somewhere in this effort and saw this confrontation as a potential step backwards. When I explained this to the supervisor, his reaction was, "What's wrong? Do you have trouble setting limits and dealing with your authority?" As any student in training will remember, a supervisor questioning your "problem" evokes a powerful response. I decided to face my responsibility, as defined by the supervisor, and went off to do combat in what I knew would be a battle of wills. Feeling upset about what I was doing only made me come on stronger.

I found the guys running and screaming in the halls, and I yelled at them to "cut it out." They slowed down for a minute and I said to them, "Look, if you guys don't cut it out, I'm going to throw you out of the building." I continued, "What kind of way is that to behave anyway? You guys know better than that. I thought I was getting somewhere with you,

but I guess I was all wrong." My words seemed to be an additional catalyst and I found myself chasing them through the building, catching them one at a time, and escorting them outside.

My mistake was a natural one. I was not clear about the meaning of deviant behavior at that time, so I did not attempt to find out what was wrong, why they were so agitated. Even if I had been clear about that, my functional confusion would have prevented me from dealing with them effectively. In the same situation today, I would be able to explain my functional role more clearly to the supervisor, suggesting that I speak to the boys to see what was going on and to try to cool them down long enough to talk to the supervisor about what was happening in the building and why. If I were unsuccessful, then the supervisor could throw the group outside and I would go with them. I would have explained that at the point they were thrown outside, I would be available to them to figure out what had happened and to find a way to deal more effectively with the Y, since they really wanted to be accepted back. The Y was concerned about this group's behavior, and this would be an opportunity to do some work on the relationship between the group and the Y. I am not suggesting there would never be a time when I felt bound to set limits on the boys and act as an agent of the agency or society. In the course of our time together there would be many such occasions. However, at this moment, when they were thrown out, they needed their worker the most. As I found out later, that day had been report card day at school and most of the boys in the group were afraid to go home that evening and face their fathers because of bad grades and similar behavior problems in school. A marvelous opportunity for work had been missed. In Chapter 16, this group-environment mediation role will be further illustrated in a number of contexts.

A group theorist who could have helped me conceptualize the problem differently is Homans.[21] In his classic book *The Human Group,* Homans presents a general theory of human interaction using five well-known field studies of social interaction to illustrate his ideas. He describes three major elements of behavior which he terms *interaction, sentiment,* and *activity.* Interaction refers to any contact between people, sentiment to feelings or drives, and activity to any action. Thus, Homans could take a descriptive social study and break it down into these three components—interactions, sentiments and activities. His interest centers on the interdependence of these elements of social behavior; for example, how sentiment in a group can affect interaction and, in turn, how interactions can feed back to affect sentiments. In the group example just described, the boys' feelings (sentiments) about their school work affected the way they related (interactions) to each other, which in turn generated many forms of behavior (activity) of the acting out type. Homans' second major theoretical contribution is important here. He viewed activities, interactions, and sentiments within two interdependent systems—one called the "internal" system and the other the "external" system. In the case of the teen group, the sentiments, interactions, and activities which made up the internal system were causing a pattern of interactions, sentiments, and activities which constituted the external system (interactions, sentiments and activities generated by the relationship with the Y). In this example, it was not possible to understand or help with the problem in the external system without dealing with what

was happening in the internal system (between the boys). I have oversimplified Homans' theory, but I think the central elements demonstrate once again how a theoretical construct can help a worker conceptualize a problem in a new way.

The second example, a sixth grade girls' group, illustrates the task of negotiating the environment in a slightly different way. The two aspects of the environment they must deal with are the school they are leaving and the high school they will be attending. The worker picks up his theme at the start of the meeting.

The girls began talking about going to a new school next year. Jean expressed her fear of leaving Bancroft, and I asked her why she felt this way. She said that she was happy at Bancroft and that she really does not want to leave. She also added that she did not know what Strathearn was like, and she had heard that they had some very strict teachers. I replied by saying that it seems as though Jean was worried about much more than just the strict teachers at Strathearn, and from what she said I got the feeling that she is telling us that it is scary to be leaving Bancroft, a school that you have been at for many years and where you know the people, and now you have to go to a completely new school with many new people and many unknown things before you. Jean agreed that she was quite scared of leaving Bancroft and having to meet new teachers and new kids. I asked the others in the group how they felt about having to go to a new school next year. All the others shared Jean's feelings and expressed their fears about leaving Bancroft. Mary said that she was worried about the first day at Strathearn and what it would be like. I asked them if any of them remembered their first day at Bancroft and what it felt like. Vera and Soula, who had come to Bancroft two years ago, said they had been frightened, but after the first few days began to feel less frightened, especially when some kids began to talk to them. Betty said that she thinks that it is harder to make friends in grade seven than in grade four or five. I asked her why, and she said that she thinks kids are friendlier when they are younger and that older kids do not always want to be friends with you. I asked Betty whether she had ever experienced this herself. She said that she had moved to a new street this year and tried to become friends with a group of girls on her street, but they did not want her as a friend. I said that she must have been hurt when this happened, and Betty replied that she felt lousy, but she was able to make friends with some other girls on the street. A few other girls related their attempts to make friends on a new street, in the hospital, with some of their attempts being successful and others unsuccessful. They were able to understand how Betty had felt.

By asking the girls to think about their first day at the elementary school, the worker was hoping to help them generalize from that experience to the new one that they faced. It was important that the worker neither underplayed the realities of their concerns nor allowed the group members to overplay them. Simply having them expressed this way was helpful, since the girls know that others feel the same way. In this case it was possible for the worker to try to arrange a visit to the school. The worker felt that the fear of the unknown was part of the problem, and by helping the group members to meet some of the high school staff and students, some of these fears might be lessened.

I said that from what they are saying, making friends can be easy at times, but sometimes it is not all that easy, and it is never a very happy thing when you try to become friends with people and they turn you down. I said that is is possible that it is harder to make friends as you get older, but I reminded them that in going to a new school they will probably be going with some of their old friends so it is a little easier than going in without any friends at all. Dmitra asked whether they would

be in the same class with their friends. I said that I really did not know but would think that some would be together whereas others would not. Taxia and some others said that they did not want to be separated from their friends. I said that I could understand their feelings of wanting to be together and this would make it less frightening for them, but the decisions for this are really not in our control but are decided by the principal and the teachers at the new school. I continued by saying that I realize that they are all worried about the unknowns of a new school and about being separated from their friends and these are real worries and I can feel for them. I told them that I had an idea which might help to reduce some of their worries and I wanted to share it with them for a few minutes. I asked them that if it was possible for us to arrange a visit to Strathearn to see the school, meet some of the teachers and students, whether they would be interested. All the girls were extremely excited and expressed their enthusiasm about the idea. I told them that I was glad that they wanted to go and I would try very hard to see if it can be arranged, but I could not assure them that we would definitely go. The girls were able to accept this and told me that they hoped it would be possible. I then said that we can talk more about this next week, once I know if it is at all possible but perhaps now we can continue our discussion where we left off before I introduced the idea. Lola began to speak and said that she wants to make some new friends next year but she is worried about what the kids at the new school will think of her. I encouraged her to elaborate this point. She was concerned with what kids might think about her looks, the way she dresses, and just her in general. I asked her how she thinks others feel about her now. She said that she thinks others like her but sometimes she is really not sure. At this point others in the group responded to what Lola said and began to express positive warm feelings towards Lola and told her that they liked her. Lola seemed to feel better when she heard this. I credited Lola and the others for being able to express and share feelings that are often difficult to express. I then asked whether others were worried about what other kids at the new school will think about them.

With this excerpt of a worker helping a school group deal with its system, I have completed my outline of the prop-

erties and dynamics related to the worker's second client, the group. In the next chapter I examine different types of groups emphasizing the identification of some of the variant elements.

NOTES

1. Margaret E. Hartford, *Groups in Social Work* (New York: Columbia University Press, 1971).

2. See William R. Bion, *Experiences in Groups* (New York: Basic Books, 1961); George Homans, *The Human Group* (New York: Harcourt Brace & Co., 1950); Warren G. Bennis and Herbert A. Shepard, "A Theory of Group Development," *Human Relations* 9 (1956):415–37.

3. Homans, *The Human Group.*

4. William Schwartz, "On the Use of Groups in Social Work Practice," in *The Practice of Group Work,* ed. William Schwartz and Serapio Zalba (New York: Columbia University Press, 1971), p. 9.

5. Bennis and Shepard, "A Theory of Group Development."

6. For discussion of T-group and sensitivity training models, see Leland P. Bradford, Jack R. Gibb, and Kenneth D. Benne (eds.), *T-Group Theory and Laboratory Method* (New York: John Wiley & Sons, 1964).

7. Bennis and Shepard, "A Theory of Group Development," p. 417.

8. Ibid.

9. A. Paul Hare, *Handbook of Small Group Research* (New York: The Free Press, 1962), p. 24.

10. Bion, *Experiences in Groups.*

11. The record of service was developed by Schwartz as a student learning device. For a

discussion of the "record of service" as a learning device, see Goodwin P. Garfield and Carol R. Irizarry, "Recording the 'Record of Service': Describing Social Work Practice," in *The Practice of Group Work,* pp. 241–65.

12. Bion, *Experiences in Groups.*

13. Ibid.

14. M. Sherif and Carolyn W. Sherif, *An Outline of Social Psychology,* rev. ed. (New York: Harper & Row, 1956).

15. S. E. Asch, "Effects of Group Pressure upon the Modification and Distortion of Judgments," in *Groups, Leadership and Men,* ed. H. Guetzkow (Pittsburgh, Pa.: Carnegie Press, 1951), pp. 177–90.

16. Hare, *Handbook of Small Group Research,* p. 9.

17. W. F. Whyte, *Street Corner Society: The Social Structure of an Italian Slum* (Chicago: University of Chicago Press, 1943).

18. A. Bavelas, "Communications Patterns in Task Oriented Groups," *Journal of Acoustical Society of America* 22 (1950):725–30.

19. M. Deutsch, "An Experimental Study of the Effects of Cooperation and Competition upon Group Process," *Human Relations* 2 (1949):199–232.

20. R. F. Bales, "Task Roles and Social Roles in Problem Solving Groups," in *Readings in Social Psychology,* Eleanor E. Maccoby, et al., 3d ed. (New York: Holt, Rinehart & Winston, 1958), pp. 437–47.

21. Homans, *The Human Group.*

CHAPTER 14

Some Variant Elements in Group Practice

While my focus has been on the common aspects of group work, there are also variant elements which must be taken into account. Four areas raised most often in my group leadership workshops are: open-ended groups, single-session groups, activity-oriented groups, and the impact of co-leadership. These four are discussed in this chapter.

THE OPEN-ENDED GROUP

The term *open-ended* refers to a group in which the membership is continuously changing. New members arrive and old members leave throughout the life of the group. This is in contrast to a "closed" or fixed-membership group where the same people meet for a defined period of time. Members may drop out and new members be added in the early sessions, but, in general, the membership of the group remains constant. The decision to run a group as open- or closed-ended depends upon a number of factors including the nature of the contract, the characteristics of the clients served, and the structure of the setting. For example, in a couples' group dealing with marital problems the difficulty of discussing personal issues such as sexual incompatibility would be compounded if membership in the group were constantly changing. A stable membership is essential for such a group to develop the necessary mutual trust and culture for work. On the other hand, an open-ended group is more appropriate for unwed mothers in a maternity home, where residents are entering and leaving at different times. The problems associated with shifting membership in this type of group are outweighed by the advantages of having all the residents present. Thus, the decision to operate open- or closed-ended groups must be made with the unique characteristics of members, purpose, and setting in mind.

There are some advantages to an open-ended group. For example, a group that has developed a sound culture for work can bring a new member in quickly. As the new members listen to the discussion, their own willingness to risk may be accelerated by the level of openness of the others. In addition, those who have been in the group for a while are able to assist new members with issues they have already dealt with. A technical problem associated with open-ended groups is that each session may be a new beginning for

328 / Group Work Skill

some members, an ending for other members, or both. In short-term groups, where members do not remain for a long period of time, the worker can take responsibility for bringing in new members and acknowledging the departure of the old ones. In groups with longer-lasting membership, the group members themselves can discuss this process and develop a system for dealing with the changing group composition. Either way, the skills involved require that the worker be able to state purpose clearly and briefly to a new member so that the ongoing work of the group can proceed in spite of the changes.

The following example of an open-ended group is on a gynecological ward of a general hospital. The women on this ward have all come for operations because of suspected cancer of the uterus. The usual routine is that they stay for two days prior to the operation, one day for the operation, and then, depending upon the results, they may be out again in as little as two days. Thus, some group members are in the preoperative state while others have completed the procedure. The worker restated the purpose at the start of each meeting.

WORKER: This group meets each day at the same time to give you a chance to talk with each other and myself about your feelings and concerns about being a patient in the hospital. We realize your illness and hospitalization have caused a great deal of stress and we feel your having a chance to discuss your reactions may help. In past groups we have discussed the food, hospital procedures, how patients get along with staff, and of course, your concerns about your illness.

The particular theme for each group changed each day with the composition of the membership. When appropriate, the worker arranged for attendance of the dietitian, nursing staff, or doctors to fa-

cilitate communication between patients and the hospital system. In the following illustration we see how one member, who has just been told she has cancer, uses the group to deal with her initial shock even though it was her first day of group attendance:

After some preliminary chatter, I turned to Mrs. B. (an elderly delicate-looking lady) who had been silent and explained to her and Mrs. D. (both new to the group) that our aim here was to bring up anything that might be of concern to them, about their illness or hospital experience, a worry that could be shared with the other members who may already have experienced the same anxiety and may be able to help them with it. Mrs. B. blurted out that she had just been told she had cancer. There was silence. I asked how she felt about hearing this. Was she expecting it? She said no, she was in a state of shock. She added that this was her first time in a hospital. They have to do a biopsy. I explained that this was another test for cancer. Was she sure that this is what the doctor had said? Then she reenacted the abruptness with which she was told that another doctor would see her this afternoon. Mrs. P., who is a private patient, joined us. I briefly outlined that we were discussing how Mrs. B. feels after having just been told she has cancer. She was really shaken by the news, and we are trying to share the feeling with her. I said that maybe if others could remember how they had felt (I knew that two others had been successfully treated for cancer) when they were first faced with the same news, it would be helpful to Mrs. B. Mrs. P. took over. She had had sixteen operations in thirteen years. She's a nurse, you have to have a hopeful outlook, etc., etc. I said maybe our previous experience with cancer shapes our attitude toward it. I asked Mrs. B. what her experience had been. She had known a young woman who had undergone all kinds of treatment including cobalt, and poof, she was gone. It did no good. She told the doctor to open her up; if it was cancer, close her, and be done with it. Mrs. L. talked of her first husband who had died of cancer of the throat. He couldn't talk about it with his family. Then came a discussion of sharing this diagnosis with your family. Mrs. G. said when she first was told, she cried, and she's not one to cry. The other ladies encouraged Mrs. B. to cry as well, but she didn't respond. I pointed out that she still seemed too shocked. They asked about her family. She said she had a son and daughter. Her son has just gone to South Africa. They said she *has* to tell her daughter. She should be told, and talking about it with family would make her feel better. She said her daughter would cry. I said it is a hard thing to face. Mrs. P. brought in having your chaplain talk to you at this time. It was helpful. She had found it supportive. Mrs. B. remarked that there was no use having the priest talk to her. She is disenchanted with her religion. Mrs. P. then went into a brief monologue on cancer being just another disease like alcoholism and other illnesses and how it used to be something to be ashamed of and now it's treated openly as a disease. She expressed her present despondency because it has reached a point where they may not be able to operate on her present cancer. Someone asked how her husband feels. He feels terrible. They asked about the children, but she has none. She said at the end she was depressed and wanting to get this all over with. It was no pleasure for her husband, and she's not getting any younger. Then she immediately changed her mood and said you need a sense of humor, to which all the ladies agreed. Our time was up.

At this point it was too difficult for Mrs. B. to take in the words because of the shock of the diagnosis. However, she had been able to begin the process of talking with others about her first reactions. The worker picked up with her after the session for individual work in this area and other group members offered their support through their informal contacts on the ward. The report of this group session was also used later for work with the medical staff on the problem of how staff communicate diagnoses to patients.

Examples of using a ward group to provide feedback to the system are shared in Chapter 16.

Just as each group meeting may be a new beginning for a member, other members are leaving, and the ending process must be taken into account. The worker can deal with this by calling attention to the departure of each member at the start of their last session or sessions, depending upon the length of their attendance. There can also be some time allowed at the end of the last session for them to say their farewells and for the group to say good-bye as well. The following excerpt illustrates a worker structuring this process at the start of session:

WORKER: This will be Mrs. L.'s and Mrs. P.'s last day with us. We have enjoyed having both of you in this group. If it's all right with the rest of you, perhaps we could leave the last five minutes of the session to say good-bye and to give both ladies a chance to share their thoughts and feelings about the group.

Open-ended groups, particularly short-term groups, are characterized by the need for more worker structure. Since the group may have little continuity, the worker has actively to provide the structural supports. The same dynamic is true in the single-session groups examined next.

THE SINGLE-SESSION GROUP

It is not uncommon for some work to be done on a short-term, even a single-session, basis. Examples include informational meetings (e.g., foster parent recruitment) or educational sessions (e.g., a session at a school designed to help parents work with their children on their homework problems). These groups will often be larger than the small, face-to-face groups I have been describing thus far. When confronted with such groups, workers often feel that the time and size limitations eliminate the possibility of group interaction or involvement. So instead they substitute direct presentation of the information or ideas to be shared followed by a question period. Sessions structured in this way can be quite effective. However, one drawback of straight didactic presentations is that people do not always remember the material presented. It is not unusual to have questions raised at follow-up sessions which suggest that, although the worker has shared the data, the group members have not taken in the ideas. The challenge for the worker is to structure a session so that information can be presented in a way that allows participants to interact with the data and make it more meaningful. My own view is that size of group and restricted time do not automatically rule out active participant involvement and that many of the principles discussed thus far can be adapted to such situations.

I start by viewing each group as if it were a "small group" and by attempting to adapt the basic model to the group's limitations. For example, the idea of phases of work is still helpful, but, of course, the beginning, work and ending/ transition phases all must be encompassed in one session. Contracting in the opening phase of a session is critical as is demonstrated in this illustration of a foster parent recruitment meeting:

I explained that the agency was holding these meetings to encourage families to consider providing a foster home for our children in care. The purpose of this first session was for us to share some information about fostering with the group, to try to answer their questions, and to discuss the concerns they may have on their minds that might help them to determine if further exploration were feasi-

ble. I pointed out that the group was large (over forty), and I realized that might make it hard for them to talk, but that I hoped we could treat this evening as a conversation rather than a lecture—I would be interested as much in hearing from them as in sharing my own information. I then asked if this is what they had understood to be the purpose of the meeting. There was a general shaking of heads, so I continued. I said I thought it might be helpful if I could begin by asking them what some of their questions were about fostering —some of the things which were on their minds. I would keep a list of these and try to make sure we covered them in our discussion. There was a silence for a moment and then a hand was raised.

In this example the worker chose to obtain feedback from the group before beginning her presentation. The advantage to this approach is that if someone has an urgent concern about the subject, it can be hard for them to listen to any other conversation until that concern is either dealt with or at least acknowledged. Once they know they are "on the agenda," energy can be freed to invest in other data. The amount of time taken to raise questions or, in other groups, swap problems is determined by the overall time available. For example, in a two-hour meeting I would not want to spend more than fifteen minutes contracting and problem swapping while in a three-hour session, I might use more time to explore issues and develop a group consensus on the agenda. Timing is always important in group sessions, but it naturally takes on a special urgency in a single-session group. The worker needs to develop the ability to keep track of time and to point out continually to the group the relationship between time and their work. For example: "You are raising so many good issues I think we could probably meet for a week. However, we only have two hours.

I wonder if it is possible for us to focus on one or two central concerns and dig into them?" In another example: "I would like some time at the end to discuss this evening's program, to evaluate the session, and to see what you feel you have gotten out of it. Can we be sure to leave the last fifteen minutes to do this?"

Workers often suggest a number of reasons for not involving clients in single-session or large groups more actively in the work. First, they are concerned that they have so much to "cover" they do not have time for group process. But as most of us have noticed in our own educational experience, a teacher who is busy "covering" the agenda does not necessarily teach us anything. We are often better off focusing the field of work and limiting our goals. Effective work with a manageable agenda is preferable to going through the motions of trying to cover a wide area. The first skill in handling such meetings, then, is to narrow down the potential area of work to suit the time available.

A second area of concern advanced by workers is that the group may raise questions they are not prepared to answer. This is particularly true with new workers who are nervous enough as it is. They may have little experience in the field and have prepared extensively to deal with the specific areas they have predetermined as important. Their notes are written out in detail and the last thing they want is someone asking a question for which they are unprepared. This is understandable, since it takes confidence to allow the group to shape the direction of the work. When workers realize they are not judged by group members on whether or not they have all the answers but rather on how well they involve the group in the process, they are often more willing to risk opening up the session in novel and unexpected directions. When they do so,

they find they can learn as much from such sessions as the group members. Each session helps the worker to tune in and prepare for the next one, so that the ability to deal with the real concerns of the group grows with experience.

A third area of concern, particularly with large groups, is that a single member may take over the group for individual or personal issues unrelated to the contract. I have already illustrated in the section on deviant members how it may be necessary for the worker to be assertive in such a situation and to guard the contract vigorously. This ability also comes with experience. Once again, the worker has to be willing to risk the hazards of such an approach if the benefits of more member involvement are to be gained.

In summary, it is my view that even a single-session group with large numbers (I have asked groups with as many as 350 people to attempt a discussion with some degree of success) can be involved actively in a group process with beneficial results. I want to be clear that there are many situations where direct didactic presentation at the beginning of a session can be extremely helpful. However, the worker must keep the presentation of material to a reasonable time (over forty minutes may be too much) and should monitor the group's reactions as the presentation progresses. The ability of group members to work effectively, with feeling, in a single-session large group, when the proper conditions are set by the worker, has never ceased to amaze me.

ACTIVITY IN GROUPS

Activity group is a term usually applied to groups involved in a range of activities other than just conversation. *Program* is another term used to describe the activities implemented in such groups, such as the expressive arts (e.g., painting, dancing), games, folk singing, social parties, cooking, in fact almost any recreational or social activity used by people in groups. In an earlier article, I attempted to examine the ways in which people relate to each other suggesting that to dichotomize "talking" and "doing" is a mistake.[1] I suggested that relationships between people were best described by a "mixed transactional model."

In the complex process of human interaction people express feelings, ideas, support, interest, and concern—an entire range of human reactions—through a variety of mediums. The concept of a mixed transactional model implies that all of these mediums—words, facial and body expressions, touch, shared experiences of various kinds, and other forms of communications (often used simultaneously)—be included when considering the means by which transactions are negotiated and consummated. We should not fragment human interactions by forcing them into such categories as "talking" and "doing" but should focus instead on the common denominators among transactions, defined here as *exchanges in which people give to and take from each other*. As group workers we are concerned with helping people who are pursuing common purposes to carry out mutually productive transactions.[2]

In analyzing the ways in which shared activity might be used by group members for mutual aid, I rejected grandiose claims that suggested specific activities might lead to "creating spontaneous or creative individuals" or "strengthened egos" and instead suggested the need to describe the specific and immediate functions that activity must play in the mutual aid process. Five of these identified were: *(a) human contact*—a meeting of a basic human need for social interaction (e.g., golden age clubs for isolated senior citizens); *(b) data gathering*—activities de-signed to help members obtain more information central to their tasks (e.g., teenagers preparing to enter the work field arranging a series of trips to business or industrial complexes); *(c) rehearsal*—a means of developing skills for specific life tasks (e.g., a teenage party in an institution creating an opportunity for members to practice the social skills necessary for the courtship phase of life); *(d) deviational allowance*—activities can create a flow of affect between members which can build up a positive relationship. This relationship may help members to deviate from the accepted norms and raise concerns and issues which might otherwise be taboo (e.g., young teenage boys who have gotten to know each other and the leader over a period of time through many shared activities might be more willing to accept a worker's invitation to discuss their real fears about sex); *(e) entry*—specific activities may be planned by a group as a way to enter an area of difficult discussion (e.g., the playacting of young children as they create roles and situations that often reveal their concerns of the moment).[3]

There are two general categories of groups in which activities are used as a medium of exchange. In the first, the activities themselves constitute the purpose of the group, as for instance, a teenage club in a community center or a patients' committee in a psychiatric hospital charged with planning recreational activities or an evening lounge program. The group exists for the purpose of implementing the activity. A second category of groups is those established for therapeutic purposes in which an activity is employed as a medium of exchange with specific therapeutic goals in mind. A dance therapy group in a psychiatric center is an example of this type of group. I will discuss these two categories separately because each raises special issues.

The first type of group, for example a teenage club, can often be found in the agencies which gave birth to group work practice in the social work field. These would be the community centers, Y's, and national youth organizations. Their use in other institutions as a vehicle for involving clients in planning their own use of leisure time activity has grown immensely. The most typical problem I have found in analyzing work with this type of group is that the worker or the agency ascribes therapeutic purposes to the group which in effect constitute a hidden agenda. While the group members may think they are attending a Y teenage club, the workers view the group as a medium through which they can use the program to effect changes in the members. This view reflects the early and still dominant view of program activity as a "tool of the worker" which was developed in the social work profession's early efforts to distinguish the social worker with groups from the recreation worker. The professional worker, so the thinking goes, would bring to bear special skills in selecting programs which would result in the desired behavior changes. Take, for instance, the problem of the child who was scapegoated in a group. In this early model, the worker might ascertain what area of skill this child had and then select or influence the group to choose the activity at which the scapegoated child would shine. This approach was rooted in a relatively unsophisticated view of group process and a sense of worker function which called for use of direct or indirect influence in the attempt to "change" the group members. It was this attitude that was mentioned earlier when I discussed the children's groups developed in schools for youngsters in trouble which attempted to aid them in their school problems by the development of "clubs" and activity groups as

mediums for the worker to "change their behavior."

My own training was rooted in this view of practice. In one setting, my agenda involved attempting to influence group members (teenagers) towards their religious association. The agency was sponsored by the Jewish community and was concerned that second generation teenagers might be "drifting away." Program was the tool through which I was to influence the members by involving them in agencywide activities, for example, in connection with religious holidays and celebrations. Unfortunately, I was so busy attempting to "influence" the membership that I ended up missing the indirect cues group members offered about their real concerns related to their identity as a minority group in a Christian culture. There were important moments when the concerns of the community and the felt needs of the group members were identical; the common ground was missed because of the misguided view that I could use program to accomplish the agency's ends.

My argument is that program is an effective tool, but that it is the members' tool, not the worker's. A group of teenagers in a community center or a residential setting sharing a "club" in which they plan their own social and recreational activity is an important service in itself. It does not have to be embellished with "professional" purposes. The worker's function in such a group is not secretly to influence members but rather to help them to develop their own club. The worker's suggestions for activities which relate to the group members' needs can be shared freely as a worker with any group would share relevant data, but it is the group members who must sort out those activities and decide which they wish to pursue. They will need the worker's help in doing so as they struggle with all of the tasks of the group as outlined in the previous chapter. If the agency has other agendas it feels are important for groups, then these must be openly presented in the contracting phase, and the group worker must attempt to find whatever common ground may exist. However, just as the worker will guard the group's contract from subversion by members, it must also be guarded from subversion by the agency. Members will learn a great deal about relationships, problem solving, and other areas as they work to create and run their groups; however, the worker must see the club as an end in itself, not a tool to be used for secret professional purposes.

The second category of activity group is the type in which specific therapeutic purposes are the major focus and the activity is used to help achieve these ends. An illustration of this work is a dance therapy group in a psychiatric setting.[4] Group members were girls aged thirteen to sixteen with various levels of disturbance. Common characteristics of the members were poor body awareness and image, concerns over their sexuality, and significant problems in expressing feelings. Staff felt these clients were "overloaded" with talking groups yet unable to make effective use of groups which were verbally oriented. The worker contracted with the members to develop a weekly dance group in which she would help them develop the ability to express their feelings through dance. She openly explained the purposes of the group and her hopes that through these activities they might discover new feelings and insights and that this could lead to their ability to talk with her and other staff about things which concerned them. She also explained that as they developed confidence in their bodies, they would find it easier to develop confidence in other areas of

their lives. Her contract included the agreement that they would select the music they wished to use and would take control over what they wanted to express, the concerns they wished to work on, and so on. They would use video equipment to record sessions and then view their tapes, and group members would be expected to provide critical feedback to each other on the dance techniques as well as the related discussion. A critical factor to be underlined at this point was that the worker was suggesting the use of activity as a tool for the members' use. The group members, not the worker, would be in control over the medium, so that they would experience the activity as something they did *with* the other group members and the worker, as opposed to something the worker was doing *to* them.

In the following illustration from this group, two of the group members are sick. The worker continued with the remaining member, Sandy, aged sixteen. The opening of the session demonstrates the group member's control as she selected the music and decided to use singing as a medium instead of dance.

Sandy arrived early today and ready for work. She noted the others were absent and said, "Good, I can have a one-to-one with you—there are some things I want to work on." I asked what, to which she replied, "The dog—with the Harmonica Man Music, but I'm a bit tight, a bit scared, can we start with something else?" I agreed that it made sense to loosen up a bit and not rush into the heavy things right away. At times Sandy becomes impatient, and there is a need to slow the process down and give her controls within which to work.

We looked at the records, and she picked out "I Can See Clearly Now" and she said she wanted to work with it. I asked if we could use the video, to which she agreed. When I asked how she wanted it, Sandy said she didn't feel like dancing but she would like to sing, but wasn't sure she would sound or look very good. I suggested that we use the music as an exercise and try it several different ways. In the first of three versions, her affect was flat, she was unable to look directly into the camera and body movements were stiff, with nervous gestures with the hand-held mike. Her voice was also flat and hushed. After looking at it on replay, Sandy was disappointed, to which I replied, "Let's keep going—add something into the next taping—pretend you're on TV, that you're a professional singer, try looking into the camera, sing to somebody, and don't worry how your voice sounds; let the feelings come out." The second version began to come alive, she smiled, looked into the camera and began to build up some confidence. Sandy became more stylized in her singing and began to move the mike back and forth. She tossed her hair and did stepping movements as she sang. On viewing the replay, Sandy was really surprised to see the changes in her appearance and wondered if she should go on to something else. I suggested she stay with this piece and do another version—putting as much as she could into it—exaggerating—really feeling the music. She shared that it is one of her wishes to be a rock singer. She liked the feeling of being the center of so much attention and of being able to really sing about what is inside. I said, "OK—let those feelings go—let them out, let's see what really does come out."

In the third version Sandy was like a person totally removed from her former identities. There was a surging sense of power in her voice, a ventilation of emotion which reached a climax in which she threw her hair back, holding the mike up over her mouth and she held a high note strongly until her energy dissipated and she gasped for air, choking forward. The jerking movement and relaxation of the tension was clearly orgasmic in quality. She appeared to be stupefied at her own power and physical reaction—grabbing her throat and trying to regain her balance and composure. She lost several lines of the music, then began again to complete the song. Her outpouring of feeling, movement, and charisma was definite

and exciting. While her voice lacked true singing quality, its impact was unmistakable. In replaying the tape she became a little giddy and excited with the results and expressed concern with the voice quality and that maybe she'd overdone it. I reassured her that we were learning and experimenting and she should not make a final decision on the results yet. I gave her feedback as to how much more animated and alive she was than the first and second version and just how much feeling she had inside. I asked how she felt after letting the feeling go, to which she replied, "I feel just exhausted—so much rushed out at once." I suggested we move on to something else and asked if she felt ready for the "Harmonica Man Music." She said she would try but wasn't sure if she could get into it now. She said the music frightens her, but she is also haunted by it and wants to understand why it has this effect on her. I replied that we must move slowly—take one step at a time.

It is interesting to note how the words of the music can be used to express, in a poetic manner, the group member's inner feelings and aspirations. For example, the words of the song Sandy selected are as follows:

I can see clearly now—the rain is gone
I can see all obstacles in my way
Gone are the dark clouds that had me blind
It's gonna be a bright, bright sunshiny day[5]

Sandy used this music to begin to express the part of her reaching for growth—the hopeful part. The second song, to which she danced later in the session, enabled her to express some of her fears which up until that point she had not felt free enough to share with staff. The discussion of these feelings followed her improvised dancing as she and the worker attempted to understand the reactions evoked by the music.

Another group, in the same setting, decided to develop a dance routine which the three members would perform at the institution's annual Christmas party concert. The dance involved dressing in Tahitian costumes and performing a somewhat sensual dance before staff and other residents. The three girls in the group had all been shy, concerned about their bodies and their sexuality. The idea of performing was quite frightening. At the last moment, Jeannine decided she could not go on, and the other two girls performed the dance with the worker. This illustration is from the first meeting after the concert. The two girls who danced are preparing to leave the institution, and the discussion at the start of the meeting began with their impending endings. The discussion shifted to the Christmas concert and revealed the learning which had taken place for the girls who danced and the one who did not.

To this point, none of the girls had mentioned the Christmas party concert or the Tahitian dance performed by Terry, Joanne, and myself. I said, "We've done a lot together over the last few months, and I'm realizing our group, *too*, will be ending, and we won't be able to continue on as we were before Christmas." There was silence. Joanne and Terry both indicated the Christmas concert had been exciting but a real struggle, and they didn't believe they could do it.

Jeannine, who had been quiet throughout the discussion, looked up, twisted her fingers, looked down, then looked straight toward Terry and Joanne and said quietly, "You looked really beautiful—I wished I had been up there with you but I couldn't stick with it—I was having a bad time before Christmas. I was scared, and I couldn't do it—but you guys did—and they [the kids in the cottage] loved it. You were good." Jeannine was choked with emotion as she spoke. She was soft-spoken and looked vulnerable. Joanne burst into smiles and chatter saying, "Were we really! Gee, I was so nervous and I made so many mistakes—you know I had to be on medica-

tion, I was so anxious I didn't think I could do it—but Sharon (the worker) came over and I did it!" Terry asked Jeannine, "Did they really like it?" She added, "It was the hardest thing I've ever done—I can move my hips to the music, but I can't do steps and I usually get mixed up." The girls went on to compare notes on their highly successful performance and remembered their encore and the kids whistling and applauding. Terry added, "I didn't believe I could do such a dance in front of the boys, especially from our own cottage. I was afraid they'd laugh." I said, "I had the jitters, too—I knew you could do it, but for a while there it was touch and go for all of us!" The girls started to laugh, saying, "*You* weren't nervous, too!" I reminded them the rehearsals had been difficult, and it was natural to get nervous before a performance.

I looked at Jeannine, who was glowing with the excitement, and said, "That was very special of you to tell Joanne and Terry they looked beautiful. I wish you could have been up there doing it with us, too." I moved and put my arm around Jeannine. "It's not easy to watch others do something you couldn't follow through on—but you know, it feels like you really were up there with us in spirit." Jeannine nodded her head, saying, "I do that all the time—I know I know the steps, but I just wouldn't do it." Terry and Joanne listened to Jeannine, attempting to reassure her by pointing out their own misgivings. I said, "I'm really proud of all of you; you've worked so hard, and it sounds like you want to get more for yourself, Jeannine."

I looked at Jeannine and asked, "What about you—do you want to continue in the dance group?" Jeannine was embarrassed and quiet but said, "If there is a group, I'd like to stay—but maybe I will be the only one." I indicated that I would be glad to work with her, even alone.

In the weeks that followed this session, Jeannine struggled to take new risks in the dancing area with the encouragement and support of the new group members. A close working relationship usually developed between the group members and the worker which encouraged them to use her for discussions in sensitive areas, such as trouble with other staff or their fears about leaving the institution. At times, the worker would point out the connections between their fears of risking new dances or exposing themselves to criticism (e.g., using the video) and similar concerns in other areas of their life. Thus, the work moved between activity and talking, and the supposed dichotomy between the two was proved to be false. Similar creative group work has been demonstrated using other mediums, showing the potential power of mutual aid offered without words.[6]

CO-WORKERS

Whenever the general subject of co-workers is raised by workers, I inquire if they have had experience working with another staff member in a group. Almost inevitably they have, and the experience was a bad one. The list of problems includes: disagreement on the basic approach to the group, subtle battles over control of group sessions, and disagreement during the group session over specific interventions—particularly those by a co-worker which seem to cut off a line of work you feel is productive. Underlying all of these problems is a lack of honest communications between co-workers both in and outside of the group sessions. Workers often feel embarrassed to confront their co-workers outside of the session and believe it would be unprofessional to disagree during the session. This stance is similar to the "not arguing in front of the children" syndrome which many parents experience. There is an unreasonable expectation that they must appear to agree at all times. This lack of honesty usually reflects the

insecurity of both workers and often leads to defensiveness and the illusion of cooperative work.

Co-leadership can be helpful in a group. A group is complex, and assistance by another worker in implementing the helping function can be a welcome aid. In my couples' group one co-worker was female. She was able to add perspectives to the work strikingly different from mine. For example, she reacted with a different mind set to issues raised in the group related to women. Our ability to work well together was based upon a number of factors. First, there was a basic agreement about an approach to the helping process. While our theoretical frameworks differed and we used different conceptual models for understanding client behavior and dynamics, our attitudes towards clients and our commitment to mutual aid and the importance of reaching for client strength were shared. Within this common framework, our different conceptual models served in fact to enrich our work with the group. Second, we structured time to discuss the group. We met before the start of the first group sessions to prepare strategy and also met before the start of each session to "tune in," using the previous session as well as any additional knowledge gained from individual contacts with couples. A time was set aside after each session to discuss the group. (In this case, the discussion took place with a group of students training at the school of social work who observed the group on a video monitor.) Every effort was made to encourage honest communications about the sessions and our reactions to each other's input. This was not simple, since I was the senior group worker, and it was not easy for co-workers to challenge me. As our relationship grew and trust developed, more direct communication was apparent. Finally, we had an understanding that we would feel free to disagree in the group. In many ways, the co-worker and I were a model of a male/female relationship in action. It would be a mockery of our effort if we supported honesty and willingness to confront while maintaining professional "courtesy" towards each other in the group. Observing co-leaders disagree, even argue, in a group and still respect and care for each other can be a powerful object lesson for group members.

Group members are very observant, and they can pick up the subtle cues of tensions between leaders no matter how hard workers try to hide them. This was pointed out in the midyear evaluation of this couples' group. A third co-worker in this group was a former student of mine, and although he participated in the session up until that point, the presence of the other co-worker and his feelings about working with a former teacher inhibited him. We had discussed this in the sessions with the student observers who had been quick to pick up his hesitancy. In the midyear evaluation session of the couples' group I inquired how the members felt we could improve our work during the second half of the year. Illustrating the perceptiveness of group members, Rose, our member in her late sixties, turned to my co-worker and said:

"I hope you don't take what I'm going to say personally. I think you have a lot to give to this group, and I would like to hear more from you. I don't think you should let Larry [the senior worker] frighten you just because he is more experienced." He responded, "You know, Rose, I've been worried about my participation, too. It is hard on me to get in as often as I want to, and I'm going to work on it."

As a final comment on co-leadership, I believe it is very difficult for two beginning group leaders to work together. Their own anxieties are so great that they often become more of a problem for each other than a help. Working with a more experienced worker provides learners with an opportunity to test their wings without taking full responsibility for the outcome. When mutual trust and sharing are developed between co-workers, they can be an important source of support for each other. The feelings of warmth and caring which develop between members and between the group worker and members must also exist between co-leaders as they tackle the complex task of working with groups. However, the problems of co-leadership, only partially elaborated in this brief discussion, must be kept in mind.

The discussion of co-leadership brings to a close this chapter on some variant elements in work with groups. The next chapter completes Part II of this book by examining the ending process in the group context.

NOTES

1. Lawrence Shulman, " 'Program' in Group Work: A Second Look," in *The Practice of Group Work*, ed. William Schwartz and Serapio Zalba (New York: Columbia University Press, 1971), p. 224.
2. Ibid.
3. Ibid., p. 225.
4. For readings related to dance therapy, see Susan Sandel, "Integrating Dance Therapy into Treatment," *Hospital and Community Psychiatry* 26 (July 1975):439–41; and Helene Lefco, *Dance Therapy: Narrative Case Histo-*

ries (Chicago: Nelson-Hall, 1975).

5. Johnny Nash (words and music), "I Can See Clearly Now" (New York: C.B.S., Inc., 1972).

6. For a seminal discussion on the use of activity in group work, see Grace L. Coyle, *Group Work with American Youth* (New York: Harper & Row, 1948).

CHAPTER 15

Endings and Transitions
with Groups

The dynamics and skills involved in the ending and transition phase, as described in Schwartz's practice theory, were discussed in detail in Chapter 5; all these processes are equally applicable to work with groups. I have summarized them in this chapter and identified the variations applicable to the group context and illustrated them by examples from group work practice. The chapter concludes with a full description of an ending meeting which demonstrates the unique aspects of endings in groups.

ENDING AND TRANSITION SUMMARY

The pain of separation described in ending work with individuals is also present in the group context. This time, however, in addition to terminating the intimacy established with the worker, the members must also deal with their feelings about separating from each other. Guilt over the way in which the group functioned is common. For example, if a member has dropped out, discussion may return to this event, suggesting a feeling that the group may have "let him down." The desire to have functioned more effec-

tively also emerges in requests for continuation of the sessions. There is often unfinished business related to both the authority and the intimacy themes. Members need to share with each other not only the angry feelings generated by their work together but also the feeling of loss they experience as the mutual aid system is dismantled.

The ending stages are also apparent in group sessions. First, there is the denial whereby group members appear to ignore the imminent end of the group. This is followed by the anger which emerges in direct and indirect forms. The mourning period is usually characterized by apathy and a general tone of sadness that one can feel in the group. Next, the group attempts to try the ending on for size. For example, one notices that group members are operating independently of the worker or spending a great deal of time talking about new groups or new workers. The "farewell-party" syndrome is also present as group members appear to protect the preciousness of the group by avoiding its negative aspects. It is not at all unusual for group members to avoid the pain of the ending itself by suggesting a real farewell party.

Worker strategies for dealing with endings are also similar to those described earlier. The worker should bring the ending to the group member's attention early to allow the process to be established. The stages should be pointed out as the group experiences them, reaching for the indirect cues and articulating the processes taking place—the denial, the anger, the mourning, and so on. The worker should also put personal feelings and recollections into the discussion, since the group ending has meaning for the worker as well. Discussion of the ending feelings should be encouraged, and the worker participate fully in the exchange of both positive and negative reactions. The worker should also attempt to make the evaluation of their work together specific. For example, when a member says, "It was a great group!" the worker should ask, "What was it about the group that made it great?" There should also be an attempt to reach past the "farewell-party" syndrome to encourage members to share negative feedback. In the group context, since members will have different reactions, the worker should encourage the expression and acceptance of differing views. The worker must also pay attention to the transitional aspect of the ending phase. For example, if members are continuing with other workers, how can they begin the relationship in a positive manner? If members have finished their work, what have they learned, and how can they use their learning in their new experiences? If they have found the group helpful, how can they find similar sources of support in their life situations? In this way, the worker can ensure that the ending discussion deals with substantive matters as well as the process of ending. In some situations help can also take the form of a physical transition (e.g., a visit to a new school or institution). Finally,

the worker should search for the subtle connections between the process of the group ending and the substantive work of the contract. For example, endings for a group of unmarried mothers may coincide with separation from their child. As a second example, foster teenagers who have provided mutual aid to each other have learned something about giving and taking help from their peer group. These and other connections can help to enrich the ending discussion. Illustrations of these dynamics and skills, drawn from the group context, follow this summary of the discussion in Chapter 5.

ENDING AND TRANSITIONS: GROUP ILLUSTRATIONS

As the ending approaches there is always unfinished business between the group and the worker which needs to be explored. In the following illustration from a maternity home group for unwed mothers we see the worker reaching for the cues that represent both the anger and the positive feelings. We also see the worker sharing her own feelings as well.

Unwed Mothers' Group

The session opened today with a review of last week. I told the girls that Mrs. B. (co-worker) and I had felt their sadness and depression last week, but only afterwards had we realized that they were angry, too. I commented that their depression seemed to be a result of their frustration and anger. I asked if they knew why they were angry. Monique said last week she was fearful of the possibility of a Caesarean section. Ginny said she had been fearful of going to hospital. Nicky said they'd felt depressed before the session. I suggested that when we left last week, Mrs. B. and I were also feeling sad and depressed, in part because of the feelings resulting from our coming separation. Alison commented that the group seemed so small, so many girls had left. I wondered if this, too, didn't give them a feeling of loss. They were coming so close to the end of their pregnancy, and for them, in addition to the loss of the group, they were also preparing for the loss of their baby. I thought it was no wonder they were feeling angry. I also said I wanted them to know we would miss them—we had become very close in the group—they had shared so much of themselves. I said, "We are a part of all that we have met." I suggested that they were a part of Mrs. B.'s and my experience and we would not forget them, nor would we forget what we had learned from them. They had shown us how they could grow and mature, they had shown us courage in reaching their decision, they had taught us the importance of communication with each other and between teenagers, and their parents, etc.

Ginny said it was hard to put into words what she had gained from the group, but she felt better about herself and better able to cope with things in the future. Alison said she had been feeling very sorry for herself when she arrived at the home. Through the group she had learned that she wasn't the only one, that she was lucky compared with some of the other girls. Nicky said she was learning to look at other people's problems, trying to understand them. Mona thought other decisions would be easier when they had made the tremendous decision about their baby.

After some discussion about what they had learned in the group, the workers asked if the members would like to have them visit them and their babies at the hospital. The responses were positive, and the group then moved into a discussion of the future. The worker acknowledged the graduation quality of the discussion as they prepared for their transitions:

Alison can hardly wait to get back home. She is very homesick. Ginny is still concerned that her parents may not be ready to let her make her own decisions. They were afraid she might

get hurt again. Mona said they couldn't stop her getting hurt. She thought parents made a mistake to make early childhood "like a fairy tale." Then when you got out in the world, you discovered the real world wasn't like that. She thought parents tried to be too protective. After all, Nicky said, you had to learn by your mistakes. I said sometimes it was hard for parents to let their children go. Alison thought it was a little like their giving up their babies when their parents had to let them grow up and go out on their own. Even when their parents knew their decision to let their children go was right, it still hurt to let them do it.

Mona and Margaret thought you had to reach the point when you made your own decisions, even if you made mistakes. Mona said she was sure now she wouldn't get too involved with a boy too quickly. Nicky agreed. She said she was going to have the "light" approach. They were going to be very sure of the boy before they entered a serious relationship. Nicky thought she didn't want to get married for a long time. She said the last nine months had taught her she wasn't ready to settle down yet. She wanted to have a job, get nice clothes, travel.

Mona said she was hoping to choose a new career, get more training. Nicky was afraid she might have made the wrong choice of course. She wasn't sure now she wanted to be a secretary. She'd like a job that would let her travel. Several of the girls thought she could travel. If she were a good secretary, she could get a job in another country, too.

I said I thought the girls were sounding much less depressed. They were already thinking about new decisions, their future, and showing their increased maturity. Alison asked when the next group would be starting. Nicky said the new group would be a bunch of "teeny-boppers." She said, even though some of the new girls in the home were eighteen or so, they acted like children. She didn't think they were showing much "respect" for the "old-timers." Alison wanted to know if they could come to the next group if they were still there. I assured her they were welcome and said we were having difficulty "ending." I said I thought they'd been one of the very best groups I'd been with. Monique, Alison, Ginny, and Nicky said they had all looked forward to their Thursdays with us, and were going to miss us. Nicky wanted to know in what way they had been a "best" group.

I said perhaps it had been because we'd been together for twelve weeks, but I felt I could see their noticeable gains in maturity. I felt very close to them all. I thought they had a better feeling about themselves and had made wise decisions for their babies. Monique said she was glad she had thought through her decision so carefully. She said on the day she left the hospital, she had felt, "I just can't leave my baby behind," but then had said to herself, "Your situation hasn't changed, you can't keep your baby." She said she had been very blue when the group began today, but was feeling ever so much better. The other girls agreed. We wished them "Good luck." The girls wondered when they'd be seeing us again. I said Mrs. B. and I would be seeing them in individual sessions and said we were having trouble stopping today. Endings were hard for all of us. Alison and Nicky commented on Mrs. B., "the silent member." We said goodbye. The girls' supper bell had rung and we were very late.

Children's Group

Sometimes the expression of anger can emerge indirectly as acting out behavior. This is particularly true in children's groups as they seem to revert to the behaviors experienced in the beginning sessions. In the following illustration, a student worker returned after a two-week absence from her group of grade-school children who had been meeting with her weekly because of trouble in school. This was only two weeks from their last meeting. The worker reached for the cues of the anger expressed in the children's behavior.

The children were sitting in the middle of the room in a circle waiting for me. This was different from usual. There was a big table at the back of the room, and we usually sat around it. The boys started cheering and clapping when I came in. I said hello and told them that I was glad to see them too. I had missed them, and it was good to be back. They asked me a lot of questions about where I had been, what I had done, etc., and I had to give them a rather detailed description of my vacation. After a while of this joking around, I said that it had been a long time since I had seen them last, and I asked what was new. They started talking about Chang, the Chinese boy in the class whom they hated, and how they had beat him up. While I was trying to get the story straight about what had happened, a couple of the kids started becoming rowdy and rude, cutting each other off more than usual and cutting me off, too. I was surprised because although they had the habit of interrupting each other and me as well, the were never so belligerent. George continued telling me about the fight he had with Chang, and how he had given him a bloody nose and sent him to the hospital for stitches. (I later found out the stitches part of the story was exaggerated.) Warren, Bobby, and a couple of others joined in and they all proudly described in detail the way they had beat Chang up. I wanted to remark on this and finally had to tell them to hold it, I wanted to say something. They quieted down a bit, and I finally was able to say what I had wanted—that I couldn't get over how excited and proud they were about what they did to Chang and I asked why? They totally ignored my question and continued in depth about the fight. I waited for a while and tried again to say something, but they were so noisy, I couldn't finish my sentence. There was a lot of horsing around, and they continued extolling the merits of beating Chang up. I tried to speak but kept getting cut off. I let them continue for a couple of minutes and kept quiet. Finally I was able to ask them what was happening. I said that I got the feeling they were mad at me because they wouldn't let me speak. Jimmy nodded yes. Costa said, "We've wasted time, we've spent enough time talking about Chang, we only have a half hour left and then next week and that's all." I said that I thought maybe they weere angry at me because I went away for two weeks, and maybe the group didn't go so well while I was away. They nodded yes. I said maybe also they were angry because the group was ending next week. John said he didn't want the group to end.

George asked why it had to end, was I leaving the school? I said no, I'd be in the school until the end of May, but did they remember the first session we all agreed that we'd have six to ten sessions and then it would end? They agreed. Costa said, "We'll miss you. I know we fool around a lot, but we'll really get down to talk about something properly." I said that I guess that they were sad the group was ending, and they thought that it was ending because I was punishing them for being noisy and rowdy. They nodded. I said that this wasn't so; it was ending because I had other things that I had to do in the school. But, I said, the group was not supposed to end, it was supposed to continue with their teacher leading it, as we had all agreed. There was a lot of complaining about their teacher and what had happened when I wasn't there, how she had made them do health instead of having a discussion.

I said that they were saying that the group wasn't the same when I wasn't there, and I got them to elaborate on how the two sessions had been during my absence. The boys felt that it was terrible. Jimmy complained that next week would be their last session, so they had better make the most of it. I said that in part they were angry with me because I was saying that I could no longer come in after next week and maybe they were feeling let down and deserted. They quietly nodded. I said that I could understand how they felt, I was also sad that I would no longer be able to come in on Tuesday mornings, because I really enjoyed working with them, but I would still be in the school for a while and they could come to see me alone if they wanted to, and I would come in from time to time to see them. One of the boys asked if I would come to their next party, and I said that I would

love to. I added that besides talking about me and them, I knew that they were angry at Mrs. M., and I wondered if we could talk about that and see if we could work something out.

Mrs. M. was a classroom teacher who had offered to continue the group. The worker focused on the transition question realizing that she might be able to help the group members continue their work after she was gone. A detailed discussion of the group sessions which occurred while she was away revealed that the youngsters were so upset at her absence that they did not give Mrs. M. a chance. They acted out, causing her to abandon the group meeting and turn to a general health discussion. The worker strategized with the boys about how they could handle things differently with Mrs. M. She also offered to meet with Mrs. M. to assist in the transition.

In these last sessions there are, in addition to issues related to the worker, questions of unfinished business between members. These issues, particularly the negative feelings, often only emerge towards the end of the group. There is a tendency for workers to pass over these issues, in order to end the group on a high note. However, the worker who trusts in the group will encourage exploration of the negative feelings as well as the positive ones, as illustrated in the next example.

Welfare Mothers' Group

In the following illustration, a group of mothers on welfare is in its twelfth and final session. Hurt feelings of one member, caused by the actions of another, were shared:

SARA: (to the worker) I gotta lot'a help here—like when I used to do this in June—I felt like you cared—(to the group)—and we helped each other. . . .

CONNIE: (to Sara—interrupting) Stop puttin' us on—I don't put nobody on and I don't want nobody puttin' me on.

SARA: (to Connie, puzzled) Me—what are you talking about?

CONNIE: (to Sara) You know perfectly well what I'm talkin' about—walkin' right out this door—that day when I was so desperate for money—

SARA: (looks down and ashamed) Oh!

CONNIE: (to Sara) To feed my kids on an' you offered me five dollars . . .

SARA: Yeah—

CONNIE: (to Sarah, anger building but controlled anger) . . . an' I called you an' asked—now if it's not gonna cut you short an' you said to come over in the morning—you said you'd loaned it to your sister an' she'd have it back in the morning—an' when I got there, I knew you was home—I heard you when I first walked up to the door—but did you answer—no—an' all you would'a had to say was Connie—I'm sorry—an' invited me in for a cup of coffee—I'd rather talked anyway—(to the group and worker)—that's why I didn't come back for so long—probably never would'a if you [the worker] hadn't keep comin' by—(laughs)

SARA: (to Connie, some anger) Well—why didn't ya say something about it last week—if you was so mad—

CONNIE: (to Sara) Oh—I just said to myself—forget it—it's not that important—an' I should'a known better than to believe ya to begin with—

WORKER: Why do you say that—

CONNIE: (to group) That's the way women are—we see one of us down, an' it seems the best thing is to stomp on 'em.

PEGGY: (to Sara, gently but firm) That hurts—if somebody promises you something an' then doesn't do it—(pause)—what was the matter with you—

SARA: (to Peggy, sheepishly) Well—I wanted to loan her the money—(to Connie)—I wanted to help you—an' I was so mad at my sister for not giving it back to me—I still don't have it back—I felt so bad—(smiles)—an' I

didn't have the guts to tell you—(pause) I wish I had—cuz I've felt real bad about it—real bad—ever since—I'm sorry—Sara smiles at Connie and Connie smiles back. Group collectively lets out its breath and relaxes.

PEGGY: (to Sara) All right—now yer even—you didn't have the guts to be the good guy—(to Connie)—an' she didn't have the guts to come back an' tell you off—(group laughter)

WORKER: I'll carry it a step further—you're each ahead. Connie did have the guts to give Sara a chance to talk about it—and Sara had the guts to be honest and say she felt sorry—

Group makes comments of general agreement with worker, "Yeah," "Better late than never," etc.

Men's Support Group

The worker must avoid the temptation to allow group members to ignore problems in the group. In the next illustration, the worker encouraged group members to share negative reactions to the helping efforts. The question was: "How can I be more helpful to groups in the future?" The group was composed of men who had beaten their wives or the women they had lived with:

WORKER: What I want to ask you is what do you think I could have done better? What did I do that I shouldn't have done? That kind of thing. I would like some feedback about me in relationship to the group and what's been going on here.

The members responded to the worker's question by referring to a co-worker, who was not present. The worker brought it back to himself.

C: I always felt like he was giving me the "third degree," but at the same time it brought out answers that probably wouldn't have come out any other time. I didn't feel like he was pushing, but at the same time he asked penetrating questions. And you had a choice, you could either lie about them or you could just fade out and go around them—or tell the truth; most of the time instead of hiding it I would answer his questions and I think I got a lot more said that way than talking on my own.

WORKER: Do you think I could have asked more questions?

C: Yeh, you could have, but ... I don't like criticizing.

A: I don't see where you could have asked that many more questions. I think you've done well at bringing things out. It always takes somebody to start it ... and I think you've tried to get it going.

C: Yeah.

A: I think it has slipped quite a few times, but I don't think that is necessarily your responsibility; I think that's the group's.

C: Yeah. For some reason we did seem to digress quite often, I felt. But I think it's my responsibility just as much as it is yours. Although, maybe we could have talked about some things more.

A: How do you mean "slipped?" Do you mean we got off the topic?

C: Yeh,

B: ... we used to bullshit a lot!

A: But I feel that's really good because you have to be comfortable with the people you're talking with, therefore you have to bullshit sometimes. You have to get off the subject in order to get back on to it because we always manage to get back onto the topics. I think it's good to get off the subject—it's a rest ...

B: I'm just questioning how much we do, that's all.

A: Yeh, well, we did quite a bit ... but I think we got things done.

C: But we always noticed it, eh? If it got carried too far, one of the group would say something about it; but I think it helped in a way because it made things more relaxed. We weren't always discussing somebody's hang-up or anything.

WORKER: I won't say that I don't mind being criticized, because I do ... (laughter) OK! But at the same time, I recognize that ... Larry, the consultant in this outfit, says, "We make mistakes, we learn from those and then

we make more sophisticated mistakes—that kind of thing." I need that kind of input, not only for me as an individual, but for other guys who are going to be leading these groups.

C: Well, I think you're OK then—you haven't reached the sophisticated stage yet.

WORKER: You mean I'm just making the gross mistakes?! (laughter)

C: No, you're just making the everyday, ordinary ones.

WORKER: Like what?

C: I don't know, I haven't noticed you making any mistakes ...

WORKER: What would you like to see me doing differently?

B: Going back to what I said earlier this evening about becoming more aware of how pervasive (maybe) this anger is, how it manifests itself in different ways, and one way is just kind of a sense of being uptight. And it seems to me that the only way I'm gonna change is that I first have to become somehow aware. I mean, I don't know how you ask questions to help another person become aware, but I think that's the kind of question that is helpful and maybe you could have asked more of those—Now, specifically, I can't say because I don't have a firm grasp on that. Do you have an idea of what I'm talking about?

J: Yes. Maybe I'm putting too much responsibility on you? I don't think so. If I could do everything myself, I wouldn't be here in a group.

WORKER: I agree with that.

B: And I'm not sophisticated enough, I guess, to have penetrating questions ... or to draw out ... to help me become aware, I guess that takes ... first of all that you have the knowledge or something and being able to see more than I can—or at least have an idea, so that you can ask the questions that will help me rather than telling me, but help me become aware of what, you know, uh ... Because I'm just seeing now that I don't think I'm very aware of all the waves in my life—and I don't know why, but I think it's important that I gain that knowledge for myself. I'm not sure how to go about it. Because I don't think that my being is just going to change in the sense of my violence towards women—just towards women; I think it has to change in other areas, it will carry over. (Pause)

WORKER: (speaking to A): I was really moved when you talked about your feeling of being set up and you were obviously very upset talking about it. Maybe I could have reached a bit more, I don't know, helped you get in touch with . . .

A: Yeh, I think that you might have and I probably showed it too, because I was uptight that night, I was getting into it—I think maybe you should have pushed me a little more. It was a very touchy subject for me, because it's a helpless . . . I never really had a totally helpless feeling in my entire life; I've always been able to do something about it, but this is one thing that I can do *nothing* about; every time I try it gets worse and the frustration that comes from that really gets me. I get hit by this almost every day . . . the feeling that I can do nothing.

By making a demand for work, the worker demonstrated that he really wanted the feedback and the members responded. Of course, the worker had to have enough confidence in himself to invite the negative responses and to stay with them when the members tested him to see if he really meant it. In addition to making the ending discussion honest and receiving important professional feedback, the worker was demonstrating a view of manhood that said it was all right to make mistakes and to accept criticism. This was critical for this group where many of their difficulties with women resulted from their inability to own up to their own mistakes.

Deaf Teenager Group

In the next illustration, a worker helps a group come to grips with her leaving and to prepare for the arrival of a new worker. The group consists of teenagers who are deaf or hard of hearing. The beginning phase of work had been difficult,

since the worker had to develop a way of communicating with the members and to help them communicate with each other. Their concern about the new leader was heightened by their fears that an "outsider" might not accept them because of their handicap. The group had operated using discussion and activities as mediums. The planned activity for that evening was tobogganing:

When I arrived, the members were already there. The usual greetings were exchanged, and we sat down to wait to see if more members would come. Billy said, "I think we should wait ten minutes and then go." Kathy said she had spoken to several members and they indicated they wouldn't be coming, as it was such an awful night. I remarked that it was pretty cold for tobogganing. It was too bad we didn't know what the weather would be like. Billy said he had brought his *touque,* which would keep him warm. He proceeded to model it, which caused all of the members to laugh.

At that point, Billy asked when the new girl (the new leader) was coming. I said that Barbara would be coming next meeting. Stephen said, "Is she like you?" I replied that she was a social work student like I was, she was young and very happy to be coming to the group. I turned to Kathy and said, "We are talking about the new leader who will be coming to our meeting next week." Kathy turned to Amelia and Anna and indicated by sign language that the new leader would be coming next week. Amelia mocked a crying gesture which brought a chorus of smiles from the other members.

Stephen said, "Has she ever worked in a group like ours, like with deaf people?" Billy turned to Stephen, and said, "Well, Lucille never worked with deaf people before us." Kathy replied, "That's right."

Amelia, Jo-Ann, and Anna were craning their necks to find out what was going on. I pointed out that some members were being left out of our conversation, and we had to try to remember to include everyone. Billy made a mock gesture to the effect "here we go again," and he motioned the three members to move in closer. I said it's tough work letting everybody know what's going on, to which Billy replied, "Yeah!"

I remarked that Billy and Stephen seemed sort of worried about the new leader coming in. Kathy smiled the sort of smile that says, you hit the nail on the head. Stephen said, "We just want to know what she's like." I said that I think Kathy was thinking that, too. I said, "Was I right, Kathy?" to which she nodded her head.

Amelia mumbled something which I didn't understand. Billy turned to her and then translated to me. Amelia had said it was like starting our group all over again. Jo-Ann asked what was starting over? Kathy explained to Jo-Ann what was going on. Jo-Ann shook her head. Anna, who is totally mute, was looking as if she were in another world; I was aware that she was understanding nothing. I smiled at her and she grinned back. Billy looked at me, and said "I'll explain to Anna."

I then turned to Amelia and said, "You're nervous like maybe it was like when you came to the meeting with me for the first time." Amelia mumbled, "Nervous? Nervous?" and turned to Stephen with a puzzled expression. Stephen very slowly said, "Remember what it was like the first time we came here?"; Amelia gave the look of "I sure do." I said I guessed it was like that again, knowing a new leader is coming. Stephen nodded and said, "How come you're going?" then in a joking way added, "I guess you don't like us any more." I said, "Of course I still like you." Stephen then patted Billy on the back. Billy said, "A good group, aren't we?" I smiled and said we'd been through an awful lot together. Kathy nodded her head and this was a message which quickly got translated to all the members. Kathy said, "Gee, I wish we could have a social worker that would stay in our group." Stephen said, "Yeah." I said I guessed maybe that people were also angry because I was going. Stephen said, "No, no, that's not right." Billy said, "We've had a good time in this group." I said, "Just the same, I understood it was a hard thing to have to face going through getting to know a new leader again."

Kathy said, "Yeah, we just got to know you." Amelia made another mock gesture of crying. In the meantime Jo-Ann and Anna were talking in sign language and I think were quite out of the conversation.

The worker's direct reaching for the anger at her leaving was too difficult a demand for the members. In flight from the painful feelings, they play a trick on her instead of responding directly:

Jo-Ann then said to Billy (in sign language), "When are we going to go tobogganing?" He translated for me. I said we had some way passed our ten minutes Billy had suggested, and I asked her, "Are you ready to go?" Jo-Ann shook her head. I said, "You had a tough time knowing what was going on," and repeated this several times until she understood. She smiled and nodded and then smiled at Anna. Billy and Stephen then said they were ready to go. Billy poked Kathy and said, "Ready?" Kathy nodded. I said I thought Anna was being left out. Billy translated it to her, and she nodded.

I said I would go and get the two office toboggans and I'd be back in a minute. When I came back, to my dismay the group had all disappeared. I looked in several rooms and then decided to sit down and wait. In several seconds, Billy came whistling in. I jumped to my feet and said, "Gee, what happened to our group?" Billy, in a mischievous way, said, "Gee, I don't know. I just went for a walk." He said, "Why don't we look in the hall?" I said I guessed the members would come back, at which point he, in an insistent way, said, "No, let's look in the hall," which we did. Five beaming faces appeared with Kathy saying, "Surprise!" Everyone laughed, as did I; however I said, "How come the group wanted to leave?"

Stephen said, "We wanted you to come look for us." Amelia grinned and said, "Were you worried?" I said, "Did you want me to be?"—to which there were several nervous titters. I then said, "I think this group wants to leave me before I leave them," to which there were vehement no's. Billy said, "We were just joking." I said, "Still, I wasn't sure that everyone knew why I was leaving." Stephen said, "You're going back to Saskatchewan, isn't that where you were from?" I said I would be working on my research till June. Kathy said, "We'll still have a good group." Stephen poked Kathy and said, "You'll still be here." Kathy said, "All of us members will be here." I said that I thought they could continue to have a good group, but that would depend a lot on them. Billy nodded his head as if he understood. Kathy said, "Like you always say, we got to work at it." The group members laughed and shared this last piece of information, and then we got ready to leave.

A TERMINATION SESSION: DETAILED ANALYSIS

To conclude the discussion of endings and transitions, I have selected a description of a group meeting with teenaged girls in a residential treatment center. The session takes place one week after the worker has told the group members that she is leaving the agency for another job. This meeting demonstrates both an advanced level of group work skill and skill in dealing with endings. Of particular interest is the impact of the worker's sharing of her own powerful feelings. The entire meeting is presented, together with a detailed analysis of the skills employed. The process in the meeting is classic, as one can see elements of all the ending dynamics in one session.

The three girls came in with each other and seemed in a very happy mood. They said that they'd had a good week in school. I said, you know, that that sounded real nice and that this was one of the enjoyments of finally being a senior, and we kind of teased about that. I asked about where Gladys and Beth were, and they said that they had to speak with some teacher about some kind of arrangements and that they'd be in in a little while. The three of

them continued talking about school and the rehearsals and the senior trip and stuff like that. Then Beth came in, and she was singing "Everything Is Beautiful," a new rock-and-roll song. She took her seat and was laughing with everyone.

The good feelings expressed by the group members were the opposite of the worker's expectations and represented a denial of the ending. Since there were only a few meetings left, the worker had strategized to reach past the denial for the opposite feelings she knew would be there. The members responded to her *demand for work.*

After a while I said, "Hey, it's great to see everybody in such a good mood, and I hate to be a party pooper, but I kind of feel that I have to say that this is our next-to-last meeting, and I guess a lot of things between you and I will be drawing to an end." Margie said, "You have a hell of a nerve." I said, "You mean about my leaving?" She said, "Yeah, that and a whole lot of things." I said, "Oh, let's hear 'em. I'm sure that my leaving and the ending of the group has caused a lot of reactions in all of you." Nobody picked up on that, and Margie said, "Are we going to have a group next year?" A couple of the girls said, "Yeah, we want to have another group next year," and Beth said, "Let's have a party in honor of your leaving."

The group's anger was expressed in Margie's comment "You have a hell of a nerve." The worker acknowledged this anger and encouraged the members to continue. The anger they felt and the pain underneath it were too much for them at this point, so they backed off. They began, instead, to discuss the continuation of the group and a "farewell party." The worker allowed them to move away from the anger, but held them to discuss the importance of the group:

There was a lot of kind of mixed-up talk, and I tried to pick up about the thing about continuing the group. I said, "You're saying that the group has meant something to you and that you want to continue even without me." Beth said, "Naw, the group wasn't all that good," and Margie said, "Sometimes it was and sometimes not. Sometimes the meeting was very good, and sometimes they were a waste of time." I said, "Can you tell me more about that?" Margie said, "Well, sometimes it just seemed like we weren't in the right mood and we couldn't get down to work." Jill said, "Yeah, we were just fooling around all over the place," and Donna said, "Like the mood we were in Sunday night," and they all began to talk about some kind of a riot that had happened in the cottage, and they were all kind of fooling around. I said, "Hey, can we get back to the thing about the group, and what you thought about it, and what it meant to you? I think it *is* important for us to take a look at it now that you're nearing the end."

The members attempted to evade the discussion once again, and it was a mark of the advanced skill of the worker that she did not let them put her off. She made another demand for work and insisted that the group discuss their specific reactions to their time together. As they described the mutual aid they had experienced, the worker attempted to explore this aspect of their learning; however, they were not ready for this discussion and still needed to express their angry feelings:

Donna said: "Well, the best meeting we had was just with three of us—me, Jill, and Gladys. That's when we really talked about ourselves." Margie said, "You mean without me and Beth, is that what you mean?" Jill said quickly, "No, I don't mean that. We did have a good meeting with everybody, but I guess that was really the best," and I said, "Well, what made it the best?" and Donna said, "Because we talked about our families, and we got to understand how we were feeling," and

Margie said, "Yeah, I agree. The best meetings were when we talked about our families, and the worst meetings were when we talked about the cottage and the cottage parents." And I said, "How come?" Gladys said, "Because we couldn't do anything about the cottage parents or even about the cottage, and at least when we talk about ourselves and about our families we can understand more, we can know why we are like we are," and Beth said, "Yeah, we can help each other." I said, "You have helped each other a lot. Is that something important that you've gotten from these meetings?" Nobody picked up on that.

Beth began talking about a party that they had been to, and all of a sudden in the midst of a whole big discussion Beth turned to me and said, "You're leaving, you God damned fink." And everybody stopped, and everybody looked at me. I said, "I'm leaving and I guess that makes me a fink." And everybody began, saying, "Why are you leaving? Why do you have to leave us? Why can't you stay?" Then a whole torrent of emotion came pouring out. Finally Jill said, "Why *are* you leaving?" I said, "I tried to explain the reasons on Friday, but if you'd like me to I'll explain them again now. But I don't know if it's the *reason* that really matters, it's more how you feel knowing that I'm leaving, for whatever the reason." They said, "No, no, we want to hear the reasons, we don't understand." I said, "OK, let me try to explain. I'm leaving because I've been here for a number of years and I feel that it's time for me to move on, to move into another situation. Working here has meant an awful lot to me and you all have meant an awful lot to me. Yet I feel that a combination of things, the long traveling, working a lot of nights, have become very hard for me and I feel like I want to work nearer to where I live, and that I want to have a new kind of experience and not work in a residential treatment school. That's pretty much the reason. If there's anything you don't understand, ask me and I'll try to explain more."

As the anger emerged, the worker struggled with her own feelings in order not to block its expression. Her acceptance of their feelings demonstrated in her response, "I'm leaving, and I guess that makes me a fink," freed them to move to their feelings of dependency and hurt which were below the surface feelings of anger. Although she had explained her reasons for leaving the week before, the group members had been too shocked to heed and understand. She agreed to explain them again while acknowledging that their feelings were what really mattered rather than her reasons. As the group members began to express their emotions towards the worker, she asked them to identify the specific things about her they found helpful. These would be the qualities they must look for in other workers. She also stayed with their hurt feelings, reached for their fears about establishing a relationship with a new worker, for their sense of rejection, and for their anger. Most important, the worker also shared her own pain at leaving them. It was the open expression of her feelings which provided the impetus for the members to respond with theirs.

Beth started to cry and said, "You can't leave. We need you." I said, "You mean you won't be able to make it without me?" Margie said, "You're the best social worker I ever had. I won't be able to talk to anybody else." I said, "We have been real close, me and everyone of you, and I guess the thought of starting over with somebody else scares the hell out of you. What do you think there was about me that made it easier for you to talk to me?" Beth said, "It's because you cared about us. It's 'cause we knew that even when you were mad at us, you were really sticking up for us, and you were really with us." Donna said in a soft voice, "Yeah, but if you cared so much, you wouldn't be leaving." And I said, "That's a thing, isn't it? How could I leave you if I really care for you?" Gladys said, "We know you care for us. We know you're leaving because you really feel that you

have to." And then she just kind of shrugged, and I said, "But the words don't help very much, huh? They don't take away the bad feeling." Beth said, "That's right, what good does it do me to know that you care if you're not here?" And Jill said, "Yeah, you've been my social worker for a whole year. I don't want anybody else." There was a lot more talk about that they didn't want anybody new. And I said, "You're angry as hell at me. You have a right to be, and even though your anger hurts me and a big piece of me wants to say 'Don't be angry at me,' I can understand that you are, and I know the kind of pain that must be underneath, and I feel some of that pain also. It's hard as hell for me to leave you." Beth said, "If it was hard for you to leave us, then you wouldn't leave us." Margie said, "No, Beth, that's just not the truth. It was hard for me to leave home...."

At this point in the session, the pain of the discussion caused the group to adopt its pattern of using a scapegoat when things got rough. Gladys, the group scapegoat, began to cry, expressing many of the emotions felt by the other members. Their anger at her was an expression of their anger at the same feelings within themselves. The worker demonstrated her group work skill, at a time when she herself was feeling somewhat overwhelmed by emotion, by paying attention to her two clients. In the next excerpt we see an illustration of the worker's functional role as outlined in the earlier discussion on scapegoating:

Gladys put her head down and began to cry, and one of the kids hollered, "Oh, cut it out. This hurts us as much as it hurts you." I said, "Maybe it hurts each of you in a different way, and this is how Gladys is reacting." She picked up her head and said, "Oh, leave me alone. None of you care about me," and Margie said, "Yes, we do, you don't want help. You just want to feel sorry for yourself." I said, "You're all getting so angry at Gladys, and it seems that all she's doing is acting out how *you* feel. Is it that you hurt so much that you don't have room for anybody else's hurt?" Jill said, "She cries all the time. Who gives a damn about her?" Donna said, "I care about her, but I don't know what to do." Beth said to her (by this time Gladys had moved away from the table where we meet and was sitting alone on a chair crying), "Gladys, why don't you come over here?" and Gladys just shrugged, and one of the other kids said, "Aw, leave her alone," and there was kind of an uncomfortable quiet in the room, and I said, "I don't think that you feel right leaving her alone," and Beth said, "Hell, what can we do?" and I said, "What do you feel like doing? Do you feel like reaching out to her?" Beth got up and walked over to Gladys and put her arms around her and said, "You're scared because everybody's leaving, right?" Gladys nodded her head. Beth said, "We're all in that situation, too. L.'s leaving us, too. Miss S.'s leaving us, too. Not only you." Beth said, "But maybe it is different for Gladys." Gladys said, "You have a mother and father. Every one of you has at least a mother or a father. Who do I have?" Beth said, "You have foster parents." Gladys said, "Big deal. They don't want me." There was a hush in the room at the pain of those words, and I said, "Wow, you really know how that feels."

The worker's trust in her group was rewarded as they reached out to Gladys to offer aid. As they spoke to Gladys, they were really speaking to each other and to the part of them that was facing the same set of problems. The faith of the worker was important at this point because with her help they were able to experience the power of mutual aid in the peer group. As they move into their young adult years, they will have to seek out support and help from their peers; this was possibly the most important learning for them.

Beth said, "I think I know how it feels. I think I know how bad it feels. And if you want to cry, that's OK, but you gotta live. You got to pick yourself up. You gotta face it." Gladys shook her head. "No," she said, "I can't." I said, "It seems that she can't pick herself up." Donna said, "Even when you're alone, you have to trust yourself." Margie said, "That's pretty hard to do." Beth said, "But you're not alone, Gladys, you have us. We'll help you, and sometimes you'll help us." Margie said, "You gotta have confidence in yourself." I said, "How do you do that, Margie? Can you tell her?" Margie said, "You gotta think of the things that you do *right*, not only the bad things. Even when people leave you, you gotta think of what you did have with them, and all that was good. And then you got to believe that you're going to have somebody else, too." Beth said, "You gotta learn to stand on your own feet. You gotta learn how to make friends." Jill said, "You gotta take responsibility for what you do, even when it's hard." I said, "It sounds like you feel that Gladys can do these things, even though now she doesn't think that she can." Beth said, "That's right, and I mean it even coming from me. Lots of times I hate her, but other times I really like her, and I remember when she was nice to me and when she helped me, and I do believe in her, and I believe she can pick herself up." Beth took Gladys' hand and brought her back to the table. Then Gladys said, "I feel real, real bad. Miss S.'s leaving hurts me more than anybody can know, but you've helped me and I want to thank you," and there were tears in everybody's eyes, and I said, "This is what it's all about. This beautiful thing that you can do in helping each other, and you've got that now. You own that. And no matter who leaves, no matter how much it hurts, you can't lose that." Beth said, "I hate you for leaving, but I know what you mean. I know you're right." Margie hung her head and I said: "Go ahead, Margie, what do you want to say?" She said, "I know what Beth means also, and I want to feel that I can go on also, that we can even have a group without you, that we can keep on helping each other just like we can in the group. I'm scared." And I said, "Sure, it's a scary thing. Can you talk a little more about what you're scared about?" Margie said, "I'm scared that we won't be able to do it alone, that we need you to help us." Beth said, "Well, maybe we'll have somebody else who can help us." Donna said, "And maybe we'll also have to help ourselves." Gladys said, "I know what you mean. I know that in the end I do have to help myself." I said to her, "But are you scared that you won't be able to do that?" She shook her head yes, and once again she began to cry. Beth said, "We'll help you, too. Just like we did here this morning." And I had tears in my eyes, too, and I said, "Wow, you kids are fantastic." And they all kind of laughed and somebody said, "Maybe we'll become social workers, too," and that kind of broke the tension of the moment, and we never really got back to the thing of them helping each other.

The feelings associated with endings stir deep and powerful emotions in all of us. When I have used this example in workshops, workers have been visibly moved by the power of the feelings expressed; they have perhaps moved you as well. Workers also react to the degree of skill demonstrated by this worker. They reflect on endings they have not handled well by missing the cues or not facing their own feelings with enough honesty. This record represents an advanced level of skill. This same worker handled endings quite differently in her training days; she would have cut and run at a number of key places in this meeting. There were many group endings along the way in which she made mistakes, learned from them, and ended her next group with more skill. This process is a painful one, but it represents the only way I know to develop professional skill. It is a process which continues throughout a professional's working life. Parts I and II of this book have been designed to aid you in thinking about your own practice with individuals and groups, to help you identify more clearly what it is you do that works well, as well as what you might be able to do differently. In Part III of this book, I examine the worker's skill in dealing with the systems clients must negotiate. You will note that the dynamics and skills identified thus far will be just as useful in describing this other aspect of the helping professional's functional role.

III. Work With The System

CHAPTER 16

Helping Clients to Negotiate the System

In Part I, I presented the helping model in the context of work with individuals and families. Much of my emphasis was on preparing and assisting clients to deal with important systems. In Part II I examined this same individual-social interaction in the context of group work, suggesting that the group was a microcosm of the larger society. In the following part of the book, I consider another level of interaction—the relationship between clients and the social institutions with which they come into contact, such as schools, hospitals, housing agencies, political systems, residential care centers, and social agencies. It should be apparent as we examine this interaction and the worker's function and skill required to implement it that much of the material already presented is applicable by analogy. My use of an approach based on systems theory makes this possible: since different levels of systems have universal properties, insights into one level can serve as hypotheses for understanding another. Hearn has pointed out the possibilities of using a systems approach as a general framework for viewing the client:

If there are principles which apply to organismic systems in general, and if individuals, groups, organizations, and communities may be regarded as such systems, then these principles collectively might find their place in a unified theory of practice. This would provide a *common* framework for conceiving the individuals, groups, organizations, and communities as "clients," or as the means by which service is rendered to "clients."[1]

Hearn is suggesting we use our understanding of one level of system to understand better another level. I would like to take his idea further and propose that such an approach is also helpful in conceptualizing the worker's function and in identifying the required skills. I will therefore examine the individual-system interaction in much the same terms I have used thus far and will use the mediation function to describe the worker's role, illustrating this function in action with examples from a number of settings showing work with clients who sometimes individually and at other times in groups are endeavoring to negotiate systems and their representatives (e.g., teachers, principals, doctors, housing authority administrators). Many of the skills already identified will prove to be as helpful in dealing with

357

system representatives as they were with clients. Since confrontation with the system and social pressure are also part of the way change takes place, these processes will also be illustrated. The worker's mediation function will be defined broadly and will include advocacy as one method of implementing it. In Chapter 17 the worker's responsibility for having professional impact on her or his own agency and other settings will be discussed. The illustrations in that chapter demonstrate how a worker can use experiences with clients to guide efforts to affect agency policies, structures, procedures, and programs to meet the needs of clients better.

THE INDIVIDUAL-SYSTEM INTERACTION

In a modern, industrial, and largely urban society, the relationship between individuals and society has taken on a very complex character. A large number of institutions and agencies have been established to deal with the individual on behalf of society. For example, welfare agencies were designed to care for those who were unable to support themselves; schools were developed to provide the education needed for individuals to become integrated into the community and to play a productive role; hospitals were established as centers for medical care for physical illness; and psychiatric centers were set up for those with emotional disorders. As is often the case, the very institutions set up to solve problems became so complex themselves that new problems were generated. Social, medical, and educational systems are difficult to negotiate, even for individuals who are well equipped to deal with them, never mind those with limited education and resources. The services established for people are often so complex that it is

difficult for individuals to make use of them.

In addition to complexity, there are other factors which compound the individual-system interaction. For example, many services inherently approach clients ambivalently. Thus, while welfare is established to meet the needs of the poor, it is often administered in a way which reflects a judgmental and punitive attitude. For example, welfare recipients are often made to feel that their checks are public "doles," gifts from a generous community rather than a right, and that acceptance of welfare is a sign that the individual is neither a productive nor an important member of society.

A third factor contributing to breakdowns in the individual-system relationship is the size of a bureaucracy. For example, finding the right department in a large government agency can be a frustrating, even overwhelming, task. Entering a large high school as just one student in a class of 2,000 can easily lead to getting "lost" in the system, thus not getting the special help needed for successful completion of a program. Another complication is the difficulty in human communication. For instance, a student may, even in a small setting such as a specific class, feel that the teacher does not care, and the teacher, in turn, may feel the same way about the student. Both may well be mistaken. I am sure you can provide numerous examples in which the size and complexity of a system, difficulties in communications, or the ambivalence of the system towards its clients cuts them off from services they require. Since the individual who needs to use the system is also complex, feels some ambivalence towards the service, and has difficulty in communications, then breakdowns are almost inevitable.

One fact of life we can all acknowledge

from our own experiences is that simply establishing a service to meet a need is no guarantee that the need will be met. Recognizing this reality led Schwartz to propose the function of the social work profession to mediate the individual-social engagement.[2] He suggests that this is the historical reason for the development of the social work profession: to stand as a buffer between clients and the systems they needed to negotiate. This functional role can be assumed by any helping professional who sees it within his or her function to deal with relevant systems when required.

MEDIATING THE INDIVIDUAL-SYSTEM INTERACTION

One of the major problems facing workers in implementing this role is their own feelings. They often tend to over-identify with the individual client against the system and its representatives. In the earlier discussion of work with the family and work with scapegoats in the group, I described how workers, because of their own life experiences, often identify with one side in an engagement. Since we have all known complex bureaucracies, authoritarian and insensitive administrators, teachers who seemed not to care, and the like, it is not difficult to understand such an initial reaction to a client's problem with a system. I have seen workers develop a fine sense of tolerance for deviant behavior on the part of clients, an ability to see past a facade and reach for clients' strength underneath, and an understanding of clients' ambivalence. However, these same workers lack tolerance for deviant behavior, are fooled by facades, and cannot accept ambivalence when they see these characteristics in a system or representatives of the system. I should hasten to point out that there are times

when anger is the only appropriate response and that workers may be faced with a situation where confrontation is the only answer. However, I believe workers often respond in this way *before* they have attempted to understand the dynamics involved and so may respond to teachers, doctors, welfare workers as if they were stereotypes. At the point when a client needs the worker's help in negotiating a system, the worker may be responding in a way which further cuts off the system from the client. The worker may then point to the system as an impossible situation rather than examining personal feelings and critically analyzing his or her own part in the proceedings.

A striking example of this process was brought home in a workshop I conducted for Native Indian women who worked as social aides for their local bands. Their job was to help the members of the band in their dealings with many white-dominated agencies and institutions (e.g., schools, welfare). One worker presented an example of her efforts to help a Native Indian teenager who was on his way to failing a course taught by a white teacher. This worker had often attacked the inadequacy of the school. The following record presents the conversation between the worker and the white teacher:

WORKER: I hear you're having problems with Albert's English.

TEACHER: It's not my problem, it's his.

WORKER: I do think you're leaning on him too hard.

TEACHER: Look, if he wants to get anywhere, he'll have to shape up. I really don't have the time to argue. If he wants to pass English, he'll have to try harder.

WORKER: Speaking about time, we do pay some of your wages, you know. I do think you could be a little more lenient.

TEACHER: I'll try to keep that in mind.

WORKER: You do that.

In discussing this brief interchange, the workshop participants, all Native Indian workers, felt that the presenter had come on too hard with the teacher. Both appeared to be defensive: the teacher may have felt the worker wanted her to let Albert pass in spite of his poor performance, and the worker felt that the teacher did not really care about Albert. There was consensus in the group that the relationship between the worker and the teacher was in poor shape and that, as a result of the interview, there was not much hope for an improved relationship between the teacher and Albert. The teacher had not gained a better idea about Albert's feelings in the class or towards the subject or of what might be making it difficult for Albert to learn. In addition, the worker interpreted the teacher's expectations for Albert's performance as a rejection of him, even though many workshop members pointed out that some teachers made no demands on Native Indian youngsters at all. They just passed them along, a real form of rejection. The workshop group members strategized how the worker might go back to meet with the teacher and negotiate a contract for their relationship and try to begin again. Although the worker seemed to agree, I sensed her hesitation, particularly in respect to the part of the strategizing in which her fellow workers suggested she admit to the teacher that she had come on too strong. I reached for her feelings:

WORKSHOP LEADER: You seem hesitant. I get the feeling you're not anxious to go back and try again. Am I right?
WORKER: (After a very long silence) It would hurt my pride to go back and talk to that teacher. (Another long silence)
WORKSHOP LEADER: Could you explain why it would hurt?
WORKER: I don't think you understand. Thirty years ago, I was one of the first of five

Indian children to go to that school when it was all white . . .

What followed was a description of her experience in a white-dominated school in which she and other Native Indian students were made to feel ashamed of their race and their heritage. They had been forbidden to speak their native language, were ridiculed by teachers and white students for their poor dress and manners, and were generally made to feel like outsiders. One example of the cultural shock was related to the use of silence. When asked questions in class, Native Indian students would take a long time to respond, either thinking about the answer (as was the custom in conversations they heard in their families) or trying to translate into their native language and then back to English. Teachers who did not understand the importance of silence would often interpret the delay as indicating they did not know the answer, and would move on to another student. After a while, the Native Indian students did not even try. Others in the workshop group added their own experiences. Some participants gently pointed out that things were not the same today, and that some of the white teachers tried hard to understand their kids. I tried to acknowledge the feelings of the worker:

WORKSHOP LEADER: I guess every time you walk into that school it must bring back a great deal of pain and feelings of humiliation. I can understand now why you would feel it would be a blow to your pride. I'm not sure if I can help right now. What is hitting me hard is that for you to work differently with this teacher, you have to deal with your feelings about the white world—all the hurt you have experienced—and that's a tall order.

Other workshop members moved in at this point, and the discussion focused on how they had to avoid the tendency to see the world the Native Indian teenagers had to face now as exactly the same one they had had to deal with. There were still many similarities, and the anger they felt towards present injustices was clearly stated. However, if they were to help things be different for their kids, they had to do something to try to change things themselves.

In this specific case, they felt it would not help Albert for the worker to simply give up on the school. If Albert were to make it, someone had to open up communications between him and his teacher. The worker agreed that she could see this and said she would have to think about what she would do. I pointed out that this example opened up a larger question about the relationship between the band children and their parents and the staff of the school. Had they thought about the possibility of trying to do something on a band- and school-wide basis? Were other Native Indian parents also feeling somewhat intimidated by the school? Perhaps the school staff felt cut off and somewhat intimidated by the band? Would this be an area to explore? Discussion continued on the implications of this specific case for the general problem of Native Indian children in the school. This line of work, moving from the specific example to more general problems, will be illustrated in the next chapter. For now, the important point is that the worker's feelings can have a powerful effect on perception of the system and its representatives. If the worker only sees that part of the system which evidences resistance, then the worker may fall into the trap of missing the part of the system which is still reaching out.

It is, of course, not necessary to have experiences such as those described by these Native Indian women to feel intimidated by a school setting. One graduate student of mine described his first day of field work. He was placed as a student social worker in the same school he had attended as a child. On his first morning he met his former fourth-grade teacher in the hall, and she said, "Terry, what are you doing here?" He replied, "I'm the new student social worker." He described her face as broadening into a maternal smile as she said, "Isn't that nice." He blushed and felt that his possibilities of doing any effective work with this teacher were finished. A first step, therefore, in functioning more effectively in systems work is for the worker to become aware of personal feelings about a system's representatives, particularly those in positions of authority. This is essential.

Work with the School System

The following example is a record of service to a youngster who has been suspended from school. It illustrates the mediation role in action. The worker demonstrates her ability to be with the youngster and the system representatives in the engagement. This was the key to her success. The client was a sixty-one-year-old woman who had contacted the worker at a community psychiatry department of the local hospital. The worker had been seeing her son in a group at the hospital and the client, Mrs. J., had called to inform the worker that she was not able to get her son Bobby accepted into school, despite a court order requiring her to do so. The worker described the client as not very adept at handling school matters and vague about why the school was failing to comply with the order. The worker felt that Mrs. J. was worried and depressed about the school. She visited the client at her home to help her talk about her problem.

WORKER: I know that with all of the criticism you have had regarding your children, it is very hard for you.

MRS. J.: (looking depressed) I am trying my best. I don't want the courts to send Bobby away, but the school won't let him return and he is getting into more trouble.

WORKER: It's like going around in circles—everyone's telling you what to do, and no one is showing you how.

MRS. J.: Now, they will say I'm neglecting Bobby. (In an exasperated manner) The court says put him in school; the school says he can't go. I don't know what to do!

She continued to talk about her inability to understand why the school has refused to allow Bobby to return. While we were talking, the other children were yelling and screaming. Mrs. J. was very edgy. Several times she grabbed the little ones violently to make them be quiet. I said she seemed overwhelmed and asked how I could help. She said I could do better if I talked to the school. She didn't understand "those people." Maybe I could. She explained how difficult it is for her to travel to school with all the other children. I said I would speak to the school and keep in close contact with her as to what was happening. She seemed relieved and thanked me.

I later talked to Bobby to see how he was feeling. He was out on the block when I spoke with him, and he seemed unhappy but perked up a little when he saw me. His immediate comment was "You going to get me in school?" I gave him some information about the steps I had in mind and added that I knew he and his mother had been trying very hard. My comment led to further discussion.

BOBBY: I know why the school doesn't want me.

WORKER: I'd like to know why.

BOBBY: The teachers don't like me, and they don't want me in that school.

He was sulking and seemed quite torn inside. He looked at me and his eyes were watery. I reached out and probed for what he was feeling:

WORKER: I know it's hard but get it out of you; tell me what you are feeling.

BOBBY: (who was crying) I want to get back into school. There's nothing to do on the block! The court is going to send me away, and my mother keeps hollering at me!

We talked at great length about his feelings, and he continued to express his fears about getting into school. If he gets into school, he is not sure he will do well. He is afraid the same experiences will repeat themselves. Mostly, I just listened, giving support where I could.

WORKER: I know it's hard, Bobby. I want to help you by trying to help your parents as well as the school to see that you want to do the right thing. But it's not easy. You'll have to help me do this.

BOBBY: I'll try.

WORKER: You're trying already. It must have been very hard for you to tell me what you were thinking.

Bobby was silent, but I felt he understood what I was saying. When I was leaving, he reminded me of the group's trip that evening, and I said I would be there.

The worker had begun the process by contracting with Mrs. J. and Bobby about how she could help. She tried to get a sense of how they saw the difficulty and attempted to encourage their expression of feeling about the problem. After these conversations it would have been easy to understand if the worker had gone to the school to do battle for Bobby. With a court order in the background, the worker might have tried to use the power of the court to force Bobby back into school. This effort might have worked, but the worker recognized it would have been a short-lived victory. If the problems between Bobby and the school system were not dealt with, they would just return to haunt him, and he would soon be suspended again. In addition, while the worker might have been able to force the school to take Bobby back, she wanted more from them—she wanted them to work to help Bobby stay in. To enlist their aid, she needed to treat the staff at the school as allies in the struggle to aid Bobby, not as the enemy. Instead of creating a "self-fulfilling prophecy" by attacking the school representatives and creating a defensive and negative response, the worker began the first contact with the school guidance counselor by contracting, employing the skill of clarifying purpose. Often, because of their hidden agendas, workers begin their systems work without a clear and direct statement of what they are about. Lack of clarity as to purpose can be just as threatening and unproductive with systems' representatives as it is in work with clients. She also encouraged the guidance counselor to elaborate her perceptions of the problem. A worker who saw the counselor as the enemy might have begun a "counter-attack" after the counselor's first responses. Returning to the worker's record of service:

I visited the school for the purpose of getting clarification on the reasons why Bobby was not allowed in school and to trace the source of his difficulty there.

I met Miss G., the guidance counselor, and after briefly describing my involvement with the family, I told her what I was after:

WORKER: The court has requested that Bobby be returned to school. Mrs. J. has informed me that the school has refused to readmit him.

COUNSELOR: I know that the court has ordered Bobby back to school. However, when he was suspended, he was done so by the district superintendent. Therefore, only that office can admit him to school.

I then asked for some clarification as to the meaning of Bobby's suspension. I wanted to know if it were common for suspended pupils to have to wait so long for readmission. She said Bobby's situation was different because he had been so disruptive (emphasis on disruptive) in school. She was emphatic about his fight with the lunchroom teacher last year.

Further discussion revealed that there was a possibility that Bobby had been provoked. This came out when I shared with her Bobby's feelings about the situation. I revealed some of Bobby's characteristics that I felt the school should know about. My purpose was twofold: (1) I knew Bobby's record at that school would follow him, and I wanted to clear it up; (2) Because of the demands placed on teachers, a child's struggles with the school and himself can often go unnoticed.

In response to the worker's direct statement of purpose and her willingness to listen, the guidance counselor began to open up with the worker. The worker listened and attempted to empathize with the counselor and her difficulties. It is in this sense that the worker tries to be "with" the client and the system at the same time. It would be easier not to hear the problems facing the system, but just as with any relationship, there must be genuine understanding before it is possible to make demands.

Miss G. was very responsive:

COUNSELOR: I have noticed that Bobby is a sensitive boy, and under all his toughness there's a scared child.

Miss G. seemed frustrated by her inability to reach for the positive aspects that Bobby has, and I suspected that she was feeling defeated and threatened by my probing into the particulars surrounding Bobby's suspension. I said to her, "There's probably a desire on your part to be more responsive. You probably feel uncomfortable about not reaching Bobby." Miss G., in a sincere but hesitant manner, had this to say:

COUNSELOR: Many of the teachers are insensitive, and there is a lack of cooperation on the part of the principal. Also, there is a large population of disruptive children who are frequently sent to the office. The lack of sufficient personnel for these children inhibits us from doing our job.

She continued for some time, talking about her frustrations. I made several unsuccessful attempts to refocus the discussion on Bobby. I then decided it was best to allow her to ventilate her feelings. I listened while she told me how she tries to help the children; and how in the past she has had some real struggles in terms of getting the teachers to relate to the disruptive student. In an exasperated manner, she said: "The pupils do need help, but it is hard for the teachers to give it to them—especially with so many!" I chose this opportunity to get back to Bobby's problem:

WORKER: Miss G., I can understand how frustrating it is for you and the teachers, but it is also frustrating for Bobby. He wants to belong to the school, and I know that the school wants to help him.

COUNSELOR: (very concerned) I will not send any record of this to Bobby's new school. I wouldn't want to prejudice the teachers against him. I will write in the records that Bobby is a sensitive boy who is bright and capable but who need some special help. I feel this will give him a better chance of adjusting. Miss G. then gave me some names at the district office. She said she enjoyed talking to me because it is rare that she gets a chance to talk about her frustration. I suggested that we could talk some more, and this comment led to a long discussion about obtaining a social worker for the school.

Because of the worker's stance and skill, the guidance counselor became an important ally in the effort to get Bobby back into school. Workers often wonder about the use of empathic skills on other staff. They ask, "Isn't it like 'social working' a staff member, and won't they resent it?" I believe that when they say this, they are using the term *social working* in its worst sense and that what they are referring to is an insincere, ritualistic empathic response, which the other staff members quickly experience as an attempt to manipulate them. In this case, there are real difficulties in dealing with children like Bobby in a school system, and if the worker expects the counselor

and the staff to "listen" to Bobby, to "understand" his difficulties, and to "empathize" with his feelings, she must do the same with them. Of course, the guidance counselor and other staff people at the school are not "clients," and the worker needs to keep clear that they are professional colleagues, each with different functions in relation to the same client. However, mutual respect and understanding between colleagues and a willingness to understand the complexities of a situation are important if the worker is to help Bobby and his mother, as well as have a positive effect on the Bobby-school interaction. Analyzing numerous process recordings of work with systems representatives, I have often found the worker running into trouble in the session just after the point where the problems in the system start to be shared. Workers demand empathy for clients despite refusing to empathize with a colleague.

The worker in this example next approached the supervisory level for further information. She sensed that there might have been some reactions to her involvement and therefore reached for reactions.

At the district office, my strategy was to find out just what or who was preventing Bobby's return to school. I spoke with Miss R., guidance coordinator. Upon introducing myself, she said she had heard of me. I was surprised and asked what she had heard. She said she saw my name on several court reports as the family social worker for St. Luke's Hospital. Miss G. had also called and told her I was coming. Miss R. seemed nervous and I decided to explore her feelings about my involvement:

WORKER: Here I am trying to get a child back in school who has been out for a long period of time. You must feel somewhat annoyed by my efforts.

COORDINATOR: At first I felt that way,

but my conversation with Miss G. changed my mind. I am impressed with anyone who is interested in listening to problems of the school as well as the child.

WORKER: You must have had some bad experiences with social workers?

COORDINATOR: (with some irritation) Too many social agencies attack the schools. They make a big STINK, and when the child is returned to school, they drop out of the picture. I don't like the fact that Bobby has been out of school so long, but I am waiting for a report from Child Guidance before returning him to school.

I began to reach for her positive feelings:

WORKER: I know you want the best for Bobby as well as for any child. With so many demands on counselors, it is easy for a child to get lost.

COORDINATOR: This is true. There are so many students like Bobby who have been out of school long periods of time. The parents think we don't care; but the children need so much and the teachers are unable to give it. We need help!

I then attempted to focus on Bobby's situation and at the same time recognize the global problems of the school system. I said I knew how difficult the school situation is.

WORKER: We need social workers, psychiatrists, etc., right in the school, and most of all we need sympathetic teachers. But I am concerned with what we can do together for Bobby.

COORDINATOR: (rather embarrassingly) Oh! Forgive me! It's just that I had said to Miss G. that I would explore the possibility of getting social services in at least one of the schools in the district.

I then invited her to a meeting Miss G. and I were having to work to secure services for the school. I then made some suggestions about what we could do for Bobby. I asked her to call Child Guidance to determine when the report would be ready. When she phoned, she discovered that Child Guidance was under the impression that the court was going to do a psychiatric. Miss R. then phoned the court and spoke to the probation officer who informed her that their psychiatric evaluation

was to be done on the parents only, and Child Guidance was to do the one on Bobby. Miss R. seemed frustrated: "No one really communicates with each other." She angrily phoned Dr. B., head of Child Guidance, and obtained a commitment to do a psychiatric on Bobby.

After acknowledging the problems, the worker made a demand for work by concentrating on the immediate problem facing Bobby. The supervisor's conversation with the probation officer was one illustration of how the complexity of the system can often lead to clients falling into the cracks. In the following excerpt the worker sensed the coordinator's underlying ambivalence and reached directly for the feelings. She wanted to be sure that her conversation with the coordinator was "real," because any unexpressed doubts would return to haunt Bobby later. An important additional step is the worker's recognition that she would have to begin a working relationship with the staff in Bobby's new school;' she thus suggested modifications in the coordinator's description of her role to prevent misunderstanding.

I told Miss R. of my earlier conversations with Bobby and Mrs. J. and expressed their desire to have him back in school right away. Miss R. said she also wanted him in school immediately, but I sensed some reservations. I reached for her ambivalent feelings:

WORKER: Part of you seems to want him back and part of you doesn't.

COORDINATOR: You're right. I'm concerned about what school to send him to. Most of the other schools in the district are loaded with problem kids. There is one school which is better than others, but they are somewhat rigid. I want Bobby to have the best possible chance, but that's the only school that has room for him.

I offered a plan of action and reached for some feedback:

WORKER: If you could introduce me to

the principal of the new school, perhaps we could work together with the teachers in a supportive role to broaden the chances of Bobby making a satisfactory adjustment.

Miss R. felt that this was a good plan. She thought the school would appreciate my help. However, she suggested that I work with the school social worker and the teachers because they might resent my working directly with the principal. I said that I didn't fully understand what she was trying to tell me. She explained that the principal and the teachers have a "pretty rocky relationship," and she didn't want to get in the way of my attempts to help. She wrote a letter to the principal explaining who I was and what role I would have in working closely with the school to help Bobby. She ended the letter by stating that I should be consulted before decisions were made regarding anything Bobby has become involved in. I suggested that the letter be reworded so as not to give the impression of taking away decision powers. I told her to simply ask that I be involved as a resource person to enable them to make more informed decisions.

I gave recognition to Miss R. for her assistance in getting movement on the reinstatement of Bobby:

WORKER: I know it isn't an easy decision to return Bobby to school. But I will be around to help when you need me.

As I was leaving, Miss R. said I should contact her about the meeting to get social services in Miss G.'s school.

This worker recognized that getting Bobby back into school was just the beginning of the work, certainly not the final solution to the problem. She managed to keep in contact with the school and to monitor Bobby's progress so that when trouble arose, she would be there to help. In this important part of her work, her earlier efforts to develop a positive working relationship with the school staff paid dividends as she had a basis of trust from which to work. The following is the worker's assessment of where things stand:

Bobby is presently in school. He is feeling quite nervous because the school is new, and he is having difficulty adjusting to a structured setting again. So far, he has not made any friends, and his relationship with classmates is strained. Bobby's teacher is kind of rigid, but she has begun to use me when she feels he is heading for difficulty. She is somewhat overexcited and afraid of not "bringing Bobby around." Her preoccupation with a good class is strong, and she lets it get in the way of reaching and understanding Bobby's needs.

The social worker in the school is in a rather dubious position. She is the only social worker in the school and is walking a rather thin line by trying to please everyone and "not rock the boat." She is also frustrated because she has strong feelings about teachers' insensitivity.

Mrs. J. is worried that Bobby might not continue in school. Therefore, she is constantly threatening him. Her threats seem to discourage Bobby and put ideas into his head about playing "hooky."

The worker continued by identifying her next steps in this case:

I want to:

(1) Meet on a regular basis with the teacher to talk with her in an attempt to help her see that her feelings about success are preventing her from reaching Bobby.

(2) Work with the social worker who is in a bind and torn between the demands of the teachers and the children. I would like to see her work more closely with Bobby.

(3) Point out to Mrs. J. that her negative attitude toward Bobby's progress in school can only complicate things for him—as well as for herself.

(4) Continue to encourage Bobby to talk about his fears and anxiety about being in a new school. Also, to support him when things are going rough and let him know I am available to him.

(5) Secure tutorial help for Bobby.

Work with a Teacher

In another example drawn from a school setting, the problem of mediating the interaction between the client and a significant system's representative is illustrated. A worker's record of service of work with an eleven-year-old, sixth-grade student and her teacher helps to focus on the sensitive area of working with fellow professionals who deal with one's client. This is a particularly difficult situation when one feels that the system's representative may be exacerbating the problem. The difficulty and embarrassment for the worker rest in the discomfort involved in providing honest feedback to another profession, particularly if the worker does not like or respect that professional's work. Because of these strong feelings, a worker will often give up on the system's person prematurely and concentrate on trying to straighten out the client's life in other areas. In this example, Wendy was referred to the worker as an acting out child who was getting into trouble in class with her teacher, Miss M., and other students (physical fights) and who seemed headed for failure that year. The worker accepted this client, as workers often do, without contracting for the part of the work involving the teacher. The two worked together during the fall term, and Wendy's acting out behavior decreased so that the worker was able to ignore the signals of ongoing tension and lack of understanding between Wendy and her teacher. Miss M. had expressed dislike of Wendy because of her irritating behavior; the worker, however, had ignored these comments. When I inquired why, the worker indicated she did not like Miss M., thought she should not be teaching, and saw her as a stereotypical, uptight teacher.

After the Christmas vacation, when Wendy got into a number of "dirty" fights while Miss M. apparently just stood by and watched, the worker was forced to recognize the difficulties in the work. She decided to face her attitude and begin to deal with the problem. The record of service begins at the point in the interview where Wendy describes Miss M.'s passive reaction during the fights:

I tried to explore Wendy's feelings re: Miss M.'s newly adopted stance toward her negative behavior—feelings which began to impede the communication between Wendy and Miss M.

I said, "I guess you're pretty angry at her for that." Wendy said, "I don't care." This was said in a tone of voice indicating the antithesis of what she had said. I challenged her and said, "I think you do care very much, Wendy." Wendy said, "Ya, I do, but if she doesn't care, why should I?" Wendy then began speaking of the position Miss M. used to take prior to Christmas, when Wendy was involved in a fight. She intervened and stopped the fighting. I then asked Wendy what it feels like when Miss M. stands there and watches you in such a painful situation. Wendy responded, "She doesn't care anymore; that's what it feel like."

On the same day that Wendy had expressed her feeling that Miss M. was no longer concerned about her, Miss M. spoke to me of being "fed up" with Wendy; that she had run out of patience with this child.

Wendy was dealing with this blockage in communication in her own way, by exhibiting very negative, irresponsible behavior (i.e., fighting) in an attempt to elicit some attention from Miss M. Unlike previously, though, Wendy's attention-seeking device was now ineffective, as Miss M. had adopted a position of seeming indifference by not intervening in the fights.

The worker began with Wendy, trying to help her understand what Miss M. might be feeling. It soon became obvious to the worker that she needed to get Wendy and Miss M. talking to each other directly, since Wendy could not understand the worker's interpretations of Miss M.'s actions. She proposed a meeting:

I then asked Wendy if she has been able to talk to Miss M. about how she's feeling. "No," Wendy replied. I said, "How about all of us meeting together so that you and Miss M. can have a chance to start talking to each other?" "OK," Wendy said, "but I think she knows how I feel by the way I look at her."

The worker then met with Miss M. to discuss Wendy's feelings and to suggest a joint meeting. Her proposal was initially resisted by Miss M.; the worker, however, tried to explain how the meeting might help and also attempted to recognize the strain Wendy had been putting on Miss M.

Miss M. was reluctant about taking part in such a meeting. I realized that in light of Miss M.'s expression of feelings of total frustration and impatience with this child and her behavior, it had to be demonstrated how she as the teacher might benefit from such a session— what she would get out of it. *I attempted to respond to Miss M.'s needs and said,* "As long as Wendy is not helped to find another outlet for some of her feelings, she may continue to use the outlet she has been using—physical fighting." I then said, "This meeting may help Wendy become aware of the existence of a more acceptable outlet and one that still meets her needs—direct verbal expression of her feelings." I continued, saying, "I know, Miss M., how rough Wendy has been on you in class, but unless you both can begin to move towards each other, the situation can't be made more pleasant for you."

Miss M. agreed to the meeting. The worker tried to clarify purpose and to encourage both Wendy and Miss M. to share their feelings:

I opened it up by saying that Miss M. and myself were so pleased with their progress—

evident by her improved class behavior before Christmas, but we are all concerned as she seems to be slipping. I pointed out that Miss M. is getting pretty fed up. I went on to say that we are all meeting together to be most helpful to you because secrets between us would not serve any purpose. Wendy spoke at this point, saying, "It's OK, I told you you could tell Miss M." (the issue of Wendy's feeling that her teacher does not care). I proceeded to bring this up at the time. Miss M. responded to this, saying that she has now decided not to intervene in Wendy's fights because she does not want to restrain the release of Wendy's pent-up anxiety and frustration. Miss M. went on to say that she is concerned about Wendy. This was said without much affect. I repeated what Miss M. had said; I suppose I wanted this concern of Miss M. for Wendy to be more strongly stated....

Wendy was on the verge of tears. I pointed this out and asked what was making her so sad. She said, "I am afraid." "Of what?" I asked. Wendy said, "That I can't do it again." I told Wendy that I could understand why she feels this way—you feel so disappointed, you were trying so very hard for a while and you did beautifully and now you're back into the fighting pattern. I then said, "Fear you can't do it, Wendy, or is it more because again you feel the girls in class are against you and don't care?" Wendy said, "I know they don't care anymore." Miss M. came in at this point, saying, "The girls are fed up just as I am with the way you have been acting." Miss M. then related to Wendy the time when some of the girls were helping Miss M. prepare Christmas cookies, and at the time the girls spoke a lot of Wendy and how they wanted to help Wendy, but were getting fed up. Miss M. continued, saying, "They even asked why you couldn't bake cookies with them." Wendy was delighted—Miss M. had given Wendy something meaningful.

Both Miss M. and I told Wendy of our understanding of her fear of failing, but we stressed the reality that this fear isn't going to go away until you begin putting in the effort you put in before Christmas and then seeing the good results.

Two weeks had gone by since the meeting between Miss M., Wendy, and myself. Both Miss M. and Wendy maintained that there has not been a single incident of Wendy being involved in a fight; further, the interaction between teacher and pupil improved. In my meeting with Wendy on this date she said, "That meeting with you and my teacher made me see that Miss M. does care." Consequently Wendy's need to elicit concern from her teacher through negative behavior has diminished.

I asked Wendy what makes her feel Miss M. cares. She responded, "I can just feel it, the way she talks to me, she hugged me yesterday!"

A common problem in such work is that workers may be deceived by apparently quick solutions. The positive response was only a honeymoon period, and the worker would have been wise to prepare both Wendy and Miss M. for the inevitable backsliding. Neither Wendy nor Miss M. was able to change so easily. The worker's purpose should be to help them find ways of dealing with the problems as they occurred. Wendy still had many difficulties in her peer-group relationships, and when these resulted in a fight, Miss M. reacted as if it were a breakdown of their agreement, cutting Wendy off once again. In addition, a serious problem with a boy in the class who was also acting out and upset, called on all of Miss M.'s energy. The boy (Mike) had attempted suicide in the school, and Miss M., who had a close relationship with the youngster, had been very upset. As she gave more time to Mike, Wendy felt further rejected and began to act out again. After an incident in which Wendy was ejected from class, the worker spoke with Miss M. to try to reopen communications between the teacher and Wendy.

I approached Miss M. to prepare her for Wendy's plan to talk with her. I said, "Miss M., Wendy wants to speak with you very much about the incident last week when you told Wendy to leave class as she was refusing to work on her geography project." Miss M. responded, saying she had no energy or desire to exert any efforts in this area (meaning around Wendy).

I attempted to deal with Miss M.'s resistance by acknowledging my understanding of what she is going through right now with Mike. I said, "You know, Miss M., I can really understand how rough it has been for you having Mike in class the past few weeks—your energy and effort have been drained by him [the child who attempted suicide]." Miss M. excused herself very abruptly and asked if I could call her at home this evening.

Miss M. was not able to share her feelings with the worker and probably felt overwhelmed by them. It has been my experience in work with teachers that their sources of support and mutual aid are limited, so that they are not able to share their real feelings with each other and the supervisory staff. Very little help is available in the way of analysis of classroom interaction and the development of interactional skills for work with children. As a result, teachers who are overwhelmed by their children's problems have very little support offered other than platitudes in the lunchroom about "how tough teaching can be." If a teacher is also under personal strain, as Miss M. appeared to be, this may emerge in her work with the children. It is important that the worker concentrate on this aspect of Miss M.'s feelings:

Miss M. thanked me for calling and then began to relate to me that Wendy did approach her to talk at 3:15 as the class was lining up to leave, when one boy "accidentally" kicked Wendy's boot. Wendy lost her temper and yelled: "You lousy . . ." Miss M. told me that at this point she said to Wendy, "I guess you're not at all ready to talk." Miss M. was feeling very guilty. She spoke of realizing she has had no patience with Wendy in particular.

I attempted to lessen her guilt feelings and empathize with the pressure she has experienced around the situation with Mike. I said "I can very well understand this, as you have been under such tremendous pressure and strain with Mike in class." Miss M. began speaking of how frightening it is with him in class. Miss M. then said, "I do want to talk with Wendy." I sensed from the way she spoke she wanted some help around it.

I tried to offer Miss M. some help and suggestions around what to say to Wendy. I said, "Try and be as open and honest as possible with Wendy; tell her as you told me that you feel you have been unfair with her lately because you have been so worried about Mike and as a result have not had patience with anyone else." I said, "It would also be helpful if you point out to Wendy that there are other children in the class needing a lot of your attention, and Wendy can't demand it all the time." Miss M. said at this point, "I think you're right—I must be honest." I pointed out to Miss M. that Wendy still needs to be assured that despite this, you're still concerned about her.

I said, "Miss M., unless you and Wendy begin talking to each other, Wendy may continue to present antagonistic behavior in the class in order to get some kind of attention from you." Miss M. thanked me for my concern and for being so helpful.

Subsequent to the talk between Wendy and Miss M., Miss M. became more receptive towards Wendy and Wendy settled down in class.

However, further problems emerged during the year: Wendy was not completing assignments, and this led to a further breakdown in the classroom, eventually resulting in her suspension. The worker met with Wendy, Miss M., and Wendy's mother to help them deal with this problem area and to get Wendy back into school. Further work involved discussions with Wendy on why she continued to provoke Miss M. about schoolwork and how she might take more responsibility for what was happening. Discussion with Miss M. dealt with how she could continue to demand work from Wendy while still offering support. The eventual success of the work would depend a great deal on the strengths brought to bear by Wendy and Miss M., and the worker's efforts accordingly were directed at this aspect of the relationship.

A part of the work which may have been overlooked in this interaction concerns the direct expression of underlying anger. Miss M. was mad at Wendy but often expressed her anger indirectly. Wendy was angry with her teacher, but taboos prevented the direct expression of her feelings. The worker attempted to smooth over the anger in the relationship, probably because she herself was so angry with Miss M. In addition to showing understanding, it might have been more helpful if the worker had allowed herself to get angry at Miss M. as well. There were a number of points in the process when the worker probably felt like sitting Wendy or Miss M. down and letting them have a piece of her mind. A misconception about working as a mediator in these relationships is that the worker must always try to smooth things out. Actually, the encouragement of honest expression of underlying anger is very much a part of the mediating function. Human relations are marked by both positive and negative feelings and it is important that both be recognized if a relationship is to grow.

Work with the Hospital System

The final excerpts in this section are drawn from work in a hospital setting.

The context is a ward group set up for the purpose of improving communications between patients and the hospital staff. In the first example, the focus is on medical questions which patients have not asked their doctors. A doctor has been invited to attend. To assist in the communications, the worker explored with the patients why they seemed hesitant to ask these questions. What emerged was an admission that the hesitancy was partly due to the doctors' rushed appearance but also to the patients' fear of the answers:

Before the doctor arrived five women had gathered; two spoke only French; one understood some English. I introduced the three new members, all English-speaking, one bilingual. I asked them not to hesitate to ask the doctor any questions they might have in mind when he comes. The general consensus was that it was a good idea, since the doctors are always too busy. Mrs. David said (re: rounds), "They come around your bed, this one and that one, take a look at you, they write something down and go away." I said, "You're left there wondering." All were in agreement. Mrs. Laflamme said: "Like this morning; I was too shy to ask them, I asked the nurse, she couldn't speak French, finally the doctor came back and explained." I openly wondered why it is that patients don't ask the doctors the score in times like that? Mrs. Dupont: "We feel his time is too precious." I said, "It is you who are precious, his patients, precious to him, and I'm sure it would take less time in the long run if you asked him, and it would probably only take two minutes of his time to answer, and it would keep you from a few hours of worry and feeling worse." Just then the doctor arrived; I told him the above. He concurred, the patient shouldn't hesitate to ask; the doctor cannot know the patient's thinking. I interjected that the not asking may be because we really don't want to know. He was gracious and smiled at this. Then I said, "Now that he was here they could ask their questions." Mrs. David started re: fibroids. He answered simply and honestly: the cancer in-

cidence was low. Mrs. Driscoll was encouraged to ask. She twisted in her chair, hung down her head and said she had no questions. I wondered why she didn't. She said: "I guess I want to know and I don't want to know. I might as well take the plunge. Doctor, what are they going to do with me?" He gave a complete explanation of curettage and bleeding that they must check for cancer, and try to eliminate it as a cause. They don't operate over the weekend do they? Can't I go home for the weekend then? You can go for the day, but you *must* be back for 8 o'clock, all smiles. Mrs. Dort asked what happens if you're a little late. You lose your bed. I asked if the doctor would translate what he had already said for the ladies who had not understood. He did so. He had made a drawing. Mrs. Dort got up, asking in French re: tubal ligation, then the other two French ladies joined in re: birth control pills after curettage, etc., sexual relations, how long after surgery, etc.

In addition to discussing the specifics of medical problems, ward groups can also be used to open up communications between patients and staff about the working relationship. Staff members also need an opportunity to tell those they work with of their frustrations and concerns. They are often inhibited about doing so, feeling it is unprofessional to share their feelings. However, it is easier for clients once they understand the realities. I have found that the process of being honest with clients about the frustrations in the system often frees the system's person to hear the concerns expressed by the client more clearly. In the following illustration, a doctor attending a ward group responded to the patients' negative feedback about communications with medical staff. The patients were surprised to find the doctor also had feelings about this.

Dr. F. began talking about clinics—the position the doctor finds himself in, with long waits and perhaps never even seeing some patients properly. I remarked that it is a problem—for both patient and doctor, and this was one of the concerns that patients bring up. Dr. F. continued to explain a doctor's viewpoint of clinic and that you hope for consistency of treatment, which is no problem in a private office because the patient sees the same doctor all the time. Mr. H. said that even that is a problem because the doctor prescribing medication and treatment goes away and another doctor replacing him prescribes something totally different. Dr. F. explained about clinic records and importance of doctor's notations. He continued discussing clinics at length and said that the problem in medical clinics was that there were too many patients to see and no time to talk with them. Mr. L. said that was exactly the problem. Dr. F. said that doctors have pride, are human beings, too, and like to do a good job. Mr. L. said that Dr. F. was dedicated, but some of the other young doctors he met were not. I remarked that it sounded like all of us—doctor and patients—talked about the need to get back to the general practitioner relationship of one doctor treating a patient all the time.

In another illustration, nurses at a ward group used the worker's invitation to share some of their frustrations:

Mr. L. talked about someone in his room who always complained and wanted to see his doctor, but when the doctor was there, the patient wasn't. I said it's hard enough to have to be here but having to put up with people you would not normally put up with makes it more difficult. He said, "It does." Mr. L. brought up the night shift staff being noisy and how hard it is to sleep; he said they seemed to be divided into cliques and always bickering between the two. Nurse 2 said that was true that the shift was like that; she rolled her eyes. I asked if she worked on it at times. She said "yes," but she didn't like it for that reason. I said that I imagined it would be hard for anyone to work under those conditions. Mr. L. asked why they have to be so noisy. Nurse 2 said that the staff had jobs to do and had to do them. I said it sounded as if the

nurses take as dim a view of some of the tasks as the patients do. Nurse 2 said, "You're not kidding—but we have to do them."

She used one example of giving a needle. She said sometimes we have to wake a patient up from his sleep to give him a needle, well, we don't like to do that. Silence. I said I bet the patient doesn't like receiving it. One patient said maybe that's why we sometimes get needles that hurt, because you don't like to do it, you jab it in and get it over with, and we get mad because we were wakened for a needle which hurt. I said, "It sounds like a vicious circle. Nurse has to give patient something she doesn't like doing, so becomes a bit angry. Patient doesn't like it either and is annoyed, he senses nurse's anger and he also gets angry and thus becomes an uncooperative patient." I said that it must be difficult for all concerned because the nurses have to maintain a professional role, which means they are not allowed to let loose and verbalize true feelings, and the patient is trying as always to be the "ideal patient." One patient said, "When you're sick, a lot of little things can get on your nerves faster than when you're well."

Nurse 1 said, "Another example is giving out juice. We're not supposed to do that, but we're made to because no one else will. I feel that if we have time to do it, that's great, we get to chat with patients, but half of the time we don't have time."

Mr. E. said, "That sounds awful. Why do nurses have to do it?" Nurse 2 said, "Because the ward aides are too lazy to. I don't mind doing it if I have time, but to be made to feel obliged to is stupid. If I wanted to push juice, I wouldn't have become a nurse—I would have been a ward aide, which I was for some time. I didn't go to school to do the same thing." I said I imagined it would be pretty frustrating and annoying. Nurse 1 said, "Yes, and while we're pushing juice, we feel guilty that patients aren't getting proper nursing care because we don't have time to practice what we're trained for." She sat rigid in her seat. I said that she looked like she could explode right now. She took a deep breath and smiled. Mr. E., Mr. N., and Mr. L. supported the nurses saying that they're put in unsatisfactory predicaments. Mr. B. said he found the nursing care excellent. I asked the patients how they felt about hearing what the nurses had to say. They looked stumped. I asked if they were surprised with what they heard. They said they were pleased to hear what the nurses had to say and they could understand how they felt.

Evaluating the sessions, the nurses felt it was the best group meeting they had attended. They felt they could understand the patients' feelings better and that, perhaps, the patients could understand theirs as well.

In this final example from a hospital setting, we see the classic conflict between professionals over "who owns the client." As the worker comes to grips with her feelings of anger towards a psychiatrist, and works to clarify her role, in her own mind and with her colleagues, she begins to play a more effective third-force role.

Problem and How It Came to My Attention. Cynthie is a 23-year-old woman, diagnosed schizophrenic, who I worked with intermittently over a course of six months. Her medical record revealed no less than eleven psychiatric admissions since the age of fourteen, three of these being at this hospital. During the time I knew her she had in fact been discharged and readmitted to our ward twice, with a serious suicide attempt in between. To say the least, the ward staff considered Cynthie to be a chronic patient. It seemed clear that they had pretty well given up on her. They felt discouraged, exasperated and disillusioned with what they interpreted as her lack of motivation, her lack of compliance to treatment (specifically, medication) and her recurrent readmissions. In my view, Cynthie had also taken on much of *their* discouragement and pessimism which compounded her already hopeless and depressed view of her life.

My task, in the narrowest sense, was to find a suitable placement for Cynthie upon discharge. However, as time progressed, I soon realized that placement was the least of Cynthie's problems. I became aware that if I was to be of any help to her at all, it would be necessary for me to re-define the problem as follows: First, by virtue of her admisson to hospital, Cynthie had been thrown into a complex maze of hospital life. Within six months, she had been subjected to no less than three psychiatrists, two psychiatrists-in-training, two psychologists, four primary nurses, an agency social worker, the ward social worker, three boarding home co-ordinators, two day-care program co-ordinators, two occupational therapists, two student nurses and myself. She had been spared being assigned to medical students only because her "case" was considered chronic and thus not very interesting from a psychiatric point of view. Here was a multilayered hierachy of staff, difficult for even the well-equipped person to deal with, let alone a frightened, depressed, sometimes-psychotic and definitely over-medicated woman like Cynthie. Second, two further issues became crucial: One being Cynthie's medication (and her refusal to take it) and the other being Cynthie's plea (revealed to me in an interview with her) that, and I quote, "I just want to be a normal human being."

Over and above the placement problem, my task became at least threefold: First, to help Cynthie negotiate this complex hospital system to her advantage; a system whose representatives were making demands of her (e.g., insistence on medication) that Cynthie saw as being incompatible with her goal of becoming "normal." Second, to help the system reach past their image of Cynthie as a chronic, amotivated and hopeless patient. Third, to persist in my efforts to reach out to both these "clients": to Cynthie, on the one hand, who much of the time was so withdrawn, depressed and uncommunicative, that it was very difficult for me to reach her; and to the staff, on the other hand, often resistant and rigid in their view of Cynthie as "sick" and definitely short of "normal." The following record of service is not comprehensive. It simply highlights some of my attempts and many of my misses in my effort to stand as a buffer between Cynthie and the system.

Early Attempts to Reach for Cynthie's Feelings. Our first few meetings revealed an image of Cynthie not unlike the one described in her chart: depressed, withdrawn, rigid-in-posture and almost mute. She rarely spoke, and when she did, she answered my questions with one or two words at best. I entered her room, having *tuned in* to her possible concerns, or so I thought. I asked if I could talk with her. No response. I sat beside her, gave a brief introduction, and *stated my purpose:* "Cynthie, I'm the social work student. I'll be helping you find a place to stay when you leave the hospital." (My sense of role was not yet clear.) Silence. "Have you thought about where you might live?" Long silence, not even looking at me. (I'm missing the boat here, I thought. Probably the hospital's concern, not hers.) "I'm sorry, Cynthie, I guess a place to stay is the least of your worries right now." No response. I continued, "I know it's been scary for you, being in hospital." No response, but now looking at me, although rather vacantly. *I reached, rather hesitantly, for the taboo issue:* "I know about Jean-Paul too, Cynthie, and I'm so sorry." (Three weeks prior to my arrival on the ward, Cynthie had been abruptly informed by a social worker that her four-year-old son, Jean-Paul, had been permanently taken into care. The loss of her son had compounded Cynthie's anxiety and depression and had precipitated two solid weeks of pacing up and down the ward's corridors, screaming and wailing, "I want my son back" and prostrating herself on the corridor floors, refusing to move, particularly when offered medication.) I felt torn: reluctant, on the one hand, to broach the subject of Jean-Paul knowing that the ward staff discouraged Cynthie's outbursts and fearing that I would precipitate one; and, on the other hand, feeling she had little opportunity to express her grief. There was no outburst. (I admit to having felt relieved about that.) Just a long silence and then, looking at me, she simply said, "Can I have my son back?" She looked so sad. I didn't know what to say. "No, Cynthie, you can't." It sounded so blunt. "I'm sorry," I said ... Long pause ... *I shared my feeling and made an offer:* "I feel sad too, Cynthie ... Do you want to talk about Jean-

Paul?" No response. Long pause. "Or maybe you'd like to be alone now?" Another long pause. Finally she said, "I'm okay, I'll be okay." I reassured her that I wanted to talk to her about Jean-Paul, if that's what she wanted. Long pause. "Perhaps tomorrow then," I said.

Making Demands for Work. In later meetings with Cynthie she continued to show little response. Her affect was blunted, her face was mask-like and vacant. Occasionally she would say "I'm sad," sometimes "I'm okay." I continued making efforts to *put her feelings into words,* to *reach inside of silences* (of which there were many) largely to no avail. I felt I was getting nowhere. Finally, I said, "I feel frustrated, Cynthie. I don't know what you're thinking. I don't know what you're feeling. I'd like to help you, Cynthie, but if you never talk to me I don't know how I can." Long silence. What was to come showed me a side of Cynthie I hadn't yet seen; one I would later convey to her psychiatrist on her behalf. "I just want to be a normal human being," she said. Now *I* was silent. Actually, I was floored. She said it without emotion. It sounded so pathetic and tragic. And not much to ask for, really. The least she deserved. I felt like saying, you're in the wrong place for that, Cynthie. (My resentment towards her treatment was surfacing.) But I didn't want to cut her off from the help she might get here. I believed, perhaps naively, that this system *could* help her be normal. I sensed her feelings of being stuck and overwhelmed. Or maybe these were my own feelings. *I partialized her concern:* "It's just hard sometimes to know where to start," I said. *I asked for clarification:* "What would normal mean to you, Cynthie?" to which she replied rather solidly, "No more psychiatrists, no more mental hospitals, no more medication."

Identifying with Both Cynthie and Her Doctor. It was unlikely I could help her negotiate these goals within the context of this system. But perhaps in some small way, I wanted her to know that there *was* a next step. I know Cynthie had become less and less compliant to taking her meds—a going concern for the staff. Having experienced a round of anti-depressants myself at one time, I recalled my own feelings: feeling numb, deadened, unreal, not myself, slowed down, too numb to talk or care. In short, not normal. I wondered if Cynthie was feeling the same way. *I shared this experience and reached for her feedback.* Long pause. "The pills make me crazy," she said. "I'm scared . . . They're trying to kill my brain. They're killing my brain." *I acknowledged her fear* and tried, with difficulty *to be with her and the system at the same time:* "The side effects *are* scary, Cynthie—I had them too—Like you can't control you own body—But the doctor gives you the pills to help you, not to kill you—Remember how you felt before?" I hoped to help Cynthie see that the pills *had* helped. She said, "Before, I thought I was Jesus. I thought demons were crawling on my body. I covered my body in paint. I felt crazy." Cynthie was unable to talk to her doctor about her fear of the pills. We agreed that I would talk to her doctor and that I would help her talk to him.

Helping Cynthie's Doctor to Understand Her Feelings. First, some background: My first encounters with Dr. X were something short of positive. I found him patronizing and condescending and wondered if Cynthie experienced him in a similar way. He was the patriarch on the ward, with the nurses, all women, seemingly willing to jump at his every command. Everyone knew their place and although there were resentments, these were never directly expressed (including my own).

From the moment I was introduced as the social work student, I sensed he had written me off as brainless. He rarely missed a chance to "put in a dig." Like the time in rounds, when we were discussing Tourette's (a central nervous system disorder). I'd studied Tourette's and knew of its treatment. To which Dr. X asked, "Oh, did you see that on Quincy, or something?" I rose to the bait, responding defensively, "No, actually, Dr. X. I read it in Harrison's" (a well-known and standard textbook in Internal Medicine). That shut him up. I had won the point, but not the war.

Dr. X insisted on seeing me as "the placement person." Therapy, as he called it, was psychiatry's domain. It frustrated him, he said, that "everyone around here wants to do therapy." He actually approached me one time

while I was talking with Cynthie in her room and demanded to know what we were talking about. I was beginning to wonder who was more paranoid, patient or doctor? Dr. X's argument was that the only one qualified to understand the patients' "complete clinical picture" was the psychiatrist. And one could not understand the so-called complete clinical picture, according to Dr. X, without medical training, of course. It started looking like a contest of "Who knows the patient best?"

It also really bothered me that Cynthie's case was always presented last or close to last in Dr. X's rounds. This indicated to me the degree of Cynthie's interest or importance to him. Or maybe his level of frustration. The focus rarely shifted from diagnostic issues and from endless discussions about which medication and in what dosage to use. Cynthie's feelings were always overlooked.

In retrospect, two things were clear: First, I had let my resentment toward Dr. X get in the way on any real work with him. I had written him off as a "jerk" and *refused to reach for his feelings,* convincing myself that he probably had very few. Second, *I missed every opportunity to clarify my role* (mostly because I wasn't yet clear on what that role was). If I didn't want to be seen simply as a "placement person," it would be my responsibility to tell Dr. X exactly how I could help. Cynthie's medication problem gave me this chance, as the following dialogue shows.

I approached Dr. X and asked if he had a few minutes to talk with me about Cynthie. "I'm still working on a placement for her," I said reminding him. "You know, I guess I've never said it this way (*in an attempt to clarify my role*), but I also think an important part of my work with Cynthie is to help *you* help her and that's why I need to talk to you." *Crediting his work* I continued, "I know how hard you've been working to stabilize Cynthie on her medication," then *empathizing with his situation,* "and how frustrating it must be for you and for the nurses with Cynthie acting out all the time and refusing her pills." I had his full attention. "Well, that's true," he said, "it isn't easy." *Sharing my own experience* I said, "I find it hard to reach her at the best of times too, but while I was talking to her today she said some incredible things I thought you should know about . . . about not taking her pills." "Oh, like what?" he asked. "Well, this probably won't surprise you, but she's really scared. She's scared of taking her pills. And do you know why? (He shook his head to say no) She thinks we're trying to kill her brain." "Did she say that?" he asked. "Yes, she did . . . *I* wouldn't take them either, if I thought that, would *you?*" "Obviously not," he said. I continued, "She also said—and this was really sad— that all she wants is to be a normal human being. Do you think she'd feel more normal without side effects? I was wondering if you thought she might be toxic?" "Well, I think you have a point. I'll check into it today," he said, "and we'll get this cleared up." I suggested a three-way meeting between Dr. X, Cynthie, and myself. "I've had *some* luck getting her to talk about her medication," I said, "but I think she needs some reassurance from you." He agreed.

Ignoring the Lurking Negative and Paying for It Later. All the while, I continued to look for a suitable placement for Cynthie. I soon came to realize that Cynthie's "private trouble" was indeed a "public issue": There was a serious shortage of suitable homes for women like Cynthie and those that did exist had incredible waiting lists. Finally, en route to a home that was willing to take her, Cynthie announced to me, "I want to live with Jurgen (her ex-husband)." Oh no, I thought, I don't want to hear this, here we go again: Cynthie had bounced back and forth from Jurgen to hospital to Jurgen to hospital. At one point, Jurgen even had Cynthie prostituting herself. I felt she needed a supportive environment, some stability in her life . . . something she'd never had. "Cynthie," I said, "I can't force you to go to the boarding home, but I really think you should give it a try." *What I failed to do* was reach for her feelings. She was probably scared stiff. Living in the boarding home was *my agenda, not hers*. Besides, what gave *me* the right to make that decision for *her* anyway? Five days later Cynthie was back in hospital having stabbed herself in the abdomen with a kitchen knife at the boarding home,

missing all her vital organs, thank God. I came away feeling that I had set her up for failure. **Sabotaged by the System.** The final blow came in early February. Cynthie, it had been decided, would be transferred to another hospital. "She's too chronic for our ward," announced Dr. X. "She needs long-term care, so I'm transferring her. And *I've* decided that she's not to be told." The orders were written in the chart, just like that. I was furious and *shared my feelings* with Dr. X: "I can't understand the transfer, Dr. X (I guess I had rationalized that perhaps *they* could help her) *but* not preparing her for it! I think that's pretty crummy! She deserves at least that, don't you think?" "Look, I know it seems crummy," he started. I interrupted, "It doesn't *seem* crummy, it *is* crummy." He went on, "Look, in my opinion, she's a serious suicide risk, and if she's told now, she'll probably elope and kill herself. I can't and won't risk that." "I see your dilemma," I said, "but I can't agree with your decision. I think you're shortchanging Cynthie." (Actually, *I* also felt shortchanged and ripped off. Without choice, my ability to help her had been cut off.) Dr. X and I agreed to disagree.

I was on the ward when they came to get Cynthie. She cried when they told her. Within ten minutes, she was gone. I did manage to stop her in the hall on her way out. I felt like a traitor. I gave her a hug. "I'm sorry you're going, Cynthie," I said. "It's okay," she said to me exactly as she had many times before. And off she went.

Where It Stands Now. Cynthie is out of the hospital and back with her parents, in another city. Fran, the student nurse who was also working with Cynthie, took it upon herself to phone Cynthie's parents. Up until now they had been unsupportive and had "written Cynthie off." Fran was "severely reprimanded" by her nursing supervisor for having acted in an unprofessional way and for putting her own needs ahead of Cynthie's. I thought what Fran did was great, and surprisingly so did Dr. X.

Specific Next Steps. 1. To continue "working on" Dr. X. I think he has potential.

If this worker is going to be able to tap the "potential" she sees in Dr. X, she will have to tune in to the implications of patient suicides in a psychiatric setting. The strong reactions of the system to Cynthie's suicide attempt can be viewed as a signal of serious, unresolved issues in this area. It is not unusual for helping systems to be very unhelpful to their own staff members at times of stress. Instead of providing support through some form of mutual aid, the defensiveness in the system is heightened by a crisis and can result in an effort to place blame. In Chapter 17 I will explore ways in which a worker can move from a specific example, such as this case, to trying to deal with the underlying problem in the system.

Summary

Helping clients to negotiate systems is a complex but important process. The worker has to be clear about personal feelings in entering the exchange and avoid overidentifying with the client versus the system. Many of the helping skills are critical in working with staff as one tries to improve the communications between clients and the system. Anger can be very much a part of these communications, and the worker has to resist the tendency to "cool out" the exchanges because of fears about the expression of negative feelings. Finally, workers can be helpful in making sure that both clients and systems' representatives have the opportunity to talk to each other about their feelings so that the interaction is a two-way process. Thus far, most of the examples have included system representatives who have appeared to be open to the worker's offer of help. With more or less resistance, most of the teachers, doctors, and nurses described were respon-

sive. What happens if workers try their best and the system does not respond? What if one cannot get the teacher to the meeting and the doctor won't even talk to the worker? In those situations where workers have tried their best and the system appears immovable, then confrontation and social pressure become part of the mediation process. As the next section suggests, these may be necessary steps essential to "unfreezing" the system, as is illustrated in the next section.

CONFRONTATION, SOCIAL PRESSURE, AND ADVOCACY

If we think of agencies and institutions as social systems, employing the organic model used in Chapter 13 to describe the group, then some of the processes observed in small groups may also apply to larger systems. One such idea is Lewin's description of systems as maintaining a "quasi-stationary equilibrium" in which "customs" and "social habits" create an "inner resistance" to change.[3] This resistance to change is found in the individual, the family, the group, the community, agencies, and institutions. In the model presented thus far, the worker has endeavored to open up communications between clients and relevant systems in order to help overcome the obstacles to the inherent common ground (e.g., the individual and the group). The worker has at all times been reaching for the desire for change of both the client and the system. However, because of the inherent forces against change, systems and their representatives do not always respond with a willingness to deal with the obstacles. Even with a worker who is understanding of the system's problems and who makes every effort to influence the system in a positive manner, there may be no progress. In such situations the use of confrontation and social pressure is required. Some additional force is needed to overcome the system's resistance to change and to bring to its attention the need to respond in new ways to the client's needs. This additional force upsets the "quasi-stationary equilibrium" and makes the system more open to change. This argument is not unlike ideas of crisis theory which suggest that individuals and families are most open to change when a crisis makes maintenance of a situation untenable. Under conditions where negotiation has failed or has not even been given a chance, something is needed to upset the dysfunctional equilibrium. The resistance part of the system's ambivalence is so strong, it dominates the interaction. In the remainder of this chapter, I describe two examples where this proved necessary. In the first, a worker helped a group of welfare mothers deal with an administrator of a public housing project who refused to meet with them. In the second, a worker acted as an advocate for an overwhelmed client facing a housing crisis without receiving help from housing agencies.

Welfare Mothers and the Housing Agency

The group was established by the state welfare agency to explore the problems presented by A.D.C. (Aid to Dependent Children) families and to provide help with these problems when necessary. Seven women, ages twenty-three to forty-five, made up the group's membership. Discussion during the group's second session indicated that their problems with the housing authority and the housing project in which they all lived were central concerns. Examples of these concerns are included in the following record excerpt from that meeting:

MRS. B.: I don't have any complaint about the building or rent, but if we get more money from welfare for any reason, they [Housing Authority] raise our rent. But if our checks are reduced, they say they can't break our lease to reduce the rent.

MRS. M.: They also make us pay for things that people not on welfare do not have to pay for.

WORKER: Like what?

MRS. S.: During the summer a man from the gas company came and put a tube on my stove so that I could move the stove, and the Housing Authority sent me a bill for $26.00.

WORKER: Did you call the gas company for repairs on your stove?

MRS. S.: No, he just came.

WORKER: Did you discuss this with the office?

MRS. M.: That doesn't do any good.

MRS. S.: I told them I couldn't pay the bill because I didn't have the money. They said I broke the pipe, so I had to pay the bill or move. So I paid it. But I didn't break any pipe.

MRS. S.B.: Last summer the children were playing in the court and broke four windows in my apartment, and I had to pay for them. I called the office when they were broken and told them how they were broken, but I had to pay for them anyway.

MRS. S.: There is no such thing as wear and tear items that most landlords have to replace for tenants when you live in the project.

MRS. B.: That's what they tell us.

MRS. M.S.: If they come into your apartment and see the shades are worn, we have to pay for them.

WORKER: Do you know of any repairs or replacements that the Welfare Board will pay for?

MRS. S.: Yes, Miss D. told us to send in these bills and the welfare would pay for plumbing, shades, oven doors, and things like that.

WORKER: What does your lease say that the Housing Authority is responsible for replacing or repairing?

MRS. S.: It has all don'ts on the back and nothing else.

MRS. M.: They make us pay for everything, and I don't think this is fair.

WORKER: Do you have a tenants' group that takes complaints to the office?

MRS. S.: Yes, but they [Housing Authority] choose the officers, and they don't do anything about the complaints. They call us trouble makers and try to keep us out of meetings. Group all agreed.

WORKER: Would you like for me to invite Mr. M. [housing project manager] to one of our meetings so that you could find out just what the Housing Authority is responsible for and what your responsibilities are?

MRS. M.: It won't do any good. He's great for listening and taking no action on complaints.

MRS. S.: Yes, let's ask him. But I don't think he'll come.

WORKER: Do you want him to come, or not?

Group all indicated yes.

As they discussed their relationship to the housing project, they found they shared many of the same complaints. Strength in numbers made them believe some change might be possible in spite of their past experiences. In her enthusiasm for moving the work forward, the worker missed the underlying fears and doubts only hinted at in the conversation. If it were going to be so easy to take on the housing project, why had they not done so before? At the next session, the worker corrected this and began by trying to determine if the housing issue was still the central concern. It is important to note that the worker has not taken it upon herself to determine which issues the group members should tackle. A common error is for workers to determine, in advance, what issues citizens should be concerned about. They see their work then involving the use of direct or indirect influence to convince the members to act on the hidden agenda. Rather, the driving force for the work must emerge from

the client's sense of urgency. The encounter may be a rough one, and the clients need to feel a commitment to the issue to carry them through. At the next meeting, their conversation reflected some of the fears and doubts which have occurred to them during the week. The silences hint at these feelings:

Worker redefined purpose of the group and gave brief summary of the concerns expressed in last three meetings before the holidays to give group some sort of perspective as to where the group was. The group was asked on what topic they would like to focus their attention.

The group agreed that their problems with the Housing Authority needed immediate attention (Fourteen welfare checks had been stolen from the mail boxes.)

WORKER: I called Mr. M.'s office and his secretary said that she thought Mr. M. would be willing to meet with the group. Maybe we should use this time to plan for the meeting with him. Make a list of questions you want to ask and what approach to use.

MRS. McI.: I would like to know if we can have more secure mail boxes or a different type of lock on them.

MRS. M.: Anybody could open these boxes—even a child with a stick or nail file.

MRS. K.: I'm there when the mailman comes, so no one gets my check.

MRS. M.: I can't sit by the box and wait for the man. I've got other things to do.

MRS. S.: Why should we have to wait? If the boxes were better, this would not be a problem.

MRS. McI.: I've complained about those boxes, but they [Housing Authority] say we talk too much about our business. He said the thieves know who gets the most money and when the checks come.

MRS. S.: That's common knowledge that the checks come on the first.

MRS. K.: I'd never tell anyone I was on welfare.

MRS. S.: People assume that you are on welfare if you live in the project.

MRS. I.S.: Why can't the police be there on

check day? Some one broke into my box, and I had to pay $2.50 for it.

MRS. McI.: That's right. They [Housing Authority] say we are responsible for the boxes whether we break them or not.

MRS. S.: That's not fair. Why should we have to pay for something we did not do?

MRS. McI.: Most people are afraid to call the police.

MRS. M.: You're right. You never know what those people [drug addicts] will do to you or your children.

MRS. McI.: You remember when that brick was thrown through my window? It was because I called the office [Housing Authority] about those big boys hanging out in the halls.

MRS. M.: They can sure make it bad for you.

MRS. McI.: The other tenants call you a trouble maker if you complain about noise or dirty halls or anything like that.

MRS. S.: I complain to the office all the time, not that it does any good. I don't care what the other tenants think. I've got my family to look out for.

MISS B.: That's right and look what happened to you last summer.
Laughter from the group.

LEADER: What happened, Mrs. S.?

MRS. S.: There were a lot of older boys outside my door making noise. I asked them to leave because my mother was sick, but they wouldn't do it. so I called the office. The police made them move, but they came back and turned the fire hose on and flooded my apartment.
Silence.

MRS. W.: They'll get you all right.
Group agreed.

The worker sensed the fear in the silence but did not reach for it. Workers in these situations are sometimes afraid to acknowledge underlying feelings of fear and ambivalence. One worker told me, "If I reach for it, I might get it, and then they would be so scared they would back out." This view underestimates the strength of people to face difficult and

frightening tasks when they have a stake in the proceedings. Rather than frightening the group members off, the acknowledgment of the fears may provide the added strength needed to make the *second* decision about the confrontation. The first decision to act for their rights was one made in the heat of the exchange of complaints. The second decision, the real one, must be made *after* the members have had a chance to react to their own bold steps. They must reflect on the risks involved and feel the fear that is associated with an action such as this. Workers who do not pay attention to helping clients with these feelings often find that when the crunch comes, clients are not ready to take the next step. It is then that a worker has to take over for the clients, become the spokesperson in a confrontation for example, when, with more help, the clients might have handled the problem themselves. In this group, the housing manager's refusal to come to the meeting and a threat against one of the members by a local welfare rights group brings the issue to a head:

Plans had been made for Mr. M., manager of the Housing Authority, to attend this meeting. Worker told of her meeting with Mr. M. and his refusal to come to the group's meeting. A general attitude of pessimism, disappointment, and "I told you so" was expressed by all members.

MRS. M.: I think we should go over his head, since he refused to come.
All agreed.

MRS. S.: Let's talk to Commissioner L. He is black and just recently appointed to the Housing Authority Board.
All agreed.

MRS. M.: I told you, Mrs. P., that he would not come. He does not care about us. None of them do.
At this point Mrs. K. came in looking upset. She apologized for being late and stated that she started not to come at all.

WORKER: I'd rather you be late than not come at all.

MRS. S.: What's the matter, B.—is R. [son] all right?

MRS. K.: He's all right, that's not it.

MRS. M.: Don't you feel all right?

MRS. K.: (Silent for a few minutes.)

WORKER: If you'd rather not discuss it, we'll go on to our discussion about the Housing Authority.

MRS. K.: No, I'll tell you.

She then explained in detail how some members of the Welfare Rights Group had come to her apartment and accused her of starting trouble with the people in the project by being in this group and that she should get out. She denied the charges but stated that she was upset when they left and was worried whether or not they would cause trouble for her because of her participation in the group. She stated that this morning she got mad with herself for letting them boss her around so she got dressed and came to the meeting.

MRS. M.: How can they cause trouble for you? They don't have any power.

MRS. S.: How did they know you belonged to this group?

MRS. K.: I don't know. I didn't know any of the people. I've seen two of them who live in my building. I don't bother anyone. I stay to myself and mind my own business.

WORKER: Were any of you approached by this group? All said no. (Two of the five present belong to the Welfare Rights Group.)

MRS. M.: Have they bothered you any more?

MRS. K.: I don't really know. I had two slips in my box to come to the office [Housing Authority]. The lady under me complained that I let water run down her walls from my apartment.

MRS. S.: I remember your telling me about that.

MRS. K.: I knocked over the pile of scrub water and it went through the holes between the radiator pipes. I said I was sorry, that it was an accident.

MRS. M.: They [Housing Authority] should close up the holes anyway.

MRS. K.: The other was that my son made too much noise.

WORKER: Have you received complaints before these?

MRS. K.: No.

GROUP: Silence (long).

This time, the worker had strategized to reach into the silence and explore the group members' feelings and ask them to face the second decision.

WORKER: I believe that this has troubled all of you and I can understand your concern. Let's take a few minutes and think about the group and your participation in it. How do you feel about it? Are you getting anything from the group?

Silence.

MRS. K.: I've been thinking about it a lot. I'm not going to let people tell me what to do. I don't really know what I'm getting from being here. I like to come and I've been able to meet some new people. I think I understand your agency better.

MRS. I.S.: You see, Mrs. P., people are afraid of reprisals. I'm older so they don't bother me. I get a lot out of these meetings. Things are clearer to me. And you helped me with those bills from the Housing Authority. Besides, this gives me a chance to get out.

MRS. D.S.: I've learned a lot. I think my attitude about the caseworkers has changed. I know now that they are not all bad, and it's my responsibility to see that they know what my family needs. Certain things that I did not know about came up and other policies were explained to me. I don't feel sorry for myself anymore because I see other people's problems are worse than mine.

MRS. M.: I like coming here; a lot of things that were on my mind about welfare are clear to me now. You have helped me a lot. Besides if we can get somewhere with the Housing Authority about our complaints, that alone will be a great deal.

MRS. K.: I've learned a lot about welfare, too, that I did not know before. I enjoy the group and I'm going to keep coming. It's too bad more people don't come. It makes me mad to know that they will benefit from all our hard work.

GROUP: That's the truth.

WORKER: Then I take it that you want to go on?

All agreed.

WORKER: I'll follow through and will let you know before the meeting if we will have a guest.

After contact was made with the city commissioners, the project manager, Mr. M., changed his mind about meeting with the group. The group members found that if they understood the political system, they could use it by applying pressure in the right places. Decisions concerning public housing are political in nature, and as long as there are no public complaints, problems can be ignored. Using the political power system as a tool for citizens is an important step for change. All too often the poor and repressed groups have given up hope of trying to deal with the "system." The "you can't fight city hall" attitude is dominant, leading citizens to give up on the institutions, structures and agencies established to meet their needs. The worker must convey the idea that there is always a next step. After the worker clarified the purpose of the meeting with Mr. M., the group members began their confrontation:

MRS. S.: I'd like to know what the Housing Authority considers wear and tear items. I don't think I should have to pay for shades that are worn when I came into my apartment or if they have been hanging for five years.

MR. M.: If the shades are worn when an apartment is vacant, we replace the shades. All apartments are in good order when you people move in.

GROUP: (All disagreed.)

MR. M.: When you move in, you sign a statement that everything is in good order. If you don't agree, don't sign it.

MRS. S.: I wrote on the list that the shades were worn. You replaced them, but you charged me for them. Ask Mrs. P. She gave me the money for them.

MR. M.: You should not have been charged for those shades.

MRS. McI.: You see, that's what we are complaining about. We don't know what we should and should not pay for. Your men make us pay for everything. Even if we disagree, you take their word for it.

GROUP: That's right.

MR. M.: You should come to me when you feel you are being charged unjustly.

GROUP: Laughter.

MRS. S.: You're never there, and no action is taken if we leave a message.

GROUP: (Agreement.)

As the meeting proceeded, the manager expressed his feelings about the tenants. It became clear that he had a stereotyped view of the tenants derived from those who had damaged property and not maintained their apartments:

MR. M.: The problem is that you people don't take care of your apartment. You let your kids wreck the place because you don't own it. You've got a responsibility, too, you know.

MRS. McI.: I resent that. Most of us keep our places clean. I know there are some people who don't care, but why should we have to suffer?

MR. M.: We clean the grounds, make repairs, paint the halls every four years. It's the tenants' responsibility to care for the upkeep of their agreements.

MRS. B.: Gin bottles, beer cans, urine, etc., stay in the halls for days, and your men don't clean it away.

MR. M.: Call me. I'll see that it gets done.

MRS. McI.: What about mail boxes? Can't we have better boxes with pick-proof locks?

Our checks are always stolen and boxes broken into, and we have to pay for them.

MR. M.: There's no such thing as a pickproof lock. I know the trouble you are having with your checks, and I'm sorry, but if we assume cost, then you people will break in every time you lose your key.

MRS. McI.: I disagree. I don't think the tenants would deliberately break into boxes.

MR. M.: They do and will do it more often if I change that rule.

When the members felt they could not get past the defensiveness of the manager, they again resorted to political pressure which had worked the first time. The manager responded by inquiring why they had not brought their complaints to him, and the issue of retribution was out in the open. The worker intervened to try to help the manager see that the residents were motivated to improve the living situation:

MRS. S.: Who makes appointments to the Housing Authority?

MR. M.: The city commissioners make the appointments.

MRS. S.: Can one of us go the commissioners to let them know our problems?

MR. M.: My board meets once a month. It's open to the public. The board is autonomous. It sets its own rules within the federal guidelines. We will listen to your complaints.

MRS. S.: We want them to take some action, too.

GROUP: (Agreed.)

MRS. M.: We don't feel that the building representatives represent us. I did not know about the elections of officers.

MR. M.: You were all told about the meeting and I know it.

GROUP: (Disagrees.)

MRS. McI.: (Member of one of the committees) Maybe the representatives do not take the time to tell all the people in his building.

MRS. S.: That man in my building does not represent me. He's not qualified, besides he does not care about us.

MR. M.: You people have lots of complaints, but you never bring them to the office.

MRS. McI.: Most people don't complain because they are afraid of trouble from the office.

MR. M.: We have not put anyone out because of your making complaints. I don't see why you should be afraid. There's no reason for it.

WORKER: What the group is saying is that the office has ways to put pressure on these people. The fear is here and cannot be changed overnight. These people are not here to attack you personally but the people who make these unjust rules. These people are motivated—that's why they are here. They want to improve their living circumstances. It's up to you and your board to help them.

MR. M.: If the tenants think the representatives do not meet their approval, then I'll see to it that new elections are held.

MRS. McI.: The people don't feel that you are willing to meet with them. They don't feel that you are interested.

MR. M.: I'll do what I can and take your complaints to the board. If you like, you may form your own committee.

MRS. S.: We will be at your next meeting. The meeting had to be called to an end, as it had run forty-five minutes over the scheduled time.

The housing manager's reaction to the confrontation was predictable—inspections were suddenly ordered for all apartments. At the next meeting, the worker again attempted to explore the members' feelings about the reactions to their assertive behavior:

MRS. S.: Everybody's talking about it [Group's meeting with Mr. M.] in the office. The janitor who came to inspect my apartment got mad because I refused to sign the inspection form. I told him why and he asked who had I been talking to, Mrs. P. [the worker]?

GROUP: (Laughter.)

MRS. B.: They think we are wrong. He [maintenance man] said that there were over

$6,000.00 in repairs this year in the projects and that we were responsible for them.

MRS. K.: Andy [maintenance man] said it's about time someone spoke up.

MRS. K.: They blame us for the inspection because they have not been inspecting apartments.

GROUP: (All agreed.)

MRS. S.: I knew Mr. M. would do something to get back at us.

GROUP: (All agreed.)

LEADER: Well, how do you feel about the things that are happening to you?

MRS. S.: I don't mind. I knew he would do something to get back at us. But with the agency (welfare) behind us he knows he cannot get away with these things anymore.

MRS. B.: I heard they were inspecting the apartments so I was ready for them. My apartment was really clean and in order.

MRS. M.: They [Housing Authority] have not inspected our apartments in two years or more. Why now?

GROUP: (Agreement. They seemed to make light of the situation and seemed to take it as a joke.)

WORKER: But you still have not told me how you feel about all this, the criticism and pressure from the Housing Authority and your friends and neighbors.

MRS. B.: I don't mind, something had to be done, so we are doing it.

MRS. S.: I don't mind either being the scapegoat. I think we can still do a lot more. We will benefit if they [Housing Authority] approve some of our requests as well as those people who call us trouble makers. It's for them too, not just us.

MRS. K.: The only thing I did not like was their going into my apartment when I was not home.

GROUP: (All agreed.)

WORKER: Were you notified of the inspection?

GROUP: No.

MRS. S.: They [Housing Authority] can come into your apartment anytime they want. It's in the lease as long as it's a reasonable hour.

MRS. K.: I still don't want them walking into my place.

WORKER: Were nonwelfare tenants' apartments inspected also?

GROUP: Yes.

MRS. K.: They wouldn't like it if it was their place.

MRS. M.: They did not miss a thing. We even had to pay for tassels on the shades and missing screws.

WORKER: In other words, they went over your apartment with a fine-tooth comb.

GROUP: (Laughter, agreement.)

MRS. B.: They even took the screens out of the windows to be cleaned and fixed. I asked the man not to take mine because those windows are high and the children might fall out, and he said I should put parachutes on all of my kids. I could tell he was mad.

There was a great deal of conversation between members about what they did and would not sign for in regard to the inspection. Their general attitude was surprisingly light and gay.

WORKER: Am I correct in assuming that you want to go on with the plans for the meeting tomorrow?

GROUP: (All agreed. Of course, why not? etc.)

MRS. S.: We all have asked the tenants in our buildings, but most people won't come because they are afraid of reprisals. They are always asking what we are doing and are interested.

WORKER: Are you afraid of the reprisals?

GROUP: (All chime in) No, of course not.

MRS. S.: No, I've always complained about things, not that it does any good. We think we are right. We are not asking for anything that is unreasonable.

MRS. B.: My friend said she would not come but would baby-sit so I could go.

Group all agreed that they were not afraid and would all be there Thursday night.

The worker then suggested that they consider their strategy for the meeting. The members were concerned about speaking in public and asked the worker to read their requests. She refused, emphasizing instead the importance of tenants' speaking for themselves. The worker's belief in them was important. She offered to be there to help, but it was their fight and she believed they could do it.

WORKER: What approach are you going to use?
MRS. M.: Can't we do like we did at our meeting?
GROUP: (All agreed.)
MRS. B.: Maybe one person should read the list of requests. Can't you do it, Mrs. P?
WORKER: No, one of you should read it. The board will want to hear from you as tenants. What I will do is make a list of your requests and have one for each of you and the board members. Then they can ask you questions. I'll be with you and give you all the support I can, but it's up to you to present your side of the picture.
MRS. K.: That's a good idea, and it will help a lot if they ask us questions.
MRS. M.: Sometimes I get all confused and can't say what I want to say.
WORKER: Let's all try to be calm and above all be polite.
GROUP: (Laughter. Personal joke on Mrs. P. told.)
Discussion continued about the painting of apartments; cheap quality of paint used; lack of color selection; penalties for not painting and differential treatment of some tenants.
Meeting adjourned with plans to meet Thursday night at 8:00 for the board meeting.

At the meeting with the board the members acquitted themselves well and the board immediately approved nine of their eleven requests. Two of the requests were complicated and required further study, but the board indicated a positive response would be forthcoming. The members of the group and the worker were elated. By using the political system, the members found they could exercise their rights. The balance of power shifted and the pattern of inaction and conformity because of fear was broken; other tenants

were encouraged by the positive reaction to the first steps taken by this group. There were, of course, still many issues to deal with. The relationship with the project manager was still poor, but the worker strategized how to help him see that it was in his own interest to recognize tenants' rights. The problem of intertenant friction also needed to be attended to, since in the last analysis, peer pressure might well be the most important factor in getting tenants to take their responsibility for better maintenance of the project. These next steps seemed more manageable to the group members after their initial success.

Client Advocacy: Helping a Client Negotiate the Housing System

In this second example a worker found it necessary to take the role of advocate of a client's right to housing when that client was ignored by an unyielding bureaucracy.[4] As with the previous example, the worker was not hired as a client advocate, but rather, considered advocacy part of his role as a worker. In this case, the worker was employed by a child welfare agency in a large Canadian city. His client was a woman of thirty-five, French-speaking, a single parent with four children. She had requested placement of her children with the agency because of severe depression after her husband left her. After a number of interviews, it appeared to the worker that one precipitating crisis was that the client, Mrs. B., had been forced to move twice within the past six months because of changes in ownership of the buildings she lived in. Adequate accommodation that she could afford was not available. As an alternative to accepting the children for placement, the worker proposed the following plan: Mrs. B. would continue seeing a psychiatrist to help her with her depression; the worker would arrange for homemaker services to give her some assistance with the children; he would also work with her to try to solve the housing problem. The client agreed. The worker felt this was a good example of a situation where, with personal support and help in dealing with the housing system, the client had the strength to maintain herself and her children. The problem seemed to be partially the responsibility of society for not providing adequate housing for this family. Thus, the worker began a four-month odyssey which provided a lesson in the complexity of the housing system and evidence of the power of persistence.

As a first step, after consulting with Mrs. B., the worker addressed a letter to the city housing authority. Excerpts of that letter follows:

Sept. 26th
This letter is on behalf of Mrs. B. and her application for a 3-bedroom unit.

Certainly this is a matter of urgency as Mrs. B. and her children have been obliged to move twice in a very short time as her landlords have sold out. There is cause for serious concern as Mrs. B.'s health demands a stable environment. Due to the limits of her financial situation and her health her choice of adequate shelter depends on your assistance.

Mrs. B., as I know her, is a quiet reserved woman with very good housekeeping standards and well-behaved children. It is my opinion that she would be a very good tenant.

To keep her family together and maintain the home it is imperative that she re-locate to a suitable unit in a French-speaking area of her choice as soon as possible.

Thank you for whatever assistance you can offer to the B. family.

As the worker developed his case for Mrs. B., he enlisted the aid of allies. The first was the psychiatrist who was treating the client. His letter to the placement manager read as follows:

Sept. 26th
The above-named client who is on your waiting list for housing, has been under my direct care for two years. She has exhausted her own possibilities in seeking housing for herself and her four children. It is imperative and urgent that suitable accommodation be found this month as otherwise her mental health may decline once again with repercussions for herself and the children.

A return letter indicated that the client did not meet the residency requirements for housing within the city limits. The area Mrs. B. lived in was technically in another municipality surrounded by the larger city. The placement manager suggested he contact the provincial government housing authority for help. The worker repeated the letters to the housing authority of the smaller municipality. Because of a shortage in housing in the French-speaking area, a shortage which the municipality had done little to rectify, the only help available to Mrs. B. was an apartment in an English-speaking area. Since Mrs. B. could not speak English, she would have been socially isolated in this area, which would compound her problems. The worker made sure to consult with Mrs. B. at each step of the process to be sure she understood and agreed with the next steps. She felt identified with her present housing area and feared moving into an English-speaking housing project. They agreed to try to have the residency requirements waived to obtain housing in the city. A second letter was sent to the placement manager of the city housing authority with additional letters of support from the homemaker service. In addition, the worker arranged a meeting with the mayor of the smaller municipality, at which time he raised the problem of Mrs. B. and received assurances that the mayor would do his best to help.

Although there were promises of help, the months dragged on with no action. The worker arranged a meeting with the placement officer of the city housing authority and his client. His impression was that the officer was not interested in the client's dilemma, but rather on applying the regulations. As the worker encountered one frustration after another, he noted his increasing depression. After only two months in the shoes of the client attempting to negotiate government bureaucracies, he felt it would not be long before he began to show clinical symptoms of depression. This increased his anger at the way his client and her children were lost in the complexity of agencies supposedly established to serve their needs. With the agreement of Mrs. B., and his supervisor, the worker wrote the following letter to the federal government representative (member of Parliament):

November 21st

I am writing on behalf of one of your constituents, Mrs. B., who is having serious difficulties in finding adequate accommodation within her budgetary limitations.

The enclosed letters indicate a series of steps that we have taken on behalf of the B. family in support of her applications of low-rent housing. I urgently requested that her doctor and visiting homemaker outline their involvement to support her request. Letters were delivered and immediate personal interviews were held with the Mayor, Mrs. J. of the Provincial Ministry and Mr. R. of the Housing Authority. Unfortunately, we have come to a dead end.

As you will note in the accompanying letter from Mrs. H., Mrs. B. has exerted many frustrating efforts on her own behalf. She, too, has been unsuccessful. She has been forced to move twice within the past year due, in both cases, simply to change of landlords through sales. Another move will occur at the end of the month as she has received a notice to vacate.

These necessary moves due to no fault of Mrs. B. and her children are very seriously affecting her health as is documented in the attached letters written by various agencies on her behalf. Needless to say, the housing problem and a resulting depression of the mother can only have negative consequences for the children. Our concern is to prevent what will inevitably occur as Mrs. B.'s health deteriorates further . . . placement of her children in foster homes.

I am asking that you intervene immediately on behalf of your constituent. I have no doubt that you will be far more effective than my efforts have been.

A phone call and the member of Parliament's secretary's promise to look into the situation followed. The urgency of the problem increased as Mrs. B. received an eviction notice. She was to be out of her apartment by the end of the week. It was at this point in the process that the worker presented this case to a workshop I was leading for his agency's staff on systems work—the skills involved in helping clients negotiate agencies and institutions. He reviewed his efforts to date, reading excerpts from the letters and describing his interviews from memory. At the end of the presentation he shared his utter frustration and anger at what was happening to his client and his feeling powerless to do anything about it. I could tell from the reactions of his colleagues, the looks in their faces, that they too were feeling the same sense of impotency as they reflected on similar cases on their caseloads. An excerpt from the workshop follows:

WORKSHOP LEADER: I can tell this case has come to mean a great deal for you. It probably symbolizes all of the cases where you feel deeply about the injustices your clients face and how little you seem to be able to do about it. It must hurt and make you feel bitter.

WORKER: What good is all the talk about systems work if Mrs. B. ends up with lousy housing and depressed, and then turns her kids over to us?

WORKSHOP LEADER: I don't think it is over yet. There is always some next step you can take. Does anyone have any ideas?

WORKSHOP PARTICIPANT: The only thing I would feel like doing is screaming about how mad I am about this.

WORKSHOP LEADER: Well, why don't you? If Mrs. B. is willing, isn't it time somebody brought her problem to the public's attention? How are they going to know about this kind of thing happening to people if you don't tell them?

WORKER: I'm a representative of the agency. How can I go to the papers?

WORKSHOP LEADER: Sounds like you need to do some work within the agency to gain support for taking a more public step. Have you spoken to the agency director about that possibility?

WORKER: No, I haven't. I assumed the agency wouldn't want this kind of publicity.

WORKSHOP LEADER: Why don't you ask your director? He's right here.

In the conversation which followed the director indicated that he felt social pressure was needed at times, and that this seemed to be one of those times. He defined the parameters within which he felt his staff could operate. He wanted to be informed about cases as they progressed and to be assured that all steps had been taken before going to the press. After that, he would cooperate with staff if they felt that public awareness was the only step left. The director and the worker agreed to meet after the workshop to plan how to use the media in this case. What I found interesting is that the worker had assumed, without asking, that the agency administration would reject going public. Workers often take this position and in some cases they would run into stiff opposition. This means that they have

some work to do within their own agency systems to obtain allies and to try to change a policy which categorically rejects the use of agency social pressure on behalf of the client. If they are unsuccessful, then they may have to consider changing jobs or taking other steps designed to bring about changes in the agency policy. What is a mistake, however, is to assume the rejection in advance without even trying. This constitutes a way of avoiding getting involved in a confrontation while being able to blame the agency as the excuse. Workers have said that it takes a lot of courage to challenge their own agency system, and I agree. The process of social change is not an easy one. However, a sense of professional identification which extends beyond affiliation as an agency staff member requires that workers take some risks along the way. The following edited excerpt is from the newspaper story on the case of Mrs. B.:

November 29th

"TAKE MY CHILDREN," MOM PLEADS

If G. B. doesn't get help within a month, she will be forced to turn her children over to the Children's Aid Society.

R. S., a Children's Aid Worker, said the separated woman's plight is critical as she and her four children continue to survive on a $464-a-month mother's allowance she receives.

This has been her only source of income since her husband left in April.

The problem is housing. The family finds itself forced to move this weekend for the third time this year because the house in which they are living has been sold.

She has two boys and two girls between the ages of eight and 12 and needs a three-bedroom accommodation that will not eat up half the monthly income, Mr. S. said.

An added problem is that Mrs. B. only speaks French and must live in a French-speaking area. She has been living in . . . which, Mr. S. said, is causing her another problem.

In living outside . . . , technically she is not eligible for a housing unit under . . . Housing Authority until she has been living in the city for a year.

"And the Provincial Housing Corp. has no units in either . . . or . . . —only further out and even then they haven't offered her anything," Mr. S. said.

"She has given up all hope," he said. She has already asked the society eight times if they cannot take the children.

"The society is trying to prevent taking them," Mr. S. said. "I have been working almost full time to find some solution to the problem."

Is there a solution?

"City Housing can waive the eligibility in December and they must do it—there is no other route to go," he said. "If it doesn't happen the society will have to take the children."

"She is a good mother and tenant," Mr. S. said. "But another month and the situation will move to emergency proportions."

A few days after the appearance of this article, the worker and Mrs. B. met with the federal representative, the member of Parliament, who was somewhat upset at the publicity. Nevertheless, he offered his support. A call was received soon after from the placement officer of the city housing authority informing the worker that the one-year residency requirement was being waived. Soon after, Mrs. B. was offered a suitable apartment. It was interesting to note that the psychiatrist treating Mrs. B. reported that during the time she and the worker were involved in the fight for housing, a period of almost four months, her psychotic symptoms disappeared. There was something very therapeutic about acting in her own self-interest and starting to affect others, rather than being passively acted on by the system. The experience appeared to be good for the worker as well, as some of his symptoms of depression, sometimes

known as the "child welfare worker blues," were also relieved.

This example has demonstrated that there are situations where mediating between a client and the social system may require the worker to act as an advocate for the client. In this example, the worker made sure that the client was involved in each step of the decision-making process. In dealing with the systems, the agencies, he was acting as if he believed they could provide the services if social pressure were employed. In a sense, he used pressure to make a demand for work and reached for the strength of the system. Another key factor was that he acted openly and honestly along the way. My view is that while tactics involving deceit may seem helpful in the short run, they always return to haunt the worker in significant ways. The worker involved allies wherever he could (the psychiatrist, homemakers, etc.). He was persistent and did not give in after encountering the first obstacles. Nor was he fooled by the system's efforts to "cool him off" by passing the buck or making vague promises of action. He made sure to involve and inform his own agency system, so that his agency (the director, supervisors) would feel part of the process. And most important, he maintained a belief in the idea that there is always some next step.

It is unfortunate that there were no detailed process recordings of the conversations between the worker and the representatives of the systems he dealt with. It is not possible to analyze the skill use, or lack of skill use, which characterized the work. This would have enriched the analysis of this example. Heymann addressed the questions related to worker skill use and the ability to establish a relationship with the system's representative at points of conflict.[5] Using the example of a social worker identified with tenants about to implement a rent strike, he describes in detail the way a worker attempted to play a mediating role and provide assistance to the landlord, which in turn, could prove helpful to his clients. The key to the worker's effectiveness was that he was always open to the side of the landlord's ambivalence which ran counter to the strong forces of resistance to accepting his help. As long as the system is not viewed as completely closed, one dimensional, and without ambivalence, then there is always the possibility of employing all of the helpful skills identified thus far.

The earlier example with the housing system raised another area of concern for the agency. Mrs. B. was one example of a client experiencing problems with public housing. There were many poor people in town who were not clients of the agency but who were also having these problems. This worker had invested a great deal of time in this case, something clearly not possible for every case on a worker's caseload. What would happen to a Mrs. B. who did not have a worker-advocate? Thus, the individual example of the problem facing Mrs. B. raised for the agency and its professional staff the general problem of housing for the poor. Almost every individual case raises some issue of public policy. Workers cannot tackle all such issues at one time; however, they have a responsibility to deal with some. In this agency, a social policy committee was established to provide leadership in identifying and developing staff programs for dealing with the social policy implications of the problems facing individual clients. The next chapter explores this aspect of the professional's dual responsibility for both clients' private troubles and societys' public issues.

NOTES

1. Gordon Hearn, *The General Systems Approach to Understanding Groups,* Health Education Monographs, no. 14 (New York: Society of Public Health Educators, 1962), p. 67.

2. William Schwartz, "The Social Worker in the Group," in *New Perspectives on Services to Groups* (New York: National Association of Social Workers, 1961).

3. Kurt Lewin, "Field Theory in Social Science," in *Frontiers in Group Dynamics,* ed. Dorwin Cartwright (New York: Harper & Row, 1951).

4. For discussions of the advocacy role, see: Ralph M. Kramer and Harry Specht, eds., *Readings in Community Organization Practice* (Englewood Cliffs, N.J.: Prentice-Hall, 1969); Charles F. Grosser, *New Directions in Community Organization* (New York: Praeger, 1973).

5. David Heymann, "A Function for the Social Worker in the Antipoverty Program," in William Schwartz and Serapio Zalba, eds., *The Practice of Group Work* (New York: Columbia University Press, 1971) pp. 157–76.

CHAPTER 17

Professional Impact
on the System

This term describes workers' activities designed to effect changes in the following two major areas:

a. Policies and services in their own agency and other agencies and institutions, as well as broader social policies which affect clients;

b. The work culture which affects interstaff relationships within their own agency and with other agencies and institutions.

This breakdown is somewhat analogous to the division cited earlier between the "content" of the work and the "process" (way of working). Interest in the first area emerges directly from the worker's practice experience. As workers relate to the concerns of individual clients, they become aware of general problems affecting categories of clients. For example, in the illustration of the work with Mrs. B., the client mentioned in Chapter 16 who was being evicted and could not find suitable alternative housing, it became clear to the worker that Mrs. B.'s particular difficulty was a specific example of the general problem of inadequate public housing. The worker's attempt to heighten his agency's interest in the problem of housing and his efforts to influence housing policies as part of his role as agency worker and as a member of a professional association are examples of professional impact on the agency, community institutions, and social policies. Similarly, a worker's bringing to the attention of the agency administration a negative effect of an agency policy on service to his clients is also an attempt to have professional impact within the system.

The second arena for professional impact is the work culture that exists within the agency staff system and between staff members of different agencies. As workers deal with clients, they are constantly brought into contact with other professionals. Services to clients are directly affected by how well interdependent staff members are able to work with each other. The staff system in an agency develops a culture similar to that of a group (see Chapter 13). The barriers to the effective development of staff culture are also similar. In fact, my observations of staff systems have indicated that difficulties between staff members often occupy the greatest portion of staff time and energy. When one inquires what the greatest source of frustration is for staff members (particularly in large and complex systems and especially if the staff is interdisciplinary), the answer is usually "interstaff relations." Similar problems often exist between staff members of different agencies within the community which are supposed to be working in partnership to meet client needs. It is not impossible to discover clients who are suffering because workers in two settings are no longer talking to each other. Efforts on the part of staff members to improve interstaff relationships and to create a more productive culture for work constitute the second area for professional impact.

It is my contention that in addition to provision of direct service to clients, helping professionals have a functional responsibility for attempting constructive impact on these two major areas—policies and services, and the work culture of the system. Of course, it is not possible to deal with every social policy, program or staff interactional issue which emerges from the work; indeed, it would be a major task even to identify all of the concerns. However, it is possible to tackle a limited number of issues, one at a time. For instance, a number of colleagues can begin working on an issue even though this may take months or even years to resolve. I have argued that the process of taking a problem and breaking it down into smaller parts (partializing) and then attacking the problem by taking a first step, followed by a second, and so on, is helpful for clients. This same process is also useful for tackling questions of professional impact.

Nonetheless, it is important to acknowledge that attempting professional impact is not easy. Let us review some of the factors which can make it hard. In addition to the magnitude of the problems, workers have to deal with many of their own feelings about change. Workers often

bring to their work situation an apathetic attitude that reflects their view of themselves as incapable of exerting meaningful influence. Our socialization experiences have generally encouraged us to conform to social structures. Families, schools, peer groups, and work settings do not always encourage individual initiative. While all systems have a profound stake in encouraging members to differentiate themselves and to make contributions by challenging the system and asserting their individuality, they have not always been aware of this need or acted upon it. Encouraging members to be an integrated part of the system is an important imperative; however, the system often achieves this at the expense of individual initiative. Efforts to integrate individuals can develop system norms which encourage conformity. The life experience of many workers tends to make them view taking responsibility for professional impact as a major change in their relationship to systems in general and people in authority in particular. Even if workers are willing to involve themselves in social change, experiences in agencies often discourage any further efforts. When workers face resistance to their first attempts, they may often fail to recognize the agency's potential for change. This potential is there, but it may require persistence on the worker's part to effect change. If workers remember that agencies are dynamic systems, open to change but also simultaneously resistant, then an initial rebuff does not necessarily mean closure to the worker's effort. Timing is also important. Workers are mistaken if they believe their agency is static and unchanging. An attempt to deal with a problem at one point in an agency's life may be blocked, while at a later stage in the agency's development, the same effort would be welcome.

In many situations workers are simply

afraid to assert themselves. If the agency culture has discouraged previous efforts, if workers feel they will be viewed as "trouble makers" and that their jobs may be on the line, then they will view raising questions about services or policies as a risky business. There are times when for a number of reasons, such as the extreme defensiveness of administrators or political pressures on the agency, these fears are well founded. Workers in such situations have to decide for themselves, in light of their personal situations and their feelings about the professional ethical issues involved in the problem, whether they feel they can take the risk. If an effort to effect a change is risky in a particular setting, then workers would be wise to be sure that they have allies before they try. In some situations I have observed workers who did not get involved because of their stereotyped attitude to an administration that they had never tested, not because any actual experience in the agency had led them to fear reprisals. Still, one should not minimize that professional impact efforts often require courage. Lack of time is also a serious factor. In some situations, where caseloads are maintained at an impossible level, the idea of becoming involved in agency or social change seems completely unrealistic. In such settings, the first efforts at social action might deal with the working situation. Often outside organizations such as professional associations or unions are the best media for effecting such changes.

In summary, the complexity and magnitude of issues tend to discourage professional impact efforts. Workers' general feelings about asserting themselves, as well as specific experiences in agencies, may act as deterrents. Fear of losing their jobs or other retribution may also be an obstacle to involvement. And finally, insufficient time plays a part in preventing attempts at professional impact efforts.

FROM INDIVIDUAL PROBLEMS TO SOCIAL ACTION

Schwartz, in developing his position on the function of the social work profession, argues that the worker must be concerned with both the specific problems faced by the client and the social issues raised by those problems.[1] Objecting to a trend he perceives in the profession of splitting these two concerns so that some professionals are only involved in dealing with the problems of the individual (clinicians) while others are concerned with problems of social change (activists), he argues that every professional has a responsibility for both concerns. He cites C. Wright Mills as one who refused to accept this dichotomy between individual concerns and the issues of policy:

In our own time, C. Wright Mills has seen most clearly into the individual-social connections identified with social struggle. He pointed up the distinction between what he called the "personal troubles of milieu" and the "public issues of social structure," and noted that *trouble* is a private matter, while *issue* is a public one. Most important, he stressed that each must be stated in the terms of the other, and of the interaction between the two.[2]

Schwartz rejects the notion of splitting responsibility within the social work profession for serving individual needs or dealing with social problems, and points out that such a split is impossible if "we understand that a private trouble is simply a specific example of a public issue, and that a public issue is made up of many private troubles."[3] Recognizing that agencies and social institutions can be complex and ambivalent, he suggests the worker's function should be a "third force" or a "hedge against the system's own complexity."[4]

Where . . . such a function originates *within the agency itself,* the image is that of a built-in monitor of the agency's effectiveness and a protection against its own rigidities. From such a position, the social worker moves to strengthen and reinforce both parties in the client-agency relationship. With the client—and with mutual aid systems of clients—the worker offers the agency service in ways designed to help them reach out to the system in stronger and more assertive ways, generalizing from their private experiences to agency policy wherever possible and avoiding the traps of conformity and inertia. In many instances, the activity thus produced is similar to that desired by the advocates—except that the movement is *towards* the service and the workers are interested in the process rather than having lost faith in it. With the system—colleagues, superiors and other disciplines—the worker feeds in his direct experience with the struggles of his clients, searches out the staff stake in reaching and innovating and brings administration wherever possible into direct contact with clients reaching for new ways of being served.[5]

In the last chapter I cited a number of examples of workers helping clients reach out to the system "in stronger and more assertive ways." The following examples show the worker raising general issues with the system which result from his experience with clients.

Illustrations of Agency Change

The worker who is alive to the dynamic tension between clients' needs and the agency service will be looking for opportunities to generalize from direct practice experience to policy issues. Noticing a particular problem emerging regularly in the caseload may be the signal for a modification in agency service. For example, one worker who dealt with groups of unmarried mothers noted the strain there seemed to be on the unwed moth-ers' parents. She shared her observations with other workers in her department, and the result was the development of a highly successful experiment in group service for parents of the clients. For a hospital worker, repeated comments from patients in his ward group about the strains of their first contact in the emergency room (e.g., lack of attention for hours, which heightened their anxiety and that of their relatives, and the difficulty in getting information) led to his exploration of the problems with the emergency room staff. The record of the start of this work follows:

I asked for a meeting with the head nurse of emergency. I met Miss T. at the end of her shift and I commented on how tired she looked. She told me it had been a particularly rough day complicated by two car accidents with four victims. I acknowledged that I could see it was really hectic and thanked her for taking some time to talk with me. I explained that I had been meeting with ward groups on 2 East and that a common theme had been patients complaining about their entry into the hospital through the emergency room. I told her I was raising this because I thought she would want to know about the problems and also to better understand the difficulty from the staff's point of view so I could handle this issue when it arose at meetings. Miss T. seemed irritated at my statement, stiffened physically, and said she and her staff didn't have time to sit and talk to patients the way social workers did. I quickly reassured her that I was not coming down to criticize her or her staff. I told her that I had worried that she would misinterpret my intentions, and I thought that she had done just that. Would she give me a chance to explain? I said, "I realize it's no picnic down here, and part of the reason I stopped in was to see if there was any way social service could be of more help. Working under pressure the way you do is rough." Miss T. seemed to relax a bit, and I asked how I might be able to help. She said she had thought it would be helpful to have a social worker around more often. I told her that might be one way. I wondered if we could arrange a meeting with the other staff members where I could share the feedback and get their reactions. I had no set ideas yet but perhaps if we put our heads together, we could come up with some. She agreed and we set a time.

The worker's directness and statement of purpose helped to clarify the boundaries for the discussion. She responded directly to the indirect cues of defensiveness by sharing her own concerns. By acknowledging the real difficulties and offering to examine how she, in her function as social worker, might help, the worker had quickly changed the situation from one staff member criticizing another to a situation where two staff members, each with their own functions, carry on the work of using patient feedback to examine their services. The meeting that followed was successful, with staff members having an opportunity to fill the social worker in on the difficulties they were facing. In addition, they were able to identify certain changes they could make in response to the patient feedback. The worker, for her part, offered to develop an open-ended group in a quiet corner of the waiting room area for relatives and patients who were waiting treatment. The group met for one half hour at midmorning to allow patients and relatives to ask questions and to deal with some of their anxieties about the emergency situation. Both staff and patients found the group to be helpful. At a later date, the worker suggested occasional meetings be held with patients before they left the hospital to discuss their experiences in the emergency room to provide feedback for hospital staff. The meetings were instituted on a bimonthly basis and were effective. Both the social worker and the other staff members in emergency approached other parts

of the hospital to enlist their aid when required. For example, a trial program was established with young volunteers to man a children's group in the adjacent outpatient clinic waiting area to cut down the problem of bored children roaming the halls.

In both the case of the parents' group for parents of unwed motheers and the example of the emergency room problems, the workers' sense of their dual responsibility for dealing with the specific problems and the policy issues led them to take their first steps. In these examples the worker made use of direct client feedback in their efforts to influence service. There are times when the feedback is more indirect and the worker has to examine the relationship between client problems and agency service closely to observe the connections. Interestingly enough, in such situations, some of the dynamics used to understand processes in the group and family can also be applied to more complex systems such as an agency or institution. For example, in Chapter 11, I pointed out how deviant group members may be signaling a problem in the group-as-a-whole. Problems in a system, such as irregular or deviant behavior on the part of groups of clients, may also be providing an indirect form of feedback. One example of this process is drawn from a rehabilitation institution for paraplegics. The institution had a rule against patients going home on weekends because of a government policy which paid for a patient only on days they slept at the hospital. Systematic work by the staff and administration, including organizing feedback by patients to government officials, led to a change in the policy, and weekend passes were authorized. Three months after implementation of the new policy, the administrator called in the worker to raise a problem. He pointed out that patients were returning to the hospital with serious bedsores and that if this continued, he would have to suspend the pass program. Before instituting such a change, however, he asked her to meet with the patients' council to discuss the issue. The administrator had been burnt before when he had instituted changes without patient consultation and was thus hoping to avoid another confrontation.

The following excerpt is from the worker's meeting with the patient council:

WORKER: Dr. M. met with me and told me that many patients are returning with bedsores. He is deeply concerned about this and feels he may have to revoke the weekend-pass policy.

LOUIS: (with great anger) He can't do that. If he takes away that privilege, we will wheel down to his office, and he'll have a sit in on his hands.

JOHN: Who does he think he is anyway? We fought hard for that right, and he can't take it away. (Others murmur in angry agreement.)

WORKER: I can understand why you are so angry. The pass is really important to you. It's important to see your families. But, tell me, I don't understand: why is it so many people come back with bedsores? (Long silence)

TERRY: (Speaking slowly and staring at the floor as he does) Here at the center the nurses turn us in our beds all the time. When we get home, our family does not.

WORKER: (suddenly understanding) And you're too ashamed to ask them, isn't that it?

In the discussion that followed, the group members talked poignantly about their feelings toward their new-found dependency. Many felt they had lost their manhood and were ashamed to need help suddenly for going to the bathroom and for turning in their beds. So, they simply did not ask for help. As they discussed

their family's reactions, it emerged that many of their wives were too embarrassed to ask what kind of help they needed. It soon became clear to the worker that the problem of bedsores was an indirect communication to the center of an important new area for service to patients and their families—the problem of dependency, their feelings about it, and how to handle it. The worker's next step was to ask for a meeting of the various department heads to report back on her session with the council.

WORKER: A most interesting issue was raised when I talked to the patients about the bedsores and I wanted to share it with you to get your reactions and ideas.

After the worker recounted the discussion, there was silence at the staff meeting as the department heads thought about the implications of this feedback for their areas. The worker suggested it might be helpful to explore this question of dependency as it was handled throughout the institution and to see if some special attention could be paid to the problem. Once again, the stance taken by the worker was one of involving her professional colleagues in mutual discussion of an issue relevant to their work. From this discussion emerged a plan for raising the issue in the various departments and developing new services to deal with the problem, for example, groups for relatives of recently paralyzed patients which would specifically focus on their reactions to the accident, their questions about their ongoing relationship and, particularly, how to handle the dependency feelings they were sure to encounter. Programs for patients were also developed and staff training implications were discussed. Because the worker was open to the idea that her setting was a dynamic system and that change was possible, she was able to enlist the aid of her colleagues to set important changes in motion.

Another example of where the worker's mind-set dramatically affects how they may describe a problem is taken from a home for the aged. At a staff conference, a ward aide raised a problem with one patient who was constantly sitting in public places and openly masturbating. This was affecting both staff and other patients and the worker was asked to speak to her about the problem. The discussion at the staff meeting was brief, and the discomfort of staff who had noticed this behavior and had been at a loss as to what to do was evident. The worker was not happy about having to see the woman and was not sure what she could do, but after some discussion with her supervisor, it began to dawn on the worker that her discomfort, and the discomfort of the staff, related to the fact that sexual issues were never raised at the home. In fact, the staff system operated as if all of its residents were past the point of sexual interest. This had a great deal to do with the staff's view of the aged and their embarrassment about even considering the question. The worker began to check out her hunch that this was a larger issue by approaching various staff members and raising her feelings. She was amazed to find that she had unlocked a number of major issues which had not been dealt with. Staff members were uncomfortable about this area and had not known how to raise the question. For example, there were elderly senile men who continually tried to get female residents and staff into bed with them. Staff tended to treat this as a joke between each other, although their real feelings about it were marked by discomfort. After a preliminary survey, the worker returned to the meeting with her findings. The result was a decision by staff to develop a survey to identify the problem as seen by staff and residents, to discuss ways to deal with the feelings of the staff, and to develop new approaches for handling the issue with residents. The worker's sense of the connection between "private trouble" and a "public issue" opened up important work in a formerly taboo area.

Social Action in the Community

Worker's contacts with clients often put them in a unique position in relation to community and social policies. Their firsthand experiences can provide insights into client needs, gaps in services, and the impact of existing policies which need to be brought to the attention of the community and policy makers. The complexities of our society often make it difficult for the wider community really to know what is happening with the many "left-out" groups. In addition, society has some stake in not finding out the real nature of the problems. Once again, the functional role of mediating between the client and the system, this time the community, can provide direction for workers' efforts. These can consist of letters to newspapers, briefs for government bodies prepared by the worker as an individual or as part of a professional organization, organized lobbying efforts in relation to specific legislation, and many other actions.

One illustration of this process is from my early practice in a small, suburban community on the outskirts of a large city. I was a youth worker in a Jewish community center serving a middle-class population. Over a period of time I noticed two teenagers attending our lounge program who were not members of the center's client population. After I made contact with these youngsters and a working relationship developed, the boys began to discuss their gang activities in town. It became obvious that they were coming to the center as a way of trying to move away from their peer group because of fear of getting seriously hurt or in trouble with the law. As a new youth worker in town, I had not been aware of the existence of this problem and had not seen any reference to it in the local press. Conversations with other teenagers in the program confirmed the extent of the problem.

At about the same time I was invited to participate in a mayor's committee on youth which had recently been established to plan the town's priorities in the area of youth programs. Over one hundred workers and volunteers in local youth organizations attended the first meeting. As I listened to the presentations, it became clear that each organization was presenting a brief in support of its own activities. It was also clear that the gang youth population was not going to be part of the discussion. In fact, because of their difficult behavior, these youngsters were usually barred from the organizations represented at the meeting. I attempted to raise the issue and was naively surprised by the reluctance of the group to admit the problem. My notes of the session describe the process:

After being recongized by the chair, I said I thought we were missing an important youth problem in town. I pointed out that no one had mentioned the gang problem, and yet it was one that must be troubling all of our organizations. There was a long silence. The chairman of the committee, a town councilman, said that he didn't think this town had a gang problem. He felt the gang trouble was usually caused by kids who came over from a neighboring town and that perhaps those were the youngsters I was referring to. He turned to the planning and research coordinator for the county government and asked if they were aware of any serious juvenile delinquency

problem or gang problem in this town. He pulled a folder from his briefcase and outlined statistics which indicated very little difficulty in this area, with the exception of some limited informal gang activity in the neighboring town. The chairman of the committee then suggested that since I was new in town, it might explain why I believed the spillover problem from X town was really our concern.

I sat down, resolving to keep my mouth shut in the future. I can still remember the embarrassment I felt in response to the patronizing tone of the chairman! A week later, after some reflection, I realized that a community was not much different from a family and that admitting a problem was not easy. Many of the members of that group were unaware of the extent of the problem and the reassurance from the officials was all they needed to return to questions such as the adequacy of the number of baseball diamonds in town. Some were aware of the problem but chose to deny the extent of the difficulty. I decided to strategize before the next session of the committee to develop a way of bringing the problem to their attention more effectively. I also decided that I needed both allies and some initial ideas about how to deal with the problem. When the two teenagers met with me that week, I explained what had happened at the meeting and asked how they felt about audiotaping a conversation with me about their gang activities which I told them I would maintain confidentially, leaving their names out; they agreed to help me. I also inquired if there were any other people in the community with whom they related well and who might be helpful in convincing the committee that the problem really existed. They mentioned a police sergeant who had been involved with the kids when there was trouble and who most of the youngsters felt was straight. I called the sergeant and met with him for lunch. My notes of that meeting follow:

I detailed my involvement in this issue including my abortive attempt to raise the problem. He told me that he had heard about it the next day and had a good laugh at the response. When I asked him why, he told me he had been raising this issue with city hall for two years and getting nowhere. I asked him what he thought needed to be done. He felt the town very badly needed a youth bureau which could concentrate on working directly with the gang kids. He tried to make contact, but this was not officially part of his job, and his being a police officer created real conflicts. I told him I thought this mayor's committee might be a great place to bring pressure to bear on city hall which would have a hard time ignoring a recommendation from its own committee. I asked if he would support me at the next meeting when I played the tape and raised the issue again. He said he could not raise it himself, for fear of sanctions, but he would attend. If the committee asked him questions directly, then he could respond. We agreed that I would raise the problem and he would respond.

My next step was to record a one-hour conversation with the two youngsters. In the first part I asked them to discuss the gang structure and activities in town. In the second, I asked them to talk about themselves, their hopes and aspirations, the problems they faced in trying to accomplish them, and what they thought might be helpful. I felt that it would be important for the committee members not only to be shocked out of their complacency but also to gain a sense of these youngsters as the community's children who also needed their help. We reviewed the tape together, with the youngsters editing out parts they felt might reveal too much about themselves and strategizing with me about which parts I should play

for the committee so as to achieve maximum effectiveness. I then made an appointment to play the tape for the police sergeant to alert him to its content. At the next session of the mayor's committee I explained what I had done and requested time to play the tape excerpts. The committee members were intrigued and agreed. They listened with attention as the two boys, in response to my questioning, described in intricate detail the gang structure in town, the names of each gang, whether they were white or black, the number of members of each gang, their relations to larger gangs in the county, and the internal structure of the gangs. They then reviewed a number of gruesome incidents in town of recent gang fights at movie theaters, in pizza parlors, and at the local high school. They gave detailed descriptions of their involvement in "stomping" kids with the currently popular hob-nail boots. I asked them how they felt about all of this, and one responded: "Lousy, but what can I do? If I don't go along with the gang, I would be on my own, with no one to back me up." The boys then talked about their future plans:

WORKER: What kind of work would you like to do?
TOM: I'd like to be something like a bank clerk, or work in an office somewhere—but you need high school for that, and I don't think I'm going to make it out.
WORKER: What do you think you will end up doing, then?
TOM: Probably, I'll end up like my brother—going to jail.

At the end of the tape there was another silence in the room, but this time the expressions of the committee members' faces indicated that they were both stunned by the description of the gang structure and moved by Tom's fatalism.

One committee member asked if all of the gang fights described had actually taken place. The police sergeant was asked if he knew about these fights, and he confirmed them. He was then asked if he knew about the gangs described, and in response detailed his experiences over the past two years with gang groups. The chairman of the committee asked him what he thought they could do about the problem. He described the possibility of a youth bureau such as had been created in other communities. The story of the gang groups received front page publicity in the town paper the next morning along with an editorial stressing the importance of dealing with this problem. A number of recommendations emerged in the final report of the commission, including the establishment of a youth bureau and the development of special programs at the other youth organizations and activity centers which would make them accessible to the gang population. The youth bureau was funded in the town's next budget, and the police sergeant accepted the job as the first director with a field staff of two.

In this instance I had the advantage of dealing with a small town which was more open to influence, the availability of a very effective ally in the sergeant, the existence of the ready-made forum provided by the mayor's committee, the support and encouragement of my agency administration and board, and the willingness of the two youngsters to risk themselves. In other situations moving from identifying a problem to changing policy would not be as easy.[6]

PROFESSIONAL IMPACT AND INTERSTAFF RELATIONSHIPS

The second area of professional impact concerns the work culture which affects staff relationships both within and between agencies. This is partially analogous to the "process" aspect of the helping relationship, but I am referring here to the way in which staff members relate to each other. It is important to be clear on a number of points. First, I am concerned with working relationships. Staff members need to deal with each other while pursuing their own functions. Personal friendships may develop within a staff system, and they may enhance the working relationship, but it is not necessary to be friendly with a colleague in order to work well together. However, when interstaff relationships are poor within a system, there is usually a strong negative effect on services to clients. For example, an interesting research project by Stanton and Schwartz indicated an association between staff tensions and evidence of psychiatric symptoms on the part of patients in a psychiatric hospital.[7] In addition, the emotional drain on staff members and the amount of time and energy expended on such issues can be extraordinary.

Second, the responsibility for strengthening staff working relationships and for dealing with obstacles which block effective collaboration rests with supervisory and administrative staff. If one thinks of the staff system as a group, then the discussion in Part II of this book can be employed to develop a model of the supervising and administrative functions.[8] In workshops I have conducted for administrative staff I have helped participants analyze problems in the staff system by using many of the constructs and models described earlier. For example, in staff systems there is often a "deviant" member who plays the same role as the deviant in the client group. In larger systems, a whole department or section may take on the scapegoat role, and one can observe the system avoiding dealing with its problems by projecting them onto its weakest part. Through analysis of process recordings, audio- or videotapes, it is possible to identify all the skills described thus far—contracting, elaborating, empathy, demand for work, and the rest—as useful for staff management functions. Helping staff members to develop a positive working culture is thus analogous to dealing with the "intimacy" theme described in Chapter 13. A discussion of the use of this model in staff management is beyond the scope of this book, but the essential point is that the functional responsibility for dealing with problems in the staff system rests with the administrative staff. Nonetheless, even though I hold this general position, I believe that each member of a staff system can make a contribution to effective staff interaction. This is part of his or her responsibility for positive professional impact, and it is this area of work I now examine.

The Agency As a Social System

In an earlier publication, I described the agency as a social system and argued for the importance of paying attention to interstaff relationships:

The complex organism called "agency" consists of two major subsystems: staff members and clients. The client subsystem is further divided into smaller units, such as families, groups, wards, cottages. The staff subsystem is subdivided along functional lines. We have administrators, social workers, supervisors, clerical staff, and so on. In order to analyze a part of a complex system we must set it off with a boundary—an artificial divider which helps focus our attention. In social work, it has been the client subsystem. We study family dynamics, ward behavior, group process, and so forth. While this is necessary, there is

the danger that we can take this boundary too seriously. We examine our client interactions as if they were in a "closed" system in which interactions with other subsystems did not have significant impact. For example, we will try to understand the deviant behavior of some hospital patients as *their* problem rather than seeing this behavior as a signal of a problem in hospital care. Or we will describe our clients as "unmotivated" when they stop coming to our agencies rather than interpreting their dropping out as "voting with their feet" against poor service.

If we view our agencies as open, dynamic systems, in which each subgroup is somewhat affected by the movement of the other subgroups with which they come in contact, then we cannot isolate our clients as discrete entities. Instead, we must see the total interaction between clients and staff as an essential part of the helping process. In turn, to the degree that staff interactions have a direct impact on the agency service they must also be placed on our agenda. *The way in which staff member relations affect the "productivity" of the agency is thus directly connected to issues of client service.* (Emphasis added.)[9]

Staff relations can have a profound impact on service. The cultural barriers which prevent open discussion of problems in the staff system are similar to those described earlier in the discussion of the group. In any complex social system there are bound to be conflicts of interest, hidden agendas, residues of bad feelings, misunderstood communications, and so forth; the system, however, treats discussion of these concerns as taboo. The organizational theorist Argyris describes how the formal organization stresses "cognitive reality" as opposed to expressions of real feelings, unilateral control in human relations, and the artificial separation of "process and task."[10] He points out how this leads to restriction of genuine interpersonal feedback; openness to new ideas, feelings, and values; owning one's own views and tolerating others; experimentation and risk taking—all factors which vitally affect the productivity of an organization. Organizations continue to function in spite of these problems, operating under what Argyris calls a "pseudoeffectiveness," which corresponds somewhat with the earlier-described illusion of work. The most important conversations about the real problems in the system then take place in the halls, over lunch, or within subgroups gathering over beers on Friday afternoons to complain about staff members they find impossible to work with. Obviously, client service must suffer under such conditions.

In recent years there has been a greater recognition of the importance of paying attention to the way in which staff members work with each other. Brager and Holloway have authored an excellent book dealing with this area of practice.[11] They have focused on the problems involved in effecting "changes from below," and focused on forces affecting stability and change, the initial assessment stage, and the change process itself.

In a contrasting approach, agency efforts to deal with such problems have included using approaches borrowed from the "sensitivity training" movement, such as weekend retreats, encounter groups, and ongoing T-groups (training groups). Outside organizational development experts are often enlisted to assist staff in developing more authentic communications. Under some circumstances, these efforts can pay important dividends, but, more often, they create more problems than they solve. Staff members may be stimulated in the artificial atmosphere created by the trainer to share thoughts and feelings which other staff members, or administrators, are unable to cope with. When the session has ended and the trainer has left, the ongoing repercussions of this honesty can deepen any rifts and intensify the bad feelings. In addition, staff members who may have felt "burned" by the experience are confirmed in their views that any attention to process is destructive and their resistance to any form of open discussions of interstaff relationships is heightened. Periodic opportunities for a general review of the working relationships in a setting can be helpful only if the setting is already operating at a sophisticated level of open communication on an ongoing basis.

However, most staff systems are not operating on that level, so that an alternative process is needed. Rather than attempt a full-scale analysis of the working relationships in a system, a very threatening process at any time, it is often more helpful to focus on specific problems directly related to service issues. By this I mean that the discussion should not deal with the general question of "How do we work together?" but rather the question of "How do we work together on this particular case or in this area of agency concern?" This discussion needs to be built into the ongoing operation of an agency as opposed to being reserved for special retreats or meetings. By keeping the discussion related to specific issues, one can avoid the trap of becoming personal (i.e., staff members dealing with each other's "personalities"), which is inappropriate for a staff session. Agency staff meetings are not "therapy" sessions, and staff members have a right to relate to each other in their own, unique ways. The only issues appropriate for discussion must be directly concerned with the business of the agency. It is precisely the fear that sessions will turn into personal encounter groups that generates resistance on the part of staff members to a discussion of process.

The idea of focusing on specific issues on an ongoing basis allows a staff to develop the skills needed to be honest with each other at their own pace. As staff find they can risk their feelings with productive results, they then will lower their defenses, building on the first experiences to increase slowly their capacity for authentic communications. As I stated earlier, this process is greatly facilitated when administrative and supervisory staff are skilled in assisting staff members to deal with each other. However, this is not always the case. In either situation, staff members can develop their own skills in relating to others individually and as a group in order to improve the agency culture for work. While the process is speeded up with strong leadership, change can begin anywhere in the system as will be illustrated in the examples which follow. Four examples have been selected which typify common situations. In the first, a staff member tries to sort out her relationship with another staff member who shares work with her with a particular client. In the second, a unit in a large organization takes a first step at opening up communications in a system and is surprised to find that this leads to major changes. In the third example, staff members in one system face their responsibility for developing a better working relationship with staff in a related agency. The final example deals with the problem of discovering that a particular client is being served by a multitude of agencies and workers, none of which ever talk to each other. Each of these problems will probably be familiar.

Interdisciplinary Work with a Client

A common area of tension between staff members occurs when different workers deal with the same client. The strains are often intensified if the workers are from different disciplines. One variation of this struggle appears in the form of a contest over "who owns the client?" In larger systems it is not unusual for one group of professionals to be quite concerned if they believe their role is being impinged upon by another group. In one example, when nurses began to lead ward groups in a hospital, other professionals felt their traditional territory threatened. Efforts to discuss the questions of role in order to resolve the conflict floundered because of the vagueness and generality used by the two professional groups when asked to describe what they did. I have witnessed meetings at which not a single sentence was spoken that was not full of incomprehensible jargon. In my experience, when a professional group is clear about its own function and the way in which that function is implemented in a particular setting and with particular clients, there is much less defensiveness and need to resort to jargon. Interprofessional conflicts over territory are often signals of lack of functional clarity within each group. A first step towards resolving such conflicts is for each professional group to work on developing its own sense of role and then attempt to share this, not with reams of jargon, but by specific examples of their work in action. In this way, different groups can become more aware of what they do with clients that is similar and what is different. Division of labor within a system can become a joint discussion of what the clients' needs are and how each group can play the most effective role.

This kind of cooperation can begin on an individual staff level as members of different professional groups clarify how they will work together with specific clients. In the example which follows, a social worker dealing with a seventeen-year-old girl attending a hospital clinic is concerned about the lack of cooperation between herself and the doctor on the case. She felt he did not respect her contribution to the work, a complaint often voiced in interdisciplinary settings. Rather than simply complaining to colleagues, the worker confronted the doctor with the issue:

I was alarmed that Cindy would cut off all contact with the clinic and thus a potential source of help. I was also concerned with how the doctor viewed the case, what his intentions were, and if he felt that my role and opinions in the case were relevant.

I confronted him with these concerns and initially he reacted defensively, stating that he felt she needed an experienced psychiatrist and not a social worker. I replied that perhaps he was correct but that I felt at present she was having enough difficulty in accepting and receiving the aid of doctors, social workers, and school counselors, let alone a psychiatrist. (She had expressed some very strong and negative feelings about psychiatrists.) He calmed down and I empathized with his difficulty in dealing with her during the interview. I then attempted to get some clarification of our roles in relation to a treatment program. We discussed at length where we might cross each other up and confuse her and decided that we would consult one another before tackling certain problem areas involved in the case.

The important result of this discussion was not that the two professionals no longer experienced conflicts in their work, but, rather, that a beginning was made to develop a working relationship in which the conflicts could be anticipated or raised with each other more quickly. The worker's taking the first step of raising the question had lifted the strong taboo against direct discussion in this sensitive area. If staff members begin joint work with the understanding that there is bound to be some conflict and confusion, then they will be more likely to build in a maintenance system for early self-correction.

Interdepartmental Communications in a Large System

A common problem in large systems is for subgroups of professionals, such as departments, to identify all the problems in the system which are caused by the inadequacies of other departments. It is even possible to observe one group of staff members being identified as scapegoats or serving the "deviant member" function as a way of avoiding facing the system's problems. Because of rules or politeness, as well as the fact that each department has some stake in maintaining the status quo, formal discussion of the problems and the "problem" department are not usually held. The talk in the informal system usually consists of speculating on how things would be much better "if only the other department straightened out." When the problem department is expressing a widely held concern, then its members will continue to bring the problem to the system's attention through indirect means. When this department finally starts to affect other departments directly, the response is often to deal with only the content of the issue. This is a mistake, since even if the specific issue is resolved, it will be replaced with another one if the underlying problems are not dealt with.

To illustrate this process and the way in which staff can use a specific confrontation to deal with the larger question of staff relations, I will draw upon an experience I had as a field instructor for a school of social work with a unit of graduate students placed in a residential institution for mildly retarded adolescents.[12] After three months in the setting, the students and I had observed many practices with which we disagreed, particularly the control procedures used by the cottage staff. The Cottage Life Department had responsibility for general resident supervision and for maintaining the rules of the institution. Staff in this department were not professionals, and a serious communications gap existed between them and the professionals (e.g., social work, psychology, education, counseling). Distaste for some of the more restrictive policies was commonly expressed by professional groups in the informal system but never directly raised in formal meetings. Our unit went along with this state of affairs, content to carve out our area of service while ignoring the general problems.

This "quasi-equilibrium" was upset when a cottage supervisor refused to allow group members to attend a session led by one of my students. Some of the residents were on restriction (a punishment for behavior offenses), and the cottage staff viewed the club group as a reward. The supervisor informed my student he could only see his members one at a time and only if he agreed to use the session to "give them a good lecture on how to behave." Our first reaction at our unit meeting the next day was one of shock at being instructed how to do our job. After reflection, however, and by applying a systematic analysis of the staff system of which we were a part, it began to be clear that this incident was a symptom of a larger problem of lack of communications between departments. While we could have easily won the battle of gaining permission to see our group members on our terms, since the administration wanted to maintain student training programs at the institution, we would have further alienated cottage staff and would probably have found our program sub-

verted in indirect ways. We chose, instead, to attack the larger communication problem, using this incident as a specific example. It was apparent to us that a major obstacle was a split in the institution between the training and therapy services, a problem that I described in an earlier publication.

The combination of overlapping boundaries and underdeveloped communications resulted in areas of conflict with limited opportunities for resolution. In such a situation, staff frustration grew, and a process of withdrawal was becoming evident. Instead of increasing lines of communications, those that were open were made less meaningful by avoiding discussion of conflict issues. Cottage Life staff, who bear the brunt of implementing the control function in the institution, became the convenient target for criticism. It became more difficult to mobilize the potential within the staff to make those adjustments which would keep the system in a "steady state." The most serious consequence of these problems was the blocking of "feedback" essential for system adjustment.[13]

Our strategy for action involved three lines of approach. First, I requested permission to attend a weekly meeting of department heads on the training side of the institution. This was the first formal bridging of the therapy-training gap and provided a forum for the discussion of conflict issues. By disregarding the taboo against real talk, I was able to raise concerns directly, and the resultant discussions served to clear up mutual misconceptions. It became clear that staff in all departments were reacting to people in other areas as if they were stereotypes, which led to consistently missed communications. Face-to-face contact made it more difficult for staff to dismiss each other out of hand. As communications opened up, the interdependence of department heads began to emerge, and the group became an arena for mutual aid. Members found they could help each other with their problems, particularly those in relation to the administration.

In a second line of work, each student in the unit requested weekly meetings with respective cottage attendants to help bridge the communication gap. One result of these meetings was that students could get a more balanced perspective on the problems faced by cottage attendants in dealing with residents. They found that their stereotypes of the attendants, developed by hearing only the residents' point of view and hardened by the general attitude towards cottage staff held in the institution, quickly faded as cottage attendants were able to share their "binds" in trying to do their job. As the students began to listen and to understand, cottage staff dramatically changed their views about student social workers. As the students better understood the realities of the attendants' jobs, they were perceived as "having their feet on the ground."

The third line of work had the most dramatic impact. In an effort to break down the isolation experienced between departments, we decided to make an effort to improve communications with the social service department itself. I outlined the problem in a meeting with the head of social service, as indicated in my notes:

I explained to Mrs. P. that I was concerned because the students felt they were an enclave in the institution and that they were even cut off from social service. I told her that we felt we had contributed to this isolation by not attending meetings and by not raising these feelings earlier. I asked if a meeting could be held with the department staff to discuss this and to see what might be done to rectify the problem. Mrs. P. told me she was glad I raised this, since she had always felt uncomfortable about the lack of connection but wasn't sure about what to do to correct it. She said she was always afraid to raise it. I asked her why, and she indicated that she didn't feel she could made demands on the unit as she would her staff, so she didn't want to seem to be pushing us for more involvement. I laughed and pointed out how we were both worried about the same thing but afraid to raise it. She agreed that other staff members might feel the same way and we decided to make it an agenda item at the next social work meeting.

The meeting provided an excellent clearing of the air as the staff members in the department and the students were able to raise their mutual concerns and to discover a number of misconceptions about each other's attitude towards student involvement. Specific strategies were discussed for more meaningful student involvement in the work of the department. I moved to generalize the question by pointing out that we felt an estrangement between social services and the rest of the institution, particularly cottage life. I gave the example of our recent experience of withholding permission from residents to attend a meeting and shared our beginning efforts to open up better communications. I asked if others felt the same way and a flood of examples and feelings emerged. It became clear that we were articulating common feelings held by the department members but never expressed. The balance of the meeting consisted of strategizing how we might reach out to the Cottage Life Department to discuss the working relationship between social workers and cottage attendants. An invitation was extended to the head of Cottage Life and his supervisors to discuss this problem and a date was mutually agreed upon. As the time approached, word of the meetings spread quickly, and the comments in the informal system revealed some clues as to why such meeting had not been held before. It was variously described as a "showdown," a "shooting match," and a "confrontation," and all staff members were tense when the meeting time arrived. To our surprise, the heads of all of the other departments also attended the meeting on their own initiative.

Three meetings were held, and those expecting fireworks were not disappointed. Many work issues were aired for the first time, often with great feeling. It was interesting to note that my attending the training department heads' weekly meetings paid dividends at this point. A beginning working relationship had been developed which led various department heads to offer support when a particular area was under attack, including the activities of my student unit. As we owned up to the ways in which we helped to make the work of others more difficult and as we attempted to be nondefensive, the defensiveness of the other staff members lessened. The focus of the discussion soon shifted from recrimination to identifying common problems, some needing to be dealt with by the departments and others requiring policy changes by the administration. As the list of concerns was drawn up, it became obvious that much work needed to be done even to begin to attack it. The group decided to form four task forces to deal with each general category of problems. Line and supervisory staff from each department sat on each task force, so that all opinions could be represented in the discussions. A steering committee was formed with a department head or supervisor from each area to monitor the process and a deadline set for reports. At this point the administration was approached and official support of this ad hoc effort requested. Some staff members had been concerned that the administrator would not value their efforts to institute change. A stereotyped view of

the administrator had previously developed, as someone not interested in anything that would disrupt the status quo, but when he was questioned, his response was, "I'm always besieged by people telling me about all of the problems. It's a relief to have the staff coming to me with some solutions, for once." A memo to all staff clearly outlined his support for the project. What had begun as our student unit raising questions about our relationship to the social service department had become an institution-wide, formally sanctioned effort to attack long-standing problems. In addition, a new structure was developed which greatly enhanced interdepartment communication at department head, supervisor, and line staff levels.

Thirty-eight recommendations for changes in policy and structure eventually emerged from the task forces. After the reports were reviewed and supported by line staff in each department, the changes were instituted. A sample of the recommendations provides a sense of the range of the topics:

1. Establishment of a representative resident council to meet monthly with the superintendent of the institution and department heads.
2. Elimination of a gold-card system which rated students of their behavior and controlled their access to the recreation program. This system had been generally described by staff as ineffective.
3. A change in the dining room procedures to allow for coed dining.
4. Allowing residents to have a degree of choice in selection of on-campus work assignments.
5. The expansion of social services into evening and weekend time when the greatest need was felt by staff and residents.
6. The combining of the training and therapy services committee into one committee.

Of course not all of the problems in the institution were solved by these changes. The crucial result was that staff members discovered that they could talk to each other and that this might yield positive results. Structural changes (e.g., resident council, combining training and therapy committees) would also increase the chances for better feedback on an ongoing basis. Most important, the experience released a flood of staff energy which had been suppressed by apathy and a related feeling of hopelessness. Staff learned that change could begin anywhere in the system and that they had to risk and invest themselves for those things they really wanted. The lesson was not lost on the social work students or myself.

Impact on Relations with Staff at Other Agencies

While providing services to clients, workers are brought into contact with staff from agencies who are also working with their clients. After repeated contacts, patterns of staff relationships develop. When these relationships are positive, they strengthen the cooperation between professionals. When they are negative, because of either direct or indirect cues of hostility or lack of mutual trust, barriers are erected which may cut a client off from the required service. In one example presented at a workshop, emergency service workers described how they had been cut off from using the services of a hospital psychiatric department which was refusing to accept their clients with drug-related psychotic episodes when they brought them to the hospital. A number of workers had had similar experiences or had experienced hostility on the part of the hospital staff, and as a result the agency had written the hospital off as non-cooperative and no longer attempted to

use it as a resource. A judgment about another agency staff can quickly become part of the agency culture. New staff members, who have had no experience with the other setting, are warned not even to try. In another illustration of this process, parole officers would not suggest that their parolees use a particular government employment service because of their past experiences which they felt indicated a bias against their clients.

When the example of the uncooperative psychiatric service was examined in some detail and the actual conversations between workers and the hospital staff analyzed, it was obvious that the workers had approached the hospital staff as if they expected to be rejected. Their aggressiveness in dealing with the nursing staff, for example, was answered by hostility and defensiveness. It was clear that nursing staff were viewing workers in an equally stereotyped way and that they began each encounter ready for a fight. When I inquired if any efforts had been made, either individually or as an agency, to explore this poor working relationship, I was not surprised to find that the answer was no. The workers sensed the tension and hostility during the encounters, but they never directly reached for it to explore the reason for the difficulty. As a staff group, it had never occurred to them to ask for a meeting with the hospital staff to discuss the obvious difficulties in communication. As often happens, the staff of each setting had decided, in advance, that the situation was hopeless.

After the analysis in the workshop, a meeting was held with the hospital staff. The skills of tuning in, contracting, and the rest were all used in developing a strategy for opening up honest discussion without backing the hospital staff into a corner. Reports from workers after this session indicated that the hospital staff had been equally upset about the state of the relationship with this agency. They had sensed the workers' hostility and particularly the workers' lack of understanding of their situation, that they were understaffed and somewhat overwhelmed by the cases brought in by the workers. The workers, in turn, were able to share their problems when faced with such cases on the emergency shift. Many of their problems were similar to those faced by the hospital staff (e.g., providing help to a spaced-out youngster, receiving a report of child abuse in progress, and being expected to be involved in both cases at the same time). The results of the session were a better delineation of the mutual responsibilities of the two settings and the working out of a system for handling the immediate problems when either system was under strain. In addition, an agreement was reached to cooperate in bringing the staffing problem to the attention of the respective agency administrations and supervisory government bodies. While the problems were not solved immediately, the hospital was once again open to agency workers. In the earlier example with the parole officers and the employment agency, a joint meeting yielded similar results with better understanding on both parts about the special problems involved in job finding for parolees and the establishment of a special group of workers to handle these referrals and to provide liaison with the parole service.

What becomes clear in many of these examples is that workers can be so overwhelmed by the demands upon them that they have little patience with problems in other systems. Communication breakdowns lead to stereotypes which then become self-fulfilling prophecies. Client service suffers in the end. Workers will argue that they do not have time for these

efforts to improve working relations between agencies; yet close analysis reveals that poor relations often result in greater loss of time than would be needed for efforts to resolve the problems.

A final example of professional impact concerns the common problem of "too many cooks." The following excerpt provides a good illustration. One worker reported an interview with a young mother of six children who was seen by the worker because of her potential for child abuse. After a good contracting interview, the worker tried to arrange a second session but, much to her amazement, she discovered another problem faced by the mother:

WORKER: I'm glad you found this interview helpful. Can we get together on Friday?
CLIENT: I would love to, but I'm afraid I'm seeing Ted's probation officer Friday morning.
WORKER: OK, how about in the afternoon?"
CLIENT: No, I have an appointment with the visiting nurse who is helping me out with my youngest.
WORKER: Would Monday be OK?
CLIENT: I don't know, the homemaker comes then, and the family support worker is here as well.
WORKER: (Beginning to feel a bit frustrated) Can you tell me your schedule next week, and maybe I can find a time?
CLIENT: Well, Tuesday I'm supposed to see Leslie's psychiatrist at the mental health center, and Wednesday the family court worker wants to speak to me ... and. ...
WORKER: My God, when do you have time for yourself?
CLIENT: You know, it's a real problem— but some of these people I have to see, and others are so nice, I don't want to hurt their feelings.
WORKER: Mrs. T., I wonder if all of these people know that you are seeing the others?
CLIENT: Probably not.
WORKER: Would it help any if I tried to call a meeting of all the workers you are see-

ing, just so we can all find out what is going on with you, and perhaps work out some way to cut down on all of this?

CLIENT: Please! Anything would help.

This interview is not unusual. Multi-problemed families often find themselves involved with such a complicated and intricate system of services that they have need of a worker just to help them sort it out. This worker called the meeting with the mother in attendance. They were all shocked to discover fourteen different services and workers involved with the family, some of whom were providing overlapping services. A plan was developed for the social worker to serve as "key worker" for the mother and for her to help coordinate the other services as needed. Discussions were also held as to how the services could do a better job of using registries to be in touch with each other's work with the same families.

Conclusions

This chapter has argued for the worker to pay attention to opportunities for professional impact both in the area of agency and community social policy and in relation to interstaff relationships. Common themes in the examples have stressed the importance of workers overcoming initial feelings of apathy and hopelessness, of not being overwhelmed by the enormity of problems, of having faith in the potential of systems to change, and of the importance of using interpersonal skills in all relationships. When I have dis-

cussed issues of professional impact in training workshops, I have noted a pattern of response from workers. First, there is a tendency to externalize and place complete blame for the problem on the "others" in the system. When I challenge this, there is usually a great deal of defensiveness and anger. Often there are charges that I simply "don't understand the particular situation." Detailed examination of the specifics of the interactions often leads to a lowering of defenses, particularly if I can be genuinely empathic with the difficulties involved and the feelings generated in the workers. Recognition that they may have had some part to play in the proceedings often leads to expressions of guilt about past or present experiences that workers feel they could have handled differently. This is followed by a renewed enthusiasm about the possibilities for action. Situations which seemed hopeless now seem very hard to deal with, but some possible next steps are evident. Workers are reassured when they realize that they only need take responsibility for their next steps and that the systems have responsibility for their own. I have come to the view that workers very much want to believe that there is a next step and that they can have some impact. Even though they may fight this idea initially, they would be very disappointed if I agreed with their apparent fatalism. I don't think I need to motivate workers to attempt professional impact on their systems. Rather, I need to reach for and free the existing impetus toward action.

NOTES

1. William Schwartz, "Private Troubles and Public Issues: One Social Work Job or Two?" *The Social Welfare Forum, 1969* (New York: Columbia University Press, 1969), pp. 22–43. This position is also argued by Schwartz in a one-hour videotape program, "Program Two:

Private Troubles and Public Issues," Lawrence Shulman (Producer), *The Helping Process in Social Work: Theory, Practice and Research* (Montreal: Instructional Communications Centre, McGill University, 1976).

2. Schwartz, "Private Troubles and Public Issues", p. 37, and C. Wright Mills, *The Sociological Imagination* (New York: Oxford University Press, 1959), p. 8.

3. Schwartz, "Private Troubles and Public Issues," p. 38.

4. Ibid., p. 40.

5. Ibid., p. 41.

6. For examples of efforts at systems change, see Zelda P. Foster, "How Social Work Can Influence Hospital Management of Fatal Illness," *Social Work* 10 (October 1965):30–35; Hyman K. Weiner, "The Hospital, the Ward and the Patients as Clients: Use of the Group Method," *Social Work* 4 (October 1959):57–64.

7. Alfred H. Stanton and Maurice F. Schwartz, *Mental Hospital: A Study of Institutional Participation in Psychiatric Illness and Treatment* (New York: Basic Books, 1954).

8. For a discussion of the adaptation of the model to staff groups, see William Schwartz, "Group Work in Public Welfare," in *Public Welfare,* 26 (October 1968), pp. 332–35.

9. Lawrence Shulman, "Client, Staff and the Social Agency," *Social Work Practice, 1970* (New York: Columbia University Press, 1970), p. 22.

10. Chris Argyris, *Integrating the Individual and the Organization* (New York: John Wiley and Sons, Inc., 1964), Chapter 3.

11. George Brager and Stephen Holloway, *Changing Human Service Organizations: Politics and Practice* (New York: The Free Press, 1978).

12. For an earlier publication describing this example, see Lawrence Shulman, *A Casebook of Social Work With Groups: The Mediating Model* (New York: Council on Social Work Education, 1968), pp. 43–50.

13. Ibid., p. 45.

EPILOGUE

This book has drawn on the practice illustrations provided by many students and workers. I have used process recordings, transcripts of audio- and videotapes, and summary devices, such as the "record of service." Each of these formats has provided insights into the moment-by-moment activities of workers in interaction with individual clients, small groups, families or the representatives of systems important to clients. This book could not have been written without these examples.

I believe the detailed analysis of our work is essential if we are to deepen our understanding of the processes involved. Examination of practice recordings provides insights into the nature of a complex process, helps to keep practice theory development close to reality, and provides hypotheses which lend themselves to empirical research. In a cyclical fashion, these insights, theoretical constructs, and research findings help us return to the analysis of practice with increased clarity. The movement from practice, to theory building and research, and then back to practice is the key to our future development.

In a like manner, workers must be continually examining the details of their interaction with clients in order to strengthen their own practice models. Caseload realities usually makes it impossible to record all practice; workers need to select some area of their work for special focus. The type of recording used for skill development can vary. The recordings shared in this book vary in type and level of sophistication. The best ones, however, usually included the following: some detail of both the beginning and the ending of the sessions described; summaries of the work, with expanded detail on key aspects of the interaction (efforts to write a complete process recording of an entire session can be overwhelming and self defeating in the long run); the worker as a participant in the action (it is not unusual for students to write their first process recordings with no mention of themselves in the interview); observations of the non-verbal signals as well as the conversation (e.g., June looked sad and seemed to turn away from the group); identification of the worker's and client's affect as an integrated part of the commentary; and finally, the worker's analysis of the action described. The ability to record process after a session is a learned skill, with students usually moving from simple statements of the interaction to deeper and richer recordings integrating the elements described above. Even in

412

those situations where more sophisticated devices for recording practice are available (e.g., video equipment), I think it is important to develop the process recording skills.

The wider availability of complex recording devices, such as videotape machines, is also having an important impact on our interest in the details of practice. We have the means of sharing our work with colleagues, and of exposing our practice to self and colleagual scrutiny. Many of us who were not trained in a culture which encouraged this form of analysis have had to overcome our fears of risking in order to benefit from critical advice. Many training institutions have recognized the importance of developing this capacity for sharing one's work and taking help from colleagues and have placed a priority on this aspect of student development. In our own program for social workers at the University of British Columbia, students are provided training in using video and audio equipment in the first weeks of class and have the opportunity to tape role plays of first interviews within two weeks of the start of the program. The analysis of these tapes in class discussion provides important handles for classroom instructors to deal with the professional "culture for work," and the importance (as well as the difficulty) of exposing one's work. The use of student practice material throughout the school year reinforces this idea.

Workers can also tap another source of help for their continued learning—their clients. For example, questionnaires developed through research can provide feedback on skill use. Clients can also be asked to listen to tape recordings of interviews with workers (or watch videotapes) and to provide their reactions as a source of help for the worker's continued learning. Most clients are quite willing to act as consultants for their worker's training. The offering of help can be a complex procedure. Every helping professional can use all the assistance available—from clients, colleagues, supervisors and teachers.

APPENDIX

Notes on Research Methodology

The purpose of this appendix is to summarize the research methodology employed by this author in the social work study cited in this book. I feel it is important for the reader to have access to the methodology employed and to be clear about the study's limitation. For a more detailed discussion, refer to other published reports.[1] The central line of inquiry of the study was to examine social work practice skill and the relationship between what workers did in their interviews and the development of a positive working relationship with clients as well as the worker's helpfulness. The approach involved starting with a number of hypotheses about the impact of worker behavior suggested by the theoretical model and developing a research design to obtain empirical data, using the findings to support, challenge, elaborate, or rethink some of the basic constructs. This in turn created a new set of theoretical generalizations which will provide hypotheses for further study. The important point is that this is an ongoing process with each step of the research viewed as tentative. Findings are seen as preliminary in nature. Only when repeated research in a range of settings replicates findings can we move from tentative hypotheses to confirmed generalization. It

is important to understand this research stance, so that a proper evaluation of the findings can be made.

INSTRUMENT DEVELOPMENT

The first phase of the work involved the development and testing of the instrument used in the study. One of these was the Social Worker Behavior Questionnaire. This consisted of twenty-seven items each describing a particular skill. The questionnaire was designed to be completed by clients who would be reporting on their worker's frequency of use of these behaviors. For example, the skill of *moving from the general to the specific* was phrased as follows: "When I raised a general concern, the worker asked me for examples." The client would choose a response from the following: "(1) often, (2) fairly often, (3) seldom, (4) never, (5) no answer." Since the study was implemented in two Canadian child welfare agencies, five versions of the questionnaire were developed to suit the particular respondents (natural parents, foster parents, unwed mothers, adolescents, and adoptive parents).[2] The items on the questionnaires were the same; only the introductions and examples used for each item varied. Items on this questionnaire constituted the independent variables in the study.

A second instrument, the Service Satisfaction Questionnaire, obtained clients' perceptions on the content of the work (e.g., the themes discussed) as well as their perceptions of their relationships with the worker ("How satisfied are you with the way you and your worker get along?") and the worker's helpfulness ("In general, how helpful has your worker been?") These two key items on the questionnaire were used as dependent variables. Both questionnaires were translated into French, since approximately 11 percent of the population of the participating agencies were French-speaking.

The instrument-development stage included testing both questionnaires for reliability and validity. While the results of these tests are summarized here, I would caution the reader to consider these instruments in an embryonic stage requiring further testing and refining.[3] Testing of the stability of the social worker behavior questionnaire was undertaken by sending them to a representative group of clients and then sending a second one two weeks after the return of the first (test-retest procedure). An average score for the total test was computed by taking the simple mean score for all items. The Pearson correlation between the average scores on the two tests was .75 (SD=.29). Individual items were also compared, with seven yielding correlations of less than .30, nine with correlations between .30 and .50, and thirteen between .51 and .86. Internal consistency of the questionnaire was examined using the split-half method. An average score for the two blocked halves of the test was computed and the score for one half correlated with the other. This yielded a correlation of .79 using the Spearman-Brown correction. In similar tests of the Service Satisfaction Questionnaire, the worker relationship item yielded a correlation of .68 in a test-retest procedure, and the helpfulness item a correlation of .56.

Validity of both questionnaires was explored through a number of procedures. Face validity was examined, using interviews with respondents, workers, and supervisors to determine the clarity of the items. In a second test, the 15 workers whose clients had given them the most positive scores on the Social Worker Behavior Questionnaire and the 15 who had received the least positive scores were selected from among the 118 workers in the study. The workers with the more positive scores on their behavior questionnaires also received more positive scores on the relationship variable ($F=5.6$, $df=29$, $p\leq.05$) and the helpfulness variable ($F=7.42$, $df=29$, $p\leq.02$). An additional analysis was conducted using trained raters who viewed videotapes of 120 hours of practice of 11 volunteer social workers and rated them employing a category observation system developed by this researcher. Rater scores were then compared with the scores assigned to the workers by the videotaped clients who completed the Social Worker Behavior Questionnaire. Although some strong correlations were found, they were not high enough to be significant with a small sample of workers. In another procedure, 20 workers scored themselves on the questionnaire and these scores were compared with the average scores they received from their clients. Workers scored themselves the same as their clients or one scale apart 81 percent of the time. However, this finding must be considered with some caution because of the low variation in responses for some items which would have contributed to agreement. In a similar validity test for the Service Satisfaction

Questionnaire, workers and clients agreed on the state of their relationship and on the worker's helpfulness or were one scale apart in their ratings 95 percent of the time. Low variations in response once again limit the interpretations possible from this finding.

METHOD

The total staffs of the two child welfare agencies participating in the study were included in the sample. Of the 118 workers, 83 percent were female, and 61 percent had some form of social work training (34 percent of the total number were MSW trained). The entire caseload (active at the time of the study) for each worker was identified, and all clients over fourteen years old were sent either a Social Worker Behavior Questionnaire *or* the Service Satisfaction Questionnaire. Random assignment was used to determine which of the two questionnaires a client received, so that each client had an equal chance to report on either their worker's behavior *or* their satisfaction with the relationship and the worker's helpfulness. This procedure was followed so that filling out one questionnaire would not influence the results on the other.

Over 4,000 questionnaires were mailed to potential respondents. The mailing took place during a Canadian mail strike, and many cases which were relatively inactive were included. In spite of these problems, the return rate was 53 percent with a respondent sample of 1,784.[4] Of this group, 82 percent had had contacts with their worker for more than two months, 70 percent had high school education or less, and 65 percent were over twenty-five. Full details on the worker and client samples are reported in the research reports as well as results of the analyses of the impact of worker and client variables

on the outcomes. Results of a telephone survey which contacted over 50 percent of the nonrespondents to determine the reasons for their lack of participation can also be found in the report.

Average scores were computed from the returns for each worker on each questionnaire. These scores were then assigned as the worker's score. The result was a measure of frequency of use of each of the twenty-seven behaviors for each worker, which reflected the average computed from his respondents' returns. In addition, an average score for relationship and helpfulness was also computed. Correlations were computed to determine the association between specific behaviors and the outcome measures of relationship and helpfulness. In addition, a partial correlation procedure was introduced which made it possible to treat the worker's score on relationship as a third variable while analyzing the association between the skills and helpfulness. This analysis allowed for interesting inferences about which skills contributed to relationship building, which ones to helpfulness, and which ones to both. Findings were then used to make inferences about the original theoretical model.

LIMITATIONS

The findings of this study must be considered in light of the limitations in the study design. The study focused on practice in two child welfare agencies and the impact of the setting on the results can be serious. For example, many clients who were contesting the agency's intervention responded to the study. However, the number was low enough to suggest that the sample may have been somewhat mellowed. Self-selection must therefore be considered a major limitation. In addition, the study was essentially of client perceptions. Although testing was implemented to determine instrument reliability and validity, further work is needed to increase our confidence in the accuracy of client perceptions. Another limitation is that the outcome data is not of the "hard" type, that is, other than client perceptions. An effort to analyze such data is reported in the study but the findings were inconclusive because of limitations in agency recording procedures. The study was also limited in that it concentrated only on the interactional skills of the worker. Other skills, such as assessment, and other factors such as client strength and motivation, caseload size, social policy which affects clients (e.g., housing, income support) all play some part in the outcome. This author's current research attempts to take these variables into account when considering the impact of worker skill. These limitations and others are reason to consider the findings of this study tentative although useful for developing the theoretical model for further testing. Replications of findings in different settings and with different clients would provide further evidence in support of the generalizations. There is already some support of this nature, since two of the skills with the strongest positive correlations, *sharing worker's feelings* and *understanding client's feelings*, are similar to those found to be helpful in similar research with other professions[5] and in follow-up research studies by this author into supervision practice and medical practice.

CATEGORY OBSERVATION SYSTEM

Mention is made in this text of the findings of a subdesign of the larger study in which videotapes of the practice of eleven workers in one of the agencies were analyzed by trained raters. You will have to refer to the other reports of this research for details; however, a brief summary will help in interpreting the findings reported in the text.[6] A category observation system provides a means for making systematic observations of interactions between workers and clients.[7] In its simplest form, a category is created by grouping together a number of associated behaviors and providing the grouping with a title and number. For example, all worker behaviors which deal with client feelings could be called empathic skills. Whenever an observer notices one of these behaviors during a session, the number representing the category of behavior can be scored. At the end of an interview one can thus have a numerical record of the worker's behaviors and the client's responses.

A category observation system was developed for this study as part of a subdesign to evaluate the validity of the Social Worker Behavior Questionnaire. From four to six individual or group sessions of each of the eleven workers were videotaped. Three trained raters reviewed these tapes and recorded every interaction observed, according to the eleven categories in the system. If a single behavior (e.g., silence) persisted for more than three seconds, the rater would continue to score it every three seconds. The resultant data rated 120 hours of practice and provided over 99,000 discrete entries for computer analysis.

Rates were tested for reliability in two ways. First, each rater independently rated a specific tape and then rated the same tape one week later. The percentages of each category scored on each of the two ratings was compared (test-retest) with the average percentage of agreement for the three raters over all categories at 89 percent. It should be pointed out that it was not possible to compare each individual score, only the agreement for the overall category. Interrater reliability was examined by having each of the three raters rate one session (different from the one used for test-retest purposes) and then comparing the raters with each other. After a period of training, average interrater reliability percentages reached 79 percent. In computing percentages of

agreement for both tests, Scott's Coefficient was used to account for the differences in the frequency of use of categories (e.g., only a very small percentage of total entries were empathic behaviors.)[8] It would be beyond the scope of this book to provide full details on the category system or the findings, and the reader is encouraged to review the other cited publications.

NOTES

1. See Lawrence Shulman, "A Study of Practice Skills," *Social Work* 23 (July 1978):274–81; Lawrence Shulman, *A Study of the Helping Process* (Vancouver, Social Work Department, University of British Columbia, 1977); Lawrence Shulman, *Identifying, Measuring and Teaching the Helping Process* (New York: Council on Social Work Education and the Canadian Association of Schools of Social Work, 1979).

2. The two agencies involved were the Children's Aid Society of Ottawa and the Children's Service Centre of Montreal.

3. Reliability and validity details can be found in the full report, *A Study of the Helping Process;* data on specific item reliability and validity can be found in the related monograph, *Identifying, Measuring and Teaching the Helping Skills.*

4. The total number of responses are less than 53 percent return rate cited because a number of respondents chose to use an option offered by the researcher to return their questionnaires without completing them if they felt they had not had sufficient contact with their workers to make a judgment. They could check a box indicating this on the return.

5. For example, see Robert R. Carkhuff, *Helping and Human Relations: A Primer for*

Lay and Professional Helpers, Vol. 1, *Selection and Training.* New York: Holt, Rinehart and Winston, 1969. See also Lawrence Shulman, Elizabeth Robinson and Anna Luckyj, *A Study of the Content, Context and Skills of Supervision* (Vancouver; Social Work Department, University of British Columbia, 1981); Lawrence Shulman and William Buchan, *The Impact of the Family Physician's Communication, Relationship and Technical Skills on Patient Compliance, Satisfaction, Reassurance, Comprehension and Improvement* (Vancouver: Social Work Department, University of British Columbia, 1982).

6. For details on the Category Observation System, see the full report in *Identifying, Measuring and Teaching the Helping Skills.*

7. For examples of other systems, see Florence Hollis, "Explorations in the Development of a Typology of Casework Treatment," *Social Casework* 48 (June 1967):335–41; Robert Bales, *Interaction Process Analysis* (Reading, Mass.: Addison-Wesley Press, 1950); Henry S. Mass, "Group Influences on Client-Worker Interaction," *Social Work* 9 (April 1964):70–79.

8. W. S. Scott, "Reliability of Content Analysis: The Case of Nominal Scale Coding," *Public Opinion Quarterly,* Fall 1955, pp. 321–25.

BIBLIOGRAPHY

Ackerman, Nathan. *Psychodynamics of Family Life.* New York: Basic Books, 1958.

Argyis, Chris. *Integrating the Individual and the Organization.* New York: John Wiley & Sons, Inc., 1964.

Asch, S. E. "Effects of Group Pressure upon the Modification and Distortion of Judgments." In *Groups, Leadership and Men,* edited by H. Guetzkow, pp. 177–90. Pittsburgh, Pa.: Carnegie Press, 1951.

Baldwin, James Mark. *The Individual and Society: or, Psychology and Sociology.* Boston: Richard G. Badger, Gorham Press, 1911.

Bales, Robert. *Interaction Process Analysis.* Reading, Mass.: Addison-Wesley Publishing, 1950.

Bales, Robert. "Task Roles and Social Roles in Problem Solving Groups." In *Readings in Social Psychology,* 3d ed., edited by Eleanor E. Maccoby et al., pp. 437–47. New York: Holt, Rinehart & Winston, 1958.

Bandler, Richard; John Grindler, and Virginia Satir. *Changing with Families.* Palo Alto, Calif.: Science and Behavior Books, 1976.

Bavelas, A. "Communications Patterns in Task Oriented Groups." *Journal of Acoustical Society of America* 22 (1950):725–30.

Bateson, Gregory; Don Jackson; Jay Haley; and John H. Weakland. "Toward a Theory of Schizophrenia." *Behavioral Science* 1 (1956):251–64.

Bell, Norman W., and Ezra F. Vogel. "The Emotionally Disturbed Child as the Family Scapegoat." In *A Modern Introduction to the Family,* edited by Norman W. Bell and Ezra F. Vogel, pp. 382–97. New York: Free Press, 1960.

Benne, Kenneth D., and Paul Sheats. "Functional Roles of Group Members." *Journal of Social Issues* 4 (1948):41–49.

Bennis, Warren G., and Herbert A. Shepard. "A Theory of Group Development." *Human Relations* 9 (1956):415–37.

Bernstein, Saul, ed. *Further Explorations in Group Work.* Boston: Boston University School of Social Work, 1970.

Bion, William R. *Experiences in Groups.* New York: Basic Books, 1961.

Block, Jack, and Norman Haan. *Lives through Time.* Berkeley, Calif.: Bancroft Books, 1971.

Bowen, Murray. "The Family as a Unit of Study and Treatment." *American Journal of Orthopsychiatry* 31 (January 1961):40–60.

Bradford, Leland P.; Jack R. Gibb; and Kenneth D. Benne, eds. *T-Group Theory and Laboratory Method.* New York: John Wiley & Sons, Inc., 1964.

Brager, George, and Stephan Holloway. *Changing Human Service Organizations: Politics and Practice.* New York: Free Press, 1978.

Carkhuff, Robert R. *Helping and Human Relations: A Primer for Lay and Professional Helpers,* Vol. 1, *Selection and Training.* New York: Holt, Rinehart & Winston, 1969.

Cox, Fred et al., *Strategies of Community Organization, A Book of Readings, Third Edition.* Itasca, Ill.: F. E. Peacock Publishers, Inc., 1979).

Coyle, Grace L. *Group Work with American Youth.* New York: Harper & Row, 1948.

Deutsch, M. "An Experimental Study of the Effects of Cooperation and Competition upon Group Process." *Human Relations* 2 (1949):199–232.

Dewey, John. *Democracy and Education; An Introduction to the Philosophy of Education.* New York: Free Press, 1916.

Erikson, Erik H. *Childhood and Society.* New York: W.W. Norton, 1950.

Flanders, Ned A. *Analyzing Teaching Behaviors.* Reading, Mass.: Addison-Wesley Publishing, 1970.

Freeman, David S. *Techniques of Family Therapy.* New York: Jason Aronson, Inc., 1981.

Freud, Sigmund. "Freud's Psychoanalytic Method," in *Standard Edition,* Vol. 7 (London: Hogarth Press, 1953).

Fried, Barbara. *The Middle-Age Crisis.* New York: Harper & Row, 1967.

Foster, Zelda P. "How Social Work Can Influence Hospital Management of Fatal Illness." *Social Work* 10 (October 1965):30–35.

Garfield, Goodwin P., and Carol R. Irizarry. "Recording the 'Record of Service': Describing Social Work Practice." In *The Practice of Group Work,* edited by William Schwartz and Serapio Zalba, pp. 241–65. New York: Columbia University Press, 1971.

Garland, James A. and Kolodny, Ralph L. "Characteristics and Resolutions of Scapegoating," *Social Work Practice, 1967.* New York: Columbia University Press, 1967.

Garvin, Charles. "Complementarity of Role Expectations in Groups: the Member-Worker Contract." *Social Work Practice, 1969,* pp. 127–45. New York: Columbia University Press, 1969.

Germain, Carel. "Teaching an Ecological Approach to Social Work Practice." In *Teaching for Competence in the Delivery of Direct Services,* pp. 31–39. New York: Council on Social Work Education, 1976.

Germain, Carel B., and Alex Gitterman. *The Life Model of Social Work Practice.* New York: Columbia University Press, 1980.

Gitterman, Alex. "Group Work in the Public Schools." In *The Practice of Group Work,* edited by William Schwartz and Serapio Zalba, pp. 45–72. New York: Columbia University Press, 1971.

Grosser, Charles F. *New Directions In Community Organization.* New York: Praeger Publishers, 1973.

Hare, Paul A. *Handbook of Small Group Research.* New York: Free Press, 1962.

Hartford, Margaret. *Groups in Social Work.* New York: Columbia University Press, 1972.

Hearn, Gordon. *Theory Building in Social Work.* Toronto: University of Toronto Press, 1958.

Hearn, Gordon. *The General Systems Approach to Understanding Groups.* Health Education Monographs, no. 14. New York: Society of Public Health Educators, 1962.

Hearn, Gordon, ed. *The General Systems Approach: Contributions toward an Holistic Conception of Social Work.* New York: Council on Social Work Education, 1969.

Heyman, David. "A Function for the Social Worker in the Antipoverty Program." In *The Practice of Group Work,* edited by William Schwartz and Serapio Zalba. New York: Columbia University Press, 1971.

Hollis, Florence. *Casework: A Psychosocial Therapy.* New York: Random House, 1964.

Hollis, Florence. "Explorations in the Development of a Typology of Casework Treatment." *Social Casework* 48 (June 1967):335–41.

Homans, George. *The Human Group.* New York: Harcourt Brace Jovanovich, 1950.

Horne, Arthur M., and Merle M. Ohlsen, eds. *Family Counseling and Therapy.* Itasca, Ill.: F. E. Peacock Publishers, Inc., 1982.

Huber, Joan, ed. *Changing Women in a Changing Society.* Chicago: University of Chicago Press, 1973.

Keith, David V., and Carl A. Whitaker. "Experiential/Symbolic Family Therapy." In *Family Counselling and Therapy,* edited by Arthur M. Horne and Merle M. Ohlsen. Itasca, Ill.: F. E. Peacock Publishers, Inc., 1982, pp. 43–74.

Klein, Alan F. *Effective Group Work.* New York: Association Press, 1972.

Konopka, Gesela. *Social Group Work: A Helping Process.* Englewood Cliffs, N.J.: Prentice-Hall, 1971.

Kropotkin, Peter. *Mutual Aid, A Factor of Evolution.* New York: Alfred A. Knopf, 1925.

Kübler-Ross, Elizabeth. *On Death and Dying.* New York: Macmillan, 1969.

Kuhn, Thomas H. *The Structure of Scientific Revolution.* Chicago: University of Chicago Press, 1962.

Lefco, Helene. *Dance Therapy: Narrative Case Histories.* Chicago: Nelson-Hall, 1975.

Levine, Baruch. *Fundamentals of Group Treatment.* Chicago: Whitehall Press, 1967.

Lewin, Kurt. *A Dynamic Theory of Personality: Selected Papers of Kurt Lewin.* New York: McGraw-Hill Book Co., Inc., 1935.

Lewin, Kurt. *Field Theory in Social Science: Selected Theoretical Papers.* New York: Harper & Row, 1951.

Lewin, Kurt. "Field Theory in Social Science." In *Frontiers in Group Dynamics,* edited by Dorwin Cartwright, pp. 221–33. New York: Harper & Row, 1951.

Linton, Ralph. *The Study of Man.* New York: Appleton-Century-Crofts, 1936.

Maas, Henry S. "Group Influences on Client-Worker Interaction." *Social Work* 9 (April 1964):70–79.

Mead, George Herbert. *Mind, Self and Society.* Chicago: University of Chicago Press, 1934.

Mills, C. Wright. *The Sociological Imagination.* New York: Oxford University Press, 1959.

Minuchin, Salvador. *Families and Family Therapy.* Cambridge, Mass.: Harvard University Press, 1974.

Minuchin, Salvador, and Herman C. Fishman. *Family Therapy Techniques.* Cambridge, Mass.: Harvard University Press, 1981.

Minuchin, Salvador; Bernice L. Rosman; and Lester Baker. *Psychosomatic Families: Anorexia Nervosa in Context.* Cambridge, Mass.: Harvard University Press, 1978.

Murphy, Gardner. *Human Potentialities.* New York: Basic Books, 1958.

Nash, Johnny (words and music). "I Can See Clearly Now." New York: C.B.S., Inc., 1972.

Norman, Elaine, and Arlene Mancuso. *Women's Issues and Social Work Practice.* Itasca, Ill.: F. E. Peacock Publishers, Inc., 1980.

Northen, Helen. *Social Work With Groups.* New York: Columbia University Press, 1969.

Petrullo, Luigi, and Bernard M. Bass. *Leadership and Interpersonal Behavior.* New York: Holt, Rinehart & Winston, 1961.

Phillips, Helen. *Essentials of Social Group Work Skill.* New York: Association Press, 1957.

Pincus, Allen, and Anne Minahan. *Social Work Practice: Model and Method.* Itasca, Ill.: F. E. Peacock Publishers, Inc., 1973.

Polansky, Norman, and Jacob Kounin. "Clients' Reactions to Initial Interviews." *Human Relations* 9 (July 1956):237–64.

Potok, Chaim. *The Chosen.* New York: Alfred A. Knopf, 1976.

Potok, Chaim. *My Name Is Asher Lev.* New York: Alfred A. Knopf, 1976.

Reid, William J., and Ann W. Shyne. *Brief and Extended Casework.* New York: Columbia University Press, 1969.

Rogers, Carl R. *On Becoming a Person.* Boston: Houghton Mifflin, 1961.

Rogers, Carl R. *Freedom to Learn.* Columbus: Charles E. Merrill, 1969.

Rose, Sheldon D. *Group Therapy: A Behavioral Approach.* Englewood Cliffs, N.J.: Prentice-Hall, 1977.

Rubington, Earl, and Martin S. Weinberg. *Deviance: The Interactionist Perspective.* Toronto: Collier-Macmillan, 1968.

Ruesch, Jurgen. *Disturbed Communications.* New York: W.W. Norton, 1957.

Sandel, Susan. "Integrating Dance Therapy into Treatment." *Hospital and Community Psychiatry* 26 (July 1975):439–41.

Satir, Virginia. *Conjoint Family Therapy.* Palo Alto, Calif.: Science and Behavior Books, Inc., 1967.

Scherz, Frances H. "Theory and Practice of Family Therapy." In *Theories of Social Casework,* edited by Robert W. Roberts and Robert H. Nee. Chicago: The University of Chicago Press, 1970.

Schwartz, William. "The Social Worker in the

Group." In *New Perspectives on Services to Groups: Theory, Organization and Practice.* New York: National Association of Social Workers, 1961, pp. 7–34; and *The Social Welfare Forum, 1961,* pp. 146–77. New York: Columbia University Press, 1961.

Schwartz, William. "Between Client and System: The Mediating Function." In *Theories of Social Work with Groups,* edited by Robert W. Roberts and Helen Northen. New York: Columbia University Press, 1976.

Schwartz, William. "Group Work in Public Welfare." *Public Welfare* 26 (October 1968):322–70.

Schwartz, William. "On the Use of Groups in Social Work Practice." In *The Practice of Group Work,* edited by William Schwartz and Serapio Zalba, pp. 3–24. New York: Columbia University Press, 1971.

Schwartz, William. "Social Group Work: The Interactionist Approach." In *Encyclopedia of Social Work,* Vol. II. Edited by John B. Turner. New York: National Association of Social Workers, 1977.

Schwartz, William. "Theory and Practice in Social Work with Groups." Transcript of a tape-recorded institute on group work practice, Columbia University School of Social Work, 1966.

Schwartz, William. "Toward a Strategy of Group Work Practice." *Social Service Review* 36 (September 1962):pp. 268–79.

Schwartz, William. "Private Troubles and Public Issues: One Social Work Job or Two?" *The Social Welfare Forum, 1969,* pp. 22–43. New York: Columbia University Press, 1969.

Scott, W.S. "Reliability of Content Analysis: The Case of Nominal Scale Coding." *Public Opinion Quarterly,* Fall 1955, pp. 321–25.

Setleis, Lloyd. "How Should We Act? How Should We Be?" *Journal of Social Work Process* 16 (1967):139–58.

Sherif, Muzafer. *The Psychology of Social Norms.* New York: Harper & Row, 1936.

Sherif, Muzafer, and Carolyn W. Sherif. *An Outline of Social Psychology,* rev. ed. New York: Harper & Row, 1956.

Shoemaker, Louise P. "The Use of Group Work Skill with Short Term Groups." In *Social Work with Groups.* New York: National Association of Social Workers, 1960.

Shulman, Lawrence, *Teaching the Helping Skills: A Field Instructor's Guide.* Itasca, Ill.: F. E. Peacock Publishers, Inc., 1983.

Shulman, Lawrence. *The Skills of Supervision and Staff Management.* Itasca, Ill.: F. E. Peacock Publishers, Inc., 1982.

Shulman, Lawrence. *The Skills of Helping.* Videotape series. Montreal: Instructional Communications Centre, McGill University, 1979.

Shulman, Lawrence. *Core Skills for Field Instructors.* Videotape series. Montreal: Instructional Communications Centre, McGill University, 1983.

Shulman, Lawrence. "A Study of Practice Skills." *Social Work* 23 (July 1978):274–81.

Shulman, Lawrence. *A Study of the Helping Process.* Vancouver: Social Work Department, University of British Columbia, 1977.

Shulman, Lawrence. *A Casebook of Social Work with Groups: The Mediating Model.* New York: Council on Social Work Education, 1968.

Shulman, Lawrence. "Social Work Skill: The Anatomy of a Helping Act." *Social Work Practice, 1969,* pp. 29–48. New York: Columbia University Press, 1969.

Shulman, Lawrence, producer. *The Helping Process in Social Work: Theory, Practice and Research.* Videotape series. Montreal: Instructional Communications Centre, McGill University, 1976.

Shulman, Lawrence. *Identifying, Measuring and Teaching the Helping Skills.* New York: Council on Social Work Education, 1979.

Shulman, Lawrence. "A Game-Model Theory of Inter-Personal Relations." *Social Work* 13 (1968):16-22.

Shulman, Lawrence. "Scapegoats, Group Workers, and the Pre-Emptive Intervention." *Social Work* 12 (April 1967):37–43.

Shulman, Lawrence. " 'Program' in Group Work: Another Look." In *The Practice of Group Work,* edited by William Schwartz and Serapio Zalba, pp. 221–40. New York: Columbia University Press, 1971.

Shulman, Lawrence. "Client, Staff and the Social Agency." *Social Work Practice, 1970,* pp. 21–40. New York: Columbia University Press, 1970.

Shulman, Lawrence; Elizabeth Robinson; and Anna Luckyj. *A Study of the Content, Context and Skills of Supervision.* Vancouver, B.C.: Social Work Department, University of British Columbia, 1981.

Shulman, Lawrence, and William Buchan. *The Impact of the Family Physician's Communication, Relationship and Technical Skills on Patient Compliance, Satisfaction, Reassurance, Comprehension and Improvement.* Vancouver, B.C.: Social Work Department, University of British Columbia, 1982.

Siporin, Max. *Introduction to Social Work Practice.* New York: Macmillan, 1975.

Smalley, Ruth E. *Theory for Social Work Practice.* New York: Columbia University Press, 1967.

Stanton, Alfred H. and Schwartz, Maurice. *Mental Hospital: A Study of Institutional Participation in Psychiatric Illness and Treatment.* New York: Basic Books, 1954.

Stark, Frances. "Barriers to Client-Worker Communications at Intake." *Social Casework* 40 (April 1959):177–83.

Strean, Herbert S. *Clinical Social Work Theory and Practice.* New York: Free Press, 1978.

Taft, Jessie. "The Relation of Function to Process in Social Casework." In *Training for Skill in Social Casework,* edited by Virginia P. Robinson, pp. 1–12. Philadelphia: University of Pennsylvania Press, 1942.

Taft, Jessie. "Time as the Medium of the Helping Process." *Jewish Social Service Quarterly* 26 (December 1949):230–43.

Taft, Jessie. "Living and Feeling." *Child Study* 10 (1933):pp. 100–12.

Taylor Kräupl, F., and J. H. Rey. "The Scapegoat Motif in Society and Its Manifestations in a Therapeutic Group." *International Journal of Psychoanalysis* 34 (1953):253–64.

Thayer, Louis. "A Person-Centered Approach to Family Therapy." In *Family Counselling and Therapy,* edited by Arthur M. Horne and Merle M. Ohlsen. Itasca, Ill.: F. E. Peacock Publishers, Inc., 1982, pp. 175–213.

Thomlison, Ray. "Outcome Effectiveness Research and Its Implications for Social Work Educators." *Canadian Journal of Social Work Education,* Vol. 7 (1980):55–92.

Truax, C. B. "Therapist Empathy, Warmth, and Genuineness, and Patient Personality Change in Group Psychotherapy: A Comparison Between Interaction Unit Measures, Time Sample Measures, and Patient Perception Measures." *Journal of Clinical Psychology* 71 (1966):1–9.

Vinter, Robert D., ed. *Readings in Group Work Practice.* Ann Arbor, Mich.: Campus Publishers, 1967.

Weakland, John H.; Richard Fisch; Paul Watzlawick; and Arthur M. Bodin. "Brief Therapy: Focussed Problem Resolution." *Family Process* 13 (1974):141–68.

Weiner, Hyman K. "The Hospital, the Ward and the Patients as Clients: Use of the Group Method." *Social Work* 4 (October 1959):57–64.

Whitaker, Dorothy Stock, and Lieberman, Morton A. *Psychotherapy Through the Group Process.* New York: Atherton Press, 1964.

Whyte, W. F. *Street Corner Society: The Social Structure of an Italian Slum.* Chicago: University of Chicago Press, 1943.

Name Index

Ackerman, Nathan, 127, 128, 129, 265, 266
Argyris, Chris, 402
Asch, S. E., 313

Bales, R. F., 318
Bevelas, A., 317
Bell, Norman W., 269
Bennis, Warren G., 293, 297, 301
Bion, William R., 293, 308, 309
Bowen, Murray, 129
Brager, George, 402

Deutsch, M., 318

Flanders, Ned A., 70
Freeman, David S., 129
Freud, Sigmund, 88

Garland, James A., 267

Hare, A. Paul, 307, 314
Hearn, Gordon, 351
Holloway, Stephen, 402
Homans, George, 293, 324

Keith, David V., 130
Kolodny, Ralph L., 267
Kubler-Ross, Elizabeth, 106
Kuhn, Thomas H., 3

Lewin, Kurt, 266, 285, 377

Mills, C. Wright, 393

Perlman, Helen Harris, 78

Rogers, Carl R., 65, 70, 130

Satir, Virginia, 130
Schwartz, William, 3, 7, 11, 12, 17, 38, 45, 51, 56, 69, 72, 79, 82, 84, 85, 91, 95, 97, 108, 109, 114, 132, 133, 163, 172, 202, 239, 249, 265, 269, 278, 295, 341, 359, 393
Setleis, Lloyd, 24
Shepard, Herbert A., 293, 297, 301
Sherif, Carolyn W., 312
Sherif, M., 312
Smalley, Ruth E., 66
Strean, Herbert S., 78, 105

Taft, Jessie, 12, 17, 65
Truax, C. B., 70

Vogel, Ezra F., 269

Whitaker, Carl A., 130
Whyte, W. F., 317

Subject Index

Activities, 324
Activity group, 331–37
  implementing the activity, 332–33
  mutual aid, 332
  therapeutic purposes, 334
Advocacy, 12, 385–90
Agency
  change, 394–97
  interstaff relations, 392, 400–410
  records and referral reports, 28–29
  as social system, 401–3
Authority, 88–91
  definition, 88
  group work, 204, 221–27, 249, 295–301
  research findings, 91
  taboos, 307
Autokinetic effect, 312

Basic assumption groups, 309
Beginning phase with groups, 195–214
  dynamics of first session, 195–97
  objectives, 196–97
Beginning skills
  contracting, 37–49
  dynamics of new relationships, 33–37
  first interview, 34
  groups, see Beginning phase with groups
Behavior, 324

Casework in the group, 239
Category observation system, 417–18
Child care worker, 40
Child welfare worker, 40
Children's group sessions, 215–21
Clarifying purpose, 38, 44, 199, 253
Clarifying role, 36, 38, 44, 199, 233
Client feedback, see Feedback
Client-system interaction, see Individual-system interaction

Clinical practice, 4
Communication, 10
  beginning phase, 34
  indirect, 11, 20–22, 26
  nonverbal, 22
  obstacles to, 10–11
Confidentiality, 137, 182–83
Confrontation
  family therapy, 129
  mutual aid, 165
  opening up the system, 378–85
Containment, 61
Content and process, 114–15, 119, 391
Contracting, 4
  clarifying purpose, 38–41, 44
  clarifying role, 39–41, 44
  client feedback, 38–44
  context of contracts as block to communi-
    cation, 20–21
  elaboration skill, 47, 59–65
  in first sessions, 37–49, 233–34
  group sessions, 199, 216, 217, 219–20,
    240–52
  over time, 41–43
  resistant clients, 43–49
  sessional skills, 57–59
Counter-dependence flight, 297
Counterdependent group member, 297
Counterpersonal group member, 301
Countertransference, 88–89, 296
Co-workers, 337–38
  tensions, 338
Crediting the client, 114
Crisis theory, 378
Culture for work, 307–14, 318–22

Data
  activity group, 332
  definition, 91

sharing skills, 91–97
Death and dying, 106
Defensive group member, 285–86
Demand for work, 44
    challenging illusion of work, 83–84
    checking for underlying ambivalence, 82–83
    holding to focus, 81–82
    partializing client concerns, 80–81
    research findings, 84–85
    resistance, 78
    skills of, 77–85
Dependence-flight, 297
Dependency, 307
Dependent group member, 297
Developmental tasks of group
    division of labor, 315–16
    formation, 294–95
    meeting individual member needs, 295
    relationships between members, 295, 301–7
    relationship with worker, 295, 296–301
    structure for work, 295, 314–22
    working culture, 295, 307–14
Deviant member, 274–80
    behavior as communication, 274–77
    as functional role, 277–80
Deviational allowance, 332
Disenchantment-flight, 301
"Doorknob" communication, 101–2
Dynamic systems theory, 4–6

Elaboration, 47, 59–65
    containment, 61
    focused listening, 62
    group work, 251
    moving from general to specific, 60–61
    questioning, 62
    reaching inside of silences, 62–65
Empathy, 17, 44–45, 65–71
    displaying understanding of client's feelings, 68–69
    mutual aid, 166–67
    putting client's feelings into words, 69–70
    reaching for feelings, 67–68
    research findings, 70–71
Enchantment-flight, 301
Endings, 105
    anger phase, 109
    crediting the client, 114
    denial phase, 108–9
    dynamics and skills of, 106
    "farewell party" syndrome, 114–15
    groups, 212–14, 262–64, 341–53

mourning period, 112–14
    skills, 97–102, 106–15
    see also Transitions
Environment of group, 322
    helping to negotiate, 322–26

Family counseling, 125
Family facade, 127, 137
Family support work, 125–27
    first session, 134–37
    native Indian family, 153–58
    parent-teen conflict, 148–53
    single-parent family, 143–48
    stepfathers' role, 138–42, 148–53
    taboos, 158–59
    two clients concept, 131–34
Family therapy, 125
    initial interview, 129
    integration and differentiation, 130
    intergenerational aspect, 129–30
    mediation, 128
    person-centered approach, 130
    theory, 127–28
"Farewell party" syndrome, 114–15
Feedback, 38
    beginning phase of work, 38
    group work, 200
    negative, 54, 90, 91, 174
    reaching for, 38–39, 44, 199, 233–34
Flight-fight group, 309
Focused listening, 62
Foster children, 216–18
Functional clarity and diffusion, 133

Gatekeeper role, 283–85
Generalizing, 98–99
Group
    adolescents and children, 215–21
    agency support, 184–85
    authority theme, 221–27
    client problem impact, 227–30
    common interest, 294
    composition, 185–87
    couples, 197–214
    defensive member, 285–86
    definition, 163
    developmental tasks, *see* Developmental tasks of group
    deviant member, 274–80
    division of labor, 315–16
    dynamics of mutual aid, 164–70
    as dynamic system, 265–67
    endings, 341–53
    fear of groups syndrome, 173–75

formation, *see* Group formation
gatekeeper role, 283–84
individual-group communication, 243–49
initial sessions, 197–238
internal leader, 280–83
mutual aid system, 163–75
negotiating the environment, 322–26
open-ended, 327–29
as an organism, 293
quiet member, 286–90
relationship to environment, 294
scapegoat, 266–74
setting of services impact, 230–34
single-session, 329–31
structure, 188–90
time impact, 234–38
timing, 187–88
versus individual work with client, 183–84
work phase; *see* Work phase in group
working with individual in group, 265–90
Group cohesion, 317
Group culture, 167, 294
Group dynamics, 266–67
Group formation
 agency support, 184–85
 composition, 187–88
 recruitment of prospective members, 190–94
  initial interview, 192–94
  strategizing for effective referrals, 191–92
 structure, 188–90
 timing, 187–88
 working with staff system, 177–78
  achieving consensus on service, 178–83
Group leader
 function, 172–73
 internal, 266, 280–83
Group norms, 307, 312
Group structure, 295, 214–18
 over time, 318–22
Group-as-a-whole, 167, 171

Helping process
 agency records and referral reports, 28–29
 preliminary phase of work
 endings, *see* Endings
 preliminary phase of work
  agency records and referral reports, ˙28–29
  beginning skills, 33–37
  clarifying purpose, 38

clarifying roles, 36
contracting, *see* Contracting
elaboration, 49
indirect communications, 20–22
preparatory empathy, 17–20
responding directly to indirect cues, 25–28
tuning in, 22–25
transitions, *see* Transitions
work phase, *see* Work phase
Hinting, 21
Human contact as function of activity group, 332
The Human Group, 324

Illusion of work, 83–84, 302, 402
Indian families, 153–58
Indirect communication, 11, 20–22
 beginning phase concerns, 34
 obstacles to, 20–21
Individual-system interaction, 357, 358–77
 bureaucratic size, 358
 complexity, 358
 dynamic systems theory, 4–5
 function of helping person, 11–13
 integration of personal and professional self, 13–15
 judgmental attitude, 358
 mediating, 359–77
 obstacles to, 9–11
 strength for change assumptions, 6–8
 symbiotic assumption, 6–8
Informal roles, 267
Intake forms, 35–36
Interaction, 324
Inter-agency staff difficulties, 391–92
 professional impact on relations with staff, 408–10
Interdependence among group members, 301
Inter-group communication problems, 316–17
Internal leadership, 266, 280–83
 threat to worker authority, 281
Interstaff relations, 392
 interdepartment communications, 404–8
 interdisciplinary work with client, 403–4
 professional impact, 400–410
Interview
 control over, 57, 59
 group formation, 192–94
 initial, 34
 intake form, 35–36
 work phase model, 51–53

Intimacy, 249
  group developmental tasks, 295, 301–6

Listening, 62

Marital counseling, 12–13
  first sessions, 39
Mediation, 12–13
  beginning phase of work, 38
  individual-group interaction, 172
  scapegoating, 269
Medical model, 4
Model, 4
Mutual aid
  all-in-the-same-boat phenomenon, 166
  confrontation, 165
  dialectical process, 165–66
  dynamics, 164
  empathy, 166–67
  healing over time, 252–60
  individual problem solving, 168, 260–62
  mutual demand, 167
  obstacles to, 170–72
  rehearsal, 168–70
  shared activities, 332
  sharing data, 164
  strength in numbers phenomenon, 170
  taboos, 166, 171

Negative behavior, 21–22
Negative feedback, 90, 91, 107, 174

Obstacles to work, 249–52
Open-ended group, 327–29
Overpersonal group member, 301

Partializing client's concern, 80–81
Person-centered therapy, 130
Personal self, 13–15
Pointing out obstacles skill, 85–91
  authority theme, 88–91
  research findings, 87–88
  taboos, 85–87, 89
Positive feedback, 107
Practice theory, definition, 3
Problem-swapping exercise, 200–204
Process and content, 114–15, 119, 391
Professional self, 13–15
Program, 331
  effectiveness, 333
Pseudoeffectiveness, 402
Purpose clarification, 38

Quiet group member, 286–90
  techniques for dealing with, 287–88

Radical social work approach, 13
Reaching inside of silence, 46, 62–65, 200, 287
Record of service, 308
Records and referral reports, 28–29
Referrals, 191
  workshop, 191–92
Reflection, 18–19
Rehearsal, 168–70
  activity groups, 332
Research methodology, 414–18
Resistance, 43–49, 78–79, 83, 250
Resolution-catharsis, 297
Resolution stage of session, 97
Role
  clarification, 36, 38, 44, 199, 233
  definition, 265
  family therapy, 129
  group, 315
  informal, 266
    defensive group member, 285–86
    deviant group member, 267, 274–80
    gatekeepers, 267, 283–84
    internal leader, 266–67, 280–83
    quiet member, 286–90
    scapegoat, 266–74
  social, 265–67

Scapegoating, 129, 266–74
  in family, 269
  history of, 268–69
  social role, 269
  work with, 273
School counselor, 40
Self-awareness, 57
Self-disclosure, 76
Sensitivity training movement, 402
Sentiments, 324
Service Satisfaction Questionnaire, 415, 416
Sessional contracting, 57–59
Sessional-ending skills, 97–102, 105
  "doorknob" communication, 101–2
  generalizing, 98–99
  identifying next step, 99–100
  rehearsal, 100–101
  summarizing, 98
  see also Endings
Sharing-data skills, 91–97
  open to examination, 94–96
  providing relevant data, 92–94
  research findings, 96

Sharing worker's feelings skills, 71–77
    research on, 76–77
Silence
    group session, 200, 287
    meaning, 63
    reaching inside of, 46, 62–65
Single-parent family, 143–48
Single-session group, 329–31
Skill, 4
Skill factors, 52
    elaborating, 59–65
    empathic skills, 65–71
    sharing worker's feelings, 71–77
    tuning in, 53–57
Social action, 393–400
    in agency, 394–97
    in community, 397–400
Social role, 265–66
Social worker, functional definition, 12
Social Worker Behavior Questionnaire, 414,
    415, 416, 417
Staff
    culture, 391
    impact on service, 401
    interstaff relations, 392, 400–410
Strength for change assumption, 8–9
Structure for work, 295, 314–22
Summarizing, 98
Symbiotic relationship
    definition, 6–8
    group, 163, 170
System
    agency, 401–3
    client-system interaction, 4–6
    dynamic systems theory, 4
    individual's interaction with, 358–90
        advocacy, 385–90
        confrontation, 378–85
        mediation, 359–77

Taboos, 20, 85–87
    activity group, 332
    family, 158–59
    group developmental tasks, 307–8
T-groups, 301
Transference, 88–89, 296

Transitions, 115–22
    group, 341–54
    identification of future work areas, 117–19
    identification of major learnings, 115–17
    initial group session, 212–14
    new experiences and support systems, 120–22
    work phase in group, 262–64
    see also Endings
Tuning in, 17, 22–25
    affective versus intellectual, 22–23
    levels of, 24–25
    self-awareness, 57
    responding directly to indirect cues, 25–28
    sessional skills, 52–57
    time, 56–57
    worker's feelings, 23–24, 54–55
Two clients concept, 131–34
    individual and group, 172, 265
    overidentifying with one part of family, 133
    worker's role, 131–34

Videotaping, 57, 198–99, 417

Work group, 308–9
Work phase in group session, 239–64
    contracting, 240–52
    endings and transitions, 262–64
    individual concerns, 239–46
    individual-group communication, 239–49
    obstacles, 249
Work phase in individual sessions
    containment, 61
    demand for work, 77–85
    interview, 51–53
    pointing out obstacles skills, 85–91
    sessional ending skills, 97–102
    sharing data skills, 91–97
    skill factors, 52, 53–77
    viewing systems people in new ways, 96–97
Working relationship, 19, 36, 47

Index of Case Illustrations

Activity group used for therapeutic purposes, 334–37
Advocacy: helping client negotiate the housing system, 385–90
Agency change, 394–95, 396–97
Authority theme
  group's relation to worker, 196–97, 298–301
  initial session, 22–23, 223–27
  worker's skill in action, 89–90

Beginning phase: clarifying reasons for referral, 34–35

Client problem impact: stating specific group concern at opening meeting, 227–30
Confrontation, 378–85
Contracting
  over time, 41–42
  resistant client, 44–48
Couple's group, first session, 197–214
Culture for work: worker's efforts to develop, 308–12

Defensive group member, 285–86
Deviant behavior, 323–24
  group member, 278–80
Division of labor problems within group, 315–16

Empathy: tuning in to client's feelings, 66–67
Endings in group work
  anger indirectly expressed by client, 110–11
  children's group, 344–45
  deaf teenager group, 348–50
  group session, 263–64
  men's support group, 346–48

mourning period, 112–14
  termination sessions: detailed analysis, 350–54
  unwed mother's group, 342–44
  welfare mother's group, 345–46
Expression of feeling by worker, 72–73

Family session with angry father, 134–37
Family support work over time: bringing stepfather into the picture, 137–42
Foster children: initial group session, 216–18

Group contract: impact of the setting of the service, 230–34
Group disagreement over chairperson's sharing of responsibility, 315–16
Group-environment interaction
  sixth graders' relationship with their school, 323–26
  teen-age boys' club, 322–23
Group formation: convincing agency of need, 178–82
Group's relationship with worker, 296–97

Indirect communication, 34–35
Inter-agency staff relations, professional impact on, 408–10
Internal leader: threat to worker authority, 281–83
Inter staff communication problem, 404–8
Intimacy theme, 249–52

Married couples group's reluctance to discuss intimate personal matters, 312
Mourning phase in termination, 112–14
Mutual aid in unwed mothers' group, 252–62

Native Indian family: impact of culture and community, 153–58

Negotiating the system
helping client negotiate the housing system, 385–90
helping hospital group communicate with doctor, 371–73
mediating between child and his school, 361–66
mediating between child and his teacher, 367–70
mediating between staff and patient in mental ward, 373–77
workshop for native Indian women, 359–61

Open-ended group, 328–29
Overidentifying with one member of the family, 133–36

Parent-teen conflict, 149–53

Quiet group member: worker's technique to draw him out, 288–90

Reaching for group response to individual, 246–49
Reaching for individual communication in the group, 241–46
Rehearsal, 100
groups, 168–69
Resistant client: contracting with, 44–48
Responding directly to indirect cues, 27–28

Scapegoat, 270–73
Sharing relevant data, skills of, 93–94
Single parent families
community care team setting, 144–48
group sessions, 234–38
Social action
in agency, 394–97
in community, 397–400

Taboos: group discussion of sexuality, 313–14
Tenant groups, initial session, 232–34
Termination session; detailed analysis, 350–54
Time impact on initial group session, 234–38
Transitions
moving to new experiences and support systems, 120–22
summing up the learning process, 116–17
synthesizing process and content, 119–20
Tuning in skills
client's sense of urgency, 53–54
showing empathy, 66–67
Two-clients concept: worker's role, 131–33, 134–36

Welfare mothers' confrontation with Housing Agency, 378–85
Withdrawal and withholding of feelings among group members, 304–6

BOOK MANUFACTURE

The Skills of Helping Individuals and Groups, Second Edition was typeset at Compositors, Cedar Rapids, Iowa. Printing and binding was by Kingsport Press, Kingsport, Tennessee. F.E. Peacock Publishers art department designed the text. The typeface is Times Roman.